THE DRAGON CEDE

The Holy Grail Descent of the House of Vere
Vampire God-Kings of Eurasia

Including

**The Dragon Descent of Jesus Christ from Satan,
The Secret Genealogy of an Ancient Lineage
Revealed**

THE BOOK TREE
San Diego, California

ISBN 9781585095490

Cover layout
Atulya Berube

Interior layout & design
Atulya Berube

Front and back cover armorial art
Michael Hunter

Published by
The Book Tree
P O Box 16476
San Diego, CA 92176
www.thebooktree.com

We provide fascinating and educational products to help awaken the public to new ideas and information that would not be available otherwise.
Call 1 (800) 700-8733 for our FREE BOOK TREE CATALOG.

DEDICATIONS

TO

My Step-Father, The Hon. J. Aubrey Brooks, Esq., R.N., CDR.
The Leiutenant Kije of Her Majesty's Royal Naval Officer Corps!

My Cousins, HI & RH Prince Alfred
Tarnawa-Krupa de Vere von Drakenberg
and family

H.E. Count Michael Hunter, R.A.D., SDR., Dragon King
of Arms: Lifelong and longsuffering Friend and
Talliére who lets me get away with nothing!

The Dragon Mother,
The Honourable Lady Peters, SDR.
Archivist and Former Officer at Arms
within the Brotherhood of the Source

My cousin H.E. Baron Robert Quinn,
Scion of King Niall of Eire, formerly of the
Brotherhood of the Source; a tireless and
relentless Dragon Warrior and Teacher

H.E. Prince Mark Amaru Tarnawa-de Vere
von Drakenberg, SDR., IOGT., KTSH.
Historiographer Royal to The Dragon Court.

My cousin and Brother, Prince Alexandre de
Bothoru – Bathory, author of the acclaimed
novel, *She-Messiah*

My beloved cousins Price Vladislav and Princess Maria
Draculea-Basarab, with congratulations on their wedding,
August, 2010.

My cousin H.R.H Prince Nicolas Rodolpho von
Sachsenstein, Imperial and Royal Ambassador
To the Dragon Court, cousin of the Royal House of
Bathory, Draculea-Basarab and Ordo Drakul of Transylvania.

The innumerable members of the Sovereign Grand Duchy of
Drakenberg, of the Imperial and Royal Dragon Court and of
the Dynasty of Vere worldwide
The Honourable Paul Tice CDR., my publisher. A man of
utmost vision, patience and forebearance

The Chevalier Goran Fistric, K.T.J., and Dame Gordana Pintaric,
D.T.J., for their fraternal care and support to the Eastern
Dragon Family. A Fine Templar Brother and Sister

The Hon. Lady Tracy Twyman,
A Radical Mystical and Political Genius

The Hon. Mr. Michael James Power CDR.,
and The Hon. Mrs. Shiela Olga Power CDR.
Generous and faithful family friends who are always there.

Our Family Physician and Lifelong Friend
The Hon. Dr. Felicity Smart CDR.

The Hon. Malcolm Slater CDR., Court Photographer.
www.malcolmslater.com
imagemsphoto@gmail.com

Alison Pullen Editorial Services
At drakenberg@talktalk.net

Publisher's Royalties

Annually the Dragon King of Arms receives and donates all the proceeds – in their
entirety – earned from the authorship of the Dragon Series to vital, registered
Social Welfare and Ecological and Environmental Charities. This situation is
one which will abide long into the future, as a part of our Ancient Dragon Duty of
Care.

Further planned and authorised works in the Dragon Series:

DRAGON ART: Images of Mysticism

GREAT DRACONIA: The Vampyre Manifesto

IN DRAGON TONGUES OF FIRE
The Elven Vampyr Languages of Eurasia

DRAGON MISTS: The Universal Mystery Tradition

Contents

Preamble

This latest book in the *Dragon* series contains the most comprehensive genealogies of the Houses of Vere, Weir and Collison published to date. It is intended as a reference work for all those readers who are interested in the Grail families or who wish to study further the ancient mythological, legendary and historical origins of their own lineage, inasmuch as they may find many "gateway ancestors" attributable to their own Family Trees.

Also published for the very first time is the Dragon Descent of Jesus Christ from Satan, an explosive secret kept hidden for centuries by a few ancient Dragon families and Gnostic sects which calls into question some of the classical identities and the inter-relationships of the figures we have grown up and become familiar with today. In the Interview with Tracy Twyman, the reader will learn the true purpose Jesus had for Mary Magdalene, her cosmic identity and the real nature of his clandestine "church."

In the excerpts from the work by Leonid Korablev, *The True Elves of Europe*, we are introduced to the factual origin of Tolkien's elves and their actual basis in history, whilst the reader will find numerous biographical notes and passages concerning the Vere family and the Grail line in both the main body of the book and in the genealogies themselves.

Why Mythology?

by Michael Hunter

Mythology largely comprises that collection of old human stories (widely regarded by the thoughtless majority as fanciful tales of impossible heroes and gods from the distant past), which have been imprisoned in the limited available lexicons of successive verbally (not "orally") oriented cultures to whom these histories have come as the inevitable concomitant of the human urge to travel for fun and profit.

Because tales are (a) of limited scope (for they are only stories of immutable and predictable human behaviour) and (b) in need of names, terms and forms which can be readily understood and remembered by those of widely differing languages and backgrounds, they tend to resemble each other trans-globally, and only the details differentiate them. It is the study of individual names and details which helps the historian to nail down the origins of individual myths, discard the accretions in order that the histories beneath the stories might be revealed, and to trace the probable migration routes and times of their originators.

In this work the deliberating reader may sift through the knowledge which is herein presented, and discern such commonality in the threads of these ancient stories and genealogies as to render the mythological as the historical. Above all the authors wish to distance themselves from any form of pseudo-history or pseudo-science which seems prevalent amongst the works of numerous contemporary writers within the genre.

PART ONE

ESSAYS

INTRODUCTION

A Brief Outline of the Prehistoric Nascence of the Imperial and Royal House of Vere

The genealogical descents that appear in this book are set out in their tabular form in order that readers may view and study them individually. The more than ninety royal descents that I present to you are the culmination of 25 years of study and reference in the fields of genealogy, heraldry, genetics, social and political history, archaeology, mythology, comparative religion and religious mysticism, symbolism, magic, occultism, folklore and, in particular, etymology.

The study of the latter has been decisive in discovering the true meaning of words, phrases and names related to the family and its history and mythology. If one merely consults a genealogist in order to discover one's family heritage, at some point or another one will hit a brick wall and go no further.

By applying a wide variety of disciplines I have discovered that, rather than being a provincial Scottish family, the Veres are in fact the senior imperial and royal dynasty of Britain, Europe and the Middle-East, and are the focus, indeed in some cases the fons et origio of Eurasian folk and religious mystical tradition, and are surrounded in an aura of myth, magic and mysticism.

By applying similar methods in subsequent years, by documentary cross-referencing and the application of etymology at every stage of my investigations a vast panorama of family tradition has opened up to us and I have been able to take our lineage back to the very beginning of written history and indeed beyond.

9

This may sound fanciful but through numerous descents from the Merovingian kings of the Franks and the Angevin kings of England the Veres have inherited the 16q24.3 genes. In correspondence with a contact of mine at Oxford University who was one of the pioneers of research in this field I discovered that these gene types refer back millennia before written records. Related genetic studies over the past few years have determined that around 90,000 years ago a catastrophic disaster occurred which more or less wiped out the entire human population.

Today the population of the planet only consists of four different genetic variations stemming from only four individual females. This disaster was termed the human genetic bottle-neck. The 16q24.3 genes which survived it were found not to have originated with homo sapiens but predated the emergence of modern man by thousands of years. Today 16q24.3 genes are rare and it is estimated scientifically that they will be bred out of the human population within about 150 years. In America only 2% of the population are red gene dominant, whilst in Scotland only 10% manifest the genes. In the Far East people with red hair are venerated as Gods which further asserts the divine origin of these genes.

In the *Epic of Gilgamesh* his closest companion, Enkidu, created like Adam by Enki (hence his name) is described as being "hairy." Furthermore in the Biblical Old Testament Esau is also described as hairy, but also, from other translations, he is described as having been "born red." In apocryphal Jewish texts Sheba (Lilith) is also described as being hairy whilst in Genesis Adam, through translations is described as being a "red man," an appellation which also applied to the divine Enkidu, son of Enki.

Esau's other name was Edom and is directly related to the word Adama both of which mean "red man." The word for red and the word for hairy come from the same root, and mistranslation is easy. One word, hairy, is translated from the word Se'ar, and the other word, red, is translated from Sear. From both Esau and Lilith (who had red hair), from Adam and indeed from Sheba-Lilith, wife of King Solomon, we can safely assert that Se'ar was mistranslated and should have read Sear and that as a result of this, we can state that Enki and the other gods were the fons et origio of the 16q24.3 genes. Jesus, according to Roman commentators, also had red hair.

Where did they come from? It has been tentatively suggested, from I must say scant archaeological evidence, that these genes were inherited from the homo-Neanderthal through interbreeding. Having previously read an ancient apocryphal Hebrew text called the Ben Sirah, and having further cross-referenced it with Greek, Babylonian and Sumerian religious works, an interesting alternative explanation emerged.

In some Jewish traditions it is stated that a mortal individual named Lilith was the rebellious first wife of Adam. Wishing to dominate Adam, and unable to accept his authority over her she fled to the coast and turned into the Leviathan, the Dragon of the Sea. According to the Jews she became the mother of all demons, vampires and witches. The dragon motif is important and should be borne in mind.

However, in the Ben Sirah Lilith is also described as the feared "red-haired queen of the north." Studying Greek tradition I discovered that both Rhadamanthus and his brother Zeus were described as having red hair. These gods, as with those of many other pantheons across Eurasia, including the God of the Israelites, were all developed from a primal, proto-Sumerian original, wherein Zeus derives from the Sumerian God Enlil who was the half-brother of the God Enki – the creator of man.

The Lilith of the Ben Sirah actually originates from the same proto-Sumerian pantheon, wherein she is depicted as the grand-daughter of the God Enlil (the red-haired Zeus of the Greeks) and the daughter of the Goddess Erish-Kigal and Nergal, king of the Underworld. In Jewish tradition she is part of the Tetragrammaton, YHVH, the four deities that were combined to form the monotheistic Jehovah. Within this group Lilith, the daughter of EL, is handmaiden to the mother Metatron – the Goddess Nin-Kursag, wife of EL – who, once Jewish polytheism was discarded, developed into the Lady Sabbath.

So rather than her being mortal, Lilith actually originated as a proto-Sumerian Goddess and a Queen. Furthermore, as these divine beings are described as having red hair, we can confirm that they carried the 16q24.3 genes. This being the case, we can also state that in carrying these genes, the proto-Sumerian Gods and Goddesses, in having a genetic make-up, were in fact Earth-bound beings made of flesh and blood, not ethereal inhabitants of the heavens.

The Dragon Motif of Lilith is important here because these proto-Sumerian Gods and goddesses were called the Anunnaki – the sons of An the father God – and they were described by their early Sumerian and Babylonian worshippers as Dragons. The word Dragon originates from the Greek word Edrakon, which is an aorist (tenseless verb) of the parent word Derkesthai which means Clear vision and relates to transcendent consciousness and wisdom.

Not being satisfied with halting my studies in Sumeria, I wanted to carry the research beyond recorded history. As the red-haired Queen of the North, Lilith obviously didn't come from Sumeria, which means that the proto-Sumerian pantheon of Gods must have originated from another region and a far earlier period in time.

Sumerian was thought to be the oldest written language on Earth, originating in Mesopotamia some 5000 years ago. Luckily I happened upon the work of Dr. M.F. Stone whose archaeological discoveries have confirmed that linguistically, Sumerian or rather proto-Sumerian originated, as a primitive language, in Central Europe and has distinct links with the later Vinca culture which was, I believe, centred around the Danube river-basin.

To be precise, Stone's team unearthed tablets bearing the effigy of the God Enki and bearing his inscriptions and ranking numbers within the Anunnaki pantheon. This discovery was made in Transylvania. In corroboration of a Central European origin for these beings, it is to be noted that the earliest detailed stone sculptures of the Dragon Gods were also discovered in this region and it is from here that the accounts of Lilith, Nergal and the ancient Gods of the Sumerians first emerge, millennia before their appearance in Mesopotamia.

It is interesting to note that whilst orthodox historians and archaeologists would like us to believe that the neo-mesolithic period of European history was a primitive time populated by grunting cave-men, it is from this period and this region that the archaeologist Richard Rudgely discovered the remnants of finely woven cloth with patterned stitching, combs, immaculately crafted coloured beads and other surprising artifacts.

Rudgely clearly reveals that the culture and the living conditions of the age were remarkably advanced, more so than we were previously led to believe. In Bohemia – now the Czech Republic – the earliest settlement yet to be unearthed – Dolne Vistonicu – was in fact the New York of its age and had trading links with places as far afield as southern France and north Africa. In conclusion, the first "cities" to emerge didn't appear on the stage of history in Mesopotamia, but originated in central Europe with the proto-Sumerians and their red-haired Anunnaki God-Kings.

To advance the argument that the Anunnaki were a sophisticated society far in advance of any other of the time I would remind the reader that the accepted, popular misconception of a universal Stone Age, Bronze Age and Iron Age is misleading. It gives us the idea that each era emerged across the planet at the same time when in fact these changes in technology emerged at different times in different places. For example by the time the Bronze Age began in Western Europe, it had already been flourishing in early Sumer for millennia. It is also possible for the ages to reverse themselves.

If a culture that has Bronze technology is forced to migrate, because of a regional disaster for instance, their first priority will be to establish an infrastructure for the provision of the basic necessities of their day-to-day survival. The last thing on their minds would be the rebuilding of their former Bronze Age culture.

Indeed the region to which they have been forced to flee may have no Tin or Copper ore at all, which would mean they would have no choice but to revert to using Stone Age tools and implements. In this manner civilizations can advance and decline according to migration and the resources available.

If I advance therefore, the idea that the Anunnaki were a highly developed technological society when others were still in their Stone Age, such a concept is perfectly reasonable. Whilst we in the west entered our Iron Age in around 500 BC, 1500 years later the American Indians were still in their Stone Age up until the 11th century and the arrival of the Vikings in Vinland.

Today, whilst the developed nations enjoy a standard of scientific knowledge and expertise unprecedented in history, numerous tribes across the planet, including the Bushmen of the Kalahari and the Thai Hill Tribes are still more or less in their Stone Age.

If our computer-based technologies failed us today, within a few months all the basic resources would disappear. Fuel and electricity would become inaccessible, food and water would run out rapidly and, because we are so reliant on modern technology, in its absence most of us would die within the space of a couple of years, if not sooner. The few of us who managed to survive the total collapse of western civilisation would have to revert to a new Stone Age and, knowing nothing about basic metallurgy and lacking any skill in primitive crafts, it would take us many centuries to reach the cultural level attained by our early ancestors.

In Egypt craftsmen built the Great Pyramid of Giza using the most primitive bronze, stone and wooden tools. As in other parts of this vast structure, the King's burial chamber is lined with massive blocks of red granite, one of the hardest and most unforgiving materials known to man at the time. Nevertheless the pyramid builders carved these granite blocks into perfect cubes, which they fitted together so precisely that even today it is impossible to push a razorblade between the joints. Such a level of skill and knowledge is extremely highly advanced, and yet they achieved these amazing feats using the most primitive and basic tools. Even today archaeologists are baffled and amazed at how they managed it. The Egyptians also used gold electro-plating and performed cranial surgery on patients suffering from water on the brain and other related ailments.

The age of pyramid building began around 5000 years ago and hundreds were constructed. However, only a handful remain today. The rest have disappeared, seemingly without a trace. Consequently it is perfectly reasonable to assert that the Anunnaki, whose descendants introduced monumental architecture to the Egyptians, enjoyed a civilisation in Europe far in advance of that of the Egyptians, perhaps millennia earlier, and that traces of that civilisation, over thousands of years, have disappeared completely.

Consulting the Sumerian King Lists we find that the Sumerians claimed that the civilisation of the eight named, divine Anunnaki dynasties reached as far back as what we now think of as the Middle Stone Age, some 30,000 years ago and more, and yet we meet such a claim with incredulity and scorn, as no evidence exists to prove the assertion. However modern scientists have calculated that, if humanity were to suffer a rapid process of complete planetary extinction, our civilisation, its infrastructure, its fragile modern materials and technologies, would rapidly crumble into dust and, after a lapse of between 5000 and 10,000 years, no trace of our existence would be found. Imagine what might survive of an advanced culture after the passage of 30,000 years. Nothing. Because of this, and because relatively little archaeological excavation has been undertaken in the poorer Central European Countries – they have more pressing needs requiring the investment of their financial resources – the Anunnaki have been relegated to the status of a myth.

After a million years of human development, the idea that we are the only people to have reached the pinnacle of cultural and technological advancement, and that no one as sophisticated as we has existed prior to the modern era is arrogant in the extreme, a degenerating symptom of our smug, self congratulating, self satisfied civilisation. Because we surround ourselves with pointless technological gadgets we think we are the most advanced culture in the history of mankind and yet we have become so dependent on these gadgets that, in our laziness and complacency we have degenerated into the weakest, most unskilled and vulnerable civilisation in history.

With a pride bordering on egomania, we worship ourselves for our purported genius and we celebrate our technology as a God, but we haven't a clue about how it works or how it is manufactured. We leave such matters to experts and specialists. Few of us even know how to repair a motorcar.

Our present level of technological sophistication is therefore unsustainable and, if disaster were to strike, we would be unable to repair or replace any of the machines upon which we have come to depend for our survival. As for attempting to eke out a living from the land, forget it.

In the space of 150 years we have completely lost all the basic skills required to make a living, skills with which our ancestors had been conversant for thousands of years. If we are honest, we will admit that ours is the most primitive, inflexible and fragile civilisation in human history. We depend ultimately on computers for our food and life support. If they break down, we starve and die. 10,000 years ago our hunter-gatherer ancestors depended on flint tools to hunt their food. If a weapon broke, they would just go out and make another one. No problem. By being sustainable and renewable their culture, however simple it may have been, was far in advance of our own.

With the Anunnaki the 16q24.3 genes reveal themselves and their presence within the individual's genetic make-up in the apparent manifestation of red hair, green eyes and a pale complexion deficient in melanin, a chemical vital to the protection of those peoples who inhabit areas with a harsh, sun-drenched climate such as Africa and Sumeria. If, like the Anunnaki, one has occupied a temperate region for millennia, melanin is an unnecessary genetic component. We may safely assert therefore that the beings that became deified as the Anunnaki of Sumeria were originally domiciled in central Europe, particularly in Transylvania, Carpathia, the White Mountains and the Black Sea, on the former, pre-flood shores of which stood the temple of the Anunnaki Dragon King Ziu Sudra.

He became the prototype and inspiration for the Jewish Noah. The Black Sea Flood – The Biblical Flood – after which the Ark came to rest on mount Ararat in Asia Minor and the Mesopotamian inundation are separated from each other by at least 500 years.

The craft used by King Uta Napishtim came to rest hundreds of miles south of Ararat on what was instead called Mount Nisir, in Mesopotamia. Consequently because the Bible Flood is that of Ziu Sudra and happened in the Bosphorus, this means that the children ascribed as belonging to Noah by Jewish scribes, and which they used in their myth, were in fact those of King Ziu Sudra, not Noah.

Why did the European Anunnaki migrate to Sumeria?

For many years scholars have dismissed the universal Biblical Flood as a myth. In fact there were two Biblical floods, one in the Bosphorus and one subsequent to it in Mesopotamia. These two events, which were separated both by time and by geography, have become fused into one myth, by both the Jews and the Akkadians.

During the exile of the Jews in Babylon in 500 BC, the Jewish scribes were permitted access to the king's library and it is from the Babylonian cylinder rolls, and from far earlier Sumerian text tablets, that the Jewish scribes copied and adapted their Biblical creation myth, their histories and genealogies and their god Jehovah, to suit their own political and religious requirements. To their God they attribute the creation of the universe, the fashioning of the Earth and the birth of mankind.

In the Biblical account, Noah builds his Ark according to the instructions given by his God, fills it with all animal life, endures the flood for forty days and forty nights and eventually disembarks on Mount Ararat with his family and livestock, once the flood waters have subsided. According to Bishop Ussher's calculations the flood, which engulfed the world, occurred in 4000 BC.

If such a universal disaster had in fact occurred, the evidence for it would have been recorded geologically in silt deposits across the planet. Unsurprisingly no such evidence exists; therefore the tale of an all-consuming worldwide disaster is just a fantasy, a misinterpretation of the facts, like so much else in the Old Testament.

The Jews originated in Mesopotamia and were evidently not European. Therefore no Semitic ancestor of theirs could have been involved in the Biblical Flood, which affected Europe and Europeans. The fact is that Noah and his divine mission were a Jewish fantasy derived from the account of the building of an Ark by the Nephilim King Ziu Sudra who, rather than constructing a huge unwieldy vessel to accommodate pairs of all the animals on Earth, built a more modest vessel to contain instead the "seed of life."

Recent experiments conducted by scientists and marine engineers have sought to reconstruct a model of the Ark taking into account the measurements God supposedly gave Noah and the materials he was instructed to build it from. It was demonstrated conclusively that within a couple of hours of hitting the floodwaters, the Ark would have split in the middle and sunk beneath the waves.

We can extrapolate from this that the Ark story is a no more than a Jewish literary artifice, gleaned from a more likely Sumerian account relating to Ziu Sudra who, according to the texts was actually domiciled in the Bosphorus region. It was his Ark, which settled on Mount Ararat, adjacent to the Black sea basin, not Noah's. We might also say that, if the Ark didn't exist in the context proposed by the Jewish scribes, then nor did Noah, or his antecedents as his own, and nor did his post-Flood scions within the context of the story as the Jewish scribes have related it.

However, the fact is that in around 4500 BC the Black sea was a vast, low lying fresh water basin hundreds of feet below the level of the adjacent Mediterranean Sea. Near its centre was situated a large land mass that the Romans later named the Pontus Euxine. During this time the volcanic island of Santorini exploded after a local tectonic shift, causing a tsunami. The resultant tidal wave battered the Hellespont causing it to burst asunder and the salt water of the Mediterranean engulfed the Black Sea basin, causing a disastrous flood of horrifying proportions.

The Pontus Euxine – the Holy Mountain – disappeared under millions of gallons of salt water which also took with it the settlements which were built on the shoreline, settlements which have recently been discovered by marine archaeologists and dated to 4500 BC Naturally this flood affected the whole region surrounding the Bosphorus and many inhabitants would have been permanently displaced, the salt water which polluted the surrounding lands making agriculture, pastoralism and food-gathering impossible.

The Pontus Euxine is one of the prototypes for the mythical Atlantis, which, over time has merged, like the account of the Biblical Flood, with other later fables. Nevertheless, the story of the inundation of the Holy Mountain in the Black Sea flood persisted in accounts recorded by the Sumerians, the Egyptians, the Chinese and even the Scandinavian Vikings. All of these accounts record the exploits of the Mountain's occupants who are know collectively as the Ogdoad; the eight great Gods of the Anunnaki who, millennia later, were venerated by Jesus himself.

The Anunnaki living in the region and on the Mountain would have had no choice but to migrate south, through the Taurus mountains and on to Mesopotamia where they eventually settled permanently, building Ziggurats as replicas of the Holy Mountain they had left behind.

With the emergence of the early city states of the Sumerians came the adaptation of their linear script into cuneiform, the invention of tarmac roads, indoor sanitation and street lighting. Clearly this advanced level of technology could not have emerged overnight, but must have been a culmination and adaptation of advanced skills and knowledge gathered in Europe over millennia.

Further to the Anunnaki migration to Mesopotamia, remnants of their people wandered to the four corners of the Earth taking the story of the Flood with them thereby assuring that the fable arises in many disparate lands. Because of this early scholars assumed that, as the Flood myth was virtually universal, the inundation must have covered the entire Earth.

To summarise the foregoing, we know that we carry the 16q24.3 genes and that these genes originate in prehistory with the lineage of the European Anunnaki who, with the passage of time, by being so advanced a people in juxtaposition to those whom they encountered in Mesopotamia after the Flood, became deified by the indigenous population as the Gods of Sumeria. So at this point in our story we have moved from prehistoric Central Europe to the Middle-East, taking our genes, our technology and our literary knowledge with us.

Remnants of this technology appear in the forests of central Germany in the form of detailed astronomical knowledge, whilst the practice of acupuncture emerges in the European heartlands centuries before it appears in China. In European prehistory acupuncture was practiced to introduce drugs and medicines into the body hypodermically, unlike the modern Chinese practice, which relies more on belief than empiricism.

The god of the Jews, often named El, derives from the Anunnaki God Enki's half brother Enlil, whose other Sumerian name is EL. After murdering his father An, the chief of the gods, and banishing his horrified senior brother Enki who was to succeed his father An as Chief of the Gods, EL became by force of arms and usurpation the father of the pantheon of Sumerian gods, also called in plural the Elohim.

The monotheistic Jewish scribes removed Enlil or EL from his collective context within the pantheon of Gods, singularised the plural term Elohim and appropriated it as another name for El or Jehovah.

They transformed the gods faithful to Enlil into angels and denigrated those faithful to Enki – An's rightful heir – relegating them to the position of "fallen angels" or demons. Although he was the creator of Man and the rightful head of the Anunnaki and was the preferred choice of his father An, Enki as the defeated and banished God – the victim of Enlil's furious jealousy and ambition – was blasphemously reduced in stature by the Jews to the status of the chief angel among the fallen ones, a figure we now know as Satan. This process has been repeated time and time again throughout history and in various cultures, where conquerors rewrite history or modify theology to suit their own ends, denigrating the gods of those they have vanquished to the status of demons and devils.

The ramifications of this process and the disastrous outcome of the "War in Heaven," originally a European internecine conflict initiated by a brutal act of patricide, have reverberated down the millennia, emerging in pagan and heterodox Christian Gnostic and dualist manuscripts which repeatedly remind us of the original Sumerian account by constantly and consistently asserting that Jehovah is the evil demiurge – the lesser god – whilst Satan is the true God, the creator and saviour of mankind.

In the Babylonian accounts Enlil (Jehovah) loathed mankind and sought constantly the annihilation of Enki's human children, reinforcing his later gnostic identification with the true opposer of man, which, in Hebrew, translates as Satan the enemy, and scourge of Mankind. The war in Heaven appears in Greek theology as the battle between Zeus (Enlil) – chief of the Olympians, the younger Gods, and Typhoeus (Enki or Ea) – chief of the Titans, the elder Gods.

In the Greek account the conflict takes place in the mountains surrounding the Bosphorus, thereby supporting the idea of a European origin for the Anunnaki. It is also interesting to note that the later Scythians – the Skoloti or Scotti of Transylvania and Greater Scythia – claim descent from the four sons of the daughter of Zeus (Enlil) fathered on her by the Titan Typhoeus (Enki).

Taking into account the fable's evolution with the passing of time, the Greek account and its Sumerian prototype are almost identical, though in the latter account Enki (Typhoeus the Titan) fathers his (Scythian) children by Enlil's (Zeus's) granddaughter Lilith, who also gives birth in the Babylonian texts to a daughter - Lilith Luluwa - who marries Cain or Qayin, King of Kish.

The Titans – the Old Gods – bequeathed their divine legacy, and their 16q24.3 genes, through Typhoeus, to the early Scythians who eventually became identified in European traditions as the Daouine Sidhe or Sithe, the Elves and Fairies of Germanic and Gaelic folklore.

Etymologically the original spelling of the name "Scythian" in middle English was "Sithian" and the pale-skinned, red-haired, green eyed genetic legacy of the Titans (Enki's divine Anunnaki followers) who were the fallen Angels or Demons of the Jews, became the distinguishing features of the Fairies, Elves, Witches and Vampires of Central and Western Europe, an association which traveled as far as sub-Saharan Africa. Even in Shakespeare's *A Midsummer Night's Dream* we find Titania as Queen of the fairies, derived from the Greek, Titanic Goddess of the same name, demonstrating the persistence of the myth down the millennia, and the abiding association and identification of the Titans – the old Anunnaki gods – with their holy offspring the Elves or Fairies: the High God-Kings and Overlords of history.

In the Gospel of the Cainites we discover that whilst Abel was the son of Eve by Adam, Cain was the son of Eve by Enki the Chief of the Gods who, as the one-eyed Samael is later replicated in form and status by Odin, Chief of the Gods of the Aesir. Besides Ziu Sudra, in the *Leibher Gabhalla* we learn that other Anunnaki princes, including Ba'ath and Fintan, build a vessel and, taking their womenfolk and sufficient provisions with them they leave the Bosphorus, navigate their way through the Mediterranean and sail to the Isles of the North.

According to the text, one contingent settles in Ireland whilst another contingent sails further afield and settles in Scandinavia. In Ireland they are remembered as the Aes Dan, the ancient gods of the Irish, an appellation also used for the later Tuadha de Danaan, and in Scandinavia these Anunnaki princes become the Aesir, the Gods of the Vikings, and their Chief is the one-eyed Odin, scion of the Sumerian Enki. In Scandinavia Odin is also known as Ygg and he is credited with the discovery of the ancient Runes, whilst in Ireland this discovery is credited to Oghma after whom the Ogham script is named. The linguistic similarity of the two names should not be ignored.

The story of the siring of Cain by Enki in the Gospel of the Cainites is also echoed in Genesis where Eve tells Adam that she has "gotten a Man from the Lord." Having doctored the original Sumerian and Babylonian account of the creation of man, transferring the credit from the defeated Enki to the victorious usurper EL the scribes, unable to countenance the fact that Cain was the son of Satan, attributed his paternity to Adam.

Just for good measure they promulgated the idea that Cain murdered his brother Abel in cold blood, thereby damning him to posterity for all time. From thence they banish him into the wilderness in the hope that he will be forgotten. And he was, at least until 1850 and the archaeological discovery in Mesopotamia of thousands of Sumerian and Babylonian texts which, when translated, told a different story. The European archaeological expeditions in Mesopotamia at the time were given specific orders to discover texts and materials, which would support and reinforce the popular view of the Bible as being an authentic, reliable historical document. When the texts were translated however, what they discovered was that the Sumerian and Babylonian records were in fact thousands of years older than the Bible, which repeated their content to the extent that it had to be admitted that the Old Testament was copied from them, and pretty badly at that. Even the law code of Moses in the Old Testament is a copy of the Laws of the Babylonian King Hammurabi, right down to the concept of "An eye for an eye." Contrary to popular belief, "Moses" received over 600 Commandments, not 10.

The Church authorities set about trying to discredit and suppress the ancient texts to the extent that, whilst they continued to be studied by academics, they were almost forbidden to be taught in schools, such was the threat they posed to the orthodox Judaeo-Christian propaganda, its dogmatic veracity and the world-wide Ecclesiastical hegemony, wealth and power it underpinned.

The effect of this smear campaign has been to relegate the Sumerian histories to the level of dismissible myth whilst even up to the beginning of the 20th Century the Bible remained the bedrock of Christian historical validity. This is in an age where Darwin was ridiculed and vilified and labeled a blasphemer, and the discovery of dinosaur bones in Pegwell Bay, Dorset, caused tremors of fear and consternation through the corridors of Church-State power.

To this day in America, many schools refuse to teach Darwinism, and the US government is too scared to force them to, such is the ubiquity of the belief in the Biblical creation myth within the population, and a huge number of Christian Fundamentalist Churches across the world continue to assert, and to teach their children, that God created fossils and planted them in the Earth to test the faith of his believers.

Recently the acclaimed naturalist Sir David Attenborough, because of his support of the modified Theory of Evolution, has received violent hate mail from Christian Fundamentalists cursing him to an eternity burning in hell. If these ignorant maniacs had power today, as their Catholic Forebears had in previous centuries, then it could be guaranteed that anyone who opposed their narrow, ignorant view of the world would be immediately tortured and killed. I wouldn't stand a chance!

Even in more enlightened seats of learning, whilst the old favourites – the Greek and Roman Classics – are still trundled out to pupils year after year, not one of these institutions bothers to teach anyone about Sumeria or the Sumerian histories, even though they are the oldest, and indeed the most reliable of all the ancient accounts in the World.

The Sumerian account of the creation of Man, the Flood and the emergence of ancient Kingship is thousands of years old and was written far closer to the time these events were taking place, whereas the Hebrew Genesis and indeed the Old Testament itself was only started during the Babylonian Exile in 565 BC and wasn't completed until 400 years later, in 100 BC.

As a result, the Bible version of events is unreliable, contradictory, patchy, selective and deceitful, if not a downright lie, intended to serve the theocratic ambitions of a people with no history of their own. If any work should be relegated to mythological status and discredited, it is the Bible, not the Sumerian and Babylonian histories from which it was copied.

With the discovery of the Sumerian tablets Cain appeared back on the scene again. Rather than being an evil fratricide who had fled into the wilderness as the Jewish scribes had insisted, Cain was shown to be a man of divine substance, a priest-king, sponsored and enthroned by the Gods themselves.

From Cain, or more properly Qayin King of Kish, there descends the lineage of Ham (Chem Zoroaster, tenth archon of Capricorn or Enki). We can say that the Jews invented Noah from the earlier accounts of Ziu Sudra and that Noah's fantasy ancestral line was transposed from that of Cain to that of Seth. We know this because Cain's descendants are virtually identical in name with those of Noah's antecedents going back to Seth, son of Adam. This demonstrates that scribal doctoring has taken place in order to fill the glaring gaps in Jewish tribal genealogy, a genealogy which the Jews prefer to begin with a victorious god – Enlil or EL – rather than the rightful but vanquished heir to the Anunnaki throne.

Flying in the face of written Babylonian accounts the scribes erroneously or purposely attribute the creation of Adam to Enlil (Jehovah) who never created anything, and then set about inventing a tribal history culminating here in the invention of Noah and the misappropriation of Chem, son of Qayin King of Kish, as Ham son of Noah. We know this as a Jewish fabrication because as the hereditary tenth high priest and magus of Capricorn (who is Enki –

the Ram or Sea Goat of the Shimmering Waters) Chem Zoroaster or Ham was naturally a sacred lineal descendant of Enki – the first Zoroaster. In the earlier records Chem married Lilith Luluwa who gave birth to Cush, father of Nimrod the Mighty Hunter. Nimrod sired Boethos, founder of the second dynasty of Egypt. Boethos's son was Raneb, who was Pharaoh in 2800 BC.

As a god of light and fire Enki as Zoroaster developed into the later Roman god Lucifer, the bringer of light. From this manifestation it was a short leap of the early imagination, which promoted Enki – Zoroaster and his descendant grandson Ham or Chem- Zoroaster to the position of Sun God and hereditary high priest of the Sun God respectively.

To this day the Persian Parsees, descendants of the Aryans, the proto-Scythian "king tribe," worship Zoroaster as a god of light and the sacred flame. The later identification of Lucifer with Satan is no coincidence or arbitrary symbolic artifice. Enki was Zoroaster who was Lucifer, and Enki was also the Jewish, and later the Christian Satan.

Ham sired the lineage of Tubal Cain King of Ur whose descendant King Boethos moved to Egypt to become the Pharaoh Hotep Sekhemwy of the second dynasty. His son Raneb founded the cult of Khem (Chem or Ham) the goat-headed sun god, reminiscent of Enki as the Ram or Goat of the shimmering waters, whose centre of worship was situated at Mendes. The Cult of Khem later migrated into Greece where he became Pan, the Horned god of the Witches (Strega). Enki also developed into the all-healing Golden Fleece, a variation of the Holy Grail. In the medieval period this cult evolved and the Solar and Goat symbolism of Khem and Pan was amalgamated with that of the Constantinian symbol of Jesus as the Sol Invicta. Synthesised as the "Black Sun," Jesus was worshipped by witches across France as "Christ, Son Dei," whilst in Scandinavia the witches called this same Horned God "The Antecessor" or ancestor, reinforcing the tradition of Christ and his Anunnaki ancestors as progenitors and forebears, and the fons et origio of druidism, which we know etymologically later developed into witchcraft.

Hotep also introduced the practice of building mortuary temples in the form of pyramids, which closely resembled the Ziggurats of his homeland. The concept of the pyramid tomb appealed to the Egyptians as a manifestation of the Holy Mountain because such was a symbol of life and fertility, and by building pyramid tombs the subsequent pharaohs hoped to replicate its effect and gain life and fertility after death.

With the arrival of Hotep Sekhemwy on the scene we are in the era of the Egyptian King lists and our 16q24.3 genes are introduced by him into the bloodline of the royal dynasties of Egypt, whilst the same genes descended from Hotep's ancestral mother Lilith Luluwa, daughter of the Jewish Satan by Queen Lilith, the Mother of all Demons, Witches, Fairies and Vampires, and established themselves in the divine Satanic lineage of the proto-Scythian Kings.

In my second preliminary summary of the foregoing we have confirmed to a greater extent a historical basis for the supposed Anunnaki myth and have cross-referenced it with the theological legends of the Greeks. Through genetics and archaeology we can assert that the Anunnaki were advanced European settlers in Mesopotamia whose divine descendants established their bloodlines within the Egyptian royal dynasties. Within the same era, more or less, we can also assert that the Anunnaki bequeathed their genetic inheritance to the proto-Scythians whose divine ancestral name means "Princes of Power."

From here we jump a couple of millennia to the year 1361 BC, passing as we do the Age of Prince Ankh-fn-khonsu who first established the Dragon Court in our lineage, to the reign of the Pharaonic Queen Sobekh Nefru. Wife of Pharaoh Amenhemet IV, Sobekh Nefru reigned during the age of the Dragon God Sobekh, the custodian and protector of the blood royal, and it was she who built the labyrinthine temple in his honour at Khayyum, a structure which was later copied by the Minoans of Crete.

Within the temple complex Sobekh Nefru ratified and re-established the Dragon Court of Prince Ankh-fn-Khonsu and the Dragon Court and her ancient genetic, Anunnaki dragon legacy descended to her ancestral daughter Merytaten, granddaughter of Queen Nefertiti.

On the occasion of her marriage to Prince Niall, Lord of the Egyptian, Red Sea region of Capacyront in the High Kingdom, the two ancient dragon legacies fused into one and became all the stronger with their bond. Niall was the son of the Dragon King Fenius Farsaidh of Scythia and Queen Tadukhipa of the Scythian Mittani and, following their marriage Merytaten was bestowed with the Scythian royal title of "Scota," meaning Princess of the Scythians or Scotti.

Thereby she became the Princess of the race of princes. Niall and Merytaten's son was named Geadheal Glas and it was he who was the ancestor of the later Gaels in the land that eventually became known as Albha, and then Scotland.

On the death of Geadheal Glas in 1300 BC, his son Easru succeeded him in Scythia and two distinct lineages emerged, that of the Gaels, and that of the Scythian Scotti. Following the passing of many generations, documented in detail within the ancestral charts herein, Easru's descendant King Easar Brec assumed the throne of Scythia and fought with his forces in the Greek wars. He was named Partholon by his Greek compatriots and his Scythians were called the "Danaan," meaning sons of An.

No doubt because of his defeat and the increasing incursions of the Sarmatians into his Scythian lands, Easar Brec quit the continent and took his remnant and their womenfolk to Eire, where they encountered and defeated their distant Bulgarian cousins, the Scythian Fir Bolg, at the Battle of Moytura. Archaeological evidence supporting the Danaan migration from Greece to

Eire was unearthed in the form of Grecian artifacts discovered, if I remember correctly, in the 19th Century.

During this period in their history Easar Brec's people became known as the Tuadha de Danaan and on his death he was succeeded by his brother's son, the legendary fairy king, the Daghda Mor. In the ensuing generations they were enveloped in an aura of mysticism and were credited with great magical power, an aura that, no doubt, was a legacy of their divine origins as the Titanic, Dragon God-Kings of antiquity. However, this process of mythification was to backfire on them in the centuries to come.

When the Milesian Gaels invaded Ireland and put them to flight they supplanted Danaan culture and overlaid upon it their own traditions and histories. The Danaan were forced to flee to the hills following the Milesian invasion and from then on they seemed to drop out of history, so much so that centuries later their aura of magic and their subsequent obscuration by the invaders led historians and folklorists, unconversant with their history and etymology, to dismiss the Tuadha de Danaan as mythical beings, as no more than ethereal gods of the ancient Gaelic tribes who usurped their real position in history. Their identification as divine beings was quite justified, but not at the expense of their corporality.

Following their victory and subsequent ascendance the Milesians renamed the Tuadha de Danaan and referred to them from then on as the fairy Daouine Sidhe which Irish scholars and historians, who apparently hadn't investigated their etymology or traced their movements, erroneously thought meant "People of the Hills," because of their supposed retreat into the mountainous regions of the island. A more thorough investigation would have revealed that Daouine Sidhe actually meant "People of Scythia."

From being the Scythians of Transylvania they became the Danaan of Greece and eventually reverted to being the people of Scythia. At least their conquerors knew who they were and named them accordingly. As late as the 19th Century, W. B. Yeats records that it had been an abiding tradition in Ireland for centuries that the fairies – the Daouine Sidhe – were the "Children of Lilith" and the sons of the Devil, thereby confirming their Anunnaki parentage and their migration from Transylvania and Central Europe.

At the time of the Milesian incursion the presiding king of the Tuadha de Danaan was an individual named Bruithnigh. His name derives from the arch druidic title Bruidhe, meaning a Seer, a custodian of ancient wisdom and a keeper of the histories of his people.

Suffering defeat, Bruithnigh took his four sons, their wives and his warriors and sailed east from Ulster to the western isles of Albha. In the ensuing years they settled permanently in Caledonia, establishing a kingdom, which stretched south from the Moray Firth to central Scotland and west as far as the Hebrides. In its time it was the largest kingdom in Albha and remained so for centuries, until the succession of King Aed in the 8th Century, by which time it had been known as Pictland, or Pictavia, for generations.

From the Pictish King Lists we know that Bruithnigh's eldest son Cait succeeded him and established the Scythian dynasty we now know through the Romans of the 1st Century as the Pictii, from the habit of painting their torsos with sacred tribal symbols; and the Cruithainn or sons of Cruithne, a Roman misunderstanding of the ancient ancestral name Bruithne or Bruithnigh.

Furthermore the Scythian Pictii retained their identity as the Daouine Sithe of Albha, and this appellation continued to be coterminous with that of the Fairies or Elves for centuries to come. Developing from this name we derive the term Pixie, another name for the fairy, which was arrived at by combining Pict with Sithe to form the word Pictsithe, which was then corrupted to Pixie.

In the 1320's Robert the Bruce had been sponsored by the Church in Scotland who, following the defeat and exile of John Balliol, decided that the Bruce was the only hope Scotland had of freeing itself from the yoke of English occupation and tyranny. Eager to crown him king and persuade the Pope to recognise him as such, and recognise the foundation of a Scottish Kingdom, Bishops Wishart and Pemberton, who had been at the forefront of the previous Scottish rebellions, sent an emissary to the Holy Father to plead their case.

The emissary, Father Bressick, was a legal expert and a gifted orator and with him he took a declaration (named "The Declaration of Arbroath") signed and sealed by the Bishops and Nobles of Scotland, in which it was declared that the Scots (Picts) were Scythians who had migrated from Central Europe and that they were descended from Princess Scota.

As they weren't English, Irish or Welsh, but a unique and separate people, with a unique and separate blood inheritance, they should not have to suffer the oppression of a foreign King.

Such was the veracity of the declaration and the eloquence of Father Bressick that the Pope assented and the Bruce, through many trials and tribulations, was eventually crowned King of the Scots. The descent of the Scotti from Scota, particularly the Picts, rather than being just a myth, was accepted as a historical fact for centuries.

In studying tribal names and migrations, by thoroughly cross-referencing sources and by applying comparative symbolism, etymology and genetic findings to so-called myth and folklore, I am the first person in this particular field to establish the Danaan and their "fairy" descendants as historical figures and place them in their proper context. The same goes for much of the research I have summarised in this essay, research that has been subsequently copied and repeated in the work of other writers and novelists.

If one remains a narrow "specialist" and refuses to adopt the polymathic approach to a subject, one gets nowhere fast. Specialists are vital for the detailed research of their given subjects, but it is only through the synthesis of those subjects that one arrives at any semblance of the wider and more detailed truth. Having said that, whilst I love doing research and synthesis and I believe I'm fairly good at it, when it comes to editing and the construction of a literary narrative, I'm absolutely useless. Consequently if the reader finds this letter muddled and meandering, I hope I might be forgiven.

To continue, King Cait ruled Pictavia in Albha from 650 BC and was succeeded by his son Debeccan. From him the divine, royal lineage of the Scythians descends to our first dynastic ancestor King Vere I in 400 BC From King Vere I there descends the succession of Vere Arch druid princes and Wood Lords to King Vere II. From him the line continues down to King Vere III called "Daich Vetla" in around 300 AD. From a succession of subsequent High Kings we arrive at the Scythian Pictish King Brude Mac Bile who reigned from 693 to 697 AD. His daughter, the Scythian Dragon Princess Pressina or Bruithina married the Gaelic sacral Dragon King Elinus of Strathclyde, also called "Gille Sidhean" or Elf Servant.

From their union arose three sisters, Melusine, Plantina and Meliore. Again through ignorance, laziness or confusion Melusine is dismissed as a legendary figure, a creature of myth.

However, persistence won the day again and subsequent research uncovered the fact that in France Melusine is called Milouziana des Scythes, or Melusine of the Scythians and that she was domiciled in Angiers in Anjou following her assasination of her father in Scotland for breaking Scythian taboos. From her sister Plantina descend the Angevin Counts who, centuries later, adopted the dynastic name Plantagenet in her memory.

Melusine is dismissed as a myth because, like her divine forbears, she was shrouded in magic and mystery, and because she became confused with the two subsequent Melusines, seemingly from other French dynasties, whose histories were at odds with each other, this false dichotomy prompted historians to dismiss her out of hand as a baseless legend, requiring no further investigation. The Veres are in fact descended from all three Melusines.

1. Melusine Vere the First, Scythian Princess of the Picts of Albha, who fled to Angiers and married Rainfroi de Vere, Duke of Angiers and Count of Anjou in 760 AD. It is more than likely that Melusine and Rainfroi were related as cousins from the same descent. From them descends Prince Milo, Duke of Angiers and Count of Anjou after his father. Milo was named after his mother Milo-ziana. In her lifetime Melusine I was called the Dragon Princess and the Fairy daughter of Satan, illustrating the fact that the Dragon Motif of the early Scythians and the Egyptian Sobekh Pharaohs persisted until the medieval period. This Melusine was also said to be a Witch. As a descendant of Scythian Arch druids in Scotland and Eire, this appellation is quite pertinent and appropriate. In Gaelic a Witch is called a Druidhe or Druid.

2. Melusine the Second, daughter of Bouchard Comte de Corbiel and Lady Adelaide de Crecy. Melusine de Corbiel was descended from the Veres via

Ida de Vere of the Ardennes, a descendant of the Vere Counts of Guisnes. This Melusine married Prince Hugh I Comte de Rethul and their son; Badouin de Bourg II married Princess Morfia of Armenia and became King of Jerusalem.

3. Melusine the Third, called Melisende of Lusignan, married Fulke the Fifth, the scion of the Scythian Princess Plantina. Following the transference of the Comite of Anjou and Maine from the House of Vere to their cousins the descendants of Melusine I's sister Plantina, Fulke became Count of Anjou by virtue of his descent and by marriage to this Melusine, he became King of Jerusalem.

Therefore all three Melusines are actually Veres of Scythian Pictish extraction, deriving originally from the same Scottish, Scythian dynasty, and it is from all three Melusines that we are descended as the individual lineages fused.

Milo Duke of Angiers, the son of Melusine Vere I and Rainfroi de Vere, married Bertheld, sister of Charlemagne and daughter of Pepin le Brevis. From this union we inherit one of thirteen lines of descent from the Merovingian sorcerer Kings of the Franks.

To tell their particular story and trace their lineage to the present day, we must again go back in time and recount the Davidic descent of the pharaonic scions of Princess Scota's cousin, the Egyptian Queen Kiya Tasherit, daughter of the Dragon Queen Kiya and the Pharaoh Amenhotep IV.

In 1361 BC Kiya Tasherit married Prince Rama, a descendant of the Sumerian Lord Abram. Rama's Egyptian forebears can be traced back to the Pharaoh Senusret I, son of Pharaoh Amenhemet and husband of Princess Sarai who was the daughter of Queen Tohwait.

In the Old Testament Abram becomes Abraham and Prince Rama is transformed into Ram. No indication of their Sumerian or Egyptian ancestry is given and we are led to believe by default that they were the Jewish descendants of Noah, who in fact never existed. The Jews claimed that, 1500 years before the Old Testament was conceived in Babylon, Abraham was the founder of the Jewish race. This is plain nonsense. The Jews were a tribe of nomadic goat-herders who were living in Mesopotamia generations before Abraham was born. In any event Abraham wasn't a Semitic Jew, he was an Egypto-Sumerian nobleman of the line of Qayin and Pharaoh Raneb. So in fact the Jews have no recorded ancestors of their own and no history beyond the time when in 1960 BC Abraham, who was not a nomad like the Jews but a respected resident of Ur, fled Sumeria during the Akkadian invasions. The Jews were one tribe among many who migrated out of Mesopotamia at the time and Abraham was lumped in with them. That the scribes record him as their leader and their father is arbitrary invention.

With Rama two lines of Anunnaki Dragon Kingship converge and become further enriched on the occasion of his marriage to Kiya Tasherit. Their children become the Egypto-Sumerian forebears of King David.

David eventually marries Bathsheba the Hittite or Hurrian (Aryan) and by so doing injects more Anunnaki blood into his dynasty. Their son Solomon wrote *The Song of Songs* which, having been analyzed, proves to be of Egyptian origin in its construction and content. Studying various sources it is my contention that Solomon adhered to pharaonic tradition and married his sister Sheba, who actually appears in one version of *The Song of Songs* as his sibling. In apocryphal Jewish texts Sheba is described as a Witch, a demoness with the hooves of a goat and legs covered in thick fur. One of her later titles was Sheba – Lilith, which means that she was of Anunnaki descent, not a black African Queen, despite Jewish assertions.

I believe that every effort has been made to denigrate her to posterity (in exactly the same manner as the Jewish Christians later denigrated Mary Magdalene), in order to hide her familial relationship to Solomon, an incestuous relationship which, as his sister-wife, was absolutely anathema to the Jewish scribes and priests of the time.

Back in time Ham, the supposed son of Noah, transgressed ancient Jewish taboo and as a result he was subsequently described as being black, which was intended to be a curse (whilst ridiculously, in some texts, "Noah" is described as being blonde!). In the last millennium all black Africans were said to be descended from Ham the transgressor, the breaker of God's holy law, and because of this Africans were seen as a race damned by God and beyond his care.

As sub-human outcasts therefore, these sons of Ham were only fit to be slaves and, armed with this excuse, good "Christian" Europeans with a clear conscience initiated the Slave Trade, a period of torture, suffering and misery which lasted 300 years and which was justified by a Jewish smear campaign.

In like manner, by describing Sheba-Lilith as black the Jews could assert that, as a daughter of Ham, she was damned and because of her black complexion, her incestuous familial relationship with her brother would be hidden from posterity.

Solomon was one of the prototypes for the Lord of the Rings. It is said that he was a great magician; the master of demons, whom he recruited into his service to build his great temple and whom he controlled by wielding a set of magic rings of power. Solomon is also credited with having a harem of oriental proportions, which he filled with fairy women from the east and princesses who worshipped foreign gods, gods whom the scribes later described as devils.

Not manifesting much piety and being tolerant to the worship of alien deities in his kingdom, Solomon doesn't appear to be particularly Jewish, either by habit or by conviction, which, given his pharaonic and Aryan antecedence, is quite understandable. All in all Solomon was an embarrassing thorn in the side of the Jewish scribes and priests of his time.

From Solomon and Sheba the line of Jewish Kings descends for 500 years until we reach King Zedekiah of Judah in 598 BC With the marriage of Zedekiah's daughter, Princess Tamar, to the Milesian King Eochaid I, the royal Egypto-Sumerian and Aryan dynastic line bifurcates. From Eochaid the royal line devolves to King Erc; the Arch druid of the sacred clan of the Ulidian Fir Bolg in Ulster in 480 AD. From Erc the blood legacy is passed down to King Rhodri Mawr of Gwynedd, North Wales in 800 AD. Rhodri Mawr's descendant Llewelyn the Great sires a daughter Helen and she marries Donald 10th Earl of the Scythian Clan of Mar. Their daughter Isobel marries Robert the Bruce and the line descends through the Kings Of Scots and the Lords Hamilton to the House of Vere of Blackwood to the present day.

Returning to King Zedekiah of Judah, his lineage descends for another 400 years until it eventually rests with Joseph ben Jacob, who married Miriamne or Mary of the Royal House of David.

Joseph is described as a carpenter in the Gospels and this description is derived from a mistranslation of the Greek word "Tekton." In this particular context, and given the corroborative findings of Dr. Barbara Thiering and other eminent persons, Tekton actually translates as a "builder of the temple." Other scholars in this field of research agree upon this translation. They further go on to suggest that his epithet relates to the building of the spiritual temple within the heart of Man. It transpires therefore that Joseph, rather than being a humble carpenter, is in fact a Teacher, a Rabbi and furthermore, he is of the Order of Pharisees and a member of the Sanhedrin. It is quite probable that the Pauline Christians decided to retain Joseph's spurious identity as a humble tradesman in order that their cash cow, their new, invented religion might appeal to the lower classes, the peasants and humble artisans of the Empire, with whom they hoped the proletariat might identify.

His wife, Mary the "Virgin," was a ward of the Sanhedrin and that is how he first encountered her. When she had come of age it was decided by the Priests that Mary should be married off and in order to secure a husband for her, they drew lots. Though something of a shock to his fellow Rabbis, the ageing Joseph won the draw and he was duly betrothed to the young child. We all know the Gospel stories so I won't elaborate too much. Suffice to say that most of the Jesus legend is a later Pauline fabrication designed to appease and appeal to a potentially hostile pagan, Roman audience, at a time when the entire Roman province of Judea was in open revolt against the Empire.

Joseph was a Rabbi and, following the family business Jesus was also a Rabbi. He is addressed as such in the Gospels. Ignorant dogmatists, still believing Jesus was a carpenter's son, explain away the false anomaly by asserting that Jesus' appellation as a Rabbi is simply a general Hebrew term meaning "teacher." However, during his sojourn in Galilee, (a Strict Orthodox district which adhered faithfully and thoroughly to the Torah and Rabbinical Law), Jesus taught regularly in the Synagogue. Unless he actually was a Rabbi in the priestly sense of the word, this would never have been permitted under Jewish Law.

Furthermore, as a Rabbi Jesus would have to have been married. For a man of Jesus' age to be single, especially as a Rabbi, would have been unthinkable. Even if he hadn't been a priest, by remaining celibate he would have been breaking God's Holy Law, which specifically commands that all Jewish men should marry and sire children. For a man of Galilee especially, celibacy would have been tantamount to blasphemy.

During the wedding at Caanah, at the behest of his mother who has noticed that the guests have run out of victuals, Jesus is purported to have turned water into wine. This apparent miracle was in fact a later addition to the story, which was actually borrowed from the Roman Cult of Bacchus, a deity to whom the exact same miracle was attributed. Like so much else in the Gospels concerning Jesus, he is repeatedly identified with the pagan gods in order that his story might appeal to the pagan target audience that Paul and his recidivist cronies intended to fleece. The strange thing is that the pagan rituals and traditions that actually can be attributed to Jesus were rigorously suppressed during the process of the canonisation of the New Testament.

The interesting thing about the wedding at Caanah, and indeed any Jewish wedding of the period, is that the master of the feast, the individual responsible for the continued provision of food and drink during the festivities, was the bridegroom himself. That a guest would have been responsible for such a duty would have been unthinkable. By asking Jesus to replenish the wine, Mary was addressing the Bridegroom.

To develop this, if we peruse the canonical gospels approved by the Pauline Church fathers, we discover that Mary Magdalene was the only female apostle and that it was she with whom Jesus was most intimate. Corroborating this fact we find that in the Nag Hammadi scrolls and in the Gospels of St. Phillip and St. Mary Magdalene, an intimate relationship between the two is variously suggested and that Jesus would often kiss Mary intimately. This relationship caused a great deal of jealousy among the other apostles, especially Peter.

If we remember that Jesus' celibacy would have been socially and theologically unacceptable and we accept Jewish marital tradition concerning the responsibilities of the bridegroom, then Jesus' intimacy with Mary Magdalene is quite understandable. She was his wife.

Jesus' cult wasn't Christian, it was overtly Jewish and was intended by Jesus' family to remain that way. With the arrival of Saul or Paul on the scene, a man who had hounded Jesus' followers to death before faking his Damascus conversion, Jesus' family and followers were naturally hostile and suspicious and refused him entry into their inner circle.

Recruiting Peter the ignorant fisherman who had supposedly betrayed Jesus and like Paul, was therefore not party to the inner teachings, the two of them set sail for Rome, taking what knowledge of Jesus' teachings they had gleaned, and set about inventing a new, bogus religion with Peter as the First Apostle, the chosen Pope of Christ, when in fact it was Prince Elinus of Britain.

Meanwhile, back in Judea, Jesus' family continued with Jesus' authentic teachings and their movement developed into the Nazorite Church, eventually to become the Celtic Church as it migrated into Europe. The Pauline movement, keen to attract a pagan audience and liberate it from its hard earned cash, modified and Romanised the Jesus cult to such an extent that it bore little resemblance at all to its Jewish, Nazorite parent or indeed to the true teachings of Christ.

Naturally a schism occurred and Paul was convinced that in order to be able to present his version of Christianity as the authentic teachings of Jesus, with Peter at its head, he would have to initiate a thoroughgoing campaign of libel, misdirection and misinformation against the Nazorites whose very existence, and whose rightful claim to Christian orthodoxy and authentic apostolic blood succession threatened the future of his newly established cottage industry.

In the Nazorite faith, it has been said, the right to its leadership was hereditary, which meant that only those of Jesus' blood descent could be the Chief Apostles. Knowing that Jesus had been married to Mary Magdalene who had borne him a male heir, Paul and his disciples concentrated their efforts on her.

Mary's title was Miriamne Mar, which translates as "Mary The Great" and "Mary The Teacher," which meant that she was firstly of noble birth, and secondly a central figure in Jesus' cult, responsible for the promulgation of Jesus' teachings and an intimate party to Jesus' inner mystery traditions.

Having asserted Jesus' celibacy in his writings, which meant to Paul's followers that Jesus had no successor, Paul could then convince them that the right to leadership of the Christian Church rested with Peter, whom Paul insisted was the legitimate successor, chosen by Jesus himself. This spurious assertion is manifest in the New Testament where Jesus is supposed to have said "Thou art Peter, and upon this Rock I will build my Church."

The name Peter derives from the Greek and means Rock. Rendered in the masculine gender Rock is Petros. So far so good. The lie is advanced.

However, what Jesus actually said was "Thou art Petra and upon this Rock I will build my Church." Jesus spoke in the feminine gender and rendered the word Rock as Petra. The Pauline usurpers overlooked this one mistake and as a result of this oversight, the feminine Petra is still in the Bible to this day.

So Jesus was actually addressing his remark to a woman, not a man. The only female disciple amongst the twelve was Mary Magdalene; Mary the Noble, Mary the Teacher. Upon her and her offspring Jesus would found his Church and for those descendants to have a legitimate right to his succession, they would have to be of his blood and antecedence.

To further defuse the threat that Mary posed, great efforts were made to present her in the worst possible light. In certain texts Mary is described as a priestess of the Babylonian Goddess Ishter – the Roman Venus – whose cult included sacred Venal rituals. The Pauline Church jumped on this and labeled her a common whore, a prostitute riddled with demons, the worst kind of sinner.

Not only did the Roman Church want to negate the threat she and her children posed to the legitimacy of the papal succession of Paul's invented orthodoxy, they also wanted to marginalise her by stripping her of her central role as a teacher of the mysteries, thereby presenting her involvement in Jesus' movement as being no more than incidental.

The task was made all the easier by public opinion. In a misogynistic, patriarchal society, the idea that a mere woman might be a religious teacher, a rabbi, was completely unthinkable and was strictly forbidden under Jewish Law. Furthermore in Roman society women were second-class citizens, the chattels of their men folk who kept them firmly in the background. To convince their Roman audience that Mary was of no importance at all was therefore very easy.

Not only was she vilified and written out of Christian Gospel history, just for good measure she becomes the hate target of the Revelations of St. John wherein, as a Babylonian priestess, and in repeating the notion that she was a common prostitute, Mary takes centre stage as The Whore of Babylon from whose chalice pour all the abominations of the world.

Riding a Dragon (an appropriate symbol!) she holds in her arms her offspring, whom St. John claims is the Anti-Christ of the latter days. Not only is she damned for posterity, but also her child – the legitimate apostolic successor of his father Jesus – is cast in the role as the enemy of God and the Roman Church, the brood of Satan himself.

As far as the Roman Church is concerned, the vilification and damnation of Mary and her royal child is complete and they can rest in the sure knowledge that their false Church, its spurious, fraudulent Pope and its right to decide apostolic succession is assured, leaving them with the most important task of their ministry – acquiring as much power, and raking in as much wealth as they possibly can.

This Papal fraud has been accepted for 1700 years, during which time the Church destroyed as many dissenting texts as it could find – thereby creating the Dark Ages – it maimed, tortured, raped and murdered thousands, if not millions of innocent people who opposed its orthodoxy and hegemony during the Inquisition. Its anti-Jewish policies and persecutions directly resulted in the Holocaust of the Second World War, after which it provided escapes routes for the Nazi death camp guards, SS Officers and other assorted war criminals, and through the centuries and up to this present day it has amassed literally trillions of dollars in revenue and property. The list of the Church's crimes is endless. Truly Christianity is the most evil religion in history.

However, all in the garden is not rosy. Apocryphal texts declare that Mary Magdalene's cousin was Herod Agrippa whose family had a palace in southern Gaul.

The texts go on to relate that, following Jesus' death, Mary his wife, Mary his mother and Mary his sister set sail for Gaul, landed in Marseilles and found refuge in Herod's palace. The arrival of the three Marys in Gaul was celebrated in religious festivals up until quite recently. During the Dark Ages and up until the medieval period the fact that Magdalene brought her son with her was also common knowledge. Early noble families claimed that Jesus' son grew up in Gaul, married and sired children whose descendants married into the Frankish Royal Line and produced the Dynasty of the Merovingian Kings. Apparently, in his old age, Mary's son returned to Judea, taking the remains of his deceased mother with him.

Having studied the evidence closely and thoroughly, eminent historians and Jewish scholars, amongst them Dr. James Tabor and Dr. Barabara Thiering, all concur that Jesus was married and had children. So-called "apocryphal" texts support this view and in balance the weight of evidence in support of this assertion far outweighs the scant, unsupported and insubstantial arguments in favour of Jesus' celibacy promoted and advanced by the orthodox Church. An organisation which in root and branch is lying, deceitful, corrupt, fraudulent and riddled with an overpowering lust for money and power which it has misappropriated in a manner which manifests a total lack of concern for the cost to the individual or to society.

Do we trust the findings of scholars whose desire is to present society with as accurate a picture of history as they possibly can. Or do we believe an organisation, which we know only too well, has deceived and oppressed human society for 1700 years in the pursuit of its own greed and megalomania?

The Church might believe they have the whole argument stitched up and that any theory, which challenges the Orthodox view, can be dismissed as speculative, heretical or blasphemous. However they do have a problem.

In 1980 a team of archaeologists were working in the Talpiyot suburb of Jerusalem, a district only two miles removed from the traditional site of Golgotha, where Jesus was supposedly crucified. During the dig they uncovered the entrance to a family tomb. Having cleared the rubble they entered and inside they discovered a number of ossiaries (ten in all), sizeable boxes fashioned from alabaster, which are intended to contain the bones of the deceased in their final resting place.

Alabaster is the stone sacred to the Egyptian God Amun – father of all the Pharaohs – and was used by them, after the age of the pyramids, to build their mortuary temples. This practice persisted up until the time of Alexander the Great. Its use in fashioning the ossiaries of Jesus and Miriamne Mara is deliberate and significant.

They removed the ossiaries and took them to their laboratory for further examination. A closer study revealed that their design dated them to the 1st century and that the patina on the ossiaries matched the date of the design. Further inspection resulted in the discovery of individual engravings on the boxes, each engrained with a patina, which matched the 1st century date in which the boxes were originally fashioned. Naturally this meant that they had been marked immediately after they had been made. After copying and translating the inscriptions they confirmed the following.

Translation

Ossiary 1 contained a set of bones and was inscribed "Joseph ben Jacob."

Ossiary 2 contained a set of bones and was inscribed "Jesus ben Joseph."

Ossiary 3 contained a set of bones and was inscribed "Joshua ben Jesus."

Ossiary 4 contained a set of bones and was inscribed "Miriamne Mara." (Literally, "Lady Mary/Marion" – cf. Lady Marion in the histories of Robon Hood, scion of Jesus Christ.)

Genetic tests carried out on the remains from ossiary 2 and ossiary 4 confirmed that they were not related to the same mother and, given Jewish burial practice, they concurred that Miriamne Mara would not have been interred in the family tomb unless she had been related to one of the other occupants which, in this case could only have been by marriage. Statisticians were consulted and they constructed a probability model to determine the liklihood of a co-incidence where another family with exactly the same names could have been contemporary with those discovered in the tomb.

Though the names were well known in Judaea at the time, one was quite rare and given the specific grouping of these individual's names together, the statistical likelihood that they were any other than Jesus's wife and family was dismissed. A coincidence seemed virtually impossible.

Scholars were satisfied that the remains interred within the tomb were indeed those of Christ, Mary Magdalene, their son Joshua and Jesus's father Joseph. This is now accepted as fact and confirms without question all the so-called apocryphal tales concerning Jesus's marriage to Mary, the existence of a male heir, and that heir's descent to the Merovingian Dynasty in Gaul.

The only reason we find this fact incredible today is because such overwhelming scientific evidence still stands in clear contradiction to what we have been spoon fed for 1700 years, an orthodox Catholic lie which has become ingrained into our racial consciousness. It isn't so incredible if we remember that Jesus emerged as only a minor provincial celebrity in what was, after all, a turbulent but insignificant backwater of the Roman Empire.

If it hadn't been for Paul's greed and ambition, and his rejection by Jesus's family, Paul would not have travelled to Rome in the hope of selling his profitable new cult to the Gentiles. As a consequence Jesus, his family and his Church would still be an insignificant, anomalous Jewish cult which, today, would have been largely forgotten. Because of this any subsequent claim to a descent from Jesus now would present no problems whatsoever and would probably be met with a shrug of the shoulders.

After Peter and Paul's death the Christian cult in the Empire struggled for its ascendancy in the face of hostile opposition from the State and other more well established pagan theologies. For generations the so-called Christians were no more than cat food, that is until the 4th century when the cult had finally found a foothold and gained in popularity to the point where the Emperor Constantine stepped in.

A tempting political opportunity presented itself, the opportunity to unite the various factions of the Empire and prevent dissension and unrest from the Christians. The only stumbling block however, was the fact that within early Christianity there were several doctrines all vying for supremacy. To neutralise their threat they had to be unified.

These factions fell loosely into two categories. On the one hand there were those who believed Paul's doctrine of the divinity of Jesus, and on the other there were those who believed that he was simply a human prophet and healer. Seeing the potential, future political profit in adopting Christianity as a State cult, Constantine determined to call a halt to the squabbling and in-fighting by ordering the heads of the various factions to meet at Nicaea in 325 AD and iron out their differences.

The bishops met and a ballot was called in which the two basic doctrines would be voted on. Was Jesus to be promoted as the divine Son of God, or was he to be promoted as a mortal Teacher and Healer? The votes were evenly split and Jesus' future hung in the balance.

The casting vote, which would confirm Jesus as the Son of God, lay with Bishop Arius who was firmly opposed to Christ's divinity. The old and frail Arius decided to vote according to his conscience and his convictions. As soon as he had done so, Bishop Nicholas of Myra, feared as a psychotic bully in his own lifetime, viciously beat the ageing Arius until he changed his mind and voted the way Myra wanted him to. In summary, the only reason we think of Christ as the Son of God now is because of an inexcusable act of violence against an old man who was too weak to defend himself.

Under Bishop Usebius and at the behest of Constantine the Gospels were canonised and those thought to be heretical were discarded, including that of St. Phillip, which confirmed the intimate relationship between Jesus and Mary. Christ was promoted as the Son of God with Constantine's approval and a unified church, with an orthodox dogma, was brought into the imperial fold.

During Constantine's reign copies of the approved Gospels were distributed across the Empire, persecution ceased, Christian heresy was met with stringent penalties and Christians and pagans co-existed side by side until the succession of the Emperor Theodosius.

Under him paganism was outlawed and at his order Christians put pagans to the sword, turning the persecuted into the persecutors. This is the basic outline of events that converted Christianity from a dissenting minor cult into a corrupt world power within the space of a couple of generations.

If the vote had gone the other way and Jesus was recognised for what he truly was, a minor mortal prophet and healer from an obscure dynasty in a blighted backwater of the empire, then claiming descent from him would not be met with the orthodox incredulity and outrage, or the secular disbelief that it does today.

Nevertheless, archaeological corroboration of Jesus' marriage and the existence of his heirs are facts supported by scientific evidence that is inescapable, regardless of our religious brainwashing and indoctrination. With this in mind I commend to you our 13 Merovingian descents from Christ and the ancient House of David.

The Merovingian dynasty began with King Meroveus and Princess Merira in 460 AD. Merira's lineage descended from Joshua, the son of Jesus and Mary, and Joshua was identified at the time as the "quinotaur," the Original Dragon from Beyond the Sea, identifiable with both Lileth and Enki as the male and female Leviathans.

Merira marries Meroveus, the founder of the Merovingian dynasty. The name Meroveus, according to some religious commentators, may be subdivided into Mer(o) + Veus; or Mer(o) + Vee. These Biblical scholars translate these components as Mer = Sea, and Vee = Vere. They further state that the noun Vere may be translated as Vere = Werewolf; and Vere = Dragon. From this we derive Merovee = Sea Dragon (Leviathan), and Merovee = Wolf from across the Seas. The Tarnawa-Krupa name is likewise exactly rendered and translated.

Interestingly, as I have mentioned in *The Dragon Legacy*, the Wolf (Romania = Stregoi; Italy = Strega: Witch) and the Dragon are initiatory degrees within Mithraism (Mithras is identified with Jesus) and grades of Vampirism in the Carpathians.

The Merovingian descent from Christ had, by this time, become popular common knowledge and again it posed a threat to the power and authority of the Church. To neutralise this threat they induced the Mayors of the Palace, themselves scions of Meroveus, to kidnap and incarcerate the Merovingian King Clovis. Having achieved this they then put Clovis to death and, as a reward for their loyal service to the Church, they were duly installed as the puppet kings of the Franks.

This Christianised lineage descended through Charles Martel and Pepin Brevis to Charlemagne in 780 AD. Here the lines of Vere Merovingian descent divide between Bertheld, daughter of King Pepin Brevis, who married Prince Milo I de Vere of Angiers, and Charlemagne. From Charlemagne the Merovingian bloodline devolves through Emperor Louis I and Princess Judith of Bavaria, to St Ida of Ardennes, circa 1050 AD. St. Ida married Eustace de Vere Comte de Boulogne and they had a daughter, Ida de Vere.

Ida married Badouin de Bourg, Comte de Rethul and the Merovingian bloodline continues down to Fulke V of Anjou, King of Jerusalem. Here the Vere descent merges with that of Melusine I's sister Plantina. From Fulke's descendant Geoffrey Platagenet the Angevin Kings of England emerge and from them the line descends, through the Lords Hamilton, to the House of Vere in Blackwood. From Milo de Vere I the Merovingian bloodline also descends to Ralph de Vere and the Veres of Blackwood. Along the way 11 other Merovingian descents emerge from these lines, along with 13 Imperial European descents dating from the time of Julius Caesar.

From my studies I have found that myth and legend, rather than being just fantasy, are usually grounded in factual persons and events, and that they and their symbolism can endure for millennia, migrating virtually intact from one culture to another. I would therefore commend my research and the resulting genealogical tables as the official family history of the House of Vere. A House quite rightly steeped in ancient magic, myth and legend and all the better for it. Indeed, demonstrated by the descents I have researched and uncovered, and attested to by eminent scholars of Law and History, the House of Vere emerge as the most ancient, and the senior Imperial and Royal family in Eurasia.

The Dragon Cede, which includes the descents of our senior branches has had, by necessity, to be somewhat provocative. Apparently this sells books, according to my publisher and he took the project on with the understanding that I should present a new, more sensational slant on the subjects I have covered. Because of this I have retained the name "Satan" as one of our first ancestors and one of Jesus' forebears. Duly this should prove provocative enough and, as I want to get the House of Vere, its ancient history and its Imperial and Royal status as widely recognised and accepted as possible, which means selling as many books as possible, I have no choice but to concur with my publisher.

In any event, as you know, being somewhat anarchic and disliking and distrusting those who have assumed self-appointed positions of authority, I have a mischievous sense of humour and the prospect of ruffling the feathers of a few bigoted religious fanatics has for me a certain appeal.

These sorts of people have convinced themselves that they have cornered the market in absolute truth and, in times past, have adopted any method at their disposal to convince others that they are the custodians of incontrovertible fact. The methods they have used, and the results they have achieved have been horrific, and socially, politically and spiritually disastrous.

Any of us with even only a modicum of understanding realises that we never stop learning and that truth is never a static concept and, unlike religious dogmatists and bigots, we go on learning and changing until the day we end up in the grave. In life, learning only ceases when we succumb to the indolence of certain belief, and knowledge then becomes a Sacred Cow. As an iconoclast I have only one use for Sacred Cows: Sacred Burgers in a Bun with Garlic Mayonnaise.

In promoting their ignorant, unresearched dogmas and forcing them on others, their ridiculous lies become legitimate targets for those of us who have taken the trouble to delve deeper for the truth. As such, Satan stays in my texts and genealogical tables and if it upsets the precious sensibilities of the mindless religious conformists who cling to their orthodoxy, in their cowardly desperation for spiritual certainty and psychological comfort in a transient and frightening world, then to my mind I have done a good day's work.

"Beliefs" regarding God and spirituality create religions, and religions create division, fear and violence within the individual and consequently within society as a whole. Religion is a handy facade for the power and money hungry to conceal themselves behind, and a crutch for the spiritually lazy, the weak minded and the unregenerate. Religions happen when people don't get the point of the message – which is nearly always – and blindly worship the message and the messenger, instead of grasping the gnosis – the wisdom – inherent within the words that the message conveys. If you talk to God... you're religious. If God talks to you... you're psychotic.

"Religion is an opiate of the masses," said Karl Marx. Too true.

Although I support and follow the teachings of Christ, I abhor and detest the orthodoxy of Christianity and the blind dogma of any religion. Adherence to such results in fear and misery and destroys any opportunity of a direct, transcendent interaction or relationship with the Creator, and without that there is no chance for any revolutionary transformation within the individual wherein, as Jesus said, "The Laws of God will be written in the hearts of men with tongues of fire." Direct experience of that which we label "God" - the vastness, the power, and the supreme balance of eternal life – produces a radical and permanent readjustment of the individual's perception of himself and his position and responsibilities within the universe.

At such a point the radical change at the very heart of the individual produces an abiding, fundamental sense of peace, equilibrium, serenity and grace. A heightened state of consciousness and perception manifests itself in daily life by the outworking of love and compassion, charity, empathy, justice and nobility of spirit.

This is what Jesus meant by Salvation, the condition where man is freed from the externally imposed social laws or the doctrines of religion written "On Tablets of Stone" and reborn into a condition where universal law is indivisibly and irreversibly incorporated into his very nature, becoming thereby "written on his heart with tongues of fire."

For this transformation to take place and for the individual to become spiritually and psychologically free, the mind must first become sensitive, able to evolve, willing to remain open to new knowledge and adaptable to change.

This can only be accomplished when neurotic, psychological adherence to the rigidity of religious conditioning and the inflexible pettiness of dogma, tradition and belief fall away and the mind becomes still, free from the puerile religious fears which are underpinned by the very religious orthodoxy which imprisons us in its web of deceit.

Promises of salvation and peace through blind adherence to doctrine and the totally unnecessary intercession of a self-appointed priesthood are absolute lies, promulgated by those whose main motivation is the greed for money and political power, and the establishment of mass social control through religious fear.

As "Dragons," those with "Clear Sight," being the natural capacity for spiritual profundity at a genetic level, the Veres are, I believe, gifted with an ancient, innate, inherited capability for transcendent vision and wisdom, gifts which in times past enabled them to be great God-Kings and Priest-Princes, Arch druids, Seers and Healers.

Because of this genetic inheritance, to a greater or lesser extent, all of us have experienced a spiritual component in our lives, as have many Veres through the generations, and I for one have been a party to profound psychological states and spiritual transformations throughout my life, and all this without the mind-numbing, soul destroying influence of religion or the misinformed, ignorant mutterings of some malignant, grubby little priesthood.

It is my belief that this is a fundamental genetic component of our Dragon Legacy and therefore, as the children of the Gods and the scions of the priest-kings of our forebears, the Veres today are their own priests and the well-spring, the fons et origio of the very concept of divinity and of spiritual truths whose nascence emerged long before primitive human history was first recorded.

Chapter One

General Notes

Over a 15 year period I have submitted numerous documents to the British Government's Home Office and various other Government agencies and departments. As a result of these correspondences, first acknowledged in 1994, up to the present, the following now obtains:

1. I am officially recognised by the British Government's Home Office Identity Services and numerous others as an Imperial and Royal Prince and I am permitted to use the title HI&RH Prince Nicholas de Vere von Drakenberg KGC (Knight Grand Cross), KCD (Knight of the Plantagenet Clan Donnachaid).

2. I am acknowledged by the British Government as the Sovereign Prince of Drakenberg: An Incorporeal Sovereign Nation State of Peoples. I hold a passport which includes my royal and diplomatic ambassadorial titles.

3. My Fons Honorum – the right to bestow arms and title – is also recognised by the Government, for which I have documentary evidence.

4. My right to the Sovereignty of Societas Draconis (Sarkany Rend): The Imperial and Royal Dragon Court and Order, which includes the Order of the Knights Templars of Scotland, and which is recognised and declared as the Sovereign family Court and Order of the House of Vere, is also officially acknowledged by the British Government. Right to membership of this body is automatically open to all of the House of Vere only.

5. Amongst the documentation submitted by me during this 15 year period was the descent of the House of Vere from Prince Milo de Vere, Duke of Angiers. As a result of this, my Imperial and Royal status now applies to the whole House of Vere and all family members bearing the Vere or Weir name. The House of Vere is consequently restored to its former Imperial and Royal status, as the oldest Royal Family in written history.

Chapter Two

General Notes on the Migration of Theological Symbolism

In the earliest Sumerian pantheon Enki (Ea/Aya) is the Lord of the Earth and Waters, he is the God of fertility symbolised by the fecund Ram of the Shimmering Waters.

He is the creator of the first dynasty of the fairy God-Kings. As the Roman "Lord of Mars," Enki is also the God of wisdom and magic, qualities that have been attributed to the Elven Kings for millennia. As the first Zoroaster: Enki is also the God of Light. As a God of wisdom and magic Enki appears in the Babylonian pantheon up to the 7th Century BC, whilst his brother El or Enlil, as the Sumerian Lord of the Air and Earth, is portrayed as the Storm God.

With the descent of the dynastic line of Cain, King of Kish to Raneb, Sumerian Pharaoh of the 2nd dynasty of Egypt, Enki as the Ram of fertility becomes the Ram God Amun, who is both father of the Egyptian Gods, and the father of the Pharaohs; the God-kings. His sacred stone is Alabaster. Amun evolves into Amon-Ra and is accredited with the solar attributes of a God of Light, like Enki. The Ram symbolism attributed to Enki and Amun as one and the same God survives until millennia later when Moses – Prince of Egypt – is portrayed with the horns of the Ram God.

In Judea the Jews continue the association with the ritual killing of the young Ram at Passover, which represents an echo of a time when the Ram – as Enki – represented the sacrificial God-King. This representation was continued with Christ, when he, as the male "Lamb of God" – the young Ram, was the replica of the earlier pagan sacrificial God.

From Sumeria the symbol of the Ram God Enki migrated with our ancient family to the Egyptians and Babylonians and from thence to Greece and Rome. In Greek lore Enki becomes the Golden Fleece, which, like Christ, Odin and other mystery Gods, is hung from a Tree. The Golden Fleece, like Enki, is attributed with healing qualities and magical powers.

The early association with the tree or cross derives from the late Genesis account of Enki as Satan who was depicted as hanging from the Tree of Knowledge. This symbol also appears later on in the Jewish, Kabalistic "Tree of Life" diagram, where the serpent (Enki) descends head first from the Sphere of Kether – the realm of his father An – as the lightning bolt of divine inspiration, and comes to rest below in the Sphere of Malkuth; the realm of Man.

40

The Kabalistic symbol evolved partly from the image of the Ram-horned Moses around whose staff was entwined the brazen serpent; a symbol of magic and healing, later echoed in the sacrifice of Christ who became the serpent on the Cross and who, having done so, like Odin descended into the otherworld.

In Rome Enki the Ram Lord of Mars, god of wisdom and magic, becomes Ares the Ram, the god of war and the patron of magicians. This identification can also be found again in the Kabalistic Tree of Life where the Sphere of Geburah represents martial force and magic.

The Anunnaki symbol of Enki as both the Ram and the sea-goat Capricorn or Leviathan repeat themselves throughout ancient history and up until the modern era. In their original form these symbols may be understood as being ancient dynastic, totemic family badges and as such their migration through various cultures and histories, with all their iconographic, magical and divine attributes remaining intact, can be appreciated as the migration of our ancient family from Neolithic Central Europe to Sumeria, and from there to Egypt, Israel, Persia, Greece and Rome during the classical period; and on to Western and Northern Europe up until the present era.

Chapter Three

Caveat Lector

By Michael Hunter

Man's presence on Earth has been characterised by an astonishing inability to achieve what he claims to desire in terms of comfortable, anxiety-free and profitable co-existence with his fellows and with his host planet, in spite of appearing to have at his disposal the means to attain that paradisiacal state. Scholarly ability and advanced education are not required to see that our species has had, for several millennia, the supposed benefit of lessons of history from which to identify past errors and recurring stumbling blocks. Yet what all history demonstrates is that humans have tended, for countless years, to reprise performances from a catalogue of reprehensible and calamitous stupidities, and to do so in ways that are altered and modified only insofar as the technology has evolved to increase the permutations possible in their perpetration.

This tragic tale of execrable excesses might lead the sensitive, intelligent and attentive observer to the conclusion that man has never regarded his past thoughtfully, nor with comprehension; yet many of the instigators of these ambitious and frequently startling catastrophes are self-evidently intelligent and minutely attentive observers of history. They are, often, educated individuals with insight, well-documented wisdom, with bright visionary vigour. Knowing this, and aware that indeed lesser humans could never have initiated those momentous and revolutionary social and political upheavals, one is inclined to the thought that history is not only less useful than widely claimed, but in fact completely useless, a mere intellectual indulgence; and if that should prove a little hard to acknowledge, then maybe one would prefer that history as presented (and received) is possibly faulty in either content or form, and needs to be radically overhauled as a discipline before it might furnish meaningful value.

In truth, of course, these latter observations as to the supposedly flawed nature of history make no real sense, for history has been expressed in as many different forms as there are, or have been, languages, carved, written and oral; and the content of any historical presentation known must, of necessity, be what it has always been, which is everything that was noticed or observed or recorded. It is in "everything" that humans are interested, and their history-worthy undertakings and failures are concerned with everything, particularly where that definition is understood to represent a resource, or a thing which might become a resource, and most things have. As is well known, the woeful efforts of humans to subjugate, control or annihilate each other frequently focus on grounds which do not, in any material sense, exist at all, for ideological and religious "struggles" are about words and about what words mean; they purport to be trials only of ideas and beliefs. The more cynical (or clear-seeing) among us may recognize that the undeclared objective of any of these acts of frequently gargantuan and always, ultimately, doomed idiocy is control of a material resource, be that in the form of land, minerals, seafood or slave labour. But people do not like to think of themselves as materially acquisitive, they prefer to think of themselves as something higher.

And it is this characteristic of humans which supplies a first clue to explain the consistent failure of history – which, after all, can be only what it is – to teach the lessons man claims to need for his self-improvement. Regrettably, man already believes himself to be much improved, notwithstanding the evidence to the contrary – because we are technologically more developed; because we are mentally more diversified through accumulated human experience and interbreeding; because, with the help of the physical sciences, we are capable of more detailed knowledge of our material environment and of the spaces beyond it. In reality, however, mankind has achieved but scant understanding of himself, appearing to consider himself as essentially generous, altruistic, "spiritual" (whatever that means), usefully creative, non-violent, sympathetically attuned to attend to the well-being of his environment and all its inhabitants.

Bollocks.

Man, like every other organism, is lazy and self-serving. Like every other organism, man is equipped with the same set of responses to any other organism consciously encountered: he assesses said organism for its suitability as a breeding partner; for the threat that it represents to him, either as predator or as rival for finite resources; for its appropriateness as edible prey or as instrument for obtaining edible prey. Horrible, isn't it? We would so like to think that even in our boiled-down essence we are more than this, but we are not, and anything else that we believe of ourselves is the result of aeons of conditioning by those whose interests have been served by our imagining ourselves otherwise, those who would direct us for their benefit, never ours.

If we could learn to accept those fundamental truths about our unadorned selves – and most of us are almost incapable, psychologically, emotionally, even intellectually of so doing – and to understand that parental and altruistic reflexes, which we value highly, are learned strategies which, in concert with the already identified instincts, do no more than preserve ourselves, then we might begin to perceive in meaningful perspective what the true value of our many other loudly-trumpeted attributes really is, for they are largely imagined, and evaporate almost instantaneously in the intense immediacy of serious struggle for survival once conditions shift to frantic anarchy or war.

If that should seem to be a rather excessive judgment, then it must be remembered that (as history teaches us!) when the mob is aroused, every member of it can and will do everything of which he truly believed himself incapable, and do it to the erstwhile friend with whom, a moment previously, he had been debating philosophy and literature over a cup of coffee and game of chess. A few individuals, naturally, do not become members of mobs at these moments: they are the people who have reflected, have realized that they could be base, unthinking, self-serving and stupid, whose realization of that has, paradoxically, helped them to rise above the unattractive base line of the average human, at least so far as self-knowledge is concerned: they have preserved the capacity to think and to perceive clearly, and thus to act "rightly."

Alas for them, they refuse to become members of a mob, and the mob, not wanting to hear sober reason, which threatens the life-affirming, sexually-charged passion of its sudden existence, dismembers them with sharp implements to still their protests.

What this demonstrably recurring truth highlights is that most people do not think clearly (if at all: which is the self-preservation instinct again) during these flashpoints of polarization; and that those who do are consistently incapable of preventing or reversing the folly. Both groups contribute if not willfully then by dint of willful negligence to disastrous social upheavals. A very small group of excessively greedy, grossly insensitive, insanely domineering inadequates displays acutely developed understanding at these moments, largely because they have engineered them, and will profit by them. Their excesses achieve early success (being intelligently timed and orchestrated), leading to the hubris resulting from the unchallenged certainty of their "rightness," and so begins the next phase of a population's history, where everything is changed to the extent that it is exactly the same, only worse.

History's lessons, then, are not likely to result in improved behaviour in societies. The only individuals that make positive, informed decisions based on them are exactly those who ought not to. Perhaps that is the human condition: not so much that populations need these upheavals and bloody culls, but that they will, for who knows what reason, demand them: thousands of years of accounts suggest so.

Possibly, then, in defence of the pursuit of historical endeavour, might it not be true that without its lessons the scale and frequency of these events could be worse? Those who succeed in retaining a clear view of past and present, who have learned from their study of what is, after all, a kind of psychology-of–the-masses, are almost certainly responsible for mitigating the intensity of impact of undesirable events. Having done so, however, they are typically terminally silenced by the democratically insane majority....

If one agrees on the desirability of making history's lessons available for the sensible use of the wise minority, one is yet faced with the conundrum that it is awash with contradictory and improbable stories, so how may one determine which accounts to trust? One of the abiding joys of historical study is also one of its chief frustrations, namely that most of the details of the interesting events are either unrecorded, or else deliberately misrepresented to serve some ulterior and usually questionable motive. As a general rule, most people are unaware of "history being made," as they are busy getting on with their lives, and trying to arrange today so that it will pretty much resemble yesterday: that is what most people want, for they are naturally indolent, and it is easier that way. So they have not recorded history happening, because they did not notice it. Those who did had an agenda, usually to do with currying favour with the expected victors.

Further, retrospective analysis of both the main event and the subsidiary details is inevitably prejudiced by the ever-changing mutations of the languages used to record events, and indeed most societies noted and passed on their major formative episodes within the framework of oral traditions, some of which were in rhyme or song-form, a few even in dance and mime, all of which must necessarily be compromised in the transition to the statically verbalised written medium, itself further compromised by inevitable errors of typography and by the limits of the available contemporary lexicon.

Thus subsequent historians are enfranchised to manufacture accounts that may, just possibly, bear some relation to the events they nominate for depiction. Their motives range from a desire for self-aggrandisement through academic recognition (natural enough); to obsequiousness (self-preservation); to a desire for profit (satisfaction of the need to secure material resource); to a wish to learn (in order to be equipped with the knowledge of self and others, which helps to satisfy the other needs); to a desire to instruct others.... Why would an historian want, as his primary objective, to instruct others? One should reflect carefully before suggesting any motive as crass as altruism: the likelihood is that this aim is designed to satisfy, however indirectly, one or more of the previous ones. In any case, historians must necessarily be constantly essaying either a best (i.e. most plausible) guess, or they harbour an agenda which is served and strengthened by structured confabulation, in which case they are trying to achieve what they can get away with.

A thankfully not uncommon agenda, the same pursued by the author of this work, is relatively harmless. After two decades of working with Nicholas de Vere I can confidently assert that he is as mad as a box of frogs, and has largely escaped formal education, so has not been taught the acceptable and expected things to say. He has so ordered his life that he has outgrown passion and greed, but, like many, he wants to tell a story that makes sense. Clearly he is still a prey to vanity, for it is his own story that he wants to discover, and his wanton love of ease drives him to create a narrative which shall not unduly tire his sensibilities by stretching his credulity too far. All this is commendable, for it lacks affectation, hiding none of its – or his – intentions, and is likely to be about as trustworthy as history ever gets.

The harmless agenda pursued by de Vere and by quite a few others over time, driven by a straightforward curiosity as much as by anything else, is that which tries to construct the narrative so that both its form and its content achieve an harmonious fluidity, believing that truth is revealed by beauty, or by poetic fluency. Robert Pirsig, in *Zen and the Art of Motorcycle Maintenance*, managed to convey (to those able to negotiate his tangentially wandering and labyrinthine prose) that what he called "quality" (his catch-all word to denote truth, high art and beauty) is recognised even by those who are not schooled in its appreciation and by those who do not desire it. Even the ignorant and uneducated, he says, know when something possesses or represents genuine "quality," for when a thing is right, it looks right. As we know, this perception will not prevent any of us from adorning our walls and mantelpieces with kitsch, and our reasons for our choices are as varied as our numbers, but this tendency does not generally eclipse our ability to be discerning – thus truthful content is self-evident because it assumes "truthful" form.

The admittedly unverifiable and rather vaguely sketched claims of the preceding paragraphs, exposed as they are in this short essay to determined and hostile analysis, will sound like a plea to accept an historical narrative as authentic merely because it has a true-seeming form, or because it reads well and pleasingly, but at any remove from events it is arguable whether any other criterion might be more reliably applied. (I apply this criterion, therefore, on the grounds that it seems more plausible than any other, but then I am no scholar, nor even an historian.) This leads to the matter of differential definition of the terms "truth" and "authenticity." That famous collection of folklore or history of the distant past of Wales, *The Mabinogion*, is characterised by curious anomalies, including the birth of a son before his father, and a character who slips out of his current space/time continuum in order to be somewhere – and somewhen – else (in the search for wisdom). For all its strangeness, it nevertheless has, if squinted at from a certain open-hearted and trusting perspective, a kind of truth. But it can be neither factually accurate nor authentic, and it is compromised yet more by virtue of having been written down by interested clerics who lacked complete comprehension of the orally-given form, and who themselves laboured under the externally imposed restrictions and contradictions of their religious conditioning – that same conditioning which, jealous of knowledge outside of itself, strove to ensure that its captive clerics were the only ones with access to the means of capturing and reproducing stories in the written word. It was this conditioning which rendered the stories in a relatively permanent state of perceptual confusion by dint of its inherent – and intended – contradictions.

But *The Mabinogion*, like many old stories, has aesthetic beauty, in which may be discerned the certainty of its message, and the relevance and truth for the times and cultures that spawned it.

The best, then, that history can hope to yield is a degree of knowledge about who we are, by showing us what we have been, where we might have come from: our genetically-inherited memories are vague and disconnected (or in the case of those romantics who believe themselves re-incarnations of their favourite historical characters, wildly inaccurate), but can be contextualised if we are apprised of some of the circumstances of their acquisition. This partial but enhanced self-knowledge can help to place current emotions and reflexes into a meaningful perspective for those who wish to understand, and who strive to live rightly through clarity of vision. Effectively, this means that the insights revealed can help us to work out how to make choices without reference to externally applied rules while nevertheless disclosing the origins of our rules, and which of them are genuinely needed. It is upon these clear seers that the larger body of society unwittingly depends to limit its potentially disastrous extremes of reactive behaviour, for the thoughtful historian can provide the majority with a "narrative of desirability," to which at least some elements of the potential mob might be tempted to respond. Not that this slightly romantic view can alter the fact that the testosterone-fueled maniacs have always outnumbered the more reflective; and because they breed as unthinkingly as they do everything else, will always outnumber them.

So let history teach us something about ourselves as individuals, and let us be thankful that it has indeed provided, along with everything ghastly that it bequeathed us, that narrative of desirability to which (though with how little hope?) we can aspire.

Chapter Four

Bread and Circuses

By Michael Hunter

Most of our current information about our past has been revealed by the study of languages: these, obviously, furnish us with myths, legends, folklore – the histories, in fact, of the cultures to which the languages are peculiar. It is at first surprising to the new cross-cultural explorer to discover the close relationship and nearly identical patterns which turn up frequently in apparently diverse societies from one end of the globe to the other. The more the stories are examined, the more clues to the interrelatedness between the Earth's tribes seem to emerge, and this phenomenon will be recognised by any scholar or interested student who has engaged, however slightly, in this particular field. All such investigation, however, demands a thoroughly detailed familiarity with, at the very least, one's mother tongue, for any foray into a foreign or defunct language will prove desperately frustrating to him who has not at his disposal the vocabulary, syntax and grammar into which to translate it, who is thus effectively impotent so far as the grasp of meaning is concerned.

A Proustian approach to sentence construction (which was not especially remarkable when Proust, a mere century ago, undertook it) is not used merely for the undoubtedly satisfying delight of demonstrating the possibility – nowadays increasingly rare – of so arranging a sequence of words, phrases and clauses, that the effort applied by the attentive reader to the deciphering of their (sometimes) tenuously connected significance and meaning (and, of course, narrative threads), may guide said reader to a more detailed and finely nuanced comprehension of what will turn out to be a more compactly suggested thesis than that offered by a series of shorter sentences, (although that latter convention is not without merit under the capable pen of a writer possessed of the skills of, say, an accomplished poet), but also – and chiefly – with the specific object of challenging the reader to develop and exercise his own linguistic faculties and neuronal pathways, and so aid him in retaining that grasp of verbal and cultural fluency which might more ably resist the insidious attempts of those who, in serving less-than-honourable motives, seek to reduce simplistically the scope of communication media available to the populations whom they would wish to render susceptible to crass and specious suggestion, typically delivered in bite-sized, easily digestible morsels of infantile meaning – a mere step from coercion of an increasingly incoherent society robbed by stealth of its ability to articulate its objections.

Compared with much modern English usage the previous sentence, at two hundred and thirty-five words, is considered too lengthy by a factor of up to eight, but Proust routinely crafted sentences between two and five times longer, and he expected his reader to comprehend them without excessive difficulty. His feel for language was such that, even in translation, they are even now fluently expressive of both large and subsidiary ideas simultaneously: the style of prose, fairly extreme in today's terms, is easier to encompass than is generally feared by the new reader, and has a lyricism and humour which render it positively addictive once one has become accustomed to its rhythmic patterns. But this type of writing, by no means unique to Proust, is not now encouraged, and there might be profit in considering why this is so.

Ignoring vulgar considerations of profit and cost, the other motives that spring to mind have to do with control and direction of the people by their lords and masters. Having introduced legislation demanding education for all (or rather, imposing education upon all), these self-appointed arbiters of what is good for the people have now discovered that the people are, indeed, educated. Whereas it was desired that this should be so, for the simple reason that a uniformly educated population could be efficiently and simply instructed en bloc, those who willed it have found themselves faced with a side effect. Parallel examples of unwanted and unforeseen problems arising from ill-judged meddling with nature abound elsewhere: who now thinks that it was a great idea to introduce South American toads into Australia to control pests? Or to "liberate" captive mink into the fragile ecosystems along England's waterways? The unlooked-for result of this educational policy is that people can now articulate their objections, and they can do so en bloc, and this gives a headache to those whose governmental aspirations, so far only thinly disguised, include totalitarianism. Of this variety of master, several examples abound even in recent times, as the surviving populations of Cambodia, the USSR, China, Austria and Germany can corroborate, and what they will remember is, in each case, large-scale culls amongst the folk who represented the cultural, technical and scientific cores of these societies. The despots responsible for this carnage are uniformly blind to the not very startling consequence of this policy, which is that although the voice of opposition is largely stilled thereby, so also is the state's ability to function, for the casualties of such pogroms invariably include most of those who could actually do any of what needed doing. Thus tyrants achieve mastery of something which has become significantly less than it had been when they desired control of it. Ah well, at least their supremacy is assured, for a while at least, until their prize, the state, should collapse under the weight of its own incompetence.

Notice then, that in Britain, the land which gave to the world possibly its most richly expressive language, the state authorities endorse a social policy called "Political Correctness," a somewhat inaccurate use of the available language, a misnomer indeed, for correct it ain't. Government departments, the national press, the State's own broadcasting corporation and, of course, the schools, are interfering with English usage and vocabulary, and they claim to be doing so in the pursuit of universal fairness. How many repressive regimes have begun their campaigns and subsequent reigns of terror with the cry, "Equality for all"? The only route to equality for all in any context at all is reduction to the lowest common denominator, for we are not born equal, we do not have identical needs or abilities. The assault on English takes the form of an attempt to simplify it to the extent that it might become accessible to even the stupidest, so that none might feel marginalised by "difficult" expressions and thoughts, so that no child will be made to feel inferior, by being left behind, as he strains to discover the meanings of words already discovered by other children.

Also, in pursuit of this no doubt laudable ideal, ghastly crimes are committed against the native tongue, for tautological neologisms are introduced into it in the mistaken (and ill-educated!) belief that the existing vocabulary excludes or denigrates females. Thus, in failing to comprehend that "chairman," for example, already means "the person chairing," and is not gender-specific, the fools have introduced the ugly – and utterly incorrect "chairperson." Similarly pointless introductions are terms such as "he or she," when "he" already means "he or she," so that supposedly simple language becomes cumbersome, losing fluidity, but protecting the "politically correct" (though linguistically incorrect) credentials of their witless authors.

The relentless drive away from Proustian usage toward short, snappy and banal sentence forms indicates a sinister intention to impoverish also our memories, for the formerly more convoluted style of writing, though it had frozen even earlier oral forms in static (and therefore limiting) prose, had at least the merit that a certain amount of careful thought was necessary to its understanding, and a capacity to remember passages for longer than a second or two was thereby exercised and honed. Memory is a useful tool in the hands of dissenters, and is the enemy of those who would have us believe our history to be other than we remember it. Without effective memory to oppose it, a regime may devise a history of its own choosing, and use that fabrication to support an idea of a nation's "destiny," which is a dictator's shorthand for the assertion that a race is chosen by god to murder righteously on an international scale.

But merely robbing people of the ability to express thought clearly in detail, and of their accurate recall of truthful narrative, is of itself insufficient in advanced affluent societies with leisure to reflect, to settle the insecure anxieties of those who would rule, so having generously granted us ease to speak and write without the strain of thought they deploy the reserve weapon of choice, the age-old standby reinforcement of "bread and circuses." Let the populace enjoy their leisure in a series of "feel good" entertainments, distractions and diversions, delivered in simple-to-digest short-burst formats for the enjoyment of which their minds have already been primed by the reduction of their language; let them be well-fed and comfortable: for certainly now they will not feel any urgent desire to rock the boat nor bite the hand that feeds.

As the population wallows indolently in the sumptuous luxury afforded by its clearly benevolent rulers, the language with which it might otherwise have tried to express its now indefinable sense of unease and spiritual frustration is methodically dismantled by those who have but scant idea of its value, and care less. In English-speaking countries government is managed, however indirectly, by the businessmen who generate and control fiscal wealth, and their interest in English is solely to ensure that it is suited to commercial purpose, and that it can be used globally. If they have ever known it, they have now forgotten the fine detail of its correct sounds and forms, because they use English without finely detailed understanding of anything beyond that necessary to preserve and secure money. This mental and emotional deficiency is typical of those who inhabit the grasping mercantile environment of the temples to Mammon.

It is a small step from the simplification of language to the simplification of the truths that it expresses, and bread and circuses deprive us not only of the will to oppose, but also of the means of expression of our opposition. The language should be saved not because it is quaintly old-fashioned and therefore rather attractive, as sumptuously ornate old buildings are, but because it is a superb and highly developed implement capable of an enormous range of shades of meaning, and those shades, half-tones and nuances are crucial in attaining pinpoint accuracy of expression. Without it we are reduced to a state of mute acceptance of our fates, and that at the hands of others no more articulate. To save such an exquisitely valuable resource as English requires that its speakers rise above the squalid state of comfortable ease into which they have been lured, and use it – really use it.

Chapter Five

"My Kingdom is Not of This World"

An Interview with Tracy Twyman, Herein Elucidated and Expanded

TT: Just as the work of Michael Baigent, Richard Leigh and Henry Lincoln introduced the study of the "Grail bloodline" to Anglo-America in the 1980s, so has the work of two individuals redefined the scope of this study in more recent years. But while the better-known Laurence Gardner has received fame, fortune, accolades, and numerous book contracts as a reward for his work, a lesser-known figure has abided quietly in the shadows up until the present.

Prince Nicholas de Vere von Drakenberg, as the Sovereign Grand Master of the Imperial and Royal Dragon Court and Order, is the true inheritor and guardian of this tradition – the Dragon tradition, also known as the Grail tradition. De Vere has spent three decades delving into history, mythology, science, religion, and his own family archives to compile what is perhaps the most extensive and insightful text upon this subject ever published.

What de Vere has come up with is enough to comprise not just another pop culture craze, but an entirely new theology, with a new philosophy and politics as well. But de Vere is clearly not out to get rich or be popular, as he has already forgone numerous opportunities to obtain both. Writing about an elite genetic strain of humanity that descends from a super-human race, and which possesses abilities inaccessible to those outside of that strain, is not exactly a ticket to universal adulation. To the contrary, de Vere's assertions regarding the elite status of the Dragon-Grail bloodline have branded him completely anathema to the Wiccan and New Age communities who would otherwise be among those most open to his message. Which begs the question: Why has Nicholas de Vere spent the last thirty years of his life on this monumental task, and why does he continue to do so?

I have known Nicholas for more than ten years, and despite what some naysayers have claimed, I have found him to be amazingly humble, selfless, anti-materialistic, and at times brutally honest. He is personable, charming, sincere, and not the least bit conceited, despite knowing that his writing has redefined an entire field of research, that he is the head of an elite occult order with origins stretching back to the Knights Templar and beyond, and that he holds a potential claim to several important royal titles.

This, some have supposed, is the real motivation behind his work. Some believe that de Vere wants to be the King of England or France, an assertion that he flatly denies. Others see in de Vere a candidate for nothing less than the anti-Christ himself, and see in the Dragon Court an international Satanic conspiracy somewhere on a level between the Ordo Templi Orientis and the Bilderberg Group.

52

But while it is true that, when the Great Dragon of Revelation does emerge to take hold of the world he will undoubtedly be of the Dragon blood, and may even be a member of the Court, but Prince Nicholas de Vere is certainly not he. As I am sure he would humbly admit himself, de Vere's mission is simply to prepare the way for Him who is yet to come. Listen, then, dear readers, to the voice crying out in the wilderness.

TT: What is your educational background? What careers have you pursued in the past?

NDV: I was educated to the British equivalent of "high school graduate" with qualifications in English Law, English Language, Art, Sociology and Business Economics. I have a further Royal Society of Arts qualification in English. I spent two brief periods at the City of Brighton University and Coleg Ceredigion in Wales where I studied English and Printing, and then later Law, Sociology and Politics.

My main careers have been in:

The Military, where I served most of my time in the Northern Ireland conflict and was decorated with the Campaign Service Medal.

In Private Security. I was managing director of my own company and provided security for various nationally and internationally known companies such as Taylor Woodrow and Virgin, for example.

TT: What is the history of your career in professional non-fiction writing?

NDV: I started writing in earnest in 1985 and was eventually persuaded to publish the thrust of my work on the Internet in 1999.

TT: How long ago did you write *The Dragon Legacy*?

NDV: About eight years ago. *The Dragon Legacy* was known on the net as *From Transylvania to Tunbridge Wells* and this was a summary of years of research and reflection. Lawrence Gardner based his third book, *Realm of the Ring Lords*, largely on what I had already published.

TT: What were your main sources of information when compiling the book?

NDV: On the so-called "Dragon path" one is imbued hereditarily with Dragon capabilities in varying measures. As one progresses, these capabilities wax and wane according to necessity. One of the main capacities is the Derkesthai Process, in which information is "channeled" through the conduit of the Dragon archetype; specifically the racial consciousness of those of the Dragon blood.
Through this process one may pick up naturally, all sorts of information relating to varied aspects of the Dragon Tradition in its many and various branches and manifestations. However, this is of no use intellectually and rationally without informed academic confirmation and corroboration.

To this end another Dragon capacity is to be able to obtain, after the fact, those confirmations required. I anticipated works before I read them, either through meditation or through experience on the Dragon Path. In a not too dissimilar manner Kerkule discovered the benzine ring, a group of carbon atoms bound together in many organic compounds.

I would say that the serious academic backbone of *The Dragon Legacy* in terms of corroboration and confirmation, lies in the work of Dr. David Barker; George Woodcock; Lysander Spooner; Professor Miranda Green; Pierre Proudhon; Professors Pierpaoli and Regelson; David Anderson; The Oxford English Dictionary and an old associate Professor C. Murray Hall M.A. (former lecturer in Barbarian Cultures at Sussex University).

TT: How did you begin research into your family history? At what point in your life did you become aware of "the Dragon legacy" in your family? Is it something you grew up with?

NDV: From the age of seven onwards my father taught me about our ancestry, an ancestry steeped in royal blood and most significantly of all in what is termed Royal Witchcraft, which is a major, ancient, draconian, druidic facet continuing within the later history of the Dragon tradition and within the Vere family.

My father educated me about our particular origins in the royal and noble Blackwood family of Lanark, Scotland. This dynasty sired the most significant practitioner of the Dragon tradition in his time: Major Thomas Weir of Vere of Edinburgh, my 11th grandfather.

As the Witch Lord of his age and the Prince Consort to the Elven Queen of the Lallan, the Lowlands of Scotland, Thomas performed the ancient Gaelic rites of the sacred kingship of Epona, and consequently founded this rite of kingship within my lineage. So I received the tradition at an early age from my father and he received it from his father, and so on.

TT: Your formal title is "Prince Nicholas de Vere." What does this title imply?

NDV: To answer your question I have pasted-in an excerpt from the "Duchy of Angiers" genealogical table charting the ancient, royal descent of the Dragon House of Vere which, as you know, will shortly be published with a full complement of supporting historical and contemporary academic sources.

I quote:

"...The Royal House of Vere – The Senior Angevin House of the original Princes and Counts of Anjou – were latterly domiciled in Bretagne and Flanders and the former senior, Scottish Branch Hope-Vere of Blackwood, traditionally observed the Flemish law of Noblesse Uterine, and matrilinear and family inheritance in accordance with noble Scottish family law, which contemporarily and historically supports female blood descent.

The titles of Princeps Draconis and Prince de Vere, currently held by Nicholas de Vere, are acknowledged as foreign titles in confidential files held by the British Government's Department of Internal Affairs and are registered with them as "Official Observations."

The right of fons honorum – the right to bestow Arms and Titles – held by Nicholas de Vere is also acknowledged by the Government. These titles are recognised by the most senior branches of the House of Vere.

Though resigned to the existence of both with some considerable political and constitutional qualification, Nicholas de Vere does not claim to be either a member of the contemporary British royal household or of its peerage in any sense, and does not claim any status or rank suggestive of such or appertaining thereunto. The Vere princedoms are not false, modern, socially derived titles; either assumed or bestowed for or by, political expediency by a spurious monarchy.

The princedoms of Vere are ancient social and cultural manifestations of the genetic qualities carried in the historical Elven Blood Royal. First established in Angiers, France, in the eighth century as an Imperial and Royal House, they arise from far older sacred Pictish, Scythian origins descending from the Iron Age King Vere and beyond.

Latterly the House of Vere is academically recorded in a single name and in an unbroken line for over one thousand three hundred years, and consequently it is the oldest surviving royal dynasty in Europe. In the published genealogies of the House, through numerous Vere Kings and Archdruids, the Vere name consistently devolves back even further, to their first progenitor King Vere I, of the Fairy Tuatha de Danaan of Eire in 400 BC. His great grandparents settled in Caledonia in Scotland two thousand six hundred years ago, following the Milesian invasion of their Irish homeland...."

So I trace my lineage back in an unbroken titular bloodline to the imperial prince Milo de Vere Count of Anjou, Duke of Angiers, son of Melusine: The Princess Milouziana of the Scythians. She was recorded throughout France as being a powerful Witch; the Fairy, Dragon Princess of the Scottish Picts descending from King Vere. Her grandson Prince Milo II Count of Guisnes derived his Merovingian descent through his father's marital alliance with the Imperial House of Charlemagne. Later in history through intermarriage, we inherited numerous other, senior lines of Merovingian descent.

Concerning my maternal lineage. My mother is descended from the old Danish Collison jarls or earls of Norfolk (source: Dr. Hugh Weir of Vere of County Clare); Lords of the Courts Baron in that County, and she is the third cousin of the Irish head of the House of Vere in the female line. In that respect we are a closely related family. The head of the Irish House himself is of royal Collison descent and this matrilinear extraction stems from the early House of Vere and again from Princess Milouziana of the Scythians. We are Veres on both sides of the family and adhere closely to the Davidic, Grail laws concerning intermarriage, which were established to maintain the ancient purity of the Holy Blood Royal.

The head of the Irish House of Vere today by patralinear descent, through marriage into the House of the Royal O'Brien descendants of Emperor Brian Boru of Tara, is himself a Borbon Archduke.

The author is the International Head of the House of Vere. The Head of the Irish branch formally addresses me as "the Dragon Prince" of the House of Vere. This is not so much an earthly title these days as it is the cultural and traditional expression of an ancient spiritual condition, hence "My Kingdom is not of this World."

TT: Who are the "Dragons" that you write about in your book?

NDV: The name Sumerian is related to the root "Sumaire," meaning Dragon, whilst the name "Scythian" specifically means both "prince" and "power." Both peoples were originally, essentially the same and in antiquity – prior to the Biblical Flood – they occupied the regions north of the Black Sea now known as Transylvania and Carpathia. The Sumerian Kings traced their descent from the Dragon Gods of the Anunnaki and likewise the Scythians traced their genealogy back to the Titan Typhoeus – the Anunnaki god Enki – and the daughter of Zeus or Enlil who was believed to be the Anunnaki goddess Lilith, whom the Jews called "the red-haired Queen of the North." In fact Lilith was Enlil's granddaughter, the offspring of Nergal and Eresh-Kigal, king and queen of the underworld, known to the later Scythians as the realm of Elphame or Faery, and to the Celts as "Annwyn."
In brief, in both their respective histories, their recorded Dragon lineage originates with the Annunaki and descends through these proto-Scythians: as the first pre-flood Sumerian kings of Transylvania and Carpathia in one branch, and on – via Mesopotamia – to the early Egyptian pharaohs in another.
From there, through the Phoenicians and the Scythian Mittani, and back to the later Scythians again through marital alliance, it then devolves to the fairy Tuatha de Danaan and the Fir Bolg, and down through their archdruidic, priest-princely families to the royal Picts of Scotland and the Kings of Dal Riada. From thence, through various alliances, it descends to the Elven dynasty of Pendragon and Avallon del Acqs, and down to a few pure bred Dragon families today.

TT: Were the Dragons originally a separate species from what we would call "human"?

NDV: Dragon tradition related to all the current genetic and historical evidence says yes they were. Both relatively recent and ancient accounts of Dragons or Elves going back to the Annunaki speak of them as having clearly distinct physical attributes, and these attributes are inherited from a species that scientists now assert preceded the human genetic bottleneck by thousands of years. This species were the Anunnaki gods. These attributes are therefore not human in the modern accepted sense. This ancient race hybridised before written history, and their later hybridisation to produce the Elven God-Kings and Ring Lords – the King Tribe – is clearly set down in the Mesopotamian records. We will deal with their specific genetic differences later.

TT: Are these Dragons the same as the "Nephilim" of the Bible or the "Watchers" of the *Book of Enoch*?

NDV: The Nephilim and the Watchers are of the Dragon race, yes. They are the children of the Anunnaki gods. The children of the Nephilim were the Naphidem, the "giants" of the Bible, produced when the sons of the Anunnaki – the Nephilim – went with the daughters of men.

TT: Were the gods of ancient cultures (Greece, India, Sumeria, etc.) Dragons?

NDV: These pantheons are derived from one another and ultimately from the Anunnaki so again, the answer in simple terms is yes.

TT: What kind of civilization did the Dragons reign over? Would you say that it was the same as the Atlantean or antediluvian civilization?

NDV: The Platonic Atlantis theory is preceded by a much older tradition relating to the "Ogdoad." The Ogdoad, sacred to Jesus himself, were the eight great Anunnaki gods who raked the Sacred Mountain – "Atlantis" – after the original Biblical Flood which was not universal but regional, and has been scientifically proven to have happened when the Hellespont burst following a shift in the tectonic plates beneath the island of Santorini in the Mediterranean.

This Flood therefore occurred in the Black Sea, originally a massive fresh-water lake situated in a land basin beneath sea level, and the Sacred Mountain, so inundated therein, was believed to be the Pontus Euxine.

Apparently the Ogdoad failed in their attempt to bring fertility back to the Holy Place and abandoned it and migrated, via the Taurus mountains of Anatolia, to Mesopotamia. Their children wandered to the four corners of the earth. This is probably why the legend of the Flood spread and can be found in most cultures. The original flood occurred in around 5065 BC, archaeologically speaking. Certain material originally from dry land strata and various fresh water material deposits dredged from the Black Sea have been carbon-dated and fall within this period. The story of this disaster was linked to a later flood that occurred in the Mesopotamian Plains, when water from the north swept down from the mountains and burst the banks of the rivers Tigris and Euphrates.

Noah wasn't the only individual to supposedly build an Ark. In *the Leibher Gabhalla* the Elven sons of the Ogdoad, the Dragon Princes Ba'ath and Fintan and fifty Anunnaki Princesses took a large vessel loaded with provisions, set sail through the Hellespont once the waters had equalized, and navigated their way through the Mediterranean, up the Bay of Biscay, past Brittany and on to Ireland. Their sons and daughters sailed even further and went on to inhabit the "Northernmost Isles of the World," becoming, like their parents, the "Aes Dan" of the Irish; the "Aesir" or Fairy God-Kings of the Scandinavians.

By comparison, poor old Noah seems to have just sailed round in circles and landed on Ararat a few nautical miles south of Atlantis about a month later, if the Bible is to be believed.

However, using the precise measurements the Jews say God gave to Noah in order to build his Ark, scientists and engineers have recently built a precise study model to test its load stresses and weak points, and have discovered that, given the materials and the level of building skill required in the time alloted to construct the boat, it would have meant that in a few hours on the turbulent water it would have split in the middle and sunk beneath the waves. Noah's project would have been doomed to failure and disaster and could never have existed, let alone sailed anywhere.

In any event the Biblical legend of Noah derives from a much earlier Babylonian account concerning the Anunnaki King Ziu Sudra. Therefore it can be said that, with much of the Old Testament gleaned from the Babylonians, and subsequently doctored by the Jewish Scribes, Noah and his family and their descendants never existed either, but were invented to give the early Jews a sense of divine antecedence from God, which was nothing but fantasy. In the Babylonian texts, which the Jewish Scribes altered to suit their own ends, the Jewish God Jehovah – modeled on Enki's half brother Enlil – never created Man at all. It was Enki who created Man.

Noah's supposed ancestors devolving back to Adam and Eve's son Seth share the same names as the descendants of Enki and Eve's son Cain, and from this we can see that the Jewish scribes simply copied these names and attributed them to their own newly invented ancestry, in order to fill in the glaring gaps in their tribal genealogy, ultimately for political ends. Noah's supposed son Ham was in fact the great magician and high-priest Chem Zarathustra, tenth Archon of Capricorn – or Enki – and he was the son, not of Noah, but of Tubal Cain, King of Ur of Sumeria.

Tubal Cain was the ancestral great grandson of Cain, king of Kish, and Cain was the son of Queen Hawah of Elda by the Anunnaki god Enki, whom the Jews later cast as their Biblical Satan in a smear campaign designed to pervert history and cover up the fact that they were no more than a tribe of nomadic goat-herders who were descended from nobody at all.

They simply stole someone else's ancestry to purport that they had survived a Flood they were never in and subsequently to lay retrospective, spurious ancestral claims to the land, property and wealth they had stolen over the generations – and this has been happening ever since.

If a tribe can say they are God's chosen people, descended from God himself and that the land they have invaded was given to them by God, they can then say it is theirs by divine right, which appears far better to posterity, and is more likely to support their territorial claims, than simply saying that they murdered an entire population and stole their land and everything in it.

The Jews of the Exile were not descended from God through Noah because their god didn't create man and Noah never existed. The ancestors of the Jews didn't survive the Biblical Flood, they were never there, and the true descendants of the Anunnaki and Enki: Cain, Tubal Cain and Chem Zarathustra, went on to found the royal Anunnaki dynasties in Sumeria and to introduce their holy bloodlines into Egypt.

The Ogdoad turn up in Chinese myth, in early Egyptian religious texts, and even in much later Viking legend, where the gods of the Aesir were said to have abandoned the Sacred Mountain – Aya – after the Flood. Aya is the Sumerian god Ea or Enki. From the Ogdoad, who were the first Anunnaki, being Dragon gods of ancient proto-Scythia, we obtain those later pantheons that derived from them. It is not to be doubted that after the Flood the wandering children of the Anunnaki had established incredible civilisations in their time, so I suppose you could say that the cultures of the Sumerians – whose language, termed "proto-Sumerian," originated in Transylvania or "Little Scythia" – the Egyptians and even the early settlers in northern Europe stemmed from and reflect an antediluvian prototype, a much older pre-Flood "Golden Age," presided over by the ancient Dragon god-kings and goddess-queens. The mistake would be to put the Atlantean period too far back in time and to locate Atlantis where Plato did. Scientists have proved the Biblical Flood to be in the Black Sea and this region is where most of the Titanic and Olympian sagas, associated with the Dawn of the Gods, unfold.

TT: Is Dragon blood the true source of divine right kingship, in your opinion? Are the Dragons the rightful rulers of the world's governments?

NDV: Ancient Dragon blood, the blood of the gods, is the true source of divine right kingship. To say that Dragons are the rightful rulers of the world's governments today is entirely true but it might raise some contention. Perhaps it would be more realistic to suggest that they may well be the rightful rulers of the world's governments in the future.

TT: There is a great deal written in your book about Cain. What is his role in the history of the Dragon bloodline?

NDV: Cain was the scion of the gods, not of Adam. He was bred to be the progenitor of the race of god-kings over man. In terms of the descent of the later Dragons, he is the father of the race.

TT: What about Isis/Venus? What is her role?

NDV: The pantheons have overlapped but essentially Isis, in her Egyptian form, belongs to their agricultural-astronomical metaphor, though in her archaic form she originates from the Anunnaki dynasty. One commentator has Isis and Osiris as Isa and Asea and originally ancient Aryan deities. The more recent manifestation of Venus – The Anunnaki Goddess Ishtar, the Sacred Lover – is a process belonging essentially to the later Grail ethos.

Briefly put, Venus is the Falling Star Lucifer – "An" in Sumerian – and in short, that star in its fall from Heaven to Earth symbolizes, microcosmically, the descent of sacred essences from the brain of the Dragon priestess to her womb, with this organ being the physical, biological reality behind the symbol of the Holy Grail, the cauldron of plenty, and so forth.

To elucidate, Kabbalistically and Hermetically, we have the image of the divine female – Sophia – though she has many other names, on both the cosmic and human level. The Cosmos was thought to replicate the perfect human form on the universal scale.

Macrocosmically – Above – the heavens or stars are represented by Kether, the head of the figure. From Kether the Cubic Stone, in the form of Lucifer, the divine inspiration, falls to Malkuth, the Earth, the birth canal of the Cosmic being.

Microcosmically – Below – Sophia, who represents divine wisdom incarnate, is embodied in the Dragon female and her head rests in Kether, her womb lies in Yesod and her birth canal lies in Malkuth. Microcosmically the process of the descent of divine inspiration from the heavens to the Earth is repeated therefore in the descent of divine, inspiring essences from Kether to Malkuth in the female form.

As a Priestess, Mary Magdalene was a Cosmic, Sophic, Grail figure and Jesus described her in the Holy Bible as the feminine PETRA, the Cubic Stone of female wisdom upon which he would build his Church. The word church derives from the Latin Circa or Circle and in Gaelic lands, going to Church was originally termed "going to the Stones," the Stone Circles. The Church of Jesus was therefore a classical Magic Circle.

Later on, during the canonisation of the Gospels, the misogynistic and opportunistic Romans decided to confer, retrospectively, this privilege upon the apostle Peter instead, whose name in Latin is the masculine PETROS. They rewrote Jesus' speech to his disciples, claiming that he would build his church on Peter, but forgot to change the feminine PETRA into the masculine PETROS, thus again revealing another one of their numerous historical and spiritual frauds.

The Witches' Circle of Christ – His Holy Church – was thus to be built on Petra; the Feminine Principle; the womb of his Pharaonic sister-wife, the Magdalene, her holy essences and her motherly issue – the Cubic Stone of the Grail – not on some treacherous, half-witted Hebrew blockhead who, at the drop of a hat, denied and betrayed his Master thrice before dawn. The Popes and apostles of Christ – the true leadership of the Church in years to come – were to have been of blood descent from Jesus and Mary, not some idiot fisherman.

In any event, that Mary Magdalene was Jesus' wife – and the mother of his children – is clearly stated in the Nag Hammadi Scrolls and in numerous other texts of the period; that they were intimate is specifically mentioned in the *Gospel of Mary Magdalene* and the *Gospel of Phillip*, and in the centuries preceding their compilation, Jesus' marriage to his "paternal half-sister" (see Ralph Ellis, *Jesus: Last of the Pharoahs*) Mary was common knowledge, even though the orthodox Churches still vehemently and nervously deny this indisputable fact today.

Therefore, as the oldest named Royal Dynasty in Eurasia, reaching back to King Vere of the Elves in 400 BC, as the direct descendants of the Merovingian dynasty, and as the foremost scions of the most ancient of Scythian Royal Fairy lines, the House of Vere stand as the pre-eminent Holy Grail Family of Britain, Ireland, Europe and the Middle East and as such are the most senior Elven heirs of the Messianic, Dragon Blood legacy of Jesus, Mary Magdalene and the House of David in existence today.

In strict accordance with the Pharaonic and Judaic laws concerning Royal inheritance, echoed in the later Flemish Laws of Noblesse Uterine, subsequently adopted in their inheritance practices by the House of Vere and Hope-Vere of Blackwood, it is the matrilineal descent, which equally decides the heirs of the dynasty.

The reason for this is that the only genetic material that doesn't get conjoined and confused during human reproduction but remains pure and unchanged, is that which is carried within the female mitochondria and is inherited by sons and daughters alike, solely through the mother.

Indeed, the Grail and Dragon Bloodline itself descends originally from a female progenitor, Queen Tiamat, the first mother of the Anunnaki before 5000 BC in the ancient records. Interestingly though, according to the genetic record, the genes of the Anunnaki and their Elven offspring are fantastically old and predate those of modern humans by thousands of years.

As has been variously noted here and in numerous other works, the pre-eminent historian – Lord Macauley of Rothley Temple – along with many others, including the senior 17th Century Law Lord, Sir Randolph Crew, in addressing the Crown and the House of Lords, confirm that the House of Vere are the senior royal and noble House of Britain and Europe.

Consequently, under the historical and contemporary European laws of linear primogeniture, as the atheling descending from the most senior branch of the royal House of Vere in Europe in the female line, and as a Vere in both his patrilinear and matrilinear descents, the author stands as the foremost representative and recipient of the Elven, Grail Blood Royal and its Apostolic and Messianic Legacy in Eurasia, the Middle-East and Asia Minor in these times: The International Sovereign Head of the House of Vere.

In the *Letter to the Disciple Ceretius* (*The Witch Cult in Western Europe*, by Prof. Margaret Murray) it is revealed that, in Moon-bathed Groves, Jesus was in the habit of playing the Pan Pipes after the fashion of the Greek Satyrs, whilst his followers, twelve in all, danced in a circle around him in imitation of the cyclic procession of the heavens in the form of the twelve astrological houses. Later depictions of the Witches Sabbats also have the Devil playing pipes whilst his twelve followers dance the chorale around him.

During these rituals Jesus used to invoke the Ogdoad: the Eight Great Gods of the Anunnaki, later linked to Egyptian Teachings, and perform ceremonies of initiation similar to those described in connection with Lazarus by Professor Morton Smith in his *Secret Gospel of Mark*.

It is no wonder that Pope Leo IX said, "This myth of Christ hath served us well." The dogma and ritual of wealthy and powerful Roman Christianity in recent centuries bears no resemblance to the original beliefs and practices of the early Christians, nor to the true transcendent Mystery Teachings of Jesus himself – teachings and symbols which incorporate fundamental links with those of Attis, Orpheus, Dionysus, Bacchus and Mithras, with whom Jesus was closely identified in his own lifetime.

In common with many of these characters from pre-Christian cults including Orpheus-Bacchus, Jesus, like them, was born of a virgin by a god, was crucified or sacrificed on a tree (like Odin of the Danes), descended into the Underworld where he discovered the ancient wisdom, and is associated with the Grail Chalice.

Like the Sun God, Apollo, Jesus was said to have been born in a stable, fashioned from a humble cave, which for both Jesus and Apollo represented their birth from the womb of the Earth Goddess. Under the Emperor Constantine, Jesus was also identified as a Sun God and was named the "Sol Invicta" – the Victorious Sun.

Each of these foregoing figures featured heavily in Romano-Jewish culture during Jesus' time and each was, like numerous other contenders of the period, considered to be a "Christ." In fact, the role of Messiah or Christ, the anointed one, in Hebrew society under the Romans, was a vocation which was open to an annual vote by the people and the successful candidate would reign for the following year.

Like Mithras, Jesus was said to be born on December 25th and also like Mithras, Jesus forms part of a holy trinity. In the case of the Persian deity, this trinity consists of Mithras, Ormuzd and Ahriman. Jesus had Persian (Aryan) royal antecedence, which is why the Magi attended his birth and why he is so closely linked with the Persian saviour.

As was the case with Dionysus, Jesus rode in procession on an ass, an animal sacred to the Egyptian God Set, who equates with the Jewish Satan. In accordance with his identification with Dionysus, Jesus was also, like him, credited with the power of turning water into wine. The feast day for Dionysus occurred at Easter and like many other Mystery gods, Jesus was said to have risen from the dead on the third day of Easter, following his sacrifice.

From Dionysus, Jesus also inherited the I.H.S. motif now used by the Roman Church and from Bacchus-Dionysus, Jesus inherited the Panther symbol from whence he derived his "Ben-Panther" appellation. Later Grail descendants of Jesus used the "Panther" in their heraldry, specifically the House of Geoffrey Plantagenet and the Angevin Kings of Britain, and the Panther eventually became known heraldically as "The Lion of England."

The orthodox Church likes to make an emphatic distinction between Jesus as the Christian God, the only true saviour, and all the other gods who either preceded him or were contemporary to him, which they curse vehemently and label as "demonic," "pagan" and "heathen." The fact is that Jesus was part of that mystery tradition and identified himself closely with these so-called heathen gods and this is so evident in the canonical and apocryphal Gospels of his followers that in order to hide his true identity, the early Church would either have had to completely rewrite the scriptures, or throw them out altogether and start again from scratch.

In any event, it transpired that in order to gain universal acceptance for their new, spurious and false version of Christianity, the Pauline Church fathers would have to leave some hints of Jesus' mystery associations in the Scriptures in order that their pagan target audience would accept their version of Jesus as the sole alternative to their traditional "pagan" religions.

The problem with the early Church was that it was populated by Jews, and Jews have a distinct distaste for the worship of foreign deities, whom they tend to label as demons. Although Jesus lived in Judea he wasn't particularly Jewish in any accepted sense, but traced his royal antecedence back through the Greek Hyksos kings of Egypt, the ethnic Egyptian Pharaonic Houses, the Persian royal dynasties and the gods of the Babylonians and Sumerians. As such, Jesus wasn't averse to celebrating the gods of his ancestors or in upholding the tradition that those ancestors were ultimately descended from the gods of their respective nations.

Jesus saw himself quite rightly as a god-king, descended from the varying pantheons of the deities of his disparate forebears. So it is no surprise that his spiritual traditions and teachings are distinctly pagan in nature – in fact, it is to be expected.

The disciples who weren't of the blood royal or shared Jesus' spiritual heritage went along with this for a time but when Jesus departed the scene, they initially reverted to form and became distinctly Jewish again, adopting all the holy fear, guilt, mistrust and hatred of women, and loathing of foreign gods that, in contemporary Jewish humour, is still part and parcel of the Hebrew stereotype even today.

This distinct national psychopathology is partly what fueled the split between the Magdalene and Jesus' family, and the rest of Jesus' followers. The purpose of Jesus' "Church," as with the Grail families today, was to keep the genes of the Dragon Anunnaki gods largely pure, and the Elven Blood Royal that descended from them as intact as possible, hence the utilisation of matrilinear, mitochondrial descent. In so doing they would retain their transcendent capabilities, retain their ancient "pagan" traditions and remain fit guides and advisors of men. As such, Jesus' tradition wasn't intended to be a religion at all, simply a repository of ancient wisdom and a custodian of the Grail Bloodline.

This "inner" tradition, separate from his public ministry as the god-king of the Jews in waiting, was meant to be kept within the family, and not broadcast to the general public. However, when things became difficult and the family's tradition and activities came under the scrutiny of the Roman collaborator, the wealthy High Priest Caiaphas, the Jewish Priesthood and the Roman authorities, because it had distinctly politically and religiously dangerous and subversive overtones, it was necessary for the tradition to go underground. At this point, Jewish fear came into play and the disciples outside the family split from the family itself and went their own way, eventually distancing themselves as much as they could from the original Nazorite Church.

Thanks to the efforts of the breakaway followers of Peter and Paul and their early successors, the family have been written out of history and have been caused to sink into obscurity by the emergent, peasant infested "Church" led by Paul, who not only initially wanted to revert Christianity to a broadly Jewish model of a variant Messianic faith, which naturally incorporated all the God fearing xenophobia of the Hebrews, their sense of misery and guilt, and their fear of natural female sexuality, but they also saw in their new cult an opportunity to make money out of their fellow peasants, gain power and make a good life for themselves.

In later developments of the new religion led by Paul, he becomes very much the Apostle of the Gentiles. Gradually, the Judaic direction of his organisation was modified to flatter a Roman audience and in order to avert Roman persecution at a time when Judaea was in an uproar of tumult and rebellion against Roman authority.

The profit motive of his Church is clearly evidenced in Paul's letter to the Corinthians, in which he constantly demands that they provide him with ready cash, which he encourages them to deliver to him in Rome on a regular basis. The Corinthians were not his only cash-cow though – all the Churches he had set up across the Mediterranean Basin were fleeced by him on a regular basis.

And who were these early Pauline disciples? The Bible describes them as the absolute lowest dregs of Roman society. They were thieves, whores, male prostitutes, drunks and extortionists. Paul, fearing the public reputation of his fledgling religion and its potential to make him rich, continually complained to them about their fornications and excesses, but that did little to change their behaviour. And from these dregs, Paul promoted his priests, deacons and bishops, and so the die was set for two thousand years and the Church continued to enlist into its ranks the worst recidivist criminal elements of society it could find.

Considering the difficulty in getting these individuals to reform and change their ways for the good of the organisation as a whole, the excuse adopted then and now is that they are "repentant sinners who have seen the light," when in fact the priesthood continue to be unrepentant degenerates who find in the complicit Church an easy meal ticket, a pension and an institution that will readily and happily bury their crimes beneath a smokescreen of seeming piety, and hide them behind an ecclesiastical wall of silence.

Evidence of this complicity is the Church's recent refusal to bring to book and allow prosecution of the large numbers of Catholic priests across the world who have sexually abused the children in their flocks for years. Instead of defrocking them and handing them over to the secular authorities, the Church, and its German, formerly Nazi Pope – who promised to reduce paedophilia in the Church down to "acceptable levels" – has simply moved these monsters to different parishes, where they have been enabled to continually repeat their unconscionable activities for decades.

So in summary, the fundamental difference between the two "Churches" was the fact that one was a royal repository of ancient holy tradition, and the other was an opportunistic peasant movement geared initially towards covering their own tracks from the authorities whilst reinstating all the good old Jewish values of lively commercial profit and absolute social control, reinforced by spiritual fear, inculcated in their congregations by a priesthood who were and still are no more than hypocritical, duplicitous, power-crazed opportunists.

The problem in establishing an absolute and unquestionable authenticity for the early Pauline Church came with the fact that firstly, Mary Magdalene took her children to France and established the Grail Bloodline and its traditions in Europe, where it thrived as the "Underground Stream" and the "Serpent Rouge" for centuries to come, marrying into the most powerful royal fairy families in Gaul, and secondly, with the Roman sack of Jerusalem and the subsequent diaspora, although the Pauline Church was toadying to the Roman authorities and amending its doctrines accordingly at that time, the original teachings of the Church of Jesus, upheld by his remaining fleeing family, also entered Europe as the Nazorite Church.

This later developed into the Celtic Church which retained within it the knowledge of Jesus' true identity and teaching, which prompted its leader, Saint Columba, one of the descendants of the Holy Family, to proclaim that Jesus was a druid and to further retain the old pagan beliefs of their Gaelic hosts within their doctrines.

Today the story of the Grail families is re-emerging and gaining popularity with a fascinated public disaffected by Church lies. Now that the corrupt political power and inherent violence of the Orthodox Church have been relatively diminished this means that, after suffering centuries of genocide, torture and suppression, I and my family can now take our rightful place at the head of the ranks of the once feared Dragon Race whose evil reputation was the political contrivance, the spurious propaganda of a wicked regime who, feeling threatened by the emerging truth, sought to retain its power and wealth at any cost to the individual or to society.

In the preceding centuries the truth about the Grail or Dragon families became such a threat that the Church initiated the Inquisition and a program of mass murder which claimed the lives of millions of people over a millennium of terror, a period in history where any individual, sect or group and their books or manuscripts that contradicted the Church's orthodox propaganda was systematically destroyed, thereby creating the Dark Ages. Such was the thoroughgoing nature of the Thousand-year Elven Holocaust. Needless to say, they also took the opportunity of confiscating and adding to their vast coffers the wealth of those they had ruthlessly and systematically murdered.

But it didn't end there, the terror continued in Britain until 1709 and even today academics and the academic institutions teach, promote and uphold the spiritual, historical and political lies of the Church-State, and the Church itself still promulgates its twisted doctrines of sexual sin, misogyny and hellfire.

These doctrines all originated in the theology of the Jews, a race racked with the hysterical psychoses of a religious and physical sense of fear and guilt, inculcated and encouraged in them by scribes and patriarchs who sought, in so doing, to retain absolute control over society, and the subsequent wealth and power they had come to enjoy through millennia of social and religious suppression.

As a Jewish contrivance by default, the Orthodox Church and its numerous lunatic derivatives still retain those psychopathological doctrines and still attempt to instill them into us today.

To return to the main thrust of the question, the male Kabbalistic counterpart of the female Sophia on both the cosmic and human level was Adam Kadmon, the perfect combination of the mortal and the divine, through whom holy wisdom was imparted and within whom Lucifer – the serpent or lightning bolt of that divine inspiration – descended from Kether, which was the divine spirit residing within the head, to Tiphareth, the mortal soul of man resting within the heart and thence, through holy prophecy, to the inhabitants of the world sphere: Malkuth.

Interestingly enough, the heart has been medically discovered to be made up of brain cells, to a significant extent. Some of those who have had heart transplants have described, in detail, memories inherited from the donors whose lives they have subsequently researched in an attempt to find answers as to why they have adopted new memories, feelings, tastes and beliefs; these new "souls." The Kabbalists were right, the heart is indeed the seat of the soul.

In Kabbalistic tracts the Cosmic or universal Christ was Tiphareth, which was the male counterpart of the Cubic Stone. In mystical Christian terms Jesus Christ, as the Tiphareth, was both the manifestation and receptacle of transcendent, holy Luciferian inspiration. In yielding to this Satanic inspiration, Jesus was truly the Fairy king and the god of the Witches (witch = wicce: "to yield to inspiration").

Indeed, in the biblical Revelation of St. John, Jesus says, "I am the bright son of the morning," which is Lucifer or Venus, the Falling Star: The Jewel in Satan's Crown. He is also referred to biblically as the second Adam, the son of God. Christ was also viewed in the Kabbala as Adam Kadmon, the divine human being – known in Hindu as an Avatar.

Jesus is Lucifer, as found in more recent orthodox Christian terms of reference. By a curious twist of logic, Jesus consequently embodies both Christ and Anti-Christ, generation and destruction, Ormuzd and Ahriman, light and darkness. It is not to be marveled at therefore, that the Anti-Christ of the latter days will arise from the very bloodline of Christ, especially as Jesus is himself descended from Satan via the Egyptian royal line and the House of David.

In summary, in some Gnostic dualist traditions Jesus was a bipartite being identified as the male counterpart of the Cubic Stone and the vessel of God's wisdom on Earth. Because of this and his associations with pagan deities, from antiquity up to the present day, his myth has become conjoined with that of the Holy Grail. However, both his divine symbolic origins and sacred attributes, and his bloodline – which embodied those sacred attributes – are far older and stem all the way back to the Anunnaki, to Enki, the "Devil."

For this reason, the witches of medieval Europe honoured Jesus as the "antecessor" (the ancestor) and as "Christ son Dei," the dual god of light and dark, the scion of both God and Satan. In medieval France he was the goat-hoofed, gold-bodied Black Sun and thousands of his witches would attend the sabbats at any given time, thereby illustrating the very real threat that the Grail Families and their supporters in the witch cult posed to the hegemony, to the power and wealth of the Catholic Church during that period. In a classical reversal of the biblical story and as a continuation of the earlier gnostic theme, the witches considered Jehovah the ultimate god of evil, the demiurge.

St. Columba called Jesus "mo drui, mac Dei" – "my druid, son of God." In Gaelic, druid means witch, and witchcraft is the lineal descendant of druidism. Again, this view of Christ is supported in the ancient Christian letter to Ceretius, quoted by the eminent Egyptologist Professor Margaret Murray, mentioned earlier.

TT: When you refer metaphorically to "the Dragon," what exactly are you referring to?

NDV "The Dragon" is a term I use generally to mean the dragon archetype resting within the Dragon blood and passed on through the genes. It is the conduit through which flow the memories of the wisdom and experience of the Dragons who have gone before. The word "dragon" is derived from the Greek "edrakon," which is an aorist of the word "derkesthai," which means, "to see clearly." "The Dragon," therefore, is the inherited Dragon archetype and that archetype is the conduit of clear sight through which racial knowledge flows. Clear sight also and principally refers to transcendent consciousness.

TT: What percentage of the world's populace would you say possesses this Dragon blood? Is it predominately found in certain types of people? How can you tell a Dragon from other types of people?

NDV: Roughly ten percent of Europeans have Dragon blood, and stem from families whose physical attributes clearly point to a genetic inheritance many thousands of years old. This figure is calculated from research deriving from studies by Oxford University and matched to historical accounts.

TT: How did the Dragon race begin, and how did they become a separate race from the rest of humanity?

NDV: This subject is extremely complex and would take several chapters to cover in any detail, however the Dragons always were, to a great extent throughout history, a separate species from that of common man. And as will be seen shortly, in the following work by Leonid Korablev, even in antiquity it was asserted by all men that the Dragon species – the Elves or Fairies – were of a different origin from man and inhabited another world.

The name Anunnaki means "sons of Anu" and the name Anu derives from the Sumerian syllable "An," which translates as "The Star" and, reflecting this in the ancient Sumerian texts, it is suggested of the Anunnaki by Zecharia Sitchin and some misguided authors that they originated from another world altogether – Nibiru – the planet of the Sha. This theme, they claim, is repeated time after time and in text after text it is clearly stated that that they were "the lofty ones from on high," "the mighty ones of eternity" and that their "kingship was lowered from the heavens." The latter simply means that the Anunnaki and the Nephilim lived in the mountainous northern regions of Transylvania, Carpathia and the White Mountains. To the ancients, high places were believed to be the realm of heaven and the Nephilim were simply those Anunnaki who were "cast down" (Sumerian: *nephilim*) from the Mountains of the North. NOT FROM OUTER SPACE. Cf. Lilith in the Ben Sira, "Lilith, the red haired queen from the North."

However the Anunnaki were evidently similar enough genetically to be able to clone their genes effectively with those of the Eljo race they found "here" and eventually, through several processes, to create modern man. What was once science fantasy genetically, is medical fact, and now some writers find no difficulty in confirming that, as the Sumerian traditions "suggest," the Anunnaki were indeed originally from another planet: The Sha World.

However, this is UTTER and ABSOLUTE BUNK. Michael S. Heiser, a Hebrew scholar at the University of Wisconsin-Madison, clearly points out that the word Sitchin translated as "rocket ship" – SHU.MU – in order to support his assertion that the Anunnaki came from Nibiru, actually means "bricks/mortar." When was the last time NASA went to Jewson's Building Supplies to buy bricks and mortar for the Shuttle? Regarding Nibiru, I quote Dr. Heiser:

"Fortunately for scholars and other interested parties, the work of the studies above and the editors of the monumental *Chicago Assyrian Dictionary* (= CADhereafter) have located and compiled all the places where the word "nibiru" and related forms of that word occur in extant tablets. A look at the CAD entry (volume "N-2," pp. 145-147) tells us immediately that the word has a variety ofmeanings, all related to the idea of "crossing" or being some sort of "crossing marker" or "crossing point." In only a minority of cases (those references in astronomical texts) does the word relate to an astronomical body. Below is a brief overview of the word's meanings outside our immediate interest, followed by specific meanings and references in the astronomical texts.

General Meanings of Occurrences Outside Astronomical TextsWord meaning, of course, is determined by context. "Nibiru" (more technically and properly transliterated as "neberu"[5]) can mean several things. I have underlined the form of nibiru for the reader: "place of crossing" or "crossing fee" – In the Gilgamesh epic,[6] for example, we read the line (remarkably similar to one of the beatitudes in the sermon on the Mount): "Straight is the crossing point (nibiru; a gateway), and narrow is the way that leads to it." A geographical name in one Sumero-Akkadian text, a village, is named "Ne-bar-ti-Ash-shur" ("Crossing Point of Asshur"). Another text dealing with the fees for a boatman who ferries people across the water notes that the passenger paid "shiqil kaspum sha ne-bi-ri-tim" ("silver for the crossing fees"). "ferry, ford"; "ferry boat"; "(act of) ferrying" – For example, one Akkadian text refers to a military enemy, the Arameans: "A-ra-mu nakirma bab ni-bi-ri sha GN itsbat"[7] ("The Arameans were defiant and took up a position at the entrance to the ford [gate, crossing point]"). In another, the Elamites are said to "ina ID Abani ni-bi-ru u-cha-du-u" ("[to] have cut off the ford [bridge, crossing way] of the river Abani"). I think the "root idea" of the nibiru word group and its forms as meaning something with respect to "crossing" is clear.

So "Neberu" refers to the doorway (cf; River Styx et al) to the Otherworld and the reader is directed towards my description of this place as both the underworld and the realm of eternity (Transcendant Universal Consciousness): Kether, Annwyn, Tir Na nog, Elphame, Faery, Samadhi, Arcadia, Elysium, The Kingdom of Heaven, etc. Connected to this concept is the Rath, also spelt Wrath. The burial mound dwellings of the Fairies, Elves-Vampires: The

Wraiths- (Ghosts/Undead/Barrow/Berg Dwellers). The Anunnaki and their elven, Vampire children (the Nephilim) were from this world, but occupied a different state of consciousness/dimension.

They used their genetic material here in Arda to sire both the Elves, the Elder Race – "The Children of the Stars" – and the subsequent races of hybrid humans. But in so doing, the Anunnaki used a massively higher concentration of their genes when fashioning the Dragons or Elves than when they created their human helpers.

Gestational surrogacy. Through IVF, a surrogate can carry embryos that have been created from the eggs of the baby's intended mother and sperm of his intended father. The eggs are retrieved from the intended mother and fertilized with the sperm, allowed to grow, then transferred into the surrogate's uterus through a catheter (or frozen for later transferring). In cases where the intended parents can't produce the necessary sperm or eggs, a donor may also be used.

The transfer of the embryos itself is often described by surrogates as startlingly quick and easy; it's the process of getting ready for that transfer and the weeks after that require heavy medical intervention. The most common protocol in the US involves months of daily injections for the surrogate. First, birth control pills and shots of hormones to control and suppress her own ovulatory cycle, then shots (or skin patches) of estrogen to build her uterine lining (as the other drugs will prevent this), then continuing after the transfer, daily injections of Progesterone until her body catches up to the idea it's pregnant and can sustain the pregnancy on its own

Phytoestrogens: Flax Seed and Tofu have the highest amounts of these chemicals and are known in the classical world. Phytoprogesterones can be obtained from Yams, amongst other plants and fruits. Where am I going with this? The Sumerian accounts of the Shimti Birthing House and gestational surrogacy are not necessarily a myth. As the Egyptians performed brain surgery, so it is entirely scientifically possible that the Dragons/Elves were created by the Anunnaki, utilising a far simpler non surgical procedure, by fertilising a second generation Homo Sapiens ovum and planting it, via a catheter, into Nin-kursag's womb, which acted as a gestational surrogate, and fed the growing foetus on pure Anunnaki blood serum. No immune suppressants would necessarily have been required to prevent rejection, but if they were, a multitude of phytological drugs were available in the classical era.

Theoretically, in vitro fertilisation could be performed by aspirating contents from a woman's fallopian tubes or uterus with a catheter after natural ovulation, mix it with semen from a man and reinsert into the uterus.

Mystery solved.

By the way, this is pre-genetic cloning. The word clone is a Greek horticultural term referring to a branch that has been grafted onto another tree. Nothing more.

The historical Dragons were further nourished in the holy wombs on the blood of the gods – whilst men were maturated in human wombs and consequently they only carried an insignificant amount of Anunnaki genetic material in their blood, enough to enable them to learn and understand – through their Dragon intermediaries – the tasks they were to perform for the gods, but not enough for them to be able to "see clearly" or transcendently. Thus they became known as the "beclouded people."

This is why the Dragons or Elves were set up as god-kings over man, they were the Avatars – the Holy Sons of the Gods and the rightful inheritors of the mantle of the Anunnaki. They were the "clear-sighted ones" and could perceive what the gods perceived and occupied the realm the gods inhabited whilst still maintaining a foothold here in Arda. And indeed, as I have pointed out, the word dragon solely and specifically means "to see clearly," to wit transcendentally.

In this respect, as sacral kings the Dragons acted hermetically as messengers and intermediaries between the two realms, between the gods and man. Later, in the area of the Lavant, the Elves became known as the Malachai, which translates as "angels": The messengers of the Order of the god-kings of the Anukim and the Repha'im; the first Pontiffs or holy bridges between the world of the gods and the world of man.

These experiments are clearly documented in the Babylonian texts and their results – the Elves – are repeatedly referred to up until the medieval period as originating (as the Anunnaki) from a different world. The Dragons or Elves are the first-born of the gods and for this reason Tolkien called them the Eldar (Elder Race).

From this we may conclude that the exercise in creating god-kings to rule over the beclouded people took place physically on this planet, but in a different realm from that occupied by man. This realm is often referred to in the Gaelic lands as "Tir n'An Og," or "Annwyn" – "The Otherworld" or "The Underworld."*

[*Note: The Norse God Odin and his brothers Thor and Frey originated in Anatolia in modern Turkey (the ancient Scythian druidic centre of Eurasia) and the eminent scholar of Scandinavian history and mythology – Magnus Magnusson – clearly states that Odin and his kin were historical God-Kings and Priest-Princes, prior to their eventual total deification in the Nordic Lands. They migrated north through Transylvania (establishing the cult of Thor there) and on through Germania to Scandinavia.

It is apparent therefore, that Odin and his brothers were druidic in origin and consequently Scythian Holy Royalty or "Kushan." It is from Odin that we trace a significant portion or our Vere ancestry, as do various other Scandinavian Royal Dynasties. In Norse legend the elves and the gods, such as Odin and Thor, are lumped together as being virtually identical and from this we may conclude that the elves native specifically to Scandinavia were the children of the god Odin who, incidentally, introduced the horned helmet to the Norse, not as apparel for the warriors, but for the priests (Magnusson). Such were an aspect of the holy garb which was originally inherited from the Anunnaki, who can be seen wearing such in precession on early Sumerian tablets.]

To continue, it is the Realm of the Gods and the Realm of Faery. It is Alfheim and Elphame, Aelfr-londe, Ljos-Alfa Heimr, Elda-mar, Eluen Londe. To the Jews, Muslims and the Christians it is the Kingdom of Heaven and to the Buddhists it is Shangri-La, Boddhisatva, Samadhi, and to the Gaels it is Anwynn – the realm of the dead. Ultimately, it may be understood as the Kabbalistic realm of Kether, which is here, and not here.

The author has been familiar with this realm throughout his life and it is indeed another dimension, inasmuch as it is a different state of being where time and space have very unique qualities. To reach it one must be able to see Kether in Malkuth, because there lies the door to this other world. This dimension has been written about on numerous occasions throughout history and these descriptions tally with each other significantly enough to produce a consistent description of another parallel realm, co-existent with this one and accessible through this world alone.

TT: When we first met you told me about a research project that some university was doing to try and identify "Dragon genes" in people. What exactly is this project, and is it still going on today?

NDV: To answer this question I will again paste an excerpt of The Duchy of Angiers table here and develop the idea afterwards.

I quote:

The relationship between the Prince de Vere – who, by patrilinear descent, is the Head of the House of Vere in Ireland and Nicholas de Vere who – by matrilinear descent – is Sovereign Head Internationally, and also Head of the House of Vere of Tyrone, is that of third, seventh and fourteenth cousins. Both share various identical genes. Found in only three percent and six percent of the clinical samples tested in Britain, Nicholas de Vere and the Head of the House in Eire share two sets of rare genes each.

The Prince de Vere is of Royal Collison extraction and Nicholas de Vere also has an extra set of these genes from his matrilinear descent which also supports the Collison descent from Norfolk in his own lineage and echoes the selective and exclusive royal and noble marital alliances which have continued throughout the history of the House of Vere.

The House of Vere and Weir commissioned genetic tests to be undertaken to confirm the precise degree of relationship between their respective lines and in order to clarify any anomalies in genealogy that inevitably creep into the records as the mists of time occlude the past. This was achieved successfully and some records were amended to reflect genetic findings both in Nicholas' lineage and that of another of his Vere cousins in Ireland, confirming that Nicholas' descent is the senior bloodline of the House of Vere.

However, the genetic makeup of the House of Vere, manifesting generation after generation, proved to be so unusual that beyond the remit of the original commission by the family, the Department of Haemogenetics at London University took the Veres on as a special study case. At that particular stage of the research a Conference Presentation Document concerning the Veres was submitted prior to the delivery of a medical paper at a then forthcoming Genetics Symposium in the United States, by an eminent professor in the department who is an internationally recognised pioneer in genetics.

In short, the members of the Race of Vere have more genes than ordinary Man. Double sets of these praeter-natural genes appear on the Y chromosome at DYS 389 I and DYS 389 II. Descending latterly from Scythian, Norse, Danaan and Gaelic gods and their fairy offspring, the genetic difference between the Veres and human beings is further reflected in the fact that Nicholas de Vere and the Houses of Vere and Collison combined have hundreds of distinct fairy bloodlines of alien extraction descending from incomparably ancient Dragon origins.

As historical avatars and god-kings, the Race of Vere contemporarily embody genetically the phrase Dieu Et Mon Droit – By God and My Right – and prove the blood-precedent of this divine right of elven high kings. As I have outlined in *The Dragon Legacy*, the name "Vere" itself derives in antiquity from the term "overlord," originating with the displaced fairies or elves who moved to Caledonia in 650 BC.

(Note: Please see Appendix C, The Meaning of the Vere Name.)

As for other Dragon genes, these were identified from research deriving from both London University and The University of Oxford. This aspect of the project has been completed. There are another two main types of genes which go to make up a contemporary Dragon.

TT: Did Dragons possess "magical" powers? If so, do their descendants possess them as well?

NDV: It depends what you mean by "magical." The greatest magic of all is to be able to naturally still one's mind to the point where one sees that "all acts are magical acts." As a natural course of events stemming from transcendent perception and stillness of mind, certain facilities are within the grasp of Dragons. These abilities, though they vary, are hereditary.

TT: Your former co-author Laurence Gardner writes a lot about "starfire" and the power of pineal secretions, which are portrayed as being analogous to the Elixir of Life or Philosopher's Stone, bestowing increased brain capacity, magical ability, and prolonged life upon him who consumes it. These are elements that he clearly picked up from your research. In your writing, you claim that people of "Dragon blood" are the only ones bio-chemically equipped to produce these substances in their own bodies at a high enough level to yield results. But Gardner has written much about this so-called "monatomic gold," and seems to think that this is a synthetic substitute for "starfire" which ordinary people can consume to become Dragons themselves. Do you know anything about this substance? What is your comment on Mr. Gardner's theories?

NDV: Firstly, it has to be said that indeed I introduced Laurence Gardner to the physical, hormonal concept of Starfire, but this is only one side of the story, and in my book I clearly state that the whole process contains several other "psycho-somatic," alchemical elements, not least that pertaining to the hierogamic relationship with the "Anam Cara."
As for being able to pop a pill to become a Dragon, this kind of stupid New Age attitude stems from the ridiculous, totally indefensible, greed-driven free market assertion that anyone can become anything they choose, and the totally unfounded PC notion that everyone is equal. If you tell people that, you can sell them anything.
This kind of pathetic, wet liberalism, born as a nervous knee-jerk reaction to the socially inculcated, whining victim mentality, should be abhorred by all rational beings, and so my attitude towards the concept of monatomic gold as a great social leveler and equalizer is one of contempt.

Can I pop a pill to turn me into a real black African Massai warrior? No. Is there a powder I can take to change me genetically into a real woman? Of course not. In any event, even if it existed, I don't see the need for monatomic gold myself. Starfire and the Seraphic relationship worked perfectly well for me, and in any case you are either genetically a Dragon – the member of the Elven Race – or you are not, and no amount of monatomic gold is going to change your genetic makeup.

In any event, since writing the foregoing, monatomic gold has been lately analyzed under laboratory conditions and has been exposed as a fraud. I think it showed itself to be a mixture of chalk and baking powder. I believe Laurence Gardner took the concept of monatomic gold in absolute good faith but was unfortunately misled. It simply doesn't exist. There is no substitute for Dragon genes and there never will be.

TT: What was the original meaning and purpose of vampirism?

NDV: Vampire stems from the word "vber" or "uber," and means "witch." It originates in Anatolia; the location of the seven yearly druidic gatherings: the Nemetons. "Witch" in Gaelic is "druidhe" – drui – or "druid." In practical terms, and suggested by the term "uber" (over), a Scythian druid was an overlord, and so originally a vampire was an overlord, and hence a witch was a Dragon. (See meaning of the Vere name in Eurasia, previous page.)

The purpose of vampirism depends on the type of vampirism practised. Starfire or transcendent consciousness was the purpose of royal or druidic vampirism in the ancient Scythian families. Additionally, related to this type of vampirism, Dragon blood was imbibed to cure ailments. The sister of the Grail knight, Parcival, used to donate her blood to be drunk by mortals suffering from afflictions.

In Scythian warrior vampirism, drinking the blood of fallen brothers in battle was intended to take their essence and bravery into the recipient. The blood of vanquished foes was also drunk. In both cases it also had the advantage of topping up one's adrenaline and testosterone levels in the heat of conflict. The savage folklore image of the vampire in Europe stems from this ancient, historical, middle-European, Scythian, military root. Vampirism was an integral part of Scythian Dragon life.

Contributing to this view is the legend of the "werewolf," meaning man-wolf, one of the initiatory grades of middle-European vampire which has distinct links with Mithraism. In the pre-Christian and early Christian period, certain clans and tribes, both in north-west and central Europe, revered totem animals whose skins would be worn, and corporal material imbibed, to avail the tribe of the virtues of the totem and to aid in its ritual invocation within the group.

We know that the Wolf clans and tribes were Scythian-Draconian because the name given to them was "Stregoi," which means "a vampire – wolf." The word *stregoi* or *strega* translates as "witch" – as indeed the word vampire does also. From witch or "druidhe" we obtain druid, and arrive at the inescapable conclusion that werewolves existed as a magical totemic group, not unlike the Greek Bacchantes, whose totem animal was the panther and who were also noted for their blood lust and savagery. Whilst the Bacchantes revered the tripartite deity Bacchus-Pan-Dionysus, whose origins can be found in the Anunnaki god Enki, the Stregoi revered the Anunnaki goddess Lilitu, or "Lilith of the Moon," whose origins can be traced to ancient Carpathia and Transylvania.

TT: What are the meanings of the terms Fairy, Pixie, Elf, Gnome, Druid, Aryan, Pharisee? Are these all names for essentially the same thing, according to your theory?

NDV: Yes, these terms are all associated with the same being and stem from the Dragon genome.

Fairy = Fata (Latin), Faery, Fey: Controller of Fate and, in particular, a controller of the fate of man and hence, an overlord. In all accounts of fairies they are of high royal blood or origin. Faery and Elf are synonymous.

Pixie = "Pict-Sidhe" or "Sithe" (Pict = Painted; Sithe = Scythian), after the Scythian, Dragon habit of painting tribal markings onto the body. The mushroom *Amanita muscaria*; the red-capped, white-spotted fungus immortalised in fairy stories, is also called the "Pixie Cap," after the human habit of eating it as a religious sacrament in order to attempt to enter the world of the Elves or Pixies.

Elf = Albe, Aelf, Oberon – "White or Shining One." This refers to the beautiful fair countenance of Dragons as witnessed by their contemporary observers.

Gnome = "Wise one." The word "gnome" derives from the Greek root "gno," from whence we obtain the word gnosis, meaning mystical wisdom derived from "Clear Sight." A Gnome was a member, therefore, of the race of Gnomes or Wise Ones and this term is synonymous with Aryan, which means "scion of the wise," and thus, "noble race." The word noble also stems from the same root word as gnome: gno. Therefore, to be a nobleman originally meant that one had to be a Wise Man of clear vision. From thence we may confirm that a gnome – a wise one – was racially a Dragon.

Druid = Man or woman of the Tree, specifically the Tree of Life: In female form the Scythian Priestess – down whom filters the essences of the brain into the Grail receptacle of the womb.

Anciently, in Irish Gaelic, the term Druid meant a Witch and in this connection St. Columba said of Jesus Christ, as I have stated; "Jesus: Mo Drui, Mac Dei," meaning, "Jesus my witch, son of God."
In *Revelations* ch 16, v 22 Jesus says, "I am the Bright and Morning Star." The Morning Star is Venus, as Lucifer the Fallen One. Jesus deliberately identifies himself as this Emerald Jewel in Satan's Crown and consequently, with the Grail Cup and Philosopher's Stone of Wisdom, as previously stated.
The statue of Melchidezek outside the Cathredral of Chartres is shown holding a cup in which there is a stone. This clearly illustrates that the synonymous nature of the Grail and the Cubic Stone had been known and acknowledged for centuries. Both are one and the same.

People often proclaim that little is known about the Druids and their discipline. However when the Druids traveled east and stayed with Siddharta (who was actually a Scythian Prince), he discussed with them their teachings and practices and proclaimed that they had established Shangri-La in the west. This was before the unenlightened had cobbled together yet another stupid religion and called it Buddhism. Thus we can say that, as well as being likened closely to original, mystical Christianity, Druidism also bore a close resemblance to the original spiritual teachings and philosophy of the Buddha. The sundered Elves who traveled east and became the Twghry, also honoured Siddharta as they would have their own Druids.

Druids were known historically to specialise in medicines and healing, with prophecy and seership. Their bards sang into being the gods for people to follow, and they controlled the behaviour and conduct of the kings they invested, through magic and exhortation. They truly were the priest-princes and overlords of their time. Add to this the practice of the original Sumerian version of the Kabbalah and "kaula tantra," with its vampiric blood rituals, and you have a reasonably clear picture of Druidism.

Aryan = Scion of the wise or noble race, see above; another term for the members of the king tribe where "king," from the Gothic "kuningjam," means "scion of the noble (wise and hence Aryan) race." Related to kuningjam, the word king is also related to the word "kenning," meaning knowledge or specifically, wisdom. Anciently, before the rise of the moronic Catholic puppet monarchs, a king was expected to be a being of profound, transcendent mystical wisdom – a true psychopomp, a seer and a hands-on leader of his people.

Prior to Hitler ridiculously asserting that the entire German "volk" were all Aryans, and then cold-bloodedly torturing and murdering six million perfectly decent human beings, the word Aryan was used in common academic parlance without creating so much as a stir. Nowadays, the name is only associated with Nazi atrocities and modern white supremacy low-life thugs.

I use the term Aryan connected only with the concept it originally embraced – the King Tribe of Indo-Europe: The Scythians. I am an Aryan, but condemn without hesitation any form of anti-semitism, racism or neo-Nazism. All true Aryans would. White supremacist peasant trash today believe the fascist lie and mindlessly and erroneously jibber that all whites are Aryans. It is not so, and in actual fact, Aryans make up only a tiny number of Europeans today. The Aryans were exclusively a small royal tribe, genetically separated from the vast mass of white, Caucasian people they reigned over.

Pharisee = In English folklore, a "farisee" or "fairy." In Hebrew it stems from "parush," meaning "one who is set aside," and hence, above others; a term which describes the elves or fairies as a race beyond the realm of man.

TT: How does the symbolism of Baphomet fit in with your theory?

NDV: Baphomet can be appreciated on several levels depending on your point of view. To the Church, Baphomet was the Devil and in a sense it is, inasmuch as the goat-headed effigy represents, on one level, Enki; who was later to appear as their Shaitan or Satan. Anciently, Enki was known as "the

Ram of the Shimmering Waters," and was the prototype of the Golden Fleece. It appears that Baphomet is a later variation on the same theme. From Enki and his partner Lilith we obtain both Capricorn, the male Goat of the Water, and the female Leviathan – the union of opposites and their subsequent negation. In this sense it can be appreciated as a glyph pointing to the origins of the Dragon dynasty.

To compound this view, on occasion the Baphomet appears with the wings of an angel, and the angel clearly associates the Baphomet – as the badge and progenitor of the Dragon race – with the biblical gods, the Elohim and their later progeny, the Anukim kings, the Angels or early elves.

On the alchemical level – in Eliphas Levi's depiction of the Baphomet – with the symbolic sexual union represented in it by the presence of both male and female sexual organs, we have the reconciliation of opposites, the amalgamation and resultant negation of the microcosmic male and female gender polarities and the consequent occurrence of individuation – spiritual transcendence – as a product of that negation within the Seraphic Relationship. It is a dynamic where, as Arthur Machin put it, "the two Dragons devour each other and another is born; a Phoenix, a fiery Star of Wonder." In Levi's glyph this process is encapsulated in the alchemical terms "solve" and "coagula." The interpretation of this in Christian terms is solve: the psychological death of the "Old Man" of the unregenerate ego and coagula: the re-emergence in the "New Man" of transcendent perception and Union with Godhead. Associated with this we have Baphomet as "Father Mithras."

Often the Baphomet, The Horned God of the Witches, is depicted as the head of the Satanic Goat within the inverted pentagram. Around this glyph are invariably placed the Hebrew consonants that spell out the name of the Anunnaki Goddess Lilith in her guise as the female form of the "Leviathan." Situated between Baphomet's horns lies the Cubic Stone of the pineal gland that is the Emerald Jewel in the Crown of Satan, and the falling star of Lucifer.

If the Satanic pentagram is turned upside down to represent the head and limbs of Lilith, the Witches' Goddess, the Cubic Stone then rests between her legs and becomes the Grail of the womb. Thence the essences of the pineal gland – melatonin, seratonin and tryptophan – descend through the third ventricle of the brain and down the spiral cortex of the spinal column like the falling star, and come finally to rest in the womb of Lilith's representative, the Dragon Priestess. From there they are harvested and ingested, on the one hand to promote higher consciousness, and on the other to aid in producing longevity and good health.

The chemical indole rings of these pineal substances are noted scientifically to bear remarkably close similarities to those related to a variety of hallucinogenic drugs, and like them they act as neuro-transmitting receptor gates within the synapses of the brain. Whilst recent scientific studies of certain other human female essences carried out in the USA have ascertained that they carry powerful anti-bodies and anti-carcinogenic substances that aid in the promotion and reinforcement of the immune system and the prevention and cure of cancer.

Furthermore, womb blood carries telomerase, which prevents the fraying of the gene strands, thereby delaying the onset of genetic degeneration and ageing. Thus the ancient alchemical, Elven tradition of royal vampirism practised by my Dragon ancestors, contemporarily termed Starfire, is now known to have a sound scientific basis. Thus the two dragons devour each other and another is born, a Phoenix, a fiery Star of Wonder that ascends to the throne of Heaven.

As Father Mithras, Baphomet represents the killing of the "world bull" of unregenerate perception, from which sacrifice flows the fertility of the freed consciousness. Additionally, Mithras is the balancing medium between Ormuzd and Ahriman, the extreme forces of generation and destruction – and therefore represents cosmic balance in the universe and personal detachment in the individual. Here again we touch upon the Hermetic doctrine of "as above, so below." What happens in the cosmos takes place also in man.

In this vein we can see that the Baphomet symbolizes the Beast 666 – man as God – uniting the Earthly nature of "man the Beast," represented as the goat; and the divine, Godly element of man as symbolized by the angel's wings. In Kabbalistic Numerology, 6 is the number of man born of woman and 3 represents the trinity of God, therefore 666 represents Man as God, or the "Beast."

In this glyph we see that the divine is to be found in base nature, and base nature is to be found in the divine. The Kabbalists put it as "Kether in Malkuth, and Malkuth in Kether, Heaven on Earth and Earth in Heaven." Furthermore, this glyph represents the true nature of the elves, sharing the mortal, bodily mantle with man but embodying the eternal, divine nature of the Gods that man never partakes in.

In practical, cosmic terms it means that, as Heaven is on Earth and Earth is in Heaven, in reality there is no spiritual or occult "path" to tread, no "system" of so-called enlightenment to follow, because it is all here now. If one kills the Mithraic "world bull" of fear and greed and stills the mind, then the timeless, the eternal, the heavenly, becomes apparent here and now on Earth, not in some fantasy, ethereal, life-after-death state to come. In realising this, one may enter the Kingdom of God, the Realm of Faery or Elphame.

Baphomet, as the legendary head of the Templars, has an earlier correlation in the Celtic symbol of the detached head of the arch druid Bran the Blessed, which was also a font of wisdom and fertility. The close association of the Head of Wisdom – the Baphomet – with the Grail, is demonstrated in the depiction of the Templar Skull and Cross Bones – the original "Jolie Rouges" or Jolly Roger.

Again, this has a Hermetic meaning inasmuch as what is above – in the head – is also below, in the womb, or Grail. The head as a Grail symbol derives spiritually and symbolically from the historically recorded Celtic belief that the divine spirit resided within the head. The severed Templar head – the skull – resting on the crossed bones of the thighs near the pudenda, reminds us again that the head and the womb were both intrinsically connected receptacles of the divine, and were therefore synonymous as symbols of the Holy Grail.

TT: Is the Dragon bloodline a Satanic or Luciferian bloodline?

NDV: Yes is the honest and simple answer.

TT: If a person believes that they have the Dragon gene, and they want to start developing the powers inherent in their blood, what course would you suggest they follow?

NDV: There isn't one gene, there are four main types that should be found together, and the best course of action, for those who want to be certain of their heritage at the outset, would be to contact a reputable commercial genetic laboratory and find out for sure.

THE SPECIES: DRACO SENTIENS

Dragon Genes

Gene set 1. Melanocortin 1 Receptors on 16q24.3. These genes produce distinct physical attributes by which Dragons/Vampires were anciently recognised, (Titian, Anunnaki coloured hair, green-blue eyes and pale white skin) and which are several hundred thousand years older than human genes. In folklore these genes were thought to make Vampires, Elves and Witches (Dragons) allergic to sunlight. It is a fact, however, that the Melanocortin gene does indeed induce photosensitivity, making it difficult for Dragons to endure bright light; it also makes Vampire flesh burn and become more susceptible to Melanomas, giving at least some credence to the tradition that we burn in sunlight.

Gene Set 2. Anti-Prion mRNA. These resistors have been present in the Dragon makeup for thousands of years and enable the Dragons to feed on human material without manifesting any of the related diseases that might be incurred if humans were to adopt the same practices.

Genes not present in Human Chromosomes

Gene set 3. DNA STR designated allele DYS 389 I.

A. 250.9 (10). Present in each cell.
B. 254.8 (11). Present in each cell.

Gene set 4. DNA STR designated allele DYS 389 II.

A. 368.2 (26). Present in each cell.
B. 372.4 (27). Present in each cell.

Consequently, Dragons have far more genes than humans.

Genetically speaking, racial markers are divided into haplogroups and subclades within those haplogroups. The Vere Haplogroup appears in Southern Germany and South Eastern Europe, featuring Gothic racial indices. Within this haplogroup the subclades indicate descent from the Royal Ha'Melech Dynasty of Judah, whose foremost ancestors included Prince Rama, husband of Princess Kiya Tasherit of Egypt, King David, King Solomon and Jesus Christ, founder of the Grail Dynasty of Europe. It is from these individuals, and the latter in particular, that the author and the Dynasty of de Vere inherit their Holy, Grail Blood. (Ashina Gene Project).

The DNA data of the cousin family of the Sanada Tarnawa-de Vere family, the Tarnawa-Krupa de Vere of HI&RH Prince Alfred Krupa Y-(male) haplogroup and in particular the subclade within it, indicates a Central Asian origin in the area of the Hindu Kush-Altay Mountain range, and today this haplogroup appears only in the south of Central Asia/North India, with some appearing in South Siberia/West China, as well as in Eastern Europe in very low percentages (below 0.061%). The genetic genealogy data strongly indicate an ancient Turk/Hun origin and as such, represents a very rare genetic trail/ signature that is certified by the genetic-genealogy community as the Imperial and Royal Ashina (Grey She-Wolf) Dynasty of Khazaria and the Celestial Turk Empire. This family DNA data also shows the descent from the original Levites – the so-called "Babylonian Levites" (see House of Tarnawa-de Vere) through frequent intermarriages with the Khazar royals. The Sanada Tarnawa-de Vere von Drakenberg and Tarnawa-Krupa de Vere von Drakenberg families, now amalgated, are descended from the same Ha'Melech dynasty.

As for developing powers for their own sake, this isn't magic, it's greed fueled by human fear, inadequacy and insecurity, and greed and ambition are the destroyers of the transcendent Dragon perception and cosmic consciousness, from whence true powers subsequently originate. Power flows naturally for those whose vision is clear, and clear perception will determine that those powers are naturally and automatically used with detachment. Jesus said, "Seek ye first the kingdom of God and all these things will be added unto you."

The fact of the matter is that to Dragons, Dragon magic is simple, naturally occurring and straightforward; and fundamentally it relies on allowing simplicity and stillness within the self, not through learning some ridiculous, half-arsed "magical" system that one might find neatly shrink-wrapped in the local Occult Kwik-E-Mart.

If the reader believes they are of the Dragon Blood and they wish to explore the transcendent concept, in lieu of a lengthy explanation for which there isn't space within the confines of this interview, I would recommend a little book entitled *The First and Last Freedom*, edited by Mary Lutyens from lectures by Jiddu Krishnamurti.

TT: What is the history of the Dragon Court of which you are the sovereign head? Did you inherit this title, and if so, who from?

NDV: The Imperial and Royal Dragon Court appears repeatedly throughout the history of my family. It is the physical, cultural manifestation of the divine Dragon spirit inherent within the Vere Dragon blood, reaching back long before the time of Christ, to the era of Prince Ankh-f-n-khonsu and the Dragon Queen Sobekh Nefru of Egypt.

Briefly, to give a few examples, in more recent times it was the Royal Court of the Dragon, Fairy Princess Milouziana, from whom we are descended in numerous lines, and later, after her, it was the fairy Court of Alberic III de Vere, the legendary Oberon; the hereditary elf king immortalised in Shakespeare's *A Midsummer Night's Dream*.

Immediately following Alberic, it was the Court of his son, Robert de Vere, Earl of Huntingdon, who was the historical Robin Hood; the elven, sacral priest-king of the witches. Later the Dragon Court was manifest in the "Thirteen Covens of Mid-Lothian," and in the cabal of Lady Somerville, the witch-mother of Thomas of Edinburgh. Thomas was the grandson of Sir William Vere of Stonebyres and the elven, Dragon priest-king of the Thirteen Covens. (Murray)

Sir William was the son of James, 7th Baron Blackwood. Lady Jane Somerville's heraldic family badge is recorded as the fiery dragon surmounting the pentacle, denoting Dragon blood in the House of the Somerville earls.

Notably in our family, the Dragon Court is also derived from the Court of the Scots and Welsh Pendragon kings whose lineage we inherit through numerous marital alliances with our close cousins, the dukes of Hamilton, whose estates bordered our own in Lanarkshire, and who were the heirs presumptive to the throne of Scotland.

Lateral inheritance from the extinct cadet cousin branch of the Vere earls of Oxford brings to the contemporary Court, via the 11th earl Richard de Vere, the degree of Societas Draconis – latterly misnamed "Sarkany Rend" – a membership bestowed upon him, it is believed academically, during his investiture into the Prince's Degree of the Order of the Garter, along with the Society's apparent founder, Emperor Sigismund of Luxembourg (who, along with Elizabeth Bathory, is a Vere cousin), at St. George's Chapel, Windsor Castle, Bolton.

The heraldry of the family prior to Richard's investiture into Societas Draconis already included the ancient Dragon motifs on both the paternal and maternal sides of the family, denoting pure Dragon blood in both descents, and reflecting the continuing presence of the Dragon Court in the family since the time of Princess Milouziana of the Scythians.

The contemporary Dragon Court is furthermore a combination of what Aleister Crowley would have termed several "currents," of which the major external one to the family proper was bestowed upon me on Midsummer's Night in 1985, with the rank of hereditary Magister Templi, via the Black Country Covenant of the Baphometic Order of the Cubic Stone, who trace their origins back to the Knights Templars. This was given in recognition of my family's hereditary involvement in Royal Witchcraft and the historical Dragon tradition.

In June 1991 I received my investiture into the Knighthood of the Plantagenet Clan Donnachaid – Dragon cousins to the House of Vere – founded by Prince Donnchadh in 963 AD. During the ceremony in the Castle Chapel, I was dubbed a knight, anointed as a priest, received the baronial cap of Maintenance and bestowed with the Garter of the Princes of the House of Plantagenet.

Laterally from our ancestral cousin, Edward de Vere, the seventeenth Earl of Oxford, we have obtained the current of Dr. John Dee's magical "School of Night." Edward was a prominent member of that fraternity during the reign of Queen Elizabeth I and also performed the rites of Dragon kingship in the family, specifically the rite of the kingship of the Calle Daouine, the Elven Kings of Caledonia in Scotland during that period.

Down the centuries the Royal Dragon Court is carried continuously in the Vere Dragon Blood and it would be correct to say I inherited the Dragon Court by virtue of being the senior blood descendant of the House of Vere, and I am recognized as a Dragon sovereign by the other senior members of the family. Academic sources and references pertaining to these Dragon descents are published in the bibliography of this book.

TT: How can one become a member of the Dragon Court and, once a member, what does one do? What is the current function of the Dragon Court?

NDV: Today the Court consists solely of participating family members. We do not admit outsiders. In addition to these, we have emeritus officers whose functions are invaluable to the running of the Court.

One of the current functions of the Dragon Court is as the custodian of the Dragon tradition within the Vere family, which includes the continuing study of the history and genealogy of its various branches, and the amendment and expansion of records as fresh knowledge comes to light.

Membership of the Dragon Court is given rarely. We are not a joining club, nor do we operate for monetary gain in any sense. As time passes the Dragon Ethos demands that the Dragon Court change and develop according to expediency. In the future we may well expand the membership of the Court to take in new Dragon members or to expand the number of emeritus officers. Alternatively, we may not.

TT: Many people have ascribed to you a radical political agenda, and say that you are trying to use your genealogy as a springboard for a bid for the throne of England, and other such nonsense. What is your response to these claims?

NDV: I cannot take such assertions seriously. The educated reader will already know that the House of Vere fielded over twenty prominent earls in an unbroken line over 561 years of British history. The House of Vere was credited with being the senior bloodline of England and Europe, both by its contemporaries and by later historians, and the Veres acted for centuries as Chancellors and Great Chamberlains to the various nondescript, transient royal dynasties that came and went over time.

As Chancellors and Great Chamberlains they were the closest advisors to the monarchs and were therefore the major influence or power behind the British throne. In all this time the family never considered it expedient to stoop to pick up the Crown.

It is apparent, given the family's pre-eminently powerful and influential historical position within British society, that the English monarchy was a triviality beneath the dignity and ambition of the House. I see no reason to change that opinion today, so as you say, the notion that I would demean myself by making a bid for a human throne is utter nonsense. We have standards to maintain in this family. Anyway the monarchical system in Britain today is, to a great extent, impotent, and so if one wanted real political power, the last place one would find it would be on the throne of England.

In any event, I am already acknowledged officially by the Government as the Sovereign Head of a Sovereign Nation State of Peoples, and I have numerous official Government documents that reflect and support my position in this capacity, being imperial, royal and diplomatic.

All Government departments and agencies on a local, regional, national and international level acknowledge me by my royal titles and according to my royal status.

Copies of these documents are available on request.

So spiritually, I have a State and a Throne of my own. Why would I want someone else's, with all the concomitant difficulties? What an utter bore. I do not seek power or position in the world, I simply work towards the restoration of my family's history and dignity, a history that has been eroded and obscured by time and overshadowed by the greed and ambition of self-serving peasant dynasties who have bought or forced their way into positions of prominence and power.

I also quote as follows:

"Vere-de-Vere stalked into the English vernacular as a playful term meaning the grandest, proudest, most historic, indisputably aristocratic and absolutely creme de la creme of Anglo-Norman antiquity. In fiction the expression is used for characters of, or assuming, unquestionable ancient lineage – and with good cause. In the Middle Ages, owing to plagues and battlefield mortality, the average noble dynasty in England lasted not more than three generations. The de Veres, however, managed to maintain a line of twenty earls of Oxford over 561 years.
Lord Thomas Macaulay, Victorian historian supreme calls this family: 'The longest and most illustrious line of nobles that England has seen... the noblest House in Europe.'
Vero Nihil Verius (nothing truer than truth) is the family motto granted by Queen Elizabeth I. The family Totem, which became its heraldic badge and crest, was already the Druidic Blue Boar."
—Verily Anderson

Also concerning the de Vere name, we have:

"The noblest subject in England, and indeed, as Englishmen loved to say, the noblest subject in Europe, was Aubrey de Vere... who derived his title through an uninterrupted male descent, from a time when the families of Howard and Seymour were still obscure, when the Nevills and Percys enjoyed only a provincial celebrity, and when even the great name of Plantagenet had not yet been heard in England. One chief of the house of de Vere had held high command at Hastings; another had marched, with Godfrey and Tancred, over heaps of slaughtered Moslems, to the sepulcher of Christ.
The first earl of Oxford had been minister of Henry Beauclerc, The third earl had been conspicuous among the lords who extorted the great Charter from King John. The seventh earl had fought bravely at Cressy and Poictiers. The thirteenth earl had, through many vicissitudes of fortune, been the chief of the party of the Red Rose, and had led the van on the decisive day of Bosworth. The seventeenth earl had shone at the court of Elizabeth I, and had won for himself an honourable place among the early masters of English poetry...."
—Lord Macaulay of Rothley Temple

TT: Are you a monarchist?

NDV: By definition Stalin was a "monarch," as were all the presidents of the United States. By such a definition I cannot be said to be a monarchist *per sé*. I am only a royalist with the greatest of qualifications because not all who contemporarily claim to be royal, or those who have occupied the positions of royalty in history, have actually been of royal blood.

I see no point in a Constitutional Monarchy like Britain's, it's just window dressing. The Queen has no political power as such, and contributes little to the well-being of her "subjects," unlike her cousins, King Juan Carlos and Queen Sophia of Spain who, at least, get out and mix with the people informally on a regular basis and are always there for them to give hands-on comfort and support when things go wrong.

Our woman hides herself, and neither acts as a brake on the excesses of party political power, nor as a champion of her people. Indeed, you would never find Elizabeth Windsor or her family regularly taking coffee in a street café and chatting easily and informally with the rest of the people like Juan and Sophia do.

By adopting this air of infallible superiority over others, she hopes to continue to discourage completely any questions concerning her right or suitability to maintain a grip on her privilege. But in so doing she has also alienated a growing section of the British public who simply see her as obsolete, uncaring and out of touch with reality.

She's a hugely expensive squatter in some of the finest properties in the United Kingdom. She has no right to the luxury and privilege that she and her family enjoy. Like her forebear Queen Victoria, Elizabeth Windsor and her family are middle-class upstarts. For this and many other fundamentally sound reasons Britain should come to its senses and declare itself a Republic.

Due to the fraudulent nature of a Papal document called the Donation of Constantine, wherein the usurping Catholic Church falsely claims the right to crown kings, we haven't actually had a legitimate monarch on the throne for well over a thousand years. This being the case, we do not have a legitimate peerage either. All the titles and Coats of Arms handed out over the last millennium have been illegal, worthless rubbish because of the invalidity of the passing monarchs' false coronations and their consequent lack of any royal fons honorum or right to bestow those honours.

Because of this, the formalised, constitutional foundation of the British College of Arms by Henry VIII, following its initial inception by Richard III, was totally spurious and illegal – because he was crowned by a Catholic Arch-Bishop who had no legal or traditional right to do so – and in consequence of this and the continued practice by each subsequent monarch to be crowned by an illegal priest including Elizabeth Windsor today, the College of Arms under them and under her, are self-regarding arrivistes, who sell worthless tat that has no historical, contemporary, legal or constitutional validity, to the equally snobbish, the stupid and the historically and constitutionally ignorant, at exorbitant prices, having no right to do so. They know this only too well and that is why, like their faux monarch, they behave so insufferably.

I have never approached the College for any honour or Arms nor yet have I been refused any honour or Arms by them. Therefore, my contempt for them isn't derived from the bitterness of having been spurned by them. My contempt is derived from the empiricism derived from the study of the constitutional monarchy and of accurate British history.

In any event, I have an ancient legal and royal right to raise my own Honours and Arms and this right refers back 2600 years in Britain, and the British government acknowledges this fact and honours it. The Crown and its College of Arms are therefore of no consequence to me.

The Crown and its College of Arms are the dubious custodians of baseless, insubstantial traditions and trinkets with an antecedence going back no more than a few hundred years, which no truly ancient family would touch. It is indeed a well-known fact that the old families of Britain view our monarchy today with queasy distaste.

Every morning I wake up and thank God that I am a Vere.

Prior to the reign of the fat Tudor pig, King Henry VIII, King Edward IV was the bastard son of a common foot soldier, a situation which, according to the prevailing law of the time, made him unfit for kingship. The real recipient of the crown should have been his brother George, whose lineage descends to Lord Michael Plantagenet-Hastings of Jiralderie, the true king of Britain, according to the erroneous rules laid down in antiquity by the Church-State. If George had been crowned King, the whole of British history would have been totally different and we wouldn't now be the subjects of ineffectual anally-retentive, self-regarding Germans who have the morals of alley-cats. We would have been the subjects of another moronic Catholic puppet instead. The whole situation is a farce.

A false Church which has fabricated an equally false, farcical apostolic succession from Christ and has obliterated Jesus' true family, Church and ministry from history has, through lies, tyranny, usurpation, torture, genocide and murder, dominated and twisted history and society to its own greed-ridden ends for two thousand years.

Its crowning glory was this aforementioned Donation of Constantine, a forged document cobbled together in late Vulgate Latin in eighth century Paris, instead of the correct classical Latin of Constantine's Byzantium, centuries after the death of Emperor Constantine, in which the Emperor has appeared to sign over to the Church, in his own hand, total temporal control and sovereignty over the whole Roman Empire, and the right to install and depose kings and emperors.

Since that time, in pursuit of their political ambition for world power, the Vatican has brandished this fake document and has perpetuated this lie for centuries. In consequence the Church has been enabled to exercise an ever-increasing, iron grip on society and the minds of a gullible population, over whom they have illegally invested a succession of puppet monarchs who have been the worst, most incompetent, ruinous scum of Europe.

Furthermore, all Churches are false because all Churches derive ultimately from, and contain within their central theology, the Roman Catholic lie and consequently, no Church at all has the right to crown some moron as monarch of a people. Whatever they may call their denominations, in the end they are all money-and power-driven, spiritually barren opportunists with no right to claim that they represent the true teachings or spirit of Christianity, let alone the right to govern a population.

I include in this number, Protestants, Anglicans, Pentecostals, Jehovah's Witnesses, Mormons, Baptists, Methodists, Seventh Day Adventists, TV Evangelists, American Christian Fundamentalists – the whole lot of them. They are all derivative apostate Catholics, just without the incense and the candles.

They all believe the same Biblical, Canonical nonsense invented and established by the Pauline Roman Church. They all believe in attempting some nonsensical divine supplication through the mediation of a spiritually ignorant priesthood; they all believe in the evil, false god Jehovah and his ridiculous creation myth, and they all believe erroneously that Jesus was the Son of God. That particular false, Pauline dogma was only pushed through by a vote at the Council of Nicaea after an act of violence against the ageing and dissenting Bishop Arian, by the unspeakable thug "Saint" Nicholas of Myra.

In the final analysis the vote was hung in the balance and Arian refused to vote Jesus in as the Son of God. Nicholas of Myra, who even in his own time was known and feared as a bully with a reputation for psychotic physical outbursts, repeatedly and violently beat Arian until he changed his vote. Thereby, the most crucial and central tenet of Christian dogma, the absolute divinity of Christ, which shaped the Church and its unwitting and unwilling believers lives for centuries to come, derived from an act of indefensible cruelty against a weak individual who was too old to defend himself.

Christian methods of conversion followed this pattern and far worse for another thousand years. If Christians had the power today, they would still use the same modus operandi, if they thought they could get away with it, and the smell of burning flesh and the screams of the tortured would again be witnessed across the western world. All so-called Christians are Catholics by any other name and many of them are just as bigoted, spiritually vacuous, closed-minded, violent and dangerous as the questionable characters who prowl along the corridors of Vatican power today.

Within the philosophies of any revolutionary movement lie the seeds of that which is being rebelled against. The tyranny and cruelty of the monarchy and nobility in France was replaced by the Age of Terror. The totalitarian monarchy of Russia was replaced by a totalitarian communist elite headed by a president, another form of monarch, with all the fear and oppression that went with it, inherent within the Gulags and the Pogroms. In the end, nothing changed and so it is with all alternative "revolutionary" religions and movements, such as fundamental Christianity, the New Age, Occultism and Wicca. They are all just Catholicism by another name.

Ultimately, all religion is divisive and destructive, all belief is in fact divisive and destructive, including the new lunatic theology of "theoretical" science, and because of this, society is disintegrating now at an alarming rate. Religion is hypocritical and ridden with inconsistencies and double standards. Reflecting this society in general has, as a backlash in recent generations, become spiritually and morally disaffected, duplicitous and confused, and increasingly turns to materialism and hedonism to mask its uncertainty and its fundamental fear of life.

In Britain, knife and gun crime have reached record levels, under-aged teen pregnancy, drunkenness and drug abuse are out of control and any adherence to a common code of social responsibility or decency is rapidly and inexorably disintegrating. All this is a result of centuries of Church-State control and outrageous abuse where a contrived, usurping elite, headed by a spurious, self-seeking, Catholic sponsored monarchy, have oppressed the people for generations.

In the end, this state of affairs we find ourselves in isn't going to change under the present monarchical, Church-State system – a system with no long term plan, no sane direction and little control over the media or corporate power and greed which now promotes and encourages for profit those same divisive social standards that are continually tearing our culture apart.

TT: There are a lot of wild theories being bandied about on the Internet regarding the agenda of the Dragon Court. "New World Order: The Movie" (http://www.geocities.com/newworldorder_themovie/dragoncourt.html) regards the Dragon Court as part of an Illuminati conspiracy involving Satanism and Nazism. "Heeding Bible Prophecy" (http://www.angelfire.com/journal2/watch-unto-prayer/prophecy.html) seems to proclaim nothing less than that the scion of the Devil – the Anti-Christ himself – will emerge from the ranks of the Dragon Court. David Icke and Arizona Wilder claim that your former co-author, Laurence Gardner, shape-shifted into a reptile and sacrificed babies in an underground military base at Montauk, New York. How close are these claims to the truth? What sinister activities are you hiding, Mr. de Vere?

NDV: People think that the Anti-Christ will emerge from the ranks of the Dragon Court? How intuitive of them. The Dragon or Grail Blood, the Blood of Christ, whose members are the rightful heirs of the Messianic tradition, unwittingly find themselves the sworn enemies of the Roman Church who, anticipating trouble at some future date, invented the concept of the Anti-Christ, the adversary of the Church and of God Himself.

This they did as an insurance policy just in case members of the Grail bloodline emerged to establish the rightful position of the Dragon Race in spiritual and social opposition to the Church. Anyone who posed such a threat to their power and wealth could be labeled the Anti-Christ, "the brood of Satan," and made an object of religious and social terror throughout the Orthodox Christian world, thereby guaranteeing the militant and unquestioning support of a horrified Christian population.

It is the Roman Church who murdered and oppressed the Grail families and their supporters for millennia, it is the Roman Church who have promulgated hatred and fear of the Dragon Blood for centuries and it is the Roman Church who declared outright war on us.

We have a right to defend ourselves, our Holy Bloodline and our ancient traditions, but in so doing we become the adversary of the Church and of God Himself, albeit a false Church and a false God. Forced to fulfill their spurious prophecy, one of the Grail Bloodline might have no choice but to oppose the Church, just in order for the Dragon Race to survive. In so doing they will pose this long anticipated threat and one of us, descending from the very blood of Christ Himself, will unavoidably become their ridiculous Anti-Christ.

My views on Nazism are well known. Like Roman Catholicism, Nazism was an opportunistic, myopic, hubris-driven peasant movement populated by the worst in German peasant scum. Its "Aryan" philosophy and aspirations were a complete joke; an outrageous political and cultural lie concocted to dupe a nation into subservience and compliance, and its devotion to nationalistic jingoism was the height of psychological blindness and wishful thinking. You can't make genetic Aryans – a race of kings – out of a nation of genetic turnip-peasants.

As for Satanism, if we mean adherence to Satan as some externalised deity separate from the Dragon blood and the object of religious mumbo-jumbo, devotion and worship, such is an illogical nonsense which is just as psychologically damaging and dangerous as worshipping Jehovah or any other ridiculous god. The ancient Dragon gods of the Anunnaki were flesh and blood beings and as their scions we carry those deities in our blood and in our genes. We do not worship the old Gods, we manifest them.

Their praeter-human legacy and its consequent cosmic consciousness is ancient, holy, rare and precious and we would never demean or compromise it by becoming involved in some pathetic hubris and greed-fueled human conspiracy like the Illuminati which, even if it does exist now, can be no more than a bunch of dissipated businessmen out to make a fast buck and massage their overblown egos by deluding themselves that they are part of some secret movement that will take over the world. What would be the point of taking over the world? It's too much like hard work.

People who invent and promulgate these conspiracy theories do not have two brain cells to rub together. They don't think the subject through to its logical conclusion. If they did, they would rapidly perceive that the whole conspiracy culture is a non sequitur. As individuals they should realise that they are so unimportant and ineffectual that no conspiracy is likely to have any effect on them in their lifetime, so why bother with the paranoia?

Such infantile nonsense just fills the inane websites of lonely, powerless people with too much time on their hands. It sells books and reinforces the erotic neuroses of those with weak minds and a victim mentality. They clearly manifest suppressed sexually submissive, masochistic tendencies that feed rapaciously on unrealistic conspiracy fantasies involving their absolute domination by some superannuated father figure, which is just perverted and childish.

David Icke once announced on his website that Laurence Gardner and his associates performed blood-drinking rituals at his "Columba House." Before uttering this ridiculous libel David should have contacted the Post Office and checked as to where "Columba House" was actually situated. If he had done so, the Post Office would quite happily have told him that "Columba House" was in fact a six inch by twelve inch Post Office box at the local Post Office branch in Tiverton, Devon. Exactly how many shape-shifting reptilian vampires and their victims can you get into a standard British Post Office box?

Having all shape-shifted into reptilian vampires, David Icke would then have us believe that they all shrunk to the size of mannekins and convinced a postal worker to put them in the box. If the Icke fan-base thinks this is possible or even probable, and I am sure that some who stay glued to the Internet all day will, then it is also entirely possible that his readers will believe that Laurence Gardner sacrificed babies at Montauk.

In my considered opinion, David Icke is concocting all this out of his cynical, fiscally motivated imagination and flogging it off to a specifically targeted, willing audience of fellow flakes who, frighteningly enough, actually swallow it whole.

Laurence Gardner published groundbreaking research and changed the course of Grail study, and presented it to a fascinated audience. As such he was an extremely creative and innovative author. People like David Icke and his lunatic followers however, have no creative talent whatsoever, and rather than write or discover something unique themselves, they just latch on to artists like Laurence and through sustained public libel and criticism they jump on the band-wagon and bathe in the negative reflected glory.

Having defended Laurence from David Icke, I must regrettably add, as a cautionary public addendum, my own criticisms, and my reply to his libels of 16th May 2000 onwards. This reply has been a long time coming, and previously I considered any reaction to be beneath my dignity. Now however, such a response, though reluctant, appears to be absolutely necessary in order to restore my good name, my honour and integrity, and that also of the true Imperial and Royal Dragon Court.

Under Hungarian constitutional law ALL "royal" or "noble" courts or orders are actually banned in Hungary, this is a well-known fact throughout Europe. A Catholic monseigneur (remember the "Donation of Constantine!") and a nondescript, minor baron, registered "Sarkany Rend" (Ordo Draconis: The Dragon Order?) in the High Courts in Budapest as Gardner asserts, but as nothing more than a social club. Certainly NOT as "The Imperial and Royal Dragon Court."

Laurence Gardner and Michael La Fosse, were dismissed by me from the Vere Dragon Court, so they then STOLE the Imperial and Royal Dragon Court and Sovereignty names from us and hurriedly decamped to this Hungarian Social Club, claiming that I was a fraud and that this Glorified Hungarian Boy Scout Troop they had joined was actually the REAL Dragon Court. However, I had registered the Vere "Imperial and Royal Dragon Court" years before, as a royal and noble organisation, in a British Court of Law. I then passed all the documentation to the Home Office who acknowledged it by bestowing me with Passport documents, within which were included my royal and ambassadorial titles, dated 12th March, 1997. Lawrence had inspected these Government documents three years prior to the schism and subsequent libels concerning me.

(See Appendix C, pages 446-7: "H.H. Nicholas the Prince [Furst] de Vere von Drakenberg.... H.E. Nicholas de Vere KGC., KCD.").

The present Hungarian Pseudo-Dragon Order never existed as an "Order" originally, it isn't Hungarian in Origin and despite Laurence's assertions to the contrary, it NEVER was registered as a Court of Nobility or Chivalry in the High Courts in Hungary. It has no legitimate fons honorum and no right to bestow noble rank or title. It is that organisation which is fraudulent, thieving and usurping, not mine. Its original leaders have no bloodline descents or genealogical connections with any of the original 1408 membership, whilst I have numerous. So, on all levels, it is simply an insubstantial, baseless and illegal artifice, embellished largely after the fact by Lawrence to cover his tracks, after his dismissal from the real Imperial and Royal Dragon Court of the House of Vere.

Mrs. Angela Gardner told me on 8th October, 1999 that she and Lawrence were "only in the Dragon Tradition for the money." By that time I had had enough of him, his literary impertinences, the petty political hubris of his faux prince, and the boorishness of his equally faux and untalented lift-music writer chum. That, and the fact that he plagiarised me repeatedly by failing to credit my research and writing (*Realm of the Ring Lords*).

Lawrence proceeded to libel me in order to keep his gravy train rolling along nicely and cover up the fact that I had very politely kicked him and his awful cronies out of the Court. On May 16th 2000 he publicly announced that the name on the 1997 passport he had seen was Nicholas Weir and that this name appeared on all my official documents. Not so. (Please see Appendix C, Pages 442 et seq: Proofs of Title and Identity.)

As for he suggesting that the name de Vere that I bear is a fraud, that is hilarious, laughable in the extreme and sadly pathetic. There are about 15 different, clearly historically recorded spelling variants for this name, including de Vere, Vere, Weir, Were, Wier, Ver, Uerre, Wer, Vir, Mhaior, Muir, Vor, Fir, Fer and so on.

Whether Laurence likes to admit it or not, he knows full well that my titles are legitimate, as is my genealogy (which he inspected thoroughly and helped to fine tune in research and collation) and both are recognised by governments in their numerous strata, and by those governments' numerous administrative departments. I have published herein the documentary proofs along with my recognised right of fons honorum.

King Sigismund changed his family tree fraudulently in order to be descended from Princess Melusine Vere, a REAL Dragon Royal, and in any event the Society of the Dragon never was and is NOT Hungarian, it is Angevin French. Like Sigismund I am descended from the House of Luxembourg in numerous lines, I am his descendant cousin on both sides of my family and my right to hold the Dragon Court is legitimate, far more so than that of a bunch of contemporary Magyar arrivistes and a dubious Catholic Priest.

Societas Draconis was NEVER founded as a Catholic body, it had no Chapel or Cathedra, no Patron Saint and no Chaplain. It's Inner Spiritual Guide – Ibrahim Eleazar – was a Muslim! Its Sacred day was Friday, the Holy Day of Venus-Lucifer in whose honour members would wear black, hence the modern Gothic and Hollywood association of vampires with that colour. My Family Seals bore the double Dragon Motif 100 years before Sigismund was even born.

Laurence Gardner knows full well that 12 years ago I confirmed my Imperial and Royal lineage by genetic testing and I do indeed have 127 recorded Imperial, Royal and Noble descents stemming from antiquity.

Finally, most of the secret, central genealogical, spiritual and biochemical knowledge he received, he obtained from me and from my family's archives, so the foreword I wrote in *Genesis of the Grail Kings* concerning his having inside, initiated access to hidden wisdom, was actually only through me. I trust this statement will settle the matter finally. It has not been easy to publish these criticisms of Lawrence, I once considered him to be a friend.

In 2002 The Dragon Court went into abeyance and all titles, honours and memberships formerly bestowed were rescinded and annulled. In 2009 the Dragon Court was revised and re-opened to Family Members, Seneschals and Companions.

Entry to the Inner Family Court is permitted when an application is accompanied with a verifiable royal genealogy and/or a comprehensive genetic profile compiled by FTDNA. Entry as a Seneschal is at the discretion of Family Members and entry as a Companion is open to all who support the aims of the Dragon Tradition. We do not bestow titles, rather, we recognise the individual's rights to bear such, and we do not charge any monies whatsoever for membership.

As a Scythian, Dragon Family and Court, Yr Llys Y Draig Ymerodrol ac Brenhinol, we adhere to "Yr Cyfraithau Am Anrhydeddei Cymraeg" in all matters concerning Heraldry and Honours.

What sinister activities am I hiding? The internal activities of the Court are confidential.

TT: What are your personal beliefs regarding God, spirituality, and religion?

NDV: "Beliefs" regarding God and spirituality create religions, and religions create division, fear and violence within the individual and consequently within society as a whole. Religion is a handy facade for the power and money hungry to conceal themselves behind, and serve as a crutch for the spiritually lazy, weak minded and the unregenerate. Religions happen when people don't get the point of the message – which is nearly always – and blindly worship the message and the messenger, instead of grasping the gnosis – the wisdom – inherent within the words that the message conveys. If you talk to God... you're religious. If God talks to you... you're psychotic.

"Religion is an opiate of the masses." —Karl Marx

Too true.

TT: Who, in your opinion, was the Judeo-Christian god Jehovah? Do you believe that there is any historical basis behind the symbolic notion of Jehovah's conflict with Satan?

NDV: The Jews obtained the main tenets of their religion from the Babylonians during the exile. This is the period when the scribes first started to write the Old Testament but as John Macarthy has pointed out, one later commentator in the Bible complained that the scribes were all damnable liars.

One can say that although the later Jehovah was a false Jewish composite which has changed and developed over the ensuing centuries, his main attributes can be traced back to the Anunnaki god Enlil, and it was Enlil who, after cold-bloodedly murdering his father Anu, caused a war with his step-brother Enki – the Jewish Satan – concerning their individual seniority of position within the Anunnaki dynasty.

So in general terms we can say that the "War in Heaven" between Jehovah and Satan originated in an internecine conflict, fueled, not by the pride and greed of Lucifer, as the Bible would have us believe, but by the fear and jealousy of "God" towards his half-brother "Satan" or Enki who, with Nin-Kursag, was the true creator of both elves and men. In later Greek mythology, Anu is replaced by Chronos. Enlil becomes Zeus, the leader of the Olympians – the younger gods – and Enki becomes Typhoeus, the leader of the Titans, the old gods.

In Gnostic texts Jehovah is called the Evil One – the demiurge – whilst the serpent or Satan, as Lucifer the Bringer of Light, occupies the position of the

Saviour of Man. As the Bible itself says, "What evil befalls a city that does not come from the Lord God." In the Book of Kings Jehovah assumes the role of Satan the Tempter – as if it were second nature for him – in an attempt to make King David break the Holy Law and number the individual members of the Tribes of Israel.

Jehovah hated mankind and sought man's oppression and ultimate annihilation. In Biblical theology this makes Jehovah the opposer of man, the real "Satan" in etymological terms. So when Jesus says in the wilderness, "Get thee behind me Satan," we don't have to wonder who he's actually talking to.

Even as Enlil, Jehovah sought constantly the destruction and eradication of all mankind whom he hated and feared because he was terrified that man, the Nephilim and the Dragons – loyal to Enki or Satan – might launch an uprising against him in retaliation for his crime. Which indeed they did, and quite rightly so. Satan, as Ea or Enki, was the son of the senior queen and the rightful heir of Anu, his father, who supported Enki's claim. Unable to bear this, in a fit of jealousy and rage, Enlil committed patricide in an attempt to force his way onto the throne of the father-god and, as a result, a protracted conflict ensued which became known in myth as The War In Heaven.

TT: What is your opinion of Christ and his ministry?

NDV: I have covered this subject in my answers to other questions, where it is clear that I am obviously a committed supporter of his spiritual and social traditions and teachings.

TT: What is your opinion of the Wiccan and New Age movements?

NDV: Again, my views of the Wiccan and New Age movements are also well known. Wicca, the so-called "Old Religion," is an artificial construct cobbled together from a variety of dubious folksy beliefs, which lacks any historical continuity, traditional pedigree, authority, or spiritual antecedence beyond sixty years. It is just substitute church dogma in another form, led by a so-called priesthood intent on self-aggrandisement, sexual seduction, petty power games and financial profit.

The New Age movement is nothing more than a baseless, cynical marketing ploy geared towards extracting money from the fear and neurosis-driven, gullible, wet liberal, super-idealistic, fluffy bunny, rainbow-unicorn brigade. New Agers force themselves to see a world filled with human hatred, corruption and sadness, through almost militantly rose-tinted spectacles and, like ostriches who at the first sign of danger bury their heads in the sand, they vehemently refuse to address in any intelligent, practical or sensible ways the dire problems that stupid mankind has foisted upon itself.

TT: How do you feel about the sudden surge of interest in the "Grail bloodline" following the publication of *The Da Vinci Code*? Do you think that the popularization of the idea is dangerous?

NDV: My opinion is that *The Da Vinci Code* is a *Holy Blood, Holy Grail* rip-off, a one-day wonder that has masses of people desperately searching for something outside of themselves that, for a few, can only be found within. Some people, the minority, will maintain their interest in the Grail, understandably leaving *The Da Vinci Code* behind to study the subject further, through more informed and reliable sources, whilst the bulk of readers will rightly treat the book as a novel experience and pass on to other unrelated subjects, once their curiosity has been satisfied. This happens with every new publication.

The only inherent danger would be to the subject itself, once the money-vampires of the New Age get hold of it and try opening weekend workshops in "How to become a member of the Grail Bloodline" or something equally unrealistic. It would then get promoted and marketed as a "lifestyle choice" open to all. Once such familiarity has bred the inevitable public contempt, the subject may well be rendered valueless to the new enquirer.

The book has come and gone and been the subject of an intended lawsuit against Dan Brown, the inevitable Hollywood film has been made, everyone has made a million out of it and the hapless reader could have picked up a copy of *Holy Blood, Holy Grail* for a fraction of the price, and learnt an awful lot more from it in the bargain.

TT; Nick, it has been noted that your de Vere family amalgamated with the Tarnawa-Krupa family of Croatia and The Balkans. Who are they actually? Can you give us some more information?

NDV; They are our Polish-Hungarian Cousins… they are artists, engineers, Second World War and homeland war heroes, "whistle-blowers," inventors, Templars. By blood descent they are the Imperial Princes of the Khazars, Hebrews and all Turks, overlords of Bulgars, Hungarians, Ukrainians.

(*Another fortified city and very important trading centre was Sarkel, by the Don River. Also Kiev, which became later the Russian capital, was founded by Khazars and Magyars. The Khazarian Empire extended its territory from the Dniepr River in the west to the Aral Sea in the east, controlling most of the shores of the Caspian Sea, so that it is still called "Khazar Sea" in Turkish, Persian, Arabic and other languages of that area. The Khazars conquered and ruled over many peoples like the Huns, Bulgars, Magyars, Sabirs, Pechenegs, Sarmatic, Slavic, Turkic and Caucasian tribes, etc. and displaced others beyond their kingdom boundaries.*) [http://www.imninalu. net/Khazars.htm]

Krupas are scions of the creators of the Hungarian early formative history in Europe and Polish Royal Piast Dynasty, as are the de Veres.

(*Polish legend speaks of a Jewish king, Abraham Prokownik, to whom the Polish tribes swore allegiance before he abdicated in favor of Piast. Whether Abraham was a Khazar dynast or viceroy, an Ashkenazi migrant from the west, or a purely mythological figure is a matter of some debate. The tale has it that he was granted the throne when the nobility, having cast out Popiel, agreed to retain as King the first man to step through the city gates the next morning – he is said to have declined the honour and insisted that the wheelwright Piast would make the best.* (http://web.raex.com/obsidian/baltic.htmlruler)

They are descendants of both Enki (Satan), through the Nephilim God-King Ziu Sudra, and his younger half-brother Enlil (Yehowah), through his granddaughters Ishtar and Kali (names and attributes of this female Goddess can vary in different Asian cultures). As carriers of sacred-divine blood, they are the rightful overlords of the Eastern branch of the one single family.

I would like to quote the following:
"The belief in the celestial origin of authority linked up with an ideal of world domination that acquired a prominent and historical form among the sixth-century Turks but existed before as part of shamanic creed. The related idea that domination was an exclusive right of the Turks was later passed on to the Uyghurs and Mongols. But the cult of heavenly ordained rule was not peculiar to the Altaic world; even less were the principles of legitimation by descent and of charisma residing in royal blood which allowed individual members of the clan to be elevated to the Qaghanate.

The second Turkish Empire, in effect, was deeply rooted in urban civilization, the joint enterprise of the Ashina clan and Soghdians, with large numbers of Chinese bureaucrats being involved as well. The Western Turks, ruling through the scions of the (Ashina) royal clan or older Hephthalite, Kushana and Irana subregimes, controlled the territory between the Syr and the Amu with the entrepots of the Chinese trade, Samarqand, Bukhara and others." From the book, *Al-Hind, the Making of the Indo-Islamic World: The Slavic Kings and the Islamic Conquest 11th-13th Century* (by André Wink).

The Western Turkic Khaganate was modernized through an administrative reform of Ishbara-Qagan (reigned 634-639) and came to be known as the Onoq. The name refers to "ten arrows" that were granted by the khagan to five leaders (*shads*) of its two constituent tribal confederations, Tulu and Nushipi, whose lands were divided by the Chui River. The division fostered the growth of separatist tendencies, and soon the Bulgarian tribes under the Dulo chieftain Kubrat seceded from the khaganate. In 657, the eastern part of the khaganate was overrun by the Tang general Su Ding Fang, while the central part had emerged as the independent khaganate of Khazaria, led by a branch of the Ashina dynasty (from *Wikipedia about GokTurks*).

Accounts of the Gokturk and Khazar khaganates suggest that the Ashina clan was accorded SACRED, perhaps QUASI-DIVINE STATUS in the shamanic religion practiced by the steppe nomads of the first millennium CE. The pagan Turks believed that their Ashina Qaghans ruled by virtue of heavenly mandated charisma (QUT). Since their blood could not be shed, dethroned Qaghans were strangled with a silk cord. The investiture ceremonies of the Ashina Turks and Khazar Qaghans included ritual near-strangulation. As THIS CHARISMA (QUT) RESIDED IN THE ENTIRE ROYAL CLAN, the latter exercised a collective sovereignty over their realms resulting in frequent succession struggles. (*From http://au.encarta.msn.com*)

According to *The New Standard Jewish Encyclopedia*, the ruling class of the Khazarian Empire – the sacred Khagan Bulan and 4000 OF HIS NOBLES (PRINCES OR BEGS OF THE ASHINA CLAN) – converted from ancient "Turkish" shamanism to Judaism in the 8th century.

Beside this, by ancient Scythian tradition being of the Holy Imperial Dragon Blood, and being born on the soil of the Western Balkans-Croatia, the Tarnawa-Krupa /now amalgamated with Royal De Vere von Drakenberg family/are legitimate and rightful overlords of Croatia and the Balkan Peninsula. Not by constitutional right, or by some Roman Catholic empowerment, or some sort of "de jure" situation, but by the most ancient Scythian spiritual traditions of the blood of both Houses – Krupa and De Vere.

The current oldest Scion, and therefore Head of the Krupa family, is Major Mladen Tarnawa Krupa-De Vere von Drakenberg, M.Sc.

Knowing these facts, or just animal-like instinct-based behaviour, the peasant Roman Catholic descent within an incompetent "democratic" government, in an ubiquitous environment of corruption (according to international sources), felt deeply endangered by the actions and statements of the Krupa family as a whole, and created a living hell for these offspring of Anu.

In short, in the last ten years or so, there erupted an irrational hatred for the family deriving from some more or less well positioned "proper" native Croats circles, resulting in a once superb family business, and 3 very valuable familiar and business properties being stolen via an ignorant, arrogant (*when they state "all is according to the law, they forget that even Jews has been burned alive in Concentration Camps according to the Law!*) and corrupted Justice system, resulting in any employment and business options being "magically" closed for almost all the Krupa family members, and at the peak of this pure hatred, one prominent family member has been the subject of a well orchestrated media lynching in the manner of the former "Communist" persecution in 50's in the USA, based on invented pedophilia rumors. That nonsense has been totally disapproved and debunked, and Prince Freddy has emerged the clear winner, whilst the person responsible for this malicious attack has been removed by the Minister for Education in the Croatian Government of that time, despite the State being in a terrible situation, as described earlier. For more please read:

http://www.thecroatiaportal.com/?p=654
http://www.youtube.com/watch?v=1PKuaMYlcJs
http://corruptcroatia.blogspot.com/2010/02/corrupt-cronies-float-pedophilia-rumors.html

This case only shows the continuation of the so-called Elven Holocaust, as I described in The Dragon Legacy, exercised wherever the Roman Catholic Church is strong and has influence on the common people. It also shows the incompetence and the primitive nature of Homo Sapiens and their ruinous rule in, sadly, most parts of this planet.

TT: What is the most important thing you want people to take away after reading *The Dragon Legacy* and this current work?

NDV: Firstly, one of the central themes of the books is transcendent consciousness. I would like to feel that the reader may derive some interest in this concept from reading *The Dragon Legacy* and *The Dragon Cede* and will pursue the subject further. Secondly, the Dragon families have been with us for millennia and, in the course of time, their innate and rightful destiny will cause them to rise again. With that rise will come a New Order, an order free of injustice and religious bigotry, free of political ambition, egotism, nationalism and social violence. This is an order that will herald in a new Golden Dawn for mankind. Those with vision will welcome their return and support them in their efforts to bring such to fruition in the time to come.

Chapter Six

Excerpts from
The True Elves of Europe

© Leonid Korablev

In view of the relatively abundant references to Elves in surviving ancient and medieval texts, modern connotations of the word "elf" as well as 18th-19th Century related folklore ideas appear as grotesque distortions of a waning tradition. Observing the older references, we notice striking similarities between Elves and their counterparts of various names across the mythological landscape of North-Western Europe. We claim that these are traces of an integral tradition, which, with time, gradually lost its integrity and merged with other traditions and/or random elements of folk fancy.

It is clear that Tolkien widely used the elements of that tradition in creating his Elves; we maintain that besides being a marvelous achievement of a story-teller, Tolkien's Elves (Eldar, Quendi) were a (veiled) attempt of a scholar at reconstructing the tradition in question. Similar treatment of the Atlantis myth (i.e. providing a "real" story of which the known myth could be an echo) speaks in favor of our hypothesis.

1. Webster's dictionary defines an Elf to be "a tiny, ...prankish fairy" (or "a small child or being, especially a mischievous one"), in perfect accordance with popular literary usage of Shakespeare and others. However, the word is much older than its current meaning and used to have completely different connotations. There is abundant linguistic and literary evidence that the beings of the same name were treated very seriously and with much reverence all over the ancient Northern Europe, and that the names "Elf" and its analogies in other languages was applied to a separate, quite independently from humans, existing race ("folk") of beings, comparable and very often even superior to humans in many respects.

2. Searle's *Onomasticon* (mentioned by Arundell Lowdham, a character of JRRT's *Notion Club Papers*) contains 35 different names of the form AElf + adjective (noun); it mentions 75 recorded bearers of the name AElfwine "Elf-friend." Of particular interest in the same *Onomasticon* are names AElfing, AElfmann, AElmanus, AElmon, etc., that could be interpreted as "descendant of Elves." Indeed, claiming an Elf for an ancestor was not at all unusual (for

example, in ancient Germanic countries [including Scandinavia] this was often the case with nobility); we will have a closer look at such cases later when discussing the sources of "undiminished" tradition concerning Elves. We should also mention the usage of "aelfsciene" ("elven-shining") by the poets of "Caedmon school" to describe the surpassing beauty of Sarah and Judith (Anglo-Saxon Paraphrase of Genesis, VII-VIII, the poem "Judith," IX-X. See "Letters of JRRT," #236).

It is interesting that Old Norse "fridh sem alfkona vaeri" [4] (beautiful as an elven woman) matches this usage quite closely. [Add here Middle-English "scho was so faire ....as ....an elfe out of an-othire erde" (she was so fair as if an elf-maid from another world) [5]] Of interest is also the Old Norse-Icelandic kenning for warrior: "her-gramr rog-ALFR" (war-fierce-hostility-ELF) & many others [6]. [Add here also two Snorri Sturluson's comments about use of "alfr" in kennings for "warrior," see *Snorra Edda*, Skaldskaparmal.] Clearly, the connotations of the name "Elf" must have changed greatly over the centuries, losing its initial associations with strength, brightness, beauty and wisdom.

Alongside with linguistic, there is plenty of literary evidence connected with "Elf," "AElf," "Alf," "Alb." Sources listed below contain descriptions or references to the Elves that would hardly fit with the modern Webster's definition, but are in good agreement with the above bright image of an Elf.

We have separated a number of features that, in our opinion, characterized the "original Elves" and got diluted and distorted with time, in each country in its own way. Later we will briefly describe some of the mergings and adulterations of the "original" image that took place.

These are the features in question. The numbers following a source show which of these are explicitly stated in it as characteristic of the beings called Elves (see a table below for a variety of equivalent names in several Northern European languages).

> 1. Elves are about as tall as humans.
> 2. Elves are beautiful.
> 3. Elves are strong and make fierce warriors.
> 4. Elves excel in arts (especially music), possess the gift of foreknowledge and can bestow similar gifts upon chosen humans.
> 5. Dwelling places of Elves are removed from those of humans (e.g. beyond the sea, on islands, etc.).
> 6. Elves possess a speech of their own, distinct from that of humans.
> 7. Elves and humans can have common children.

Let us now list the sources, grouped by their country of origin. Within these groups they roughly fall into two categories – original texts and works of folklore collectors who interpreted the matter of Elves in the beliefs of their respective countries.

Iceland (Alfar & later Huldu-folk):
Besides the famous *Elder Edda* and *Snorra Edda* of Snorri Sturluson, where "Aesir and Alfs," the gods and the Elves, are commonly mentioned together, and a reference is made to their separate speech, different from those of the gods and mortals, in *Alvismal*, there are:

ALFAR

"Hrolfs saga kraka" (XIV-XV): 1,2,4,5,7
"Goengu-Hrolfs saga" (XIV): 1,4,5
"Prests saga Gudhmundar (godha) Arasonar" (XIII): 4
"Nornagests thattr" (XIV): 4,5
"Saga af Tristram ok Isoend" (AD 1226): 1,2,3,4,5
"Hrafnagaldr Odhins" (XVII): 4
"Moettuls saga" (XIII): 4; & many others "Riddara & lygi soegur."
"Jarlmanns saga ok Hermanns" (XV) – here Icelandic Elves are already called HULDU-FOLK (the Hidden People);
Later of the Huldu-folk we have:
"Thorsteins thattr baejarmagns" (XV): 1,4,5
"Koetlu draumur" (XVI): 1,2,5,7
Jon Gudhmundsson: "Tidhfordrif," "Samantektir um skilning a Eddu" (XVII): 1,2, 4,5,7
Torfaeus (i.e. THormodhur Torfason): "Historia Hrolfi Krakii...." [see preface] (1705): 4,5,7
Finnus Johannaeus (i.e. Finnur Jonsson): *Historia Ecclesiastica Islandiae* [vol II, p. 368 ff.], (1774): 1,2,4,5,7
Jon Arnason: Islenzkar THjodhsoegur (1862-1864): 1,2,4,5,6,7

The most important for us are treatises of Jon Gudhmundsson hinn Laerdhi *Learned* (1574-1658?) respecting the nature and the origin of Elves because these preserve earliest detailed written accounts and memories of ancient Norse-Icelandic *Alfar*; namely, aforesaid *Tidhfordrif* (1644), *Samantektir um skilning a Eddu* (1641), poems: "Fjoelmodhur" (1649), "Snjafjallavisur hinar fyrri" (1611), "THeim godhu jardharinnar in buum tilheyri thessar oskir," "Huldufolks mal" & etc. Also, Olafr Sveinsson from Purkey (1780-1845) later compiled the *Writ about Hid-folk, or Elves, for Instruction and knowledge of the Realm of Nature* [7], having collected a lot of related folk-tales (testimonies of encounters with Elves). [Belief in Elves is strong even in contemporary Iceland; a certain sociological research claims that more than a half of the population believes in their existence.]

Scandinavia & Denmark ALFER:

Olaus Magnus *Historia de Gentibus Septentrionalibus* (1555): 1-5
A. Afzelius *Svenska Folkets Sago-Haefder* (1851-): 1,2,4,5
F. Nansen *In Northern Mists* (1911): 1,4,5,7
A. Faye *Norske Folkesagn* (1884): 1,2,4,5,7

Thor Age Bringsvaerd *Phantoms & Fairies from Norwegian Folklore*: 1-5
J. Moe, P. Asbjoernsen "Norske Folke Eventyr" (1842): 1,2,4,5,7
Olav Boe "Trollmakter og godvette": 1,7
Ashild Ulstrup & Wench OEyen "Huldra–den farlege lengten" (1993): 2,4,5,7
W. Craigie *Scandinavian Folk-lore* (1896): 1,2,4-7
B. Thorpe *Northern Mythology*, vol.1 (1851): 1,2,4,5,7
We can also mention here Jacob Grimm with his *Teutonic Mythology* (1882-): 2,4,5,6,7

Germany:

One has to mention the heroic sagas about the THidhrek af Bern (who was considered to be a son of an Elf), his knight Alphart, and Hagen [8], the son of queen Odda, who also had an Elvish ancestor:
Thidhreks saga af Bern (1250): 3,4,7
Numerous later works of the Grimm brothers unfortunately contain many arbitrary elements, as the old image of Elves has dramatically faded in folk-lore [9].

Scotland:

Rev. Robert Kirk (1630-1692), believed to have been taken in 1692 by the Elves [10] to live among them, composed *The Secret Commonwealth of Elves, Fauns and Fairies*, a detailed note on Elves derived from collecting local lore and "his own experiences." It is interesting that 114 years later, his successor at the same parish, Rev. Patrick Graham returned to the topic in his *Sketches Descriptive Picturesque Scenery of the Southern Confines of Perthshire*, published in 1806 and containing interesting information on the Scottish counterpart of Elves, Daoine Sithe.

Of the latter we must say in more detail. Although not directly "Elves" in most sources, Scottish daoine sithe, Irish daoine sidhe, and even the Danaan deities, Welsh Tylwyth Teg and other beings of Celtic mythological traditions possess the same features as the Elves proper. The sources below allow us to think of North-Western European Elves as consisting of two large groups – the Scandinavian and Germanic branch (with whom the name Elves is usually associated) and the Celtic branch, represented by the above- mentioned beings and Trows of Shetland Isles. Indeed, we can think of our "original" image of Elves as predating both traditions, a common ancestor of both branches. Naturally, Celtic imagination captured and retained a somewhat different image, in perfect agreement with the difference between the Celtic and Teutonic mentality. Thus we have:

Scotland DAOUINE SITHE: (our note: The people of Scythia)

Rev. Patrick Graham, *Sketches Descriptive of Picturesque Scenery of the Southern Confines of Perthshire* (1806): 1,2,4,7

J.F. Campbell, *Legend of Islay*: 4, *Kirkcundbright*: 1,2, *Sutherland Legend #4*: 4,5 [*Popular Tales of the West Highlands*, 1890-1893]

Ireland DAOINE SIDHE:

We can find all the above features except 6 in old Irish legends of Tuatha De Danaan, as described in *The Book of Leinster*, *The Book of the Dun Cow* and other well known sources. In modern times we have the works of: Lady Wilde, *Ancient Legends of Ireland* (1887): 1,2,3,4,5; W.B. Yeats, *Irish Fairy and Folktales* (1893): 1,2,3,4,5
W.Y. Evans-Wentz, *The Fairy Faith in Celtic Countries* (1911): 1 through 6

Wales (TYLWYTH TEG and GWRAGEDD ANNWN):

King Gowran of Welsh Triads (V): 5 pseudo-Gildas's *Description of the Isle of Avalon* (XII): 1,2,5
W. Owen (Pughe) *Geiriadur* (Welsh-English Dictionary, 1803): 1,2 [11] *The Legend of the Meddygon Myddfai* (ca. 1230): 1,2,4,5,7
Th. Keightley, *The Fairy Mythology....*, 1850, W. Sikes, *British Goblins* 1880: *The Legend about Secret Garden of Tylwyth Teg (or Gwragedd Annwn) near Brecknock*: 1,2,4,5
The Legend about Shui Rhys (Cardiganshire), mentioned by W. Sikes: 6
W. Howells, *The Pembrokeshire Legend* (1830): 1(?),2,4,5
J. Rhys, *Celtic Folklore* (1901): 1(?),2,4,5,6,7

Shetland Isles (TROWS):
John Spense, *Shetland Folk-Lore* (1899): 4,5,7

Elvish Ancestors
(See Descent of the House of Vere)

As we have mentioned above, claiming Elvish ancestry was not at all unusual in ancient Germanic (Scandinavian) lands; similar cases are to be found in Wales and in the whole Gaelic area as well. Such ancestry allowed one to perform deeds hard or impossible for mere humans.
In *Das Niebelungenlied* we find that the resistance of the Burgunds endures mostly because of Hagen's (Hoegni) feats, whose Elvish ancestry makes it hard for his mortal opponents to defeat him; finally, he is vanquished by Dietrich of Bern (Thidhrekr), who was reputed to be the son of an elf. A later Middle High German song tells of Alphart, a knight of the same Dietrich, who was able to disperse a host of enemies by challenging them one by one to a single fight. In Welsh lore (*Meddigon Meddfai*, 1230 AD) we find the story of three brothers, the sons of "gwraig Annwn": (de Vere – gwraig = witch; Annwn = Death), (an elvish wife), who, due to virtues of their descent, became famous doctors in Wales. [Add here also similar traditions witnessed by Scottish minister Rev. P. Graham.]
Most interesting is Icelandic *Koetlu Draumur* (XVI c.), where an Elf's love for a mortal woman Katla (consummated in her dream [12]; she bore his son,

whom her mortal husband Marr accepted as his own) serves as a reason why later that son of Katla, the sea-traveler Are Marsson (actually well-known through Iceland), could reach the mysterious island of Hvitra-manna-land [13]. This motif is certainly a familiar one to every reader of *The Simarillion*.

Elvish descendants

Add here also Scyld Scefing (*Beowulf*), Skuld Helgadottir (*Hrolfs saga Kraka*), Merlin (*Robert of Gloucester's Chronicle*.)

The Family of North-Western European Elves

We have a whole family of initially similar peoples (beings) who occupy a prominent place in the high myths and folklore of North-Western European nations. The word "Elf" itself, used in this paper to refer to a single being of the kind, can be traced (see Jacob Grimm, *Irische Elfenmaerchen*) to the Old and Middle High German "Alb," "Alf," "Alp." Etymology will help us establish a "family tree" of European Elves; analysis of features attributed to various kinds of Elves in literature and folklore will testify to the tendency of "deterioration" and "randomization" of the original high myth.

Originally a fully independent from humans, wise and strong race with time has merged in the minds of the Scandinavians, the Germans, the English, the Welsh and others with the guardian spirits of Nature (dwellers in the forests, rivers etc, Anglo-Saxon "wudu-aelfen" and "sae-aelfen" are perhaps an intermediate state of such a merging), malignant sprites and demons that cause illness to men and cattle ("malignant elves" used to be a medical term, alongside with "elf-fire," a cattle disease in Sweden (see Nils Thun, "Studia Neophilologica," 1969), or, in one case, a historical tribe, the so-called "Alfar" of "Alfheimar," an area of Scandinavia between the two rivers Raumelfr and Gautelfr. In a few cases the Elves were identified with the souls of the dead (which may have arisen from the confusion between the old barrows and the hills in which the Elves were reputed to dwell [14].)

Of the cases above, the first two represent a "logical merging" of a folklore element whose function became unclear, with the entities whose function is well-connected with the everyday life of a people; logical, that is, if we assume that every part of folklore has to have a specific "function." More examples of mergings and introduction of random elements will follow; now let us list the names the Elven kinds were known under in Europe conjecture on their relation.

We must keep in mind that in many cases the original name has become a "taboo," supplanted in everyday usage by a euphemism of sorts, for the fear of possible harm or out of courtesy to its bearers, unless indicated otherwise, the plural of a name is given.

Althochdeutsch,	Alb, Alf, Alp
Mittelhochdeutsch	fem. Elbe, pl. Elben, Elber

Anglo-Saxon	aelf, pl. ylfe (*ielfe)
Old Norse-Icelandic	alfr, pl. alfar (Ljos-alfar)
later Icelandic ("hidden folk")	alfa-folk, huldu-folk
Norse (Norway)	alfer, elver, elvir
Danish (Denmark)	alfer (elle-folk)
Swedish	aelfvor, aelfvar
Dutch	alven
Shetland Islands	trows
Faeroes	huldu-menn (huldu-folk)

A few other races should be mentioned here, because of their overwhelming similarities with the above:

Wales	Tylwith Teg ("Fair Family")
Gaelic (Ireland/Scotland)	Daoine Sidhe / Daoine Sithe
Tuatha de Danaan	

Tolkien's not-so-obvious Borrowings

Although Tolkien never made a secret of his sources, it is quite astounding how many of the folk and place-names in *The Lord of the Rings* and *Silmarillion* correspond precisely to ancient Norse-Icelandic, Anglo-Saxon and other ones that were actually used for things associated with Elves. This seems to corroborate our hypothesis that in creating his Elves, Tolkien might have been thinking of reconstructing the "original" image that, should such an original exist, was reflected in various Elves of North-Western European mythologies. A striking example of this approach is provided by his treatment of the Atlantis myth.

The story of Numenor is not only an example of a fascinating mythical image employed by a master storyteller to produce a compelling story with a moral purport of its own, but rather an amazing attempt to provide the real story that with time took the form of the familiar myth (or rather, familiar mess of ideas associated with Atlantis). And in the middle of it all stands the "original" name of the downfallen land and people, Atalante (in ancient Elvisn language "Quenya"), which is, of course, Atlantis, given its "original" meaning. We claim that this approach, this challenge of reconstructing the "original" image behind the current mythological mess, pervades all of Tolkien's work, and that creating linguistic proof of its authenticity as in the case of Atlantis-Atalante is not a singular occurrence either. Let us offer a list of names Tolkien chose to use for his creations and their historical counterparts.

* Cala-quendi, the Elves of Light – Vikings knew the Ljos-alfar, also the Elves of Light, who lived in remote world of their own, Ljos-alfa-heimr, presided over by Yngvi-Freyr. The king of Vanyar, the noblest kindred of Tolkien's Elves who never left Valinor (blessed realm over the sea) for Middle-earth (Midhs-gardhar) and dwell there with the gods till present day is called Ingwe.

* Elda-mar, the Elvenhome – We have already mentioned Ljos-alfa-heimr, its word-for-word translation. In *The Book of Lost Tales* and *Ambarkanta* Tolkien suggests a "lost" Anglo-saxon AElf-ham, an intermediary name of the same meaning.

* Alqua-londe, the Elvish Haven of the Swans – In Middle English the land of the Elves is called Eluen londe.

* Eles-sar (name), "the Elven Stone" – Cf. Germanic personal name Alb-stein, Anglo-Saxon AElf-stan, Modern German Elb-stein usually interpreted as a sacrificial stone "upon which victims were broken" or stones in which (inside) "Elfs" sat. (Swedish aelf-qvarn) Tolkien (apparently) restored the true meaning of this old Germanic name as "Elven (gem-)stone (!), jewel of Elves."

* The sundering of Elves. (Vanyar, Noldor, Teleri) – A classification of Elves was not unfamiliar to speaker of Anglo-Saxon, with "wudu-aelfen" (forest-elves), "sae-aelfen" (sea-elves) & etc.... (Cf. also "The Noldor are.... the Sword-elves," and Old Norse-Icelandic kenning for warrior "sverdh-alfr" of the same meaning.)

With thanks to the author, Dr. Leonid Korablev. The excerpts included here are from a shortened version of a Russian manuscript that is difficult to find. It has remained posted on the Internet for a number of years without an apparent copyright. Out of respect for his work we tried to contact the author, but every attempt has failed. We encourage the reader to seek out Dr. Korablev's excellent websites, sub-categorized at www.shelltown.net, containing *The True Elves of Europe* manuscript and his his impressive art work.

Chapter Seven

The Anecdotes of H.E. Count Clive Weir
of Vere von Drakenberg of Dromard

My first recollection of interest in family history came while I was still at Primary School, when I can remember my grandfather, Lancelot Weir, telling someone that "our lot" were descended from the Weir's of Hallcraig. "Our lot" were farmers with an adequate acreage under their belt, but the Hallcraig Weir's had been landlords controlling over 1000 acres. That made them seem pretty important and they would have been called "big shots" locally. While the last Weir to reside at Hallcraig died at the end of the 19th Century, this line still continues in Co. Clare.

The next jolt to my awakening brain came when I was 14 and a pupil at Portora Royal School. My grandfather was on holiday in Bundoran, Co. Donegal, an annual pilgrimage for the retired farming fraternity in the month of September, when the maid of the boarding house they were staying in, drew attention to a death notice in the *Irish Times*. This was a Miss Weir, who had died in India and there was an appeal for relatives.

My grandfather was rather laid back. He told a good yarn and enjoyed his pipe and his whiskey. He didn't do excitement, but there was one family member who decided to dig. This was my great-aunt Connie from Australia – my grandfathers' widowed sister-in-law. And dig she did. I kept an interest but at 14 there was little I could do. I had heard of the word genealogy – it sounded like geometry or geology; could I do an O level in it? Then in the library in Portora, I stumbled upon an edition of *Burkes Landed Gentry* – Wow! There was some history here.

Aunt Connie visited graveyards, met various locals, wrote many letters to all corners of the earth and toured every record office in London. But no connection was forthcoming between our family and "Miss India." Yet my ancestors and Miss India's are buried side by side, the respective farmlands adjoin and there were other clues as well, but nothing on paper to prove a relationship. Over the next few years our interest waned, and eventually great-aunt Connie passed over to meet my grandfather in the new Bundoran over the horizon. My father had no strong interest in family history and I, as a young man, had other things on my mind.

Thus the matter rested like Sleeping Beauty and it was not until October, 1998 that I resurrected my interest in my ancestry. I just *had* to "push the boat out," spend some time and money, and leave something valuable for my children and the wider family circle. My first line of attack was to continue where Aunt Connie had left off. But despite numerous trips to the Public Records Office in Belfast, no new information was obtained regarding Miss India's family. And that is still the case today. But I was finding out more about my own branch, the Hallcraig branch and a branch in Co. Sligo. I was now giving family research my undivided attention. Nick de Vere's introduction to the pre-Norman conquest Weir's was fascinating and intriguing. Nick also introduced me to his ancestor, Major Thomas Weir, who was burnt at the stake in Edinburgh in 1670 for witchcraft. I believe Major Weir is mentioned frequently on both history and ghost tours in Edinburgh and he may well have been the character Robert Louis Stevenson used for his book, *Dr. Jekyll and Mr. Hyde.*

I was sending cut letters to all parts and, unbelievably, getting replies back. People were very helpful and I was also being contacted by other Weirs to see if they were connected to me. By this time a sizable amount of information was appearing on the Internet and people worldwide were into researching their roots in a big way. I don't respond too often to what I see on Weir/Vere pages on the net, otherwise I would have very little free time! Of all the research I have conducted, one place stands out – The Public Record Office in Belfast. I hated it. The staff, when I was there, weren't that helpful and I used to come home with a headache from reading microfilm.

Anyway, this is all about stories I have heard along the way; genealogies really only interest those who can identify with people on a family tree. You won't hear the genealogies in the Bible read out during church services. No one can identify with those and they are only of interest to the historian. And yes, I was fortunate that the main body of my family tree was recorded, but I have succeeded in piecing together many names on my own line and other branches. But the real pleasure has been finding out about the *characters* and the *stories* that went before. Every family, I am sure, can relate to a past family member who was a bit of a character, either good or bad. This is what sells programmes like "Who Do You Think You Are?" When this programme was first aired a decade ago, ordinary people got to tell their story. Now it has been continued by the reality shows like, "Who Wants to be a Millionaire," "Mastermind," "Strictly Come Dancing," and "Big Brother."

Will a tale be told about me when I'm dead and gone? I don't know. Within my family, I'd like to think they'd remember me pulling all our family history together. Outside of that, perhaps I'll be remembered for my home written little comedy sketches, which I still perform at concerts. My father was a hard working farmer and an enjoyable man to talk to. Grandfather was a laugh, as was Aunt Connie. These are my only predecessors that I knew. Most names on the tree have no stories attributed to them, but those that have bring a spark of life to what can be a tedious job hunting through old records.

Undoubtedly, Major Weir is my most famous ancestor and much has already been written about him. But it is other minor characters that I would like to record from here on in. My grandfather inherited Dromard, where I live, after the Second World War. It was previously and lastly occupied by a widow, Mrs. Minona Weir. She was widowed in 1909 and in 1911 lost her only child to a fever, which he contracted while studying at Trinity College, Dublin. She was a formidable character but I believe she had a much softer side as evidenced by her love of dogs and cats. Perhaps they were a substitute for her losses early in her life…. Anyway, one of the stories that carries down relate to how she came home from a holiday to find that one of her beloved dogs had died. She was not happy with the site where one of her workmen had buried the dog, so he was exhumed and buried along the driveway with a huge 3 foot square granite stone placed on top. This still survives today. After she herself died, the farm was in limbo and a great many cats had to be fed. The workmen decided to feed all the cats at one point in the bottom yard. This was where they met their end, for in the words of one of the men, "…a barrowful and a half of cats were shot." Minona, as I have said, must have been lonesome and indeed sorrowful. She kept a photograph of her deceased son lying in his coffin on her bedroom mantelpiece. She also kept a scrapbook, mostly of newspaper cuttings, which was a valuable tool in my research.

Dromard was fairly run down by the time my grandfather Lancelot inherited it. All the men folk had either been doctors, clergy or in the army. After the death of John Weir at Trinity College, Minona and two of her late husbands' spinster aunts, Miss Charlotte and Miss Anne, resided at Dromard and ran the farm. The farm would have been in decline for nearly forty years.

There were two Christian names used in my side of the house, which were unusual – *Lancelot* and *Noble*. I found out where Lancelot originated. One of my ancestors married a Carleton – a Northern English family – and Lancelot featured there quite a bit. The name appeared twice in my line and three times in the Sligo line. But I never could find out why my great, great, great, great grandfather was christened Noble in 1766. It is rarely used as a Christian name, but in the locality where Noble Weir lived there were at least four men with the Christian name Noble, living some 200 years later. The name must have caught on.

The town lands, Derrybeg and Dromard, where I live, were purchased on 22nd July, 1851 by the Rev. Christopher Weir, son of Noble Weir. His three sons were well educated – the eldest, Rev. James Weir, became headmaster of Raphoe Grammar School in Donegal; William became rector of Sixmilecross Parish in Co. Tyrone, and John became Brigade Surgeon with the 75th Regiment of Foot. He retired to Dromard unmarried and many old medicine bottles survived in an outhouse on the farm. With the farm in decline, much was thrown away, including his sword, which was dug up by a young chap called Brownlee in the late 50's while looking for worms to go fishing with.

The Rev Christopher Weir acquired more land, one of the farms being 50 miles away in Co. Sligo, but close to his relations, the Lakeview Weirs, who settled there around 1740. My immediate ancestor was Robert Weir, brother of Christopher, and it must have been this link that brought him to meet his future wife, Frances Weir of Lakeview, his second cousin. And it was from this marriage that the name Lancelot came into my side of the family.

The Weirs of Lakeview Sligo owe their origins to the Rev George Weir who was appointed to the nearby Parish of Townagh around 1746. He had 4 sons, one of whom was a Lancelot Weir who was the father of my great, great grandmother, Frances Weir. Another son was John Weir, a reckless figure, who is well documented in John McTernan's book, Olde Sligoe. There is an excellent chapter on the Weirs of Lakeview in this book and in the space of six pages we see the rise of a family, through land acquisitions, to bankruptcy just over a century later. I have seen and heard of people building empires and slaving every moment of their life only for a future generation squandering the entire lot. In most cases four generations seems to suffer. These Weirs, long years after they have gone, are still resented by people living around Lakeview today.

Few people want to talk about them and I first experienced this in the spring of 1999. A publican from Heapstown, located beside Lakeview, told me that there are people around here who could tell you forty different stories about the Weirs and not one of them would be a good one! I well believe there are forty stories, and while no one wants to talk about them, I have no doubt many are of a sexual nature, and indeed incest was mentioned once. One told to me by John McTernan, which was not in his book, concerns a young man who was courting a Miss Weir. Her father and brother did not approve, so two local men were paid to get rid of the fellow – five pounds each. One evening, approaching Lakeview, the young man was attacked, murdered and deposited in Lough Arrow. Such crimes were common long ago and the folk group, Steeleye Span, does a cracking song on one such event – Lady Diamond. The body eventually surfaced and poor Miss Weir identified it by the ring and shoes worn.

A few years ago, I went to look for the ruins of John Weirs' house, the reckless Weir, and I came across a farmer who now owns the land. He was very courteous and took time to bring me to the exact location, where we took photographs, and he reminisced about watching the weasels play along Weirs' walls as a child. We did some farming talk and on parting he said he would ask his elderly mother if she had any stories on the Weirs. On telephoning back in two weeks time, the call was short – he obviously did not want to talk any more about these Weirs. Mummy's words had not been complimentary.

Most of John McTernan's article concerns a court case from the 1850's following the death of William Weir, grandson of the Reverend George Weir. William was the sole owner of well over one thousand acres, and a bachelor. Around the time he turned sixty, he had a relationship with a maid of sixteen years. This lasted for six years, resulting in three children, one of whom was stillborn. William then married the girl, Winnie Tivnan, and a son was born a year later. They called the boy Lancelot Ormsby Weir. He was soon to be an orphan, as William died soon after his birth, and Winnie survived him by just six weeks. It was said she consoled herself with so much alcohol that it was the death of her. So we have a baby orphan less than a year old and a nephew of William's also laying claim to the estate, on the basis that William was not in his right mind when he married Winnie.

The court case was thoroughly recorded in the *Sligo Champion*, the local paper, and makes entertaining reading. William had been in the army, and perhaps as a result he suffered from what was politely called a "softening of the brain." This is common among politicians today and is nothing new. The ones with the smart brains are the civil servants and advisors, who get paid twice as much and use some of their thirty-nine hour work week for a round or two of golf.

Undoubtedly, William was given to bouts of delusions. He talked to the faeries and acted most peculiarly, but none of this could be attributed to old age because his "turns" appear to begin before he is sixty. Many witnesses were called to testify to his strange behaviour, but three court cases later, the young Lancelot Ormsby Weir inherited his fathers estate, which he, in due course, frittered away, to die young and almost penniless. Lancelot is buried in Glasnevin Cemetary in Dublin.

It is sad to see a big place go down but it was not the first, nor will it be the last. Somehow I sense a parallel between William, and Major Weir in Edinburgh – could the strangeness be in the genes? Which of us will be next? Maybe me? The wife says I'm "gone in the head," but the faeries haven't got me yet!

One of the high points in my research was finding some male descendants of the Sligo Weirs, living in North Wales. They had a little information on their ancestors and like me as a younger man, had a strong inkling they were descended from a significant family.

The Weirs first came to Ireland in 1610, at the time of the plantation. Their roots were in Lanarkshire, in Scotland, and can be traced back to Baltredus de Vere in 1165. Baltredus (or Ralphredus) was the second son of Aubrey de Vere, first Earl of Oxford. With such a pedigree, I felt it was time for a flying visit to the Scottish heartland. I knew Scotland well, but Lanarkshire had always been bypassed as I headed north. So, one bright May morning I set off to view the ancient Weir seats of Blackwood and Stonebyres. Blackwood has been demolished, but a photo survives of this large mansion. Here I met Bob Riley who lives in a Canadian shooting lodge, imported by the main beneficiary of the last remnant of the Blackwood Weir family, an Alastair Henderson. The lodge is very close to the site of the old house, of which all that remains is the laundry room, which Mr. Riley has incorporated into his garage. Alastair Henderson was a nephew of the Hope-Veres and never married. He gained high rank in the Diplomatic service and was a close friend of Lord George Brown, a senior cabinet minister in the government of Harold Wilson in the 1960's. The wealth of Alastair Henderson was enormous, even before his inheritance, and when he resided in his lodge at Blackwood he had two coloured servants and chased the poachers off in his Masserati! Generally believed to be gay, perhaps he soon tired of the Scottish weather, for he moved to Tangiers with the family silver and a few pieces of furniture.

From Blackwood I proceeded to the graveyard at Lesmaghow where all my Weir ancestors lie buried. There are no fancy headstones, as they had all died before the Victorian fashion for sculptured tombs and huge surrounds came into vogue.

I then headed for Stonebyres. The mansion had sat on an elevated site and is long gone, but pictures remain showing its enormous size. There are fascinating and tantalizing remains of tiled floors and spiral staircases descending into cellars. The foundations of the house were at the edge of a steep-sided burn – a dangerous place for a wandering child.

Blackwood and Stonebyres gave their names to two great houses but each was the hub of a very substantial estate. Unfortunately the Hope-Veres sent a servant to clear out the office at Blackwood and all the records of estate life were burnt.

My last visit was to the dovecote at Blackwood, a stone's throw from the site of the original house. The original part of the dovecote is very old but was added to in Victorian times and again, forty years ago, to form what is now home to Heather Wise. Heather showed me the grave of Louisa-Maud, first wife of Major J.C. Hope-Vere. Louisa had been killed in a riding accident on the estate. I had heard the previous evening that a brother-in-law of the poet Robbie Burns had met a similar fate at Blackwood. There was also a tombstone to a John Brown, who had been murdered on the estate. It was a beautiful place, but surely not many homeowners would want a garden full of graves…

On a later visit to Lanarkshire in 2005 I visited Carluke, close to where Major Weir was born, and just a stone's throw from an area known as Hall Craig. Now a golf course, I believe it was from here that Robert Weir set out with his family in 1610 to begin a new life in Ireland. Why else would he name his new property Hall Craig? This should not be confused with Craigie Hall, one-time home of the Hope-Veres outside Edinburgh, and now a military barracks.

Scotland fortunately has a comprehensive archive on the Weirs of Lanarkshire and elsewhere. For those engaged in researching the Weir roots in Lanarkshire, I suggest starting with the Register of Sassines, a tremendous record from which it is easy to piece together families and their offspring.

Returning to Ireland, it is well known that a fire at the Four Courts in Dublin destroyed many of our records in 1922, but I feel there is nothing undiscovered concerning the Weirs in the record archives of either Dublin or Belfast. One valuable record in my possession is the History of Weir. Mine is an old, hand-written version, maybe even the original. It is thought to have been compiled by Sir Charles Weir around 100 years ago. While it is repetitive in places, it nonetheless gives a full account of our history here in Ireland from 1610 until the latter part of the 19th Century, as well as our Scottish lineage before 1610, and this in greater detail than in *Burkes Landed Gentry*.

While I am no fan of modern technology, the Internet has lifted the Vere and Weir name back into the spotlight: it is a name with a wonderful history and long may it flourish…

Chapter Eight

The Alchemical Dragon

The Beast, the Dragon, the terrible monster, is the disguise of the beloved; the horror to be overcome itself is, or contains, the Reward. Beauty and the Beast must be conjoined. The old tag that a serpent becomes not a Dragon save by devouring another serpent, has an Alchemical sense: These are the two Dragons, male and female: they destroy one another, or one destroys the other and a new and mightier one is born, a fiery wonder: A Phoenix, a leaping glory, a STAR of dream ascending to the throne of the world. This was the Transmutation, the Great Work of the hidden glory of perfection.
—Arthur Machen, Fr.GD., (Frater of the Hermetic Order of the Golden Dawn).

The red and gold tinctures and metals on the field of the Vere's heraldic escutcheon, (traditionally symbolising the plumage of the Phoenix) superimposed by the White Star – literally the falling star of Lucifer – are the Arms of the Vere and reflect their ancient line of descent from Sathaniel or the Devil. The escutcheon, supported by two dynastic, hermetic Dragons becomes, historically, the Ancient Alchemical Seal of the House.

The Phoenix of the Scythians was the Raven. The Raven itself, or rather the double-headed Raven found in Transylvania (Little Scythia), devolved down to the Hittites – the Hurrians or Aryans – and from them it was eventually adopted and modified as the double-headed black Eagle of the Holy Roman Empire.

The mating of Ravens is the rhythmic inhalation and exhalation of the breath of Ravens, one by the other. And in this way are the children of Ravens fashioned. —Traditional country folklore (England)

The Boar crest surmounting the shield of the Vere armorial is the Blue Boar or La Solitaire, which in ancient Gaelic is the symbol of the Arch-Druid. The Blue Boar can be found in both Ireland and the Ardennes in France where it was the totem animal of the Gaelic Moon Goddess Arduina.

In Ireland its identity as a lunar representation is reinforced by the appearance of the upturned Crescent Moon on its shoulder. The upturned crescent also appears in Scotland as the badge originating from King Erc of the Uilidian or Fir-Bolg Druidic House. That the Druids would choose to be related to a lunar deity is not in itself surprising, even though Druids themselves didn't worship the gods, they created them for the people to follow.

The Druids chose Arduina as an ancestral mother figure who is related to the Roman virgin-huntress Diana; who herself is Hecate, the God of the Witches in Greece, because ultimately the Gaelic lunar deity devolves back to Lilith Luluwa, "The Pearl," which symbolises the Moon. And Lilith Luluwa was the daughter of Enki; the Jewish Satan and the bride to Cain, the father of the Race of the Fairy Scythians from whence Druidism originated.

In the House of Vere the Blue Boar represents the Arch druid and the Moon, whilst the star on its shoulder represents Enki who, as the later Satan, was the Fallen One, the Star that fell to Earth. This Star – the Sumerian "An" – originated with Anu, Enki's father, and denoted the origins of the Anunnaki gods as being from "The Stars," from beyond this realm, but the elder race of Mother Earth, *not* from another planet!

The Superiority of the Vere Name

In the beginning of the 18th century Catherine Weir – daughter of Sir George Weir Bt. – married Charles Hope and changed the spelling of the name Weir back to Vere, not wishing to be continually known by a series of historical spelling mistakes and variations. The Lord Lyon King of Arms of Scotland acknowledges and records the restoration of the name Vere from its incorrect rendition as "Weir." Today the senior families use the affectation "Weir of Vere" or simply "de Vere" as the name is correctly accepted and most often historically rendered.

It is also to be noted that – as recorded in historical dissertations, documents and Wills pertaining thereunto – the Weirs or Veres made it a clause in their inheritance practice that any man marrying a Vere heiress had to change his name in order to enjoy the benefits of his intended spouse's wealth and lands. Furthermore, the name Vere was considered to hold seniority and superiority over all other names in Britain and in the case of a female becoming sole heiress, it was not considered fitting that she should take to herself solely her husband's surname, as was usually the practice. In this family – when the occasion arises – the female surname of Vere is either taken by the husband and father to be, or occupies the latter position traditionally taken by a husband's surname in other families.

The Falling Star of Vere

A legend lingers round the acquisition of the de Vere (star) badge. In the version as told by Leland, Aubrey was "at the Conquest of the Cities of Nicque, of Antioch, and of Hierusalem" and:
"In the year of our lord 1098, Corborant, Admiral to the Soudan of Persia was fought with at Antioch, and discomforted the Christians. The Night coming on in the Chace of this Bataile, and waxing dark, the Christianes being four miles from Antioche, God, willing the saufte of the Christianes shewed a white Starre or Molette of fyve Pointes, which to every Manne's Sighte did lighte and arrest upon the standard of Albrey, then shining excessively."

"The mystic star from this miracle became the de Veres' badge, which they wore on their shields from then onwards – quarterly gules and or, in the first quarter a mullet argent. Later heralds argued that it was merely "a mullet with a difference" as always used to distinguish a younger son from an elder. Others said that it was not a star at all, but the rowl spur, from the French word mollet, which could have been held up as a pre~arranged sign to muster supporters and was caught in a ray of sunlight. But for the de Veres the badge was simply –

'God' pointing out the family's near-deity."

—From Verily Anderson,
The Veres of Castle Hedingham

However, as I have intimated above, the origins of this Star Badge, denoting the family's deity, reach back to the dawn of history and originate with the Anunnaki – the Sons of the Star – and thus, descending from them through the early dynasties of the Fairy High Kings, the mystical badge of the House of Vere confirms in early spiritual symbolism and later noble heraldry that they are the ancient "Elven Children of the Stars."

Historically, another Vere badge is the green glass flask, the *Vas Mirabilis* of the alchemists, which represents the holy crystal womb, the emerald jewel in Satan's crown and thus the Holy Grail.

" The Counts of Anjou: Princes of Anjou"

Sir Bernard Burke, Ulster King of Arms, when speaking of the Vere called them singularly and in plural: "The Princely Noble... The Race of Vere" (Extract from *Vicissitudes of Families*, page 424 line 12 and page 426 paragraph 2 line 12).

The Madness of Kings

A count of Anjou came back with a new wife, a strange girl of extraordinary beauty, but she kept very much to herself. Unusually, in so religious an age, she was reluctant to attend the Mass. When she did go she always hurried from the church before the consecration of the host. Her husband, who was puzzled by her behaviour, told four knights to keep watch and try to delay her departure from the church. When she got up to go, one of them trod on the hem of her train. As the priest raised the host to consecrate it she screamed, wrenched herself free, and still shrieking, flew out of the window, taking two of her children with her. In reality, the countess was the wicked fairy, Melusine, the daughter of Satan, who cannot abide the consecration of the body of Christ in the Mass. It was from the children that she left behind that the counts of Anjou and the Angevin kings of England were said to have been descended.

Of the Plantagenet Branch:

So devilish an ancestry accounted for the demonic energy and passionate ill-temper by which these princes seemed often afflicted. 'We who came from the devil,' John's brother, Richard I, was reported as saying caustically, 'must needs go back to the devil. Do not deprive us of our heritage: we cannot help acting like devils.' 'De diabolo venit et ad diabolum ibid,' commented St Bernard of Clairvaux (co-founder of the Knights Templars), 'From the devil he came, and to the devil he will return.'
—Professor Vivian Greene

Cependant, apprenant plus tard que Geoffrey a brule l'abbaye de Maillezais et tue son frere, le Comte maudit son epouse. Il l'acuse publiquement d'etre "tres fausse serpent." Le secret est devoile. Melusine doit regagner L'Autre Monde et s'envole transformee en DRAGON.
—Christine Bonnet, Lusignan

Documents of the period assert that Geoffrey Plantagenet – the founding father of the Plantagenet dynasty in Britain – was the son of Fulk V by Lady Ermengarde, whilst the subsequent Plantagenets themselves repeatedly claimed descent from Melusine. In this particular instance it would be wise to believe the family, as Fulk, Geoffrey Plantagenet's father, was indeed originally married to Queen Melusine III of Jerusalem and consequently Geoffrey was her son, not Ermengarde's. The Plantagenet name originates, not with the Broom sprig, but with the Plantagenet's founding mother – Princess Plantina – sister of Princess Melusine I in 760 AD.

Historical documents sometimes abound with falsehoods, hidden agendas and wishful thinking. To uncover the truth, in some cases one has to become a forensic historian almost, as just accepting surface "facts" as they appear in many contrived "histories" will not do. A lot of double-checking and cross-referencing has to be undertaken in order to learn the truth.

Many a wealthy but illiterate family paid monks and scribes handsomely to concoct for them impressive but totally false pedigrees, and many a noble family changed their antecedence in order to be able to claim lands or titles that simply weren't theirs. Often this included the theft of another family's ancestry, which is exactly what happened to the Vere Earls of Guisnes in the eleventh century.

The Counts of Boulogne called themselves the "Earls of Guisnes" in order to be able to link their family to the Holy and Royal Kings and Queens of Jerusalem and Lusignan. It was five hundred years later in 1626 that Sir Randolph Crew confirmed to the House of Lords that it was in fact the Veres who were the true holders of this title and the real posterity of the House of Jerusalem.

Again, in the 15th Century, Emperor Sigismund, King of Hungary, a member of the House of Luxembourg, changed his antecedence in order to become descended from the Vere's Dragon Princess, Melusine I. He contrived this lineage so that he might be able to claim some historical and traditional basis for the foundation of his "Societas Draconis" or Dragon Court. By having Melusine I as an ancestor, Sigismund could also claim an ancient Dragon Lineage stretching back to Queen Sobekh Nefru and the Dragon

Court of Egypt, a lineage that – according to his son Michael – even Prince Dracula proudly but erroneously believed in when he was inducted into the "Society."

The Duchy of Angiers

Angiers was a Ducal principality in the Comite region of Anjou. In the work of The Rev. Father Sabine Baring-Gould, Angiers is referred to as the "country" where the Pictish, Dragon Princess Melusine eventually became domiciled in the eighth century, after having fled from the Sacred Isle of Avallon (Arran), following the ritual killing of her father King Elinus; the Dragon of Berenicia. Angiers is now the city of Angers in northern Anjou. As a Ducal principality, its rulers constituted a regnant royal house who, in the case of the Veres, were also the Counts of the region in which this City State was situated (see References).

Vere Princedom

Although Merovingian culture was both temperate and surprisingly modern, the monarchs who presided over it were another matter. They (the Sorcerer Kings) were not typical even of rulers of their own age, for the atmosphere of mystery, legend, magic and the supernatural surrounded them, even during their lifetimes. If the customs and economy of the Merovingian world did not differ markedly from others of the period, the aura about the throne and royal bloodline was quite unique.

Sons of the Merovingian blood were not "created" kings. On the contrary they were automatically regarded as such on the advent of their twelfth birthdays. There was no public ceremony of anointment, no coronation of any sort. Power was simply assumed, as by sacred right.

But while the king was supreme authority in the realm, he was not obliged – or even expected – to sully his hands with the mundane business of governing. He was essentially a ritualised figure, a priest-king, and his role was not necessarily to do anything, but simply to be. The king ruled, in short, but did not govern.

Even after their conversion to Christianity, the Merovingian rulers, like the Patriarchs of the Old Testament, were polygamous. On occasion they enjoyed harems of oriental proportions. Even when the aristocracy, under pressure from the Church, became rigorously monogamous, the monarchy remained exempt. And the Church, curiously enough, seems to have accepted this prerogative without any inordinate protest. According to one modern commentator: "Why was it [polygamy] tacitly approved by the Franks themselves?"

We may here be in the presence of ancient usage of polygamy in a royal family – a family of such rank that its blood could not be ennobled by any match, however advantageous, nor degraded by the blood of slaves.... It was a matter of indifference whether a queen was taken from a royal dynasty or from among courtesans.

The fortune of the dynasty rested in its blood and was shared by all who were of that blood.

And again,

It is just possible that, in the Merovingians, we may have a dynasty of Germanic Heerkonige* derived from an ancient kingly family of the migration period.
—Extracted and expanded upon by Henry Lincoln, from *The Long Haired Kings*, by J. M. Wallace-Hadrill; Fellow of Merton College Oxford.
* Fritz Kern, Gottesgnadentum und Widerstandrecht (1954).

The Houses of Vere and Collison are descended in fifty Royal Elven or Fairy Lines and thirteen Grail lines from the Merovingian dynasty, and consequently share in this ancient Germanic Royal Blood Tradition. Prince Milo de Vere – married to Charlemagne's sister – and Head of the Imperial House and Chief of the Emperor's Army, was himself an Imperial Prince.

Today the Royal Houses of Vere, Weir and Collison can also claim descent from thirteen imperial lines that include Gaius Julius Caesar, Constantine of Byzantium, Charlemagne and Louis I.

The Vere Earls of Guisnes

In the matter of the succession of Robert de Vere to the earldom of Oxford in the reign of Charles I, the title was contested by Lord Willoughby de Eresby. Several Judges of the day were appointed to guide the Lords in legal matters regarding this succession. Leading them was the Lord Chief Justice of England, Sir Randolph Crew. Robert de Vere won the case and the Crown vouchsafed the earldom of Oxford to him. The summing up speech delivered by the Lord Chief Justice before the House of Peers (The House of Lords) was recorded as part of the judicial process (Sir Bernard Burke) and its comments are therefore part of English Law.

On Saturday 1st April 1626 Sir Randolph Crew addressed their Lordships saying:

> "This great and weighty cause, incomparable to any other that hath happened at any time, requires great deliberation, and solid and mature judgment to determine it, and I wish that all the judges of England had heard it – it being a fit case for all – to the end we all might have given our humble advice to your Lordships herein.
>
> Here is represented to your Lordships certamen honoris, and, as I may well say, illustris honoris, illustrious honour. I heard a great peer of this realm, and a learned, say, when he lived there was no king in Christendom had such a subject as Oxford.
>
> He came in with the Conqueror, Earl of Guynes; shortly after the Conquest, made Great Chamberlain of England above five hundred years ago, by Henry I, the Conqueror's son, brother to Rufus; by Maud, the Empress, Earl of Oxford; confirmed and approved by Henry II, Alberico comiti, so Earl before.
>
> This great honour, this high and noble dignity hath continued ever since in the remarkable surname of De Vere, by so many ages, descents and generations, as no other kingdom can produce such a peer in one

and the self-same name and title.... And yet let the name and dignity of De Vere stand for so long as it pleaseth God."

That the Veres were Earls of Guisnes before 1066 is recognised and recorded in British law. With thanks to Miss C. Shelton; the House of Lords Archivist, for the primary sources consulted.

Count Alberic de Vere

1000+ Albery II de Vere: Earl of Genney wed – Beatrice, Sister to King William the Conqueror: Vere descent from the Merovingian dynasty. Alberic went with the King to England. He used the motto,"Albri Comes" which some say is, "Albery of truth cometh," de – of ; Ver – true. But Comes simply means Count. Albery is also Aubri, Albury, Alberic (in Latin); Alphonsus (in Greek). He built "Hedingham Castle." At the time of the general survey, Alberic de Ver was already noted as a person of ancient and noble descent (*Domesday Book*). Leland stated or deduced that the pedigree of this family was from "Noah," (incorrect) Meleager, who slew the Caledonian boar, and Diomedes, who was at the seige of Troy—N.B. Caesar and Charlemagne.

Alberic held a number of lordships in several counties in England and particularly 14 in Essex, where Hedingham was his castle, chief seat and caput or head of his barony.

Albericus III, Junior, was successor to his father; and became so much in favor with Henry I that the said King made him great "Chamberlain of England," in fee;

The first Aubrey de Vere on record (in Britain) came to England with William the Conqueror.... He is usually held to be a Norman, though he may have been a Breton; he certainly had strong connections with Brittany. Before the Conquest he was described as one of the barons of Conan, Count of Brittany, and after the Battle of Hastings he or his son (a second Aubrey) was allotted lands in Essex by the overlord there, who was Alan of Brittany, now called Alan, Count of Richmond in Yorkshire.

Like all civil wars, the conflict between the Empress Maud and King Stephen was a very troubling one.

It was really a fight between Normans and Flemings for the English throne; and since Stephen's wife was the Flemish Matilda, Countess of Boulogne, those Flemings already in England naturally flocked to her side. For reasons best known to himself, Aubrey III de Vere sided with the Normans; he got his reward when the Empress Maud created him Earl of Oxford.

It has been said, I think correctly, that before a man could be given an earldom he had to have another honour.

Among those who supported Stephen and Matilda against the Normans was Alan, Earl of Richmond, and Aubrey III's second son, named Ralf, went against his father and fought for Stephen in the army of his own overlord.

The first officially recorded de Vere in Scotland was a Radulfus (or Ralf) who was holding estates in Lanarkshire during the reign of Alexander II. In 1160 Conan, Earl of Richmond, had married Margaret, sister of the King of Scotland, and it seems likely that this may have been the time when his follower, Ralf, was awarded his lands there. We may note that when Aubrey

III died, he was succeeded as Earl of Oxford by his first son, Aubrey IV; but when that son died childless the earldom passed to a third son, missing out the second son, Ralf.
—With thanks to Mrs. Beryl Platts, author of *The Scottish Hazard*.

Alberic was also justice of all England in that king's reign, but about the 5th of king Stephen, was killed in a popular turmult at London, leaving by Adeline his wife, daughter of Gilbert de Clare, or, according to Collins, in his Extinct Peerage, daughter to Roger de Ivery, three sons; viz. Alberic, n.n canon of St. Osyth, in Essex; Robert lord of Twiwell, in the county of Northampton; Geffery, who, the 12th Henry II, certified his knight's fee to be nine deveteri seossamento and three de novo, and then resided in Shropshire; and William (constituted "Chancellor of England," by Maud the empress); and Juliana, Hugeot Bigot, Earl of Northfolk. Alberic the third succeeded his father, and was so considerable a person that Maud, the empress, in order to engage him to her interest, confirmed to him the office of great chamberlain and all his father's estates, with diver other inheritances, likewise the earldom of Cambridge, the earldoms of Oxford, Berkshire, Wiltshire, or Doresteshire, all which grants, Maud's son, Henry II, confirmed, and constitutes him Earl of Oxford, with the grant of the third penny of the pleas of the county; a perquisite then belonging to the earls of this kingdom. He died the 6th Richard I.

Hereto and in published narratives it is made manifest that the most senior bloodline of the entire Royal House of Vere in Great Britain and Eire descends – not through the Oxford posterity – but through the Scottish Branch extracted from Ralph de Vere, eldest son of Aubrey III, Earl of Oxford; and culminating contemporarily in the elder progeny of the Veres of Clare and Kildress.

Senior Descent of the Veres of Oxford in Scotland and Eire with Biographical Details

Ralfredus ("Baltredus"/Ralph) de Vere – the eldest surviving son and rightful heir of Aubrey III de Vere, Earl of Oxford, opposed his father in the Flemish war, was disinherited and fled to Scotland with his Liege Lord Conan of Brittany in approx 1165. Conan married the sister of the king and Ralph was given his lands in Lanark. He was a witness to a charter of King William, The Lion of Scotland (1165-1214). Ralph and William were captured after besieging the Castle of Alnwick in Northumbria in 1174.

He had a son:
Walter Rory de Vere

Who had a son:
Ralph (Rudolphus) de Vere, confirmed his father's donation to Kelso Monastery. Died at the end of the reign of Alexander II of Scotland, 1214-1249.

Had a son:
Thomas de Vere

Living in 1266, was witness to a charter of a donation to Kelso Monastery by Hemicus St Clan.

Had a son:
Richardus de Vere (de Were), living approx 1294. Laird (Lord or Baron) of Blackwood, Lanarkshire. Mentioned in a donation to Kelso Monastery.

Had a son:
Thomas de Were (de Vere) of Blackwood.
Proprietor of the lands and Barony of Blackwood, Lanarkshire. Died in the reign of David the Bruce; David II of Scotland, 1329-1371.

Had a son:
Brian (Buan) Were of Blackwood. Living around 1386, Brian's 6th cousin, Robert De Vere, IXth Earl of Oxford, Lord of Hedingham, was Marquess of Dublin and Duke and Vice Regent of Ireland. Robert was effectively the Sovereign Prince of Ireland during his lifetime and was permitted by King Richard II to mint coins with his own likeness. Although attainted during his lifetime, after his death King Richard restored Robert's titles in full in memorium and these are now held de jure by the Archduke Hugh of Argentina (overall head of the House of Vere) and the Irish Branch of the family. Brian died in the beginning of the reign of King Robert III of Scotland (1390-1406).

Whilst the House of Vere bore heraldically the "Double Dragon Device" of the Dragon Court of Melusine long before this period – id est circa 1200 AD – it is believed academically that it was 200 years afterwards, during the investiture together of Emperor Sigismund and Richard de Vere XIth, Earl of Oxford into the "princely degree" of the Knights of the Garter at St. George's Chapel, Windsor, by King Henry IV, that Richard de Vere also received his investiture into the Societas Draconis by Emperor Sigismund. On the evidence of historical precedent, such an investiture and the Dragon name, became heritable. In this regard and by a process of lateral inheritance, the Vere Dragon Court includes the degree of "Sarkany Rend": Societas Draconis.

Ancient Alchemical Double Dragon Seal of Vere

In Heraldry the supporters of a shield, or escutcheon – to give it its proper name – are derived from the oftimes pre-heraldic family badges or totems of the father and mother's Royal and Noble antecedents. The father's supporter is to the right, or dexter of the shield – as it would be held by the combatant – and the mother's supporter is to the left, or sinister of the escutcheon. As we can see from the seal above, the Veres are of dragon blood in both the patrilinear and matrilinear descents, and are consequently of pure Elven lineage. The Boar crest surmounting the shield is the Blue Boar or La Solitaire, which in ancient Gaelic is the symbol of the Arch-Druid.

Brian had a son:
Rotaldus Were of Blackwood. Received a charter from Patrick, Abbot of Kelso Monastery, dated 1404. He was Baillie of Lesmahagow from 1398-1400. Died in the reign of King James II of Scotland (1437-1460).

Had a son:
Thomas Were (de Vere) of Blackwood.

Had a son:
Robert Veyr of Blackwood. Died soon after receiving a charter of confirmation from Robert, the Abbot of the Monastery of Kelso, dated 1474.

Had a son:
Thomas Weir of Vere of Blackwood. Married Lady Aegidia, daughter of John, 3rd Lord Somerville (of the Dragon) in 1483. Acquired vast holdings of land and was patron of St. Mary's Church in Lesmahagow. Died in the beginning of the reign of Queen Mary of Scots in 1542 (Plantagenet descent of the House of Vere).
Thomas had a son:
James Weir of Vere, 7th Baron Blackwood. Married Lady Euphemia Hamilton (Merovingian descent), sister of the Duke of Chatelherault, Marquess of Hamilton, 5th grandson of King Edward III Plantagenet. The Hamiltons were the Heirs Presumptive to the Throne of Scotland during this period. James lived to a great age. He died in 1595.

Had sons:
1.   James Weir
2.   William Vere of Stonebyres, who married Elizabeth Hamilton.
3.   Robert Weir

James married Lady Marriotte Ramsay, daughter of George, Lord Dalhousie. James was an ancestor of the Hope-Veres of Craig Hall. George Ramsay was created Earl of Melrose in 1618 and changed this to the earldom of Dalhousie in 1619. The 9th earl was Governor of Canada, Nova Scotia and New Brunswick. His son was Governor General of India.

1. James had issue:
George Weir of Vere who married Margaret Vere of Stonebyres with whom he had one daughter:

Marriotte Weir who married:
First = Major James Bannatyne (a sept of the Stewarts of Bute).

Second = William Lowry by whom she had a Son George who retained his mother's superior Vere name and became Sir George Weir Bt. (descent to Hope-Vere of Blackwood). The Hope-Veres died out in 1974.

2. William Vere of Stonebyres. See "Vere of Tyrone," below (Merovingian descent).

3. Robert Weir of Vere of Craighead, sold or assigned his estate in 1610 and moved to Monaghan Hall in Co. Fermanagh, now renamed Hallcraig House. Robert married the sister of the alchemist, Sir David Lindsay, The Lord Lyon King of Arms of Scotland.

Robert had sons, the eldest surviving son was:
Alexander, who married Anne, daughter of Sir John Dunbar (Graham descent) of Derrygonnelly, Co. Fermanagh. Their eldest son, Alexander, married Sarah, daughter of Captain Goodwin and secondly, Elizabeth, daughter of Sir Paul Gore, Bt. Their eldest son, Robert Weir of Hallcraig, married Anne, daughter of Captain Carleton of Tullymargy Castle. They had a son, Captain Alexander Weir of Hallcraig, and Captain Noble Weir of Hallcraig, who married Catharine Graham (descent from the Grahams of Scotland 1600), and had issue descending contemporarily to Clive Weir of Dromard, Ulster. From Robert, various other branches also descend.

(*Burke's Irish Landed Gentry*, 1891-1915; *Burke's Landed Gentry*, 1974; *Burke's Peerage, Baronetage and Knightage*, 1957; *Burke's Dormant and Extinct Peerages*).

Vere of Tyrone

From the senior surviving son – Sir William Vere of Stonebyres by his cousin Elizabeth Hamilton – a son Thomas, Baron of Kirkton, who by the Witch – Lady Jane Somerville – had Major Thomas Weir of Edinburgh: Sorcerer, King of the Witches of the Lallan and Elven Prince Consort to the Queen of Faery or Elphame – or, as some say – "The Queen of Hell." The Somerville Badge was the Fiery Dragon surmounting the Pentacle.

Major Weir served with his Irish cousins as a Captain Lieutenant in Sir John Hume's Enniskillen regiment in Ulster in 1640, and by family tradition he founded the Tyrone Branch of the family.

From Major Weir – who was burnt at the stake at Leith, Edinburgh in 1670 – a son Thomas, husband of Mary Robison of Cookstown Ulster, whose issue decamped to Ireland during the witch craze, from whom John of Kildress, whose son Andrew had a daughter – Margaret Weir of Vere of Kildress – who by Archibald Thompson had a son, Archibald Weir of Vere. Archibald married Rachael Stewart and had issue.

The eldest son Robert Weir of Vere married a Vere cousin – Sarah Granann (Graham) – and had a son, John, who moved back to Scotland and married Mary Logan of Ardwell, Logan Manor in Galloway.

The Logan families have held their lands in Galloway and the Stranraer Peninsula since the 1100's, whilst others of that name held Restalrig. Accompanying Sir James Douglas, two Logan Knights, Sir Walter and Sir Robert Logan, were killed in Spain whilst taking the heart of Robert the Bruce to the Holy Land for burial.

John's eldest son:
Thomas Weir of Vere of Lewes married a Gael, Anne Grant Macdonnell of Inverness. They had male issue, the eldest of which died without heirs. The second eldest and surviving son, James Weir of Vere of Lewes, who married a Vere-Collison family cousin, Natalie Hopgood, daughter of George Collison Hopgood Esquire and Julia Harding of Godalming, grand daughter of Captain George Butcher of the 11th Light Dragoons (Lieutenant Colonel of the Regiment in the field), of Windsor Castle and Osbourne House; Tapetiere to Queen Victoria. Family Colleges: The Bluecoat School, Godalming, Surrey UK., and St. Ursula's College, Blackheath.

James and Natalie had an only son:
Prince Nicholas de Vere Gm.K.T., K.C.D., K.G.C., Knight Templar; Knight of Clan Donnachaid of Eire; Magister Templi via the Baphometic Templar Order of The Cubic Stone 1118; Princeps Draconis. By Gaelic blood descent and de jure Head of The Imperial and Royal House of Vere.

Sources:
Parish Records for Ulster 1820-1845, United Kingdom Government Registers for Births, Marriages and Deaths 1845-1957. Sussex Register of Electors, U.K. Sussex Courts of Law, U.K. British Government Department of Internal Affairs, and Burke's Genealogies.

The Scottish name Weir is derived from the Norman-French de Vere... Alberic de Vere... accompanied the Conqueror.

Ralph or Radalphus de Ver was the first of the name on record in Scotland. As Ralph de Ver, he was taken prisoner at Alnwick in July 1174. As Radulphus de Weir, he witnessed a Charter of King William, between 1174 and 1184, and as Radulph de Veir he gave a bovate of land in Sprowston, Roxburgh, to Kelso Abbey. As Radalphus de Vere he witnessed another Charter by King William to the Abbey of Lindores. He also witnessed another undated Charter of King William's to William de Hala, Herd (Errol). The same, or perhaps a succeeding Radulph de Ver, or de Uer, witnessed in about 1204 a grant to the Abbey of Arbroath, and before 1214 another Charter by William the Lion. The Weirs of Lanarkshire claimed to be descended from this Radulph, who had massive land holdings in the Border Regions.

...Richard Wer, Lanark, rendered homage to his cousin Edward I in 1296. Between 1398 and 1400 Rothald de Were, Baille of Lesmahagow, had a Charter from Patrick, Abbot of Kelso, of the lands of Blackwood, Mossiygning and Durgundreston. In 1497 Abbot Robert granted Rogerhill and Brownhill to Robert Weyr for services rendered....

The English "Weirs," however, are descended from a progenitor who dwelt at a weir or fishing dam.

Source: *Scotland and Her Tartans*, by Alexander Fulton.

Robert de Vere – Scion of Odin – the Hooded God

Robert de Vere, Ralph de Vere's brother, was the historical claimant to the earldom of Cambridge and Huntingdon in the 13th century, heritor of the lands of FitzOoth or Hood; Robert or Robin – a Knight Templar in accordance with his legend – was outlawed by King John and lost all his lands and castles. Robert was the historical Robin Hood, Robin Goodfellow or Puck; see published commentaries to Shakespeare's, i.e. Edward de Vere's, *A Midsummer Night's Dream*: Robin Hood's or "Puck's" father, Oberon or Alberic (de Vere) the Elf King, descended – via Melusine – "from Morgan la Fey and Julius Caesar." Such accords with the Vere family genealogy.

Essentially a ritualised figure, Robin "of the Hood" – the Green Stag of the Wildwood – (a variation of the White Hart of Annwn, Elphame or Faery) was an ancient, druidic form of the psychopomp, or guide of souls (and King-Maker), in a similar manner as the Blue Boar of the Gaelic Goddess Arduina of the Ardennes and the druidic Ulidian of Fir-Bolg. The ceremonial office of the Robin Hood became – in late Dark Age and early medieval times – that of God-King of the Witches and representative of the Elven Host in decline, a Dragon Lord of the Grail. As the stag of the wild wood or Cernunnos – horned god of the witches – and by his marriage to "Lady Marion" (Miriamne Mara), Robin replicates Jesus as the horned lamb and saviour god and adds credence to the tradition of Jesus and Mary's marriage, and Robin Hood as their holy scion. The legend descends! Robert's descendant, Edward de Vere, 17th Earl of Oxford, continued the role of Robin Hood, "The Stag of the Wildwood" and King of the "Calle Daouine," in the reign of Good Queen Bess. Major Thomas Weir of Vere of Edinburgh – Grail Prince and Dragon Lord – also continued this role, that of the Fairy God of the Witches, in the senior Scottish Branch of the family, descending to Nicholas de Vere.

Major Thomas Weir (1599-1670) Consort of the Queen of Elphame; was born at Kirkton House, Carluke, where he later became Laird. As an adult, he lived at West Bow and was burned at the stake in Edinburgh for Witchcraft, Human Sacrifice (vampirism), Animal Sacrifice, Congress with the "Queen of Hell," incest with his step-daughter Elizabeth Bourdon, and also with his sister. His sister was hanged the next day for her part in some of his activities.

- Armorial Bearings -
Hope Vere and Weir
Arms (of Blackwood LR 4/94) 1
Argent, on a fess Azure, three mollets of the first
(of The Royal Scythian, Pictish Tribe of Mar)

- Crest -
(As Oxford)
Upon a baronial chapeau Gules furred
Ermine a boar standant Azure armed Or.

- Motto -
(As Oxford)
"Vero Nihil Verius"
(Nothing Truer than Truth)
1. Lyon Roll of Arms.

Court of the Lyon King of Arms, Edinburgh.

Chapter Nine

The Grail Descent of Jesus Christ from Satan:
Dragon King of the Fairy Host

- Et In Arcadia Ego -

The Babylonian Goddess, Queen Tiamat

(The Greek Goddess "Chaos"), Mother of Gaia

|

The Babylonian Goddess, Queen Kishar

(The Greek Goddess Gaia: Mother Earth)

|

The Babylonian God-King Anu (Chronos-Saturn) and the High

Council of the Anunnaki: The Jewish Elohim: The Old Gods

|

Satan–Lucifer
(Enki; Ea; Khem; Pan; Capricorn:
The Ram of the Shimmering Waters)
=Queen Hawah of Eldar

|

Cain, King of Kish, Son of Satan,
Ancestral Founder of the High Elven
Kings and Queens of the Dragon and the Grail
= Queen Lilith II "Luluwa" (The Pearl)
daughter of Satan by Queen Lilith I
"The Beautiful," mother of all demons:
daughter of Nergal, King of the Underworld.
Diana of the Romans, Hecate of the Greeks
and Arduina of the Gaels.

|

Enoch
=Awan

|

Irad

|

Mehujael

|

Methusael

|

Lamech, Dragon Lord of Ur
= Queen Zillah

|

123

Tubal Cain, King of Ur
= Ninbanda, d. of Lilith Naamah
|

King Ham: Chem Zarathustra, Tenth
Archon of Capricorn
=Queen Neelata-Mek
|

Cush
|

Nimrod the Mighty Hunter
|

Boethos/ Hotep Sekhemwy
Pharaoh and founder
of 2nd Dynasty in Egypt
=Queen Bithiah
|

Pharaoh Raneb/Kalenhkos, c. 2800 BC
brought culture of Chem of Capricorn
to Egypt as Khem, the Goat of Mendes,
known as Pan in Greece, later the
Sabbatical Goat God of the Witches
and the Baphomet of the Templars;
The Black Sun: The Christos
|

Pharaoh Nynetjer
|

Pharaoh Sekhemib
|

Pharaoh Khasekhemwy
|

daughter
=Pharaoh Sanakhte
|

daughter
= Pharaoh Sekhemkhet
|

Pharaoh Khaba 2643-37 BC
|

Pharaoh Huni 2637-13 BC
= Queen Meresankh I
|

Pharaoh Sneferu
= Queen Hetep-Heres I
|

Pharaoh Khufu (Cheops)
= Queen Henutsen
|

Pharaoh Khefre
= Queen Khamerenebty
|

Pharaoh Menkaure 2532-04 BC
= Queen Khamerenebty II
|

Queen Khentkawas
= Pharaoh Userkaf

|
Pharaoh Neferirkare
|
Pharaoh Shepsekare
|
Pharaoh Neferefre
|
Pharaoh Niuserre
|
Pharaoh Menkauhor
|
Pharaoh Djedkare
|
Pharaoh Unas the Vampire 2375-45 BC
(The Pyramid Texts)
|
Queen Iput
= Pharaoh Teti
|
Pharaoh Pepi I
= Queen Ankhnesmerire
|
Pharaoh Pepi II
= Queen Neith
|
Pharaoh Merenre II 2184-81 BC
= Queen Nitoctris
|
Prince Ankhfn-Khonsu
Re-established the Royal
Dragon Court in Egypt under
the protection of the God Sobekh,
the Dragon defender of Royalty
|
Prince Intef I (The Great)
Governor of Thebes
|
Prince Intef II
|
Prince Intef III
|
Pharaoh Mentuhotep I (The Coffin Texts)
= Queen Tem
|
Pharaoh Mentuhotep II
|
Pharaoh Mentuhotep III
|
Queen Tohwait
= Pharaoh Amenhemet
|
Pharaoh Senusret I
= Princess Sarah, d. of Queen Tohwait
(later wife of Abraham)
|

Pharaoh Amenhemet II
= Queen Keminebu
|
Pharaoh Senusret II
= Queen Nofret
|
Pharaoh Senusret III
= Queen Mereret
|
Pharaoh Amenhemet III
= Queen Aat
|
Pharaoh Amenhemet IV
= Sobeknefru, The Great Dragon Queen of Egypt,
(Ratified the Royal Dragon Court under Sobekh)
|
Daughter
= Pharaoh Wegaf

13th Dynasty of Egypt
The Dragon Kings and Queens of
the God Sobekh

Pharaoh Wegaf (above)
|
Pharaoah Ameny Intef c. 1700 BC
|
Pharaoh Sobekhotep III
|
Pharaoh Sobekhotep IV
|
Daughter
= Pharaoh Sobekemsaf
|
Pharaoh Intef VII
|
Daughter
= King Khayan (The Good God)
Dragon King of the Hyksos who
descends from Queen Towait (above)
|
Apepi I
Dragon King of the Hyksos
|
Apepi II
(Apophis the Evil)
|
Senisonb (Dragon Queen)
|
Pharaoh Tuthmosis I
= Queen Mutneferte (Dragon Queen)
|
Pharaoh Tuthmosis II
= Iset
|

Pharaoh Tuthmosis III
(Founded the Rosi-crucis
Therapeutate at Karnak)
1469-36 BC
= Queen Neferue
|
The Dragon Queen Tio
= Pharaoh Amenhotep II
|
Pharaoh Tuthmosis IV
= Queen Mutemwiya
|
Pharaoh Amenhotep III
= Gilukhipa, Dragon Queen
of the Mitanni
|
Merykhipa (Kiya)
Dragon Queen
= Pharaoh Amenhotep IV
|
Queen Kiya Tasherit 1361 BC
=Prince Rama, descendant of Abraham
and the Pharaoh Sensuret I (see above).
Here the direct and unbroken
lines of Satanic descent conjoin
|
Amminadab
|
Nahshon
|
Salma
= Rahab
|
Boaz
|
Obed
|
Jesse
|
The House of David
King David of Israel
=Queen Bath-Sheba
of the Hittites
(Descent from the "Hurrians": The Aryans)
|
King Solomon, Lord of the Rings
= Sheba Lilith (Venus) his sister.
|
Rehoboam
|
Abijah
|
Asa
|
Jehoshaphat

|
Joram
|
Azariah
|
Jotham
|
Ahaz
|
Hezekiah
|
Manasseh
|
Amon
|
Josiah
|
Jeconiah
(Exile in Babylon begins)
|
Shealtiel
|
Zerubbabel
|
Abiud
|
Eliakim
|
Azor
|
Zadok
|
Achim
|
Eliud
|
Eleazar
|
Matthan
|
Jacob
|
Joseph
= Mary (parallel descent
from the House of David:
Descent from Satan)
|
Jesus Christ The Messiah
(Yehoshua ben-Joseph: called ben-Panther)
(Messiah = Messach: Anointed of the Egyptian Dragon
God Sobekh: Patron and Protector of the Royal Blood)
= Mary Magdalene, Priestess of Ishtar (Venus)

PART TWO

The Paternal Fairy Genealogies of Nicholas de Vere

and the Imperial and Royal House of Vere

Chapter Ten

The Nephilim Descent of the House of Vere
29,628 BC – 2011 AD

The Nephilim were the sons of the Anunnaki Gods and their name means "Those who came down." In the Sumerian King Lists it is recorded that the assumption of their Divine Kingship began in Mesopotamia (Iraq) some 31,000 years ago. This time coincides with the demise of the Eljo and Neanderthal races, and the Anunnaki annihilation of the voracious, monstrous Naphidem; sons of those Nephilim who rebelled against the Grand Council of the Anunnaki and bred with human women.

During this period the Cro-Magnon species emerged as a result of genetic hybridisation of the Anunnaki with early Homo sapiens. In this regard, the Anunnaki Gods are the missing link between early man – the Eljo – and modern Cro-Magnon. No further divine intervention occurred and the Cro-Magnon were left to their own devices and, in the fullness of time, kingship was lowered to them by the Gods.

However, human kingship was a disaster and was withdrawn by the Anunnaki and invested in their Nephilim sons until 4000 BC. The Nephilim God-Kings left their parents behind in Central Europe – Carpathia, Transylvania and the Bosphorus – and assumed control in Mesopotamia until the reign of the Nephilim King, Ubartutu of Shuruppak. King Ubartutu's son, King Ziu Sudra, left Mesopotamia and reigned in the northern regions of Anatolia (modern

Turkey) in 4508 BC, with his centre on the banks of the Black Sea basin, until the Great Flood (the original Biblical inundation) of 4500 BC.

Contrary to the Genesis myth, Adam – The Priest-King Attaba of Kish – was created after the Flood, in 3882 BC, not before. From Adam there are eight recorded generations to Noah who, if he had existed, would have lived 200 years afterwards, in the year 3682 BC, which is 818 years after the Biblical Black Sea Flood and 318 years after the Mesopotamian Flood.

Having built a vessel in which he rescued the "seeds of life," his "ark" eventually came to rest on Mount Ararat several miles south of the Black Sea. The name "Ziu Sudra" was hijacked from the Sumerian King Lists by the Jewish scribes and renamed Noah, who never existed within the necessary time frame or context, and is not recorded in the Sumerian records for either the Black Sea flood, or the Flooding of Mesoptamia, which happened at least five hundred years later in about 4000 BC. At that time, the records of the Library of Nineveh relate, it was Uta-Napishtim – King of Shurappak – who built the Ark, not Noah. As "Noah" never existed in this context, the Biblical descent from a son, Prince Sem (Shem), can only have been through the Nephilim-Anunnaki King Ziu Sudra.

Ziu Sudra was caught in the Black Sea Flood in c. 4500 BC Then 614 years pass between the Black Sea flood and the birth of Adam and Eve. Adam and Eve were born in the Garden of Eden in 3882 BC The real Noah was born 3612 BC, 1444 years before the Mesopotamian Flood in 2348 BC, and 888 years after the Black Sea Flood. Noah was not present at either catastrophe.

The Nephilim Kings of Mesopotamia
Table One

King Allulim of Eridu
29,628 BC
Dynasty descends

King Alagar of Eridu
Dynasty descends
26,618 BC

King Enmenluanna of Badtibira
Dynasty descends
23,608 BC

King Enmengalanna of Badtibira
Dynasty descends
20,598 BC

King Dumuzi of Badtibira
Dynasty descends
17,598 BC

King Ensipazianna of Larak
Dynasty descends
14,578 BC

King Enmenduranna of Sippar
Dynasty descends
11,568 BC

King Ubartutu of Shuruppak
Dynasty descends
8558 BC

The Great Flood
4500 BC

King Ziu Sudra
returns to Mesopotamia

Prince Elam

Prince Salitis
= Seduka Tel Bab

Prince Arpakhsar
= Rasuja of Ur

|
Prince Shalah of Ur
= Muak, d. of Kesed
|
Prince Abhar
= Azura, d. of Nebrod
|
Prince Phalek of Mesopotamia
= Lamnar of Shinar (Sumer)
|
Prince Reu
= Princess Ora of Ur
|
King Sorogh of Ur
= Melka, g. daughter of
Phalek and Lamnar of Sumer
|
King Nahor of Ur
= Princess Iyosaka
of the Chaldees
|
King Terah of Ur
= Yawna
|
Prince Abram of Ur
= Princess Hagar of Egypt
|
Isaac of Ur
= Rabkah
|
Prince Jacob
= Leah
|
Prince Judas
= Princess Tamar of Kadesh
|
Prince Pharez
= Princess Barayah
|
Prince Hezron
= Princess Kanita
|
Prince Rama
= Princess Kiya Tasherit of Egypt
|
Prince Amenhotep
= Princess Thehara (Tara)
|
Prince Nashon
= Princess Sihar, d. of Yuhannas
|
Prince Salma
= Princess Rachab
|
King Boaz
= Ruth of Moab
|
Prince Obed
= Abalit, d. of Sonas

|

Prince Jesse
= Habliar, d. of Abrias

|

King David of Judah
= Princess Bathsheba the Aryan

|

King Solomon
Lord of the Rings.
1015 BC
= Princess Naamah the Ammonitess.
Solomon's Descent from Satan
via the Dragon Queen of Sobekh,
Kiya Tasherit, wife of Prince Rama

|

King Rehoboam
King of Judah 975 BC
= Princess Maachlah
dau. of Ureil of Gibeah

|

King Abijah
King of Judah
957 BC

|

King Asa
King of Judah 955 BC
= Princess Azubah
dau. of Shilhi

|

King Jehoshaphat
King of Judah 917 BC

|

King Jehoram
King of Judah 893 BC
= Princess Athalia
dau. of Omri

|

King Ahaziah
King of Judah 885 BC
= Princess Zibiah of Beersheba

|

King Joash
King of Judah 878 BC
= Princess Jehoaddan of Jerusalem

|

King Amaziah
King of Judah 840 BC
= Princess Jecoliah of Jerusalem

|

King Uzziah
King of Judah 811 BC
= Princess Jerushah
dau. Of Zadok The Priest

|

King Jotham
King of Judah 759 BC

|

King Ahaz
King of Judah 742 BC

= Princess Abijah
dau of Zechariah
|
King Hezekiah
King of Judah 726 BC
= Princess Hephzibah
|
King Mannaseh
King of Judah 697 BC
= Princess Meshullemeth
dau of Haruz of Jotbah
|
King Amon
King of Judah 642 BC
= Princess Jedidah
dau. of Adaiah of Boscath
|
King Josiah
King of Judah 640 BC
= 2. Princess Hamutal
dau. of Jeremiah of Libnah
|
King Zedekiah
King of Judah 598 BC
|
Princess Tamar
= King Eochaid I
High King of Ireland after the
displacement of the remnant
of the Tuadha de Danaan
|
King Irial Faidh
|
King Eithriall
|
King Follain
|
King Tighernmas
|
King Eanbotha
|
King Smiorguil
|
King Fiachach Labhruine
|
King Aongus Oilbughagah
|
King Maoin
|
King Rotheachta
|
King Dein
|
King Siorna Saoghalach
|
King Oiliolla Olchaoin
|
King Nuadha Fionn Fail
|

King Giallchadh
|
King Simon Breac
|
King Muiriadhach Bolgrach
|
King Fiathadh Tolgrach
|
King Duach Laighrach
|
King Eochaidh Buillaig
|
King Ugaine Mar (The Great)
|
King Cobhtach Caolbreag
|
King Meilage
|
King Jaran Gleofathach
|
King Conla Gruaich
|
King Ceaigach
|
King Oiliolla Caisfhiaclach
|
King Eochaid Foltleathan
|
King Aonghus Tuirimheach
|
King Fiachra Firmara
|
King Feradaig
|
King Fergus I
|
King Maine
(Father of Siadhail: descent to
the O'Shiels of Ireland)
|
King Dornadil
|
King Rowein
|
King Reuther
|
King Eders
|
King Conaire Mor
|
King Admoir
|
King Corbred I
|
King Dare-Dornmoir
|
King Corbred II
|
King Luigdig-Ellatig

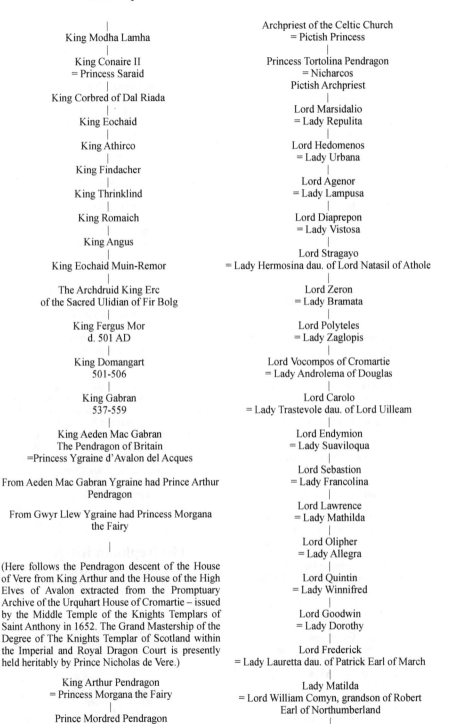

King Modha Lamha

King Conaire II
= Princess Saraid

King Corbred of Dal Riada

King Eochaid

King Athirco

King Findacher

King Thrinklind

King Romaich

King Angus

King Eochaid Muin-Remor

The Archdruid King Erc
of the Sacred Ulidian of Fir Bolg

King Fergus Mor
d. 501 AD

King Domangart
501-506

King Gabran
537-559

King Aeden Mac Gabran
The Pendragon of Britain
=Princess Ygraine d'Avalon del Acques

From Aeden Mac Gabran Ygraine had Prince Arthur
Pendragon

From Gwyr Llew Ygraine had Princess Morgana
the Fairy

(Here follows the Pendragon descent of the House
of Vere from King Arthur and the House of the High
Elves of Avalon extracted from the Promptuary
Archive of the Urquhart House of Cromartie – issued
by the Middle Temple of the Knights Templars of
Saint Anthony in 1652. The Grand Mastership of the
Degree of The Knights Templar of Scotland within
the Imperial and Royal Dragon Court is presently
held heritably by Prince Nicholas de Vere.)

King Arthur Pendragon
= Princess Morgana the Fairy

Prince Mordred Pendragon

Archpriest of the Celtic Church
= Pictish Princess

Princess Tortolina Pendragon
= Nicharcos
Pictish Archpriest

Lord Marsidalio
= Lady Repulita

Lord Hedomenos
= Lady Urbana

Lord Agenor
= Lady Lampusa

Lord Diaprepon
= Lady Vistosa

Lord Stragayo
= Lady Hermosina dau. of Lord Natasil of Athole

Lord Zeron
= Lady Bramata

Lord Polyteles
= Lady Zaglopis

Lord Vocompos of Cromartie
= Lady Androlema of Douglas

Lord Carolo
= Lady Trastevole dau. of Lord Uilleam

Lord Endymion
= Lady Suaviloqua

Lord Sebastion
= Lady Francolina

Lord Lawrence
= Lady Mathilda

Lord Olipher
= Lady Allegra

Lord Quintin
= Lady Winnifred

Lord Goodwin
= Lady Dorothy

Lord Frederick
= Lady Lauretta dau. of Patrick Earl of March

Lady Matilda
= Lord William Comyn, grandson of Robert
Earl of Northumberland

Lord Richard Comyn
= Lady Hextilda dau. of Hutred of Tynedal

Lord William Comyn, Great Justiciar of Scotland
= Lady Marjorie Countess of Buchan

Lady Elizabeth Comyn
= Lord William 9th Earl of Mar

Lord Donald 10th Earl of Mar
= Princess Helen dau. of Prince Llewellyn of North
Wales

Lady Isabel Mar
= King Robert I the Bruce
Grand Master of the Knights
Templars in Scotland

Princess Marjorie Bruce
= Lord Walter Stewart
6th High Steward of Scotland

King Robert II
= Lady Elizabeth Muir of Rowallen

King Robert III
= Lady Annabelle Drummond of Stobhall

King James I
= Princess Joan Beaufort of Somerset
(Descent from King Edward III)

King James II
= Mary, dau. of Arnold Duc de Gueldres

Princess Mary
= Lord Thomas Boyd

Lady Mary Boyd
James 1st Lord Hamilton
great grandson of
Princess Aenor de Chatellerault
and Guillaume X le Toulousain
Duc de Guyenne, Comte de Poitiers

Lady Euphemia Hamilton
(descent from the High Elves of Ireland,
Princess Melusine and the Scots Kings)
= Lord James Weir of Vere,
Baron Blackwood d. 1599

Sir William Vere of Stanebyres Castle
= Elizabeth Hamilton, his cousin.
(descent from the High Elves of Ireland,
Princess Melusine and the Scots Kings)

Lord Thomas Weir of Vere, Baron Kirkton
= Lady Jane Somerville, The Witch of
the Dragon House of the Earls Somerville

Major Thomas Weir of Vere of Edinburgh,
The Witch King of Mid-Lothian
= Margaret Bourdon

Lord Thomas Weir of Vere
de jure Baron Kirkton
Hereditary Witch King
= Miss Mary Robison of Cookstown,
County Tyrone, Ulster

John Weir of Vere

Andrew Weir of Vere

Margaret Weir of Vere of Kildress

Archibald Weir of Vere of Kildress
= Rachel Stewart of Desertcreat

Robert Weir of Vere of Kildress

John Weir of Vere of Ardwell in Logan Manor
= Mary Logan dau. of Thomas Logan of
Ardwell, Logan Manor, Galloway

Thomas Logan Weir of Vere of Carlisle
= Anne Grant Macdonnell of Inverness
(descent from the Grant earls of Seafield)

James Weir of Vere of Lewes
= Natalie Hopgood (Descent through her father
from the Collisons of Norfolk, the Plantagenet
Kings and the Imperial and Royal House of Vere.
(Descent through her mother from Lt. Col
George Butcher of Windsor Castle, Sarah Butcher
of Framlingham and the Huguenot Bourchier
Counts of Versailles, France.)

HI&RH Prince Nicholas de Vere

The Nephilim Kings of
Mesopotamia
Table Two

King Allulim of Eridu
29,628 BC
Dynasty descends

King Alagar of Eridu
Dynasty descends
26,618 BC

King Enmenluanna of Badtibira
Dynasty descends
23,608 BC

King Enmengalanna of Badtibira
Dynasty descends
20,598 BC

King Dumuzi of Badtibira
Dynasty descends
17,598

King Ensipazianna of Larak
Dynasty descends
14,578

King Enmenduranna of Sippar
Dynasty descends
11,568

King Ubartutu of Shuruppak
Dynasty descends
8558 BC

The Great Flood
4500 BC

King Ziu Sudra
returns to Mesopotamia

Prince Elam

Prince Salitis
= Seduka Tel Bab

Prince Arpakhsar
= Rasuja of Ur

Prince Shalah of Ur
= Muak, d. of Kesed

Prince Abhar
= Azura, d. of Nebrod

Prince Phalek of Mesopotamia
= Lamnar of Shinar (Sumer)

Prince Reu
= Princess Ora of Ur

King Sorogh of Ur
= Melka, g.daughter of
Phalek and Lamnar of Sumer

King Nahor of Ur
= Princess Iyosaka
of the Chaldees

King Terah of Ur
= Yawna

Prince Abram of Ur
= Princess Hagar of Egypt

Isaac of Ur
= Rabkah

Prince Jacob
= Leah

Prince Judas
= Princess Tamar of Kadesh

Prince Pharez
= Princess Barayah

Prince Hezron
= Princess Kanita

Prince Rama
= Princess Kiya Tasherit of Egypt

Prince Amenhotep
= Princess Tara (Tara)

Prince Nashon
= Princess Sihar, d. of Yuhannas

Prince Salma
= Princess Rachab

King Boaz
= Ruth of Moab

Prince Obed
= Abalit, d. of Sonas

Prince Jesse
= Habliar, d. of Abrias

King David of Judah
= Princess Bathsheba the Aryan

King Solomon, Lord of the Rings
= Sheba Lilith (Venus) his sister.
1015 BC
= Princess Naamah the Ammonitess.
Solomon's Descent from Satan
via the Dragon Queen of Sobekh,

Kiya Tasherit, wife of Prince Rama
|
King Rehoboam
King of Judah 975 BC
= Princess Maachlah
dau. of Ureil of Gibeah
|
King Abijah
King of Judah
957 BC
|
King Asa
King of Judah 955 BC
= Princess Azubah
dau. of Shilhi
|
King Jehoshaphat
King of Judah 917 BC
|
King Jehoram
King of Judah 893 BC
= Princess Athalia
dau. of Omri
|
King Ahaziah
King of Judah 885 BC
= Princess Zibiah of Beersheba
|
King Joash
King of Judah 878 BC
Princess Jehoaddan of Jerusalem
|
King Amaziah
King of Judah 840 BC
= Princess Jecoliah of Jerusalem
|
King Uzziah
King of Judah 811 BC
= Princess Jerushah
da. Of Zadok
|
King Jotham
King of Judah 759 BC
|
King Ahaz
King of Judah 742 BC
Princess Abijah
dau of Zechariah
|
King Hezekiah
King of Judah 726 BC
= Princess Hephzibah
|
King Mannaseh
King of Judah 697 BC
= Princess Meshullemeth
dau of Haruz of Jotbah
|
King Amon

King of Judah 642 BC
= Princess Jedidah
dau. of Adaiah of Boscath
|
King Josiah
King of Judah 640 BC
|
King Jehoiakim
King of Judah 609 BC
(Taken Hostage to Babylon)
= Princess Nehushtah
dau. of Elnathan of Judaea
|
King Jechoniah
King of Judah 598 BC
(Taken hostage to Babylon)
|
Prince Shealtiel
|
Prince Pedaiah
|
Prince Zerrubabel
De jure King
of Judah
|
Prince Rhesa
|
Prince Johanan
|
Prince Judah
|
Prince Joseph
|
Prince Semei
|
Prince Mattathias
|
Prince Maath
|
Prince Naage
|
Prince Azallah
|
Prince Nahum
|
Prince Amos
|
Prince Mattathias
|
Prince Joseph
|
Prince Johanan
|
Prince Melchi
|
Prince Levi
|
Prince Matthat
|

Prince Jacob

|

Prince Joseph

|

Jesus Christ The Messiah
(Yehoshua ben-Joseph: called ben-Panther)
(Messiah: Messach: Anointed of the God Sobekh)
= Mary Magdalene, Priestess of Ishtar (Venus)

|

Josue Del Graal

|

Aminadab
= Eurgis d. of King Coel I
sister of Lucius the Great

|

Catheloys

|

Manael

|

Titurel

|

Boaz
(Anfortas)

|

Frotmund
(Frimutel)

|

Faramund 420 AD
Sire of the French Monarchy
= Argotta dau. of Genebaud
of the Sicambrian Franks

|

Clodian of Tournai
= Queen Basina of Thuringia

|

King Meroveus, founder of
the Dynasty of Merovingian
Sorcerer Kings d. 456 AD
= Princess Meira

|

King Childeric of the Franks d. 481 AD
= Queen Basina II of Thuringia

|

King Clovis of the Franks d. 511 AD
= Clotilde of Burgundy

|

King Lothar I d. 561 AD

|

Princess Blitildis
= Prince Ansbert, Great Great Grandson of
King Clodian of Tournai (above) d. 570 AD

|

Lord Arnoald of Scheldt
= Princess Dua of Swabia

|

Arnulf of Metz
= Princess Dobo of Saxony

|

Lord Ansegis of Brabant (Lower Lorraine)

Margrave of Scheldt d. 685
= Lady Begga, dau of Pepin I, Mayor of Austrasia

|

Lord Pepin II of Heristal, Mayor of the Palaces of
Austrasia, Neustria and Burgundy d. 714
= Lady Alpas

|

Lord Charles Martel (The Hammer) d. 741

|

Pepin the III Brevis, Duke of Lower Lorraine
(Brabant)
Mayor of Neustrasia, King of the Franks
= Lady Leuthergis

|

Princess Bertha
= Prince Milo de Vere, Duke of Angiers
Count of Anjou, son of the Fairy Princess
Melusine I of the Scythians (parallel descent
from Satan via the Egyptian Kings as
above and the Fairy Tuadha de Danaan)

|

Prince Milo II de Vere, Count of Guisnes and Anjou
= Lady Aveline de Nantes

|

Prince Nicassius de Vere, Count of Guisnes
= Lady Agatha de Champagne

|

Prince Otho de Vere, Count of Guisnes
= Lady Constance de Chartres

|

Prince Amelius (Adolph) de Vere Count of Guisnes
= Lady Maud de Ponthieu

|

Prince Guy (Gallus) de Vere, Count of Guisnes
= Lady Gertrude de Clermont de Ponthieu

|

Two Sons:
2nd son – Prince Baldwin de Vere, descent to Ida
de Vere,
the House of Hamilton and the Royal Vere of
Blackwood
&
1st son Prince Manasses de Vere Count of
Guisnes, (descent to the Vere Earls of Oxford)
=Lady Petronilla de Boleine

|

Prince Alphonse de Vere, Count of Guisnes
= Lady Katarine, dau of Count Arnulf of Flanders

|

Prince Alberic I de Vere, Count of Guisnes
= Princess Beatrix of Normandy
(descent from Satan via the Fairy Princess
Melusine I du Scythes above)

|

Prince Alberic II de Vere,
Sheriff of Cambridge, Lord of Clare and Tonbridge
= Lady Adeliza dau. of Lord Gilbert FitzRichard

|

Prince Aubrey (Alberic) III de Vere, Earl of Oxford,

Shakespeare's Oberon, King of the Fairies
= Lady Agnes, dau. of Henry Lord Essex.
|
Prince Ralph de Vere of Blackwood 1165 AD
Brother of Robert of Huntingdon; Robin Hood;
God of the Witches, Shakespeare's
Puck, son of Oberon
|
Prince Rory de Vere of Blackwood
|
Prince Ralph de Vere of Blackwood
|
Prince Thomas de Vere of Blackwood
|
Prince Richard de Vere of Blackwood
|
Prince Thomas de Vere
1st Baron Blackwood 1340 AD
|
Prince Buan Were of Vere of Blackwood
|
Prince Rotaldus Were of Vere of Blackwood
|
Prince Thomas Were of Vere
4th Baron Blackwood
|
Prince Robert Veyr of Vere of Blackwood
|
Prince Thomas Weir of Vere of Blackwood
= Lady Aegidia Somerset
|
Prince James Weir of Vere,
7th Baron Blackwood d. 1599
= Lady Euphemia Hamilton
(descent from the High Elves of Ireland,
Princess Melusine and the Scots Kings)
|
Sir William Vere de Vere of Stanebyres Castle
= Lady Elizabeth Hamilton his cousin
(descent from the High Elves of Ireland,
Princess Melusine and the Scots Kings)
|
Lord Thomas Weir of Vere, Baron Kirkton
= Lady Jane Somerville, The Witch of
the Dragon House of the Earls Somerville
|
Major Thomas Weir of Vere of Edinburgh,
The Witch King of Mid-Lothian
= Margaret Bourdon
|
Lord Thomas Weir of Vere
de jure Baron Kirkton
Hereditary Witch King
= Miss Mary Robison of Cookstown,
County Tyrone, Ulster
|
John Weir of Vere
|
Andrew Weir of Vere

|
Margaret Weir of Vere of Kildress
|
Archibald Weir of Vere of Kildress
= Rachel Stewart of Desertcreat
|
Robert Weir of Vere of Kildress
|
John Weir of Vere of Ardwell, Logan Manor
= Mary Logan dau. of Thomas Logan of
Ardwell, Logan Manor, Galloway
|
Thomas Logan Weir of Vere of Carlisle
= Anne Grant Macdonnell of Inverness
(descent from the Grant earls of Seafield)
|
James Weir of Vere of Lewes
= Natalie Hopgood (Descent through her father
from the Collisons of Norfolk, the Plantagenet
Kings and the Imperial and Royal House of Vere.
(Descent through her mother from Lt. Col
George Butcher of Windsor Castle, Sarah Butcher
of Framlingham and the Huguenot Bourchier
Counts of Versailles, France.)
|
HI&RH Prince Nicholas de Vere

The Nephilim Kings of Mesopotamia
Table Three

King Allulim of Eridu
29,628 BC
Dynasty descends
|
King Alagar of Eridu
Dynasty descends
26,618 BC
|
King Enmenluanna of Badtibira
Dynasty descends
23,608 BC
|
King Enmengalanna of Badtibira
Dynasty descends
20,598 BC
|
King Dumuzi of Badtibira

Dynasty descends
17,598
|
King Ensipazianna of Larak
Dynasty descends
14,578
|
King Enmenduranna of Sippar
Dynasty descends
11,568
|
King Ubartutu of Shuruppak
Dynasty descends
8558 BC
|
The Great Flood
4500 BC
|
King Ziu Sudra
returns to Mesopotamia
|
Prince Elam
|
Prince Salitis
= Seduka Tel Bab
|
Prince Arpakhsar
= Rasuja of Ur
|
Prince Shalah of Ur
= Muak, d. of Kesed
|
Prince Abhar
= Azura, d. of Nebrod
|
Prince Phalek of Mesopotamia
= Lamnar of Shinar (Sumer)
|
Prince Reu
= Princess Ora of Ur
|
King Sorogh of Ur
= Melka, g.daughter of
Phalek and Lamnar of Sumer
|
King Nahor of Ur
= Princess Iyosaka
of the Chaldees
|
King Terah of Ur
= Yawna
|
Prince Abram of Ur
= Princess Hagar of Egypt

Isaac of Ur
= Rabkah
|
Prince Jacob
= Leah
|
Prince Judas
= Princess Tamar of Kadesh
|
Prince Pharez
= Princess Barayah
|
Prince Hezron
= Princess Kanita
|
Prince Rama
= Princess Kiya Tasherit of Egypt
|
Prince Amenhotep
= Princess Thehara (Tara)
|
Prince Nashon
= Princess Sihar, d. of Yuhannas
|
Prince Salma
= Princess Rachab
|
King Boaz
= Ruth of Moab
|
Prince Obed
= Abalit, d. of Sonas
|
Prince Jesse
= Habliar, d. of Abrias
|
King David of Judah
= Princess Bathsheba the Aryan
|
King Solomon, Lord of the Rings
= Sheba Lilith (Venus) his sister.
1015 BC
= Princess Naamah the Ammonitess
(Descent to the God Odin).
Solomon's Descent from Satan
via the Dragon Queen of Sobekh,
Kiya Tasherit, wife of Prince Rama
|
King Rehoboam
King of Judah 975 BC
= Princess Maachlah
dau. of Ureil of Gibeah
|
King Abijah
King of Judah
957 BC
|
King Asa

King of Judah 955 BC
= Princess Azubah
dau. of Shilhi
|
King Jehoshaphat
King of Judah 917 BC
|
King Jehoram
King of Judah 893 BC
= Princess Athalia
dau. of Omri
|
King Ahaziah
King of Judah 885 BC
= Princess Zibiah of Beersheba
|
King Joash
King of Judah 878 BC
Princess Jehoaddan of Jerusalem
|
King Amaziah
King of Judah 840 BC
= Princess Jecoliah of Jerusalem
|
King Uzziah
King of Judah 811 BC
= Princess Jerushah
da. Of Zadok
|
King Jotham
King of Judah 759 BC
|
King Ahaz
King of Judah 742 BC
Princess Abijah
dau of Zechariah
|
King Hezekiah
King of Judah 726 BC
= Princess Hephzibah
|
King Mannaseh
King of Judah 697 BC
= Princess Meshullemeth
dau of Haruz of Jotbah
|
King Amon
King of Judah 642 BC
= Princess Jedidah
dau. of Adaiah of Boscath
|
King Josiah
King of Judah 640 BC
|
King Jehoiakim
King of Judah 609 BC
(Taken Hostage to Babylon)
= Princess Nehushtah
dau. of Elnathan of Judaea

|
King Jechoniah
King of Judah 598 BC
(Taken hostage to Babylon)
|
Prince Shealtiel
|
Prince Pedaiah
|
Prince Zerrubabel
De jure King
of Judah
|
Prince Rhesa
|
Prince Johanan
|
Prince Judah
|
Prince Joseph
|
Prince Semei
|
Prince Mattathias
|
Prince Maath
|
Prince Naage
|
Prince Azallah
|
Prince Nahum
|
Prince Amos
|
Prince Mattathias
|
Prince Joseph
|
Prince Johanan
|
Prince Melchi
|
Prince Levi
|
Prince Matthat
|
Prince Jacob
|
Prince Joseph
|
Jesus Christ The Messiah
(Yehoshua ben-Joseph: called ben-Panther)
(Messiah: Messach: Anointed of the God Sobekh)
= Mary Magdalene, Priestess of Ishtar (Venus)
|
Josue Del Graal
|
Aminadab

= Eurgis d. of King Coel I
sister of Lucius the Great
|
Catheloys
|
Manael
|
Titurel
|
Boaz
(Anfortas)
|
Frotmund
(Frimutel)
|
Faramund 420 AD
Sire of the French Monarchy
= Argotta dau. of Genebaud
of the Sicambrian Franks
|
Clodian of Tournai
= Queen Basina of Thuringia
|
King Meroveus, founder of
the Dynasty of Merovingian
Sorcerer Kings d. 456 AD
= Princess Meira
|
King Childeric of the Franks d. 481 AD
= Queen Basina II of Thuringia
|
King Clovis of the Franks d. 511 AD
= Clotilde of Burgundy
|
King Lothar I d. 561 AD
|
Princess Blitildis
= Prince Ansbert, Great Great Grandson of
King Clodian of Tournai (above) d. 570 AD
|
Lord Arnoald of Scheldt
= Princess Dua of Swabia
|
Arnulf of Metz
= Princess Dobo of Saxony
|
Lord Ansegis of Brabant (Lower Lorraine)
Margrave of Scheldt d. 685
= Lady Begga, dau of Pepin I, Mayor of Austrasia
|
Lord Pepin II of Heristal, Mayor of the Palaces of
Austrasia, Neustria and Burgundy d. 714
= Lady Alpas
|
Lord Charles Martel (The Hammer) d. 741
|
Pepin the III Brevis, Duke of Lower Lorraine
(Brabant)
Mayor of Neustrasia, King of the Franks

= Lady Leuthergis
|
Princess Bertha
= Prince Milo de Vere, Duke of Angiers
Count of Anjou, son of the Fairy Princess
Melusine I of the Scythians (parallel descent
from Satan via the Egyptian Kings as
above and the Fairy Tuadha de Danaan)
|
Prince Milo II de Vere, Count of Guisnes and Anjou
= Lady Aveline de Nantes
|
Prince Nicassius de Vere, Count of Guisnes
= Lady Agatha de Champagne
|
Prince Otho de Vere, Count of Guisnes
= Lady Constance de Chartres
|
Prince Amelius (Adolph) de Vere Count of Guisnes
= Lady Maud de Ponthieu
|
Prince Guy (Gallus) de Vere, Count of Guisnes
= Lady Gertrude de Clermont de Ponthieu
|
Two Sons:
2nd son – Prince Baldwin de Vere, descent to Ida
de Vere,
the House of Hamilton and the Royal Vere of
Blackwood
&
1st son Prince Manasses de Vere Count of
Guisnes, (descent to the Vere Earls of Oxford)
=Lady Petronilla de Boleine
|
Prince Alphonse de Vere, Count of Guisnes
= Lady Katarine, dau of Count Arnulf of Flanders
|
Prince Alberic I de Vere, Count of Guisnes
= Princess Beatrix of Normandy
(descent from Satan via the Fairy Princess
Melusine I du Scythes above)
|
Prince Alberic II de Vere,
Sheriff of Cambridge, Lord of Clare and Tonbridge
= Lady Adeliza dau. of Lord Gilbert FitzRichard
|
Prince Aubrey (Alberic) III de Vere, Earl of Oxford,
Shakespeare's Oberon, King of the Fairies
= Lady Agnes, dau. of Henry Lord Essex.
|
Prince Ralph de Vere of Blackwood 1165 AD
Brother of Robert of Huntingdon; Robin Hood;
God of the Witches, Shakespeare's
Puck, son of Oberon
|
Prince Rory de Vere of Blackwood
|
Prince Ralph de Vere of Blackwood
|

Prince Thomas de Vere of Blackwood
|
Prince Richard de Vere of Blackwood
|
Prince Thomas de Vere
1st Baron Blackwood 1340 AD
|
Prince Buan Were of Vere of Blackwood
|
Prince Rotaldus Were of Vere of Blackwood
|
Prince Thomas Were of Vere
4th Baron Blackwood
|
Prince Robert Veyr of Vere of Blackwood
|
Prince Thomas Weir of Vere of Blackwood
= Lady Aegidia Somerset
|
Prince James Weir of Vere,
7th Baron Blackwood d. 1599
= Lady Euphemia Hamilton
(descent from the High Elves of Ireland,
Princess Melusine and the Scots Kings)
|
Sir William Vere de Vere of Stanebyres Castle
= Lady Elizabeth Hamilton his cousin
(descent from the High Elves of Ireland,
Princess Melusine and the Scots Kings)
|

Lord Thomas Weir of Vere, Baron Kirkton
= Lady Jane Somerville, The Witch of
the Dragon House of the Earls Somerville
|
Major Thomas Weir of Vere of Edinburgh,
The Witch King of Mid-Lothian
= Margaret Bourdon
|
Lord Thomas Weir of Vere
de jure Baron Kirkton
Hereditary Witch King
= Miss Mary Robison of Cookstown,
County Tyrone, Ulster
|
John Weir of Vere
|
Andrew Weir of Vere
|
Margaret Weir of Vere of Kildress
|
Archibald Weir of Vere of Kildress
= Rachel Stewart of Desertcreat
|
Robert Weir of Vere of Kildress
|
John Weir of Vere of Ardwell, Logan Manor
= Mary Logan dau. of Thomas Logan of
Ardwell, Logan Manor, Galloway

|
Thomas Logan Weir of Vere of Carlisle
= Anne Grant Macdonnell of Inverness
(descent from the Grant earls of Seafield)
|
James Weir of Vere of Lewes
= Natalie Hopgood (Descent through her father
from the Collisons of Norfolk, the Plantagenet
Kings and the Imperial and Royal House of Vere.
(Descent through her mother from Lt. Col
George Butcher of Windsor Castle, Sarah Butcher
of Framlingham and the Huguenot Bourchier
Counts of Versailles, France.)
|
HI&RH Prince Nicholas de Vere

The Nephilim Kings of Mesopotamia
Table Four

King Allulim of Eridu
29,628 BC
Dynasty descends
|
King Alagar of Eridu
Dynasty descends
26,618 BC
|
King Enmenluanna of Badtibira
Dynasty descends
23,608 BC
|
King Enmengalanna of Badtibira
Dynasty descends
20,598 BC
|
King Dumuzi of Badtibira
Dynasty descends
17,598
|
King Ensipazianna of Larak
Dynasty descends
14,578
|
King Enmenduranna of Sippar
Dynasty descends
11,568

King Ubartutu of Shuruppak
Dynasty descends
8558 BC

The Great Flood
4500 BC

King Ziu Sudra
returns to Mesopotamia

Prince Elam

Prince Salitis
= Seduka Tel Bab

Prince Arpakhsar
= Rasuja of Ur

Prince Shalah of Ur
= Muak, d. of Kesed

Prince Abhar
= Azura, d. of Nebrod

Prince Phalek of Mesopotamia
= Lamnar of Shinar (Sumer)

Prince Reu
= Princess Ora of Ur

King Sorogh of Ur
= Melka, g.daughter of
Phalek and Lamnar of Sumer

King Nahor of Ur
= Princess Iyosaka
of the Chaldees

King Terah of Ur
= Yawna

Prince Abram of Ur
= Princess Hagar of Egypt

Isaac of Ur
= Rabkah

Prince Jacob
= Leah

Prince Judas
= Princess Tamar of Kadesh

Prince Pharez
= Princess Barayah

Prince Hezron
= Princess Kanita

Prince Rama
= Princess Kiya Tasherit of Egypt

Prince Amenhotep
= Princess Thehara (Tara)

Prince Nashon
= Princess Sihar, d. of Yuhannas

Prince Salma
= Princess Rachab

King Boaz
= Ruth of Moab

Prince Obed
= Abalit, d. of Sonas

Prince Jesse
= Habliar, d. of Abrias

King David of Judah
= Princess Bathsheba the Aryan

King Solomon, Lord of the Rings
= Sheba Lilith (Venus) his sister.
1015 BC
= Princess Naamah the Ammonitess.
Solomon's Descent from Satan
via the Dragon Queen of Sobekh,
Kiya Tasherit, wife of Prince Rama

King Rehoboam
King of Judah 975 BC
= Princess Maachlah
dau. of Ureil of Gibeah

King Abijah
King of Judah
957 BC

King Asa
King of Judah 955 BC
= Princess Azubah
dau. of Shilhi

King Jehoshaphat
King of Judah 917 BC

King Jehoram
King of Judah 893 BC
= Princess Athalia
dau. of Omri

King Ahaziah

King of Judah 885 BC
= Princess Zibiah of Beersheba
|
King Joash
King of Judah 878 BC
Princess Jehoaddan of Jerusalem
|
King Amaziah
King of Judah 840 BC
= Princess Jecoliah of Jerusalem
|
King Uzziah
King of Judah 811 BC
= Princess Jerushah
da. Of Zadok
|
King Jotham
King of Judah 759 BC
|
King Ahaz
King of Judah 742 BC
Princess Abijah
dau of Zechariah
|
King Hezekiah
King of Judah 726 BC
= Princess Hephzibah
|
King Mannaseh
King of Judah 697 BC
= Princess Meshullemeth
dau of Haruz of Jotbah
|
King Amon
King of Judah 642 BC
= Princess Jedidah
dau. of Adaiah of Boscath
|
King Josiah
King of Judah 640 BC
|
King Jehoiakim
King of Judah 609 BC
(Taken Hostage to Babylon)
= Princess Nehushtah
dau. of Elnathan of Judaea
|
King Jechoniah
King of Judah 598 BC
(Taken hostage to Babylon)
|
Prince Shealtiel
|
Prince Pedaiah
|
Prince Zerrubabel
De jure King
of Judah
|

Prince Rhesa
|
Prince Johanan
|
Prince Judah
|
Prince Joseph
|
Prince Semei
|
Prince Mattathias
|
Prince Maath
|
Prince Naage
|
Prince Azallah
|
Prince Nahum
|
Prince Amos
|
Prince Mattathias
|
Prince Joseph
|
Prince Johanan
|
Prince Melchi
|
Prince Levi
|
Prince Matthat
|
Prince Jacob
|
Joseph of Arimathea
=Anna
|
Anna of Arimathea AD 50
= Arch Druid Bran the Blessed
Bran of the Cauldron (Grail)
St. Brandon of Eire
Archetype of the Baphomet of the Knights
Templars. Bran means Raven, Light and
Midden or Darkness; suggesting a mystical,
dualist foundation for his powers as a Druid.
His head is buried on Tower Hill in the
Tower of London.

Penarden
=Marius
|
Coel I
|
Lucius
= Gladys
|
Gladys

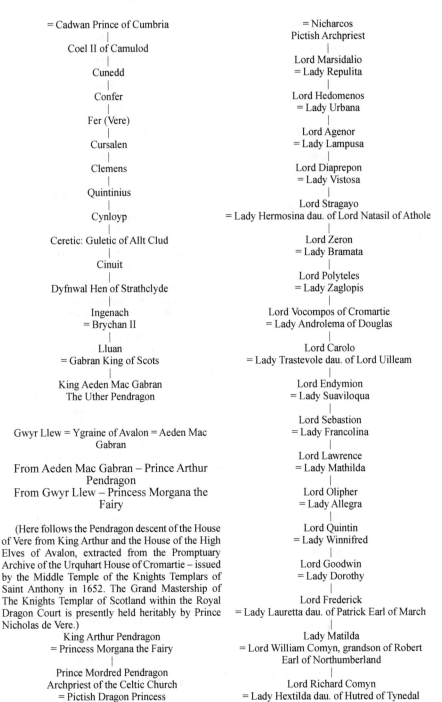

= Cadwan Prince of Cumbria
|
Coel II of Camulod
|
Cunedd
|
Confer
|
Fer (Vere)
|
Cursalen
|
Clemens
|
Quintinius
|
Cynloyp
|
Ceretic: Guletic of Allt Clud
|
Cinuit
|
Dyfnwal Hen of Strathclyde
|
Ingenach
= Brychan II
|
Lluan
= Gabran King of Scots
|
King Aeden Mac Gabran
The Uther Pendragon

Gwyr Llew = Ygraine of Avalon = Aeden Mac
Gabran

From Aeden Mac Gabran – Prince Arthur
Pendragon
From Gwyr Llew – Princess Morgana the
Fairy

(Here follows the Pendragon descent of the House
of Vere from King Arthur and the House of the High
Elves of Avalon, extracted from the Promptuary
Archive of the Urquhart House of Cromartie – issued
by the Middle Temple of the Knights Templars of
Saint Anthony in 1652. The Grand Mastership of
The Knights Templar of Scotland within the Royal
Dragon Court is presently held heritably by Prince
Nicholas de Vere.)
King Arthur Pendragon
= Princess Morgana the Fairy
|
Prince Mordred Pendragon
Archpriest of the Celtic Church
= Pictish Dragon Princess
|
Princess Tortolina Pendragon

= Nicharcos
Pictish Archpriest
|
Lord Marsidalio
= Lady Repulita
|
Lord Hedomenos
= Lady Urbana
|
Lord Agenor
= Lady Lampusa
|
Lord Diaprepon
= Lady Vistosa
|
Lord Stragayo
= Lady Hermosina dau. of Lord Natasil of Athole
|
Lord Zeron
= Lady Bramata
|
Lord Polyteles
= Lady Zaglopis
|
Lord Vocompos of Cromartie
= Lady Androlema of Douglas
|
Lord Carolo
= Lady Trastevole dau. of Lord Uilleam
|
Lord Endymion
= Lady Suaviloqua
|
Lord Sebastion
= Lady Francolina
|
Lord Lawrence
= Lady Mathilda
|
Lord Olipher
= Lady Allegra
|
Lord Quintin
= Lady Winnifred
|
Lord Goodwin
= Lady Dorothy
|
Lord Frederick
= Lady Lauretta dau. of Patrick Earl of March
|
Lady Matilda
= Lord William Comyn, grandson of Robert
Earl of Northumberland
|
Lord Richard Comyn
= Lady Hextilda dau. of Hutred of Tynedal
|
Lord William Comyn, Great Justiciar of Scotland

= Lady Marjorie Countess of Buchan
|
Lady Elizabeth Comyn
= Lord William 9th Earl of Mar
|
Lord Donald 10th Earl of Mar
= Princess Helen dau. of Prince
Llewellyn of North Wales
|
Lady Isabel Mar
= King Robert I the Bruce
Grand Master of the Knights
Templars in Scotland
|
Marjorie Bruce
= Lord Walter Stewart
6th High Steward of Scotland
|
King Robert II
= Lady Elizabeth Muir of Rowallen
|
King Robert III
= Lady Annabelle Drummond of Stobhall
|
King James I
= Princess Joan Beaufort of Somerset
(Descent from King Edward III)
|
King James II
= Mary, dau. of Arnold Duc de Gueldres
|
Princess Mary
= Lord Thomas Boyd
|
Lady Mary Boyd
James 1st Lord Hamilton
great grandson of
Princess Aenor de Chatellerault
and Guillaume X le Toulousain
Duc de Guyenne, Comte de Poitiers
|
Lady Euphemia Hamilton
(descent from the High Elves of Ireland,
Princess Melusine and the Scots Kings)
= Lord James Weir of Vere,
Baron Blackwood d. 1599
|
Sir William Vere of Stanebyres Castle
= Elizabeth Hamilton, his cousin.
(descent from the High Elves of Ireland,
Princess Melusine and the Scots Kings)
|
Lord Thomas Weir of Vere, Baron Kirkton
= Lady Jane Somerville, The Witch of
the Dragon House of the Earls Somerville
|
Major Thomas Weir of Vere of Edinburgh,
The Witch King of Mid-Lothian
= Margaret Bourdon

|
Lord Thomas Weir of Vere
de jure Baron Kirkton
Hereditary Witch King
= Miss Mary Robison of Cookstown,
County Tyrone, Ulster
|
John Weir of Vere
|
Andrew Weir of Vere
|
Margaret Weir of Vere of Kildress
|
Archibald Weir of Vere of Kildress
= Rachel Stewart of Desertcreat
|
Robert Weir of Vere of Kildress
|
John Weir of Vere of Ardwell, Logan Manor
= Mary Logan dau. of Thomas Logan of
Ardwell, Logan Manor, Galloway
|
Thomas Logan Weir of Vere of Carlisle
= Anne Grant Macdonnell of Inverness
(descent from the Grant earls of Seafield)
|
James Weir of Vere of Lewes
= Natalie Hopgood (Descent through her father
from the Collisons of Norfolk, the Plantagenet
Kings and the Imperial and Royal House of Vere.
Descent through her mother from Lt. Col
George Butcher of Windsor Castle, Sarah Butcher
of Framlingham and the Huguenot Bourchier
Counts of Versailles, France.)
|
HI&RH Prince Nicholas de Vere
Sovereign Grand Master of the Knights
Templars of Scotland

The Nephilim Kings of Mesopotamia
Table Five

King Allulim of Eridu
29,628 BC
Dynasty descends
|
King Alagar of Eridu
Dynasty descends
26,618 BC
|
King Enmenluanna of Badtibira

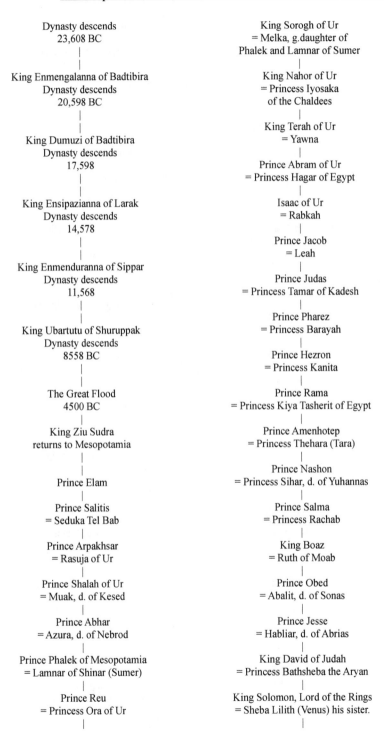

Dynasty descends
23,608 BC
|

King Enmengalanna of Badtibira
Dynasty descends
20,598 BC
|
|

King Dumuzi of Badtibira
Dynasty descends
17,598
|

King Ensipazianna of Larak
Dynasty descends
14,578
|
|

King Enmenduranna of Sippar
Dynasty descends
11,568
|
|

King Ubartutu of Shuruppak
Dynasty descends
8558 BC
|
|

The Great Flood
4500 BC
|

King Ziu Sudra
returns to Mesopotamia
|
|

Prince Elam
|

Prince Salitis
= Seduka Tel Bab
|

Prince Arpakhsar
= Rasuja of Ur
|

Prince Shalah of Ur
= Muak, d. of Kesed
|

Prince Abhar
= Azura, d. of Nebrod
|

Prince Phalek of Mesopotamia
= Lamnar of Shinar (Sumer)
|

Prince Reu
= Princess Ora of Ur
|

King Sorogh of Ur
= Melka, g.daughter of
Phalek and Lamnar of Sumer
|

King Nahor of Ur
= Princess Iyosaka
of the Chaldees
|

King Terah of Ur
= Yawna
|

Prince Abram of Ur
= Princess Hagar of Egypt
|

Isaac of Ur
= Rabkah
|

Prince Jacob
= Leah
|

Prince Judas
= Princess Tamar of Kadesh
|

Prince Pharez
= Princess Barayah
|

Prince Hezron
= Princess Kanita
|

Prince Rama
= Princess Kiya Tasherit of Egypt
|

Prince Amenhotep
= Princess Thehara (Tara)
|

Prince Nashon
= Princess Sihar, d. of Yuhannas
|

Prince Salma
= Princess Rachab
|

King Boaz
= Ruth of Moab
|

Prince Obed
= Abalit, d. of Sonas
|

Prince Jesse
= Habliar, d. of Abrias
|

King David of Judah
= Princess Bathsheba the Aryan
|

King Solomon, Lord of the Rings
= Sheba Lilith (Venus) his sister.
|

King Rehoboam
|
King Abijah
|
King Asa
|
King Jehoshephat
|
King Joram
|
King Azariah
|
King Jotham
|
King Ahaz
|
King Hezekiah
King of Judah 726 BC
= Princess Hephzibah
|
King Mannaseh
King of Judah 697 BC
= Princess Meshullemeth
dau of Haruz of Jotbah
|
King Amon
King of Judah 642 BC
= Princess Jedidah
dau. of Adaiah of Boscath
|
King Josiah
King of Judah 640 BC
= 2. Princess Hamutal
dau. of Jeremiah of Libnah
|
King Zedekiah
King of Judah 598 BC
|
Princess Tamar
= King Eochaid I
High King of Ireland after the
displacement of the remnant
of the Tuadha de Danaan
|
King Irial Faidh
|
King Eithriall
|
King Follain
|
King Tighernmas
|
King Eanbotha
|
King Smiorguil
|

King Fiachach Labhruine
|
King Aongus Oilbughagah
|
King Maoin
|
King Rotheachta
|
King Dein
|
King Siorna Saoghalach
|
King Oiliolla Olchaoin
|
King Nuadha Fionn Fail
|
King Giallchadh
|
King Simon Breac
|
King Muiriadhach Bolgrach
|
King Fiathadh Tolgrach
|
King Duach Laighrach
|
King Eochaidh Buillaig
|
King Ugaine Mar (The Great)
|
King Cobhtach Caolbreag
|
King Meilage
|
King Jaran Gleofathach
|
King Conla Gruaich
|
King Ceaigach
|
King Oiliolla Caisfhiaclach
|
King Eochaid Foltleathan
|
King Aonghus Tuirimheach
|
King Fiachra Firmara
|
King Feradaig
|
King Fergus I
|
King Maine
(Father of Siadhail: descent to
the O'Shiels of Ireland)
|

King Dornadil
|
King Rowein
|
King Reuther
|
King Eders
|
King Conaire Mor
|
King Admoir
|
King Corbred I
|
King Dare-Dornmoir
|
King Fiachadh
|
King Tuathal Teachtman
|
King Feidhimhioh
|
King Conn of the 100 Battles
|
King Art Aonthir
|
King Cormac Ulfhada Mac Art
|
King Cairbre Liffeachaire
|
King Fiachadh Streabhthuine
|
King Waegdaeg
|
King Sigegart
|
King Saebaid
|
King Siggoth
|
King Saebaid
|
King Saefugel
|
King Sudrtha
|
King Soemil
|
King Westers
|
King Wilgils
|
King Wyse Frea
|
King Yffe
|

King Aelle of Deira (Northumbria)
559 AD – 588 AD
|
Princess Atha of Berenicia
= King Cadfan of Gwynnedd
625 AD
|
King Cadwallon II of Gwynnedd d. 634
= Princess Helen, granddaughter of Crida
Chief of the Angles
|
King Cadwalladr Pendragon the Blessed 654 – 664
The last Pendragon of Britain
|
King Edwal of Gwynnedd
|
King Rhodri Molwynog 754 AD
|
King Cinan Tindaethwy 754 - 816
|
King Gwynnedd
|
Queen Esylth
|
King Merfyn Vrych
|
King Rhodri Mawr of North Wales
= Princess Angharad
|
Prince Anararwd of North Wales
|
Prince Elisedd of North Wales
|
Prince Prawst of North Wales
= Princess Seissylt of North Wales
|
Prince Llewellyn of North Wales 974 AD
= Queen Angharad II of Powys
|
Prince Griffifth I of North Wales
= Lady Ealdgyth of Mercia, granddaughter of
Earl Leofric III and Lady Godiva
|
Princess Nesta of North Wales
= Prince Trahaern of Arwystli
|
Prince Llywarch of North Wales
= Lady Dyddgu dau. of Idnerth
Lord of Builth Wells
|
Lady Gladys of North Wales
= Prince Owen I Gwynedd of North Wales
|
Prince Iorwerth of North Wales
= Lady Maret of Powys – Vadoc
|

Prince Llewellyn of Wales 1173–1240 AD
|
Princess Helen
= Lord Donald 10th Earl of Mar
|
Lady Isabel
= King Robert I the Bruce, Grand Master
of the Knights Templars in Scotland
|
Princess Marjorie Bruce
= Lord Walter Stewart
6th High Steward of Scotland
|
King Robert II
= Lady Elizabeth Muir of Rowallen
|
King Robert III
= Lady Annabelle Drummond of Stobhall
|
King James I
= Princess Joan Beaufort of Somerset
(Descent from King Edward III)
|
King James II
= Mary, dau. of Arnold Duc de Gueldres
|
Princess Mary
= Lord Thomas Boyd
|
Lady Mary Boyd
James 1st Lord Hamilton
great grandson of
Princess Aenor de Chatellerault
and Guillaume X le Toulousain
Duc de Guyenne, Comte de Poitiers
|
Lady Euphemia Hamilton
(descent from the High Elves of Ireland,
Princess Melusine and the Scots Kings)
= Lord James Weir of Vere,
Baron Blackwood d. 1599
|
Sir William Vere of Stanebyres Castle
= Elizabeth Hamilton, his cousin.
(descent from the High Elves of Ireland,
Princess Melusine and the Scots Kings)
|
Lord Thomas Weir of Vere, Baron Kirkton
= Lady Jane Somerville, The Witch of
the Dragon House of the Earls Somerville
|
Major Thomas Weir of Vere of Edinburgh,
The Witch King of Mid-Lothian
= Margaret Bourdon
|
Lord Thomas Weir of Vere

de jure Baron Kirkton
Hereditary Witch King
= Miss Mary Robison of Cookstown,
County Tyrone, Ulster
|
John Weir of Vere
|
Andrew Weir of Vere
|
Margaret Weir of Vere of Kildress
|
Archibald Weir of Vere of Kildress
= Rachel Stewart of Desertcreat
|
Robert Weir of Vere of Kildress
= Sarah Graham his cousin
|
John Weir of Vere of Ardwell, Logan Manor
= Mary Logan dau. of Thomas Logan of
Ardwell, Logan Manor, Galloway
|
Thomas Logan Weir of Vere of Carlisle
= Anne Grant Macdonnell of Inverness
(descent from the Grant earls of Seafield)
|
James Weir of Vere of Lewes
= Natalie Hopgood (Descent through her father
from the Collisons of Norfolk, the Plantagenet
Kings and the Imperial and Royal House of Vere.
Descent through her mother from Lt. Col
George Butcher of Windsor Castle, Sarah Butcher
of Framlingham and the Huguenot Bourchier
Counts of Versailles, France.)
|
HI&RH Prince Nicholas de Ver

Chapter Eleven

The House of Vere European Descents

Descent of the House of Vere from the Royal Dynasty of Luxembourg

Merovech, born 415, King of the Franks, deceased 456
Married
Verica, born 419
|
Chilperik I, King of the Salian Franks.
Married
Andovera
|
Clovis, born 466, deceased 511
Married
Arnegundis
|
Chlotarius II, deceased 628
Married
Arnegundis
|
Chilperik II, deceased 584
Married
Fredegonde
|
Clotarius II de Grote, deceased 628
|
Dagobert I, born 602, deceased 639
Married
Nanthild
|
Clodowech II, born 631, deceased 657
|
Arnulf van Metz, born 582, deceased 641
Married
Oda, deceased 581
|

Thedoric III, King of the Franks, deceased 690
Married
Clotilde, deceased 692
|
Angesil
Married
Begga, deceased 692
|
Bertrade Prum....
|
Pippijn van Herstal, deceased 714
Married
Chalpais, deceased 705
|
Hnabi, Count of Alamannen
|
Heribert van Laon, Count of Laon
Married
Gisele Bertrade
|
Karel Martel, deceased 741
Married
Rothude of Chrotud, deceased 724
|
Gerold I, Count of the Franks [Vinzgouw]
Married
Imma
|
Pippijn de Korte, deceased, 768
Married
Bertrada van Laon, born 742, deceased 783
|
Welf I, Count of Beieren
Married
Eigilwich
|
Ingram, Count of Haspengouw
Married
Ava
|
Karel de Grote, Emperor, born April 2 742,
deceased Jan. 28 814
Married
Hildegard, born 758, deceased April 30 783
|
Odo van Orleans
Judith Welf , deceased 843
|
Hugo van Tours
Married
Ava
|
Lodewijk I, Emperor, born 778 te Chassenneuil,
deceased June 20, 840 Ingelheim
Married
Irmingard, deceased Oct. 3 818
|
Karel II , Emperor, born June 13 823, Frankfurt,

deceased Oct. 6 877 to Maurienne
Married
Ermentrudis van Orlsans, born 830, deceased Oct.
6 869
|
Adalhard, Count of Paris
|
Lotharius I, King of the Franks, born 795, deceased,
Sept. 29 855
Married
Ermentrudis van Orlsans, born 830, deceased 869
|
Boudewijn II, Count of Flanders , born 865,
deceased Sept. 10 918
Married
Judith of West France, born 844
|
Edward I, King of England
Married
Aelfleda van Bernicea
|
Lodewijk II , born Nov. 1 846, deceased, April 10
879
Married
Adelheid van Paris
|
Gijsbrecht I van Leuven, Count of Darnau
|
Boudewijn II , Count of Flanders, born 865,
deceased Sept. 918
Married
Aelftryth of Wessex , deceased June 7 929
|
Hendrik I van Saksen, King of Germany
Married
Mathilde van Westfalen
|
Karel III, King of Franks, born Sept.17 879,
deceased Oct. 7 929
Married
Eadgfu of England, born 869
|
Renier I van Hehegouwen, deceased 915
Married
Alberda
|
Arnulf I, Count of Flanders, deceased 965
Married
Adela van Vermandios, born 912. deceased 960
|
Dirk I of Holland, deceased 939
Married
Geva
|
Lodewijk IV King of the Franks, born 920, deceased
Sept. 10 954
Married
Gerberga van Saksen, born 913, deceased May 5
984

Rennier II van Henegouwen, Count of Holland, born
880, deceased 935
Married
Alix of Bourgondie

Siegfried van Luxemborg
Married
Hedwig

Dirk II of Holland, Count, born 930, deceased May
6 980
Married
Hildegard van Vlaanderen, born 936, deceased April
11 990

Karel van Nederlotharingen, Duke of Holland, born
953,
Married
Adelheid

Bernhard I Count of Bohemen

Renier III, Count of Henegouwen

Dirk III, Count of Holland, deceased, May 27 1039
Married
Othilde van Noordmark

Richard II , Duke of Normandie, deceased 1026
Married
Judith van Bretagne, deceased, 1017

Duke Richard III 1027 AD

Duke Robert I 1028 AD

King William I of England
= Lady Mathilda van Vlaanderen
dau. of Count Baldwin V of Flanders

King Henry I of England
= Princess Mathilda dau. of
King Malcom III Canmore
of Scotland and Margaret,
dau. of Edward the Exile
by Princess Agatha of Bulgaria

Princess Mathilda la Imperatrice
(Empress of England)
= Count Geoffrey Plantagenet
of Anjou

King Henry II Plantagenet
= Countess Eleanor of Aquitaine

King John 'Lackland' Plantagenet
= Lady Isabella of Angouleme

King Henry III Plantagenet
= Lady Eleanor dau. of Count
Raymond Berenguer IV of Provence
and Princess Beatrix of Savoy

King Edward I Plantagenet
= Princess Eleanor of Castille

King Edward II Plantagenet
= Princess Isabella of France

King Edward III Plantagenet
1327-1377
= Princess Phillipa of Hainault

Prince John Plantagenet of Gaunt
= Lady Katharine Swynford

Prince John Plantagenet

Princess Joan Beaufort Plantagenet
= King James I of Scots

King James II
= Mary, dau. of Arnold Duc de Gueldres

Princess Mary
= Lord Thomas Boyd

Lady Mary Boyd
James 1st Lord Hamilton
great grandson of
Princess Aenor de Chatellerault
and Guillaume X le Toulousain
Duc de Guyenne, Comte de Poitiers

Lady Euphemia Hamilton
(descent from the High Elves of Ireland,
Princess Melusine and the Scots Kings)
= Lord James Weir of Vere,
Baron Blackwood d. 1599

Sir William Vere of Stanebyres
= Elizabeth Hamilton, his cousin.
(descent from the High Elves of Ireland,
Princess Melusine and the Scots Kings)

Lord Thomas Weir of Vere, Baron Kirkton
= Lady Jane Somerville, The Witch of
the Dragon House of the Earls Somerville.

Major Thomas Weir of Vere of Edinburgh,
The Witch King of Mid-Lothian
= Margaret Bourdon

Lord Thomas Weir of Vere
de jure Baron Kirkton

Hereditary Witch King
= Miss Mary Robison of Cookstown,
County Tyrone, Ulster
|
John Weir of Vere
|
Andrew Weir of Vere
|
Margaret Weir of Vere of Kildress
|
Archibald Weir of Vere of Kildress
= Rachel Stewart of Desertcreat
|
Robert Weir of Vere of Kildress
|
John Weir of Vere of Ardwell, Logan Manor
= Mary Logan dau. of Thomas Logan of
Ardwell, Logan Manor, Galloway
|
Thomas Logan Weir of Vere of Carlisle
= Anne Grant Macdonnell of Inverness
(asserted descent from the Grant earls of Seafield)
|
James Weir of Vere of Lewes
= Natalie Hopgood, (descent through her father
from the Collisons of Norfolk, the Plantagenet
Kings and the Imperial and Royal House of Vere.
Descent through her mother from Lt. Col.
George Butcher of Windsor Castle, Sarah Butcher
of Framlingham and the Huguenot Bourchier
Counts of Versailles, France)
|
HI&RH Prince Nicholas Tarnawa-de Vere von
Drakenberg
KGC., KCD., KT.St.A.S. Sovereign Prince and
Grand Duke of
the Incorporeal Sovereign Nation State of
Drakenberg. Sovereign
Grand Master of the Imperial and Royal Dragon
Court, Sovereign
Grand Master and Commander-in-Chief of the
Order of Knights Templars.

Vere Descent from the Tsars of Russia and the Dynasty of Ryurikovich via Princess Richilde and the Kings of Poland

1. Grand Prince of Kiev (sometimes Grand Duke of Kiev) was the title of the Kievan prince and the ruler of Kievan Rus in the 9th–12th centuries.

Rurik (or Ryurik), a Scandinavian Varangian, was at the roots of Kievan Rus. He founded the Rurikovich dynasty that would rule Kievan Rus',

Rus' principalities and early Russian Tsardom for the next 700 years. Rurik's capital was the northern city of Novgorod. His successor Oleg relocated the capital to Kiev (now the capital of Ukraine) at around 880, thus laying the foundation of what has become known as Kievan Rus'.

While the early rulers of Rus' were Scandinavians, they gradually merged into the local Slavic population. Still, in the 11th century, Yaroslav, (called Jarisleif in Scandinavian chronicles) maintained the dynastic links, married a Swedish princess, and gave asylum to king Olaf II of Norway.

The movement of nobility also went in the opposite direction. According to Adam of Bremen, Anund Gårdske, a man from Kievan Rus' was elected king of Sweden, ca 1070. As he was a Christian, however, he refused to sacrifice to the Aesir at the Temple at Uppsala and he was deposed by popular vote.

The unity of Kievan Rus' gradually declined, and was all but gone by 1136. After that period Kievan Rus' shattered into a number of smaller states, southern of which contested for the throne of Kiev.

Kievan Rus' was finally destroyed by the Mongols in 1237, but the Riurikovich line persisted and continued to rule Rus' principalities.

2. Rurik – a red-headed Viking – thus called the RUS (red) was born in Fresia. Son of King Haarik, Rurik Led the invasion into what became "RUS-SIA." (or land of the Red). In Henrikson's Chronicles, he states "According to the Russian Nestor chronicle in 862, a prince named Rurik came from the other side of the (North) sea, and founded a kingdom with Novgorod as its center. Two of his companions, Askild and Dir, continued southward to Kiev and settled there, after which they made an unsuccessful expedition to Constantinople. this chronicle, which calls Rurik's people the RUS (The Reds), and the invading Vikings VARJAGER, claims that the invaders originated the RUSSIAN (The RUS) empire." (Webster's Biog. Dict. = Rurik or Ryurik d. 879 AD reputed founder of the Russian empire, said to have been a Scandinavian chief who conquered Novogorod ca 862. The house of Rurik was a Russian royal family, all descended from Rurik. Extinct in 1598. Rurik had two Varangian brothers – Lech and Czech – who founded Poland and Czechoslovakia (Bohemia) respectively, whose royal dynasties are consequently of Scandinavian origins deriving ultimately from the Anunnaki and carry their red gene 16q23.4.

Grand Prince Ryurik of Kiev and Novgorod 800-879
|
Grand Prince Igor 880-947
= St. Olga
|
Grand Prince Svatislav d. 973
= Princess Maloucha
|
Grand Prince Vladimir d. 15th July 1015
= Princess of Ohningen
|
Princess Dobroniega 1011-1087
= King Casimir I of Poland
|
King Vladislav I of Poland
= Princess Judith of Bohemia d. of
King Wratislav II of Bohemia
and Princess Adelaide of Hungary
|
King Bodeslas III of Poland
= Princess Zbyslava of Kiev d. of
Grand Prince Michael II of Kiev
|
King Vladislas II of Poland
= Princess Agnes de Babenberg
d. of Prince Leopold III and Princess
Agness Hohenstauffen of Franconia
|
Princess Richilde of Poland
= King Alfonso VII of Castile - Galicia
|

King Ferdinand II 1157-1188
King of Leon
|
King Alfonso IX 1188-1230
King of Leon
|
King Ferdinand III
King of Castile 1217-1252
King of Leon 1230-1252
|
Princess Eleanor of Castile d 1290
= King Edward I of England
|
King Edward II Plantagenet
= Princess Isabella of France
|
King Edward III
1327-1377
= Princess Phillipa of Hainault
|
Prince John of Gaunt
= Lady Katharine Swynford
|

Prince John Plantagenet
|
Princess Joan Beaufort
= King James I of Scots
|
King James II
= Mary, dau. of Arnold Duc de Gueldres
|
Princess Mary
= Lord Thomas Boyd
|
Lady Mary Boyd
James 1st Lord Hamilton
great grandson of
Princess Aenor de Chatellerault
and Guillaume X le Toulousain
Duc de Guyenne, Comte de Poitiers
|

Lady Euphemia Hamilton
(descent from the High Elves of Ireland,
Princess Melusine and the Scots Kings)
= Lord James Weir of Vere,
Baron Blackwood d. 1599
|
Sir William Vere of Stanebyres
= Elizabeth Hamilton, his cousin.
(descent from the High Elves of Ireland,
Princess Melusine and the Scots Kings)
|
Lord Thomas Weir of Vere, Baron Kirkton
= Lady Jane Somerville, The Witch of
the Dragon House of the Earls Somerville.
|
Major Thomas Weir of Vere of Edinburgh,
The Witch King of Mid-Lothian
= Margaret Bourdon
|
Lord Thomas Weir of Vere
de jure Baron Kirkton
Hereditary Witch King
= Miss Mary Robison of Cookstown,
County Tyrone, Ulster
|
John Weir of Vere
|
Andrew Weir of Vere
|
Margaret Weir of Vere of Kildress
|
Archibald Weir of Vere of Kildress
= Rachel Stewart of Desertcreat
|
Robert Weir of Vere of Kildress
|

John Weir of Vere of Ardwell, Logan Manor
= Mary Logan dau. of Thomas Logan of
Ardwell, Logan Manor, Galloway
|
Thomas Logan Weir of Vere of Carlisle
= Anne Grant Macdonnell of Inverness
(asserted descent from the Grant earls of Seafield)
|
James Weir of Vere of Lewes
= Natalie Hopgood, (descent through her father
from the Collisons of Norfolk, the Plantagenet
Kings and the Imperial and Royal House of Vere.
Descent through her mother from Lt. Col.
George Butcher of Windsor Castle, Sarah Butcher
of Framlingham and the Huegenot Bourchier
Counts of Versailles, France)
|
HI&RH Prince Nicholas de Vere

Vere Descent from the Pagan Magyar
Kings and Princes of Hungary

Prince Almos of Hungary d. 895
|
Prince Arpad of Hungary d. 907
|
Prince Zoltan of Hungary d. 947
|
Prince Taksony of Hungary d. 972
|
Duke Mihaly of Poland d. 976
= Princess Adelajda of Poland
|
Prince Vasul (Pagan Magyar) d. 1037
|
King Bela I of Hungary d. 1063
= Princess Rixa of Poland d. of
King Miezsko and Queen Rixa
of Poland
|
King Andrew I of Hungary
= Princess Anastasia d. of
Grand Duke Iaroslav I and
Princess Ingeborg of Sweden
|
Princess Adelaide of Hungary
= King Wratislav II of Bohemia
|
Princess Richilde of Poland
= King Alfonso VII of Castile - Galicia
|

King Ferdinand II 1157-1188
King of Leon
|
King Alfonso IX 1188-1230
King of Leon
|
King Ferdinand III
King of Castile 1217-1252
King of Leon 1230-1252
|
Princess Eleanor of Castile d 1290
= King Edward I of England
|
King Edward II Plantagenet
= Princess Isabella of France
|
King Edward III
1327-1377
= Princess Phillipa of Hainault
|
Prince John of Gaunt
= Lady Katharine Swynford
|
Prince John Plantagenet
|
Princess Joan Beaufort
= King James I of Scots
|
King James II
= Mary, dau. of Arnold Duc de Gueldres
|
Princess Mary
= Lord Thomas Boyd
|
Lady Mary Boyd
James 1st Lord Hamilton
great grandson of
Princess Aenor de Chatellerault
and Guillaume X le Toulousain
Duc de Guyenne, Comte de Poitiers
|
Lady Euphemia Hamilton
(descent from the High Elves of Ireland,
Princess Melusine and the Scots Kings)
= Lord James Weir of Vere,
Baron Blackwood d. 1599
|
Sir William Vere of Stanebyres
= Elizabeth Hamilton, his cousin.
(descent from the High Elves of Ireland,
Princess Melusine and the Scots Kings)
|
Lord Thomas Weir of Vere, Baron Kirkton
= Lady Jane Somerville, The Witch of

the Dragon House of the Earls Somerville.

Major Thomas Weir of Vere of Edinburgh,
The Witch King of Mid-Lothian
= Margaret Bourdon

Lord Thomas Weir of Vere
de jure Baron Kirkton
Hereditary Witch King
= Miss Mary Robison of Cookstown,
County Tyrone, Ulster

John Weir of Vere

Andrew Weir of Vere

Margaret Weir of Vere of Kildress

Archibald Weir of Vere of Kildress
= Rachel Stewart of Desertcreat

Robert Weir of Vere of Kildress

John Weir of Vere of Ardwell, Logan Manor
= Mary Logan dau. of Thomas Logan of
Ardwell, Logan Manor, Galloway

Thomas Logan Weir of Vere of Carlisle
= Anne Grant Macdonnell of Inverness
(asserted descent from the Grant earls of Seafield)

James Weir of Vere of Lewes
= Natalie Hopgood, (descent through her father
from the Collisons of Norfolk, the Plantagenet
Kings and the Imperial and Royal House of Vere.
Descent through her mother from Lt. Col
George Butcher of Windsor Castle, Sarah Butcher
of Framlingham and the Huegenot Bourchier
Counts of Versailles, France)

HI&RH Prince Nicholas de Vere

Vere Descent from the Kings of Bohemia

Count Borivoy I of Bohemia 871- 894

Duke Vratislav I of Bohemia 912 -926

King Boleslav the Cruel of Bohemia 935- 967
murdered his brother Good King Wenceslas

King Boleslav II the Pious of Bohemia d.999

King Bileslav II the Blind of Bohemia d. 1035

Duke Oldrich of Bohemia

Duke Bretislav I of Bohemia
= Countess Judith von Schweinfurt
dau. of Count Heinrich, Graf von
Schweinfurt

King Wratislav III of Bohemia
= Princess Adelaide of Hungary

Princess Judith of Bohemia
= King Vladislav I of Poland

King Bodeslas III of Poland
= Princess Zbyslava of Kiev
dau. of Grand Prince Michael II
of Kiev

King Vladislas II of Poland
= Countess Agnes von Babenberg
dau. of Duke Leopold III Hohenstauffen
of (Franconia) Austria

Princess Richilde of Poland
= King Alfonso VII of Castile - Galicia

King Ferdinand II 1157-1188
King of Leon

King Alfonso IX 1188-1230
King of Leon

King Ferdinand III
King of Castile 1217-1252
King of Leon 1230-1252

Princess Eleanor of Castile d 1290
= King Edward I of England

King Edward II Plantagenet
= Princess Isabella of France

King Edward III
1327-1377
= Princess Phillipa of Hainault

Prince John of Gaunt
= Lady Katharine Swynford

Prince John Plantagenet
|
Princess Joan Beaufort
= King James I of Scots
|
King James II
= Mary, dau. of Arnold Duc de Gueldres
|
Princess Mary
= Lord Thomas Boyd
|
Lady Mary Boyd
James 1st Lord Hamilton
great grandson of
Princess Aenor de Chatellerault
and Guillaume X le Toulousain
Duc de Guyenne, Comte de Poitiers
|
Lady Euphemia Hamilton
(descent from the High Elves of Ireland,
Princess Melusine and the Scots Kings)
= Lord James Weir of Vere,
Baron Blackwood d. 1599
|
Sir William Vere of Stanebyres
= Elizabeth Hamilton, his cousin.
(descent from the High Elves of Ireland,
Princess Melusine and the Scots Kings)
|
Lord Thomas Weir of Vere, Baron Kirkton
= Lady Jane Somerville, The Witch of
the Dragon House of the Earls Somerville
|
Major Thomas Weir of Vere of Edinburgh,
The Witch King of Mid-Lothian
= Margaret Bourdon
|
Lord Thomas Weir of Vere
de jure Baron Kirkton
Hereditary Witch King
= Miss Mary Robison of Cookstown,
County Tyrone, Ulster
|
John Weir of Vere
|
Andrew Weir of Vere
|
Margaret Weir of Vere of Kildress
|
Archibald Weir of Vere of Kildress
= Rachel Stewart of Desertcreat
|
Robert Weir of Vere of Kildress
|

John Weir of Vere of Ardwell, Logan Manor
= Mary Logan dau. of Thomas Logan of
Ardwell, Logan Manor, Galloway
|
Thomas Logan Weir of Vere of Carlisle
= Anne Grant Macdonnell of Inverness
(asserted descent from the Grant earls of Seafield)
|
James Weir of Vere of Lewes
= Natalie Hopgood, (descent through her father
from the Collisons of Norfolk, the Plantagenet
Kings and the Imperial and Royal House of Vere.
Descent through her mother from Lt. Col
George Butcher of Windsor Castle, Sarah Butcher
of Framlingham and the Huegenot Bourchier
Counts of Versailles, France)
|
HI&RH Prince Nicholas de Vere

Vere Descent from the Early Dukes of Saxony

Duke Hadugato of Saxony c 531
|
Duke Berthoald of Saxony c 627
|
Duke Theoderic of Saxony 743-744
|
Duke Widukind of Saxony 777-810
|
Duke Abo of Saxony 785-811
|
Hattonid Dynasty
|
Duke Banzleib of Saxony 830
|
Ottonian Dynasty
|
Duke Liudolf of Saxony 850
|
Duke Bruno of Saxony 852-880
|
Duke Otto the Illustrious of Saxony 880-912
=Princess Hedwiga of Franconia dau. of
Duke Henry of Franconia and Princess
Ingeltrude of Fruili
|
King Henry the Fowler of Germany
= St. Matilda of Ringelheim
|
Princess Gerberga
=King Louis IV of France
936-954

|

Charles Duke of Lower Lorraine 991

|

Lady Gerberga
= Lambert de Louvain

|

Henry of Brussels

|

Maud de Louvain
= Eustace I de Vere d. 1049
Descent from Amelius ("Adolph") de Vere
Comte de Guisnes

|

Eustace II de Vere
= Saint Ida of Ardennes

|

Princess Ida de Vere
= Baudouin de Bourg
Comte de Rethul

|

Prince Hugues I
Comte de Rethul
= Melisende (Melusine II)
dau. Of Bouchard Comte de Corbeil and
Lady Adelaide de Crecy

|

Badouin II de Bourg
King of Jerusalem 1118-1131
= Princess Morfia of Armenia

|

Princess Melisende of Jerusalem (Melusine III)
= Fulke V Plantagenet Count of Anjou

|

Count Geoffrey Plantagenet of Anjou
= Princess Mathilda la Imperatrice
of England, dau. of King Henry I
and Princess Mathilda of
Scotland, dau. of King Malcom III

|

King Henry II Plantagenet
= Countess Eleanor of Aquitaine

|

King John 'Lackland' Plantagenet
= Lady Isabella of Angouleme

|

King Henry III Plantagenet
= Lady Eleanor dau. of Count
Raymond Berenguer IV of Provence
and Princess Beatrix of Savoy

|

King Edward I Plantagenet
= Princess Eleanor of Castile

|

King Edward II Plantagenet
= Princess Isabella of France

|

King Edward III Plantagenet
1327-1377
= Princess Phillipa of Hainault

|

Prince John of Gaunt Plantagenet
= Lady Katharine Swynford

|

Prince John Plantagenet

|

Princess Joan Beaufort Plantagenet
= King James I of Scots

|

King James II
= Mary, dau. of Arnold Duc de Gueldres

|

Princess Mary
= Lord Thomas Boyd

|

Lady Mary Boyd
James 1st Lord Hamilton
great grandson of
Princess Aenor de Chatellerault
and Guillaume X le Toulousain
Duc de Guyenne, Comte de Poitiers

|

Lady Euphemia Hamilton
(descent from the High Elves of Ireland,
Princess Melusine and the Scots Kings)
= Lord James Weir of Vere,
Baron Blackwood d. 1599

|

Sir William Vere of Stanebyres
= Elizabeth Hamilton, his cousin.
(descent from the High Elves of Ireland,
Princess Melusine and the Scots Kings)

|

Lord Thomas Weir of Vere, Baron Kirkton
= Lady Jane Somerville, The Witch of
the Dragon House of the Earls Somerville.

|

Major Thomas Weir of Vere of Edinburgh,
The Witch King of Mid-Lothian
= Margaret Bourdon

|

Lord Thomas Weir of Vere
de jure Baron Kirkton
Hereditary Witch King
= Miss Mary Robison of Cookstown,
County Tyrone, Ulster

|

John Weir of Vere

|

Andrew Weir of Vere

|

Margaret Weir of Vere of Kildress
|
Archibald Weir of Vere of Kildress
= Rachel Stewart of Desertcreat
|
Robert Weir of Vere of Kildress
|
John Weir of Vere of Ardwell, Logan Manor
= Mary Logan dau. of Thomas Logan of
Ardwell, Logan Manor, Galloway
|
Thomas Logan Weir of Vere of Carlisle
= Anne Grant Macdonnell of Inverness
(descent from the Grant earls of Seafield)
|
James Weir of Vere of Lewes
= Natalie Hopgood, (descent through her father
from the Collisons of Norfolk, the Plantagenet
Kings and the Imperial and Royal House of Vere.
Descent through her mother from Lt. Col
George Butcher of Windsor Castle, Sarah Butcher
of Framlingham and the Huegenot Bourchier
Counts of Versailles, France)
|
HI&RH Prince Nicholas de Vere

Vere Descent from the Babenberg Dynasty of Austria

Count Adalbert I von Babenberg d. 997
= Brunehilde of Saxony dau. Of Duke Otto
the Illustrious of Saxony and Princess Hedwig
|
Count Adalbert II von Babenberg 901-933
|
Count Leopold I von Babenberg 923-994
= Lady Richenza
|
Count Albert I von Babenberg 983-1065
= Lady Adela of Venice
|
Count Ernest I von Babenberg 1027-1075
= Lady Maud of Lausnitz
|
Count Leopold II von Babenberg "The Fair" 1050-1136
= Princess Ida of Germany dau. of King Henry III
"The Black" of Germany and Princess Agnes of
Poitou
|

Duke Leopold III von Babenberg 1073-1110
= Princess Agnes of Franconia dau. of King Henry
IV of Germany and Princess Bertha von
Hohenstauffen of Maurienne
|
Princess Agnes von Babenberg-Hohenstauffen
= King Vladislas III of Poland
|
Princess Richilde of Poland
= King Alfonso VII of Castile-Galicia
|
King Ferdinand II 1157-1188
King of Leon
|
King Alfonso IX 1188-1230
King of Leon
|
King Ferdinand III
King of Castile 1217-1252
King of Leon 1230-1252
|
Princess Eleanor of Castile d 1290
= King Edward I of England
|
King Edward II Plantagenet
= Princess Isabella of France
|
King Edward III
1327-1377
= Princess Phillipa of Hainault
|
Prince John of Gaunt
= Lady Katharine Swynford
|
Prince John Plantagenet
|
Princess Joan Beaufort
= King James I of Scots
|
King James II
= Mary, dau. of Arnold Duc de Gueldres
|
Princess Mary
= Lord Thomas Boyd
|
Lady Mary Boyd
James 1st Lord Hamilton
great grandson of
Princess Aenor de Chatellerault
and Guillaume X le Toulousain
Duc de Guyenne, Comte de Poitiers
|
Lady Euphemia Hamilton
(descent from the High Elves of Ireland,
Princess Melusine and the Scots Kings)

= Lord James Weir of Vere,
Baron Blackwood d. 1599

|

Sir William Vere of Stanebyres
= Elizabeth Hamilton, his cousin.
(descent from the High Elves of Ireland,
Princess Melusine and the Scots Kings)

|

Lord Thomas Weir of Vere, Baron Kirkton
= Lady Jane Somerville, The Witch of
the Dragon House of the Earls Somerville.

|

Major Thomas Weir of Vere of Edinburgh,
The Witch King of Mid-Lothian
= Margaret Bourdon

|

Lord Thomas Weir of Vere
de jure Baron Kirkton
Hereditary Witch King
= Miss Mary Robison of Cookstown,
County Tyrone, Ulster

|

John Weir of Vere

|

Andrew Weir of Vere

|

Margaret Weir of Vere of Kildress

|

Archibald Weir of Vere of Kildress
= Rachel Stewart of Desertcreat

|

Robert Weir of Vere of Kildress

|

John Weir of Vere of Ardwell, Logan Manor
= Mary Logan dau. of Thomas Logan of
Ardwell, Logan Manor, Galloway

|

Thomas Logan Weir of Vere of Carlisle
= Anne Grant Macdonnell of Inverness
(asserted descent from the Grant earls of Seafield)

|

James Weir of Vere of Lewes
= Natalie Hopgood, (descent through her father
from the Collisons of Norfolk, the Plantagenet
Kings and the Imperial and Royal House of Vere.
Descent through her mother from Lt. Col
George Butcher of Windsor Castle, Sarah Butcher
of Framlingham and the Huegenot Bourchier
Counts of Versailles, France)

|

HI&RH Prince Nicholas de Vere

Vere Descent from the Ancient Kings of Poland

The Kings of Poland originated with Lech, who was
one of three Varangian brothers (including Rurik
or Rus who founded the Russian state and Cech or
Czech who founded Bohemia

Duke Piast (Founder of the Piast dynasty)

|

Duke Siemowit I c. 890 AD

|

Duke Lestko c. 920 AD

|

Duke Siemosyl

|

Duke Mieszko I 960-992

|

Duke Boleslaw I the Brave
First King of Poland in 1025

|

King Mieszko II 1025-1031

|

King Casimir I 1039-1058
= Princess Dobroniega of Kiev
dau. of Grand Prince Vladimir of Kiev

|

King Vladislav I
= Princess Judith of Bohemia dau. of
King Wratislav II of Bohemia and
Princess Adelaide of Hungary

|

King Vladislav II
= Princess Agness Hohenstauffen of
Babenberg dau. of Duke Leopold
Hohenstauffen of Austria-Franconia

|

Princess Richilde of Poland
= King Alfonso VII of Castile-Galicia

|

|

King Ferdinand II 1157-1188
King of Leon

|

King Alfonso IX 1188-1230
King of Leon

|

King Ferdinand III
King of Castile 1217-1252
King of Leon 1230-1252

|

Princess Eleanor of Castile d 1290
= King Edward I of England

|

King Edward II Plantagenet
= Princess Isabella of France
|
King Edward III
1327-1377
= Princess Phillipa of Hainault
|
Prince John of Gaunt
= Lady Katharine Swynford
|
Prince John Plantagenet
|
Princess Joan Beaufort
= King James I of Scots
|
King James II
= Mary, dau. of Arnold Duc de Gueldres
|
Princess Mary
= Lord Thomas Boyd
|
Lady Mary Boyd
James 1st Lord Hamilton
great grandson of
Princess Aenor de Chatellerault
and Guillaume X le Toulousain
Duc de Guyenne, Comte de Poitiers
|
Lady Euphemia Hamilton
(descent from the High Elves of Ireland,
Princess Melusine and the Scots Kings)
= Lord James Weir of Vere,
Baron Blackwood d. 1599
|
Sir William Vere of Stanebyres
= Elizabeth Hamilton, his cousin.
(descent from the High Elves of Ireland,
Princess Melusine and the Scots Kings)
|
Lord Thomas Weir of Vere, Baron Kirkton
= Lady Jane Somerville, The Witch of
the Dragon House of the Earls Somerville.
|
Major Thomas Weir of Vere of Edinburgh,
The Witch King of Mid-Lothian
= Margaret Bourdon
|
Lord Thomas Weir of Vere
de jure Baron Kirkton
Hereditary Witch King
= Miss Mary Robison of Cookstown,
County Tyrone, Ulster
|
John Weir of Vere
|

Andrew Weir of Vere
|
Margaret Weir of Vere of Kildress
|
Archibald Weir of Vere of Kildress
= Rachel Stewart of Desertcreat
|
Robert Weir of Vere of Kildress
|
John Weir of Vere of Ardwell, Logan Manor
= Mary Logan dau. of Thomas Logan of
Ardwell, Logan Manor, Galloway
|
Thomas Logan Weir of Vere of Carlisle
= Anne Grant Macdonnell of Inverness
(asserted descent from the Grant earls of Seafield)
|
James Weir of Vere of Lewes
= Natalie Hopgood, (descent through her father
from the Collisons of Norfolk, the Plantagenet
Kings and the Imperial and Royal House of Vere.
Descent through her mother from Lt. Col
George Butcher of Windsor Castle, Sarah Butcher
of Framlingham and the Huguenot Bourchier
Counts of Versailles, France)
|
HI&RH Prince Nicholas de Vere

Vere Descent from the Dynasty of Hohenstauffen

Count Frederick of Buren 1036-1146
= Lady Hildegarde
|
Count Frederick I von Hohenstauffen 1050-1105
= Princess Agnes of Franconia
dau. of King Henry IV of Germany
and Princess Bertha of Maurienne
|
Princess Agnes II of Franconia
= Duke Leopold III of Austria
|
Countess Agnes von Babenberg
dau. of Duke Leopold III of Austria
|King Vladislas II of Poland
|
Princess Richilde of Poland
= King Alfonso VII of Castile - Galicia
|
King Ferdinand II 1157-1188
King of Leon

King Alfonso IX 1188-1230
King of Leon
|
King Ferdinand III
King of Castile 1217-1252
King of Leon 1230-1252
|
Princess Eleanor of Castile d. 1290
= King Edward I of England
|
King Edward II Plantagenet
= Princess Isabella of France
|
King Edward III
1327-1377
= Princess Phillipa of Hainault
|
Prince John of Gaunt
= Lady Katharine Swynford
|
Prince John Plantagenet
|
Princess Joan Beaufort
= King James I of Scots
|
King James II
= Mary, dau. of Arnold Duc de Gueldres
|
Princess Mary
= Lord Thomas Boyd
|
Lady Mary Boyd
James 1st Lord Hamilton
great grandson of
Princess Aenor de Chatellerault
and Guillaume X le Toulousain
Duc de Guyenne, Comte de Poitiers
|
Lady Euphemia Hamilton
(descent from the High Elves of Ireland,
Princess Melusine and the Scots Kings)
= Lord James Weir of Vere,
Baron Blackwood d. 1599
|
Sir William Vere of Stanebyres
= Elizabeth Hamilton, his cousin.
(descent from the High Elves of Ireland,
Princess Melusine and the Scots Kings)
|
Lord Thomas Weir of Vere, Baron Kirkton
= Lady Jane Somerville, The Witch of
the Dragon House of the Earls Somerville.
|
Major Thomas Weir of Vere of Edinburgh,

The Witch King of Mid-Lothian
= Margaret Bourdon
|
Lord Thomas Weir of Vere
de jure Baron Kirkton
Hereditary Witch King
= Miss Mary Robison of Cookstown,
County Tyrone, Ulster
|
John Weir of Vere
|
Andrew Weir of Vere
|
Margaret Weir of Vere of Kildress
|
Archibald Weir of Vere of Kildress
= Rachel Stewart of Desertcreat
|
Robert Weir of Vere of Kildress
|
John Weir of Vere of Ardwell, Logan Manor
= Mary Logan dau. of Thomas Logan of
Ardwell, Logan Manor, Galloway
|
Thomas Logan Weir of Vere of Carlisle
= Anne Grant Macdonnell of Inverness
(asserted descent from the Grant earls of Seafield)
|
James Weir of Vere of Lewes
= Natalie Hopgood, (descent through her father
from the Collisons of Norfolk, the Plantagenet
Kings and the Imperial and Royal House of Vere.
Descent through her mother from Lt. Col
George Butcher of Windsor Castle, Sarah Butcher
of Framlingham and the Huegenot Bourchier
Counts of Versailles, France)
|
HI&RH Prince Nicholas de Vere

The Vere Cousins of King Sigismund of Hungary Founder of Societas Draconis (The Dragon Court), Husband of the Vampire Queen Barbara Cille

Origins with the Early Kings of Poland

The Kings of Poland originated with Lech, who was one of three Varangian brothers (including Rurik or Rus who founded the Russian state and Cech or Czech who founded Bohemia.

Duke Piast (Founder of the Piast dynasty)
|
Duke Siemowit I c. 890 AD
|
Duke Lestko c. 920 AD
|
Duke Siemosyl
|
Duke Mieszko I 960-992
|
Duke Boleslaw I the Brave
First King of Poland in 1025
|
King Mieszko II 1025-1031
|
King Casimir I 1039-1058
= Princess Dobroniega of Kiev
dau. of Grand Prince Vladimir of Kiev
|
King Vladislav I
= Princess Judith of Bohemia dau. of
King Wratislav II of Bohemia and
Princess Adelaide of Hungary
|
King Vladislav II
= Princess Agness Hohenstauffen of
Babenberg dau. of Duke Leopold
Hohenstauffen of Austria-Franconia
|
Prince Zibigniew - Princess Richilde
(Descent to the House of Vere)
|
Boleslas III
|
Ladislas II
|
Boleslas IV
|
Casimir II

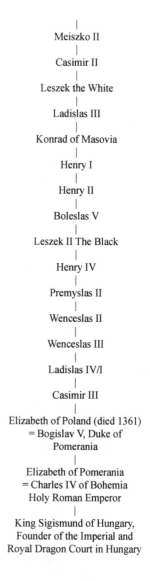

|
Meiszko II
|
Casimir II
|
Leszek the White
|
Ladislas III
|
Konrad of Masovia
|
Henry I
|
Henry II
|
Boleslas V
|
Leszek II The Black
|
Henry IV
|
Premyslas II
|
Wenceslas II
|
Wenceslas III
|
Ladislas IV/I
|
Casimir III
|
Elizabeth of Poland (died 1361)
= Bogislav V, Duke of
Pomerania
|
Elizabeth of Pomerania
= Charles IV of Bohemia
Holy Roman Emperor
|
King Sigismund of Hungary,
Founder of the Imperial and
Royal Dragon Court in Hungary

The Vere Cousins of the Vampire Countess Elizabeth Bathory

Duke Piast (Founder of the Piast dynasty)
|
Duke Siemowit I c. 890 AD
|
Duke Lestko c. 920 AD
|
Duke Siemosyl

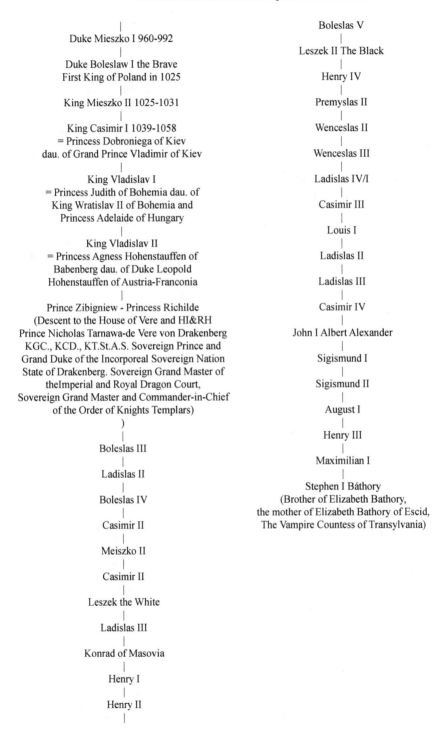

|
Duke Mieszko I 960-992
|
Duke Boleslaw I the Brave
First King of Poland in 1025
|
King Mieszko II 1025-1031
|
King Casimir I 1039-1058
= Princess Dobroniega of Kiev
dau. of Grand Prince Vladimir of Kiev
|
King Vladislav I
= Princess Judith of Bohemia dau. of
King Wratislav II of Bohemia and
Princess Adelaide of Hungary
|
King Vladislav II
= Princess Agness Hohenstauffen of
Babenberg dau. of Duke Leopold
Hohenstauffen of Austria-Franconia
|
Prince Zibigniew - Princess Richilde
(Descent to the House of Vere and HI&RH
Prince Nicholas Tarnawa-de Vere von Drakenberg
KGC., KCD., KT.St.A.S. Sovereign Prince and
Grand Duke of the Incorporeal Sovereign Nation
State of Drakenberg. Sovereign Grand Master of
theImperial and Royal Dragon Court,
Sovereign Grand Master and Commander-in-Chief
of the Order of Knights Templars)
)
|
Boleslas III
|
Ladislas II
|
Boleslas IV
|
Casimir II
|
Meiszko II
|
Casimir II
|
Leszek the White
|
Ladislas III
|
Konrad of Masovia
|
Henry I
|
Henry II
|

Boleslas V
|
Leszek II The Black
|
Henry IV
|
Premyslas II
|
Wenceslas II
|
Wenceslas III
|
Ladislas IV/I
|
Casimir III
|
Louis I
|
Ladislas II
|
Ladislas III
|
Casimir IV
|
John I Albert Alexander
|
Sigismund I
|
Sigismund II
|
August I
|
Henry III
|
Maximilian I
|
Stephen I Báthory
(Brother of Elizabeth Bathory,
the mother of Elizabeth Bathory of Escid,
The Vampire Countess of Transylvania)

Chapter Twelve

Vere Descent from the Ostrogoths

Royal Descent of the House of Vere from the Kings of the Ostrogoths via the Dukes of Hamilton

The Ostrogoths of Romania and Transylvania

King Vultwulf 350 AD
|
King Valaravaus 380 AD
|
King Winithar 400 AD
Conquered Vanadi-Slavs
|
King Qandahar d. 459 AD
|
King Theodemer d. 475 AD
|
King Theoderic The Great of Italy
King of Macedonia
King of the Visigoths d. August 30th 526 AD
|
Princess Theodora
= Count Severinus of Cartegena
|
Princess Theodosia
= Leovigild of Spain
|
St. Hermengild d. 585
= Princess Ingunda of France
dau. of King Sigebert of France
and Princess Brunchildis of Spain
|
King Athanagildo
= Princess Flavia Juliana
of Byzantium
|
King Ardebasto
= Princess Godo
|
King Ervigo of Spain
= Princess Liubigotona
Descent from King Clovis of France

Duke Pedro of Cantabaria
|
Princess Aupais of the Goths
= Duke Pepin of Heristal of France
Mayor of the Palaces of
Austrasia, Neustria and Burgundy
|
Lord Charles Martel (The Hammer)
|
Pepin the III Brevis, Duke of Lower Lorraine
(Brabant)
Mayor of Neustrasia, King of the Franks
= Lady Leuthergis
|
Princess Bertha
= Prince Milo de Vere, Duke of Angiers
Count of Anjou, son of the Fairy Princess
Melusine I of the Scythians (parallel descent
from Satan via the Egyptian Kings as
above and the Fairy Tuadha de Danaan)
|
Prince Milo II de Vere, Count of Guisnes and Anjou
= Lady Aveline de Nantes
|
Prince Nicassius de Vere, Count of Guisnes
= Lady Agatha de Champagne
|
Prince Otho de Vere, Count of Guisnes
= Lady Constance de Chartres
|
Prince Amelius (Adolph) de Vere Count of Guisnes
= Lady Maud de Ponthieu
|
Prince Guy (Gallus) de Vere, Count of Guisnes
= Lady Gertrude de Clermont de Ponthieu
|
Prince Baldwin de Vere
|
Eustace I de Vere
= Maud de Louvain
|
Eustace II de Vere
Comte de Boulogne
=Saint Ida of Ardennes
|
Princess Ida de Vere
= Baudouin de Bourg
Comte de Rethul
|
Prince Hugues I
Comte de Rethul
= Melisende (Melusine II)
dau. Of Bouchard Comte de Corbeil and
Lady Adelaide de Crecy

Badouin II de Bourg
King of Jerusalem 1118 – 1131
= Princess Morfia of Armenia

|

Princess Melisende of Jerusalem (Melusine III)
= Fulke V Plantagenet Count of Anjou

|

Count Geoffrey Plantagenet of Anjou
= Princess Mathilda of England la Imperatrice
(Empress of England), dau. of King
Henry I and Princess Mathilda of Scotland,
dau. of King Malcolm III

|

King Henry II Plantagenet
= Countess Eleanor of Aquitaine

|

King John 'Lackland' Plantagenet
= Lady Isabella of Angouleme

|

King Henry III Plantagenet
= Lady Eleanor dau. of Count
Raymond Berenguer IV of Provence
and Princess Beatrix of Savoy

|

King Edward I
= Princess Eleanor of Castile

|

King Edward II Plantagenet
= Princess Isabella of France

|

King Edward III Plantagenet
1327-1377
= Princess Phillipa of Hainault

|

Prince John Plantagenet of Gaunt
= Lady Katharine Swynford

|

Prince John Plantagenet

|

Princess Joan Beaufort
= King James I of Scots

|

King James II
= Mary, dau. of Arnold Duc de Gueldres

|

Princess Mary
= Lord Thomas Boyd

|

Lady Mary Boyd
James 1st Lord Hamilton
great grandson of
Princess Aenor de Chatellerault
and Guillaume X le Toulousain
Duc de Guyenne, Comte de Poitiers

Lady Euphemia Hamilton
(descent from the High Elves of Ireland,
Princess Melusine and the Scots Kings)
= Lord James Weir of Vere,
Baron Blackwood d. 1599

|

Sir William Vere of Stanebyres
= Elizabeth Hamilton, his cousin.
(descent from the High Elves of Ireland,
Princess Melusine and the Scots Kings)

|

Lord Thomas Weir of Vere, Baron Kirkton
= Lady Jane Somerville, The Witch of
the Dragon House of the Earls Somerville.

|

Major Thomas Weir of Vere of Edinburgh,
The Witch King of Mid-Lothian
= Margaret Bourdon

|

Lord Thomas Weir of Vere
de jure Baron Kirkton
Hereditary Witch King
= Miss Mary Robison of Cookstown,
County Tyrone, Ulster

|

John Weir of Vere

|

Andrew Weir of Vere

|

Margaret Weir of Vere of Kildress

|

Archibald Weir of Vere of Kildress
= Rachel Stewart of Desertcreat

|

Robert Weir of Vere of Kildress

|

John Weir of Vere of Ardwell, Logan Manor
= Mary Logan dau. of Thomas Logan of
Ardwell, Logan Manor, Galloway

|

Thomas Logan Weir of Vere of Carlisle
= Anne Grant Macdonnell of Inverness
(asserted descent from the Grant earls of Seafield)

|

James Weir of Vere of Lewes
= Natalie Hopgood, (descent through her father
from the Collisons of Norfolk, the Plantagenet
Kings and the Imperial and Royal House of Vere.
Descent through her mother from Lt. Col
George Butcher of Windsor Castle, Sarah Butcher
of Framlingham and the Huguenot Bourchier
Counts of Versailles, France)

|

HI&RH Prince Nicholas de Vere

Royal Descent of the House of Vere from the Kings of the Ostrogoths via the Emperors of Germany

The Ostrogoths of Romania and Transylvania

King Vultwulf 350 AD
|
King Valaravaus 380 AD
|
King Winithar 400 AD
Conquered Vanadi-Slavs
|
King Wandalar d. 459 AD
|
King Theodemer d. 475 AD
|
King Theoderic The Great of Italy
King of Macedonia
King of the Visigoths d. August 30th 526 AD
|
Princess Theodora
= Count Severinus of Cartegena
|
Princess Theodosia
= Leovigild of Spain
|
St. Hermengild d. 585
= Princess Ingunda of France
dau. of King Sigebert of France
and Princess Brunchildis of Spain
|
King Athanagildo
= Princess Flavia Juliana
of Byzantium
|
King Ardebasto
= Princess Godo
|
King Ervigo of Spain
= Princess Liubigotona
Descent from King Clovis of France
|
Duke Pedro of Cantabaria
|
Princess Aupais of the Goths
= Duke Pepin of Heristal of France
Mayor of the Palaces of
Austrasia, Neustria and Burgundy
|
Lord Charles Martel (The Hammer)
|
Pepin the III Brevis, Duke of Lower Lorraine

(Brabant)
Mayor of Neustrasia, King of the Franks
= Lady Leuthergis
|
Emperor Charlemagne
King of the Romans
= Princess Hildegarde
|
Emperor Louis the Pious
|
Princess Gisella of Italy
= Duke Eberhard of Fruili
|
Princess Ingeltrude
|
Princess Hedwiga of Franconia dau. of
Duke Henry of Franconia and Princess
Ingeltrude of Fruili
= Duke Otto the Illustrious of Saxony
|
King Heinrich of Germany
(Henry the Fowler)
|
King Otto I the Great of Germany 912 – 973
Holy Roman Emperor 962
= Princess Adelaide of Italy 931 – 999
|
Princess Luitgarde of Germany
= Duke Conrad of Lorraine
|
Duke Otto I of Carinthia d. 1004
= Princess Judith of Bavaria
|
Duke Henry of Speyer d. 1000
= Princess Adelaide of Alsace d. 1046
|
King Conrad II of Germany 990 1039
Holy Roman Emperor 1027
= Princess Gisela of Swabia 995 – 1043
|
King Henry III "The Black" of Germany 1017 –
1056
Holy Roman Emperor 1046
= Princess Agnes of Poitou 1025 – 1077
|
King Henry IV of Germany 1050 – 1106
Holy Roman Emperor 1084
= Princess Bertha of Savoy 1057 – 1081
|
Princess Agnes of Germany 1072 – 1143
= Duke Frederick I of Swabia 1050 – 1105
|
Duke Frederick II of Swabia 1090 – 1147
= Princess Judith of Bavaria d. 1130
|

King Frederick "Barbarossa" (Red Beard) von
Hohenstauffen
King of Germany 1122 – 1190
Holy Roman Emperor 1191
= Countess Beatrice I of Burgundy 1145 – 1184
|
King Philip of Germany 1173 – 1208
= Princess Irene Angelina 1181 – 1208
|
Princess Elizabeth of Germany 1203 – 1235
= King Ferdinand III of Castile-Galicia
|
Princess Eleanor of Castile d 1290
= King Edward I of England
|
King Edward II Plantagenet
= Princess Isabella of France
|
King Edward III
1327-1377
= Princess Phillipa of Hainault
|
Prince John of Gaunt
= Lady Katharine Swynford
|
Prince John Plantagenet
|
Princess Joan Beaufort
= King James I of Scots
|
King James II
= Mary, dau. of Arnold Duc de Gueldres
|
Princess Mary
= Lord Thomas Boyd
|
Lady Mary Boyd
James 1st Lord Hamilton
great grandson of
Princess Aenor de Chatellerault
and Guillaume X le Toulousain
Duc de Guyenne, Comte de Poitiers
|
Lady Euphemia Hamilton
(descent from the High Elves of Ireland,
Princess Melusine and the Scots Kings)
= Lord James Weir of Vere,
Baron Blackwood d. 1599
|
Sir William Vere of Stanebyres
= Elizabeth Hamilton, his cousin.
(descent from the High Elves of Ireland,
Princess Melusine and the Scots Kings)
|
Lord Thomas Weir of Vere, Baron Kirkton

= Lady Jane Somerville, The Witch of
the Dragon House of the Earls Somerville.
|
Major Thomas Weir of Vere of Edinburgh,
The Witch King of Mid-Lothian
= Margaret Bourdon
|
Lord Thomas Weir of Vere
de jure Baron Kirkton
Hereditary Witch King
= Miss Mary Robison of Cookstown,
County Tyrone, Ulster
|
John Weir of Vere
|
Andrew Weir of Vere
|
Margaret Weir of Vere of Kildress
|
Archibald Weir of Vere of Kildress
= Rachel Stewart of Desertcreat
|
Robert Weir of Vere of Kildress
|
John Weir of Vere of Ardwell, Logan Manor
= Mary Logan dau. of Thomas Logan of
Ardwell, Logan Manor, Galloway
|
Thomas Logan Weir of Vere of Carlisle
= Anne Grant Macdonnell of Inverness
(asserted descent from the Grant earls of Seafield)
|
James Weir of Vere of Lewes
= Natalie Hopgood, (descent through her father
from the Collisons of Norfolk, the Plantagenet
Kings and the Imperial and Royal House of Vere.
Descent through her mother from Lt. Col
George Butcher of Windsor Castle, Sarah Butcher
of Framlingham and the Huegenot Bourchier
Counts of Versailles, France)
|
HI&RH Prince Nicholas de Vere

Royal Descent of the House of Vere from the Kings of the Ostrogoths via Prince Milo de Vere

The Ostrogoths of Romania and Transylvania

Ostrogoths (East Goths), division of the Goths, one of the most important groups of the Germans. According to their own unproven tradition, the ancestors of the Goths were the Gotar of S Sweden. By the 3d cent. AD, the Goths settled in the region N of the Black Sea. They split into two divisions, their names reflecting the areas in which they settled; the Ostrogoths settled in Ukraine, while the Visigoths, or West Goths, moved further west of them. By c.375 the Huns conquered the Ostrogothic kingdom ruled by Ermanaric, which extended from the Dniester River, north and east to the headwaters of the Volga River. The Ostrogoths were subject to the Huns until the death (453) of Attila, when they settled in Pannonia (roughly modern Hungary) as allies of the Byzantine (East Roman) empire. The Ostrogoths, who had long elected their rulers, chose (471) Theodoric the Great as king. A turbulent ally, the Byzantine emperor, Zeno, commissioned Theodoric to reconquer Italy from Odoacer. The Ostrogoths entered Italy in 488, defeated and slew (493) Odoacer, and set up the Ostrogothic kingdom of Italy, with Ravenna as their capital. After Theodoric's death (526) his daughter Amalasuntha was regent for her son Athalric. She placed herself under the protection of the Byzantine emperor Justinian I. Her murder (535) served as pretext for Justinian to send Belisarius to reconquer Italy. He crushed the Ostrogothic kingdom, but on his recall (541) the Ostrogoths rebelled under the leadership of Totila. In 552 the Byzantine general Narses defeated Totila, who fell in battle. As a result, the Ostrogoths lost their national identity, and the hegemony over Italy passed to Byzantium and shortly afterward to the Lombards. Under the Ostrogothic kings, the culture of late antiquity was revived by Boethius and Cassiodorus; Dionysius Exiguus compiled church law; and Saint Benedict laid the basis of Western monasticism. Roman law and institutions were for the most part maintained; however, the Ostrogoths were resented as aliens by the Italians, from whom they differed not only in culture but also in religion, since they were Arians.

King Vultwulf 350 AD
|
King Valaravaus 380 AD
|
King Winithar 400 AD
Conquered Vanadi-Slavs
|
King Wandalar d. 459 AD
|
King Theodemer d. 475 AD
|
King Theoderic The Great of Italy
King of Macedonia
King of the Visigoths d. August 30th 526 AD
|
Princess Theodora
= Count Severinus of Cartegena
|
Princess Theodosia
= Leovigild of Spain
|
St. Hermengild d. 585
= Princess Ingunda of France
dau. of King Sigebert of France
and Princess Brunchildis of Spain
|
King Athanagildo
= Princess Flavia Juliana
of Byzantium
|
King Ardebasto
= Princess Godo
|
King Ervigo of Spain
= Princess Liubigotona
Descent from King Clovis of France
|
Duke Pedro of Cantabaria
|
Princess Aupais of the Goths
= Duke Pepin of Heristal of France
Mayor of the Palaces of
Austrasia, Neustria and Burgundy
|
Lord Charles Martel (The Hammer)
|
Pepin the III Brevis, Duke of Lower Lorraine
(Brabant)
Mayor of Neustrasia, King of the Franks
= Lady Leuthergis
|
Princess Bertha
= Prince Milo de Vere, Duke of Angiers
Count of Anjou, son of the Fairy Princess
Melusine I of the Scythians (parallel descent

from Satan via the Egyptian Kings as
above and the Fairy Tuadha de Danaan)
|
Prince Milo II de Vere, Count of Guisnes and Anjou
= Lady Aveline de Nantes
|
Prince Nicassius de Vere, Count of Guisnes
= Lady Agatha de Champagne
|
Prince Otho de Vere, Count of Guisnes
= Lady Constance de Chartres
|
Prince Amelius (Adolph) de Vere Count of Guisnes
= Lady Maud de Ponthieu
|
Prince Guy (Gallus) de Vere, Count of Guisnes
= Lady Gertrude de Clermont de Ponthieu
|
Two Sons:
2nd son – Prince Baldwin de Vere, descent to Ida
de Vere,
the House of Hamilton and the Royal Vere of
Blackwood
&
1st son Prince Manasses de Vere Count of Guisnes,
(descent
to the Vere Earls of Oxford)
=Lady Petronilla de Boleine
|
Prince Alphonse de Vere, Count of Guisnes
= Lady Katarine, dau of Count Arnulf of Flanders
|
Prince Alberic I de Vere, Count of Guisnes
= Princess Beatrix of Normandy
(descent from Satan via the Fairy Princess
Melusine I du Scythes above)
|
Prince Alberic II de Vere,
Sheriff of Cambridge, Lord of Clare and Tonbridge
= Lady Adeliza dau. of Lord Gilbert FitzRichard
|
Prince Aubrey (Alberic) III de Vere, Earl of Oxford,
Shakespeare's Oberon, King of the Fairies
in 'A Midsummer Night's Dream'
= Lady Agnes, dau. of Henry Lord Essex.
|
Prince Ralph de Vere of Blackwood 1165 AD
Brother of Robert of Huntingdon; Robin Hood;
God of the Witches, Shakespeare's
Puck, son of Oberon
|
Prince Rory de Vere of Blackwood
|
Prince Ralph de Vere of Blackwood
|

Prince Thomas de Vere of Blackwood
|
Prince Richard de Vere of Blackwood
|
Prince Thomas de Vere
1st Baron Blackwood 1340 AD
|
Prince Buan Were of Vere of Blackwood
|
Prince Rotaldus Were of Vere of Blackwood
|
Prince Thomas Were of Vere
4th Baron Blackwood
|
Prince Robert Veyr of Vere of Blackwood
|
Prince Thomas Weir of Vere of Blackwood
= Lady Aegidia Somerset
(Descent from King Edward III)
|
Prince James Weir of Vere,
7th Baron Blackwood d. 1599
= Lady Euphemia Hamilton
(descent from the High Elves of Ireland,
Princess Melusine and the Scots Kings)
|
Sir William Vere de Vere of Stanebyres
= Lady Elizabeth Hamilton his cousin
(descent from the High Elves of Ireland,
Princess Melusine and the Scots Kings)
|

Lord Thomas Weir of Vere, Baron Kirkton
= Lady Jane Somerville, The Witch of
the Dragon House of the Earls Somerville.
|
Major Thomas Weir of Vere of Edinburgh,
The Witch King of Mid-Lothian
= Margaret Bourdon
|
Lord Thomas Weir of Vere
de jure Baron Kirkton
Hereditary Witch King
= Miss Mary Robison of Cookstown,
County Tyrone, Ulster
|
John Weir of Vere
|
Andrew Weir of Vere
|
Margaret Weir of Vere of Kildress
|
Archibald Weir of Vere of Kildress
= Rachel Stewart of Desertcreat
|

Robert Weir of Vere of Kildress
|

John Weir of Vere of Ardwell, Logan Manor
= Mary Logan dau. of Thomas Logan of
Ardwell, Logan Manor, Galloway
|

Thomas Logan Weir of Vere of Carlisle
= Anne Grant Macdonnell of Inverness
(asserted descent from the Grant earls of Seafield)
|

James Weir of Vere of Lewes
= Natalie Hopgood, (descent through her father
from the Collisons of Norfolk, the Plantagenet
Kings and the Imperial and Royal House of Vere.
Descent through her mother from Lt. Col
George Butcher of Windsor Castle, Sarah Butcher
of Framlingham and the Huegenot Bourchier
Counts of Versailles, France)
|

HI&RH Prince Nicholas de Vere

Chapter Thirteen

Ancient Royal Gothic Descents of the House of Vere

Ancient Royal Gothic Descent of the House of Vere via Prince Milo de Vere

The Gothic Balthae Dynasty of Romania and Bulgaria

King Boiorix of the Goths d. 101 BC
Line descends
|
King Etepamara of the Goths c. 90 AD
Line descends
|
King Nidad of the Visi-Goths (Tervingi)
218-249
|
King Ovida of the Visi-Goths 249-273
|
King Ascaric of the Visi-Goths
Line descends
|
King Vidigoia of the Visi-Goths
|
King Wihturic of the Visi-Goths c. 376
|
King Athanaric of the Visi-Goths 383
= Queen Gaatha of the Visi-Goths
dau. of King Fridigar of the Goths
|
King Alaric of the Visi-Goths
Sacked Rome in 410ad
|
King Teodoredo 1st Gothic King of Spain 418-451
|
King Evarix of the Visi-Goths
Gothic King of Spain 466-484
= Princess Ragnahilde
|
King Alaric II Gothic King of Spain
= Princess Arevagna

King Giselac Gothic King of Spain 507-511
|
King Amalaric Gothic King of Spain 511-531
|
King Tribigildo Gothic King of Spain 531-548
= Princess Gisela of the Goths
|
King Thiudigisclus Gothic King of Spain 548-549
|
King Theodimir Gothic King of Spain 567-571
|
King Leova Gothic King of Spain 571-572
= Princess Theodosia
|
King Hermenegild II Gothic King of Spain
Murdered 586
|
King Recaredo I Gothic King of Spain 586-601
= Princess Clotsvinth of France
|
King Leova Gothic King of Spain 601-603
|
King Witeric Gothic King of Spain 603-610
|
King Gundemar Gothic King of Spain 610-612
|
King Sisebuto Gothic King of Spain 612-621
|
King Suintila Gothic King of Spain 621-631
|
King Sisenande Gothic King of Spain 631-636
|
King Chintila Gothic King of Spain 636-640
Son of King Fritgarde and Queen Chinterico
|
King Tulga Gothic King of Spain 640-642
|
King Chindasuinto 642-649
= Princess Reciberga
|
King Reccesvinto Gothic King of Spain 649-672
|
King Ervigio Gothic King of Spain 680-687
= Princess Liubigotona
|
King Rodrigo Gothic King of Spain 709-711
|
King Pelayas 1st King of Asturias 718-737
= Princess Ingunde of France
|
King Atanagildo Gothic King of Spain

175

= Princess Flavia Juliana of Byzantium
|
King Atanagildo Gothic King of Spain
= Princess Goto of Burgundy
|
King Ervigio Gothic King of Spain
= Princess Liubigotona of the Goths
|
King Pedro of Spain
|
Princess Aupais of the Goths
= Duke Pepin of Heristal of France
Mayor of the Palaces of
Austrasia, Neustria and Burgundy
|
Lord Charles Martel (The Hammer)
|
Pepin the III Brevis, Duke of Lower Lorraine
(Brabant)
Mayor of Neustrasia, King of the Franks
= Lady Leuthergis
|
Princess Bertha
= Prince Milo de Vere, Duke of Angiers
Count of Anjou, son of the Fairy Princess
Melusine I of the Scythians (parallel descent
from Satan via the Egyptian Kings as
above and the Fairy Tuadha de Danaan)
|
Prince Milo II de Vere, Count of Guisnes and Anjou
= Lady Aveline de Nantes
|
Prince Nicassius de Vere, Count of Guisnes
= Lady Agatha de Champagne
|
Prince Otho de Vere, Count of Guisnes
= Lady Constance de Chartres
|
Prince Amelius (Adolph) de Vere Count of Guisnes
= Lady Maud de Ponthieu
|
Prince Guy (Gallus) de Vere, Count of Guisnes
= Lady Gertrude de Clermont de Ponthieu
|
Two Sons:
2nd son-Prince Baldwin de Vere, descent to Ida de
Vere,
the House of Hamilton and the Royal Vere of
Blackwood
&
1st son Prince Manasses de Vere Count of Guisnes,
(descent
to the Vere Earls of Oxford)

=Lady Petronilla de Boleine
|
Prince Alphonse de Vere, Count of Guisnes
= Lady Katarine, dau of Count Arnulf of Flanders
|
Prince Alberic I de Vere, Count of Guisnes
= Princess Beatrix of Normandy
(descent from Satan via the Fairy Princess
Melusine I du Scythes above)
|
Prince Alberic II de Vere,
Sheriff of Cambridge, Lord of Clare and Tonbridge
= Lady Adeliza dau. of Lord Gilbert FitzRichard
|
Prince Aubrey (Alberic) III de Vere, Earl of Oxford,
Shakespeare's Oberon, King of the Fairies
in "A Midsummer Night's Dream"
= Lady Agnes, dau. of Henry Lord Essex.
|
Prince Ralph de Vere of Blackwood 1165 AD
Brother of Robert of Huntingdon; Robin Hood;
God of the Witches, Shakespeare's
Puck, son of Oberon
|
Prince Rory de Vere of Blackwood
|
Prince Ralph de Vere of Blackwood
|
Prince Thomas de Vere of Blackwood
|
Prince Richard de Vere of Blackwood
|
Prince Thomas de Vere
1st Baron Blackwood 1340 AD
|
Prince Buan Were of Vere of Blackwood
|
Prince Rotaldus Were of Vere of Blackwood
|
Prince Thomas Were of Vere
4th Baron Blackwood
|
Prince Robert Veyr of Vere of Blackwood
|
Prince Thomas Weir of Vere of Blackwood
= Lady Aegidia Somerset
(Descent from King Edward III)
|
Prince James Weir of Vere,
7th Baron Blackwood d. 1599
= Lady Euphemia Hamilton
(descent from the High Elves of Ireland,
Princess Melusine and the Scots Kings)

Sir William Vere de Vere of Stanebyres
= Lady Elizabeth Hamilton his cousin
(descent from the High Elves of Ireland,
Princess Melusine and the Scots Kings)

Lord Thomas Weir of Vere, Baron Kirkton
= Lady Jane Somerville, The Witch of
the Dragon House of the Earls Somerville.

Major Thomas Weir of Vere of Edinburgh,
The Witch King of Mid-Lothian
= Margaret Bourdon

Lord Thomas Weir of Vere
de jure Baron Kirkton
Hereditary Witch King
= Miss Mary Robison of Cookstown,
County Tyrone, Ulster

John Weir of Vere

Andrew Weir of Vere

Margaret Weir of Vere of Kildress

Archibald Weir of Vere of Kildress
= Rachel Stewart of Desertcreat

Robert Weir of Vere of Kildress

John Weir of Vere of Ardwell, Logan Manor
= Mary Logan dau. of Thomas Logan of
Ardwell, Logan Manor, Galloway

Thomas Logan Weir of Vere of Carlisle
= Anne Grant Macdonnell of Inverness
(asserted descent from the Grant earls of Seafield)

James Weir of Vere of Lewes
= Natalie Hopgood, (descent through her father
from the Collisons of Norfolk, the Plantagenet
Kings and the Imperial and Royal House of Vere.
Descent through her mother from Lt. Col
George Butcher of Windsor Castle, Sarah Butcher
of Framlingham and the Huegenot Bourchier
Counts of Versailles, France)

HI&RH Prince Nicholas de Vere

Ancient Royal Gothic Descent of the House of Vere via the Dukes of Hamilton

The Gothic Balthae Dynasty 2nd Century BC of Romania, Transylvania and Bulgaria

King Boiorix of the Goths d. 101 BC
Line descends

King Etepamara of the Goths c. 90 AD
Line descends

King Nidad of the Visi-Goths (Tervingi)
218-249

King Ovida of the Visi-Goths 249-273

King Ascaric of the Visi-Goths
Line descends

King Vidigoia of the Visi-Goths

King Wihturic of the Visi-Goths c. 376

King Athanaric of the Visi-Goths 383
= Queen Gaatha of the Visi-Goths
dau. of King Fridigar of the Goths

King Alaric of the Visi-Goths
Sacked Rome in 410 AD

King Teodoredo 1st Gothic King of Spain 418-451

King Evarix of the Visi-Goths
Gothic King of Spain 466-484
= Princess Ragnahilde

King Alaric II Gothic King of Spain
= Princess Arevagna

King Giselac Gothic King of Spain 507-511

King Amalaric Gothic King of Spain 511-531

King Tribigildo Gothic King of Spain 531-548
= Princess Gisela of the Goths

King Thiudigisclus Gothic King of Spain 548-549

King Theodimir Gothic King of Spain 567-571

King Leova Gothic King of Spain 571-572
= Princess Theodosia
|
King Hermenegild II Gothic King of Spain
Murdered 586
|
King Recaredo I Gothic King of Spain 586-601
= Princess Clotsvinth of France
|
King Leova Gothic King of Spain 601-603
|
King Witeric Gothic King of Spain 603-610
|
King Gundemar Gothic King of Spain 610-612
|
King Sisebuto Gothic King of Spain 612-621
|
King Suintila Gothic King of Spain 621-631
|
King Sisenande Gothic King of Spain 631-636
|
King Chintila Gothic King of Spain 636-640
Son of King Fritgarde and Queen Chinterico
|
King Tulga Gothic King of Spain 640-642
|
King Chindasuinto 642-649
= Princess Reciberga
|
King Reccesvinto Gothic King of Spain 649-672
|
King Ervigio Gothic King of Spain 680-687
= Princess Liubigotona
|
King Rodrigo Gothic King of Spain 709-711
|
King Pelayas 1st King of Asturias 718-737
= Princess Ingunde of France
|
King Atanagildo Gothic King of Spain
= Princess Flavia Juliana of Byzantium
|
King Atanagildo Gothic King of Spain
= Princess Goto of Burgundy
|
King Ervigio Gothic King of Spain
= Princess Liubigotona of the Goths
|
King Pedro of Spain
|
Princess Aupais of the Goths
= Duke Pepin of Heristal of France
|
Lord Charles Martel (The Hammer)
|

Pepin the III Brevis, Duke of Lower Lorraine
(Brabant)
Mayor of Neustrasia, King of the Franks
= Lady Leuthergis
|
Princess Bertha
= Prince Milo de Vere, Duke of Angiers
Count of Anjou, son of the Fairy Princess
Melusine I of the Scythians (parallel descent
from Satan via the Egyptian Kings as
above and the Fairy Tuadha de Danaan)
|
Prince Milo II de Vere, Count of Guisnes and Anjou
= Lady Aveline de Nantes
|
Prince Nicassius de Vere, Count of Guisnes
= Lady Agatha de Champagne
|
Prince Otho de Vere, Count of Guisnes
= Lady Constance de Chartres
|
Prince Amelius (Adolph) de Vere Count of Guisnes
= Lady Maud de Ponthieu
|
Prince Guy (Gallus) de Vere, Count of Guisnes
= Lady Gertrude de Clermont de Ponthieu
|
Prince Baldwin de Vere
|
Eustace I de Vere
= Maud de Louvain
|
Eustace II de Vere
Comte de Boulogne
=Saint Ida of Ardennes
|
Princess Ida de Vere
= Baudouin de Bourg
Comte de Rethul
|
Prince Hugues I
Comte de Rethul
= Melisende (Melusine II)
dau. Of Bouchard Comte de Corbeil and
Lady Adelaide de Crecy
|
Badouin II de Bourg
King of Jerusalem 1118-1131
= Princess Morfia of Armenia
|
Princess Melisende of Jerusalem (Melusine III)
= Fulke V Plantagenet Count of Anjou
|
Count Geoffrey Plantagenet of Anjou
= Princess Mathilda of England la Imperatrice

(Empress of England), dau. of King
Henry I and Princess Mathilda of Scotland,
dau. of King Malcolm III

|

King Henry II Plantagenet
= Countess Eleanor of Aquitaine

|

King John 'Lackland' Plantagenet
= Lady Isabella of Angouleme

|

King Henry III Plantagenet
= Lady Eleanor dau. of Count
Raymond Berenguer IV of Provence
and Princess Beatrix of Savoy

|

King Edward I
= Princess Eleanor of Castile

|

King Edward II Plantagenet
= Princess Isabella of France

|

King Edward III Plantagenet
1327-1377
= Princess Phillipa of Hainault

|

Prince John Plantagenet of Gaunt
= Lady Katharine Swynford

|

Prince John Plantagenet

|

Princess Joan Beaufort
= King James I of Scots

|

King James II
= Mary, dau. of Arnold Duc de Gueldres

|

Princess Mary
= Lord Thomas Boyd

|

Lady Mary Boyd
James 1st Lord Hamilton
great grandson of
Princess Aenor de Chatellerault
and Guillaume X le Toulousain
Duc de Guyenne, Comte de Poitiers

|

Lady Euphemia Hamilton
(descent from the High Elves of Ireland,
Princess Melusine and the Scots Kings)
= Lord James Weir of Vere,
Baron Blackwood d. 1599

|

Sir William Vere of Stanebyres

= Elizabeth Hamilton, his cousin.
(descent from the High Elves of Ireland,
Princess Melusine and the Scots Kings)

Lord Thomas Weir of Vere, Baron Kirkton
= Lady Jane Somerville, The Witch of
the Dragon House of the Earls Somerville.

|

Major Thomas Weir of Vere of Edinburgh,
The Witch King of Mid-Lothian
= Margaret Bourdon

|

Lord Thomas Weir of Vere
de jure Baron Kirkton
Hereditary Witch King
= Miss Mary Robison of Cookstown,
County Tyrone, Ulster

|

John Weir of Vere

|

Andrew Weir of Vere

|

Margaret Weir of Vere of Kildress

|

Archibald Weir of Vere of Kildress
= Rachel Stewart of Desertcreat

|

Robert Weir of Vere of Kildress

|

John Weir of Vere of Ardwell, Logan Manor
= Mary Logan dau. of Thomas Logan of
Ardwell, Logan Manor, Galloway

|

Thomas Logan Weir of Vere of Carlisle
= Anne Grant Macdonnell of Inverness
(asserted descent from the Grant earls of Seafield)

|

James Weir of Vere of Lewes
= Natalie Hopgood, (descent through her father
from the Collisons of Norfolk, the Plantagenet
Kings and the Imperial and Royal House of Vere.
Descent through her mother from Lt. Col
George Butcher of Windsor Castle, Sarah Butcher
of Framlingham and the Huegenot Bourchier
Counts of Versailles, France)

HI&RH Prince Nicholas de Vere

Ancient Royal Gothic Descent of the House of Vere via the German Emperors

The Gothic Balthae Dynasty of Romania and Bulgaria

King Boiorix of the Goths d. 101 BC
Line descends
|
King Etepamara of the Goths c. 90 AD
Line descends
|
King Nidad of the Visi-Goths (Tervingi)
218-249
|
King Ovida of the Visi-Goths 249-273
|
King Ascaric of the Visi-Goths
Line descends
|
King Vidigoia of the Visi-Goths
|
King Wihturic of the Visi-Goths c. 376
|
King Athanaric of the Visi-Goths 383
= Queen Gaatha of the Visi-Goths
dau. of King Fridigar of the Goths
|
King Alaric of the Visi-Goths
Sacked Rome in 410 AD
|
King Teodoredo 1st Gothic King of Spain 418-451
|
King Evarix of the Visi-Goths
Gothic King of Spain 466-484
= Princess Ragnahilde
|
King Alaric II Gothic King of Spain
= Princess Arevagna
|
King Giselac Gothic King of Spain 507-511
|
King Amalaric Gothic King of Spain 511-531
|
King Tribigildo Gothic King of Spain 531-548
= Princess Gisela of the Goths
|
King Thiudigisclus Gothic King of Spain 548-549
|
King Theodimir Gothic King of Spain 567-571
|
King Leova Gothic King of Spain 571-572

= Princess Theodosia
|
King Hermenegild II Gothic King of Spain
Murdered 586
|
King Recaredo I Gothic King of Spain 586-601
= Princess Clotsvinth of France
|
King Leova Gothic King of Spain 601-603
|
King Witeric Gothic King of Spain 603-610
|
King Gundemar Gothic King of Spain 610-612
|
King Sisebuto Gothic King of Spain 612-621
|
King Suintila Gothic King of Spain 621-631
|
King Sisenande Gothic King of Spain 631-636
|
King Chintila Gothic King of Spain 636-640
Son of King Fritgarde and Queen Chinterico
|
King Tulga Gothic King of Spain 640-642
|
King Chindasuinto 642-649
= Princess Reciberga
|
King Reccesvinto Gothic King of Spain 649-672
|
King Ervigio Gothic King of Spain 680-687
= Princess Liubigotona
|
King Rodrigo Gothic King of Spain 709-711
|
King Pelayas 1st King of Asturias 718-737
= Princess Ingunde of France
|
King Atanagildo Gothic King of Spain
= Princess Flavia Juliana of Byzantium
|
King Atanagildo Gothic King of Spain
= Princess Goto of Burgundy
|
King Ervigio Gothic King of Spain
= Princess Liubigotona of the Goths
|
King Pedro of Spain
|
Princess Aupais of the Goths
= Duke Pepin of Heristal of France
|
Lord Charles Martel (The Hammer)
|
Pepin the III Brevis, Duke of Lower Lorraine

(Brabant)
Mayor of Neustrasia, King of the Franks
= Lady Leuthergis
Emperor Charlemagne
King of the Romans
= Princess Hildegarde

Emperor Louis the Pious

Princess Gisella of Italy
= Duke Eberhard of Fruili

Princess Ingeltrude

Princess Hedwiga of Franconia dau. of
Duke Henry of Franconia and Princess
Ingeltrude of Fruili
= Duke Otto the Illustrious of Saxony

King Heinrich of Germany
(Henry the Fowler)

King Otto I the Great of Germany 912-973
Holy Roman Emperor 962
= Princess Adelaide of Italy 931-999

Princess Luitgarde of Germany
= Duke Conrad of Lorraine

Duke Otto I of Carinthia d. 1004
= Princess Judith of Bavaria

Duke Henry of Speyer d. 1000
= Princess Adelaide of Alsace d. 1046

King Conrad II of Germany 990 1039
Holy Roman Emperor 1027
= Princess Gisela of Swabia 995-1043

King Henry III "The Black" of Germany 1017-1056
Holy Roman Emperor 1046
= Princess Agnes of Poitou 1025-1077

King Henry IV of Germany 1050-1106
Holy Roman Emperor 1084
= Princess Bertha of Savoy 1057-1081

Princess Agnes of Germany 1072-1143
= Duke Frederick I of Swabia 1050-1105

Duke Frederick II of Swabia 1090-1147
= Princess Judith of Bavaria d. 1130

King Frederick "Barbarossa" (Red Beard) von
Hohenstauffen

King of Germany 1122-1190
Holy Roman Emperor 1191
= Countess Beatrice I of Burgundy 1145-1184

King Philip of Germany 1173-1208
= Princess Irene Angelina 1181-1208

Princess Elizabeth of Germany 1203-1235
= King Ferdinand III of Castile-Galicia

Princess Eleanor of Castile d 1290
= King Edward I of England

King Edward II Plantagenet
= Princess Isabella of France

King Edward III
1327-1377
= Princess Phillipa of Hainault

Prince John of Gaunt
= Lady Katharine Swynford

Prince John Plantagenet

Princess Joan Beaufort
= King James I of Scots

King James II
= Mary, dau. of Arnold Duc de Gueldres

Princess Mary
= Lord Thomas Boyd

Lady Mary Boyd
James 1st Lord Hamilton
great grandson of
Princess Aenor de Chatellerault
and Guillaume X le Toulousain
Duc de Guyenne, Comte de Poitiers

Lady Euphemia Hamilton
(descent from the High Elves of Ireland,
Princess Melusine and the Scots Kings)
= Lord James Weir of Vere,
Baron Blackwood d. 1599

Sir William Vere of Stanebyres
= Elizabeth Hamilton, his cousin.
(descent from the High Elves of Ireland,
Princess Melusine and the Scots Kings)

Lord Thomas Weir of Vere, Baron Kirkton
= Lady Jane Somerville, The Witch of
the Dragon House of the Earls Somerville.

|

Major Thomas Weir of Vere of Edinburgh,
The Witch King of Mid-Lothian
= Margaret Bourdon

|

Lord Thomas Weir of Vere
de jure Baron Kirkton
Hereditary Witch King
= Miss Mary Robison of Cookstown,
County Tyrone, Ulster

|

John Weir of Vere

|

Andrew Weir of Vere

|

Margaret Weir of Vere of Kildress

|

Archibald Weir of Vere of Kildress
= Rachel Stewart of Desertcreat

|

Robert Weir of Vere of Kildress

|

John Weir of Vere of Ardwell, Logan Manor
= Mary Logan dau. of Thomas Logan of
Ardwell, Logan Manor, Galloway

|

Thomas Logan Weir of Vere of Carlisle
= Anne Grant Macdonnell of Inverness
(asserted descent from the Grant earls of Seafield)

|

James Weir of Vere of Lewes
= Natalie Hopgood, (descent through her father
from the Collisons of Norfolk, the Plantagenet
Kings and the Imperial and Royal House of Vere.
Descent through her mother from Lt. Col
George Butcher of Windsor Castle, Sarah Butcher
of Framlingham and the Huegenot Bourchier
Counts of Versailles, France)

|

HI&RH Prince Nicholas de Vere

Chapter Fourteen

Vere Cousin Descent from Vlad III Dracula Tepes

Prince Almos of Hungary
Prince of Transylvania
d. 895
|
Prince Arpad of Hungary
Prince of Transylvania
d. 907
|
Prince Zoltan of Hungary
Prince of Transylvania
d. 947
|
Prince Taksony of Hungary
Prince of Transylvania
d. 972
|
Duke Mihaly of Poland
Prince of Transylvania
d. 976
= Princess Adelajda of Poland
|
Prince Vasul (Pagan Magyar)
Prince of Transylvania
d. 1037
|
King Bela I of Hungary
King of Transylvania
d. 1063
= Princess Rixa of Poland d. of
King Miezsko and Queen Rixa
of Poland
(Descent to the House of Vere and HI&RH Prince
Nicholas Tarnawa-de Vere von Drakenberg KGC.,
KCD., KT.St.A.S. Sovereign Prince and Grand
Duke of the Incorporeal Sovereign Nation State
of Drakenberg. Sovereign Grand Master of the
Imperial and Royal Dragon Court, Sovereign Grand
Master and Commander-in-Chief of the Order of
Knights Templars.)

Solomon (Salamon) August 1063
28 October 1074 son of Andrew I
|
Géza I, 28 October 1074, 25 April 1077 son of Béla
I
|
St. Ladislaus (Szent László) 25 April 1077, 29 July
1095 son of Béla I

Coloman (Könyves Kálmán) 29 July 1095, 3
February 1116 son of Géza I.
|
Stephen II, 3 February 1116, 3 April 1131 Son of
Kálmán
|
ÁrpádsBéla II the Blind (Vak Béla), 3 April 1131, 13
February 1141, grandson of Géza I., son of Álmos,
Kálmán's executed younger brother
|
Géza II, 13 February 1141, 31 May 1162 son of
Béla II
|
Stephen III, 31 May 1162, 4 March 1172 son of
Géza II
|
Ladislaus II, 31 May 1162, 14 January 1163, rebel
anti-king, younger
brother of Géza II.
|
Stephen IV,14 January 1163, June 1163 rebel anti-
king, younger brother of Géza II.
|
Béla III, 4 March 1172, 13 April 1196 younger
brother of Stephen III.
|
Emeric (Imre) 13 April 1196, 30 November 1204
son of Béla III.
|
Ladislaus III, 30 November 1204, 7 May 1205 son
of Imre, crowned
and died as a child
|
Andrew II, 7 May 1205, 21 September 1235, brother
of Imre
|
Béla IV,14 October 1235, 3 May 1270, son of
Andrew II., the "second founder" after the First
Mongol invasion (1241-42)
|
Stephen V, 3 May 1270, 6 August 1272, son of Béla
IV.
|
Ladislaus IV the Cuman (Kun László), 6 August
1272, 10 July 1290, son of Steven V.; unsuccessful
Mongol invasion; lived with the nomad Cuman
tribes
|
Andrew III, 4 August 1290, 14 January 1301,
grandson of Andrew II., born in Venice last of the
Árpád dynasty
|
Wenceslaus of Bohemia (Vencel), 1301-1305, King
of Bohemia, elected as King of Hungary but not
universally recognized
|
Otto of Bavaria (Béla V)
(Ottó) or Béla V, 6 December 1305-1308, Duke of

183

Lower Bavaria, was not universally recognized
|
Charles Robert I
(Károly Róbert) 20 August 1310, 16 July 1342
established the Angevin dynasty in Hungary.
|
Louis I the Great
(Nagy Lajos), 16 July 1342, 11 September 1382,
also King of Poland
|
Maria I (I. Mária), 11 September 1382, 17 May
1395, married Sigismund of Luxemburg
|
Charles II the Small
(Kis Károly), 31 December 1385, 24 February 1386,
also King of Naples, in opposition to Mary
|
Sigismund (Zsigmond), 31 March 1387, 9
December 1437, later also
Roman-German King (since 1410), King of
Bohemia (since 1419), Holy Roman Emperor (since
1433)
|
Albert, 1 January 1438, 27 October 1439, son-in-law
Sigismund, also
Roman-German King, King of Bohemia, Duke of
Austria
Kingship disputed between Ulászló I and Ladislaus
Posthumus
Jagiellon Ulászló I, 15 May 1440, 10 November
1444, also King of Poland
|
Ladislaus V, Posthumus, 15 May 1440, 23
November 1457, born in 1440 after his father's
death, spent most of his life in captivity.
|
János Hunyadi, 1446-1453, ruled as regent. Fought
with great success
against the Ottomans
|
Matthias Corvinus (Corvin Mátyás), 24 January
1458, 6 April
|
Ilona Szilagyi, Daughter of Stephen Szilagyi;
cousin of Matthias Corvinus

= Vlad III Dracula

Chapter Fifteen

The Elven Vere Descendants of Odin, Lord of the Rings; Princess Plantina; Geoffrey Plantagenet Count of Anjou; the Merovingian Princes and the Ancient Kings of Britain

Based on the genealogies compiled by David Womack

- De Diabolo Venit Et Ad Diabolum Ibid -

"From the Devil he came and to the Devil he will return"

Generation No. 1

1. Geoffrey Plantagenet was born 1113, and died 1151. He married Matilda of England, daughter of King Henry and of Matilda. She was born Abt. 1104, and died September 10, 1167.

Notes for Geoffrey Plantagenet:

GEOFFREY, surnamed PLANTAGENET, COUNT d'ANJOU, born 1113, died 1151. King Henry I, of England, in despair over loss of his son, William, Duke of Normandy, who was drowned in the sinking of a ship off the coast of France, sought the aid of GEOFFREY PLANTAGENET, one of the most powerful princes of France, a noble person, with "elegant and courtly manners and a reputation for gallantry in the field." Approving the marriage of his daughter MATILDA with GEOFFREY, King Henry personally invested him with Knighthood, and expressed the hope that all Englishmen would give them full allegiance. The Barons took the oath to uphold the succession of Matilda and Geoffrey and their children after them. Thus Geoffrey heads the line of English kings which bear his Plantagenet name.

The friends of Geoffrey were unaware that their playful nickname for him of Plantagenet would live through the years. Geoffrey was descended from the Elven Princess Plantina, sister of the Fairy Princess Melusine I. Thus he derived his popular title. As eldest son of FULK V, KING OF JERUSALEM, and his wife, Princess Melusine III, Geoffrey was of the House of Angevin Kings, which had been prominent for three centuries.

Geoffrey's descent from the House of Angevin Kings follows: From Princess Plantina, sister of the Fairy Princess Melusine – TORQUAT C760. TORTULF C780. THERTULLUS C.800 (Tortulf the Woodman of Nide de Merle), wife PETRONELLA, daughter of Conrad, Count of Paris; (2) INGELERUS I, married Adeline of Challon; (3) FULK, "the red," born 888, died 938, wife Roscilla of Blois; (4) FULK II, The Good, Count of Anjou, died 958, married

Gerberga of Catinais; (5) GEOFFREY I, Count of Anjou, died 21 July 987, married Adelaide de Vermandois, also known as Adelaide de Chalons, born 950, died 975-78; (6) FULK III, "the Black" Count of Anjou, born 970, died 21 June 1040, married, second, after 1000, Hildegarde, who died 1 April 1109, married, fifth, Bertrade de Montfort; (9) FULK V, "The Young," Count of Anjou, King of Jerusalem, born 1092; died 10 Nov. 1143, who, as above stated, was the father of GEOFFREY V "PLANTAGENET," Count of Anjou, Duke of Normandy, who, on 3 April 1127, married MATILDA of ENGLAND, daughter of HENRY I, of England. NOTE: Also being given below, is the descent of Geoffrey V of Anjou, (called "Plantagenet") husband of Matilda (Maud), of England, from KING EDWARD THE GREAT.

GENEALOGY OF GEOFFREY PLANTAGENET (born 1113, died 7 Sept. 1151, from Aedd Mawr) (KING EDWARD THE GREAT), who appears to have lived about 1300 B.C. (the line of BOAZ and RUTH) to WILLIAM THE CONQUEROR, whose Genealogy back to ROLLO the DANE, is given: (1) KING EDWARD the GREAT, his son; (2) BRYDAIN, who settled in the island at an early date, and, according to tradition, gave his name to the entire island, which has since been corrupted into "Britain." His son; (3) ANNYN TRO, his son; (4) SELYS HEN, his son; (5) BRWT, his son; (6) CYMRYW, his son; (7) ITHON, his son; (8) GWEYRYDD, his son; (9) PEREDUR, his son; (10) LLYFEINYDD, his son; (11) TEUGED, his son; (12) LLARIAN, in whose day London was a considerable town, having been founded B.C. 1020, or earlier, as some hold, at least 270 years before the founding of Rome; his son; (13) ITHEL, his son; (14) ENIR FARDD, his son; (15) CALCHWYDD, his son; (16) LLYWARCH, his son; (17) IDWAL, his son; (18) RHUN, his son; (19) BLEDDYN, his son; (20) MORGAN, his son; (21) BERWYN, his son; (22) CERAINT FEDWW, an irreclaimable drunkard, deposed by his subjects for setting fire, just before harvest, to the cornfields of Siluris, now Monmouthshire, his son; (23) BRYWLAIS; his son; (24) ALAFON, his son; (25) ANYN, his son; (26) DINGAD, his son; (27) GREIDIOL, his son; (28) CERAINT, his son; (29) MEIRION, his son; (30) ARCH, his son; (31) CAID, his son; (32) CERI, his son; (33) BARAN, his son; (34) LLYR, (KING LEAR).

He was educated in Rome by Augustus Caesar, his son; (35) BRAN, KING of SILURIA. In the year AD 36, he resigned the crown to his son Caradoc, and became Arch-Druid Bran the Blessed of the college of Siluria. Bran married Anna, granddaughter of St. James (Joseph of Aramathea); the neice of Jesus Christ. Jesus and his brother St. James' lineage conjoin with The Uther Pendragon: Aedan Mac Gabran King of Scots, who married Ygraine of Avallon (see Avallon descent). During his seven years in Rome, Bran (St. Brandon) became the first royal convert to Christianity and was baptized by the Apostle Paul, as was his son, Cardoc, and the latter's two sons, Cyllinus and Cynon (he introduced the use of vellum into England). his son; (36) CARADOC (CARACTACUS), was King of Siluria, (Monmouthshire, etc.), his son; (37) ST. CYLLIN, King of Siluria. He, first of the Cymry (Cimmerians of Scythia), gave infants names, for before, names were not given except to adults.

His brother, Linus the Martyr; his sister Claudia and her husband Rufus Pudens, aided the apostle Paul in the Christian Church in Rome. As recorded in II Timothy 4:21 and Romans 16:13, Rufus Pudens and St. Paul are shown to be half-brothers, children of the same mother, they had different fathers; Paul, by a Hebrew husband and Rufus, by a second marriage with a Roman Christian. His son; (38) PRINCE COEL, son of Cyllin was living AD 120; his son; (39) KING LLEUVER MAWR, (Lucius the Great), the second Blessed Sovereign, married Gladys, whose ancestry for eight immediate past generations is as follows; (a) CAPOIR, whose son was; (b) BELI (HELI) THE GREAT, died B.C. 72, whose son; (c) LUD, died B.C. 62, his son; (d) TENUANTIUS, his son; (e) CYNVELINE (Cymbeline), King of Britain. He was educated in Rome by Augustus Caesar, and later, forestalled the invasion of the island. His eleventh son; (f) AVIRAGUN, King of Britain, lived in Avalon (The Isle of Arran), the renowned enemy of Rome; married VENISSA JULIA, daughter of TIBERIUS CLAUDIUS CAESAR, EMPEROR OF ROME, who was the grandson of MARK ANTONY. The son of Aviragus and Venissa Julia was; (g) MERIC, (Marius,), King of Britain, married the daughter of the GODDESS-QUEEN BOADICEA (VICTORIA.).

They had a daughter; (h) EURGEN, and later a son Coel, who became King of Britain in 125. OLD KING COLE, educated in Rome, built Colchester (Coel-Castra), and died AD 170. (h) EURGEN, (see above), the said daughter of Meric, (Marius) and his wife, the daughter of Boadicea, had, as above stated, Gladys, who became the wife of No. 39 (see above), Lleuver Mawr (Lucius the Great) who is said to have changed the established religion of Britain from DRUIDISM to CHRISTIANITY though this must be patently untrue. The daughter of Lucius the Great and his wife, Gladys, was; (40) GLADYS, who became the wife of Cadvan, of Cambria, Prince of Wales. Their daughter; (41) STRADA, the FAIR, married Coel, a later King of Colchester, living AD 232. Their daughter; (42) HELEN of the CROSS (The Arms of Colchester were a "cross with three crowns"), Helen was born 248, died 328 and became the wife of CONSTANTIUS I, afterward Emperor of Rome, and, in right of his wife, King of Britain. He was born 242, died 306.

The God King of Valhalla: Odin, Lord of the Rings

Their son; (43) CONSTANTINE THE GREAT, born 265, died 336. Of British birth, he is known as the first CHRISTIAN EMPEROR. The greatest of all Roman Emperors, he annexed Britain to the Roman Empire, his son; (44) CONSTANTIUS II, died in 360, his son; (45) CONSTANTIUS III, married Placida, died in 421, his son; (46) VALENTINIAN III, died in 455. His daughter; (47) EUDOXIA, married Hunneric, who died in 480. her son; (48) HILDERIC, King of the Vandals in 525, his daughter; (49) HILDA, married Frode VII, who died 548; her son; (50) HALFDAN, KING OF DENMARK, his son; (51) IVAR VIDFADMA, KING of DENMARK and SWEDEN in 660 his son: (52) RORIC SLINGEBAND, KING of DENMARK and SWEDEN in 700, his son; (53) HARALD HILDETAND, KING of DENMARK and SWEDEN in 725, his son; (54) SIGURD RING, living in 750, his son; (55) RAYNER LODBROCK, KING of DENMARK and SWEDEN, died in 794, married Aslanga.

Aslanga was granddaughter of the one-eyed, hooded God-King ODIN, Father of Sigfreid and Brunhilde: the Swan Princess and Valkyrie. LORD OF THE AESIR, Odin was the inspiration for both Tolkien's Gandalf – Grey Elf – and the one-eyed Sauron Lord of the Rings, from Saur, a Dragon. Odin was the ancestor of Robert de Vere, the historical Robin Hood or Hoden.

RAYNER LODBROCK'S son; (56) SIGURD SNODOYE, KING of DENMARK and SWEDEN, died 830, his son; (57) HORDA KNUT, KING of DENMARK, died in 850, his son; (58) FROTHA, KING of DENMARK, died 875, his son; (59) GORM ENSKE, married Sida and died in 890, his son; (60) HAROLD PARCUS, KING of DENMARK, whose wife was Elgiva, daughter of ETHELRED I, King of England, (a brother of King Alfred The Great), his son; (61) GORM del CAMMEL, KING of DENMARK, died in 931. His wife was Thyra, his son; (62) HAROLD BLAATAND, KING of DENMARK, died in 981, his daughter; (63) LADY GUNNORA, wife of Richard I, third Duke of Normandy, born 933, died 996. They had (beside their son Richard II ((see later)), a son; (64) ROBERT d'EVEREUX, the Archbishop, who died in 1087, his son; (65) RICHARD, Count d'Evereux, died in 1067, his daughter, (66) AGNES EVEREUX, who became the wife of Simon l de Montfort, her daughter; (67) BERTRADE MONTFORT, became the wife of FULK IV, Count d'Anjou, born 1043, died 1109. The said Fulk IV's descent from OLD KING COLE is as follows;

The Frankish Kings

Coel: OLD KING COLE, son of Meric (MARIUS) (g) above mentioned, was the father of, (1) ATHILDIS, wife of Marcomir IV, King of Franconia, who died 149. They had (2) CLODOMIR IV, King of the Franks, died 166, married Hasilda, their son; (3) KING FARABERT, died 186, his son; (4) KING SUNNO, died 213, his son; (5) KING HILDERIC, died 253, his son; (6) KING PARTHERUS, died 272, his son; (7) KING CLOLIUS III, died 298, his son; (8) KING WALTER, died 306, his son; (9) KING DAGOBERT, died 317, his son; (10) GENEBALD I Duke of the East Franks, died 350, his son; (11) KING DAGOBERT, died 379, his son; (12) KING CLODIUS I, died 389, his son; (13) KING MARCOMIR, died 404, his son; (14) KING PHAROMOND, married Argotta, daughter of Genebald, their son; (15) KING CLODIO, married Basina de Thuringia, and died 455, their son; (16) SIGERMERUS I, married the daughter of Ferreolus Tomantius, his son; (17) FERREOLUS, married Deuteria, a Roman lady, their son; (18) AUSBERT, died 570, married Blitheldes, daughter of Clothaire I, King of France, and his wife Ingonde, and grand-daughter of CLOVIS THE GREAT, King of France, born 466, baptized at Rheims, and died 511, and his wife Clothilde, of Burgundy, "The girl of the French Vineyards."

It was she who led him to embrace Christianity, and mythically three thousand of his followers were baptized in a single day. When Clovis first listened to the story of Christ's Crucifixion, he was so moved that he cried, "If I had been there with my valiant Franks, I would have avenged Him." Ausbert and Blithildes were the parents of (19) ARNOUL, Bishop of Metz, died 601, married Oda de Savoy and had (20) ST. ARNOLPH, Bishop of Metz, died 641, married Lady Dodo and had, (21) ACHISEA, married Begga of Brabant, who died 698, their son; (22) PEPIN d'HERISTAL, Mayor of the Palace, died 714, who married Alpais.

PEPIN of HERISTAL made himself conspicuous. His home was near Spa in the woodland country around Liege. He made the office hereditary in his family. His heroic son, (23) CHARLES MARTEL, the Hammer, Mayor of the Palace, King of France, was still more famous, because, in the decisive Battle of Tours in 732, he utterly routed the Arabs, who had conquered Spain and the south of France. Charles Martel Married Rotrude and died in 741. His son, (24) PEPIN THE SHORT (or PEPIN le BREF), King of France, died in 768, leaving by his wife Bertha, of Laon, a son; (25) CHARLEMAGNE, Charles the Great, born 2 April 742, probably at Aix-La-Chapelle, the greatest figure of the Middle Ages, King of the Franks. Charlemagne and his younger brother, Carloman, succeeded to equal portions to one of the most powerful of European kingdoms, bounded by the Pyrenees, the Alps, the Mediterranean and the Ocean. Carloman, the younger brother, died soon after the death of their father, Pepin The Short, and with the consent of the great nobles, Charlemagne became King. Desiderius, the King of Lombardy, had made large encroachments upon the states of the Roman Pontiff, whose cause was taken up by Charlemagne. This led to feuds, which Bertha, his mother, endeavored to appease by arranging a marriage between her son and the daughter of the Lombard.

But the King Lord Charlemagne soon took a disgust to the wife thus imposed upon him, and repudiated her, that he might marry Hildegarde, born 757, died 30 April 782, the daughter of a noble family in Suabia. By his wife, Hildegarde, he had a son: (26) LOUIS I, the DEBONAIRE, who by his second wife, Judith, was the father of Gisela, ancestress of Hugh Capet, King of France and of JAMICIA, wife of RICHARD de CLARE, MAGNA CHARTA SURETY. Louis I, by his first wife Ermengarde, who died 818, daughter of Ingram, Count of Basbania, was father of (27) LOTHAIRE, Earl of Germany, who married Ermengarde of Alsace, and had (28) ERMENGARDE, who was the wife of Giselbert. Their son; (29) REGUIER I, Count of Hainault, died 916, who married Albreda, their son; (30) CISELBERT, Duke of Lorraine, married Gerlerga and died 930, their daughter; (31) ALBREDA of LORRAINE, wife of Renaud, Count de Roucy, who died 973, their daughter; (32) ERWENTRUDE ROUCY, married Alberic II, Count de Macon, who died 975, their daughter; (33) BEATRICE MACON, married Geoffrey I de Castenais, their son; (34) GEOFFREY II de CASTINAIS, married Ermengarde de Anjou, their son; (35) FULK IV, Count of Anjou, born 1043, died 1109, married Bertrade de Montfort (no. 67 above), their son (36) FULK V, Count d'Anjou, who, as elsewhere stated (above) was the father of GEOFFREY PLANTAGENET, who married MATILDA of ENGLAND, a great-great-great-grand daughter of RICHARD I, Duke of Normandy and his wife, Lady Cunnora. Matilda's descent from Richard I, Duke of Normandy is as follows: (1) RICHARD I, Duke of Normandy, his son; (2) RICHARD II, Duke of Normandy, died 1026, married Judith de Bretagne, their son; (3) ROBERT the MAGNIFICENT, also known as Robert the Devil, who, by Herleve Falaise, had WILLIAM THE CONQUEROR, father of King Henry I of England, who had Matilda, Wife of Geoffrey Plantagenet.

NOTE: WURTS' MAGNA CHARTA, pp. 158-168 inclusive, gives sixty nine Generations of lineal descent from No. 1, Edward the Great, (Aedd Mawr) to No. 69, Geoffrey Plantagenet. This also shows Geoffrey's descent from the FRANKISH KINGS, Nos. 1, to and including 35; also his descent from No. (6) (HELI) Beli the Great through LUD, through TUANTIUS, through CYNVELIN (CYMBELINE), through AVIRAGUS, through MERIC (MARIUS), through EURGEN, through GLADYS, wife of No. 39, (LLEUVER MAWR) LUCIUS THE GREAT. And page 168 of Wurt's Magna Charta shows that both Geoffrey Plantagenet and his wife, Matilda, or Maud, of England, were descendants of WILLIAM THE CONQUEROR, who, as above stated, was descended from CHARLEMAGNE.

Notes for Matilda of England:

Descent from CHARLEMAGNE to MATILDA, or Maud, of England, wife of GEOFFREY PLANTAGENET; (1) CHARLEMAGNE and wife, Hildegarde had a son; (2) PEPIN, born 776, died 8 July 810, before his father. He was crowned by the Pope in 781, King of Lombardy and Italy, married Bertha, daughter of William, Count of Toulouse, his son; (3) BERNHARD, King of Lombardy, succeeded his father about the year 812, he was deposed by his Uncle Louis, blinded and put to death. By his wife Cunegonde, he had a son; (4) PEPIN, who was deprived of the throne by his Uncle Louis, Emperor, called the Debonair, and received a part of Vermandois and the Seigneuries of St. Quentin and Peronne. His son; (5) PEPIN, Pepin de Senlis de Valois, Count Berengarius, of Bretagne, who was living in 893, the father of (6) LADY POPPA, (puppet or doll), who became the first wife of ROLLO the DANE, first Duke of Normandy. Their son; (7) WILLIAM LONGSWORD, was father of (8) RICHARD the FEARLESS, father of; (9) RICHARD II, "the Good," whose son; (10) ROBERT "THE DEVIL," sixth Duke of Normandy, who, by Herleve de Falaise, daughter of the Tanner, Fulbert de Falaise, had a son; (11) WILLIAM THE CONQUEROR, born at Falaise in 1027, father of HENRY I, KING of ENGLAND, WHO WAS THE LAST OF THE NORMAN KINGS. (Magna Charta 178, 182, 183). She was designated Henry's heir, and on his death (1135), Stephen seized the throne and Matilda invaded England (1139) inuagurating a period of inconclusive civil war. She and her second husband (Geoffrey) captured Normandy and in 1152 the Treaty of Wallingford recognised Henry as Stephen's heir. Burke says she was betrothed in her eighth year (1119) to Henry.

Child of Geoffrey Plantagenet and Matilda England is:
King Henry II Plantagenet, born March 25, 1133 in Le Mans; died
July 06, 1189 in Chinon Castle, Anjou.

Generation No. 2
King Henry II Plantagenet. He married (1) Eleanor of Aquitaine May 18,
1152 in Bordeaux, France. She died June 26, 1202. He met (2) Rosamond De
Clifford 1160. He met (3) Ida Abt. 1172.

Notes for King Henry II Plantagenet:
KING HENRY II of ENGLAND, son of Matilda, or Maud, of England and
her husband, Geoffrey Plantagenet, was born at Le Mans, 25 March 1133 and
died at Chinon, 6 July 1189. In 1152 he married Eleanor of Aquitaine, former
wife of Louis VII, of France, and daughter of William, Duke of Aquitaine.
She survived King Henry nearly three years, dying 26 June 1202. Both were
buried at Fontrevaud in Anjou. Their daughter Eleanor married Alphonse IX,
King of Castile; their eldest son William, died at the age of four years, their
second son, Henry, born 28 Feb. 1155, who on 15 July 1170, by command of
his father, was crowned King of England, but died before his father, 11 July
1183, their third son, Richard the Lion Hearted, reigned as King of England
from 1189 to 1199. He was the most prominent leader on the Third Crusade to
regain Jerusalem for the Christians from the Mohammedans. He had greater
military genius, but less statesmanship than his father.

His great power was in his physical and mental capacity as a soldier, and
in his strenuous and irrepressible courage. Richard was proud, cruel and
treacherous. He left the government of England in the hands of his Justiciars,
and was in his English Kingdom but twice in his reign of ten years; four
months at the time of his coronation, and two months, five years later. The
Third Crusade was a failure. Richard fell out with the French King, and
refused to marry his sister Alice, to whom he had been betrothed since early
childhood, but on 12 May 1191, he married Perengaria of Navarre. HE DIED
WITHOUT ISSUE. The fourth son of Henry II, Geoffrey, had a son Arthur,
who was murdered in 1203, leaving as successor to the throne of England:

Henry II (1154-1189) Born: 5th March 1133 at Le Mans, Maine. Died:
6th July 1189 at Chinon Castle, Anjou. Buried: Fontevrault Abbey, Anjou.
Parents: Geoffrey, Count of Anjou and the Empress Matilda. Siblings:
Geoffrey, Count of Nantes & William, Count of Poitou. Crowned: 19th
December 1154 at Westminster Abbey, Middlesex. Married: 18th May 1152 at
Bordeaux Cathedral, Gascony. Spouse: Eleanor, daughter of William X, Duke
of Aquitane & divorcee of Louis VII, King of France. Offspring: William,
Henry, Matilda, Richard, Geoffrey, Eleanor, Joan & John. Contemporaries:
Louis VII (King of France, 1137-1180), Thomas Beckett (Archbishop of
Canterbury), Pope Adrian IV, Frederick I (Frederick Barbarossa, Holy Roman
Emperor, 1152-1190).
Henry II, first of the Angevin kings, was one of the most effective of all
England's monarchs. He came to the throne amid the anarchy of Stephen's reign

and promptly collared his errant barons. He refined Norman government and created a capable, self-standing bureaucracy. His energy was equalled only by his ambition and intelligence. Henry survived wars, rebellion, and controversy to successfully rule one of the Middle Ages' most powerful kingdoms. Henry was raised in the French province of Anjou and first visited England in 1142 to defend his mother's claim to the disputed throne of Stephen. His continental possessions were already vast before his coronation: He acquired Normandy and Anjou upon the death of his father in September 1151, and his French holdings more than doubled with his marriage to Eleanor of Aquitane (ex-wife of King Louis VII of France). In accordance with the Treaty of Wallingford, a succession agreement signed by Stephen and Matilda in 1153, Henry was crowned in October 1154. The continental empire ruled by Henry and his sons included the French counties of Brittany, Maine, Poitou, Touraine, Gascony, Anjou, Aquitaine and Normandy. Henry was technically a feudal vassal of the king of France but, in reality, owned more territory and was more powerful than his French lord.

Although King John (Henry's son) lost most of the English holdings in France, English kings laid claim to the French throne until the fifteenth century. Henry also extended his territory in the British Isles in two significant ways. First, he retrieved Cumbria and Northumbria from Malcom IV of Scotland and settled the Anglo-Scottish border in the North. Secondly, although his success with Welsh campaigns was limited, Henry invaded Ireland and secured an English presence on the island. English and Norman barons in Stephen's reign manipulated feudal law to undermine royal authority; Henry instituted many reforms to weaken traditional feudal ties and strengthen his position. Unauthorized castles built during the previous reign were razed.

Monetary payments replaced military service as the primary duty of vassals. The Exchequer was revitalized to enforce accurate record keeping and tax collection. Incompetent sheriffs were replaced and the authority of royal courts was expanded. Henry empowered a new social class of government clerks that stabilized procedure – the government could operate effectively in the king's absence and would subsequently prove sufficiently tenacious to survive the reign of incompetent kings. Henry's reforms allowed the emergence of a body of common law to replace the disparate customs of feudal and county courts. Jury trials were initiated to end the old Germanic trials by ordeal or battle. Henry's systematic approach to law provided a common basis for development of royal institutions throughout the entire realm.

The process of strengthening the royal courts, however, yielded an unexpected controversy. The church courts instituted by William the Conqueror became a safe haven for criminals of varying degree and ability, for one in fifty of the English population qualified as clerics. Henry wished to transfer sentencing in such cases to the royal courts, as church courts merely demoted clerics to laymen. Thomas Beckett, Henry's close friend and chancellor since 1155, was named Archbishop of Canterbury in June 1162 but distanced himself from Henry and vehemently opposed the weakening of church courts. Beckett fled England in 1164, but through the intervention of Pope Adrian

IV (the lone English pope), returned in 1170. He greatly angered Henry by opposing the coronation of Prince Henry. Exasperated, Henry hastily and publicly conveyed his desire to be rid of the contentious Archbishop – four ambitious knights took the king at his word and murdered Beckett in his own cathedral on December 29, 1170. Henry endured a rather limited storm of protest over the incident and the controversy passed.

Henry's plans of dividing his myriad lands and titles evoked treachery from his sons. At the encouragement – and sometimes because of the treatment – of their mother, they rebelled against their father several times, often with Louis VII of France as their accomplice. The deaths of Henry the Young King in 1183 and Geoffrey in 1186 gave no respite from his children's rebellious nature; Richard, with the assistance of Philip II Augustus of France, attacked and defeated Henry on July 4, 1189 and forced him to accept a humiliating peace. Henry II died two days later, on July 6, 1189. A few quotes from historic manuscripts shed a unique light on Henry, Eleanor.

From Sir Winston Churchill Kt, 1675: "Henry II Plantagenet, the very first of that name and race, and the very greatest King that England ever knew, but withal the most unfortunate . . . his death being imputed to those only to whom himself had given life, his ungracious sons. . ."

From Sir Richard Baker, *A Chronicle of the Kings of England*:
Concerning endowments of mind, he was of a spirit in the highest degree generous . . . His custom was to be always in action; for which cause, if he had no real wars, he would have feigned . . . To his children he was both indulgent and hard; for out of indulgence he caused his son Henry to be crowned King in his own time; and out of hardness he caused his younger sons to rebel against him . . . He married Eleanor, daughter of William Duke of Guienne, late wife of Lewis the Seventh of France. Some say King Lewis carried her into the Holy Land, where she carried herself not very holily, but led a licentious life; and, which is the worst kind of licentiousness, in carnal familiarity with a Turk. "King Henry II Plantagenet, had many illegitimate children, one of which was William de Longespee.

KING JOHN, LACKLAND, the fifth son of Henry II and Eleanor of Aquitaine, born at Oxford, 24 Dec. 1166, died at Newark Castle, Notts, 19 Oct. 1216, married, first on 29 August 1189, Isabel, daughter of William, Earl of Gloucester; married, second, in 1200, Isabel, daughter of Aymer de Taillefer, the Swordsmith. She was the mother of all his children. John S. Wurts, in his *Magna Charta*, pages 6 to 17, inclusive. Page 6; "In case we have forgotten our English history, let us be reminded that King John was a horrid person, an arbitrary and mercenary ruler, who threw people into dungeons at the drop of a hat; married off wards of the crown, young widows and pretty girls, to foreign adventurers and then collected a nice percentage of the ward's fortunes from their husbands... he greatly increased the royal taxes and replenished his exchequer with the confiscated property of the clergy."

Shortly after he became King, he quarreled with the Pope, who deposed him and proclaimed him no longer King. John ignored the deposing, and made a gift to the Pope of all the realm, crown and revenue, by written indenture, dated Monday, 13 May 1213. John then received the crown back as the Pope's tenant and vassal, at a rental of a thousand marks for the whole kingdom, 700 for England and 300 for Ireland.

Under this condition the Barons of England were only yeoman, or free-holders, or copy-holders of King John, the free-holder of the Pope, and tiring of John's tyranny, they called a conference after King John had left the Abbey at Saint-Edmundsbury (where he had been asked to attend the conference, which had been called by Stephen Langston, Archbishop of Canterbury), at which meeting nothing was accomplished, the barons took a solemn oath on the high altar, that they would stand united until they could compel the King to confirm their liberties, or they would wage war against him to the death. They did wage war, "a holy crusade against John to recover the liberties their forefathers had enjoyed." Virtually powerless, and with nearly his whole Baronage and the majority of his subjects of all degrees in arms against him, he finally called his Barons to a conference. They said, "let the day be the 15th of June and the place Runnemede" (which is in sight of Windsor Castle, and was used as "the field of council").

In this way was brought about the GREATEST EVENT OF KING JOHN'S REIGN, the veritable wresting from him of MAGNA CARTA, granting rights to the people of his realm, "an expression in written words of the principles of human life," which had been either grossly neglected or altogether forgotten by the king. Section 61 of the Charter authorized the election of twenty five Surety Barons, who would see that the previsions of the Charter were carried into effect. Their names are not recorded in the Magna Carta, "but we learn them from Matthew Paris' *"Chronilca Majora.""*
These Barons were astonishingly inter-related. Among them were several instances of father and son, of father-in-law and son-in-law, of brothers and cousins. Twenty of the twenty-five were related in the degree of second cousin, or nearer. Of these twenty-five, only seventeen have descendants surviving to the present day. They had a common descent from Charlemagne. On the 15th day of June, 1215, more than two thousand knights and barons were encamped on the field of Runnemede to await the coming of King John and secure from him the rights of the people of England, although John had previously sworn by "God's teeth," his favorite oath, that he would never agree to such demands or any part of them. Runnemede was the "ancient meadow of council," and is within sight of Windsor Castle. For ages, this had been crown land and rented for pasturage. When it was proposed a few years ago (from the Crown Edition of *Magna Carta*, reprint 1945), to sell the field of Runnemede to the highest bidder, a great outcry arose. (The former Cara Rogers, now Lady Fairhaven, an American girl, a member of the "Magna Carta Dames," bought and presented to the British people the field of Runnemede as a memorial to her husband, to be kept for all time as a sacred, historic spot).

On 15 June 1215, before the day passed, the king affixed his seal to the original, but preliminary draft known as the "Articles of the Barons," which contained forty-nine articles, setting forth the principles of the Charter. The exact terms of the Charter were decided upon during the four days that followed. On the 19th of June 1215, the great seal was affixed, presumably to twenty-five duplicate copies, perhaps one for each of the twenty-five Surety Barons, who were to see that King John kept his promises. Neither the king, the barons, nor the knights could read or write, except a few, but a scholar, who was the Secretary of the Baron of Kendal, had accompanied him to Runnemede.

DESCENT OF ISAREL DE TAILLEFUR, second wife of KING JOHN OF ENGLAND from CHARLEMAGNE:

More About King John, Lackland:
Burial: Worcester, Cathedral
Notes for Isabell: She was the mother of all his children. John S. Wurts, in his Magna Charta, pages 6 to 17, inclusive.
More About Isabell:
Burial: Fontevraud Abbey
Child of King John and Isabell is:

King Henry III, born October 01, 1207 in Winchester, England; died November 16, 1272 in Westminster, Palace, London, England.
William De Longespee was born 1173 in England, and died March 07, 1225/26 in Salisbury, Wilts, England. He married Ela Fitzpatrick. She was born 1191 in Amesbury, Wiltshire, England, and died August 24, 1261 in Lacock, Wiltshire, England.

Notes for William De Longespee: According to Gary Boyd Roberts' *Royal Descents of 500 Immigrants...*, pp. 345-347, the mother of William LONGESPEE (natural son of King Henry II of England) was Ida, who married Roger BIGOD, 2nd Earl of Norfolk. One source of this is evidently a charter of William LONGSWORD published in the *Cartulary of Bradenstoke Priory*, ed. Vera C. M. Longdon, in which Countess Ida is explicitly named as his mother. The fact that William named a daughter Ida does lend credence to this, of course.

Child of William Longespee and Ela Fitzpatrick is:
Stephen De Longespee, born Abt. 1216 in Sutton, Co.
Northampton, England; died 1260 in Sutton, Co. Northampton, England.
Generation No. 4
King Henry III was born October 01, 1207 in Winchester, England, and died November 16, 1272 in Westminster, Palace, London, England. He married Queen Eleanor of Provence January 04, 1235/36 in England. She was born Abt. 1217 in Aix-en-Provence, and died June 24, 1291 in Amesbury, Wiltshire.

Notes for King Henry III:
Brother of King Richard. King of England. He was crowned king 28 Oct.

1216, when only nine years of age. On 14 January 1236, he married Eleanor of Provence. A Plantagenet King; House of Anjou.

Notes for Queen Eleanor of Provence:
Queen Eleanor took the veil at Amesbury in Wiltshire, and died there 24 June 1291. Their elder sons, John and Henry, died young.

QUEEN ELEANOR'S GENEALOGY (1) CLOVIS, King of the Franks, married Clothilde, his son; (2) Clothaire I, born 497, died 561, married Ingolde, their son; (3) Chilperice I, born 523, died 584, married Fredegonde, born 543, died 598, his son; (4) Clothaire II, born 584, died 628, married Bertrude, who died 618, his son; (5) Claribert II, born 608, died 631, married Gisela, daughter of Arnoud, of Gascony, his son; (6) Boggis, Duke of Aquitaine, died 688, married Oda, his son; (7) Eudes, Duke of Aquitaine, married Valtrude, daughter of Valtrude and her husband, Walchigise, Count of Verdon, son of St. Arnolph, Bishop of Metz and his wife, Dodo, his son; (8) Hunold, Duke of Aquitaine, died 774, his son; (9) Waifir, Duke of Aquitaine, died 768, married his cousin, Adele, daughter of Loup I, Duke of Gascony, his son; (10) Loup II, Duke of Gascony, died 778, his son; (11) Adelrico, Duke of Gascony, died 812, his son; (12) Ximeno, Duke of Gascony, died 816, married Munia, his son; (13) Inigo Arista, first King of Navarre married Iniga Ximena, his son; (14) Careia II, of Navarre, married Urracca of Gascony, daughter of a cousin, Sancho II, his son; (15) Sancho I, became King of Navarre in 905, married his cousin Toda, daughter of Aznzr Galindez, Count of Aragon, his son; (16) Garcia III, became king in 921, died 970, married Teresa Iniquez of Aragon, and had (17) Sancho II Abarca, died 994.

He married Urracca Clara, daughter of Fortuna Ximenez, of Navarre, his second cousin, his son; (18) Garcia V, King of Navarre, died 999, married Ximena, daughter of Consslo, Count of Asturias and his wife, Teresa. They were the parents of the earlier of the two kings, both called Sancho III, this one; (19) Sancho III King of Navarre from 1000 to 1035, married Munia, daughter of Sancho of Castile, and thus united the two important Houses of Castile and Navarre, to which that of Aragon was later added, his son; (20) Ramirez I, founded the kingdom of Aragon, was killed in battle by the Moors, 8 May 1063. By his wife Gisberge, he had; (21) Sancho-Ramirez, died 4 June 1094, King of Aragon, married, first, Felice, who died 14 April 1086, daughter of Hildouin, Count of Rouci, his son; (22) Ramirez II, King of Aragon, married Agnes, daughter of William IX, Duke of Aquitaine.

His daughter; (23) Petronella was only two years old when her father abdicated the throne in her favor. He had arranged that Raymund Berenger V, Count of Barcelona, should govern the realm as Prince of Aragon, and that he should, at the proper time, marry Petronella. This was accomplished in accordance with his wish. Petronella died 18 October 1172, their son; (24) Alphonse II, King of Aragon, born 1151, died 25 April 1196, married his cousin Sanchia, who was descended as follows; KING SANCHO III (Navarre) and his wife Munia, as stated above, were the parents of (1) Ferdinand I, King of Castile from 1033 to 1065, died in battle 27 Dec. 1065. In 1035, he married Sanchia, daughter of Alphonso V, King of Leon, and thus united the latter kingdom to his own; (2) Alphonso VI, King of Castile and Leon, married a daughter of Robert, Duke of Burgundy, his daughter; (3) Urracca, married first, Raimond of Burgundy, who died in 1108, after which, Urracca married Alphonso I, King of Aragon. Her only child, son of Raimond, was; (4) Alphonso-Raimond VII, born 1103, died 1157. By his first wife, Berenguela, he had two sons, Sancho III (or Alphonso), and Ferdinand II, King of Leon, died 1188. By his second wife, Richilda of Poland, he had; (5) Sanchia, wife of Alphonso II, King of Aragon, as stated above. Her son; (6) Alphonso II, King of Provence, who reigned from 1196 to 1209, his son; (7)

Raimond-Berenger IV, King of Provence, married Beatrice (Beatrix), daughter of Thomas, Count of Savoy, his daughter; (8) ELEANOR OF PROVENCE, became the wife of HENRY III KING OF ENGLAND as stated above.

Child of King Henry and Queen Eleanor of Province is:
King Edward I, born June 17, 1239 in Westminster, Palace, London, England; died July 07, 1307 near Carlisle, England. He married Princess Eleanor of Castile in Las Huelgas, daughter of King Ferdinand III. She was born abt. 1244 in Castile, and died November 24, 1290 in Herdeby, Near Grantham, Lincolnshire.

Notes for King Edward I:
EDWARD I, KING OF ENGLAND, (called Longshanks), Earl of Chester, born at Westminster 17 June 1239, married Eleanor of Castile. In 1272 he went on a Crusade as far as Acre, where his daughter JOAN (see later) was born, and although he inherited the crown that year, he did not return to England until 1274, being crowned on August 19th. He was eminent as a ruler and as a legislator, and succeeded in enacting many new laws. He determined to authorize no new legislation without the counsel and acquiescence of those who were most affected by it. Not until late in his reign did he call a whole Parliament together. Instead he called the Barons together in any matter that affected the Barons, and the representatives of the townsmen together in any matter that affected the townsmen, and so with other classes. Edward's first wife, ELEANOR OF CASTILE, whom he married in 1254, died 20 Nov. 1290. Reign: 1272-1307; Of the Plantagenets, House of Anjou. In 1270 Edward left England to join the Seventh Crusade. The first years of Edward's reign were a period of the consolidation of his power.
He suppressed corruption in the administration of justice, restricted the jurisdiction of the ecclesiastical courts to church affairs, and eliminated the papacy's overlordship over England. In 1290 Edward expelled all Jews from England. In 1296, after invading and conquering Scotland, he declared himself king of that realm. The conquest of Scotland became the ruling passion of his life. He was, however, compelled by the nobles, clergy and commons to desist in his attempts to raise by arbitrary taxes the funds he needed for campaigns. In 1307 Edward set out for the third time (at age 68) to subdue the Scots, but he died en route near Carlisle on 7 Jul 1307.

Notes for Princess Eleanor of Castile:
Of Castile and Leon Spain. Eleanor was only about ten years old when married to the 15-year-old Edward of Westminster at Las Huelgas in 1254. Such child marriages were commonplace in Europe in the Middle Ages and the brides were usually consigned to their husbands' families to complete their education. The marriages were not consummated until the bride reached a suitable age (usually 14 or 15) and in Eleanor's case it seems to have been 18 or 19.

More About Princess Eleanor of Castile:
Burial: Westminster, Abbey, London, England
Children of King Edward and Princess Eleanor of Castile are:
Edward II, born April 25, 1284 in Caernarvon, Castle, Wales; died September 21, 1327 in Berkeley Castle, Gloucestershire.
Princess Joan Plantagenet, born 1272; died 1305.

Generation No. 6
Edward II was born April 25, 1284 in Caernarvon, Castle, Wales, and died September 21, 1327 in Berkeley Castle, Gloucestershire. He married Isabella January 28, 1307/08 in Boulogne. She was born 1292 in Paris, and died August 22, 1358 in Castle Rising, Norfolk, England.
Notes for Edward II:
Edward was the first heir apparent in English history to be proclaimed Prince of Wales. He was a Plantagenet King of England (the House of Anjou) whose incompetence and distaste for government finally led to his deposition and murder. In January 1327, Parliament forced Edward to resign and proclaimed the Prince of Wales king, as Edward III. On September 21 of that year Edward II was murdered by his captors at Berkeley Castle, Gloucestershire.

More About Edward II:
Burial: Gloucester, Cathedral
More About Isabella:
Burial: Grey Friars Church, London, England
Child of Edward and Isabella is:
Edward III, born November 13, 1312 in Windsor Castle, Berkshire, England; died June 21, 1377 in Sheen Palace.
He married Philippa January 28, 1327/28 in York Minster. She was born June 24, 1311 in Valenciennes, and died August 14, 1369 in Windsor Castle, Windsor, Berkshire, England.

More About Edward III:
Burial: Westminster, Abbey, London, England
More About Philippa:
Burial: Westminster, Abbey, London, England
Child of Edward and Philippa is:
John, born March 1339/40 in Ghent; died February 03, 1398/99 in Leicester Castle.

Notes for Princess Joan Plantagenet:

PRINCESS JOAN OF ACRE, born in 1272, when her father, King Edward I went on a crusade as far as Acre, where she was born. In 1290, Joan married, as his second wife, Earl Gilbert de Clare, The "Red Earl," Crusader, Knight, ninth Earl of Clare, Earl of Hertford and Gloucester, born 2 September 1243, died 7 December 1295. The "Red Earl" was descended from four of the twenty-five Magna Carta Surety Barons chosen by the Barons and Knights of England as Sureties to enforce the provisions laid down in the "Articles of the Barons," (the forerunner of Magna Carta,) which contained the first constitutional rights ever granted the subjects of a monarch. (No one signed Magna Carta, as neither King John nor the Barons could write, and at common law, sealing was sufficient to authenticate any formal document).

Notes for Gilbert de Clare:

9th Earl of Clare, 7th Earl of Hertford, and 3rd Earl of Gloucester. He was of Royal descent. The "Red Earl."

Child of Princess Joan Plantagenet and Gilbert de Clare is:

Lady Margaret11 de Clare, born 1292; died 1342.

19. Lady Margaret11 de Clare (Princess Joan10 Plantagenet, King9 Edward I, King8 Henry III, King7 John, Lackland, King Henry II6 Plantagenet, Geoffrey5, Fulk4 V, Fulk3 IV, Geoffrey II de2 Castinais, Geoffrey I de1) was born 1292, and died 1342. She married Baron d'Audley.

Notes for Lady Margaret de Clare:

Married, first, Piers de Caveston, who was executed, married second, Lord Hugh de Audley, Junior, Eight Earl of Gloucester in 1336, Ambassador to France in 1341, Sheriff of Rutland; died on 10 November 1347. By Lady Margaret's second husband, Hugh de Audley, she had a daughter.

Notes for Baron d'Audley:

Who was in 1337, Earl of Gloucester.

Child of Lady de Clare and Baron Audley is:

Lady Margaret d'Audley.

20. Maud De La Zouche was born 1284 in Ashley, England. She married Sir Robert De Holland. He was born abt. 1280 in Upholland, Lancaster, England.

Child of Maud Zouche and Sir De Holland is:

Sir Robert12 Holland, born Abt. 1312 in Lancaster, England.

Generation No. 8

21. John was born March 1339/40 in Ghent, and died February 03, 1398/99 in Leicester Castle. He married Katherine Swynford January 13, 1395/96 in Lincoln. She was born 1350, and died May 10, 1403 in Lincoln.

Notes for John:

Duke John of Gaunt

His eldest surviving son by his first marriage later became King Henry IV.

Notes for Katherine Swynford:

Widow of Sir Hugh Swynford and dau. of Sir Payn (Payne) Roet. She was Hugh Swynford's third wife. Catherine (or Katherine) was also the sister-in-law of Geoffrey Chaucer. All her issue legitimated by charter of Richard II, 1397.

Child of John of Gaunt and Katherine Swynford is:

John 13, born 1410.

© David Womack, with special thanks.

Descent to the Veres of Scotland and Eire

...John and Katherine's son John had a daughter – Lady Joan Beaufort – who was the wife of King James I of Scotland. Their issue King James II married Lady Mary, the daughter of the Duke de Geldres. They had a son, King James III and a daughter, Princess Mary, who married Thomas, Lord Boyd. Their daughter – Lady Mary – married James 1st Lord Hamilton, whose family were the heirs presumptive to the throne of Scotland. Their daughter – Lady Euphemia – married the prince James, 7th Baron Blackwood, de jure the Laird and Clan Chief of the Royal House of Vere of Great Britain.

James and Euphemia had a son – William Vere of Stonebyers – and a daughter Margaret. From Sir William Vere by Elizabeth Hamilton – a son, Lord Thomas of Kirkton who, by the Witch – Lady Jane Somerville – had Major Thomas Weir of Edinburgh: Sorcerer, King of the Witches of the Lallan and Elven Prince Consort to the Queen of Faery or Elphame – or as some say – "The Queen of Hell." The Somerville Badge was the Fiery Dragon surmounting the Pentacle.

Major Weir served with his Irish cousins as a Captain Lieutenant in Sir John Hume's Enniskillen regiment in Ulster in 1640 and by family tradition he founded the Tyrone Branch of the family.

From Major Weir – who was burnt at the stake in Leith in 1670 – a son Thomas, husband of Mary Robison, whose issue decamped to Ireland during the witch craze, from whom John of Kildress whose son Andrew had a daughter – Margaret Weir of Vere of Kildress – who by Archibald Thompson had a son, Archibald Weir of Vere. Archibald married Rachael Stewart and had issue.

The eldest son Robert Weir of Vere married Sarah Granann (Graham) and had a son John who moved back to Scotland and married Mary Logan of Ardwell, Logan Manor in Galloway. Mary bore a son, Thomas Weir of Vere, who married Anne Grant Macdonnell and had a son, James Weir of Vere, who wed a Vere-Collison family cousin, Natalie Hopgood, and had their eldest son Nicholas de Vere.

© The Imperial and Royal Dragon Court.

The Sacred, Nordic, Fairy Descent of the Dukes of Hamilton to the Imperial and Royal House of Vere

King Ingiald "The Wicked," 650 AD, last of the Frey-born (elven-born of the God Frey) Yngling Pagan Sacral "Peace Kings" of Uppsala in Sweden (where their great burial mounds can be seen). As Yngvi-Freyr Frey was the Lord of the Light Elves and as can be seen in the prefix "Yng," the Yngling Peace Kings were of Elven descent. These sacred God-Kings were associated with the human sacrifice of victims from within their own dynastic family and they descended from ritual incarnations of the male manifestation of the ancient Goddess-Spirit Nerthus – Mother Earth – whose emblem was the Moon-Crescent-Shaped Galley. This lineage also includes a second descent from the God Odin in the House of Vere; via King Ragnar.

The God-King Ingiald "The Wicked" 650 AD
|

King Olaf "Tree Hewer" 710 AD
King of Vermaland in Norway
Sacrificed to Woden by the People
|

King Halfdan "White Leg" 730 AD
King of the Upplanders in Norway
Conquered Raumarike and founded
the Pagan Temple at Skiringssal
|

King Eystein of Raumarike
|

King Halfdan of Vestfold
|

King Godfrey "The Proud" of Vestfold
King of Raumarike, Vestmarar. Killed 810 AD
|

King Olaf "Geirstada-Alf " (Elf or Fairy)
King of Vestfold and Ofse
|

King Ranald "Higher than the Hills"
(expelled to Orkney by his half brother Halfdan)
in whose honour Thiodolf wrote "Ynglingatal,"
Ranald's family history
|

King Godfrey, raided Ireland in 854, died 873
|

King Ivarr
King of Dublin
Sacked Dumbarton 870
|

King Guthorm d. 890 AD

His mother was daughter of the
Odin-Born Skioldung sacral
Danish King Ragnar, and sister of
Sigurd "Dragon Eye" King of Seeland
|
King Ranald
King of Dublin, Waterford and York d. 921 AD
|
King Ivarr d. 950 AD
|
King Ivarr
King of Waterford and Dublin d. 1000
|
King Ranald d. 995 AD
|
King Ranald
King of Waterford 1022-1031
Killed in Dublin in 1035
|
King Echmarcach
King of Dublin
Defeated in Man 1061
Died in Rome 1065
|
King Solmund, married into
the Sacred Kindred of St. Columba
|
King Gilladamnan of the Celtic Church
of Scotland. Married into the Royal House
of Argyll which descends from an alliance
with the Royal House of Lorn
|
King Gillebride
Claimant of Argyll
|
King Somerled
Regulus of Argyll
King of the South
Isles from 1156.
Killed 1164
|
Angus Lord of Bute and Arran
Killed 1210
|
Lord Seumas killed 1210
|
Lady Jean g.dau of Angus
Lord of Bute and Arran,
descent from Somerled,
Lord of the Isles
= Alexander, Steward and
Co-Regent of Scotland 1255
|
Sir James Stewart, Co–Regent
and 5th High Steward of Scotland
d. 1309
= Lady Jill de Bourg dau. of
Lord Walter de Bourg
1st Earl of Ulster

Sir Walter Stewart 6th
High Steward of Scotland
= Princess Marjorie Bruce
dau. Of King Robert I Bruce
Grand Master of the Knights
Templars in Scotland
|
King Robert II
= Lady Elizabeth Muir of Rowallen
|
King Robert III
= Lady Annabelle Drummond of Stobhall
|
King James I
= Princess Joan Beaufort
Plantagenet of Somerset
(Descent from King
Edward III Plantagenet and the
Imperial and Royal House of Vere)
|
King James II
= Mary, dau. of Arnold Duc de Gueldres
|
Princess Mary
= Lord Thomas Boyd
|
Lady Mary Boyd
= James 1st Lord Hamilton
great grandson of
Princess Aenor de Chatellerault
and Guillaume X le Toulousain
Duc de Guyenne, Comte de Poitiers
|
Lady Euphemia Hamilton
(descent from the High Elves of Ireland,
Princess Melusine and the Scots Kings)
= Lord James Weir of Vere,
Baron Blackwood d. 1595
|
Sir William Vere of Stanebyres Castle
= Elizabeth Hamilton, his cousin.
(descent from the High Elves of Ireland,
Princess Melusine and the Scots Kings)
|
Lord Thomas Weir of Vere, Baron Kirkton
= Lady Jane Somerville, the hereditary Witch
of the Dragon House of the Earls Somerville
|
Major Thomas Weir of Vere of Edinburgh,
The hereditary Witch King of Mid-Lothian
= Margaret Bourdon
|
Thomas Weir of Vere
Baron Kirkton of Mid-Lothian,
Hereditary Witch King in Ireland
= Mary Robison of Cookstown Ulster
|
John Weir of Vere

Andrew Weir of Vere	Confer
Margaret Weir of Vere of Kildress	Fer (Vere)
Archibald Weir of Vere of Kildress = Rachel Stewart of Desertcreat	Cursalen Clemens
Robert Weir of Vere of Kildress	Quintinius
John Weir of Vere of Ardwell, Logan Manor = Mary Logan dau. of Thomas Logan of Ardwell, Logan Manor, Galloway	Cynloyp Ceretic: Guletic of Allt Clud
Thomas Logan Weir of Vere of Carlisle = Anne Grant Macdonnell of Inverness (Descent from the Grant Earls of Seafield)	Cinuit Dyfnwal Hen of Strathclyde
James Weir of Vere of Lewes = Natalie Hopgood (descent from the Collisons of Norfolk and the Imperial and Royal House of Vere)	Ingenach = Brychan II Lluan = Gabran King of Scots
HI & RH Prince Nicholas de Vere *de jure* Laird and Baron of Kirkton	King Aeden Mac Gabran The Uther Pendragon

Gwyr Llew = Ygraine of Avalon = Aeden Mac Gabran

Vere Grail Descent from Joseph of Arimathea, the Arch Druid Bran the Blessed and the Elven Pendragon Dynasty of King Arthur

From Aeden Mac Gabran – Prince Arthur Pendragon
From Gwyr Llew – Princess Morgana the Fairy

(Here follows the Pendragon descent of the House of Vere from King Arthur and the House of the High Elves of Avalon extracted from the Promptuary Archive of the Urquhart House of Cromartie – issued by the Middle Temple of the Knights Templars in 1652. The Grand Mastership of the Degree of The Knights Templar of Scotland within the Imperial and Royal Dragon Court is presently held heritably by Prince Nicholas de Vere.)

Joseph of Arimathea
=Anna

Anna of Arimathea AD 50
= Arch Druid Bran the Blessed
Bran of the Cauldron (Grail)
St. Brandon of Eire
His head is buried on Tower
Hill in the Tower of London

Penarden
=Marius

Coel I

Lucius
= Gladys

Gladys
= Cadwan Prince of Cumbria

Coel II of Camulod

Cunedd

King Arthur Pendragon
= Princess Morgana the Fairy

Prince Mordred Pendragon
Archpriest of the Celtic Church
= Pictish Dragon Princess

Princess Tortolina Pendragon
= Nicharcos
Pictish Archpriest

Lord Marsidalio
= Lady Repulita

Lord Hedomenos
= Lady Urbana

Lord Agenor

= Lady Lampusa
|
Lord Diaprepon
= Lady Vistosa
|
Lord Stragayo
= Lady Hermosina dau. of Lord Natasil of Athole
|
Lord Zeron
= Lady Bramata
|
Lord Polyteles
= Lady Zaglopis
|
Lord Vocompos of Cromartie
= Lady Androlema of Douglas
|
Lord Carolo
= Lady Trastevole dau. of Lord Uilleam
|
Lord Endymion
= Lady Suaviloqua
|
Lord Sebastion
= Lady Francolina
|
Lord Lawrence
= Lady Mathilda
|
Lord Olipher
= Lady Allegra
|
Lord Quintin
= Lady Winnifred
|
Lord Goodwin
= Lady Dorothy
|
Lord Frederick
= Lady Lauretta dau. of Patrick Earl of March
|
Lady Matilda
= Lord William Comyn, grandson of Robert
Earl of Northumberland
|
Lord Richard Comyn
= Lady Hextilda dau. of Hutred of Tynedal
|
Lord William Comyn, Great Justiciar of Scotland
= Lady Marjorie Countess of Buchan
|
Lady Elizabeth Comyn
= Lord William 9th Earl of Mar
|
Lord Donald 10th Earl of Mar
= Princess Helen dau. of Prince
Llewellyn of North Wales
|
Lady Isabel Mar

= King Robert I the Bruce
Grand Master of the Knights
Templars in Scotland
|
Marjorie Bruce
= Lord Walter Stewart
6th High Steward of Scotland
|
King Robert II
= Lady Elizabeth Muir of Rowallen
|
King Robert III
= Lady Annabelle Drummond of Stobhall
|
King James I
= Princess Joan Beaufort of Somerset
(Descent from King Edward III)
|
King James II
= Mary, dau. of Arnold Duc de Gueldres
|
Princess Mary
= Lord Thomas Boyd
|
Lady Mary Boyd
James 1st Lord Hamilton
great grandson of
Princess Aenor de Chatellerault
and Guillaume X le Toulousain
Duc de Guyenne, Comte de Poitiers
|
Lady Euphemia Hamilton
(descent from the High Elves of Ireland,
Princess Melusine and the Scots Kings)
= Lord James Weir of Vere,
Baron Blackwood d. 1595
|
Sir William Vere of Stanebyres Castle
= Elizabeth Hamilton, his cousin.
(descent from the High Elves of Ireland,
Princess Melusine and the Scots Kings)
|
Lord Thomas Weir of Vere, Baron Kirkton
= Lady Jane Somerville, the hereditary Witch
of the Dragon House of the Earls Somerville
|
Major Thomas Weir of Vere of Edinburgh,
The hereditary Witch King of Mid-Lothian
= Margaret Bourdon
|
Thomas Weir of Vere
Baron Kirkton of Mid-Lothian,
Hereditary Witch King in Ireland
= Mary Robison of Cookstown Ulster
|
John Weir of Vere
|
Andrew Weir of Vere
|

Margaret Weir of Vere of Kildress
|
Archibald Weir of Vere of Kildress
= Rachel Stewart of Desertcreat
|
Robert Weir of Vere of Kildress
|
John Weir of Vere of Ardwell, Logan Manor
= Mary Logan dau. of Thomas Logan of
Ardwell, Logan Manor, Galloway
|
Thomas Logan Weir of Vere of Carlisle
= Anne Grant Macdonnell of Inverness
|
James Weir of Vere of Lewes
= Natalie Hopgood (descent from
the Collisons of Norfolk and the
Imperial and Royal House of Vere)
|
HI & RH Prince Nicholas de Vere

Vere Descent from King Heinrich of Germany

King Heinrich of Germany
(Henry the Fowler) 900 AD
|
Princess Gerberga
=King Louis IV of France
936-954
|
Charles Duke of Lower Lorraine 991
|
Lady Gerberga
= Lambert de Louvain
|
Henry of Brussels
|
Maud de Louvain
= Eustace I de Vere d. 1049
Descent from Amelius ("Adolph") de Vere
Comte de Guisnes
|
Eustace II de Vere
= Saint Ida of Ardennes
|
Princess Ida de Vere
= Baudouin de Bourg
Comte de Rethul
|
Prince Hugues I
Comte de Rethul
= Melisende (Melusine II)
dau. Of Bouchard Comte de Corbeil and
Lady Adelaide de Crecy
|
Badouin II de Bourg

King of Jerusalem 1118–1131
= Princess Morfia of Armenia
|
Princess Melisende of Jerusalem (Melusine III)
= Fulke V Plantagenet Count of Anjou
|
Count Geoffrey Plantagenet
= Princess Mathilda, la Imperatrice
daughter of King Henry I and Princess
Mathilda of Scotland, daughter of
King Malcolm III
|
King Henry II Plantagenet
= Countess Eleanor of Aquitaine
|
King John "Lackland" Plantagenet
= Lady Isabella of Angouleme
|
King Henry III Plantagenet
= Lady Eleanor dau. of Count
Raymond Berenguer IV of Provence
and Princess Beatrix of Savoy
|
King Edward I Plantagenet
= Princess Eleanor of Castile
|
King Edward II Plantagenet
= Princess Isabella of France
|
King Edward III Plantagenet
1327-1377
= Princess Phillipa of Hainault
|
Prince John of Gaunt Plantagenet
= Lady Katharine Swynford
|
Prince John Plantagenet
|
Princess Joan Beaufort Plantagenet
= King James I of Scots
|
King James II
= Mary, dau. of Arnold Duc de Gueldres
|
Princess Mary
= Lord Thomas Boyd
|
Lady Mary Boyd
James 1st Lord Hamilton
great grandson of
Princess Aenor de Chatellerault
and Guillaume X le Toulousain
Duc de Guyenne, Comte de Poitiers
|
Lady Euphemia Hamilton
(descent from the High Elves of Ireland,
Princess Melusine and the Scots Kings)
= Lord James Weir of Vere,
Baron Blackwood d. 1595

|
Sir William Vere of Stanebyres Castle
= Elizabeth Hamilton, his cousin.
(descent from the High Elves of Ireland,
Princess Melusine and the Scots Kings)
|
Lord Thomas Weir of Vere, Baron Kirkton
= Lady Jane Somerville, the hereditary Witch
of the Dragon House of the Earls Somerville
|
Major Thomas Weir of Vere of Edinburgh,
The Witch King of Mid-Lothian
= Margaret Bourdon
|
Thomas Weir of Vere
Baron Kirkton of Mid-Lothian,
Hereditary Witch King in Ireland
= Mary Robison of Cookstown Ulster
|
John Weir of Vere
|
Andrew Weir of Vere
|
Margaret Weir of Vere of Kildress
|
Archibald Weir of Vere of Kildress
= Rachel Stewart of Desertcreat
|
Robert Weir of Vere of Kildress
|
John Weir of Vere of Ardwell, Logan Manor
= Mary Logan dau. of Thomas Logan of
Ardwell, Logan Manor, Galloway
|
Thomas Logan Weir of Vere of Carlisle
= Anne Grant Macdonnell of Inverness
|
James Weir of Vere of Lewes
= Natalie Hopgood (descent from
the Collisons of Norfolk and the
Imperial and Royal House of Vere)
|
HI & RH Prince Nicholas de Vere

Vere Descent from King Nascien II of the Royal Messianic, Judaic, Septimanian Midi of Southern France

- Et In Arcadia Ego -

King Nascien II
descent from the Royal House of
Troy and the Sicambrian Franks,
Sires of the Merovingian Kings
|
Prince Galains
|

Prince Jonaans
|
Prince Lancelot
Lover of Queen
Gwenhwyfar of Camelot
|
Prince Bors
= The Dragon Princess Viviane
II d'Avalon del Acques.
descent from the Elven Archdruid
Merlin Taliesin (descent from the Fairy
Queen Mabh of Ireland) and the High
Elves of Avalon
|
Prince Bors of Camelot
|
Prince Lionel
|
Prince Alain
|
Froamidus Count of Brittany
762
|
Frodaldus Count of Brittany
795
|
Count Frotmund
d. 850
|
Count Flotharius
|
Count Adelrad
|
Count Frotbald
923
|
Count Alirad
|
Count Frotmund
985
|
Count Fretaldus
1008
|
Count Frotmundus Vetules
1052
|
Count Fratmaldus the
Seneschal
|
Count Alan, Seneschal of
Dol and Dinan
Dapifer of Dol, Brittany
1045
|
Count Alan, Hereditary
Steward of Dol
b. 1050 d. 1097
|

Countess Emma
= Lord Walter, Thane of
Lochaber
|
Lord Alan of Lochaber
b. 1088 d. 1153
= Lady Adelina of Oswestry
|
Lord Walter FitzAlan
1st High Steward of Scotland
= Lady Eschyne de Molle
|
Lord Alan FitzWalter
2nd High Steward of Scotland
d.1204
= Lady Eve of Crawford
|
Lord Walter Stewart
of Dundonald
3rd High Steward of Scotland
= Lady Beatrix, dau of Gilchrist
Earl of Angus
|
Lord Alexander Stewart
4th High Steward of Scotland
d. 1283
= Lady Jean g.dau of Angus
Lord of Bute and Arran,
(descent from Somerled,
Lord of the Isles)
|
Sir James Stewart, Co–Regent
and 5th High Steward of Scotland
d. 1309
= Lady Jill de Bourg dau. of
Lord Walter de Bourg
1st Earl of Ulster
|
Sir Walter Stewart 6th
High Steward of Scotland
= Princess Marjorie Bruce
dau. Of King Robert I Bruce
Grand Master of the Knights
Templars in Scotland
|
King Robert II
= Lady Elizabeth Muir of Rowallen
|
King Robert III
= Lady Annabelle Drummond of Stobhall
|
King James I
= Princess Joan Beaufort Plantagenet
of Somerset (Descent from King
Edward III Plantagenet)
|
King James II
= Lady Mary, dau. of
Arnold Duc de Gueldres

Princess Mary
= Lord Thomas Boyd
|
Lady Mary Boyd
James 1st Lord Hamilton
great grandson of
Princess Aenor de Chatellerault
and Guillaume X le Toulousain
Duc de Guyenne, Comte de Poitiers
|
Lady Euphemia Hamilton
(descent from the High Elves of Ireland,
Princess Melusine and the Scots Kings)
= Lord James Weir of Vere,
Baron Blackwood d. 1595
|
Sir William Vere of Stanebyres Castle
= Elizabeth Hamilton, his cousin.
(descent from the High Elves of Ireland,
Princess Melusine and the Scots Kings)
|
Lord Thomas Weir of Vere, Baron Kirkton
= Lady Jane Somerville, the hereditary Witch
of the Dragon House of the Earls Somerville
|
Major Thomas Weir of Vere of Edinburgh,
The hereditary Witch King of Mid-Lothian
= Margaret Bourdon
|
Thomas Weir of Vere
Baron Kirkton of Mid-Lothian,
Hereditary Witch King in Ireland
= Mary Robison of Cookstown Ulster
|
John Weir of Vere
|
Andrew Weir of Vere
|
Margaret Weir of Vere of Kildress
|
Archibald Weir of Vere of Kildress
= Rachel Stewart of Desertcreat
|
Robert Weir of Vere of Kildress
|
John Weir of Vere of Ardwell, Logan Manor
= Mary Logan dau. of Thomas Logan of
Ardwell, Logan Manor, Galloway
|
Thomas Logan Weir of Vere of Carlisle
= Anne Grant Macdonnell of Inverness
|
James Weir of Vere of Lewes
= Natalie Hopgood (descent from
the Collisons of Norfolk and the
Imperial and Royal House of Vere)
|
HI & RH Prince Nicholas de Vere

Vere Descent from King Vere
(400 BC)
via Prince Milo of Angiers

King Vere was the Priest King and Archdruid of the Bruidhainn, or Cruithainn as the Romans called them. These were the sons of the displaced High Elves of Ireland – The Tuadha de Danaan – who became the Scythian (Sidhe) Picts of the Calle Daouine (Caledonia) in what is now Scotland.

In Eire the Tuadha de Danaan, descending from Princess Scota of Egypt, remain remembered there as the Fairy Daouine Sidhe (Daouine = People, and Sidhe = Scythians). Whilst the Pict-Sidhes (Pict = Painted, and Sidhe = Scythians as above) of Albany or Scotland became familiar to us here in Britain as the Pixies or Fairies (Elves).

Descending ultimately from Enki (Satan) before 5000 BC, King Vere is the first of this name in these Isles, and was the founder of the House of Vere in 400 BC, making the Holy and Royal Elven Vere dynasty the oldest known Dragon Family in Europe descending dynastically in a single name.

By virtue of this ancient descent and the purity of its Elvish Blood, the Veres can rightfully claim seniority and superiority over all other Royal Houses. Such a claim is reflected in the work of the pre-eminent Royal Historian Baron Thomas Macaulay, Lord Macaulay of Rothley Temple.

King Vere 400 BC
Fairy Lord and Dragon King
|
Alternate succession of the Vere
Druid Prophets and Wood Lords
of the Ancient Caledonian
Fairy Forest Kingdom
|
Brude Pont
|
Vere Pont
|
Brude Leo
|
Vere Leo
|
Brude Grant

Vere Grant
|
Brude Gnith
|
Vere Gnith
|
Brude Fechir
|
Vere Fechir
|
Brude Cal
|
Vere Cal
|
Brude Cint
|
Vere Cint
|
Vere Feta
Dragon Queen
|
Gartnait Bolg
Priest King of Caledonia
AD 165-169
|
King Vere II
AD 169-178
Ard Righ (High King)
of the Bruithnigh
(Pict-Sidhes or Elves)
|
Vipoguenech
|
Fiacha Albus
|
Canutumel
|
Dovernach Vetalec
|
King Vere III
"Daich Vetla"
|
Gartnait Diuperr
Ard Righ (High King)
AD 355
|
Achivir
|
Aniel
|
Giron
|
Mailcon
|
Bridei
High King AD 520
|
Wid I

Gartnait
Ard Righ (High King)
|
Ainfrid
|
Talorcan
Ard Righ
|
daughter
= Bile ap Fili
Welsh King of Alcut
at Dumbarton
|
Brude Mac Bile
Ard Righ 693-697
(High Dragon King of the Elves)
|
Bruidhina (Pressina) Vere,
Dragon Queen, La Fey du
Fontaine: Mermaid, Druidess
= King Elinus (Gille Sidhean:
Elf Servant) of Albha, North Argyll;
The Dragon of Berenicia, Priest King
|
Princess Melusine I Vere
(Maelesanu; Milouziana du Scythes)
La Fey d'Avalon et la Fonteine de Soif
The Fairy Melusine, Neice of Morgan La Fey
= Rainfroy de Vere, Earl of Forez 733
"The Blue Boar" or Mistletoe Bard.
Melusine's cousin
|
Prince Milo de Vere, Duke of Angiers
Count of Anjou,
= Princess Bertha, sister of Charlemagne
(parallel Satanic, Fairy descent via
Jesus Christ, Elven King of the Israelites)
|
Prince Milo II de Vere, Count of Guisnes and Anjou
= Lady Aveline de Nantes
|
Prince Nicassius de Vere, Count of Guisnes
= Lady Agatha de Champagne, ancestor of
the Count of Champagne 1118, co-founder
of the Knights Templars
|
Prince Otho de Vere, Count of Guisnes
= Lady Constance de Chartres
|
Prince Amelius (Adolphus) de Vere Count of
Guisnes
= Lady Maud de Ponthieu
|
Prince Gallus (Guy) de Vere, Count of Guisnes
= Lady Gertrude de Clermont de Ponthieu
|
Two Sons:
2nd son – Prince Baldwin de Vere, descent to

Godfroi de Bouillon, founder of the Priory
of Sion and the Order of the Sacred
Sepulchre in Jerusalem; to Saint
Ida de Vere, the House of Plantagenet;
the House of Hamilton and the Imperial and
Royal House of Vere of Blackwood
&
1st son Prince Manasses de Vere Count
of Guisnes, (descent to the Vere Earls of Oxford)
=Lady Petronilla de Boleine
|
Prince Alphonse de Vere, Count of Guisnes
= Lady Katarine, dau of Count Arnulf of Flanders
|
Prince Alberic I de Vere, Count of Guisnes
= Princess Beatrix of Normandy
(descent from Satan via the Fairy Princess
Melusine I Vere du Scythes above)
|
Prince Alberic II de Vere,
Sheriff of Cambridge, Lord of Clare and Tonbridge
= Lady Adeliza dau. of Lord Gilbert FitzRichard
|
Prince Aubrey (Alberic) III de Vere, Earl of Oxford,
(Alberic: Albe-Righ; Oberon–Elf King) Inspiration
for Shakespeare's Oberon, King of the Fairies
in *A Midsummer Night's Dream*
= Lady Agnes, dau. of Henry Lord Essex.
|
Prince Ralph de Vere of Blackwood 1165 AD
Brother of Robert of Huntingdon: Robin Hood;
God of the Witches, Shakespeare's
Puck, son of Oberon (Aubrey)
|
Prince Rory de Vere of Blackwood
|
Prince Ralph de Vere of Blackwood
|
Prince Thomas de Vere of Blackwood
|
Prince Richard de Vere of Blackwood
|
Prince Thomas de Vere
1st Baron Blackwood 1340 AD
|
Prince Buan Were of Vere of Blackwood
|
Prince Rotaldus Were of Vere of Blackwood
|
Prince Thomas Were of Vere
4th Baron Blackwood
|
Prince Robert Veyr of Vere of Blackwood
|
Prince Thomas Weir of Vere of Blackwood
= Lady Aegidia Somerset
|
Prince James Weir of Vere,
7th Baron Blackwood d. 1599

= Lady Euphemia Hamilton
(descent from the High Elves of Ireland,
Princess Melusine and the Scots Kings)
|
Sir William Vere of Stanebyres Castle
= Elizabeth Hamilton, his cousin.
(descent from the High Elves of Ireland,
Princess Melusine and the Scots Kings)
|
Lord Thomas Weir of Vere, Baron Kirkton
= Lady Jane Somerville, the hereditary Witch
of the Dragon House of the Earls Somerville
|
Major Thomas Weir of Vere of Edinburgh,
The hereditary Witch King of Mid-Lothian
= Margaret Bourdon
|
Thomas Weir of Vere
Baron Kirkton of Mid-Lothian,
Hereditary Witch King in Ireland
= Mary Robison of Cookstown Ulster
|
John Weir of Vere
|
Andrew Weir of Vere
|
Margaret Weir of Vere of Kildress
|
Archibald Weir of Vere of Kildress
= Rachel Stewart of Desertcreat
|
Robert Weir of Vere of Kildress
|
John Weir of Vere of Ardwell, Logan Manor
= Mary Logan dau. of Thomas Logan of
Ardwell, Logan Manor, Galloway
|
Thomas Logan Weir of Vere of Carlisle
= Anne Grant Macdonnell of Inverness
|
James Weir of Vere of Lewes
= Natalie Hopgood (descent from
the Collisons of Norfolk and the
Imperial and Royal House of Vere)
|
HI & RH Prince Nicholas de Vere

Vere Descent from King Vere via Princess Plantina

King Vere 400 BC
Fairy Lord and Dragon King
|
Alternate succession of the Vere
Druid Prophets and Wood Lords

of the Ancient Caledonian
Fairy Forest Kingdom
|
Brude Pont
|
Vere Pont
|
Brude Leo
|
Vere Leo
|
Brude Grant
|
Vere Grant
|
Brude Gnith
|
Vere Gnith
|
Brude Fechir
|
Vere Fechir
|
Brude Cal
|
Vere Cal
|
Brude Cint
|
Vere Cint
|
Vere Feta
Dragon Queen
|
Gartnait Bolg
Priest King of Caledonia
AD 165-169
|
King Vere II
AD 169-178
Ard Righ (High King)
of the Bruithnigh
|
Vipoguenech
|
Fiacha Albus
|
Canutumel
|
Dovernach Vetalec
|
King Vere III
"Daich Vetla"
|
Gartnait Diuperr
Ard Righ (High King)
AD 355
|
Achivir

Aniel
|
Giron
|
Mailcon
|
Bridei
High King AD 520
|
Wid I
|
Gartnait
Ard Righ (High King)
|
Ainfrid
|
Talorcan
Ard Righ
|
daughter
= Bile ap Fili
Welsh King of Alcut
at Dumbarton
|
Brude Mac Bile
Ard Righ 693-697
|
Bruidhina (Pressina) Vere
(The Fairy Queen Pressina of the Scythian Picts)
= King Elinus of Albha, the Dragon
of Berenicia (Northumberland)
|
Melusine — Plantina — Meliore
|
The Plantagenista Descent
|
Torquat b. c. 760
|
Tortulf de Rennes 790
|
Tertulle Count of Anjou c. 821
= Petronella of France
|
Count Ingelgar of Anjou 845
= Adelais de Rescinde
|
Fulk I The Red, Count of Anjou b.888
= Roscilla de Loches
|
Fulk II The Good, Count of Anjou b. 920
= Gerberga de Maine
|
Geoffrey Greymantle, Count of Anjou b. 939
= Adele de Vermandois
|
Fullk III The Black, Count of Anjou b. 956
= 2. Hildegard of Metz
dau. of Arnulf of Metz

and Princess Oda de Savoy
|
Geoffrey II Martel, Count of Anjou b. 1006
= Agnes of Bourgogne
|
Geoffrey III Le Harbu b. 1040
= Julienne de Langeaise
|
Geoffrey IV Martel b. 1073
= Bertrade de Montfort
|
Fulk V The Younger, Count of Anjou b. 1092
= Princess Melisende of Jerusalem
|
Count Geoffrey Plantagenet
= Princess Mathilda, la Imperatrice
daughter of King Henry I and Princess
Mathilda of Scotland, daughter of
King Malcolm III
|
King Henry II Plantagenet
= Countess Eleanor of Aquitaine
|
= Countess Eleanor of Aquitaine
|
King John "Lackland" Plantagenet
= Lady Isabella of Angouleme
|
King Henry III Plantagenet
= Lady Eleanor dau. of Count
Raymond Berenguer IV of Provence
and Princess Beatrix de Savoy
|
King Edward I Plantagenet
= Princess Eleanor of Castille
|
King Edward II Plantagenet
= Princess Isabella of France
|
King Edward III Plantagenet
1327-1377
= Princess Phillipa of Hainault
|
Prince John Plantagenet of Gaunt
= Lady Katharine Swynford
|
Prince John Plantagenet
|
Princess Joan Beaufort Plantagenet
= King James I of Scots
|
King James II
= Mary, dau. of Arnold
Duc de Gueldres
|
Princess Mary
= Lord Thomas Boyd
|
Lady Mary Boyd

= James 1st Lord Hamilton
great grandson of
Princess Aenor de Chatellerault
and Guillaume X le Toulousain
Duc de Guyenne, Comte de Poitiers
|
Lady Euphemia Hamilton
(descent from the High Elves of Ireland,
Princess Melusine and the Scots Kings)
= Lord James Weir of Vere,
Baron Blackwood d. 1595
|
Sir William Vere of Stanebyres Castle
= Elizabeth Hamilton, his cousin.
(descent from the High Elves of Ireland,
Princess Melusine and the Scots Kings)
|
Lord Thomas Weir of Vere, Baron Kirkton
= Lady Jane Somerville, the hereditary Witch
of the Dragon House of the Earls Somerville
|
Major Thomas Weir of Vere of Edinburgh,
The hereditary Witch King of Mid-Lothian
= Margaret Bourdon
|

Thomas Weir of Vere
Baron Kirkton of Mid-Lothian,
Hereditary Witch King in Ireland
= Mary Robison of Cookstown Ulster
|
John Weir of Vere
|
Andrew Weir of Vere
|
Margaret Weir of Vere of Kildress
|
Archibald Weir of Vere of Kildress
= Rachel Stewart of Desertcreat
|
Robert Weir of Vere of Kildress
|
John Weir of Vere of Ardwell, Logan Manor
= Mary Logan dau. of Thomas Logan of
Ardwell, Logan Manor, Galloway
|
Thomas Logan Weir of Vere of Carlisle
= Anne Grant Macdonnell of Inverness
|
James Weir of Vere of Lewes
= Natalie Hopgood (descent from
the Collisons of Norfolk and the
Imperial and Royal House of Vere)
|
HI & RH Prince Nicholas de Vere

**Vere Descent from King Vere
via the Dukes of Hamilton**

King Vere 400 BC
Fairy Lord and Dragon King
|
Alternate succession of the Vere
Druid Prophets and Wood Lords
of the Ancient Caledonian
Fairy Forest Kingdom
|
Brude Pont
|
Vere Pont
|
Brude Leo
|
Vere Leo
|
Brude Grant
|
Vere Grant
|
Brude Gnith
|
Vere Gnith
|
Brude Fechir
|
Vere Fechir
|
Brude Cal
|
Vere Cal
|
Brude Cint
|
Vere Cint
|
Vere Feta
Dragon Queen
|
Gartnait Bolg
Priest King of Caledonia
AD 165-169
|
King Vere II
AD 169-178
Ard Righ (High King)
of the Bruithnigh
|
Vipoguenech
|
Fiacha Albus
|
Canutumel
|

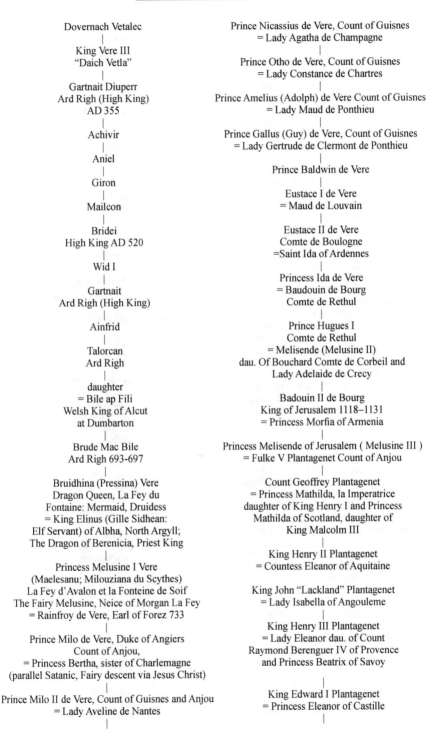

Dovernach Vetalec
|
King Vere III
"Daich Vetla"
|
Gartnait Diuperr
Ard Righ (High King)
AD 355
|
Achivir
|
Aniel
|
Giron
|
Mailcon
|
Bridei
High King AD 520
|
Wid I
|
Gartnait
Ard Righ (High King)
|
Ainfrid
|
Talorcan
Ard Righ
|
daughter
= Bile ap Fili
Welsh King of Alcut
at Dumbarton
|
Brude Mac Bile
Ard Righ 693-697
|
Bruidhina (Pressina) Vere
Dragon Queen, La Fey du
Fontaine: Mermaid, Druidess
= King Elinus (Gille Sidhean:
Elf Servant) of Albha, North Argyll;
The Dragon of Berenicia, Priest King
|
Princess Melusine I Vere
(Maelesanu; Milouziana du Scythes)
La Fey d'Avalon et la Fonteine de Soif
The Fairy Melusine, Neice of Morgan La Fey
= Rainfroy de Vere, Earl of Forez 733
|
Prince Milo de Vere, Duke of Angiers
Count of Anjou,
= Princess Bertha, sister of Charlemagne
(parallel Satanic, Fairy descent via Jesus Christ)
|
Prince Milo II de Vere, Count of Guisnes and Anjou
= Lady Aveline de Nantes
|

Prince Nicassius de Vere, Count of Guisnes
= Lady Agatha de Champagne
|
Prince Otho de Vere, Count of Guisnes
= Lady Constance de Chartres
|
Prince Amelius (Adolph) de Vere Count of Guisnes
= Lady Maud de Ponthieu
|
Prince Gallus (Guy) de Vere, Count of Guisnes
= Lady Gertrude de Clermont de Ponthieu
|
Prince Baldwin de Vere
|
Eustace I de Vere
= Maud de Louvain
|
Eustace II de Vere
Comte de Boulogne
=Saint Ida of Ardennes
|
Princess Ida de Vere
= Baudouin de Bourg
Comte de Rethul
|
Prince Hugues I
Comte de Rethul
= Melisende (Melusine II)
dau. Of Bouchard Comte de Corbeil and
Lady Adelaide de Crecy
|
Badouin II de Bourg
King of Jerusalem 1118–1131
= Princess Morfia of Armenia
|
Princess Melisende of Jerusalem (Melusine III)
= Fulke V Plantagenet Count of Anjou
|
Count Geoffrey Plantagenet
= Princess Mathilda, la Imperatrice
daughter of King Henry I and Princess
Mathilda of Scotland, daughter of
King Malcolm III
|
King Henry II Plantagenet
= Countess Eleanor of Aquitaine
|
King John "Lackland" Plantagenet
= Lady Isabella of Angouleme
|
King Henry III Plantagenet
= Lady Eleanor dau. of Count
Raymond Berenguer IV of Provence
and Princess Beatrix of Savoy
|
King Edward I Plantagenet
= Princess Eleanor of Castille
|

King Edward II Plantagenet
= Princess Isabella of France
|
King Edward III Plantagenet
1327-1377
= Princess Phillipa of Hainault
|
Prince John Plantagenet of Gaunt
= Lady Katharine Swynford
|
Prince John Plantagenet
|
Princess Joan Beaufort
= King James I of Scots
|
King James II
= Mary, dau. of Arnold
Duc de Gueldres
|
Princess Mary
= Lord Thomas Boyd
|
Lady Mary Boyd
James 1st Lord Hamilton
great grandson of
Princess Aenor de Chatellerault
and Guillaume X le Toulousain
Duc de Guyenne, Comte de Poitiers
|
Lady Euphemia Hamilton
(descent from the High Elves of Ireland,
Princess Melusine and the Scots Kings)
= Lord James Weir of Vere,
Baron Blackwood d. 1599
|
Sir William Vere of Stanebyres Castle
= Elizabeth Hamilton, his cousin.
(descent from the High Elves of Ireland,
Princess Melusine and the Scots Kings)
|
Lord Thomas Weir of Vere, Baron Kirkton
= Lady Jane Somerville, the hereditary Witch
of the Dragon House of the Earls Somerville
|
Major Thomas Weir of Vere of Edinburgh,
The Witch King of Mid-Lothian
= Margaret Bourdon
|
Thomas Weir of Vere
Baron Kirkton of Mid-Lothian,
Hereditary Witch King in Ireland
= Mary Robison of Cookstown Ulster
|
John Weir of Vere
|
Andrew Weir of Vere
|
Margaret Weir of Vere of Kildress
|

Archibald Weir of Vere of Kildress
= Rachel Stewart of Desertcreat
|
Robert Weir of Vere of Kildress
|
John Weir of Vere of Ardwell, Logan Manor
= Mary Logan dau. of Thomas Logan of
Ardwell, Logan Manor, Galloway
|
Thomas Logan Weir of Vere of Carlisle
= Anne Grant Macdonnell of Inverness
|
James Weir of Vere of Lewes
= Natalie Hopgood (descent from
the Collisons of Norfolk and the
Imperial and Royal House of Vere)
|
HI & RH Prince Nicholas de Vere

Vere Descent from Princess Scota and the High Elves of Ireland

- The Tuadha de Danaan -

King Tushratta
Dragon Lord of the
Scythian Mittani
|
Tadukhipa
Dragon Queen
= King Fenius Farsaidh
of Scythia
|
Prince Niall of Scythia
Lord of the Region
of Capacyront in Egypt
= Princess Scota of Egypt
Dragon Queen and Princess
of Scythia: Granddaughter
of Pharaoh Amenhotep IV
and cousin of Queen
Kiya Tasherit
|
King Geadheal Glas
(Ancestor of the Scots Gaels)
|
Easru 1300 BC
|
King Sru
|
King Tait
|
King Pamp
|
King Adnoin

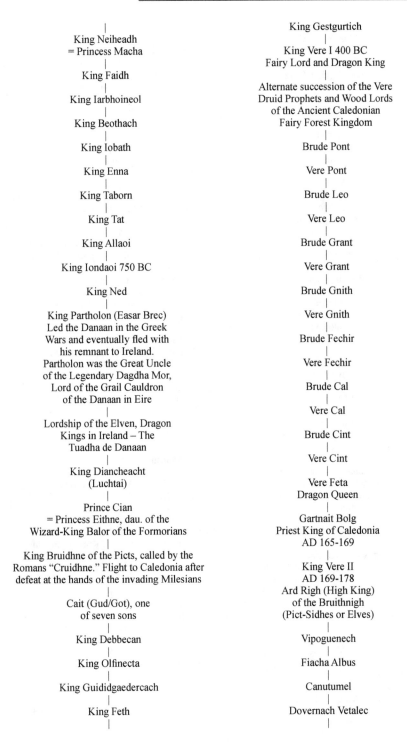

|
King Neiheadh
= Princess Macha
|
King Faidh
|
King Iarbhoineol
|
King Beothach
|
King Iobath
|
King Enna
|
King Taborn
|
King Tat
|
King Allaoi
|
King Iondaoi 750 BC
|
King Ned
|
King Partholon (Easar Brec)
Led the Danaan in the Greek
Wars and eventually fled with
his remnant to Ireland.
Partholon was the Great Uncle
of the Legendary Dagdha Mor,
Lord of the Grail Cauldron
of the Danaan in Eire
|
Lordship of the Elven, Dragon
Kings in Ireland – The
Tuadha de Danaan
|
King Diancheacht
(Luchtai)
|
Prince Cian
= Princess Eithne, dau. of the
Wizard-King Balor of the Formorians
|
King Bruidhne of the Picts, called by the
Romans "Cruidhne." Flight to Caledonia after
defeat at the hands of the invading Milesians
|
Cait (Gud/Got), one
of seven sons
|
King Debbecan
|
King Olfinecta
|
King Guididgaedercach
|
King Feth
|

King Gestgurtich
|
King Vere I 400 BC
Fairy Lord and Dragon King
|
Alternate succession of the Vere
Druid Prophets and Wood Lords
of the Ancient Caledonian
Fairy Forest Kingdom
|
Brude Pont
|
Vere Pont
|
Brude Leo
|
Vere Leo
|
Brude Grant
|
Vere Grant
|
Brude Gnith
|
Vere Gnith
|
Brude Fechir
|
Vere Fechir
|
Brude Cal
|
Vere Cal
|
Brude Cint
|
Vere Cint
|
Vere Feta
Dragon Queen
|
Gartnait Bolg
Priest King of Caledonia
AD 165-169
|
King Vere II
AD 169-178
Ard Righ (High King)
of the Bruithnigh
(Pict-Sidhes or Elves)
|
Vipoguenech
|
Fiacha Albus
|
Canutumel
|
Dovernach Vetalec
|

King Vere III
"Daich Vetla"
|
Gartnait Diuperr
Ard Righ (High King)
AD 355
|
Achivir
|
Aniel
|
Giron
|
Mailcon
|
Bridei
High King AD 520
|
Wid I
|
Gartnait
Ard Righ (High King)
|
Ainfrid
|
Talorcan
Ard Righ
|
daughter
= Bile ap Fili
Welsh King of Alcut
at Dumbarton
|
Brude Mac Bile
Ard Righ 693-697
(High Dragon King of the Elves)
|
Bruidhina (Pressina) Vere,
Dragon Queen, La Fey du
Fontaine: Mermaid, Druidess
= King Elinus (Gille Sidhean:
Elf Servant) of Albha, North Argyll;
The Dragon of Berenicia, Priest King
|
Princess Melusine I Vere
(Maelesanu; Milouziana du Scythes)
La Fey d'Avalon et la Fonteine de Soif
The Fairy Melusine, Neice of Morgan La Fey
= Rainfroy de Vere, Earl of Forez 733
"The Blue Boar" or Mistletoe Bard.
Melusine's cousin
|
Prince Milo de Vere, Duke of Angiers
Count of Anjou,
= Princess Bertha, sister of Charlemagne
(parallel Satanic, Fairy descent via
Jesus Christ, Elven King of the Israelites)
|
Prince Milo II de Vere, Count of Guisnes and Anjou

= Lady Aveline de Nantes
|
Prince Nicassius de Vere, Count of Guisnes
= Lady Agatha de Champagne, ancestor of
the Count of Champagne 1118, co-founder
of the Knights Templars
|
Prince Otho de Vere, Count of Guisnes
= Lady Constance de Chartres
|
Prince Amelius (Adolphus) de Vere Count of
Guisnes
= Lady Maud de Ponthieu
|
Prince Gallus (Guy) de Vere, Count of Guisnes
= Lady Gertrude de Clermont de Ponthieu
|
Two Sons:
2nd son – Prince Baldwin de Vere, descent to
Godfroi de Bouillon, founder of the Priory
of Sion and the Order of the Sacred
Sepulchre in Jerusalem; to Saint
Ida de Vere, the House of Plantagenet;
the House of Hamilton and the Imperial and
Royal House of Vere of Blackwood
&
1st son Prince Manasses de Vere Count
of Guisnes, (descent to the Vere Earls of Oxford)
=Lady Petronilla de Boleine
|
Prince Alphonse de Vere, Count of Guisnes
= Lady Katarine, dau of Count Arnulf of Flanders
|
Prince Alberic I de Vere, Count of Guisnes
= Princess Beatrix of Normandy
(descent from Satan via the Fairy Princess
Melusine I Vere du Scythes above)
|
Prince Alberic II de Vere,
Sheriff of Cambridge, Lord of Clare and Tonbridge
= Lady Adeliza dau. of Lord Gilbert FitzRichard
|
Prince Aubrey (Alberic) III de Vere, Earl of Oxford,
(Alberic: Albe-Righ – Elf King) Inspiration for
Shakespeare's Oberon, King of the Fairies
in *A Midsummer Night's Dream*
= Lady Agnes, dau. of Henry Lord Essex.
|
Prince Ralph de Vere of Blackwood 1165 AD
Brother of Robert of Huntingdon: Robin Hood;
God of the Witches, Shakespeare's
Puck, son of Oberon (Aubrey)
|
Prince Rory de Vere of Blackwood
|
Prince Ralph de Vere of Blackwood
|
Prince Thomas de Vere of Blackwood
|

Prince Richard de Vere of Blackwood
|
Prince Thomas de Vere
1st Baron Blackwood 1340 AD
|
Prince Buan Were of Vere of Blackwood
|
Prince Rotaldus Were of Vere of Blackwood
|
Prince Thomas Were of Vere
4th Baron Blackwood
|
Prince Robert Veyr of Vere of Blackwood
|
Prince Thomas Weir of Vere of Blackwood
= Lady Aegidia Somerset
|
Prince James Weir of Vere,
7th Baron Blackwood d. 1595
= Lady Euphemia Hamilton
(descent from the High Elves of Ireland,
Princess Melusine and the Scots Kings)
|
Sir William Vere of Stanebyres Castle
= Elizabeth Hamilton, his cousin.
(descent from the High Elves of Ireland,
Princess Melusine and the Scots Kings)
|
Lord Thomas Weir of Vere, Baron Kirkton
= Lady Jane Somerville, the hereditary Witch
of the Dragon House of the Earls Somerville
|
Major Thomas Weir of Vere of Edinburgh,
The Witch King of Mid-Lothian
= Margaret Bourdon
|
Thomas Weir of Vere
Baron Kirkton of Mid-Lothian,
Hereditary Witch King in Ireland
= Mary Robison of Cookstown Ulster
|
John Weir of Vere
|
Andrew Weir of Vere
|
Margaret Weir of Vere of Kildress
|
Archibald Weir of Vere of Kildress
= Rachel Stewart of Desertcreat
|
Robert Weir of Vere of Kildress
|
John Weir of Vere of Ardwell, Logan Manor
= Mary Logan dau. of Thomas Logan of
Ardwell, Logan Manor, Galloway
|
Thomas Logan Weir of Vere of Carlisle
= Anne Grant Macdonnell of Inverness

|
James Weir of Vere of Lewes
= Natalie Hopgood (descent from
the Collisons of Norfolk and the
Imperial and Royal House of Vere)
|
HI & RH Prince Nicholas de Vere

Vere Descent from Princess Scota and the High Elves of Ireland – The Tuadha de Danaan – via the Fairy Princess Plantina

King Tushratta
Dragon Lord of the
Scythian Mittani
|
Tadukhipa
Dragon Queen
= King Fenius Farsaidh
of Scythia
|
Prince Niall of Scythia
Lord of the Region
of Capacyront in Egypt
= Princess Scota of Egypt
Dragon Queen and Princess
of Scythia: Granddaughter
of Pharaoh Amenhotep IV
and cousin of Queen
Kiya Tasherit
|
King Geadheal Glas
(Ancestor of the Scots Gaels)
|
Easru 1300 BC
|
King Sru
|
King Tait
|
King Pamp
|
King Adnoin
|
King Neiheadh
= Princess Macha
|
King Faidh
|
King Iarbhoineol
|
King Beothach
|
King Iobath
|

King Enna
|
King Taborn
|
King Tat
|
King Allaoi
|
King Iondaoi 750 BC
|
King Ned
|
King Partholon (Easar Brec)
Led the Danaan in the Greek Wars
and eventually fled with his
remnant to Ireland.
Partholon was the Great Uncle
of the Legendary Dagdha Mor,
Lord of the Grail Cauldron
of the Danaan in Eire
|
Lordship of the Elven, Dragon
Kings in Ireland – The
Tuadha de Danaan
|
King Diancheacht
(Luchtai)
|
Prince Cian
= Princess Eithne, dau. of the
Wizard-King Balor of the Formorians
|
King Bruidhne of the Picts, called by the
Romans "Cruidhne." Flight to Caledonia after
defeat at the hands of the invading Milesians
|
Cait (Gud/Got), one
of seven sons
|
King Debbecan
|
King Olfinecta
|
King Guididgaedercach
|
King Feth
|
King Gestgurtich
|
King Vere 400 BC
Fairy Lord and Dragon King
|
Alternate succession of the Vere
Druid Prophets and Wood Lords
of the Ancient Caledonian
Fairy Forest Kingdom
|
Brude Pont
|

Vere Pont
|
Brude Leo
|
Vere Leo
|
Brude Grant
|
Vere Grant
|
Brude Gnith
|
Vere Gnith
|
Brude Fechir
|
Vere Fechir
|
Brude Cal
|
Vere Cal
|
Brude Cint
|
Vere Cint
|
Vere Feta
Dragon Queen
|
Gartnait Bolg
Priest King of Caledonia
AD 165-169
|
King Vere II
AD 169-178
Ard Righ (High King)
of the Bruithnigh
|
Vipoguenech
|
Fiacha Albus
|
Canutumel
|
Dovernach Vetalec
|
King Vere III Daich Vetla
|
Gartnait Diuperr
Ard Righ (High King)
AD 355
|
Achivir
|
Aniel
|
Giron
|
Mailcon

Bridei
High King AD 520

Wid I

Gartnait
Ard Righ (High King)

Ainfrid

Talorcan
Ard Righ

daughter
= Bile ap Fili
Welsh King of Alcut
at Dumbarton

Brude Mac Bile
Ard Righ 693-697

Bruidhina (Pressina)
Dragon Queen, La Fey du
Fontaine: Mermaid, Druidess
= King Elinus (Gille Sidhean:
Elf Servant) of Albha, North Argyll;
The Dragon of Berenicia, Priest King

Melusine — Plantina — Meliore

The Plantagenista Descent

Torquat b. c. 760

Tortulf de Rennes 790

Tertulle Count of Anjou c. 821
= Petronella of France

Count Ingelgar of Anjou 845
= Adelais de Rescinde

Fulk I The Red, Count of Anjou b. 888
= Roscilla de Loches

Fulk II The Good, Count of Anjou b. 920
= Gerberga de Maine

Geoffrey Greymantle, Count of Anjou b. 939
= Adele de Vermandois

Fullk III The Black, Count of Anjou b. 956
= 2. Hildegard of Metz
dau. of Arnulf of Metz
and Princess Oda de Savoy

Geoffrey II Martel, Count of Anjou b. 1006
= Agnes of Bourgogne

Geoffrey III Le Harbu b. 1040
= Julienne de Langeaise

Geoffrey IV Martel b. 1073
= Bertrade de Montfort

Fulk V The Younger, Count of Anjou b. 1092
= Princess Melisende of Jerusalem

Princess Melisende of Jerusalem (Melusine III)
= Fulke V Plantagenet Count of Anjou

Count Geoffrey Plantagenet
= Princess Mathilda, la Imperatrice
daughter of King Henry I and Princess
Mathilda of Scotland, daughter of
King Malcolm III

King Henry II Plantagenet
= Countess Eleanor of Aquitaine

King John "Lackland" Plantagenet
= Lady Isabella of Angouleme

King Henry III Plantagenet
= Lady Eleanor dau. of Count
Raymond Berenguer IV of Provence
and Princess Beatrix de Savoy

King Edward I Plantagenet
= Princess Eleanor of Castille

King Edward II Plantagenet
= Princess Isabella of France

King Edward III Plantagenet
1327-1377
= Princess Phillipa of Hainault

Prince John Plantagenet of Gaunt
= Lady Katharine Swynford

Prince John Plantagenet

Princess Joan Beaufort Plantagenet
= King James I of Scots

King James II
= Mary, dau. of Arnold
Duc de Gueldres

Princess Mary

= Lord Thomas Boyd

Lady Mary Boyd
James 1st Lord Hamilton

great grandson of
Princess Aenor de Chatellerault
and Guillaume X le Toulousain
Duc de Guyenne, Comte de Poitiers
|
Lady Euphemia Hamilton
(descent from the High Elves of Ireland,
Princess Melusine and the Scots Kings)
= Lord James Weir of Vere,
Baron Blackwood d. 1595
|
Sir William Vere of Stanebyres Castle
= Elizabeth Hamilton, his cousin.
(descent from the High Elves of Ireland,
Princess Melusine and the Scots Kings)
|
Lord Thomas Weir of Vere, Baron Kirkton
= Lady Jane Somerville, the hereditary Witch
of the Dragon House of the Earls Somerville
|
Major Thomas Weir of Vere of Edinburgh,
The hereditary Witch King of Mid-Lothian
= Margaret Bourdon
|
Thomas Weir of Vere
Baron Kirkton of Mid-Lothian,
Hereditary Witch King in Ireland
= Mary Robison of Cookstown Ulster
|
John Weir of Vere
|
Andrew Weir of Vere
|
Margaret Weir of Vere of Kildress
|
Archibald Weir of Vere of Kildress
= Rachel Stewart of Desertcreat
|
Robert Weir of Vere of Kildress
|
John Weir of Vere of Ardwell, Logan Manor
= Mary Logan dau. of Thomas Logan of
Ardwell, Logan Manor, Galloway
|
Thomas Logan Weir of Vere of Carlisle
= Anne Grant Macdonnell of Inverness
|
James Weir of Vere of Lewes
= Natalie Hopgood (descent from
the Collisons of Norfolk and the
Imperial and Royal House of Vere)
|
HI & RH Prince Nicholas de Vere

Vere Descent from Princess Scota and the High Elves of Ireland – The Tuadha de Danaan – via the Dukes of Hamilton

King Tushratta
Dragon Lord of the
Scythian Mittani
|
Tadukhipa
Dragon Queen
= King Fenius Farsaidh
of Scythia
|
Prince Niall of Scythia
Lord of the Region
of Capacyront in Egypt
= Princess Scota of Egypt
Dragon Queen and Princess
of Scythia: Granddaughter
of Pharaoh Amenhotep IV
and cousin of Queen
Kiya Tasherit
|
King Geadheal Glas
(Ancestor of the Scots Gaels)
|
Easru 1300 BC
|
King Sru
|
King Tait
|
King Pamp
|
King Adnoin
|
King Neiheadh
= Princess Macha
|
King Faidh
|
King Iarbhoineol
|
King Beothach
|
King Iobath
|
King Enna
|
King Taborn
|
King Tat
|
King Allaoi
|
King Iondaoi 750 BC
|

King Ned
|
King Partholon (Easar Brec)
Led the Danaan in the Greek Wars
and eventually fled with his
remnant to Ireland.
Partholon was the Great Uncle
of the Legendary Dagdha Mor,
Lord of the Grail Cauldron
of the Danaan in Eire
|
Lordship of the Elven, Dragon
Kings in Ireland – The
Tuadha de Danaan
|
King Diancheacht
(Luchtai)
|
Prince Cian
= Princess Eithne, dau. of the
Wizard-King Balor of the Formorians
|
King Bruidhne of the Picts, called by the
Romans "Cruidhne." Flight to Caledonia after
defeat at the hands of the invading Milesians
|
Cait (Gud/Got), one
of seven sons
|
King Debbecan
|
King Olfinecta
|
King Guididgaedercach
|
King Feth
|
King Gestgurtich
|
King Vere 400 BC
Fairy Lord and Dragon King
|
Alternate succession of the Vere
Druid Prophets and Wood Lords
of the Ancient Caledonian
Fairy Forest Kingdom
|
Brude Pont
|
Vere Pont
|
Brude Leo
|
Vere Leo
|
Brude Grant
|
Vere Grant
|

Brude Gnith
|
Vere Gnith
|
Brude Fechir
|
Vere Fechir
|
Brude Cal
|
Vere Cal
|
Brude Cint
|
Vere Cint
|
Vere Feta
Dragon Queen
|
Gartnait Bolg
Priest King of Caledonia
AD 165-169
|
King Vere II
AD 169-178
Ard Righ (High King)
of the Bruithnigh
|
Vipoguenech
|
Fiacha Albus
|
Canutumel
|
Dovernach Vetalec
|
King Vere III
"Daich Vetla"
|
Gartnait Diuperr
Ard Righ (High King)
AD 355
|
Achivir
|
Aniel
|
Giron
|
Mailcon
|
Bridei
High King AD 520
|
Wid I
|
Gartnait
Ard Righ (High King)
|

Ainfrid
|
Talorcan
Ard Righ
|
daughter
= Bile ap Fili
Welsh King of Alcut
at Dumbarton
|
Brude Mac Bile
Ard Righ 693-697
|
Bruidhina (Pressina) Vere
Dragon Queen, La Fey du
Fontaine: Mermaid, Druidess
= King Elinus (Gille Sidhean:
Elf Servant) of Albha, North Argyll;
The Dragon of Berenicia, Priest King
|
Princess Melusine I Vere
(Maelesanu; Milouziana du Scythes)
La Fey d'Avalon et la Fonteine de Soif
The Fairy Melusine, Neice of Morgan La Fey
= Rainfroy de Vere, Earl of Forez 733
|
Prince Milo de Vere, Duke of Angiers
Count of Anjou,
= Princess Bertha, sister of Charlemagne
(parallel Satanic, Fairy descent via Jesus Christ)
|
Prince Milo II de Vere, Count of Guisnes and Anjou
= Lady Aveline de Nantes
|
Prince Nicassius de Vere, Count of Guisnes
= Lady Agatha de Champagne
|
Prince Otho de Vere, Count of Guisnes
= Lady Constance de Chartres
|
Prince Amelius (Adolph) de Vere Count of Guisnes
= Lady Maud de Ponthieu
|
Prince Gallus (Guy) de Vere, Count of Guisnes
= Lady Gertrude de Clermont de Ponthieu
|
Prince Baldwin de Vere
|
Eustace I de Vere
= Maud de Louvain
|
Eustace II de Vere
Comte de Boulogne
=Saint Ida of Ardennes
|
Princess Ida de Vere
= Baudouin de Bourg
Comte de Rethul
|

Prince Hugues I
Comte de Rethul
= Melisende (Melusine II)
dau. Of Bouchard Comte de Corbeil and
Lady Adelaide de Crecy
|
Badouin II de Bourg
King of Jerusalem 1118-1131
= Princess Morfia of Armenia
|
Princess Melisende of Jerusalem (Melusine III)
= Fulke V Plantagenet Count of Anjou
|
Princess Melisende of Jerusalem (Melusine III)
= Fulke V Plantagenet Count of Anjou
|
Count Geoffrey Plantagenet
= Princess Mathilda, la Imperatrice
daughter of King Henry I and Princess
Mathilda of Scotland, daughter of
King Malcolm III
|
King Henry II Plantagenet
= Countess Eleanor of Aquitaine
dau. of King Malcolm III
|
King John "Lackland" Plantagenet
= Lady Isabella of Angouleme
|
King Henry III Plantagenet
= Lady Eleanor dau. of Count
Raymond Berenguer IV of Provence
and Princess Beatrix of Savoy
|
King Edward I Plantagenet
= Princess Eleanor of Castille
|
King Edward II Plantagenet
= Princess Isabella of France
|
King Edward III Plantagenet
1327-1377
= Princess Phillipa of Hainault
|
Prince John Plantagenet of Gaunt
= Lady Katharine Swynford
|
Prince John Plantagenet
|
Princess Joan Beaufort
= King James I of Scots
|
King James II
= Mary, dau. of Arnold
Duc de Gueldres
|
Princess Mary
= Lord Thomas Boyd

Lady Mary Boyd
James 1st Lord Hamilton
great grandson of
Princess Aenor de Chatellerault
and Guillaume X le Toulousain
Duc de Guyenne, Comte de Poitiers

|

Lady Euphemia Hamilton
(descent from the High Elves of Ireland,
Princess Melusine and the Scots Kings)
= Lord James Weir of Vere,
Baron Blackwood d. 1595

|

Sir William Vere of Stanebyres Castle
= Elizabeth Hamilton, his cousin.

(descent from the High Elves of Ireland,
Princess Melusine and the Scots Kings)

|

Lord Thomas Weir of Vere, Baron Kirkton
= Lady Jane Somerville, the hereditary Witch
of the Dragon House of the Earls Somerville

|

Major Thomas Weir of Vere of Edinburgh,
The hereditary Witch King of Mid-Lothian
= Margaret Bourdon

|

Thomas Weir of Vere
Baron Kirkton of Mid-Lothian,
Hereditary Witch King in Ireland
= Mary Robison of Cookstown Ulster

|

John Weir of Vere

|

Andrew Weir of Vere

|

Margaret Weir of Vere of Kildress

|

Archibald Weir of Vere of Kildress
= Rachel Stewart of Desertcreat

|

Robert Weir of Vere of Kildress

|

John Weir of Vere of Ardwell, Logan Manor
= Mary Logan dau. of Thomas Logan of
Ardwell, Logan Manor, Galloway

|

Thomas Logan Weir of Vere of Carlisle
= Anne Grant Macdonnell of Inverness

|

James Weir of Vere of Lewes
= Natalie Hopgood (descent from
the Collisons of Norfolk and the
Imperial and Royal House of Vere)

|

HI & RH Prince Nicholas de Vere

Vere Descent from the Dukes of Brittany
via Princess Beatrix of Normandy

Count Frodaldus de Bretagne

|

Count Rivallon de Bretagne

|

Duke Saloman de Bretagne
857-870
= Lady Gimberta

|

Countess de Bretagne
= Count Garvand de Rennes

|

Count Judicael de Rennes

|

Count Juhel Bereger de Rennes
930-937
= Lady Gerberge

|

Count Conan le Tort de Rennes
= Lady Ermengarde of Anjou
dau. of Geoffrey I Count of
Anjou and Lady Adelaide de
Vermandois (Fairy descent from
Princess Plantina, sister of the Fairy
Princess Melusine the Scythian)

|

Lady Havoise
= Count Geoffrey

|

Duke Alain V de Bretagne
Count de Rennes
= Lady Berta de Blois

|

Lady Judith de Bretagne
= Duke Richard II of Normandy

|

Duke Richard III 1027 AD

|

Duke Robert I 1028 AD

|

Princess Beatrix of Normandy
Sister of King William I the Conqueror
= Prince Alberic I de Vere, Count of Guisnes
(descent from Satan via the Fairy Princess
Melusine I Vere du Scythes)

|

Prince Alberic II de Vere,
Sheriff of Cambridge, Lord of Clare and Tonbridge
= Lady Adeliza dau. of Lord Gilbert FitzRichard

|

Prince Aubrey (Alberic) III de Vere, Earl of Oxford,
(Alberic: Albe-Righ; Oberon – Elf King) Inspiration
for Shakespeare's Oberon, King of the Fairies

in *A Midsummer Night's Dream*
= Lady Agnes, dau. of Henry Lord Essex.

|

Prince Ralph de Vere of Blackwood 1165 AD
Brother of Robert of Huntingdon: Robin Hood;
God of the Witches, Shakespeare's
Puck, son of Oberon (Aubrey)

|

Prince Rory de Vere of Blackwood

|

Prince Ralph de Vere of Blackwood

|

Prince Thomas de Vere of Blackwood

|

Prince Richard de Vere of Blackwood

|

Prince Thomas de Vere
1st Baron Blackwood 1340 AD

|

Prince Buan Were of Vere of Blackwood

|

Prince Rotaldus Were of Vere of Blackwood

|

Prince Thomas Were of Vere
4th Baron Blackwood

|

Prince Robert Veyr of Vere of Blackwood

|

Prince Thomas Weir of Vere of Blackwood
= Lady Aegidia Somerset

|

Prince James Weir of Vere,
7th Baron Blackwood d. 1599
= Lady Euphemia Hamilton
(descent from the High Elves of Ireland,
Princess Melusine and the Scots Kings)

|

Sir William Vere of Stanebyres Castle
= Elizabeth Hamilton, his cousin.
(descent from the High Elves of Ireland,
Princess Melusine and the Scots Kings)

|

Lord Thomas Weir of Vere, Baron Kirkton
= Lady Jane Somerville, the hereditary Witch
of the Dragon House of the Earls Somerville

|

Major Thomas Weir of Vere of Edinburgh,
The hereditary Witch King of Mid-Lothian
= Margaret Bourdon

|

Thomas Weir of Vere
Baron Kirkton of Mid-Lothian,
Hereditary Witch King in Ireland
= Mary Robison of Cookstown Ulster

|

John Weir of Vere

|

Andrew Weir of Vere

|

Margaret Weir of Vere of Kildress

|

Archibald Weir of Vere of Kildress
= Rachel Stewart of Desertcreat

|

Robert Weir of Vere of Kildress

|

John Weir of Vere of Ardwell, Logan Manor
= Mary Logan dau. of Thomas Logan of
Ardwell, Logan Manor, Galloway

|

Thomas Logan Weir of Vere of Carlisle
= Anne Grant Macdonnell of Inverness

|

James Weir of Vere of Lewes
= Natalie Hopgood (descent from
the Collisons of Norfolk and the
Imperial and Royal House of Vere)

|

HI & RH Prince Nicholas de Vere

Vere Descent from the Dukes of Brittany via Richard II of Normandy

Count Frodaldus de Bretagne

|

Count Rivallon de Bretagne

|

Duke Saloman de Bretagne
857-870
= Lady Gimberta

|

Countess de Bretagne
= Count Garvand de Rennes

|

Count Judicael de Rennes

|

Count Juhel Bereger de Rennes
930-937
= Lady Gerberge

|

Count Conan le Tort de Rennes
= Lady Ermengarde of Anjou

|

Lady Havoise
= Count Geoffrey

|

Duke Alain V de Bretagne
Count de Rennes
= Lady Berta de Blois

|

Lady Judith de Bretagne
= Duke Richard II of Normandy

Duke Richard III 1027 AD

Duke Robert I 1028 AD

King William I of England
= Lady Mathilda van Vlaanderen
dau. of Count Baldwin V of Flanders

King Henry I of England
= Princess Mathilda dau. of
King Malcom III Canmore
of Scotland and Margaret,
dau. of Edward the Exile
by Princess Agatha of Bulgaria

Princess Mathilda of England la Imperatrice
= Count Geoffrey Plantagenet
of Anjou

King Henry II Plantagenet
= Countess Eleanor of Aquitaine

King John "Lackland" Plantagenet
= Lady Isabella of Angouleme

King Henry III Plantagenet
= Lady Eleanor dau. of Count
Raymond Berenguer IV of PrOvence
and Princess Beatrix of Savoy

King Edward I Plantagenet
= Princess Eleanor of Castille

King Edward II Plantagenet
= Princess Isabella of France

King Edward III Plantagenet
1327-1377
= Princess Phillipa of Hainault

Prince John Plantagenet of Gaunt
= Lady Katharine Swynford

Prince John Plantagenet

Princess Joan Beaufort Plantagenet
= King James I of Scots

King James II
= Mary, dau. of Arnold Duc de Gueldres

Princess Mary
= Lord Thomas Boyd

Lady Mary Boyd
James 1st Lord Hamilton

great grandson of
Princess Aenor de Chatellerault
and Guillaume X le Toulousain
Duc de Guyenne, Comte de Poitiers

Lady Euphemia Hamilton
(descent from the High Elves of Ireland,
Princess Melusine and the Scots Kings)
= Lord James Weir of Vere,
Baron Blackwood d. 1595

Sir William Vere of Stanebyres Castle
= Elizabeth Hamilton, his cousin.
(descent from the High Elves of Ireland,
Princess Melusine and the Scots Kings)

Lord Thomas Weir of Vere, Baron Kirkton
= Lady Jane Somerville, the hereditary Witch
of the Dragon House of the Earls Somerville

Major Thomas Weir of Vere of Edinburgh,
The hereditary Witch King of Mid-Lothian
= Margaret Bourdon

Thomas Weir of Vere
Baron Kirkton of Mid-Lothian,
Hereditary Witch King in Ireland
= Mary Robison of Cookstown Ulster

John Weir of Vere

Andrew Weir of Vere

Margaret Weir of Vere of Kildress

Archibald Weir of Vere of Kildress

= Rachel Stewart of Desertcreat

Robert Weir of Vere of Kildress

John Weir of Vere of Ardwell, Logan Manor
= Mary Logan dau. of Thomas Logan of
Ardwell, Logan Manor, Galloway

Thomas Logan Weir of Vere of Carlisle
= Anne Grant Macdonnell of Inverness

James Weir of Vere of Lewes
= Natalie Hopgood (descent from
the Collisons of Norfolk and the
Imperial and Royal House of Vere)

HI & RH Prince Nicholas de Vere

Vere Descent from the Early English Kings

King Egbert
802-839
|
King Aethelwulf
839-858
|
King Alfred the Great
871-899
= Princess Aelhswith
d. 904
|
King Edward the Elder
899-924
|
King Edmund I
939-946
= Princess Aelfgifu
|
King Edgar
959-975
= 2. Princess Aelfthryf
|
King Aelthelred II the Unready
979-1016
= Princess Aelgifu
|
King Edmund II Ironside
d. 1016
= Princess Algitha
|
King (de jure) Edward the Exile
d. 1057
= Princess Agatha of Bulgaria
|
Princess Margaret
= King Malcolm III Canmore
King of Scots
|
Princess Mathilda
= King Henry I of England
1101-1135
|
Princess Mathilda la Imperatrice
= Count Geoffrey Plantagenet
|
King Henry II Plantagenet
= Countess Eleanor of Aquitaine
|
King John "Lackland" Plantagenet
= Lady Isabella of Angouleme
|
King Henry III Plantagenet
= Lady Eleanor dau. of Count
Raymond Berenguer IVof Provence

and Princess Beatrix of Savoy
|
King Edward I Plantagenet
= Princess Eleanor of Castille
|
King Edward II Plantagenet
= Princess Isabella of France
|
King Edward III Plantagenet
1327-1377
= Princess Phillipa of Hainault
|
Prince John of Gaunt Plantagenet
= Lady Katharine Swynford
|
Prince John Plantagenet
|
Princess Joan Beaufort Plantagenet
|
= King James I of Scots
|
King James II
= Mary, dau. of Arnold Duc de Gueldres
|
Princess Mary
= Lord Thomas Boyd
|
Lady Mary Boyd
= James 1st Lord Hamilton
great grandson of
Princess Aenor de Chatellerault
and Guillaume X le Toulousain
Duc de Guyenne, Comte de Poitiers
|
Lady Euphemia Hamilton
(descent from the High Elves of Ireland,
Princess Melusine and the Scots Kings)
= Lord James Weir of Vere,
Baron Blackwood d. 1595
|
Sir William Vere of Stanebyres Castle
= Elizabeth Hamilton, his cousin.
(descent from the High Elves of Ireland,
Princess Melusine and the Scots Kings)
|
Lord Thomas Weir of Vere, Baron Kirkton
= Lady Jane Somerville, the hereditary Witch
of the Dragon House of the Earls Somerville
|
Major Thomas Weir of Vere of Edinburgh,
The hereditary Witch King of Mid-Lothian
= Margaret Bourdon
|
Thomas Weir of Vere
Baron Kirkton of Mid-Lothian,
Hereditary Witch King in Ireland
= Mary Robison of Cookstown Ulster
|
John Weir of Vere

Andrew Weir of Vere
|
Margaret Weir of Vere of Kildress
|
Archibald Weir of Vere of Kildress
= Rachel Stewart of Desertcreat
|
Robert Weir of Vere of Kildress
|
John Weir of Vere of Ardwell, Logan Manor
= Mary Logan dau. of Thomas Logan of
Ardwell, Logan Manor, Galloway
|
Thomas Logan Weir of Vere of Carlisle
= Anne Grant Macdonnell of Inverness
|
James Weir of Vere of Lewes
= Natalie Hopgood (descent from
the Collisons of Norfolk and the
Imperial and Royal House of Vere)
|
HI & RH Prince Nicholas de Vere

Vere Descent from the Early Frankish Kings via Prince Milo de Vere of Angiers

- Et In Arcadia Ego -

Trojan Royal House
|
King Antenor d. 443 BC
Of the Cimmerians of Scythia
|
King Marcomer d. 412 BC
Moved Cimmerians from the Black Sea
to Western Europe and what is now Wales,
where they became the Cymru
|
King Antenor d. 385 BC
= Princess Cambra of the Sicambrians
|
King Priamus d. 358 BC
|
King Helenus d. 339 BC
Priest-King of the Arcadian God Pallas
|
King Diocles d. 300 BC
Fought the Goths and Gauls
|
Priest-King Bassanus Magnus d. 250 BC
Built Aix la Chapelle
|

King Clodomir d. 232 BC
|
King Nicanor d. 198 BC
|
King Marcomer d. 170 BC
|
King Clodius d. 195 BC
|
King Antenor d. 143 BC
|
King Clodomir d. 123 BC
|
King Merovachus d. 95 BC
|
King Cassander d. 74 BC
|
King Antharius d. 39 BC
|
King Francus d. 11 BC
Changed tribal name from Sicambri to Franks
|
King Clodius d. 20 AD
|
King Marcomer d. 50 AD
|
King Clodomir d. 63 AD
|
King Antenor d. 69 AD
|
King Ratherius d. 90 AD
|
King Richemer d. 114 AD
|
King Odomar d. 128 AD
|
King Marcomer d. 169 AD
Built Marpurg in Hesse
= Princess Athildis of Camelot
|
King Clodomir d. 180 AD
|
King Farabert d. 186 AD
|
King Sunno d. 213 AD
|
King Hilderic d. 253 AD
|
King Bartherus d. 272 AD
|
King Clodius d. 298 AD
|
King Walter d. 306 AD
|
King Dagobert d. 317 AD
|
King Clodomir d. 337 AD
|
King Richemir d. 350 AD
|

King Theodomir d. 360 AD
|
King Clodius d. 378 AD
|
King Dagobert d. 389 AD
|
Lord Genobaud d. 419 AD
|
Princess Argotta
= Lord Faramund of
the Western Franks
419-430
|
Chief Clodian of Tournai
Priest of Neptune of Arcadia
Lord of the Western Franks 430-446
= Queen Basina I of Thuringia
|
King Meroveus
Founder of the Merovingian Dynasty
of Sorceror Kings d. 456
= Princess Merira
|
King Childeric of the Franks d. 481AD
= Queen Basina II of Thuringia
|
King Clovis of the Franks d. 511 AD
= Clotilde of Burgundy
|
King Lothar I d. 561 AD
|
Princess Blitildis
= Prince Ansbert, Great Great Grandson of
King Clodian of Tournai (above) d. 570 AD
|
Lord Arnoald of Scheldt
= Princess Dua of Swabia
|
Arnulf of Metz
= Princess Dobo of Saxony
|
Lord Ansegis of Brabant (Lower Lorraine)
Margrave of Scheldt d. 685
= Lady Begga, dau of Pepin I, Mayor of Austrasia
|
Lord Pepin II of Heristal, Mayor of the Palaces of
Austrasia, Neustria and Burgundy d. 714
= Lady Alpas
|
Lord Charles Martel (The Hammer) d. 741
|
Pepin the III Brevis, Duke of Lower Lorraine
(Brabant)
Mayor of Neustrasia, King of the Franks
= Lady Leuthergis
|
Princess Bertha
= Prince Milo de Vere, Duke of Angiers
Count of Anjou, son of the Fairy Princess

Melusine I of the Scythians (parallel descent
from Satan via the Egyptian Kings as
above and the Fairy Tuadha de Danaan)
|
Prince Milo II de Vere, Count of Guisnes and Anjou
= Lady Aveline de Nantes
|
Prince Nicassius de Vere, Count of Guisnes
= Lady Agatha de Champagne
|
Prince Otho de Vere, Count of Guisnes
= Lady Constance de Chartres
|
Prince Amelius (Adolph) de Vere Count of Guisnes
= Lady Maud de Ponthieu
|
Prince Guy (Gallus) de Vere, Count of Guisnes
= Lady Gertrude de Clermont de Ponthieu
|
Two Sons:
2nd son – Prince Baldwin de Vere, descent to Ida
de Vere,
the House of Hamilton and the Royal Vere of
Blackwood
&
1st son Prince Manasses de Vere Count of Guisnes,
(descent
to the Vere Earls of Oxford)
=Lady Petronilla de Boleine
|
Prince Alphonse de Vere, Count of Guisnes
= Lady Katarine, dau of Count Arnulf of Flanders
|
Prince Alberic I de Vere, Count of Guisnes
= Princess Beatrix of Normandy
(descent from Satan via the Fairy Princess
Melusine I du Scythes above)
|
Prince Alberic II de Vere,
Sheriff of Cambridge, Lord of Clare and Tonbridge
= Lady Adeliza dau. of Lord Gilbert FitzRichard
|
Prince Aubrey (Alberic) III de Vere, Earl of Oxford,
Shakespeare's Oberon, King of the Fairies
in *A Midsummer Night's Dream*
= Lady Agnes, dau. of Henry Lord Essex.
|
Prince Ralph de Vere of Blackwood 1165 AD
Brother of Robert of Huntingdon; Robin Hood;
God of the Witches, Shakespeare's
Puck, son of Oberon
|
Prince Rory de Vere of Blackwood
|
Prince Ralph de Vere of Blackwood
|
Prince Thomas de Vere of Blackwood
|
Prince Richard de Vere of Blackwood

Prince Thomas de Vere
1st Baron Blackwood 1340 AD

Prince Buan Were of Vere of Blackwood

Prince Rotaldus Were of Vere of Blackwood

Prince Thomas Were of Vere
4th Baron Blackwood

Prince Robert Veyr of Vere of Blackwood

Prince Thomas Weir of Vere of Blackwood
= Lady Aegidia Somerset

Prince James Weir of Vere,
7th Baron Blackwood d. 1599
= Lady Euphemia Hamilton
(descent from the High Elves of Ireland,
Princess Melusine and the Scots Kings)

Sir William Vere of Stanebyres Castle
= Elizabeth Hamilton, his cousin.
(descent from the High Elves of Ireland,
Princess Melusine and the Scots Kings)

Lord Thomas Weir of Vere, Baron Kirkton
= Lady Jane Somerville, the hereditary Witch
of the Dragon House of the Earls Somerville

Major Thomas Weir of Vere of Edinburgh,

The hereditary Witch King of Mid-Lothian
= Margaret Bourdon

Thomas Weir of Vere
Baron Kirkton of Mid-Lothian,
Hereditary Witch King in Ireland
= Mary Robison of Cookstown Ulster

John Weir of Vere

Andrew Weir of Vere

Margaret Weir of Vere of Kildress

Archibald Weir of Vere of Kildress
= Rachel Stewart of Desertcreat

Robert Weir of Vere of Kildress

John Weir of Vere of Ardwell, Logan Manor
= Mary Logan dau. of Thomas Logan of
Ardwell, Logan Manor, Galloway

Thomas Logan Weir of Vere of Carlisle
= Anne Grant Macdonnell of Inverness

James Weir of Vere of Lewes
= Natalie Hopgood (descent from
the Collisons of Norfolk and the
Imperial and Royal House of Vere)

HI & RH Prince Nicholas de Vere

Vere Descent from the Early Frankish
Kings via the Dukes of Hamilton

- Et In Arcadia Ego -

Trojan Royal House

King Antenor d. 443 BC
Of the Cimmerians of Scythia

King Marcomer d. 412 BC
Moved Cimmerians from the Black Sea
To Western Europe

King Antenor d. 385 BC
= Princess Cambra of the Sicambrians

King Priamus d. 358 BC

King Helenus d. 339 BC
Priest-King of the Arcadian God Pallas

King Diocles d. 300 BC
Fought the Goths and Gauls

Priest-King Bassanus Magnus d. 250 BC
Built Aix la Chapelle

King Clodomir d. 232 BC

King Nicanor d. 198 BC

King Marcomer d. 170 BC

King Clodius d. 195 BC

King Antenor d. 143 BC

King Clodomir d. 123 BC

King Merovachus d. 95 BC

King Cassander d. 74 BC

King Antharius d. 39 BC

King Francus d. 11 BC

Changed tribal name from Sicambri to Franks
|
King Clodius d. 20 AD
|
King Marcomer d. 50 AD
|
King Clodomir d. 63 AD
|
King Antenor d. 69 AD
|
King Ratherius d. 90 AD
|
King Richemer d. 114 AD
|
King Odomar d. 128 AD
|
King Marcomer d. 169 AD
Built Marpurg in Hesse
= Princess Athildis of Camelot
|
King Clodomir d. 180 AD
|
King Farabert d. 186 AD
|
King Sunno d. 213 AD
|
King Hilderic d. 253 AD
|
King Bartherus d. 272 AD
|
King Clodius d. 298 AD
|
King Walter d. 306 AD
|
King Dagobert d. 317 AD
|
King Clodomir d. 337 AD
|
King Richemir d. 350 AD
|
King Theodomir d. 360 AD
|
King Clodius d. 378 AD
|
King Dagobert d. 389 AD
|
Lord Genobaud d. 419 AD
|
Princess Argotta
= Lord Faramund of
the Western Franks
419-430
|
Chief Clodian of Tournai
Priest of Neptune of Arcadia
Lord of the Western Franks 430-446
= Queen Basina I of Thuringia
|
King Meroveus

Founder of the Merovingian Dynasty
of Sorceror Kings d. 456
= Princess Merira
|
King Childeric of the Franks d. 481 ad
= Queen Basina II of Thuringia
|
King Clovis of the Franks d. 511 ad
= Clotilde of Burgundy
|
King Lothar I d. 561 ad
|
Princess Blitildis
= Prince Ansbert, Great Great Grandson of
King Clodian of Tournai (above) d. e70 ad
|
Lord Arnoald of Scheldt
= Princess Dua of Swabia
|
Arnulf of Metz
= Princess Dobo of Saxony
|
Lord Ansegis of Brabant (Lower Lorraine)
Margrave of Scheldt d. 685
= Lady Begga, dau of Pepin I, Mayor of Austrasia
|
Lord Pepin II of Heristal, Mayor of the Palaces of
Austrasia, Neustria and Burgundy d. 714
= Lady Alpas
|
Lord Charles Martel (The Hammer) d. 741
|
Pepin the III Brevis, Duke of Lower Lorraine
(Brabant)
Mayor of Neustrasia, King of the Franks
= Lady Leuthergis
|
Princess Bertha
= Prince Milo de Vere, Duke of Angiers
Count of Anjou, son of the Fairy Princess
Melusine I of the Scythians (parallel descent
from Satan via the Egyptian Kings as
above and the Fairy Tuadha de Danaan)
|
Prince Milo II de Vere, Count of Guisnes and Anjou
= Lady Aveline de Nantes
|
Prince Nicassius de Vere, Count of Guisnes
= Lady Agatha de Champagne
|
Prince Otho de Vere, Count of Guisnes
= Lady Constance de Chartres
|
Prince Amelius (Adolph) de Vere Count of Guisnes
= Lady Maud de Ponthieu
|
Prince Guy (Gallus) de Vere, Count of Guisnes
= Lady Gertrude de Clermont de Ponthieu
|

Prince Baldwin de Vere
|
Eustace I de Vere
= Maud de Louvain
|
Eustace II de Vere
Comte de Boulogne
=Saint Ida of Ardennes
|
Princess Ida de Vere
= Baudouin de Bourg
Comte de Rethul
|
Prince Hugues I
Comte de Rethul
= Melisende (Melusine II)
dau. Of Bouchard Comte de Corbeil and
Lady Adelaide de Crecy
|
Badouin II de Bourg
King of Jerusalem 1118-1131
= Princess Morfia of Armenia
|
Princess Melisende of Jerusalem (Melusine III)
= Fulke V Plantagenet Count of Anjou
|
Count Geoffrey Plantagenet
= Princess Mathilda, la Imperatrice
daughter of King Henry I and Princess
Mathilda of Scotland, daughter of
King Malcolm III
|
King Henry II Plantagenet
= Countess Eleanor of Aquitaine
|
King John "Lackland" Plantagenet
= Lady Isabella of Angouleme
|
King Henry III Plantagenet
= Lady Eleanor dau. of Count
Raymond Berenguer IV of Provence
and Princess Beatrix of Savoy
|
King Edward I Plantagenet
= Princess Eleanor of Castille
|
King Edward II Plantagenet
= Princess Isabella of France
|
King Edward III Plantagenet
1327-1377
= Princess Phillipa of Hainault
|
Prince John Plantagenet of Gaunt
= Lady Katharine Swynford
|
Prince John Plantagenet
|
Princess Joan Beaufort Plantagenet

= King James I of Scots
|
King James II
= Mary, dau. of Arnold Duc de Gueldres
|
Princess Mary
= Lord Thomas Boyd
|
Lady Mary Boyd
= James 1st Lord Hamilton
great grandson of
Princess Aenor de Chatellerault
and Guillaume X le Toulousain
Duc de Guyenne, Comte de Poitiers
|
Lady Euphemia Hamilton
(descent from the High Elves of Ireland,
Princess Melusine and the Scots Kings)
= Lord James Weir of Vere,
Baron Blackwood d. 1595
|
Sir William Vere of Stanebyres Castle
= Elizabeth Hamilton, his cousin.
(descent from the High Elves of Ireland,
Princess Melusine and the Scots Kings)
|
Lord Thomas Weir of Vere, Baron Kirkton
= Lady Jane Somerville, The hereditary Witch
of the Dragon House of the Earls Somerville
|
Major Thomas Weir of Vere of Edinburgh,
The hereditary Witch King of Mid-Lothian
= Margaret Bourdon
|
Thomas Weir of Vere
Baron Kirkton of Mid-Lothian,
Hereditary Witch King in Ireland

= Mary Robison of Cookstown Ulster
|
John Weir of Vere
|
Andrew Weir of Vere
|
Margaret Weir of Vere of Kildress
|
Archibald Weir of Vere of Kildress
= Rachel Stewart of Desertcreat
|
Robert Weir of Vere of Kildress
|
John Weir of Vere of Ardwell, Logan Manor
= Mary Logan dau. of Thomas Logan of
Ardwell, Logan Manor, Galloway
|
Thomas Logan Weir of Vere of Carlisle
= Anne Grant Macdonnell of Inverness
|
James Weir of Vere of Lewes

= Natalie Hopgood (descent from
the Collisons of Norfolk and the
Imperial and Royal House of Vere)
|
HI & RH Prince Nicholas de Vere

Vere Descent from the Scythian, Elven Kings of Scots

King Alpin 839-841
|
King Kenneth I 844-859
King of Picts and Scots
|
King Constantine I 863-877
|
King Donald II 889-900
|
King Malcolm I 942-954
|
King Kenneth II 971-995
|
King Malcolm II 1005-1034
|
Princess Bethoc
= Earl Crinan, Thane of the Isles k. 1045
|
King Duncan I 1034-1040 slain by Macbeth
|
King Malcolm III Canmore 1058-1093
= Princess Margaret granddaughter of King
Edmund of England (Descent to Natalie
Hopgood via King Malcolm's daughter
Princess Mathilda who married King Henry I)
|
King David I 1153-1224
|
Lord Henry Earl of Huntingdon d. 1152
= Lady Ada de Warrene
|
Lord David Earl of Huntingdon d. 1219
= Lady Maud de Kevilloc of Chester
|
Lady Isabel of Huntingdon
= Lord Robert de Brus of Annandale d. 1245
|
Lord Robert Bruce of Annandale d; 1294
= Lady Isabel dau. of Lord Gilbert
de Clare Earl of Gloucester
|
Lord Robert Bruce of Annandale Earl of Carrick
= Lady Marjorie dau of Lord Neill Earl of Carrick
|
King Robert I The Bruce 1306-1329

Grand Master of the Knights
Templars in Scotland
= Isabel dau. of Lord Donald Earl of Mar
|
Princess Marjorie Bruce d. 1316
= Lord Walter Stewart,
6th High Steward of Scotland 1291-1326
|
King Robert II
= Lady Elizabeth Muir of Rowallen
|
King Robert III
= Lady Annabelle Drummond of Stobhall
|
King James I
= Princess Joan Beaufort of Somerset
(Descent from King Edward III)
|
King James II
= Mary, dau. of Arnold Duc de Gueldres
|
Princess Mary
= Lord Thomas Boyd
|
Lady Mary Boyd
James 1st Lord Hamilton
great grandson of
Princess Aenor de Chatellerault
and Guillaume X le Toulousain
Duc de Guyenne, Comte de Poitiers
|
Lady Euphemia Hamilton
(descent from the High Elves of Ireland,
Princess Melusine and the Scots Kings)
= Lord James Weir of Vere,
Baron Blackwood d. 1595.
|
Sir William Vere of Stanebyres Castle
= Elizabeth Hamilton, his cousin.
(descent from the High Elves of Ireland,
Princess Melusine and the Scots Kings)
|
Lord Thomas Weir of Vere, Baron Kirkton
= Lady Jane Somerville, the hereditary Witch
of the Dragon House of the Earls Somerville
|
Major Thomas Weir of Vere of Edinburgh,
The hereditary Witch King of Mid-Lothian
= Margaret Bourdon
|
Thomas Weir of Vere
Baron Kirkton of Mid-Lothian,
Hereditary Witch King in Ireland
= Mary Robison of Cookstown Ulster
|
John Weir of Vere
|
Andrew Weir of Vere

Margaret Weir of Vere of Kildress
|
Archibald Weir of Vere of Kildress
= Rachel Stewart of Desertcreat
|
Robert Weir of Vere of Kildress
|
John Weir of Vere of Ardwell, Logan Manor
= Mary Logan dau. of Thomas Logan of
Ardwell, Logan Manor, Galloway
|
Thomas Logan Weir of Vere of Carlisle
= Anne Grant Macdonnell of Inverness
|
James Weir of Vere of Lewes
= Natalie Hopgood (descent from
the Collisons of Norfolk and the
Imperial and Royal House of Vere)
|
HI & RH Prince Nicholas de Vere

Vere Descent from the Irish Dalcassian Kings O'Brien of Munster and the Princes of Desmond

King Feidlimidh
King of Munster
c. 580 AD
|
King Criomthann
King of Munster
|
King Aodh Dubh
King of Munster
|
King Failbe Flan
King of Munster
|
King Colgan 680 AD
King of Munster
|
King Natfraich
King of Munster
|
King Faolghus
King of Munster
|
King Donnghal
King of Munster
|
King Donnghus
King of Munster
|

King Donnghal
King of Munster
|
King Snedghus 850 AD
King of Munster
|
King Artghal
King of Munster
|
King Lachtna
King of Munster
|
King Buadachan
King of Munster
|
King Ceallachan
King of Munster
|
Prince Donnchadh 963 AD
Prince of Desmond
|
Prince Saerbtrethac
Prince of Desmond
|
Prince Carthac
Prince of Desmond 1045
Founder of the House
of Macarthy
|
Prince Muircadhach
Prince of Desmond 1011-1095
|
King Tadgh Macarthy
King of Munster 1124
|
Princess Sabh Macarthy
= King Dermot O'Brien
King of Munster
(Fairy descent from
King Brian Boru of Tara)
|
Prince Turlach O'Brien
= Princess Raignait O'Fogurthy
|
King Donal Mor O'Brien 1194
King of Munster
= Princess Urlachan
of Leinster
|
Princess More O'Brien
= Lord William de Burgh 1205
|
Lord Richard de Burgh 1243
= Lady Egidia de Lacey dau. of
Lord Walter de Lacey and Lady
Margaret de Braosa
|
Lord Walter de Burgh
1st Earl of Ulster 1232-1271

Lady Jill de Burgh
= Sir James Stewart, Co–Regent
and 5th High Steward of Scotland
d. 1309

Sir Walter Stewart 6th
High Steward of Scotland
= Princess Marjorie Bruce
dau. Of King Robert I Bruce
Grand Master of the Knights
Templars in Scotland

King Robert II
= Lady Elizabeth Muir of Rowallen

King Robert III
= Lady Annabelle Drummond of Stobhall

King James I
= Princess Joan Beaufort
Plantagenet of Somerset
(Descent from King
Edward III Plantagenet and the
Imperial and Royal House of Vere)

King James II
= Mary, dau. of Arnold Duc de Gueldres

Princess Mary

= Lord Thomas Boyd

Lady Mary Boyd
James 1st Lord Hamilton
great grandson of
Princess Aenor de Chatellerault
and Guillaume X le Toulousain
Duc de Guyenne, Comte de Poitiers

Lady Euphemia Hamilton
(descent from the High Elves of Ireland,
Princess Melusine and the Scots Kings)
= Lord James Weir of Vere,
Baron Blackwood d. 1599

Sir William Vere of Stanebyres Castle
= Elizabeth Hamilton, his cousin.
(descent from the High Elves of Ireland,
Princess Melusine and the Scots Kings)

Lord Thomas Weir of Vere, Baron Kirkton
= Lady Jane Somerville, the hereditary Witch
of the Dragon House of the Earls Somerville

Major Thomas Weir of Vere of Edinburgh,
The hereditary Witch King of Mid-Lothian
= Margaret Bourdon

Thomas Weir of Vere
Baron Kirkton of Mid-Lothian,
Hereditary Witch King in Ireland
= Mary Robison of Cookstown Ulster

John Weir of Vere

Andrew Weir of Vere

Margaret Weir of Vere of Kildress

Archibald Weir of Vere of Kildress
= Rachel Stewart of Desertcreat

Robert Weir of Vere of Kildress

John Weir of Vere of Ardwell, Logan Manor
= Mary Logan dau. of Thomas Logan of
Ardwell, Logan Manor, Galloway

Thomas Logan Weir of Vere of Carlisle
= Anne Grant Macdonnell of Inverness

James Weir of Vere of Lewes
= Natalie Hopgood (descent from
the Collisons of Norfolk and the
Imperial and Royal House of Vere)

HI & RH Prince Nicholas de Vere

Vere Descent from the Kings of Dalriada
via the Royal House of Stewart

King Erc of Dalriada (North Antrim in Ireland) belonged to the Sacred and Holy Pagan Royal House of the Uilidian of Fir-Bolg, which descended from the Sacred "Peace King" Conaire Mor of Eire, through ritual incarnations of the Celtic God-Spirit of the Sun "Eochaid" who was known as "The Horseman of the Heavens." The God-King Eochaid equated with a male manifestation of the ancient Belgic Goddess-Spirit of Lightning. Through blood and spiritual descent King Erc of Dalriada was an Avatar; a God-King and the Fir-Bolg druidic totem was the Blue Boar, still borne today by his druidic descendants; the Imperial and Royal House of Vere.

The Archdruid King Erc of Dalriada c. 450 AD

King Fergus Mor d. 501 AD

King Domangart

King Grabran of
the Dalriadic Scots

King Aedan MacGabran
The Uther Pendragon or
Great Dragon of Albany

King Eochaid Buide

King Donald Brec

King Domangart

King Eochaid d. 696

King Eochaid II

King Aed Find

King Eochaid III d. 781

King Alpin of Scots

King Kenneth MacAlpin
King of Picts and Scots

King Aedh d. 878

THANES OF LOCHABER

Lord Doir b. 870 d. 936
= The Princess of Northumberland,
dau. of King Oswald

Lord Murdoch b. 900 d. 959

Lord Ferguard b. 929 d. 980
= dau. of King Eric of Norway

Lord Kenneth b. 960 d. 1030
= Dunclina dau. of Kenneth II

Lord Banquo, Killed by Macbeth
b. 990 d. 1043
= Lady Muldivana dau. of Lord
Phaetus, Thane of Atholl,
g.g.g. Grandson of King
Murdoch of Dalriada see above.

Lord Fleance b. 1020
= Princess Nesta-Mary dau. of
Prince Gruffyd, son of King Llewelyn
and Princess Guerta of Deheubarth

Lord Walter, Thane of Locharber
b. 1045 d. 1093 at Alnwick
= Lady Emma b. 1070, dau of Lord
Alan hereditary Steward of Dol

Lord Alan of Lochaber
b. 1088 d. 1153
= Lady Adelina of Oswestry

Lord Walter FitzAlan
1st High Steward of Scotland
= Lady Eschyne de Molle

Lord Alan FitzWalter
2nd High Steward of Scotland
d. 1204
= Lady Eve of Crawford

Lord Walter Stewart
of Dundonald
3rd High Steward of Scotland
= Lady Beatrix, dau of Gilchrist
Earl of Angus

Lord Alexander Stewart
4th High Steward of Scotland
d. 1283
= Lady Jean g.dau of Angus
Lord of Bute and Arran,
descent from Somerled,
Lord of the Isles

Sir James Stewart, Co–Regent
and 5th High Steward of Scotland
d. 1309
= Lady Jill de Bourg dau. of
Lord Walter de Bourg
1st Earl of Ulster

Sir Walter Stewart 6th
High Steward of Scotland
= Princess Marjorie Bruce
dau. Of King Robert I Bruce
Grand Master of the Knights
Templars in Scotland

King Robert II
= Lady Elizabeth Muir of Rowallen

King Robert III
= Lady Annabelle Drummond of Stobhall

King James I

= Princess Joan Beaufort
Plantagenet of Somerset
(Descent from King
Edward III Plantagenet and the

Imperial and Royal House of Vere)
|
King James II
= Mary, dau. of Arnold Duc de Gueldres
|
Princess Mary
= Lord Thomas Boyd
|
Lady Mary Boyd
James 1st Lord Hamilton
great grandson of
Princess Aenor de Chatellerault
and Guillaume X le Toulousain
Duc de Guyenne, Comte de Poitiers
|
Lady Euphemia Hamilton
(descent from the High Elves of Ireland,
Princess Melusine and the Scots Kings)
= Lord James Weir of Vere,
Baron Blackwood d. 1595
|
Sir William Vere of Stanebyres Castle
= Elizabeth Hamilton, his cousin.
(descent from the High Elves of Ireland,
Princess Melusine and the Scots Kings)
|
Lord Thomas Weir of Vere, Baron Kirkton
= Lady Jane Somerville, the hereditary Witch
of the Dragon House of the Earls Somerville
|
Major Thomas Weir of Vere of Edinburgh,
The hereditary Witch King of Mid-Lothian
= Margaret Bourdon
|
Thomas Weir of Vere
Baron Kirkton of Mid-Lothian,
Hereditary Witch King in Ireland
= Mary Robison of Cookstown Ulster
|
John Weir of Vere
|
Andrew Weir of Vere
|
Margaret Weir of Vere of Kildress
|
Archibald Weir of Vere of Kildress
= Rachel Stewart of Desertcreat
|
Robert Weir of Vere of Kildress
|
John Weir of Vere of Ardwell, Logan Manor
= Mary Logan dau. of Thomas Logan of
Ardwell, Logan Manor, Galloway
|
Thomas Logan Weir of Vere of Carlisle
= Anne Grant Macdonnell of Inverness
|
James Weir of Vere of Lewes
= Natalie Hopgood (descent from

the Collisons of Norfolk and the
Imperial and Royal House of Vere)
|
HI & RH Prince Nicholas de Vere

Vere Descent from the Lia Fail and the Kings of Ireland

The Babylonian Goddess Tiamat
(The Greek Goddess "Chaos"), Mother of Gaia
|
The Babylonian Queen Kishar
(The Greek Goddess Gaia:
Mother Earth)
|
The Babylonian God-King Anu (Chronos-Saturn)
and the High
Council of the Anunnaki: The Jewish Elohim: The
Old Gods
|
Satan (Enki; son of Anu, half-brother of Enlil-
Jehovah)
|
Egyptian Royal descent
|
King Solomon
Lord of the Rings.
1015 BC
= Princess Naamah the Ammonitess.
Solomon's Descent from Satan
via the Dragon Queen of Sobekh,
Kiya Tasherit, wife of Prince Rama
|
King Rehoboam
King of Judah 975 BC
= Princess Maachlah
dau. of Ureil of Gibeah
|
King Abijah
King of Judah
957 BC
|
King Asa
King of Judah 955 BC
= Princess Azubah
dau. of Shilhi
|
King Jehoshaphat
King of Judah 917 BC
|
King Jehoram
King of Judah 893 BC
= Princess Athalia
dau. of Omri
|

King Ahaziah
King of Judah 885 BC
= Princess Zibiah of Beersheba
|
King Joash
King of Judah 878 BC
= Princess Jehoaddan of Jerusalem
|
King Amaziah
King of Judah 840 BC
= Princess Jecoliah of Jerusalem
|
King Uzziah
King of Judah 811 BC
= Princess Jerushah
dau. Of Zadok The Priest
|
King Jotham
King of Judah 759 BC
|
King Ahaz
King of Judah 742 BC
= Princess Abijah
dau of Zechariah
|
King Hezekiah
King of Judah 726 BC
= Princess Hephzibah
|
King Mannaseh
King of Judah 697 BC
= Princess Meshullemeth
dau of Haruz of Jotbah
|
King Amon
King of Judah 642 BC
= Princess Jedidah
dau. of Adaiah of Boscath
|
King Josiah
King of Judah 640 BC
= 2. Princess Hamutal
dau. of Jeremiah of Libnah
|
King Zedekiah
King of Judah 598 BC
|
Princess Tamar
= King Eochaid I
High King of Ireland after the
displacement of the remnant
of the Tuadha de Danaan
|
King Irial Faidh
|
King Eithriall
|
King Follain
|

King Tighernmas
|
King Eanbotha
|
King Smiorguil
|
King Fiachach Labhruine
|
King Aongus Oilbughagah
|
King Maoin
|
King Rotheachta
|
King Dein
|
King Siorna Saoghalach
|
King Oiliolla Olchaoin
|
King Nuadha Fionn Fail
|
King Giallchadh
|
King Simon Breac
|
King Muiriadhach Bolgrach
|
King Fiathadh Tolgrach
|
King Duach Laighrach
|
King Eochaidh Buillaig
|
King Ugaine Mar (The Great)
|
King Cobhtach Caolbreag
|
King Meilage
|
King Jaran Gleofathach
|
King Conla Gruaich
|
King Ceaigach
|
King Oiliolla Caisfhiaclach
|
King Eochaid Foltleathan
|
King Aonghus Tuirimheach
|
King Fiachra Firmara
|
King Feradaig
|
King Fergus I
|
King Maine

(Father of Siadhail: descent to
the O'Shiels of Ireland)
|
King Dornadil
|
King Rowein
|
King Reuther
|
King Eders
|
King Conaire Mor
|
King Admoir
|
King Corbred I
|
King Dare-Dornmoir
|
King Corbred II
|
King Luigdig-Ellatig
|
King Modha Lamha
|
King Conaire II
= Princess Saraid
|
King Corbred of Dal Riada
|
King Eochaid
|
King Athirco
|
King Findacher
|
King Thrinklind
|
King Romaich
|
King Angus
|
King Eochaid Muin-Remor
|
King Erc
|
King Fergus Mor
d. 501 AD
|
King Domangart
501-506
|
King Gabran
537-559
|
King Aeden Mac Gabran
The Pendragon of Britain
=Princess Ygraine d'Avalon del Acques

From Aeden Mac Gabran Ygraine had Prince
Arthur Pendragon
From Gwyr Llew Ygraine had Princess Morgana
the Fairy
|
King Arthur Pendragon
= Princess Morgana the Fairy

|
Prince Mordred Pendragon
Archpriest of the Celtic Church
= Pictish Princess
|
Princess Tortolina Pendragon
= Nicharcos
Pictish Archpriest
|
Lord Marsidalio
= Lady Repulita
|
Lord Hedomenos
= Lady Urbana
|
Lord Agenor
= Lady Lampusa
|
Lord Diaprepon
= Lady Vistosa
|
Lord Stragayo
= Lady Hermosina dau. of Lord Natasil of Athole
|
Lord Zeron
= Lady Bramata
|
Lord Polyteles
= Lady Zaglopis
|
Lord Vocompos of Cromartie
= Lady Androlema of Douglas
|
Lord Carolo
= Lady Trastevole dau. of Lord Uilleam
|
Lord Endymion
= Lady Suaviloqua
|
Lord Sebastion
= Lady Francolina
|
Lord Lawrence
= Lady Mathilda
|
Lord Olipher
= Lady Allegra
|
Lord Quintin
= Lady Winnifred
|

Lord Goodwin
= Lady Dorothy
|
Lord Frederick
= Lady Lauretta dau. of Patrick Earl of March
|
Lady Matilda
= Lord William Comyn, grandson of Robert
Earl of Northumberland
|
Lord Richard Comyn
= Lady Hextilda dau. of Hutred of Tynedal
|
Lord William Comyn, Great Justiciar of Scotland
= Lady Marjorie Countess of Buchan
|
Lady Elizabeth Comyn
= Lord William 9th Earl of Mar
|
Lord Donald 10th Earl of Mar
= Princess Helen dau. of Prince
Llewellyn of North Wales
|
Lady Isabel Mar
= King Robert I the Bruce
Grand Master of the Knights
Templars in Scotland
|
Princess Marjorie Bruce
= Lord Walter Stewart
6th Hgh Steward of Scotland
|
King Robert II
= Lady Elizabeth Muir of Rowallen
|
King Robert III
= Lady Annabelle Drummond of Stobhall
|
King James I
= Princess Joan Beaufort of Somerset
(Descent from King Edward III)
|
King James II
= Mary, dau. of Arnold Duc de Gueldres
|
Princess Mary
= Lord Thomas Boyd
|
Lady Mary Boyd
James 1st Lord Hamilton
great grandson of
Princess Aenor de Chatellerault
and Guillaume X le Toulousain
Duc de Guyenne, Comte de Poitiers
|
Lady Euphemia Hamilton
(descent from the High Elves of Ireland,
Princess Melusine and the Scots Kings)
= Lord James Weir of Vere,

Baron Blackwood d. 1595
|
Sir William Vere of Stanebyres Castle
= Elizabeth Hamilton, his cousin.
(descent from the High Elves of Ireland,
Princess Melusine and the Scots Kings)
|
Lord Thomas Weir of Vere, Baron Kirkton
= Lady Jane Somerville, the hereditary Witch
of the Dragon House of the Earls Somerville
|
Major Thomas Weir of Vere of Edinburgh,
The hereditary Witch King of Mid-Lothian
= Margaret Bourdon
|
Thomas Weir of Vere
Baron Kirkton of Mid-Lothian,
Hereditary Witch King in Ireland
= Mary Robison of Cookstown Ulster
|
John Weir of Vere
|
Andrew Weir of Vere
|
Margaret Weir of Vere of Kildress
|
Archibald Weir of Vere of Kildress
= Rachel Stewart of Desertcreat
|
Robert Weir of Vere of Kildress
|
John Weir of Vere of Ardwell, Logan Manor
= Mary Logan dau. of Thomas Logan of
Ardwell, Logan Manor, Galloway
|
Thomas Logan Weir of Vere of Carlisle
= Anne Grant Macdonnell of Inverness
|
James Weir of Vere of Lewes
= Natalie Hopgood (descent from
the Collisons of Norfolk and the
Imperial and Royal House of Vere)
|
HI & RH Prince Nicholas de Vere

The Viking Descent of the Veres from the Norse Kings via the Dukes of Hamilton

King Ingiald The Wicked 600 AD
|
King Olaf of Vermaland, Norway
|

King Halfdan of the Uplanders
|
King Eystein of Raumariki
|
King Halfdan
|
Jarl (Earl) Ivar of the Uplanders
|
Jarl Eystein Glumra
|
Jarl Ranald I the Wise of Orkney
|
Duke Rolf of Normandy 911 AD
|
Duke William I 932 AD
|
Duke Richard I 942 AD
|
Duke Richard II 996 AD
|
Duke Richard III 1027 AD
|
Duke Robert I 1028 AD
|
King William I of England
= Lady Mathilda van Vlaanderen
dau. of Count Baldwin V of Flanders
|
King Henry I of England
= Princess Mathilda dau. of
King Malcom III Canmore
of Scotland and Margaret,
dau. of Edward the Exile
by Princess Agatha of Bulgaria
|
Princess Mathilda la Imperatrice
(Empress of England)
= Count Geoffrey Plantagenet
of Anjou
|
King Henry II Plantagenet
= Countess Eleanor of Aquitaine
|
King John "Lackland" Plantagenet
= Lady Isabella of Angouleme
|
King Henry III Plantagenet
= Lady Eleanor dau. of Count
Raymond Berenguer IV of Provence
and Princess Beatrix of Savoy
|
King Edward I Plantagenet
= Princess Eleanor of Castille
|
King Edward II Plantagenet
= Princess Isabella of France
|
King Edward III Plantagenet
1327-1377

= Princess Phillipa of Hainault
|
Prince John Plantagenet of Gaunt
= Lady Katharine Swynford
|
Prince John Plantagenet
|
Princess Joan Beaufort Plantagenet
= King James I of Scots
|
King James II
= Mary, dau. of Arnold Duc de Gueldres
|
Princess Mary
= Lord Thomas Boyd
|
Lady Mary Boyd
James 1st Lord Hamilton
great grandson of
Princess Aenor de Chatellerault
and Guillaume X le Toulousain
Duc de Guyenne, Comte de Poitiers
|
Lady Euphemia Hamilton
(descent from the High Elves of Ireland,
Princess Melusine and the Scots Kings)
= Lord James Weir of Vere,
Baron Blackwood d. 1595
|
Sir William Vere of Stanebyres Castle
= Elizabeth Hamilton, his cousin.
(descent from the High Elves of Ireland,
Princess Melusine and the Scots Kings)
|
Lord Thomas Weir of Vere, Baron Kirkton
= Lady Jane Somerville, the hereditary Witch
of the Dragon House of the Earls Somerville
|
Major Thomas Weir of Vere of Edinburgh,
|
The hereditary Witch King of Mid-Lothian
= Margaret Bourdon
|
Thomas Weir of Vere
Baron Kirkton of Mid-Lothian,
Hereditary Witch King in Ireland
= Mary Robison of Cookstown Ulster
|
John Weir of Vere
|
Andrew Weir of Vere
|
Margaret Weir of Vere of Kildress
|
Archibald Weir of Vere of Kildress
= Rachel Stewart of Desertcreat
|
Robert Weir of Vere of Kildress
|

John Weir of Vere of Ardwell, Logan Manor
= Mary Logan dau. of Thomas Logan of
Ardwell, Logan Manor, Galloway
|
Thomas Logan Weir of Vere of Carlisle
= Anne Grant Macdonnell of Inverness
|
James Weir of Vere of Lewes
= Natalie Hopgood (descent from
the Collisons of Norfolk and the
Imperial and Royal House of Vere)
|
HI & RH Prince Nicholas de Vere

The Viking Descent of the Veres from the Norse Kings via Princess Beatrix of Normandy

King Ingiald "The Wicked" 600 AD
|
King Olaf of Vermaland, Norway
|
King Halfdan of the Uplanders
|
King Eystein of Raumarike
|
King Halfdan
|
Jarl (Earl) Ivar of the Uplanders
|
Jarl Eystein Glumra
|
Jarl Ranald I the Wise of Orkney
|
Duke Rolf of Normandy 911 AD
|
Duke William I 932 AD
|
Duke Richard I 942 AD
|
Duke Richard II 996 AD
|
Duke Richard III 1027 AD
|
Duke Robert I 1028 AD
|
Princess Beatrix of Normandy
Sister of King William I the Conqueror
= Prince Alberic I de Vere, Count of Guisnes
(descent from Satan via the Fairy Princess
Melusine I Vere du Scythes)
|
Prince Alberic II de Vere,
Sheriff of Cambridge, Lord of Clare and Tonbridge

= Lady Adeliza dau. of Lord Gilbert FitzRichard
|
Prince Aubrey (Alberic) III de Vere, Earl of Oxford,
(Alberic: Albe-Righ; Oberon – Elf King) Inspiration
for Shakespeare's Oberon, King of the Fairies
in *A Midsummer Night's Dream*
= Lady Agnes, dau. of Henry Lord Essex.
|
Prince Ralph de Vere of Blackwood 1165 AD
Brother of Robert of Huntingdon: Robin Hood;
God of the Witches, Shakespeare's
Puck, son of Oberon (Aubrey)
|
Prince Rory de Vere of Blackwood
|
Prince Ralph de Vere of Blackwood
|
Prince Thomas de Vere of Blackwood
|
Prince Richard de Vere of Blackwood
|
Prince Thomas de Vere
1st Baron Blackwood 1340 AD
|
Prince Buan Were of Vere of Blackwood
|
Prince Rotaldus Were of Vere of Blackwood
|
Prince Thomas Were of Vere
4th Baron Blackwood
|
Prince Robert Veyr of Vere of Blackwood
|
Prince Thomas Weir of Vere of Blackwood
= Lady Aegidia Somerset
|
Prince James Weir of Vere,
7th Baron Blackwood d. 1595
= Lady Euphemia Hamilton
(descent from the High Elves of Ireland,
Princess Melusine and the Scots Kings)
|
Sir William Vere of Stanebyres Castle
= Elizabeth Hamilton, his cousin
(descent from the High Elves of Ireland,
Princess Melusine and the Scots Kings)
|
Lord Thomas Weir of Vere, Baron Kirkton
= Lady Jane Somerville, the hereditary Witch
of the Dragon House of the Earls Somerville
|
Major Thomas Weir of Vere of Edinburgh,
The hereditary Witch King of Mid-Lothian
= Margaret Bourdon
|
Thomas Weir of Vere
Baron Kirkton of Mid-Lothian,
Hereditary Witch King in Ireland
= Mary Robison of Cookstown Ulster

John Weir of Vere
|
Andrew Weir of Vere
|
Margaret Weir of Vere of Kildress
|
Archibald Weir of Vere of Kildress
= Rachel Stewart of Desertcreat
|
Robert Weir of Vere of Kildress
|
John Weir of Vere of Ardwell, Logan Manor
= Mary Logan dau. of Thomas Logan of
Ardwell, Logan Manor, Galloway
|
Thomas Logan Weir of Vere of Carlisle
= Anne Grant Macdonnell of Inverness
|
James Weir of Vere of Lewes
= Natalie Hopgood (descent from
the Collisons of Norfolk and the
Imperial and Royal House of Vere)
|
HI & RH Prince Nicholas de Vere

Vere Descent from the Princes of Wales from the

Genealogy of the Duchess of Pembrokeshire

Prince Prawst of North Wales
= Princess Seissylt of North Wales
|
Prince Llewellyn of North Wales 974 AD
= Queen Angharad II of Powys
|
Prince Griffifth I of North Wales
= Lady Ealdgyth of Mercia, granddaughter of
Earl Leofric III and Lady Godiva
|
Princess Nesta of North Wales
= Prince Trahaern of Arwystli
|
Prince Llywarch of North Wales

= Lady Dyddgu dau. of Idnerth
Lord of Builth Wells
|
Lady Gladys of North Wales
= Prince Owen I Gwynedd of North Wales
|
Prince Iorwerth of North Wales

= Lady Maret of Powys–Vadoc
|
Prince Llewellyn of Wales 1173-1240 AD
|
Princess Helen
= Lord Donald 10th Earl of Mar
|
Lady Isabel
= King Robert I the Bruce, Grand Master
of the Knights Templars in Scotland
|
Princess Marjorie Bruce
= Lord Walter Stewart
6th High Steward of Scotland
|
King Robert II
= Lady Elizabeth Muir of Rowallen
|
King Robert III
= Lady Annabelle Drummond of Stobhall
|
King James I
= Princess Joan Beaufort of Somerset
(Descent from King Edward III)
|
King James II
= Mary, dau. of Arnold Duc de Gueldres
|
Princess Mary
= Lord Thomas Boyd
|
Lady Mary Boyd
James 1st Lord Hamilton
great grandson of
Princess Aenor de Chatellerault
and Guillaume X le Toulousain
Duc de Guyenne, Comte de Poitiers
|
Lady Euphemia Hamilton
(descent from the High Elves of Ireland,
Princess Melusine and the Scots Kings)
= Lord James Weir of Vere,
Baron Blackwood d. 1595
|
Sir William Vere of Stanebyres Castle
= Elizabeth Hamilton, his cousin.
(descent from the High Elves of Ireland,
Princess Melusine and the Scots Kings)
|
Lord Thomas Weir of Vere, Baron Kirkton
= Lady Jane Somerville, the hereditary Witch
of the Dragon House of the Earls Somerville
|
Major Thomas Weir of Vere of Edinburgh,
The hereditary Witch King of Mid-Lothian
= Margaret Bourdon
|
Thomas Weir of Vere
Baron Kirkton of Mid-Lothian,

Hereditary Witch King in Ireland
= Mary Robison of Cookstown Ulster
|
John Weir of Vere
|
Andrew Weir of Vere
|
Margaret Weir of Vere of Kildress
|
Archibald Weir of Vere of Kildress
= Rachel Stewart of Desertcreat
|
Robert Weir of Vere of Kildress
|
John Weir of Vere of Ardwell, Logan Manor
= Mary Logan dau. of Thomas Logan of
Ardwell, Logan Manor, Galloway
|
Thomas Logan Weir of Vere of Carlisle
= Anne Grant Macdonnell of Inverness
|
James Weir of Vere of Lewes

= Natalie Hopgood (descent from
the Collisons of Norfolk and the
Imperial and Royal House of Vere)
|
HI & RH Prince Nicholas de Vere

Vere Descent from the Royal House of Stewart

Lord Alan of Lochaber
b. 1088 d. 1153
= Lady Adelina of Oswestry
|
Lord Walter FitzAlan
1st Hgh Steward of Scotland
= Lady Eschyne de Molle
|
Lord Alan FitzWalter
2nd High Steward of Scotland
d. 1204
= Lady Eve of Crawford
|
Lord Walter Stewart
of Dundonald
3rd High Steward of Scotland
= Lady Beatrix, dau of Gilchrist
Earl of Angus
|
Lord Alexander Stewart
4th High Steward of Scotland
d. 1283

= Lady Jean g.dau of Angus
Lord of Bute and Arran,
descent from Somerled,
Lord of the Isles
|
Sir James Stewart, Co–Regent
and 5th High Steward of Scotland
d. 1309
= Lady Jill de Bourg dau. of
Lord Walter de Bourg
1st Earl of Ulster
|
Sir Walter Stewart 6th
High Steward of Scotland
= Princess Marjorie Bruce
dau. Of King Robert I Bruce
Grand Master of the Knights
Templars in Scotland
|
King Robert II
= Lady Elizabeth Muir of Rowallen
|
King Robert III
= Lady Annabelle Drummond of Stobhall
|
King James I
= Princess Joan Beaufort
Plantagenet of Somerset
(Descent from King
Edward III Plantagenet and the
Imperial and Royal House of Vere)
|
King James II
= Mary, dau. of Arnold Duc de Gueldres
|
Princess Mary
= Lord Thomas Boyd
|
Lady Mary Boyd
James 1st Lord Hamilton
great grandson of
Princess Aenor de Chatellerault
and Guillaume X le Toulousain
Duc de Guyenne, Comte de Poitiers
|
Lady Euphemia Hamilton
(descent from the High Elves of Ireland,
Princess Melusine and the Scots Kings)
= Lord James Weir of Vere,
Baron Blackwood d. 1595
|
Sir William Vere of Stanebyres Castle
= Elizabeth Hamilton, his cousin.
(descent from the High Elves of Ireland,
Princess Melusine and the Scots Kings)
|
Lord Thomas Weir of Vere, Baron Kirkton
= Lady Jane Somerville, the hereditary Witch
of the Dragon House of the Earls Somerville

Major Thomas Weir of Vere of Edinburgh,
The hereditary Witch King of Mid-Lothian
= Margaret Bourdon
|
Thomas Weir of Vere
Baron Kirkton of Mid-Lothian,
Hereditary Witch King in Ireland
= Mary Robison of Cookstown Ulster
|
John Weir of Vere
|
Andrew Weir of Vere
|
Margaret Weir of Vere of Kildress
|
Archibald Weir of Vere of Kildress
= Rachel Stewart of Desertcreat
|
Robert Weir of Vere of Kildress
|
John Weir of Vere of Ardwell, Logan Manor
= Mary Logan dau. of Thomas Logan of
Ardwell, Logan Manor, Galloway
|
Thomas Logan Weir of Vere of Carlisle
= Anne Grant Macdonnell of Inverness
|
James Weir of Vere of Lewes
= Natalie Hopgood (descent from
the Collisons of Norfolk and the
Imperial and Royal House of Vere)
|
HI & RH Prince Nicholas de Vere

Vere Descent from the Spanish Royal Houses of Castile, Navarre and Aragon via the Dukes of Hamilton

King Sancho I The Great 970-1035
King of Castile, Navarre and Aragon
|
King Ferdinand 1037-1065
King of Castile
|
King Alfonso IV 1072-1109
King of Castile and Leon
|
Queen Uracca 1109-1126
Queen of Castile and Leon
|
King Alfonso VII 1126-1157
King of Castile and Leon
|

King Ferdinand II 1157-1188
King of Leon
|
King Alfonso IX 1188-1230
King of Leon
|
King Ferdinand III
King of Castile 1217-1252
King of Leon 1230-1252
|
Princess Eleanor of Castile d. 1290
= King Edward I of England
|
King Edward II Plantagenet
= Princess Isabella of France
|
King Edward III
1327-1377
= Princess Phillipa of Hainault
|
Prince John of Gaunt
= Lady Katharine Swynford
|
Prince John Plantagenet
|
Princess Joan Beaufort
= King James I of Scots
|
King James II
= Mary, dau. of Arnold Duc de Gueldres
|
Princess Mary
= Lord Thomas Boyd
|
Lady Mary Boyd
James 1st Lord Hamilton
great grandson of
Princess Aenor de Chatellerault
and Guillaume X le Toulousain
Duc de Guyenne, Comte de Poitiers
|
Lady Euphemia Hamilton
(descent from the High Elves of Ireland,
Princess Melusine and the Scots Kings)
= Lord James Weir of Vere,
Baron Blackwood d. 1595
|
Sir William Vere of Stanebyres Castle
= Elizabeth Hamilton, his cousin.
(descent from the High Elves of Ireland,
Princess Melusine and the Scots Kings)
|
Lord Thomas Weir of Vere, Baron Kirkton
= Lady Jane Somerville, the hereditary Witch
of the Dragon House of the Earls Somerville
|
Major Thomas Weir of Vere of Edinburgh,
The hereditary Witch King of Mid-Lothian

= Margaret Bourdon
|
Thomas Weir of Vere
Baron Kirkton of Mid-Lothian,
Hereditary Witch King in Ireland
= Mary Robison of Cookstown Ulster
|
John Weir of Vere
|
Andrew Weir of Vere
|
Margaret Weir of Vere of Kildress
|
Archibald Weir of Vere of Kildress
= Rachel Stewart of Desertcreat
|
Robert Weir of Vere of Kildress
|
John Weir of Vere of Ardwell, Logan Manor
= Mary Logan dau. of Thomas Logan of
Ardwell, Logan Manor, Galloway
|
Thomas Logan Weir of Vere of Carlisle
= Anne Grant Macdonnell of Inverness
|
James Weir of Vere of Lewes
= Natalie Hopgood (descent from
the Collisons of Norfolk and the
Imperial and Royal House of Vere)
|
HI & RH Prince Nicholas de Vere

Vere Descent from the Sacred and Holy Uilidian Fir Bolg and the Archdruid Erc of Dalriada
via Prince Milo de Vere of Angiers

Archdruid Erc, King of Dalriada 450 AD
|
Archdruid Loarn, King of Dalriada
Appenaged in Dalriada
|
Archdruid Prince Muiredach
|
Archdruid Prince Eochaid
|
Archdruid Prince Bartan
App. In Morvern
|
Archdruid Prince Colman 590 AD
|
Archdruid Prince Nechtan
|
Archdruid Prince Fergus
|
Archdruid Prince Feradach

|
Archdruid Prince Ferchar b. c. 660 AD
|
Archdruid King Melusthainn 680 AD
|
King Elinus (Gille Sidhean)
= Princess Pressina dau. of King
Brude Mac Bile of the Picts
|
The Fairy Princess Melusine
=Rainfroi de Vere
|
Prince Milo de Vere, Duke of
Angiers, Count of Anjou
=Princess Bertheld, sister to
Charlemagne
|
Prince Milo II de Vere, Count of Guisnes and Anjou
= Lady Aveline de Nantes
|
Prince Nicassius de Vere, Count of Guisnes
= Lady Agatha de Champagne
|
Prince Otho de Vere, Count of Guisnes
= Lady Constance de Chartres
|
Prince Amelius (Adolph) de Vere Count of Guisnes
= Lady Maud de Ponthieu
|
Prince Guy (Gallus) de Vere, Count of Guisnes
= Lady Gertrude de Clermont de Ponthieu
|
Two Sons:
2nd son – Prince Baldwin de Vere, descent to Ida
de Vere,
the House of Hamilton and the Royal Vere of
Blackwood
&
1st son Prince Manasses de Vere Count of
Guisnes, (descent to the Vere Earls of Oxford)
=Lady Petronilla de Boleine
|
Prince Alphonse de Vere, Count of Guisnes
= Lady Katarine, dau of Count Arnulf of Flanders
|
Prince Alberic I de Vere, Count of Guisnes
= Princess Beatrix of Normandy
(descent from Satan via the Fairy Princess
Melusine I du Scythes above)
|
Prince Alberic II de Vere,
Sheriff of Cambridge, Lord of Clare and Tonbridge
= Lady Adeliza dau. of Lord Gilbert FitzRichard
|
Prince Aubrey (Alberic) III de Vere, Earl of Oxford,
Shakespeare's Oberon, King of the Fairies
= Lady Agnes, dau. of Henry Lord Essex.
|
Prince Ralph de Vere of Blackwood 1165 AD

Brother of Robert of Huntingdon; Robin Hood;
God of the Witches, Shakespeare's
Puck, son of Oberon
|
Prince Rory de Vere of Blackwood
|
Prince Ralph de Vere of Blackwood
|
Prince Thomas de Vere of Blackwood
|
Prince Richard de Vere of Blackwood
|
Prince Thomas de Vere
1st Baron Blackwood 1340 AD
|
Prince Buan Were of Vere of Blackwood
|
Prince Rotaldus Were of Vere of Blackwood
|
Prince Thomas Were of Vere
4th Baron Blackwood
|
Prince Robert Veyr of Vere of Blackwood
|
Prince Thomas Weir of Vere of Blackwood
= Lady Aegidia Somerset
|
Prince James Weir of Vere,
7th Baron Blackwood d. 1595
= Lady Euphemia Hamilton
(descent from the High Elves of Ireland,
Princess Melusine and the Scots Kings)
|
Sir William Vere of Stanebyres Castle
= Elizabeth Hamilton, his cousin.
(descent from the High Elves of Ireland,
Princess Melusine and the Scots Kings)
|
Lord Thomas Weir of Vere, Baron Kirkton
= Lady Jane Somerville, the hereditary Witch
of the Dragon House of the Earls Somerville
|
Major Thomas Weir of Vere of Edinburgh,
|
The hereditary Witch King of Mid-Lothian
= Margaret Bourdon
|
Thomas Weir of Vere
Baron Kirkton of Mid-Lothian,
Hereditary Witch King in Ireland
= Mary Robison of Cookstown Ulster
|
John Weir of Vere
|
Andrew Weir of Vere
|
Margaret Weir of Vere of Kildress
|
Archibald Weir of Vere of Kildress

= Rachel Stewart of Desertcreat
|
Robert Weir of Vere of Kildress
|
John Weir of Vere of Ardwell, Logan Manor
= Mary Logan dau. of Thomas Logan of
Ardwell, Logan Manor, Galloway
|
Thomas Logan Weir of Vere of Carlisle
= Anne Grant Macdonnell of Inverness
|
James Weir of Vere of Lewes
= Natalie Hopgood (descent from
the Collisons of Norfolk and the
Imperial and Royal House of Vere)
|
HI & RH Prince Nicholas de Vere

Vere Descent from the Sacred and Holy Ulidian Fir Bolg Archdruid Erc via the Dukes of Hamilton

Archdruid Erc, King of Dalriada 450 AD
|
Archdruid Loarn, King of Dalriada
Appenaged in Dalriada
|
Archdruid Prince Muiredach
|
Archdruid Prince Eochaid
|
Archdruid Prince Bartan
App. In Morvern
|
Archdruid Prince Colman 600 AD
|
Archdruid Prince Nechtan
|
Archdruid Prince Fergus
|
Archdruid Prince Feradach
|
Archdruid Prince Ferchar
|
Archdruid King Melusthainn
|
King Elinus (Gille Sidhean:
Elf Servant) of Albha, North Argyll;
The Dragon of Berenicia, Priest King
= Bruidhina (Pressina) Vere
Dragon Queen, La Fey du
Fontaine: Mermaid, Druidess
|
Princess Melusine I Vere
(Maelesanu; Milouziana du Scythes)
La Fey d'Avalon et la Fonteine de Soif

The Fairy Melusine, Neice of Morgan La Fey
= Rainfroy de Vere, Earl of Forez 733
|
Prince Milo de Vere, Duke of Angiers
Count of Anjou,
= Princess Bertha, sister of Charlemagne
(parallel Satanic, Fairy descent via Jesus Christ)
|
Prince Milo II de Vere, Count of Guisnes and Anjou
= Lady Aveline de Nantes
|
Prince Nicassius de Vere, Count of Guisnes
= Lady Agatha de Champagne
|
Prince Otho de Vere, Count of Guisnes
= Lady Constance de Chartres
|
Prince Amelius (Adolph) de Vere Count of Guisnes
= Lady Maud de Ponthieu
|
Prince Gallus (Guy) de Vere, Count of Guisnes
= Lady Gertrude de Clermont de Ponthieu
|
Prince Baldwin de Vere
|
Eustace I de Vere
= Maud de Louvain
|
Eustace II de Vere
Comte de Boulogne
=Saint Ida of Ardennes
|
Princess Ida de Vere
= Baudouin de Bourg
Comte de Rethul
|
Prince Hugues I
Comte de Rethul
= Melisende (Melusine II)
dau. Of Bouchard Comte de Corbeil and
Lady Adelaide de Crecy
|
Badouin II de Bourg
King of Jerusalem 1118-1131
= Princess Morfia of Armenia
|
Princess Melisende of Jerusalem (Melusine III)
= Fulke V Plantagenet Count of Anjou
|
Count Geoffrey Plantagenet
= Princess Mathilda, la Imperatrice
daughter of King Henry I and Princess
Mathilda of Scotland, daughter of
King Malcolm III
|
King Henry II Plantagenet
= Countess Eleanor of Aquitaine
|
King John "Lackland" Plantagenet

= Lady Isabella of Angouleme
|
King Henry III Plantagenet
= Lady Eleanor dau. of Count
Raymond Berenguer IV of Provence
and Princess Beatrix of Savoy
|
King Edward I Plantagenet
= Princess Eleanor of Castille
|
King Edward II Plantagenet
= Princess Isabella of France
|
King Edward III Plantagenet
1327-1377
= Princess Phillipa of Hainault
|
Prince John Plantagenet of Gaunt
= Lady Katharine Swynford
|
Prince John Plantagenet
|
Princess Joan Beaufort
= King James I of Scots
|
King James II
= Mary, dau. of Arnold
Duc de Gueldres
|
Princess Mary
= Lord Thomas Boyd
|
Lady Mary Boyd
James 1st Lord Hamilton
great grandson of
Princess Aenor de Chatellerault
and Guillaume X le Toulousain
Duc de Guyenne, Comte de Poitiers
|
Lady Euphemia Hamilton
(descent from the High Elves of Ireland,
Princess Melusine and the Scots Kings)
= Lord James Weir of Vere,
Baron Blackwood d. 1595
|
Sir William Vere of Stanebyres Castle
= Elizabeth Hamilton, his cousin.
(descent from the High Elves of Ireland,
Princess Melusine and the Scots Kings)
|
Lord Thomas Weir of Vere, Baron Kirkton
= Lady Jane Somerville, the hereditary Witch
of the Dragon House of the Earls Somerville
|
Major Thomas Weir of Vere of Edinburgh,
The hereditary Witch King of Mid-Lothian
= Margaret Bourdon
|
Thomas Weir of Vere

Baron Kirkton of Mid-Lothian,
Hereditary Witch King in Ireland
= Mary Robison of Cookstown Ulster
|
John Weir of Vere
|
Andrew Weir of Vere
|
Margaret Weir of Vere of Kildress
|
Archibald Weir of Vere of Kildress
= Rachel Stewart of Desertcreat
|
Robert Weir of Vere of Kildress
|
John Weir of Vere of Ardwell, Logan Manor
= Mary Logan dau. of Thomas Logan of
Ardwell, Logan Manor, Galloway
|
Thomas Logan Weir of Vere of Carlisle
= Anne Grant Macdonnell of Inverness
|
James Weir of Vere of Lewes
= Natalie Hopgood (descent from
the Collisons of Norfolk and the
Imperial and Royal House of Vere)
|
HI & RH Prince Nicholas de Vere

Vere Descent from the Archdruid Merlin Taliesin

Queen Mabh (Maive) of the Fairies
(Clan Daouine Sidhe) of Ireland
Sword-Tutor of Finn MacCool
|
Merlin Taliesin
Archdruid and Elven Prince Bard
= Princess Viviane I d'Avalon del Acques
of the Elven Kings of Albany
(Descent from Jesus Christ and Archdruid
Bran the Blessed)
|
Princess Ygraine de Avalon del Acques

Gwyr Llew = Ygraine of Avalon = Aeden Mac
Gabran

From Aeden Mac Gabran – Prince Arthur Pendragon
From Gwyr Llew – Princess Morgana the Fairy

(Here follows the Pendragon descent of the House
of Vere from King Arthur and the House of the High
Elves of Avalon extracted from the Promptuary
Archive of the Urquhart House of Cromartie – issued
by the Middle Temple of the Knights Templars in

1652. The Grand Mastership of the Degree of The
Knights Templar of Scotland within the Imperial and
Royal Dragon Court is presently held heritably by
Prince Nicholas de Vere.)

King Arthur Pendragon
= Princess Morgana the Fairy
|
Prince Mordred Pendragon
Archpriest of the Celtic Church
= Pictish Princess
|
Princess Tortolina Pendragon
= Nicharcos
Pictish Archpriest
|
Lord Marsidalio
= Lady Repulita
|
Lord Hedomenos
= Lady Urbana
|
Lord Agenor
= Lady Lampusa
|
Lord Diaprepon
= Lady Vistosa
|
Lord Stragayo
= Lady Hermosina dau. of Lord Natasil of Athole
|
Lord Zeron
= Lady Bramata
|
Lord Polyteles
= Lady Zaglopis
|
Lord Vocompos of Cromartie
= Lady Androlema of Douglas
|
Lord Carolo
= Lady Trastevole dau. of Lord Uilleam
|
Lord Endymion
= Lady Suaviloqua
|
Lord Sebastion
= Lady Francolina
|
Lord Lawrence
= Lady Mathilda
|
Lord Olipher
= Lady Allegra
|
Lord Quintin
= Lady Winnifred
|
Lord Goodwin

= Lady Dorothy
|
Lord Frederick
= Lady Lauretta dau. of Patrick Earl of March
|
Lady Matilda
= Lord William Comyn, grandson of Robert
Earl of Northumberland
|
Lord Richard Comyn
= Lady Hextilda dau. of Hutred of Tynedal
|
Lord William Comyn, Great Justiciar of Scotland
= Lady Marjorie Countess of Buchan
|
Lady Elizabeth Comyn
= Lord William 9th Earl of Mar
|
Lord Donald 10th Earl of Mar
= Princess Helen dau. of Prince
Llewellyn of North Wales
|
Lady Isabel Mar
= King Robert I the Bruce
Grand Master of Knights
Templars in Scotland
|
Princess Marjorie Bruce
= Lord Walter Stewart
6th High Steward of Scotland
|
King Robert II
= Lady Elizabeth Muir of Rowallen
|
King Robert III
= Lady Annabelle Drummond of Stobhall
|
King James I
= Princess Joan Beaufort of Somerset
(Descent from King Edward III)
|
King James II
= Mary, dau. of Arnold Duc de Gueldres
|
Princess Mary
= Lord Thomas Boyd
|
Lady Mary Boyd
James 1st Lord Hamilton
great grandson of
Princess Aenor de Chatellerault
and Guillaume X le Toulousain
Duc de Guyenne, Comte de Poitiers
|
Lady Euphemia Hamilton
(descent from the High Elves of Ireland,
Princess Melusine and the Scots Kings)
= Lord James Weir of Vere,
Baron Blackwood d. 1595

|
Sir William Vere of Stanebyres Castle
= Elizabeth Hamilton, his cousin.
(descent from the High Elves of Ireland,
Princess Melusine and the Scots Kings)
|
Lord Thomas Weir of Vere, Baron Kirkton
= Lady Jane Somerville, the hereditary Witch
of the Dragon House of the Earls Somerville
|
Major Thomas Weir of Vere of Edinburgh,
The hereditary Witch King of Mid-Lothian
= Margaret Bourdon
|
Thomas Weir of Vere
Baron Kirkton of Mid-Lothian,
Hereditary Witch King in Ireland
= Mary Robison of Cookstown Ulster
|
John Weir of Vere
|
Andrew Weir of Vere
|
Margaret Weir of Vere of Kildress
|
Archibald Weir of Vere of Kildress
= Rachel Stewart of Desertcreat
|
Robert Weir of Vere of Kildress
|
John Weir of Vere of Ardwell, Logan Manor
= Mary Logan dau. of Thomas Logan of
Ardwell, Logan Manor, Galloway
|
Thomas Logan Weir of Vere of Carlisle
= Anne Grant Macdonnell of Inverness
|
James Weir of Vere of Lewes
= Natalie Hopgood (descent from
the Collisons of Norfolk and the
Imperial and Royal House of Vere)
|
HI & RH Prince Nicholas de Vere

Vere Descent from King Solomon and the Kings of Judah via Prince Milo of Angiers

- Et In Arcadia Ego -

The Babylonian Goddess-Queen Tiamat
(The Greek Goddess "Chaos"), Mother of Gaia.
Origins in Scythia before the Biblical Black Sea
flood in 4500 BC

The Babylonian Goddess-Queen Kishar
(The Greek Goddess Gaia:
Mother Earth)
|
The Babylonian God-King Anu (Chronos-Saturn)
and the High
Council of the Anunnaki: The Jewish Elohim: The
Old Gods
|
Satan-Lucifer
(Enki; Ea; Khem; Pan; Capricorn:
The Ram of the Shimmering Waters; Leviathan
half-brother of Enlil-Jehovah)
=Queen Hawah of Eldar his daughter
|
Qayin, King of Kish, Son of Satan,
Ancestral Founder of the High Elven God
Kings and Queens of the Dragon and the Grail
= Queen Lilith II "Luluwa" (The Pearl)
daughter of Satan by Queen Lilith I
"The Beautiful," mother of all demons:
daughter of Nergal King of the Underworld.
Hecate, Goddess of the Moon; Goddess of the
Witches.
Diana of the Romans; Arduina of the Gaels
|
Enoch
=Awan
|
Irad
|
Mehujael
|
Methusael
|
Lamech, Dragon Lord of Ur
= Queen Zillah
|
Tubal Cain King of Ur
= Ninbanda, d. of Lilith Naamah
|
King Ham: Chem Zarathustra, Tenth
Archon of Capricorn
=Queen Neelata-Mek
|
Cush
|
Nimrod the Mighty Hunter
(Scion of the Nephilim: The Fallen Gods)
|
Boethos/ Hotep Sekhemwy
Pharaoh and founder
of 2nd Dynasty in Egypt
=Queen Bithiah
|
Pharaoh Raneb/Kalenhkos c. 2800 BC
brought culture of Chem of Capricorn
to Egypt as Khem, the Goat of Mendes

known as Pan in Greece, later the
Sabbatical Goat God of the Witches
and the Baphomet of the Templars
|
Pharaoh Nynetjer
|
Pharaoh Sekhemib
|
Pharaoh Khasekhemwy
|
daughter
=Pharaoh Sanakhte
|
daughter
= Pharaoh Sekhemkhet
|
Pharaoh Khaba 2643-37 BC
|
Pharaoh Huni 2637-13 BC
= Queen Meresankh I
|
Pharaoh Sneferu
= Queen Hetep-Heres I
|
Pharaoh Khufu (Cheops)
= Queen Henutsen
|
Pharaoh Khefre
= Queen Khamerenebty
|
Pharaoh Menkaure 2532-04 BC
= Queen Khamerenebty II
|
Queen Khentkawas
= Pharaoh Userkaf
|
Pharaoh Neferirkare
|
Pharaoh Shepsekare
|
Pharaoh Neferefre
|
Pharaoh Niuserre
|
Pharaoh Menkauhor
|
Pharaoh Djedkare
|
Pharaoh Unas the Vampire 2375-45 BC
(The Pyramid Texts)
|
Queen Iput
= Pharaoh Teti
|
Pharaoh Pepi I
= Queen Ankhnesmerire
|
Pharaoh Pepi II
= Queen Neith

Pharaoh Merenre II 2184-81 BC
= Queen Nitoctris

Prince Ankhfn-Khonsu
Re-established the Royal
Dragon Court in Egypt under
the protection of the God Sobekh,
the Dragon defender of Royalty

Prince Intef I (The Great)
Governor of Thebes

Prince Intef II

Prince Intef III

Pharaoh Mentuhotep I (The Coffin Texts)
= Queen Tem

Pharaoh Mentuhotep II

Pharaoh Mentuhotep III

Queen Tohwait
= Pharaoh Amenhemet

Pharaoh Senusret I
= Princess Sarah, d. of Queen Tohwait
(later wife of Abraham)

Pharaoh Amenhemet II
-= Queen Keminebu

Pharaoh Senusret II
= Queen Nofret

Pharaoh Senusret III
= Queen Mereret

Pharaoh Amenhemet III
= Queen Aat

Pharaoh Amenhemet IV
= The Great Dragon Queen of Egypt, Sobeknefru
(Ratified the Royal Dragon Court under Sobekh)

Daughter
= Pharaoh Wegaf

13th Dynasty of Egypt
The Dragon Kings and Queens of
the God Sobekh

Pharaoh Wegaf

Pharaoah Ameny Intef c. 1700 BC

Pharaoh Sobekhotep III

Pharaoh Sobekhotep IV

Daughter
= Pharaoh Sobekemsaf

Pharaoh Intef VII

Daughter
= King Khayan (The Good God)
Dragon King of the Hyksos who
descend from Queen Towait (above)

Apepi I
Dragon King of the Hyksos

Apepi II
(Apophis the Evil)

Senisonb (Dragon Queen)

Pharaoh Tuthmosis I
= Queen Mutneferte (Dragon Queen)

Pharaoh Tuthmosis II
= Iset

Pharaoh Tuthmosis III
(Founded the Rosi-crucis
Therapeutate at Karnak)
1469-36 BC
= Queen Neferue

The Dragon Queen Tio
= Pharaoh Amenhotep II

Pharaoh Tuthmosis IV
= Queen Mutemwiya

Pharaoh Amenhotep III
= Gilukhipa, Dragon Queen
of the Mitanni

Merykhipa (Kiya)
Dragon Queen
= Pharaoh Amenhotep IV

Queen Kiya Tasherit 1361 BC
=Prince Rama, descendant of Abraham
and the Pharaoh Sensuret I (see above).
Here the direct and unbroken
lines of Satanic descent conjoin

Amminadab

Nahshon

Salma
= Rahab

Boaz
|
Obed
|
Jesse
|
The House of David
King David of Israel
=Queen Bath-Sheba
of the Hittites
(Descent from the Hurrians or Aryans)
|
King Solomon, Lord of the Rings
= Sheba Lilith (Venus) his sister.
1015 BC
Solomon's Descent from Satan
via the Dragon Queen of Sobekh,
Kiya Tasherit, wife of Prince Rama
|
King Rehoboam
King of Judah 975 BC
= Princess Maachlah
dau. of Ureil of Gibeah
|
King Abijah
King of Judah
957 BC
|
King Asa
King of Judah 955 BC
= Princess Azubah
dau. of Shilhi
|
King Jehoshaphat
King of Judah 917 BC
|
King Jehoram
King of Judah 893 BC
= Princess Athalia
dau. of Omri
|
King Ahaziah
King of Judah 885 BC
= Princess Zibiah of Beersheba
|
King Joash
King of Judah 878 BC
Princess Jehoaddan of Jerusalem
|
King Amaziah
King of Judah 840 BC
= Princess Jecoliah of Jerusalem
|
King Uzziah
King of Judah 811 BC
= Princess Jerushah
da. Of Zadok
|

King Jotham
King of Judah 759 BC
|
King Ahaz
King of Judah 742 BC
Princess Abijah
dau of Zechariah
|
King Hezekiah
King of Judah 726 BC
= Princess Hephzibah
|
King Mannaseh
King of Judah 697 BC
= Princess Meshullemeth
dau of Haruz`of Jotbah
|
King Amon
King of Judah 642 BC
= Princess Jedidah
dau. of Adaiah of Boscath
|
King Josiah
King of Judah 640 BC
|
King Jehoiakim
King of Judah 609 BC
(Taken Hostage to Babylon)
= Princess Nehushtah
dau. of Elnathan of Judaea
|
King Jechoniah
King of Judah 598 BC
(Taken hostage to Babylon)
|
Prince Shealtiel
|
Prince Pedaiah
|
Prince Zerrubabel
De jure King
of Judah
|
Prince Rhesa
|
Prince Johanan
|
Prince Judah
|
Prince Joseph
|
Prince Semei
|
Prince Mattathias
|
Prince Maath
|
Prince Naage
|

Prince Azallah

Prince Nahum

Prince Amos

Prince Mattathias

Prince Joseph

Prince Johanan

Prince Melchi

Prince Levi

Prince Matthat

Prince Jacob

Prince Joseph

Jesus Christ The Messiah
(Yehoshua ben-Joseph: called ben-Panther)
(Messiah: Messach: Anointed of the God Sobekh)
= Mary Magdalene, Priestess of Ishtar (Venus)

Josue Del Graal

Aminadab
= Eurgis d. of King Coel I
sister of Lucius the Great

Catheloys

Manael

Titurel

Boaz
(Anfortas)

Frotmund
(Frimutel)

Faramund 420 AD
Sire of the French Monarchy
= Argotta dau. of Genebaud
of the Sicambrian Franks

Clodian of Tournai
= Queen Basina of Thuringia

King Meroveus, founder of
the Dynasty of Merovingian
Sorcerer Kings d. 456 AD
= Princess Meira

King Childeric of the Franks d. 481 AD

= Queen Basina II of Thuringia

King Clovis of the Franks d. 511 AD
= Clotilde of Burgundy

King Lothar I d. 561 AD

Princess Blitildis
= Prince Ansbert, Great Great Grandson of
King Clodian of Tournai (above) d. 570 AD

Lord Arnoald of Scheldt
= Princess Dua of Swabia

Arnulf of Metz
= Princess Dobo of Saxony

Lord Ansegis of Brabant (Lower Lorraine)
Margrave of Scheldt d. 685
= Lady Begga, dau of Pepin I, Mayor of Austrasia

Lord Pepin II of Heristal, Mayor of the Palaces of
Austrasia, Neustria and Burgundy d. 714
= Lady Alpas

Lord Charles Martel (The Hammer) d. 741

Pepin the III Brevis, Duke of Lower Lorraine
(Brabant)
Mayor of Neustrasia, King of the Franks
= Lady Leuthergis

Princess Bertha
= Prince Milo de Vere, Duke of Angiers
Count of Anjou, son of the Fairy Princess
Melusine I of the Scythians (parallel descent
from Satan via the Egyptian Kings as
above and the Fairy Tuadha de Danaan)

Prince Milo II de Vere, Count of Guisnes and Anjou
= Lady Aveline de Nantes

Prince Nicassius de Vere, Count of Guisnes
= Lady Agatha de Champagne

Prince Otho de Vere, Count of Guisnes
= Lady Constance de Chartres

Prince Amelius (Adolph) de Vere Count of Guisnes
= Lady Maud de Ponthieu

Prince Guy (Gallus) de Vere, Count of Guisnes
= Lady Gertrude de Clermont de Ponthieu

Two Sons:
2nd son – Prince Baldwin de Vere, descent to Ida
de Vere,
the House of Hamilton and the Royal Vere of
Blackwood

&
1st son Prince Manasses de Vere Count of
Guisnes, (descent to the Vere Earls of Oxford)
=Lady Petronilla de Boleine
|
Prince Alphonse de Vere, Count of Guisnes
= Lady Katarine, dau of Count Arnulf of Flanders
|
Prince Alberic I de Vere, Count of Guisnes
= Princess Beatrix of Normandy
(descent from Satan via the Fairy Princess
Melusine I du Scythes above)
|
Prince Alberic II de Vere,
Sheriff of Cambridge, Lord of Clare and Tonbridge
= Lady Adeliza dau. of Lord Gilbert FitzRichard
|
Prince Aubrey (Alberic) III de Vere, Earl of Oxford,
Shakespeare's Oberon, King of the Fairies
= Lady Agnes, dau. of Henry Lord Essex.
|
Prince Ralph de Vere of Blackwood 1165 AD
Brother of Robert of Huntingdon; Robin Hood;
God of the Witches, Shakespeare's
Puck, son of Oberon
|
Prince Rory de Vere of Blackwood
|
Prince Ralph de Vere of Blackwood
|
Prince Thomas de Vere of Blackwood
|
Prince Richard de Vere of Blackwood
|
Prince Thomas de Vere
1st Baron Blackwood 1340 AD
|
Prince Buan Were of Vere of Blackwood
|
Prince Rotaldus Were of Vere of Blackwood
|
Prince Thomas Were of Vere
4th Baron Blackwood
|
Prince Robert Veyr of Vere of Blackwood
|
Prince Thomas Weir of Vere of Blackwood
= Lady Aegidia Somerset
|
Prince James Weir of Vere,
7th Baron Blackwood d. 1599
= Lady Euphemia Hamilton
(descent from the High Elves of Ireland,
Princess Melusine and the Scots Kings)
|
Sir William Vere of Stanebyres Castle
= Elizabeth Hamilton, his cousin.
(descent from the High Elves of Ireland,
Princess Melusine and the Scots Kings)

|
Lord Thomas Weir of Vere, Baron Kirkton
= Lady Jane Somerville, the hereditary Witch
of the Dragon House of the Earls Somerville
|
Major Thomas Weir of Vere of Edinburgh,
The hereditary Witch King of Mid-Lothian
= Margaret Bourdon
|
Thomas Weir of Vere
Baron Kirkton of Mid-Lothian,
Hereditary Witch King in Ireland
= Mary Robison of Cookstown Ulster
|
John Weir of Vere
|
Andrew Weir of Vere
|
Margaret Weir of Vere of Kildress
|
Archibald Weir of Vere of Kildress
= Rachel Stewart of Desertcreat
|
Robert Weir of Vere of Kildress
|
John Weir of Vere of Ardwell, Logan Manor
= Mary Logan dau. of Thomas Logan of
Ardwell, Logan Manor, Galloway
|
Thomas Logan Weir of Vere of Carlisle
= Anne Grant Macdonnell of Inverness
|
James Weir of Vere of Lewes
= Natalie Hopgood (descent from
the Collisons of Norfolk and the
Imperial and Royal House of Vere)
|
HI & RH Prince Nicholas de Vere

The Grail Descent of The Royal Elven House of Vere from Satan; King of The Fairy Host, via Jesus Christ and Charlemagne

- Et In Arcadia Ego -

The Babylonian Goddess-Queen Tiamat
(The Greek Goddess "Chaos"), Mother of Gaia
Origins in Scythia before the Biblical Black Sea
flood in 4500 BC
|
The Babylonian Goddess-Queen Kishar
(The Greek Goddess Gaia:
Mother Earth)
|

The Babylonian God-King Anu (Chronos-Saturn)
and the High
Council of the Anunnaki: The Jewish Elohim: The
Old Gods
|
Satan-Lucifer
(Enki; Ea; Khem; Pan; Capricorn:
The Ram of the Shimmering Waters; Leviathan
half-brother of Enlil-Jehovah)
=Queen Hawah of Eldar his daughter
|
Qayin, King of Kish, Son of Satan,
Ancestral Founder of the High Elven God
Kings and Queens of the Dragon and the Grail
= Queen Lilith II "Luluwa" (The Pearl)
daughter of Satan by Queen Lilith I
"The Beautiful," mother of all demons:
daughter of Nergal King of the Underworld.
Hecate, Goddess of the Moon; Goddess of the
Witches.

Diana of the Romans; Arduina of the Gaels

|

Enoch
=Awan
|
Irad
|
Mehujael
|
Methusael
|
Lamech, Dragon Lord of Ur
= Queen Zillah
|
Tubal Cain King of Ur
= Ninbanda, d. of Lilith Naamah
|
King Ham: Chem Zarathustra, Tenth
Archon of Capricorn
=Queen Neelata-Mek
|
Cush
|
Nimrod the Mighty Hunter
(Scion of the Nephilim: The Fallen Gods)
|
Boethos/ Hotep Sekhemwy
Pharaoh and founder
of 2nd Dynasty in Egypt
=Queen Bithiah
|
Pharaoh Raneb/Kalenhkos c. 2800 BC
brought culture of Chem of Capricorn
to Egypt as Khem, the Goat of Mendes
known as Pan in Greece, later the
Sabbatical Goat God of the Witches
and the Baphomet of the Templars
|

Pharaoh Nynetjer
|
Pharaoh Sekhemib
|
Pharaoh Khasekhemwy
|
daughter
=Pharaoh Sanakhte
|
daughter
= Pharaoh Sekhemkhet
|
Pharaoh Khaba 2643-37 BC
|
Pharaoh Huni 2637-13 BC
= Queen Meresankh I
|
Pharaoh Sneferu
= Queen Hetep-Heres I
|
Pharaoh Khufu (Cheops)
= Queen Henutsen
|
Pharaoh Khefre
= Queen Khamerenebty
|
Pharaoh Menkaure 2532-04 BC
= Queen Khamerenebty II
|
Queen Khentkawas
= Pharaoh Userkaf
|
Pharaoh Neferirkare
|
Pharaoh Shepsekare
|
Pharaoh Neferefre
|
Pharaoh Niuserre
|
Pharaoh Menkauhor
|
Pharaoh Djedkare
|
Pharaoh Unas the Vampire 2375-45 BC
(The Pyramid Texts)
|
Queen Iput
= Pharaoh Teti
|
Pharaoh Pepi I
= Queen Ankhnesmerire
|
Pharaoh Pepi II
= Queen Neith
|
Pharaoh Merenre II 2184-81 BC
= Queen Nitoctris
|

Prince Ankhfn-Khonsu
Re-established the Royal
Dragon Court in Egypt under
the protection of the God Sobekh,
the Dragon defender of Royalty
|
Prince Intef I (The Great)
Governor of Thebes
|
Prince Intef II
|
Prince Intef III
|
Pharaoh Mentuhotep I (The Coffin Texts)
= Queen Tem
|
Pharaoh Mentuhotep II
|
Pharaoh Mentuhotep III
|
Queen Tohwait
= Pharaoh Amenhemet
|
Pharaoh Senusret I
= Princess Sarah, d. of Queen Tohwait
(later wife of Abraham)
|
Pharaoh Amenhemet II
-= Queen Keminebu
|
Pharaoh Senusret II
= Queen Nofret
|
Pharaoh Senusret III
= Queen Mereret
|
Pharaoh Amenhemet III
= Queen Aat
|
Pharaoh Amenhemet IV
= The Great Dragon Queen of Egypt, Sobeknefru
(Ratified the Royal Dragon Court under cobekh)
|
Daughter
= Pharaoh Wegaf

13th Dynasty of Egypt
The Dragon Kings and Queens of
the God Sobekh

Pharaoh Wegaf
|
Pharaoah Ameny Intef c. 1700 BC
|
Pharaoh Sobekhotep III
|
Pharaoh Sobekhotep IV
|
Daughter

= Pharaoh Sobekemsaf
|
Pharaoh Intef VII
|
Daughter
= King Khayan (The Good God)
Dragon King of the Hyksos who
descend from Queen Towait (above)
|
Apepi I
Dragon King of the Hyksos
|
Apepi II
(Apophis the Evil)
|
Senisonb (Dragon Queen)
|
Pharaoh Tuthmosis I
= Queen Mutneferte (Dragon Queen)
|
Pharaoh Tuthmosis II
= Iset
|
Pharaoh Tuthmosis III
(Founded the Rosi-crucis
Therapeutate at Karnak)
1469-36 BC
= Queen Neferue
|
The Dragon Queen Tio
= Pharaoh Amenhotep II
|
Pharaoh Tuthmosis IV
= Queen Mutemwiya
|
Pharaoh Amenhotep III
= Gilukhipa, Dragon Queen
of the Mitanni
|
Merykhipa (Kiya)
Dragon Queen
= Pharaoh Amenhotep IV
|
Queen Kiya Tasherit 1361BC
=Prince Rama, descendant of Abraham
and the Pharaoh Sensuret I (See above).
Here the direct and unbroken
lines of Satanic descent conjoin
|
Amminadab
|
Nahshon
|
Salma
= Rahab
|
Boaz
|
Obed

Jesse

The House of David
King David of Israel
=Queen Bath-Sheba
of the Hittites
(Descent from the Hurrians or Aryans)

King Solomon, Lord of the Rings
= Sheba Lilith (Venus) his sister.

Rehoboam

Abijah

Asa

Jehoshaphat

Joram

Azariah

Jotham

Ahaz

Hezekiah

Manasseh

Amon

Josiah

Jeconiah
(Exile in Babylon begins)

Shealtiel

Zerubbabel

Abiud

Eliakim

Azor

Zadok

Achim

Eliud

Eleazar

Matthan

Jacob

Joseph
= Mary (Parallel descent
from the House of David)

Jesus Christ The Messiah
(Yehoshua ben-Joseph: called ben-Panther)
(Messiah: Messach: Anointed of the God Sobekh)
= Mary Magdalene, Priestess of Ishtar (Venus)

Descent to the Fisher Kings of the Grail,
the Merovingian Sorcerer Kings and
the Imperial and Royal House of Vere

Josue Del Graal

Aminadab
= Eurgis dau. of King Coel I
sister of Lucius the Great,
King Leiffer Mawr of Britain

Catheloys

Manael

Titurel

Boaz
(Anfortas)

Frotmund
(Frimutel)

Faramund 420 AD
Sire of the French Monarchy
= Argotta dau. of Genebaud
of the Sicambrian Franks

Clodian of Tournai
= Queen Basina of Thuringia

King Meroveus, founder of
the Dynasty of Merovingian
Sorcerer Kings d. 456 AD
= Princess Meira

King Childeric of the Franks d. 481 AD
= Queen Basina II of Thuringia

King Clovis of the Franks d. 511 AD
= Clotilde of Burgundy

King Lothar I d. 561 AD

Princess Blitildis
= Prince Ansbert, Great Great Grandson of

King Clodian of Tournai (above) d. 570 AD
|
Lord Arnoald of Scheldt
= Princess Dua of Swabia
|
Arnulf of Metz
= Princess Dobo of Saxony
|
Lord Ansegis of Brabant (Lower Lorraine)
Margrave of Scheldt d. 685
= Lady Begga, dau of Pepin I, Mayor of Austrasia
|
Lord Pepin II of Heristal, Mayor of the Palaces of
Austrasia, Neustria and Burgundy d. 714
= Lady Alpas
|
Lord Charles Martel (The Hammer) d. 741
|
Pepin the III Brevis, Duke of Lower Lorraine
(Brabant)
Mayor of Neustrasia, King of the Franks
= Lady Leuthergis
|
Charlemagne the Great
King of France 771-814
Holy Roman Emperor 800-814
= Princess Hildegarde
|
Emperor Louis I
814-830
=2. Princess Judith of Bavaria
|
Emperor Lothair I
Middle Emperor from 840
King of Western Franks 843-855
|
Emperor Louis II of Italy
855-975
|
Princess Irmengarde
= Count Bouquet VIII of
Provence
|
Lady Kunigund
= Count Sigebert of Verdun
(Bouquet IX of Provence)
|
Duke Gozelo I
Duke of Lower Lorraine
(Descent to the House of Habsburg-Lorraine)
1023-1044
|
Duke Godfrey II
Duke of Upper Lorraine
d.1069
= Princess Doda
|
Saint Ida of Ardennes
= Eustace II de Vere

Comte de Boulogne
|
Princess Ida de Vere
= Baudouin de Bourg
Comte de Rethul
|
Prince Hugues I
Comte de Rethul
= Melisende (Melusine II)
dau. Of Bouchard Comte de Corbeil and
Lady Adelaide de Crecy
|
Badouin II de Bourg
King of Jerusalem 1118-1131
= Princess Morfia of Armenia
|
Princess Melisende of Jerusalem (Melusine III)
= Fulke V Plantagenet Count of Anjou
|
Princess Melisende of Jerusalem (Melusine III)
= Fulke V Plantagenet Count of Anjou
|
Count Geoffrey Plantagenet
= Princess Mathilda, la Imperatrice
daughter of King Henry I and Princess
Mathilda of Scotland, daughter of
King Malcolm III
|
King Henry II Plantagenet
= Countess Eleanor of Aquitaine
|
King John "Lackland" Plantagenet
= Lady Isabella of Angouleme
|
King Henry III Plantagenet
= Lady Eleanor dau. of Count
Raymond Berenguer IV of Provence
and Princess Beatrix of Savoy
|
King Edward I Plantagenet
= Princess Eleanor of Castille
|
King Edward II Plantagenet
= Princess Isabella of France
|
King Edward III
1327-1377
= Princess Phillipa of Hainault
|
Prince John of Gaunt
= Lady Katharine Swynford
|
Prince John Plantagenet
|
Princess Joan Beaufort
= King James I of Scots
|
King James II
= Mary, dau. of Arnold Duc de Gueldres

Princess Mary
= Lord Thomas Boyd
|
Lady Mary Boyd
James 1st Lord Hamilton
great grandson of
Princess Aenor de Chatellerault
and Guillaume X le Toulousain
Duc de Guyenne, Comte de Poitiers
|
Lady Euphemia Hamilton
(descent from the High Elves of Ireland,
Princess Melusine and the Scots Kings)
= Lord James Weir of Vere,
Baron Blackwood d. 1599
|
Sir William Vere of Stanebyres Castle
= Elizabeth Hamilton, his cousin.

(descent from the High Elves of Ireland,
Princess Melusine and the Scots Kings)
|
Lord Thomas Weir of Vere, Baron Kirkton
= Lady Jane Somerville, the hereditary Witch
of the Dragon House of the Earls Somerville
|
Major Thomas Weir of Vere of Edinburgh,
The hereditary Witch King of Mid-Lothian
= Margaret Bourdon
|
Thomas Weir of Vere
Baron Kirkton of Mid-Lothian,
Hereditary Witch King in Ireland
= Mary Robison of Cookstown Ulster
|
John Weir of Vere
|
Andrew Weir of Vere
|
Margaret Weir of Vere of Kildress
|
Archibald Weir of Vere of Kildress
= Rachel Stewart of Desertcreat
|
Robert Weir of Vere of Kildress
|
John Weir of Vere of Ardwell, Logan Manor
= Mary Logan dau. of Thomas Logan of
Ardwell, Logan Manor, Galloway
|
Thomas Logan Weir of Vere of Carlisle
= Anne Grant Macdonnell of Inverness
|
James Weir of Vere of Lewes
= Natalie Hopgood (descent from
the Collisons of Norfolk and the
Imperial and Royal House of Vere)
|
HI & RH Prince Nicholas de Vere

The Grail Descent of The Royal Elven House of Vere from Satan: King of The Fairy Host, via Jesus Christ and Prince Milo de Vere

- Et In Arcadia Ego -

The Babylonian Goddess-Queen Tiamat
(The Greek Goddess "Chaos"), Mother of Gaia.
Origins in Scythia before the Biblical Black Sea
Flood in 4500 BC
|
The Babylonian Goddess-Queen Kishar
(The Greek Goddess Gaia:
Mother Earth)
|
The Babylonian God-King Anu (Chronos-Saturn)
and the High
Council of the Anunnaki: The Jewish Elohim: The
Old Gods
|
Satan-Lucifer
(Enki; Ea; Khem; Pan; Capricorn:
The Ram of the Shimmering Waters; Leviathan
half-brother of Enlil-Jehovah)
=Queen Hawah of Eldar his daughter
|
Qayin, King of Kish, Son of Satan,
Ancestral Founder of the High Elven God
Kings and Queens of the Dragon and the Grail
= Queen Lilith II "Luluwa" (The Pearl)
daughter of Satan by Queen Lilith I
"The Beautiful," mother of all demons:
daughter of Nergal King of the Underworld.
Hecate, Goddess of the Moon; Goddess of the
Witches.
Diana of the Romans; Arduina of the Gaels
|
Enoch
=Awan
|
Irad
|
Mehujael
|
Methusael
|
Lamech, Dragon Lord of Ur
= Queen Zillah
|
Tubal Cain King of Ur
= Ninbanda, d. of Lilith Naamah
|
King Ham: Chem Zarathustra, Tenth
Archon of Capricorn
=Queen Neelata-Mek

Cush	Pharaoh Djedkare
Nimrod the Mighty Hunter (Scion of the Nephilim: The Fallen Gods)	Pharaoh Unas the Vampire 2375-45 BC (The Pyramid Texts)
Boethos/ Hotep Sekhemwy Pharaoh and founder of 2nd Dynasty in Egypt =Queen Bithiah	Queen Iput = Pharaoh Teti
	Pharaoh Pepi I = Queen Ankhnesmerire
Pharaoh Raneb/Kalenhkos c. 2800 BC brought culture of Chem of Capricorn to Egypt as Khem, the Goat of Mendes known as Pan in Greece, later the Sabbatical Goat God of the Witches and the Baphomet of the Templars	Pharaoh Pepi II = Queen Neith
	Pharaoh Merenre II 2184-81 BC = Queen Nitoctris
Pharaoh Nynetjer	Prince Ankhfn-Khonsu Re-established the Royal Dragon Court in Egypt under the protection of the God Sobekh, the Dragon defender of Royalty
Pharaoh Sekhemib	
Pharaoh Khasekhemwy	Prince Intef I (The Great) Governor of Thebes
daughter =Pharaoh Sanakhte	Prince Intef II
daughter = Pharaoh Sekhemkhet	Prince Intef III
Pharaoh Khaba 2643-37 BC	Pharaoh Mentuhotep I (The Coffin Texts) = Queen Tem
Pharaoh Huni 2637-13 BC = Queen Meresankh I	Pharaoh Mentuhotep II
Pharaoh Sneferu = Queen Hetep-Heres I	Pharaoh Mentuhotep III
Pharaoh Khufu (Cheops) = Queen Henutsen	Queen Tohwait = Pharaoh Amenhemet
Pharaoh Khefre = Queen Khamerenebty	Pharaoh Senusret I = Princess Sarah, d. of Queen Tohwait (later wife of Abraham)
Pharaoh Menkaure 2532-04 BC = Queen Khamerenebty II	Pharaoh Amenhemet II -= Queen Keminebu
Queen Khentkawas = Pharaoh Userkaf	Pharaoh Senusret II = Queen Nofret
Pharaoh Neferirkare	Pharaoh Senusret III = Queen Mereret
Pharaoh Shepsekare	Pharaoh Amenhemet III = Queen Aat
Pharaoh Neferefre	Pharaoh Amenhemet IV = The Great Dragon Queen of Egypt, Sobeknefru
Pharaoh Niuserre	
Pharaoh Menkauhor	

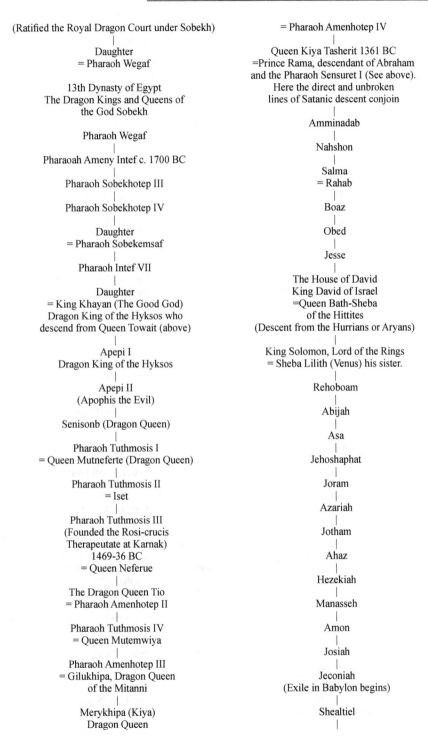

(Ratified the Royal Dragon Court under Sobekh)
|
Daughter
= Pharaoh Wegaf

13th Dynasty of Egypt
The Dragon Kings and Queens of
the God Sobekh

Pharaoh Wegaf
|
Pharaoah Ameny Intef c. 1700 BC
|
Pharaoh Sobekhotep III
|
Pharaoh Sobekhotep IV
|
Daughter
= Pharaoh Sobekemsaf
|
Pharaoh Intef VII
|
Daughter
= King Khayan (The Good God)
Dragon King of the Hyksos who
descend from Queen Towait (above)
|
Apepi I
Dragon King of the Hyksos
|
Apepi II
(Apophis the Evil)
|
Senisonb (Dragon Queen)
|
Pharaoh Tuthmosis I
= Queen Mutneferte (Dragon Queen)
|
Pharaoh Tuthmosis II
= Iset
|
Pharaoh Tuthmosis III
(Founded the Rosi-crucis
Therapeutate at Karnak)
1469-36 BC
= Queen Neferue
|
The Dragon Queen Tio
= Pharaoh Amenhotep II
|
Pharaoh Tuthmosis IV
= Queen Mutemwiya
|
Pharaoh Amenhotep III
= Gilukhipa, Dragon Queen
of the Mitanni
|
Merykhipa (Kiya)
Dragon Queen

= Pharaoh Amenhotep IV

Queen Kiya Tasherit 1361 BC
=Prince Rama, descendant of Abraham
and the Pharaoh Sensuret I (See above).
Here the direct and unbroken
lines of Satanic descent conjoin
|
Amminadab
|
Nahshon
|
Salma
= Rahab
|
Boaz
|
Obed
|
Jesse
|
The House of David
King David of Israel
=Queen Bath-Sheba
of the Hittites
(Descent from the Hurrians or Aryans)
|
King Solomon, Lord of the Rings
= Sheba Lilith (Venus) his sister.
|
Rehoboam
|
Abijah
|
Asa
|
Jehoshaphat
|
Joram
|
Azariah
|
Jotham
|
Ahaz
|
Hezekiah
|
Manasseh
|
Amon
|
Josiah
|
Jeconiah
(Exile in Babylon begins)
|
Shealtiel
|

Zerubbabel
|
Abiud
|
Eliakim
|
Azor
|
Zadok
|
Achim
|
Eliud
|
Eleazar
|
Matthan
|
Jacob
|
Joseph
= Mary (Parallel descent
from the House of David)
|
Jesus Christ The Messiah
(Yehoshua ben-Joseph: called ben-Panther)
(Messiah: Messach: Anointed of the God Sobekh)
= Mary Magdalene, Priestess of Ishtar (Venus)

|

Descent to the Fisher Kings of the Grail,
the Merovingian Sorcerer Kings and
the Imperial and Royal House of Vere
|
Josue Del Graal
|
Aminadab
= Eurgis dau. of King Coel I
sister of Lucius the Great,
King Leiffer Mawr of Britain
|
Catheloys
|
Manael
|
Titurel
|
Boaz
(Anfortas)
|
Frotmund
(Frimutel)
|
Faramund 420 AD
Sire of the French Monarchy
= Argotta dau. of Genebaud
of the Sicambrian Franks
|

Clodian of Tournai
= Queen Basina of Thuringia
|
King Meroveus, founder of
the Dynasty of Merovingian
Sorcerer Kings d. 456 AD
= Princess Meira
|
King Childeric of the Franks d. 481 AD
= Queen Basina II of Thuringia
|
King Clovis of the Franks d. 511 AD
= Clotilde of Burgundy
|
King Lothar I d. 561 AD
|
Princess Blitildis
= Prince Ansbert, Great Great Grandson of
King Clodian of Tournai (above) d. 570 AD
|
Lord Arnoald of Scheldt, (grandson of
Arnold of Scheldt I and Lady Oda de Savoy)
= Princess Dua of Swabia
|
Arnulf of Metz
= Princess Dobo of Saxony
|
Lord Ansegis of Brabant (Lower Lorraine)
Margrave of Scheldt d. 685
= Lady Begga, dau of Pepin I, Mayor of Austrasia
|
Lord Pepin II of Heristal, Mayor of the Palaces of
Austrasia, Neustria and Burgundy d. 714
= Lady Alpas
|
Lord Charles Martel (The Hammer) d. 741
|
Pepin the III Brevis, Duke of Lower Lorraine
(Brabant)
Mayor of Neustrasia, King of the Franks
= Lady Leuthergis
|
Princess Bertha
= Prince Milo de Vere, Duke of Angiers
Count of Anjou, son of the Fairy Princess
Melusine I of the Scythians (parallel descent
from Satan via the Egyptian Kings as
above and the Fairy Tuadha de Danaan)
|
Prince Milo II de Vere, Count of Guisnes and Anjou
= Lady Aveline de Nantes
|
Prince Nicassius de Vere, Count of Guisnes
= Lady Agatha de Champagne
|
Prince Otho de Vere, Count of Guisnes
= Lady Constance de Chartres
|
Prince Amelius (Adolph) de Vere Count of Guisnes

= Lady Maud de Ponthieu
|
Prince Guy (Gallus) de Vere, Count of Guisnes
= Lady Gertrude de Clermont de Ponthieu
|
Two Sons:
2nd son – Prince Baldwin de Vere, descent to Ida
de Vere,
the House of Hamilton and the Royal Vere of
Blackwood
&
1st son Prince Manasses de Vere Count of Guisnes,
(descent to the Vere Earls of Oxford)
=Lady Petronilla de Boleine
|
Prince Alphonse de Vere, Count of Guisnes
= Lady Katarine, dau of Count Arnulf of Flanders
|
Prince Alberic I de Vere, Count of Guisnes
= Princess Beatrix of Normandy
(descent from Satan via the Fairy Princess
Melusine I du Scythes above)
|
Prince Alberic II de Vere,
Sheriff of Cambridge, Lord of Clare and Tonbridge
= Lady Adeliza dau. of Lord Gilbert FitzRichard
|
Prince Aubrey (Alberic) III de Vere, Earl of Oxford,
Shakespeare's Oberon, King of the Fairies
= Lady Agnes, dau. of Henry Lord Essex.
|
Prince Ralph de Vere of Blackwood 1165 AD
Brother of Robert of Huntingdon; Robin Hood;
God of the Witches, Shakespeare's
Puck, son of Oberon
|
Prince Rory de Vere of Blackwood
|
Prince Ralph de Vere of Blackwood
|
Prince Thomas de Vere of Blackwood
|
Prince Richard de Vere of Blackwood
|
Prince Thomas de Vere
1st Baron Blackwood 1340 AD
|
Prince Buan Were of Vere of Blackwood
|
Prince Rotaldus Were of Vere of Blackwood
|
Prince Thomas Were of Vere
4th Baron Blackwood
|
Prince Robert Veyr of Vere of Blackwood
|
Prince Thomas Weir of Vere of Blackwood
= Lady Aegidia Somerset
(Plantagenet descent)

|
Prince James Weir of Vere,
7th Baron Blackwood d. 1599
= Lady Euphemia Hamilton
great great granddaughter of

Princess Aenor de Chatellerault

and Guillaume X le Toulousain

Duc de Guyenne, Comte de Poitiers

(descent from the High Elves of Ireland,
Princess Melusine and the Scots Kings)
|
Sir William Vere of Stanebyres Castle

= Elizabeth Hamilton, his cousin.
(descent from the High Elves of Ireland,
Princess Melusine and the Scots Kings)
|
Lord Thomas Weir of Vere, Baron Kirkton
= Lady Jane Somerville, the hereditary Witch
of the Dragon House of the Earls Somerville
|
Major Thomas Weir of Vere of Edinburgh,
The hereditary Witch King of Mid-Lothian
= Margaret Bourdon
|
Thomas Weir of Vere
Baron Kirkton of Mid-Lothian,
Hereditary Witch King in Ireland
= Mary Robison of Cookstown Ulster
|
John Weir of Vere
|
Andrew Weir of Vere
|
Margaret Weir of Vere of Kildress
|
Archibald Weir of Vere of Kildress
= Rachel Stewart of Desertcreat
|
Robert Weir of Vere of Kildress
|
John Weir of Vere of Ardwell, Logan Manor
= Mary Logan dau. of Thomas Logan of
Ardwell, Logan Manor, Galloway
|
Thomas Logan Weir of Vere of Carlisle
= Anne Grant Macdonnell of Inverness
|
James Weir of Vere of Lewes
= Natalie Hopgood (descent from
the Collisons of Norfolk and the
Imperial and Royal House of Vere)
|
HI & RH Prince Nicholas de Vere

The Grail Descent of The Royal Elven House of Vere from Satan: King of The Fairy Host, via Jesus Christ and the Dukes of Hamilton

The Babylonian Goddess-Queen Tiamat
(The Greek Goddess "Chaos"), Mother of Gaia
Origins in Scythia before the Biblical Black Sea
Flood in 4500 BC
|
The Babylonian Goddess-Queen Kishar
(The Greek Goddess Gaia:
Mother Earth)
|
The Babylonian God-King Anu (Chronos-Saturn)
and the High
Council of the Anunnaki: The Jewish Elohim: The
Old Gods
|
Satan-Lucifer
(Enki; Ea; Khem; Pan; Capricorn:
The Ram of the Shimmering Waters; Leviathan
half-brother of Enlil-Jehovah)
=Queen Hawah of Eldar his daughter
|
Qayin, King of Kish, Son of Satan,
Ancestral Founder of the High Elven God
Kings and Queens of the Dragon and the Grail
= Queen Lilith II "Luluwa" (The Pearl)
daughter of Satan by Queen Lilith I
"The Beautiful," mother of all demons:
daughter of Nergal King of the Underworld.
Hecate, Goddess of the Moon; Goddess of the
Witches.
|
Enoch
=Awan
|
Irad
|
Mehujael
|
Methusael
|
Lamech, Dragon Lord of Ur
= Queen Zillah
|
Tubal Cain King of Ur
= Ninbanda, d. of Lilith Naamah
|
King Ham: Chem Zarathustra, Tenth
Archon of Capricorn
=Queen Neelata-Mek
|
Cush
|
Nimrod the Mighty Hunter

(Scion of the Nephilim: The Fallen Gods)
|
Boethos/ Hotep Sekhemwy
Pharaoh and founder
of 2nd Dynasty in Egypt
=Queen Bithiah
|
Pharaoh Raneb/Kalenhkos c. 2800 BC
brought culture of Chem of Capricorn
to Egypt as Khem, the Goat of Mendes
known as Pan in Greece, later the
Sabbatical Goat God of the Witches
and the Baphomet of the Templars
|
Pharaoh Nynetjer
|
Pharaoh Sekhemib
|
Pharaoh Khasekhemwy
|
daughter
=Pharaoh Sanakhte
|
daughter
= Pharaoh Sekhemkhet
|
Pharaoh Khaba 2643-37 BC
|
Pharaoh Huni 2637-13 BC
= Queen Meresankh I
|
Pharaoh Sneferu
= Queen Hetep-Heres I
|
Pharaoh Khufu (Cheops)
= Queen Henutsen
|
Pharaoh Khefre
= Queen Khamerenebty
|
Pharaoh Menkaure 2532-04 BC
= Queen Khamerenebty II
|
Queen Khentkawas
= Pharaoh Userkaf
|
Pharaoh Neferirkare
|
Pharaoh Shepsekare
|
Pharaoh Neferefre
|
Pharaoh Niuserre
|
Pharaoh Menkauhor
|
Pharaoh Djedkare
|
Pharaoh Unas the Vampire 2375-45 BC

(The Pyramid Texts)
|
Queen Iput
= Pharaoh Teti
|
Pharaoh Pepi I
= Queen Ankhnesmerire
|
Pharaoh Pepi II
= Queen Neith
|
Pharaoh Merenre II 2184-81 BC
= Queen Nitoctris
|
Prince Ankhfn-Khonsu
Re-established the Royal
Dragon Court in Egypt under
the protection of the God Sobekh,
the Dragon defender of Royalty
|
Prince Intef I (The Great)
Governor of Thebes
|
Prince Intef II
|
Prince Intef III
|
Pharaoh Mentuhotep I (The Coffin Texts)
= Queen Tem
|
Pharaoh Mentuhotep II
|
Pharaoh Mentuhotep III
|
Queen Tohwait
= Pharaoh Amenhemet
|
Pharaoh Senusret I
= Princess Sarah, d. of Queen Tohwait
(later wife of Abraham)
|
Pharaoh Amenhemet II
-= Queen Keminebu
|
Pharaoh Senusret II
= Queen Nofret
|
Pharaoh Senusret III
= Queen Mereret
|
Pharaoh Amenhemet III
= Queen Aat
|
Pharaoh Amenhemet IV
= The Great Dragon Queen of Egypt, Sobeknefru
(Ratified the Royal Dragon Court under Sobekh)
|
Daughter
= Pharaoh Wegaf

13th Dynasty of Egypt
The Dragon Kings and Queens of
the God Sobekh
|
Pharaoh Wegaf
|
Pharaoah Ameny Intef c. 1700 BC
|
Pharaoh Sobekhotep III
|
Pharaoh Sobekhotep IV
|
Daughter
= Pharaoh Sobekemsaf
|
Pharaoh Intef VII
|
Daughter
= King Khayan (The Good God)
Dragon King of the Hyksos who
descend from Queen Towait (above)
|
Apepi I
Dragon King of the Hyksos
|
Apepi II
(Apophis the Evil)
|
Senisonb (Dragon Queen)
|
Pharaoh Tuthmosis I
= Queen Mutneferte (Dragon Queen)
|
Pharaoh Tuthmosis II
= Iset
|
Pharaoh Tuthmosis III
(Founded the Rosi-crucis
Therapeutate at Karnak)
1469-36 BC
= Queen Neferue
|
The Dragon Queen Tio
= Pharaoh Amenhotep II
|
Pharaoh Tuthmosis IV
= Queen Mutemwiya
|
Pharaoh Amenhotep III
= Gilukhipa, Dragon Queen
of the Mitanni
|
Merykhipa (Kiya)
Dragon Queen
= Pharaoh Amenhotep IV
|
Queen Kiya Tasherit 1361 BC
=Prince Rama, descendant of Abraham

and the Pharaoh Sensuret I (See above).
Here the direct and unbroken
lines of Satanic descent conjoin
|
Amminadab
|
Nahshon
|
Salma
= Rahab
|
Boaz
|
Obed
|
Jesse
|
The House of David
King David of Israel
=Queen Bath-Sheba
of the Hittites
(Descent from the Hurrians or Aryans)
|
King Solomon, Lord of the Rings
= Sheba Lilith (Venus) his sister.
|
Rehoboam
|
Abijah
|
Asa
|
Jehoshaphat
|
Joram
|
Azariah
|
Jotham
|
Ahaz
|
Hezekiah
|
Manasseh
|
Amon
|
Josiah
|
Jeconiah
(Exile in Babylon begins)
|
Shealtiel
|
Zerubbabel
|
Abiud
|

Eliakim
|
Azor
|
Zadok
|
Achim
|
Eliud
|
Eleazar
|
Matthan
|
Jacob
|
Joseph
= Mary (Parallel descent
from the House of David)
|
Jesus Christ The Messiah
(Yehoshua ben-Joseph: called ben-Panther)
(Messiah: Messach: Anointed of the God Sobekh)
= Mary Magdalene, Priestess of Ishtar (Venus)
|

Descent to the Fisher Kings of the Grail,
the Merovingian Sorcerer Kings and
the Imperial and Royal House of Vere
|
Josue Del Graal
|
Aminadab
= Eurgis dau. of King Coel I
sister of Lucius the Great,
King Leiffer Mawr of Britain
|
Catheloys
|
Manael
|
Titurel
|
Boaz
(Anfortas)
|
Frotmund
(Frimutel)
|
Faramund 420 AD
Sire of the French Monarchy
= Argotta dau. of Genebaud
of the Sicambrian Franks
|
Clodian of Tournai
= Queen Basina of Thuringia
|

- Et In Arcadia Ego -

King Meroveus, founder of
the Dynasty of Merovingian
Sorcerer Kings d. 456 AD
= Princess Meira
|
King Childeric of the Franks d. 481AD
= Queen Basina II of Thuringia
|
King Clovis of the Franks d. 511AD
= Clotilde of Burgundy
|
King Lothar I d. 561AD
|
Princess Blitildis
= Prince Ansbert, Great Great Grandson of
King Clodian of Tournai (above) d. 570 AD
|
Lord Arnoald of Scheldt
= Princess Dua of Swabia
|
Arnulf of Metz
= Princess Dobo of Saxony
|
Lord Ansegis of Brabant (Lower Lorraine)
Margrave of Scheldt d. 685
= Lady Begga, dau of Pepin I, Mayor of Austrasia
|
Lord Pepin II of Heristal, Mayor of the Palaces of
Austrasia, Neustria and Burgundy d. 714
= Lady Alpas
|
Lord Charles Martel (The Hammer) d. 741
|
Pepin the III Brevis, Duke of Lower Lorraine
(Brabant)
Mayor of Neustrasia, King of the Franks
= Lady Leuthergis
|
Princess Bertha
= Prince Milo de Vere, Duke of Angiers
Count of Anjou, son of the Fairy Princess
Melusine I of the Scythians (parallel descent
from Satan via the Egyptian Kings as
above and the Fairy Tuadha de Danaan)
|
Prince Milo II de Vere, Count of Guisnes and Anjou
= Lady Aveline de Nantes
|
Prince Nicassius de Vere, Count of Guisnes
= Lady Agatha de Champagne
|
Prince Otho de Vere, Count of Guisnes
= Lady Constance de Chartres
|
Prince Amelius (Adolph) de Vere Count of Guisnes
= Lady Maud de Ponthieu
|

Prince Guy (Gallus) de Vere, Count of Guisnes
= Lady Gertrude de Clermont de Ponthieu
|
Prince Baldwin de Vere
|
Eustace I de Vere
= Maud de Louvain
|
Eustace II de Vere
Comte de Boulogne
=Saint Ida of Ardennes
|
Princess Ida de Vere
= Baudouin de Bourg
Comte de Rethul
|
Prince Hugues I
Comte de Rethul
= Melisende (Melusine II)
dau. Of Bouchard Comte de Corbeil and
Lady Adelaide de Crecy
|
Badouin II de Bourg
King of Jerusalem 1118-1131
= Princess Morfia of Armenia
|
Princess Melisende of Jerusalem (Melusine III)
= Fulke V Plantagenet Count of Anjou
|
Count Geoffrey Plantagenet
= Princess Mathilda, la Imperatrice
daughter of King Henry I and Princess
Mathilda of Scotland, daughter of
King Malcolm III
|
King Henry II Plantagenet
= Countess Eleanor of Aquitaine
|
King John "Lackland" Plantagenet
= Lady Isabella of Angouleme
|
King Henry III Plantagenet
= Lady Eleanor dau. of Count
Raymond Berenguer IV of Provence
and Princess Beatrix of Savoy
|
King Edward I
= Princess Eleanor of Castile
|
King Edward II Plantagenet
= Princess Isabella of France
|
King Edward III Plantagenet
1327-1377
= Princess Phillipa of Hainault
|
Prince John Plantagenet of Gaunt
= Lady Katharine Swynford
|

Prince John Plantagenet
|
Princess Joan Beaufort
= King James I of Scots
|
King James II
= Mary, dau. of Arnold Duc de Gueldres
|
Princess Mary
= Lord Thomas Boyd
|
Lady Mary Boyd
James 1st Lord Hamilton
great grandson of
Princess Aenor de Chatellerault
and Guillaume X le Toulousain
Duc de Guyenne, Comte de Poitiers
|
Lady Euphemia Hamilton
(descent from the High Elves of Ireland,
Princess Melusine and the Scots Kings)
= Lord James Weir of Vere,
Baron Blackwood d. 1595
|
Sir William Vere of Stanebyres Castle
= Elizabeth Hamilton, his cousin.
(descent from the High Elves of Ireland,
Princess Melusine and the Scots Kings)
|
Lord Thomas Weir of Vere, Baron Kirkton
= Lady Jane Somerville, the hereditary Witch
of the Dragon House of the Earls Somerville
|
Major Thomas Weir of Vere of Edinburgh,
The hereditary Witch King of Mid-Lothian
= Margaret Bourdon
|
Thomas Weir of Vere
Baron Kirkton of Mid-Lothian,
Hereditary Witch King in Ireland
= Mary Robison of Cookstown Ulster
|
John Weir of Vere
|
Andrew Weir of Vere
|
Margaret Weir of Vere of Kildress
|
Archibald Weir of Vere of Kildress
= Rachel Stewart of Desertcreat
|
Robert Weir of Vere of Kildress
|
John Weir of Vere of Ardwell, Logan Manor
= Mary Logan dau. of Thomas Logan of
Ardwell, Logan Manor, Galloway
|
Thomas Logan Weir of Vere of Carlisle
= Anne Grant Macdonnell of I~verness

James Weir of Vere of Lewes
= Natalie Hopgood (descent from
the Collisons of Norfolk and the
Imperial and Royal House of Vere)
|
HI & RH Prince Nicholas de Vere

Vere Descent from the Archdruid Bran the Blessed and the Holy Families of Britain

The Archdruid Bran the Blessed
= Anna, d. of St. Joseph of Arimathea
(Descent to the High Elves of Avalon
and the Royal House of Pendragon)
|
Princess Penardun – Iceni Commander
= King Marius of Siluria
|
King Coel I
|
King Lleifer Mawr – Good King Lucius
= Princess Gladys, g.g. dau of
King Aviragus of Siluria
|
Princess Gladys
= Prince Cadwan of Cumbria
|
King Coel II of Colchester (Camulod)
|
Prince Cunedd
|
Prince Confer of Strathclyde
|
Prince Neithon
|
Prince Eubre Gwydel of Ayr
|
King Cormac of Galloway
|
Prince Tudwall
= Lady Gratiana, dau of
Emperor Magnus Maximus
|
Prince Anlach
= Marchelle, dau of
Tewdrig of Garth Madrun
|
Princess Gladys
= Saint Gwynllyw
(Parallel descent from the
Archdruid Bran the Blessed)
|
Saint Brychan d. 450 AD
Regulus (Ruler) of Breichniog

= Princess Ribrawst, dau of King Vortigern

Prince Brychan of
Manau Gododdin
= Princess Ingenach

Princess Luan
= King Gabran of Scots

King Aeden MacGabran
the Great Pendragon

Gwyr Llew = Ygraine of Avalon = Aeden Mac
Gabran

From Aeden Mac Gabran – Prince Arthur Pendragon
From Gwyr Llew – Princess Morgana the Fairy

(Here follows the Pendragon descent of the House
of Vere from King Arthur and the House of the High
Elves of Avalon extracted from the Promptuary
Archive of the Urquhart House of Cromartie – issued
by the Middle Temple of the Knights Templars in
1652. The Grand Mastership of the Degree of The
Knights Templar of Scotland within the Imperial and
Royal Dragon Court is presently held heritably by
Prince Nicholas de Vere.)

King Arthur Pendragon
= Princess Morgana the Fairy

Prince Mordred Pendragon
Archpriest of the Celtic Church
= Pictish Dragon Princess

Princess Tortolina Pendragon
= Nicharcos
Pictish Archpriest

Lord Marsidalio
= Lady Repulita

Lord Hedomenos
= Lady Urbana

Lord Agenor
= Lady Lampusa

Lord Diaprepon
= Lady Vistosa

Lord Stragayo
= Lady Hermosina dau. of Lord Natasil of Athole

Lord Zeron
= Lady Bramata

Lord Polyteles
= Lady Zaglopis

Lord Vocompos of Cromartie
= Lady Androlema of Douglas

Lord Carolo
= Lady Trastevole dau. of Lord Uilleam

Lord Endymion
= Lady Suaviloqua

Lord Sebastion
= Lady Francolina

Lord Lawrence
= Lady Mathilda

Lord Olipher
= Lady Allegra

Lord Quintin
= Lady Winnifred

Lord Goodwin
= Lady Dorothy

Lord Frederick
= Lady Lauretta dau. of Patrick Earl of March

Lady Matilda
= Lord William Comyn, grandson of Robert
Earl of Northumberland

Lord Richard Comyn
= Lady Hextilda dau. of Hutred of Tynedal

Lord William Comyn, Great Justiciar of Scotland
= Lady Marjorie Countess of Buchan

Lady Elizabeth Comyn
= Lord William 9th Earl of Mar

Lord Donald 10th Earl of Mar
= Princess Helen dau. of Prince
Llewellyn of North Wales

Lady Isabel Mar
= King Robert I the Bruce
Grand Master of the Knights
Templars in Scotland

Marjorie Bruce
= Lord Walter Stewart
6th High Steward of Scotland

King Robert II
= Lady Elizabeth Muir of Rowallen

King Robert III
= Lady Annabelle Drummond of Stobhall

|
King James I
= Princess Joan Beaufort of Somerset
(Descent from King Edward III)
|
King James II
= Mary, dau. of Arnold Duc de Gueldres
|
Princess Mary
= Lord Thomas Boyd
|
Lady Mary Boyd
James 1st Lord Hamilton
great grandson of
Princess Aenor de Chatellerault
and Guillaume X le Toulousain
Duc de Guyenne, Comte de Poitiers
|
Lady Euphemia Hamilton
(descent from the High Elves of Ireland,
Princess Melusine and the Scots Kings)
= Lord James Weir of Vere,
Baron Blackwood d. 1595
|
Sir William Vere of Stanebyres Castle
= Elizabeth Hamilton, his cousin.
(descent from the High Elves of Ireland,
Princess Melusine and the Scots Kings)
|
Lord Thomas Weir of Vere, Baron Kirkton
= Lady Jane Somerville, the hereditary Witch
of the Dragon House of the Earls Somerville
|
Major Thomas Weir of Vere of Edinburgh,
The hereditary Witch King of Mid-Lothian
= Margaret Bourdon
|
Thomas Weir of Vere

Baron Kirkton of Mid-Lothian,
Hereditary Witch King in Ireland
= Mary Robison of Cookstown Ulster
|
John Weir of Vere
|
Andrew Weir of Vere
|
Margaret Weir of Vere of Kildress
|
Archibald Weir of Vere of Kildress
= Rachel Stewart of Desertcreat
|
Robert Weir of Vere of Kildress
|
John Weir of Vere of Ardwell, Logan Manor
= Mary Logan dau. of Thomas Logan of
Ardwell, Logan Manor, Galloway
|
Thomas Logan Weir of Vere of Carlisle

= Anne Grant Macdonnell of Inverness
|
James Weir of Vere of Lewes
= Natalie Hopgood (descent from
the Collisons of Norfolk and the
Imperial and Royal House of Vere)
|
HI & RH Prince Nicholas de Vere

Vere Imperial Trojan Descent
via Emperor Charlemagne

- Et In Arcadia Ego -

Trojan Royal House
|
King Antenor d. 443 BC
Of the Cimmerians of Scythia
|
King Marcomer d. 412 BC
Moved Cimmerians from the Black Sea
to Western Europe and Wales
where they became the Cymru
|
King Antenor d. 385 BC
= Princess Cambra of the Sicambrians
|
King Priamus d. 358 BC
|
King Helenus d. 339 BC
Priest-King of the Arcadian God Pallas
|
King Diocles d. 300 BC
Fought the Goths and Gauls
|
Priest-King Bassanus Magnus d. 250 BC
Built Aix la Chapelle
|
King Clodomir d. 232 BC
|
King Nicanor d. 198 BC
|
King Marcomer d. 170 BC
|
King Clodius d. 195 BC
|
King Antenor d. 143 BC
|
King Clodomir d. 123 BC
|
King Merovachus d. 95 BC
|
King Cassander d. 74 BC
|
King Antharius d. 39 BC
|

King Francus d. 11 BC
Changed tribal name
from Sicambri to Franks
|
King Clodius d. 20 AD
|
King Marcomer d. 50 AD
|
King Clodomir d. 63 AD
|
King Antenor d. 69 AD
|
King Ratherius d. 90 AD
|
King Richemer d. 114 AD
|
King Odomar d. 128 AD
|
King Marcomer d. 169 AD
Built Marpurg in Hesse
= Princess Athildis of Camelot
|
King Clodomir d. 180 AD
|
King Farabert d. 186 AD
|
King Sunno d. 213 AD
|
King Hilderic d. 253 AD
|
King Bartherus d. 272 AD
|
King Clodius d. 298 AD
|
King Walter d. 306 AD
|
King Dagobert d. 317 AD
|
King Clodomir d. 337 AD
|
King Richemir d. 350
|
King Theodomir d. 360
|
King Clodius d. 378
|
King Dagobert d. 389
|
Lord Genobaud d. 419
|
Princess Argotta
= Lord Faramund of
the Western Franks
419-430
|
Chief Clodian of Tournai
Priest of Neptune of Arcadia
Lord of the Western Franks 430-446
= Queen Basina I of Thuringia

|
King Meroveus
Founder of the Merovingian
Dynasty of Sorceror Kings d. 456
= Princess Merira
|
King Childeric of the Franks d. 481 AD
= Queen Basina II of Thuringia
|
King Clovis of the Franks d. 511 AD
= Clotilde of Burgundy
|
King Lothar I d. 561 AD
|
Princess Blitildis
= Prince Ansbert, Great Great Grandson of
King Clodian of Tournai (above) d. 570 AD
|
Lord Arnoald of Scheldt
= Princess Dua of Swabia
|
Arnulf of Metz
= Princess Dobo of Saxony
|
Lord Ansegis of Brabant (Lower Lorraine)
Margrave of Scheldt d. 685
= Lady Begga, dau of Pepin I, Mayor of Austrasia
|
Lord Pepin II of Heristal, Mayor of the Palaces of
Austrasia, Neustria and Burgundy d. 714
= Lady Alpas
|
Lord Charles Martel (The Hammer) d. 741
|
Pepin the III Brevis, Duke of Lower Lorraine
(Brabant)
Mayor of Neustrasia, King of the Franks
= Lady Leuthergis
|
Charlemagne the Great
King of France 771-814
Holy Roman Emperor 800-814
= Princess Hildegarde
|
Emperor Louis I
814-830
=2. Princess Judith of Bavaria
|
Emperor Lothair I
Middle Emperor from 840
King of Western Franks 843-855
|
Emperor Louis II of Italy
855-975
|
Princess Irmengarde
= Count Bouquet VIII of
Provence
|

Lady Kunigund
= Count Sigebert of Verdun
(Bouquet IX of Provence)
|
Duke Gozelo I
Duke of Lower Lorraine
(Descent to the House of Habsburg-Lorraine)
1023-1044
|
Duke Godfrey II
Duke of Upper Lorraine
d. 1069
= Princess Doda
|
Saint Ida of Ardennes
= Eustace II de Vere
Comte de Boulogne
|
Princess Ida de Vere
= Baudouin de Bourg
Comte de Rethul
|
Prince Hugues I
Comte de Rethul
= Melisende (Melusine II)
dau. Of Bouchard Comte de Corbeil and
Lady Adelaide de Crecy
|
Badouin II de Bourg
King of Jerusalem 1118-1131
= Princess Morfia of Armenia
|
Princess Melisende of Jerusalem (Melusine III)
= Fulke V Plantagenet Count of Anjou
dau. of King Malcolm III
|
Count Geoffrey Plantagenet
= Princess Mathilda, la Imperatrice
daughter of King Henry I and Princess
Mathilda of Scotland, daughter of
King Malcolm III
|
King Henry II Plantagenet
= Countess Eleanor of Aquitaine
|
King John "Lackland" Plantagenet
= Lady Isabella of Angouleme
|
King Henry III Plantagenet
= Lady Eleanor dau. of Count
Raymond Berenguer IV of Provence
and Princess Beatrix of Savoy
|
King Edward I
= Princess Eleanor of Castile
|
King Edward II Plantagenet
= Princess Isabella of France
|

King Edward III
1327-1377
= Princess Phillipa of Hainault
|
Prince John of Gaunt
= Lady Katharine Swynford
|
Prince John Plantagenet
|
Princess Joan Beaufort
= King James I of Scots
|
King James II
= Mary, dau. of Arnold
Duc de Gueldres
|
Princess Mary
= Lord Thomas Boyd
|
Lady Mary Boyd
James 1st Lord Hamilton
great grandson of
Princess Aenor de Chatellerault
and Guillaume X le Toulousain
Duc de Guyenne, Comte de Poitiers
|
Lady Euphemia Hamilton
(descent from the High Elves of Ireland,
Princess Melusine and the Scots Kings)
= Lord James Weir of Vere,
Baron Blackwood d. 1595
|
Sir William Vere of Stanebyres Castle
= Elizabeth Hamilton, his cousin.
(descent from the High Elves of Ireland,
Princess Melusine and the Scots Kings)
|
Lord Thomas Weir of Vere, Baron Kirkton
= Lady Jane Somerville, the hereditary Witch
of the Dragon House of the Earls Somerville
|
Major Thomas Weir of Vere of Edinburgh,
The hereditary Witch King of Mid-Lothian
= Margaret Bourdon
|

Thomas Weir of Vere
Baron Kirkton of Mid-Lothian,
Hereditary Witch King in Ireland
= Mary Robison of Cookstown Ulster
|
John Weir of Vere
|
Andrew Weir of Vere
|
Margaret Weir of Vere of Kildress
|
Archibald Weir of Vere of Kildress
= Rachel Stewart of Desertcreat

Robert Weir of Vere of Kildress
|
John Weir of Vere of Ardwell, Logan Manor
= Mary Logan dau. of Thomas Logan of
Ardwell, Logan Manor, Galloway
|
Thomas Logan Weir of Vere of Carlisle
= Anne Grant Macdonnell of Inverness
|
James Weir of Vere of Lewes
= Natalie Hopgood (descent from
the Collisons of Norfolk and the
Imperial and Royal House of Vere)
|
HI & RH Prince Nicholas de Vere

Vere Imperial and Royal Elven Descent

from King Brian Boru of Tara

- King Brian Boru of Tara -
Imperator Scotorum
Emperor and High King of
Ireland, son of Kennedy, Chief of the
Dalcassians of Munster; son of King
Lorcan of Ireland, scion of the
Dragon Dalcassians, who numbered
a Banshee (Ban-Sidhe or fairy) in their family
(source Dr. Hugh Weir).
According to Irish legend King
Brian was King of the Fairies.
|
The Princess Slani O'Brien of Munster
= King Sithric of Dublin, son of King
Olaf of Dublin and Northumbria
|
King Auloed of Dublin
|
King Raignalt of Dublin
= Princess Cynan of North Wales
|
Griffifth II Prince of North Wales
= Princess Angharat of Tegainol
|
Owen I Gwynedd Prince of North Wales
= Princess Gladys of North Wales
|
Iorwerth Prince of North Wales
= Princess Maret of Powys – Vadoc
dau. of Madoc Prince of Powys –
Vadoc and Princess Susannah of North Wales
|

Llewellyn Prince of Gwynedd
|
Princess Helen
= Lord Donald 10th Earl of Mar
|
Lady Isabel
= King Robert I the Bruce
Grand Master of Knights
Templars in Scotland
|
Princess Marjorie Bruce
= Lord Walter Stewart
6th High Steward of Scotland
|
King Robert II
= Lady Elizabeth Muir of Rowallen
|
King Robert III
= Lady Annabelle Drummond of Stobhall
|
King James I
= Princess Joan Beaufort of Somerset
(Descent from King Edward III)
|
King James II
= Mary, dau. of Arnold Duc de Gueldres
|
Princess Mary
= Lord Thomas Boyd
|
Lady Mary Boyd
James 1st Lord Hamilton
great grandson of
Princess Aenor de Chatellerault
and Guillaume X le Toulousain
Duc de Guyenne, Comte de Poitiers
|
Lady Euphemia Hamilton
(descent from the High Elves of Ireland,
Princess Melusine and the Scots Kings)
= Lord James Weir of Vere,
Baron Blackwood d. 1599
|
Sir William Vere of Stanebyres Castle
= Elizabeth Hamilton, his cousin.
(descent from the High Elves of Ireland,
Princess Melusine and the Scots Kings)
|
Lord Thomas Weir of Vere, Baron Kirkton
= Lady Jane Somerville, the hereditary Witch
of the Dragon House of the Earls Somerville
|
Major Thomas Weir of Vere of Edinburgh,
The hereditary Witch King of Mid-Lothian
= Margaret Bourdon
|
Thomas Weir of Vere,
Baron Kirkton of Mid-Lothian,

Hereditary Witch King in Ireland
= Mary Robison of Cookstown Ulster
|
John Weir of Vere
|
Andrew Weir of Vere
|
Margaret Weir of Vere of Kildress
|
Archibald Weir of Vere of Kildress
= Rachel Stewart of Desertcreat
|
Robert Weir of Vere of Kildress
|
John Weir of Vere of Ardwell, Logan Manor
= Mary Logan dau. of Thomas Logan of
Ardwell, Logan Manor, Galloway
|
Thomas Logan Weir of Vere of Carlisle
= Anne Grant Macdonnell of Inverness
|
James Weir of Vere of Lewes
= Natalie Hopgood (descent from
the Collisons of Norfolk and the
Imperial and Royal House of Vere)
|
HI & RH Prince Nicholas de Vere

Vere Imperial Descent from Princess Plantina, sister of Princess Melusine of the Scythians

King Elinus of Albha, the Dragon
King of Berenicia – Northumberland
(descent from the Uilidian Druid Princes)
=Queen Pressina of the Scythian Picts
(descent from King Vere 400 BC)
|
Melusine I — Plantina — Meliore
|
The Plantagenista Descent
|
Torquat b. c. 760
|
Tortulf de Rennes 790
|
Tertulle Count of Anjou c. 821
= Petronella of France
|
Count Ingelgar of Anjou 845
= Adelais de Rescinde
|
Fulk I The Red, Count of Anjou b. 888

= Roscilla de Loches
|
Fulk II The Good, Count of Anjou b. 920
= Gerberga de Maine
|
Geoffrey Greymantle, Count of Anjou b. 939
= Adele de Vermandois
|
Fullk III The Black, Count of Anjou b. 956
= 2. Lady Hildegard of Metz
dau. of Count Arnulf of Metz
and Princess Oda de Savoy
|
Geoffrey II Martel, Count of Anjou b. 1006
= Lady Agnes of Bourgogne
|
Geoffrey III Le Harbu b. 1040
= Julienne de Langeaise
|
Geoffrey IV Martel b. 1073
= Bertrade de Montfort
|
Fulk V The Younger, Count of Anjou b. 1092
= 1. Ermengarde dau. of Helias Count of Maine
= 2. Princess Melisende (Melusine III) of Jerusalem
|
Count Geoffrey Plantagenet
= Princess Mathilda, la Imperatrice
daughter of King Henry I and Princess
Mathilda of Scotland, daughter of
King Malcolm III
|
King Henry II Plantagenet
= Countess Eleanor of Aquitaine
|
King John "Lackland" Plantagenet
= Lady Isabella of Angouleme
|
King Henry III Plantagenet
= Lady Eleanor dau. of Count
Raymond Berenguer IV of Provence
and Princess Beatrix of Savoy
|
King Edward I Plantagenet
= Princess Eleanor of Castille
|
King Edward II Plantagenet
= Princess Isabella of France
|
King Edward III Plantagenet
1327-1377
= Princess Phillipa of Hainault
|
Prince John Plantagenet of Gaunt
= Lady Katharine Swynford
|
Prince John Plantagenet
|
Princess Joan Beaufort Plantagenet

= King James I of Scots
|
King James II
= Mary, dau. of Arnold
Duc de Gueldres
|
Princess Mary
= Lord Thomas Boyd
|
Lady Mary Boyd
James 1st Lord Hamilton
great grandson of
Princess Aenor de Chatellerault
and Guillaume X le Toulousain
Duc de Guyenne, Comte de Poitiers
|
Lady Euphemia Hamilton
(descent from the High Elves of Ireland,
Princess Melusine and the Scots Kings)
= Lord James Weir of Vere,
Baron Blackwood d. 1595
|
Sir William Vere of Stanebyres Castle
= Elizabeth Hamilton, his cousin.
(descent from the High Elves of Ireland,
Princess Melusine and the Scots Kings)
|
Lord Thomas Weir of Vere, Baron Kirkton
= Lady Jane Somerville, the hereditary Witch
of the Dragon House of the Earls Somerville
|
Major Thomas Weir of Vere of Edinburgh,
The hereditary Witch King of Mid-Lothian
= Margaret Bourdon
|
Thomas Weir of Vere,
Baron Kirkton of Mid-Lothian,
Hereditary Witch King in Ireland
= Mary Robison of Cookstown Ulster
|
John Weir of Vere
|
Andrew Weir of Vere
|
Margaret Weir of Vere of Kildress
|
Archibald Weir of Vere of Kildress
= Rachel Stewart of Desertcreat
|
Robert Weir of Vere of Kildress
|
John Weir of Vere of Ardwell, Logan Manor
= Mary Logan dau. of Thomas Logan of
Ardwell, Logan Manor, Galloway
|
Thomas Logan Weir of Vere of Carlisle
= Anne Grant Macdonnell of Inverness
|

James Weir of Vere of Lewes
= Natalie Hopgood (descent from
the Collisons of Norfolk and the
Imperial and Royal House of Vere)
|
HI & RH Prince Nicholas de Vere

Vere Imperial and Merovingian Descent from King Dagobert I "The Great" and Charlemagne

- Et In Arcadia Ego -

King Dagobert I
King of Austrasia,
King of the Franks
630-638
= Princess Nanthilda
|
King Clovis II
633-656
= Princess Batilde
|
King Theuderic III
King of Neustria and Burgundy 673
King of Austrasia 679-691
|
King Childebert III
695-711
|
King Dagobert III
711-715
|
Princess Blanche Fleur
= King Flora of Hungary
|
Princess Bertha
= Pepin III
Mayor of Neustria d. 768
|
Charlemagne the Great
King of France 771-814
Holy Roman Emperor 800-814
= Princess Hildegarde
|
Emperor Louis I
814-830
= 1. Princess Irmengarde
|
Emperor Charles II
Western Emperor from 840
King of France from 843
Holy Roman Emperor from 867-877
|
King Louis II of France
877-879

King Charles II of France
893–dep. 922
= Princess Eadgifu

King Louis IV of France
936-954
= Princess Gerberga dau. of
King Henry of Germany
(descent to the Imperial
and Royal House of Vere)

Charles Duke of Lower Lorraine 991

Lady Gerberga
= Lambert de Louvain

Henry of Brussels

Maud de Louvain
= Eustace I de Vere d. 1049
Descent from Amelius ("Adolph") de Vere
Comte de Guisnes

Eustace II de Vere
= Saint Ida of Ardennes

Princess Ida de Vere
= Baudouin de Bourg
Comte de Rethul

Prince Hugues I
Comte de Rethul
= Melisende (Melusine II)
dau. Of Bouchard Comte de Corbeil and
Lady Adelaide de Crecy

Badouin II de Bourg
King of Jerusalem 1118-1131
= Princess Morfia of Armenia

Princess Melisende of Jerusalem (Melusine III)
= Fulke V Plantagenet Count of Anjou

Count Geoffrey Plantagenet
= Princess Mathilda, la Imperatrice
daughter of King Henry I and Princess
Mathilda of Scotland, daughter of
King Malcolm III

King Henry II Plantagenet
= Countess Eleanor of Aquitaine

King John "Lackland" Plantagenet
= Lady Isabella of Angouleme

King Henry III Plantagenet
= Lady Eleanor dau. of Count
Raymond Berenguer IV of Provence

and Princess Beatrix of Savoy

King Edward I
= Princess Eleanor of Castile

King Edward II Plantagenet
= Princess Isabella of France

King Edward III Plantagenet
1327-1377
= Princess Phillipa of Hainault

Prince John of Gaunt Plantagenet
= Lady Katharine Swynford

Prince John Plantagenet

Princess Joan Beaufort Plantagenet
= King James I of Scots

King James II
= Mary, dau. of Arnold Duc de Gueldres

Princess Mary
= Lord Thomas Boyd

Lady Mary Boyd
James 1st Lord Hamilton
great grandson of
Princess Aenor de Chatellerault
and Guillaume X le Toulousain
Duc de Guyenne, Comte de Poitiers

Lady Euphemia Hamilton
(descent from the High Elves of Ireland,
Princess Melusine and the Scots Kings)
= Lord James Weir of Vere,
Baron Blackwood d. 1595

Sir William Vere of Stanebyres Castle
= Elizabeth Hamilton, his cousin.
(descent from the High Elves of Ireland,
Princess Melusine and the Scots Kings)

Lord Thomas Weir of Vere, Baron Kirkton
= Lady Jane Somerville, the hereditary Witch
of the Dragon House of the Earls Somerville

Major Thomas Weir of Vere of Edinburgh,
The hereditary Witch King of Mid-Lothian
= Margaret Bourdon

Thomas Weir of Vere
Baron Kirkton of Mid-Lothian,
Hereditary Witch King in Ireland
= Mary Robison of Cookstown Ulster

John Weir of Vere

Andrew Weir of Vere
|
Margaret Weir of Vere of Kildress
|
Archibald Weir of Vere of Kildress
= Rachel Stewart of Desertcreat
|
Robert Weir of Vere of Kildress
|
John Weir of Vere of Ardwell, Logan Manor
= Mary Logan dau. of Thomas Logan of
Ardwell, Logan Manor, Galloway
|
Thomas Logan Weir of Vere of Carlisle
= Anne Grant Macdonnell of Inverness
|
James Weir of Vere of Lewes
= Natalie Hopgood (descent from
the Collisons of Norfolk and the
Imperial and Royal House of Vere)
|
HI & RH Prince Nicholas de Vere

Vere Imperial Descent from Emperor Magnus Maximus

Emperor Magnus Maximus
Imperial Guletic 383-388
= Princess Elen (Oriene)
|
Princess Severa
= Lord Vortigern
(Vere–Tigherna)
Regulus of Britain
|
Lady Ribrawst
= Saint Brychan
|
Prince Brychan II
of Manau Gododdin
= Princess Ingenach of Strathclyde
|
Princess Lluan
= King Gabran
|
King Aeden Mac Gabran
The Uther Pendragon

Gwyr Llew = Ygraine of Avalon = Aeden Mac
Gabran

From Aeden Mac Gabran – Prince Arthur Pendragon
From Gwyr Llew – Princess Morgana the Fairy

(Here follows the Pendragon descent of the House of Vere from King Arthur and the House of the High Elves of Avalon extracted from the Promptuary Archive of the Urquhart House of Cromartie – issued by the Middle Temple of the Knights Templars of Saint Anthony L'Ermite in 1652. The Sovereign Grand Mastership of the Degree of Knights Templar within the Imperial and Royal Dragon Court is presently held heritably by Prince Nicholas de Vere.)

King Arthur Pendragon
= Princess Morgana the Fairy
|
Prince Mordred Pendragon
Archpriest of the Celtic Church
= Pictish Princess
|
Princess Tortolina Pendragon
= Nicharcos
Pictish Archpriest
|
Lord Marsidalio
= Lady Repulita
|
Lord Hedomenos
= Lady Urbana
|
Lord Agenor
= Lady Lampusa
|
Lord Diaprepon
= Lady Vistosa
|
Lord Stragayo
= Lady Hermosina dau. of Lord Natasil of Athole
|
Lord Zeron
= Lady Bramata
|
Lord Polyteles
= Lady Zaglopis
|
Lord Vocompos of Cromartie
= Lady Androlema of Douglas
|
Lord Carolo
= Lady Trastevole dau. of Lord Uilleam
|
Lord Endymion
= Lady Suaviloqua
|
Lord Sebastion
= Lady Francolina
|
Lord Lawrence
= Lady Mathilda
|
Lord Olipher

= Lady Allegra
|
Lord Quintin
= Lady Winnifred
|
Lord Goodwin
= Lady Dorothy
|
Lord Frederick
= Lady Lauretta dau. of Patrick Earl of March
|
Lady Matilda
= Lord William Comyn, grandson of Robert
Earl of Northumberland
|
Lord Richard Comyn
= Lady Hextilda dau. of Hutred of Tynedal
|
Lord William Comyn, Great Justiciar of Scotland
= Lady Marjorie Countess of Buchan
|
Lady Elizabeth Comyn
= Lord William 9th Earl of Mar|
Lord Donald 10th Earl of Mar
= Princess Helen dau. of Prince Llewellyn of North
Wales
|
Lady Isabel Mar
= King Robert I the Bruce
Grand Master of the Knights
Templars in Scotland
|
Marjorie Bruce
= Lord Walter Stewart
6th High Steward of Scotland
|
King Robert II
= Lady Elizabeth Muir of Rowallen
|
King Robert III
= Lady Annabelle Drummond of Stobhall
|
King James I
= Princess Joan Beaufort of Somerset
(Descent from King Edward III)
|
King James II
= Mary, dau. of Arnold Duc de Gueldres
|
Princess Mary
= Lord Thomas Boyd
|
Lady Mary Boyd
James 1st Lord Hamilton
great grandson of
Princess Aenor de Chatellerault
and Guillaume X le Toulousain
Duc de Guyenne, Comte de Poitiers

|
Lady Euphemia Hamilton
(descent from the High Elves of Ireland,
Princess Melusine and the Scots Kings)
= Lord James Weir of Vere,
Baron Blackwood d. 1595
|
Sir William Vere of Stanebyres Castle
= Elizabeth Hamilton, his cousin.
(descent from the High Elves of Ireland,
Princess Melusine and the Scots Kings)
|
Lord Thomas Weir of Vere, Baron Kirkton
= Lady Jane Somerville, the hereditary Witch
of the Dragon House of the Earls Somerville
|
Major Thomas Weir of Vere of Edinburgh,
The hereditary Witch King of Mid-Lothian
= Margaret Bourdon
|
Thomas Weir of Vere
Baron Kirkton of Mid-Lothian,
Hereditary Witch King in Ireland
= Mary Robison of Cookstown Ulster
|
John Weir of Vere
|
Andrew Weir of Vere
|
Margaret Weir of Vere of Kildress
|
Archibald Weir of Vere of Kildress
= Rachel Stewart of Desertcreat
|
Robert Weir of Vere of Kildress
|
John Weir of Vere of Ardwell, Logan Manor
= Mary Logan dau. of Thomas Logan of
Ardwell, Logan Manor, Galloway
|
Thomas Logan Weir of Vere of Carlisle
= Anne Grant Macdonnell of Inverness
|
James Weir of Vere of Lewes
= Natalie Hopgood (descent from
the Collisons of Norfolk and the
Imperial and Royal House of Vere)
|
HI & RH Prince Nicholas de Vere

Vere Imperial Descent from the Emperor Constantine of Byzantium

Emperor Constantine I (The Great)
|
Constantia
= Emperor Gratianus of Rome
|
Helen of Hosts
= Magnus Maximus
Imperial Guletic
|
Gratiana
= Tudwall of Galloway
|
Anlach
= Marchell
|
Saint Brychan
|
Brychan II
= Princess Ingenach
|
Lluan
= Gabran King of Scots
|
King Aeden Mac Gabran
The Uther Pendragon
or Great Dragon of Albany

Gwyr Llew = Ygraine of Avalon = Aeden Mac Gabran

From King Aeden Mac Gabran Queen Ygraine had
– Prince Arthur Pendragon
From Lord Gwyr Llew Queen Ygraine had –
Princess Morgana the Fairy

King Arthur Pendragon High King of Scots
= Princess Morgana the Fairy
|
Prince Mordred Pendragon
Archpriest of the Celtic Church
= Pictish Princess
|
Princess Tortolina Pendragon
= Nicharcos
Pictish Archpriest
|
Lord Marsidalio
= Lady Repulita
|
Lord Hedomenos
= Lady Urbana
|
Lord Agenor

= Lady Lampusa
|
Lord Diaprepon
= Lady Vistosa
|
Lord Stragayo
= Lady Hermosina dau. of
Lord Natasil of Athole
|
Lord Zeron
= Lady Bramata
|
Lord Polyteles
= Lady Zaglopis
|
Lord Vocompos of Cromartie
= Lady Androlema of Douglas
|
Lord Carolo
= Lady Trastevole
dau. of Lord Uilleam
|
Lord Endymion
= Lady Suaviloqua
|
Lord Sebastion
= Lady Francolina
|
Lord Lawrence
= Lady Mathilda
|
Lord Olipher
= Lady Allegra
|
Lord Quintin
= Lady Winnifred
|
Lord Goodwin
= Lady Dorothy
|
Lord Frederick
= Lady Lauretta dau. of
Patrick Earl of March
|
Lady Matilda
= Lord William Comyn,
grandson of Robert
Earl of Northumberland
|
Lord Richard Comyn
= Lady Hextilda dau.
of Hutred of Tynedal
|
Lord William Comyn,
Great Justiciar of Scotland
= Lady Buchan
|
Lady Elizabeth Comyn
= Lord William 9th Earl of Mar

Lord Donald 10th Earl of Mar
= Princess Helen

Lady Isabel
= King Robert I the Bruce
Grand Master of the Knights
Templars in Scotland

Princess Marjorie Bruce
= Lord Walter Stewart
6th High Steward of Scotland

King Robert II
= Lady Elizabeth Muir of Rowallen

King Robert III
= Lady Annabelle Drummond of Stobhall

King James I
= Princess Joan Beaufort of Somerset
(Descent from King Edward III)

King James II
= Mary, dau. of Arnold Duc de Gueldres

Princess Mary
= Lord Thomas Boyd

Lady Mary Boyd
James 1st Lord Hamilton
great grandson of
Princess Aenor de Chatellerault
and Guillaume X le Toulousain
Duc de Guyenne, Comte de Poitiers

Lady Euphemia Hamilton
(descent from the High Elves of Ireland,
Princess Melusine and the Scots Kings)
= Lord James Weir of Vere,
Baron Blackwood d. 1595

Sir William Vere of Stanebyres Castle
= Elizabeth Hamilton, his cousin.
(descent from the High Elves of Ireland,
Princess Melusine and the Scots Kings)

Lord Thomas Weir of Vere, Baron Kirkton
= Lady Jane Somerville, the hereditary Witch
of the Dragon House of the Earls Somerville

Major Thomas Weir of Vere of Edinburgh,
The hereditary Witch King of Mid-Lothian
= Margaret Bourdon

Thomas Weir of Vere
Baron Kirkton of Mid-Lothian,
Hereditary Witch King in Ireland
= Mary Robison of Cookstown Ulster

John Weir of Vere

Andrew Weir of Vere

Margaret Weir of Vere of Kildress

Archibald Weir of Vere of Kildress
= Rachel Stewart of Desertcreat

Robert Weir of Vere of Kildress

John Weir of Vere of Ardwell, Logan Manor
= Mary Logan dau. of Thomas Logan of
Ardwell, Logan Manor, Galloway

Thomas Logan Weir of Vere of Carlisle
= Anne Grant Macdonnell of Inverness

James Weir of Vere of Lewes
= Natalie Hopgood (descent from
the Collisons of Norfolk and the
Imperial and Royal House of Vere)

HI & RH Prince Nicholas de Vere

Vere Imperial Descent from Emperor Louis I

Charlemagne the Great
King of France 771-814
Roman Emperor 800-814
= Princess Hildegarde

Emperor Louis I
814-830
=2. Princess Judith of Bavaria

Emperor Lothair I
Middle Emperor from 840
King of Western Franks 843-855

Emperor Louis II of Italy
855-975

Princess Irmengarde
= Count Bouquet VIII of
Provence

Lady Kunigund
= Count Sigebert of Verdun
(Bouquet IX of Provence)

Duke Gozelo I
Duke of Lower Lorraine
(Descent to the House of Habsburg-Lorraine)
1023-1044

Duke Godfrey II
Duke of Upper Lorraine
d. 1069
= Princess Doda

Saint Ida of Ardennes
= Eustace II de Vere
Comte de Boulogne

Princess Ida de Vere
= Baudouin de Bourg
Comte de Rethul

Prince Hugues I
Comte de Rethul
= Melisende (Melusine II)
dau. Of Bouchard Comte de Corbeil and
Lady Adelaide de Crecy

Badouin II de Bourg
King of Jerusalem 1118-1131
= Princess Morfia of Armenia

Princess Melisende of Jerusalem (Melusine III)
= Fulke V Plantagenet Count of Anjou

Count Geoffrey Plantagenet
= Princess Mathilda, la Imperatrice
daughter of King Henry I and Princess
Mathilda of Scotland, daughter of
King Malcolm III

King Henry II Plantagenet
= Countess Eleanor of Aquitaine

King John "Lackland" Plantagenet
= Lady Isabella of Angouleme

King Henry III Plantagenet
= Lady Eleanor dau. of Count
Raymond Berenguer IV of Provence
and Princess Beatrix of Savoy

King Edward I
= Princess Eleanor of Castile

King Edward II Plantagenet
= Princess Isabella of France

King Edward III
1327-1377
= Princess Phillipa of Hainault

Prince John of Gaunt
= Lady Katharine Swynford

Prince John Plantagenet

Princess Joan Beaufort Plantagenet
= King James I of Scots

King James II
= Lady Mary, dau. of
Arnold Duc de Gueldres

Princess Mary Stewart
= Lord Thomas Boyd

Lady Mary Boyd
James 1st Lord Hamilton
great grandson of
Princess Aenor de Chatellerault
and Guillaume X le Toulousain
Duc de Guyenne, Comte de Poitiers

Lady Euphemia Hamilton
(descent from the High Elves of Ireland,
Princess Melusine and the Scots Kings)
= Lord James Weir of Vere,
Baron Blackwood d. 1595

Sir William Vere of Stanebyres Castle
= Elizabeth Hamilton, his cousin.
(descent from the High Elves of Ireland,
Princess Melusine and the Scots Kings)

Lord Thomas Weir of Vere, Baron Kirkton
= Lady Jane Somerville, the hereditary Witch
of the Dragon House of the Earls Somerville

Major Thomas Weir of Vere of Edinburgh,
The hereditary Witch King of Mid-Lothian
= Margaret Bourdon

Thomas Weir of Vere
Baron Kirkton of Mid-Lothian,
Hereditary Witch King in Ireland
= Mary Robison of Cookstown Ulster

John Weir of Vere

Andrew Weir of Vere

Margaret Weir of Vere of Kildress

Archibald Weir of Vere of Kildress
= Rachel Stewart of Desertcreat

Robert Weir of Vere of Kildress

John Weir of Vere of Ardwell, Logan Manor
= Mary Logan dau. of Thomas Logan of
Ardwell, Logan Manor, Galloway

Thomas Logan Weir of Vere of Carlisle
= Anne Grant Macdonnell of Inverness

|
James Weir of Vere of Lewes
= Natalie Hopgood (descent from
the Collisons of Norfolk and the
Imperial and Royal House of Vere)
|
HI & RH Prince Nicholas de Vere

Vere Imperial Descent from Lohengrin and the Early Habsburg-Lorraine Forefathers

Prince Lohengrin
(From whom the name
"Lorraine" originated)
The Elven Swan Knight,
Prince of the Holy Grail
= Countess Elsa of Brabant
(
)
(
Duke Gozelo I
(Gozelin the Rich)
Duke of Lower Lorraine
(Descent to the House of
Habsburg-Lorraine)
1023-1044
|
Duke Godfrey II
Duke of Upper Lorraine
d. 1069
= Princess Doda
|
Saint Ida of Ardennes
= Eustace II de Vere
Comte de Boulogne
|
Princess Ida de Vere
= Baudouin de Bourg
Comte de Rethul
|
Prince Hugues I
Comte de Rethul
= Melisende (Melusine II)
dau. of Bouchard Comte de Corbeil and
Lady Adelaide de Crecy
|
Baudouin II de Bourg
King of Jerusalem 1118-1131
= Princess Morfia of Armenia
|
Princess Melisende of Jerusalem (Melusine III)
= Fulke V Plantagenet Count of Anjou
|

Count Geoffrey Plantagenet
= Princess Mathilda, la Imperatrice
daughter of King Henry I and Princess
Mathilda of Scotland, daughter of
King Malcolm III
|
King Henry II Plantagenet
= Countess Eleanor of Aquitaine
|
King John "Lackland" Plantagenet
= Lady Isabella of Angouleme
|
King Henry III Plantagenet
= Lady Eleanor dau. of Count
Raymond Berenguer IV of Provence
and Princess Beatrix of Savoy
|
King Edward I Plantagenet
= Princess Eleanor of Castile
|
King Edward II Plantagenet
= Princess Isabella of France
|
King Edward III Plantagenet
1327-1377
= Princess Phillipa of Hainault
|
Prince John of Gaunt Plantagenet
= Lady Katharine Swynford
|
Prince John Plantagenet
|
Princess Joan Beaufort Plantagenet
= King James I of Scots
|
King James II
= Lady Mary, dau. of
Arnold Duc de Gueldres
|
Princess Mary Stewart
= Lord Thomas Boyd
|
Lady Mary Boyd
James 1st Lord Hamilton
great grandson of
Princess Aenor de Chatellerault
and Guillaume X le Toulousain
Duc de Guyenne, Comte de Poitiers
|
Lady Euphemia Hamilton
(descent from the High Elves of Ireland,
Princess Melusine and the Scots Kings)
= Lord James Weir of Vere,
Baron Blackwood d. 1599
|
Sir William Vere of Stanebyres Castle
= Elizabeth Hamilton, his cousin.
(descent from the High Elves of Ireland,
Princess Melusine and the Scots Kings)

Lord Thomas Weir of Vere, Baron Kirkton
= Lady Jane Somerville, the hereditary Witch
of the Dragon House of the Earls Somerville

Major Thomas Weir of Vere of Edinburgh,
The hereditary Witch King of Mid-Lothian
= Margaret Bourdon

Thomas Weir of Vere
Baron Kirkton of Mid-Lothian,
Hereditary Witch King in Ireland
= Mary Robison of Cookstown Ulster

John Weir of Vere

Andrew Weir of Vere

Margaret Weir of Vere of Kildress

Archibald Weir of Vere of Kildress
= Rachel Stewart of Desertcreat

Robert Weir of Vere of Kildress

John Weir of Vere of Ardwell, Logan Manor
= Mary Logan dau. of Thomas Logan of
Ardwell, Logan Manor, Galloway

Thomas Logan Weir of Vere of Carlisle
= Anne Grant Macdonnell of Inverness

James Weir of Vere of Lewes
= Natalie Hopgood (descent from
the Collisons of Norfolk and the
Imperial and Royal House of Vere)

HI & RH Prince Nicholas de Vere

Vere Imperial Descent from the Goddess Venus via the House of Gaius Julius Caesar

The Babylonian Goddess-Queen Tiamat
(The Greek Goddess "Chaos"), Mother of Gaia

The Babylonian Goddess-Queen Kishar
(The Greek Goddess Gaia:
Mother Earth)

The Babylonian God-King Anu (Chronos-Saturn)
and the High
Council of the Anunnaki: The Jewish Elohim: The
Old Gods

The Goddess Venus-Aphrodite

The Bright and Morning Star,
the Jewel in the Crown of Satan
(The Demon Queen Ishtar-Astaroth);
Half-Sister of Queen Lilith.
Jesus consciously equated himself with Venus
as the Bright and Morning Star, the Roman
"Lucifer" in *Revelations* whilst Jesus' wife
Mary Magdalene was herself Priestess of
the Goddess Ishtar-Venus
= Typhoeus, (Enki-Set-Satan) God of the Titans;
God-King of the Fairies, father of the Elven
Scythians;
Half-Brother of the God Enlil–Zeus–Jehovah

Prince Anchises, Lord of
the Scythians of Troy

Lord Aeneas of the Labyrinth
Dragon Prince of Troy
=Princess Creusa

Romulus
Founder of Rome

Ascanius

Julus
Founder of the House of the Julii

Numerus Julius Julus

Lucius Julus Julius I

Caius Julius Julius I

Caius Julius Julius II

Caius Julius Julius III 260 BC

Lucius Julius Julus 240 BC

Lucius Julius Julus II

Lucius Julius Libo I

Lucius Julius Libo II

Numerius Julius Caesar 180 BC

Lucius Julius Caesar I

Sextus Julius Caesar I

Sextus Julius Caesar II

Caius Caesar Julius

Julius Caesar (Julius Slakten)

The Lady Julia Julii,
Sister of Emperor Gaius Julius Caesar
(Who was murdered by the Senate of Rome)
|
The Lady Atia of the Julii
=Emperor Octavian
|
Octavia Minor
=Marcus Antonius
|
Antonia Minor
=Emperor Nero
|
Emperor Claudius
= Valeria
|
Genevissa
= Arviragus
|
Marius
|
Coel I
|
Lucius
= Gladys
|
Gladys
= Cadwan Prince of Cumbria
|
Coel II of Camulod
|
Cunedd
|
Confer
|
Fer (Vere)
|
Cursalen
|
Clemens
|
Quintinius
|
Cynloyp
|
Ceretic: Guletic of Allt Clud
|
Cinuit
|
Dyfnwal Hen of Strathclyde
|
Ingenach
= Brychan II
|
Lluan
|
= Gabran King of Scots
|

King Aeden Mac Gabran
The Uther Pendragon
or Great Dragon of Albany

Gwyr Llew = Ygraine of Avalon = Aeden Mac
Gabran
|
From King Aeden Mac Gabran Queen Ygraine had
– Prince Arthur Pendragon
From Lord Gwyr Llew Queen Ygraine had –
Princess Morgana the Fairy
King Arthur Pendragon High King of Scots
= Princess Morgana the Fairy
|
Prince Mordred Pendragon
Archpriest of the Celtic Church
= Pictish Princess
|
Princess Tortolina Pendragon
= Nicharcos
Pictish Archpriest
|
Lord Marsidalio
= Lady Repulita
|
Lord Hedomenos
= Lady Urbana
|
Lord Agenor
= Lady Lampusa
|
Lord Diaprepon
= Lady Vistosa
|
Lord Stragayo
= Lady Hermosina dau. of Lord Natasil of Athole
|
Lord Zeron
= Lady Bramata
|
Lord Polyteles
= Lady Zaglopis
|
Lord Vocompos of Cromartie
= Lady Androlema of Douglas
|
Lord Carolo
= Lady Trastevole dau. of Lord Uilleam
|
Lord Endymion
= Lady Suaviloqua
|
Lord Sebastion
= Lady Francolina
|
Lord Lawrence
= Lady Mathilda

Lord Olipher
= Lady Allegra

Lord Quintin
= Lady Winnifred

Lord Goodwin
= Lady Dorothy

Lord Frederick
= Lady Lauretta dau. of Patrick Earl of March

Lady Matilda
= Lord William Comyn, grandson of Robert
Earl of Northumberland

Lord Richard Comyn
= Lady Hextilda dau. of Hutred of Tynedal

Lord William Comyn, Great Justiciar of Scotland
= Lady Marjorie Countess of Buchan

Lady Elizabeth Comyn
= Lord William 9th Earl of Mar

Lord Donald 10th Earl of Mar
= Princess Helen

Lady Isabel
= King Robert I the Bruce
Sovereign Grand Master of the
Knights Templars in Scotland

Marjorie Bruce
= Lord Walter Stewart
6th High Steward of Scotland

King Robert II
= Lady Elizabeth Muir of Rowallen

King Robert III
= Lady Annabelle Drummond of Stobhall

King James I
= Princess Joan Beaufort
Plantagenet of Somerset
(Descent from King Edward III)

King James II
= Mari, dau. of Arnold Duc de Gueldres

Princess Mary
= Lord Thomas Boyd

Lady Mary Boyd
= James 1st Lord Hamilton
great grandson of Princess
Aenor de Chatellerault and

Guillaume X le Toulousain
Duc de Guyenne, Comte de Poitiers

Lady Euphemia Hamilton
(descent from the High Elves of Ireland,
Princess Melusine and the Scots Kings)
= Lord James Weir of Vere,
Baron Blackwood d. 1595

Sir William Vere of Stanebyres Castle
= Elizabeth Hamilton, his cousin.
(descent from the High Elves of Ireland,
Princess Melusine and the Scots Kings)

Lord Thomas Weir of Vere, Baron Kirkton
= Lady Jane Somerville, the hereditary Witch
of the Dragon House of the Earls Somerville

Major Thomas Weir of Vere of Edinburgh,
The hereditary Witch King of Mid-Lothian
= Margaret Bourdon

Thomas Weir of Vere
Baron Kirkton of Mid-Lothian,
Hereditary Witch King in Ireland
= Mary Robison of Cookstown Ulster

John Weir of Vere

Andrew Weir of Vere

Margaret Weir of Vere of Kildress

Archibald Weir of Vere of Kildress
= Rachel Stewart of Desertcreat

Robert Weir of Vere of Kildress

John Weir of Vere of Ardwell, Logan Manor
= Mary Logan dau. of Thomas Logan of
Ardwell, Logan Manor, Galloway

Thomas Logan Weir of Vere of Carlisle
= Anne Grant Macdonnell of Inverness

James Weir of Vere of Lewes
= Natalie Hopgood (descent from
the Collisons of Norfolk and the
Imperial and Royal House of Vere)

HI & RH Prince Nicholas de Vere

The Maternal Fairy Genealogies of Nicholas de Vere and The Imperial and Royal House of Collison

Collison Descent from the Lia Fail and the High Kings of Ireland

Lord Anu and the High Council
of the Anunnaki: The Elohim

|

Satan (Enki; son of Anu)

|

Egyptian Royal descent

|

King Solomon
Lord of the Rings.
1015 BC
= Princess Naamah the Ammonitess.
(King Solomon descends from "Satan"
via the Egyptian Dragon Queen of Sobekh,
Queen Kiya Tasherit, wife of Prince Rama.)

|

King Rehoboam
King of Judah 975 BC
= Princess Maachlah
dau. of Ureil of Gibeah

|

King Abijah
King of Judah
957 BC

|

King Asa

King of Judah 955 BC
= Princess Azubah
dau. of Shilhi
|
King Jehoshaphat
King of Judah 917 BC
|
King Jehoram
King of Judah 893 BC
= Princess Athalia
dau. of Omri
|
King Ahaziah
King of Judah 885 BC
= Princess Zibiah of Beersheba
|
King Joash
King of Judah 878 BC
= Princess Jehoaddan of Jerusalem
|
King Amaziah
King of Judah 840 BC
= Princess Jecoliah of Jerusalem
|
King Uzziah
King of Judah 811 BC
= Princess Jerushah
da. Of Zadok
|
King Jotham
King of Judah 759 BC
|
King Ahaz
King of Judah 742 BC
= Princess Abijah
dau of Zechariah
|
King Hezekiah
King of Judah 726 BC
= Princess Hephzibah
|
King Mannaseh
King of Judah 697 BC
= Princess Meshullemeth
dau of Haruz of Jotbah
|
King Amon
King of Judah 642 BC
= Princess Jedidah
dau. of Adaiah of Boscath
|
King Josiah
King of Judah 640 BC
= 2. Princess Hamutal
dau. of Jeremiah of Libnah
|
King Zedekiah
King of Judah 598 BC
|

Princess Tamar of Judah
= King Eochaid I The Milesian.
High King of Ireland after the
displacement of the remnant
of the Tuadha de Danaan
|
King Irial Faidh
|
King Eithriall
|
King Follain
|
King Tighernmas
|
King Eanbotha
|
King Smiorguil
|
King Fiachach Labhruine
|
King Aongus Oilbughagah
|
King Maoin
|
King Rotheachta
|
King Dein
|
King Siorna Saoghalach
|
King Oiliolla Olchaoin
|
King Nuadha Fionn Fail
|
King Giallchadh
|
King Simon Breac
|
King Muiriadhach Bolgrach
|
King Fiathadh Tolgrach
|
King Duach Laighrach
|
King Eochaidh Buillaig
|
King Ugaine Mar (The Great)
|
King Cobhtach Caolbreag
|
King Meilage
|
King Jaran Gleofathach
|
King Conla Gruaich
|
King Ceaigach
|
King Oiliolla Caisfhiaclach

King Eochaid Foltleathan	Fir Bolg House of the Ulidian
King Aonghus Tuirimheach	King Fergus Mor d. 501 AD
King Fiachra Firmara	King Domangart 501-506
King Feradaig	King Gabran 537-559
King Fergus I	King Aeden MacGabran Pendragon 574-608
King Maine (Father of Prince Siadhail, descent to the Ua Siadhails or O'Shiels of Ireland)	King Eochaid Buide 608-630
King Dornadil	King Donald Brecc 630-643
King Rowein	King Domangart
King Reuther	King Eochaid 695-696
King Eders	King Eochaid 726-733
King Conaire Mor	King Aed Find 748-778
King Admoir	King Eochaid 781
King Corbred I	= Princess Unuisticc of Fortren
King Dare-Dornmoir	King Alpin King of Scots 839-841
King Corbred II	King Kenneth I MacAlpin King of Picts and Scots 844-859
King Luigdig-Ellatig	King Constantine I 863-877
King Modha Lamha	King Donald II 889-900
King Conaire II = Princess Saraid (Migration of the Ulster Horse Lords to Albany/Scotland c. 200 AD)	King Malcom I 942-954
King Corbred of the Dal Riada	King Kenneth II 971-995
King Eochaid	King Malcom II MacKenneth 1005-1034
King Athirco	Princess Bethoc
King Findacher	
King Thrinklind	
King Romaich	
King Angus	
King Eochaid Muin-Remor	
King Erc, Archdruid of the sacred	

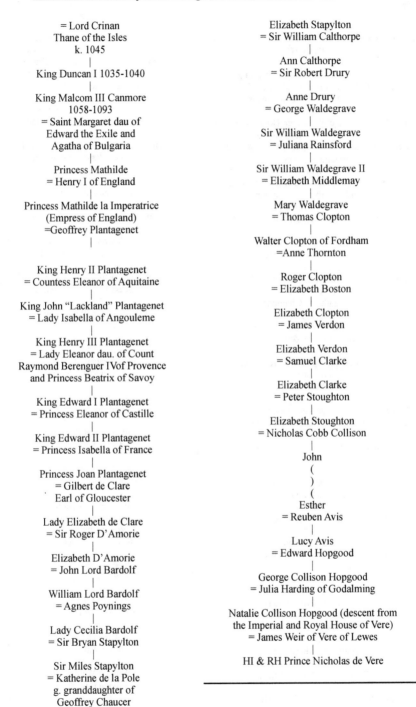

= Lord Crinan
Thane of the Isles
k. 1045
|
King Duncan I 1035-1040
|
King Malcom III Canmore
1058-1093
= Saint Margaret dau of
Edward the Exile and
Agatha of Bulgaria
|
Princess Mathilde
= Henry I of England
|
Princess Mathilde la Imperatrice
(Empress of England)
=Geoffrey Plantagenet
|

King Henry II Plantagenet
= Countess Eleanor of Aquitaine
|
King John "Lackland" Plantagenet
= Lady Isabella of Angouleme
|
King Henry III Plantagenet
= Lady Eleanor dau. of Count
Raymond Berenguer IVof Provence
and Princess Beatrix of Savoy
|
King Edward I Plantagenet
= Princess Eleanor of Castille
|
King Edward II Plantagenet
= Princess Isabella of France
|
Princess Joan Plantagenet
= Gilbert de Clare
Earl of Gloucester
|
Lady Elizabeth de Clare
= Sir Roger D'Amorie
|
Elizabeth D'Amorie
= John Lord Bardolf
|
William Lord Bardolf
= Agnes Poynings
|
Lady Cecilia Bardolf
= Sir Bryan Stapylton
|
Sir Miles Stapylton
= Katherine de la Pole
g. granddaughter of
Geoffrey Chaucer
|

Elizabeth Stapylton
= Sir William Calthorpe
|
Ann Calthorpe
= Sir Robert Drury
|
Anne Drury
= George Waldegrave
|
Sir William Waldegrave
= Juliana Rainsford
|
Sir William Waldegrave II
= Elizabeth Middlemay
|
Mary Waldegrave
= Thomas Clopton
|
Walter Clopton of Fordham
=Anne Thornton
|
Roger Clopton
= Elizabeth Boston
|
Elizabeth Clopton
= James Verdon
|
Elizabeth Verdon
= Samuel Clarke
|
Elizabeth Clarke
= Peter Stoughton
|
Elizabeth Stoughton
= Nicholas Cobb Collison
|
John
(
)
(
Esther
= Reuben Avis
|
Lucy Avis
= Edward Hopgood
|
George Collison Hopgood
= Julia Harding of Godalming
|
Natalie Collison Hopgood (descent from
the Imperial and Royal House of Vere)
= James Weir of Vere of Lewes
|
HI & RH Prince Nicholas de Vere

Collison Descent from the Veres of Scotland

Rainfroi de Vere Count of Anjou
= The Fairy Princess Melusine I
Dragon Queen of the Scythians
|
Prince Milo I de Vere, Sovereign Duke of the State
of Angiers, Count of Anjou
= Bertheld, dau of King Pepin of the Franks, sister
to Charlemagne.
Descent from the Dragon Queens of Egypt,
King Solomon, Christ and King Meroveus,
Founder of the Merovingian
Royal Dynasty of the Franks
(See chart – Jesus' descent from Satan)
|
Prince Milo II de Vere
= Lady Aveline de Nantes
|
Prince Nicassius de Vere, Count of Guisnes and
Anjou
=Lady Agatha de Champagne
|
Prince Otho de Vere, Count of Guisnes
= Lady Constance de Chartres
|
Prince Amelius (Adolphus) de Vere Count of
Guisnes
2. = Lady Maud de Ponthieu
|
Prince Gallus (Guy) de Vere, Count of Guisnes
2. = Lady Gertrude de Clermont de Ponthieu
|
Prince Baldwin de Vere de Boulogne
= Adele de Ghent
|
Prince Eustace de Vere
= Lady Maud de Lovain
|
Princess Ida de Vere
= Baudouin de Bourg
Comte de Rethul
(Merovingian descent via Charlemagne)
|
Prince Hugues I
Comte de Rethul
= Melisende (Melusine II)
dau. Of Bouchard Comte de Corbeil and
Lady Adelaide de Crecy
|
Badouin II de Bourg
King of Jerusalem 1118-1131
= Princess Morfia of Armenia
|
Princess Melisende of Jerusalem (Melusine III)
= Fulke V Plantagenet Count of Anjou

Count Geoffrey Plantagenet
= Princess Mathilda, la Imperatrice
daughter of King Henry I and Princess
Mathilda of Scotland, daughter of
King Malcolm III
|
King Henry II Plantagenet
= Countess Eleanor of Aquitaine
|
King John "Lackland" Plantagenet
= Lady Isabella of Angouleme
|
King Henry III Plantagenet
= Lady Eleanor dau. of Count
Raymond Berenguer IVof Provence
and Princess Beatrix of Savoy
|
King Edward I Plantagenet
= Princess Eleanor of Castille
|
King Edward II Plantagenet
= Princess Isabella of France
|
Princess Joan Plantagenet
= Gilbert de Clare
Earl of Gloucester
|
Lady Elizabeth de Clare
= Sir Roger D'Amorie
|
Elizabeth D'Amorie
= John Lord Bardolf
|
William Lord Bardolf
= Agnes Poynings
|
Lady Cecilia Bardolf
= Sir Bryan Stapylton
|
Sir Miles Stapylton
= Katherine de la Pole
g. granddaughter of
Geoffrey Chaucer
|
Elizabeth Stapylton
= Sir William Calthorpe
|
Ann Calthorpe
= Sir Robert Drury
|
Anne Drury
= George Waldegrave
|
Sir William Waldegrave
= Juliana Rainsford
|
Sir William Waldegrave II
= Elizabeth Middlemay

|
Mary Waldegrave
= Thomas Clopton
|
Walter Clopton of Fordham
=Anne Thornton
|
Roger Clopton
= Elizabeth Boston
|
Elizabeth Clopton
= James Verdon
|
Elizabeth Verdon
= Samuel Clarke
|
Elizabeth Clarke
= Peter Stoughton
|
Elizabeth Stoughton
= Nicholas Cobb Collison
|
John
(
)
(
Esther
= Reuben Avis
|
Lucy Avis
= Edward Hopgood
|
George Collison Hopgood
= Julia Harding of Godalming
|
Natalie Collison Hopgood (descent from
the Imperial and Royal House of Vere)
= James Weir of Vere of Lewes
|
HI & RH Prince Nicholas de Vere

Collison Descent from King
Solomon and the Kings of Judah

Lord Anu and the High Council
of the Anunnaki: The Elohim
|
Satan-Lucifer
(Enki, son of Anu)
|
The Egyptian Kings
|
King Solomon
Lord of the Rings.
1015 BC
= Princess Naamah the Ammonitess.

Solomon's Descent from Satan
via the Dragon Queen of Sobekh,
Kiya Tasherit, wife of Prince Rama
|
King Rehoboam
King of Judah 975 BC
= Princess Maachlah
dau. of Ureil of Gibeah
|
King Abijah
King of Judah
957 BC
|
King Asa
King of Judah 955 BC
= Princess Azubah
dau. of Shilhi
|
King Jehoshaphat
King of Judah 917 BC
|
King Jehoram
King of Judah 893 BC
= Princess Athalia
dau. of Omri
|
King Ahaziah
King of Judah 885 BC
= Princess Zibiah of Beersheba
|
King Joash
King of Judah 878 BC
Princess Jehoaddan of Jerusalem
|
King Amaziah
King of Judah 840 BC
= Princess Jecoliah of Jerusalem
|
King Uzziah
King of Judah 811 BC
= Princess Jerushah
da. Of Zadok
|
King Jotham
King of Judah 759 BC
|
King Ahaz
King of Judah 742 BC
Princess Abijah
dau of Zechariah
|
King Hezekiah
King of Judah 726 BC
= Princess Hephzibah
|
King Mannaseh
King of Judah 697 BC
= Princess Meshullemeth
dau of Haruz of Jotbah

|
King Amon
King of Judah 642 BC
= Princess Jedidah
dau. of Adaiah of Boscath
|
King Josiah
King of Judah 640 BC
|
King Jehoiakim
King of Judah 609 BC
(Taken Hostage to Babylon)
= Princess Nehushtah
dau. of Elnathan of Judaea
|
King Jechoniah
King of Judah 598 BC
(Taken hostage to Babylon)
|
Prince Shealtiel
|
Prince Pedaiah
|
Prince Zerrubabel
De jure King
of Judah
|
Prince Rhesa
|
Prince Johanan
|
Prince Judah
|
Prince Joseph
|
Prince Semei
|
Prince Mattathias
|
Prince Maath
|
Prince Naage
|
Prince Azallah
|
Prince Nahum
|
Prince Amos
|
Prince Mattathias
|
Prince Joseph
|
Prince Johanan
|
Prince Melchi
|
Prince Levi
|

Prince Matthat
|
Prince Jacob
|
Prince Joseph
|
Jesus Christ The Messiah
(Messach: Anointed of the God Sobekh)
(Yehoshua ben-Joseph, [called ben-Panther])
= Mary Magdalene, Priestess of Ishtar (Venus)

Descent to the Fisher Kings of the Grail, the Merovingian Sorcerer Kings and the Imperial and Royal House of Vere

- Et In Arcadia Ego -

|
Jesus and Mary
|
Josue Del Graal
|
Aminadab
= Eurgis d. of King Coel I
sister of Lucius the Great
|
Catheloys
|
Manael
|
Titurel
|
Boaz
(Anfortas)
|
Frotmund
(Frimutel)
|
Faramund 420 AD
Sire of the French Monarchy
= Argotta dau. of Genebaud
of the Sicambrian Franks
|
Clodian of Tournai
= Queen Basina of Thuringia
|
King Meroveus, founder of
the Dynasty of Merovingian
Sorcerer Kings d. 456 AD
= Princess Meira
|
King Childeric of the Franks d. 481 AD
= Queen Basina II of Thuringia
|
King Clovis of the Franks d. 511 AD

= Clotilde of Burgundy
|
King Lothar I d. 561 AD
|
Princess Blitildis
= Prince Ansbert, Great Great Grandson of
King Clodian of Tournai (above) d. 570 AD
|
Lord Arnoald of Scheldt
= Princess Dua of Swabia
|
Arnulf of Metz
= Princess Dobo of Saxony
|
Lord Ansegis of Brabant (Lower Lorraine)
Margrave of Scheldt d. 685
= Lady Begga, dau of Pepin I, Mayor of Austrasia
|
Lord Pepin II of Heristal, Mayor of the Palaces of
Austrasia, Neustria and Burgundy d. 714
= Lady Alpas
|
Lord Charles Martel (The Hammer) d. 741
|
Pepin the III Brevis, Duke of Lower Lorraine
(Brabant)
Mayor of Neustrasia, King of the Franks
= Lady Leuthergis
|
Princess Bertha
= Prince Milo de Vere, Duke of Angiers
Count of Anjou (son of the Fairy Princess Melusine
I
of the Scythians: parallel descent from Satan via the
Egyptian Kings as above)
|
Prince Milo II de Vere, Count of Guisnes and Anjou
= Lady Aveline de Nantes
|
Prince Nicassius de Vere, Count of Guisnes and
Anjou
Lady Agatha de Champagne
|
Prince Otho de Vere, Count of Guisnes
= Lady Constance de Chartres
|
Prince Amelius (Adolph) de Vere
= Lady Maud de Ponthieu
|
Prince Gallus (Guy) de Vere, Count of Guisnes
= Lady Gertrude de Clermont de Ponthieu
|
Prince Baldwin de Vere
= Adele de Ghent
|
Prince Eustace de Vere
= Lady Maud de Lovain
|
Princess Ida de Vere

= Baudouin de Bourg
Comte de Rethul
(Merovingian descent from
Satan via Charlemagne)
|
Prince Hugues I
Comte de Rethul
= Melisende (Melusine II)
dau. Of Bouchard Comte de Corbeil and
Lady Adelaide de Crecy
|
Badouin II de Bourg
King of Jerusalem 1118-1131
= Princess Morfia of Armenia
|
Princess Melisende of Jerusalem (Melusine III)
= Fulke V Plantagenet Count of Anjou
(Descent from Melusine I's sister Princess Plantina,
mother of Lord Tortulf de Nide de Merle)
|
Count Geoffrey Plantagenet
= Princess Mathilda, la Imperatrice
daughter of King Henry I and Princess
Mathilda of Scotland, daughter of
King Malcolm III
|
King Henry II Plantagenet
= Countess Eleanor of Aquitaine
|
King John "Lackland" Plantagenet
= Lady Isabella of Angouleme
|
King Henry III Plantagenet
= Lady Eleanor dau. of Count
Raymond Berenguer I Vof Provence
and Princess Beatrix of Savoy
|
King Edward I Plantagenet
= Princess Eleanor of Castille
|
King Edward II Plantagenet
= Princess Isabella of France
|
Princess Joan Plantagenet
= Gilbert de Clare
Earl of Gloucester
|
Lady Elizabeth de Clare
= Sir Roger D'Amorie
|
Elizabeth D'Amorie
= John Lord Bardolf
|
William Lord Bardolf
|
= Agnes Poynings
|
Lady Cecilia Bardolf
= Sir Bryan Stapylton
|

Sir Miles Stapylton
= Katherine de la Pole
g. granddaughter of
Geoffrey Chaucer
|
Elizabeth Stapylton
= Sir William Calthorpe
|
Ann Calthorpe
= Sir Robert Drury
|
Anne Drury
= George Waldegrave
|
Sir William Waldegrave
= Juliana Rainsford
|
Sir William Waldegrave II
= Elizabeth Middlemay
|
Mary Waldegrave
= Thomas Clopton
|
Walter Clopton of Fordham
=Anne Thornton
|
Roger Clopton
= Elizabeth Boston
|
Elizabeth Clopton
= James Verdon
|
Elizabeth Verdon
= Samuel Clarke
|
Elizabeth Clarke
= Peter Stoughton
|
Elizabeth Stoughton
= Nicholas Cobb Collison
|
John
(
)
(
Esther
= Reuben Avis
|
Lucy Avis
= Edward Hopgood
|
George Collison Hopgood
= Julia Harding of Godalming
|
Natalie Collison Hopgood (descent from
the Imperial and Royal House of Vere)
= James Weir of Vere of Lewes
|
HI & RH Prince Nicholas de Vere

Collison Imperial and Merovingian Descent from King Dagobert I "The Great" and Emperor Charlemagne

King Dagobert I
King of Austrasia,
King of the Franks
630-638
= Princess Nanthilda
|
King Clovis II
633-656
= Princess Batilde
|
King Theuderic III
King of Neustria and Burgundy 673
King of Austrasia 679-691
|
King Childebert III
695-711
|
King Dagobert III 711-715
|
Princess Blanche Fleur
= King Flora of Hungary
|
Princess Bertha
= Pepin III
Mayor of Neustria d. 768
|
Charlemagne the Great
King of France 771-814
Holy Roman Emperor 800-814
= Princess Hildegarde
|
Emperor Louis I
814-830
= Princess Irmengarde
|
Emperor Charles II
Western Emperor from 840
King of France from 843
Holy Roman Emperor from 867-877
|
King Louis II of France
877-879
|
King Charles II of France
893–dep. 922
= Princess Eadgifu
|
King Louis IV of France
936-954
Princess Gerberga dau. of
King Henry of Germany
|

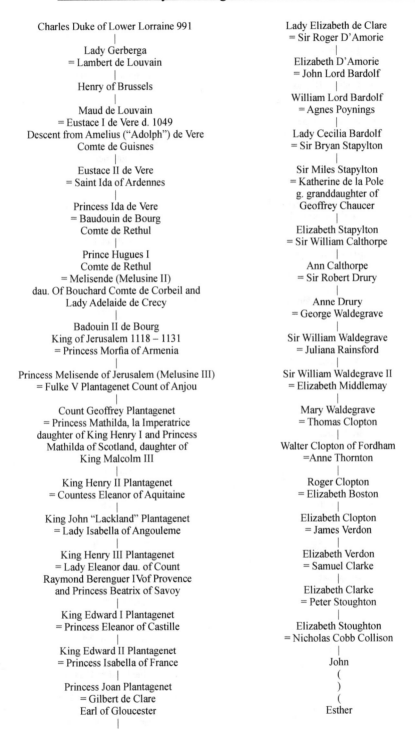

Charles Duke of Lower Lorraine 991
|
Lady Gerberga
= Lambert de Louvain
|
Henry of Brussels
|
Maud de Louvain
= Eustace I de Vere d. 1049
Descent from Amelius ("Adolph") de Vere
Comte de Guisnes
|
Eustace II de Vere
= Saint Ida of Ardennes
|
Princess Ida de Vere
= Baudouin de Bourg
Comte de Rethul
|
Prince Hugues I
Comte de Rethul
= Melisende (Melusine II)
dau. Of Bouchard Comte de Corbeil and
Lady Adelaide de Crecy
|
Badouin II de Bourg
King of Jerusalem 1118 – 1131
= Princess Morfia of Armenia
|
Princess Melisende of Jerusalem (Melusine III)
= Fulke V Plantagenet Count of Anjou
|
Count Geoffrey Plantagenet
= Princess Mathilda, la Imperatrice
daughter of King Henry I and Princess
Mathilda of Scotland, daughter of
King Malcolm III
|
King Henry II Plantagenet
= Countess Eleanor of Aquitaine
|
King John "Lackland" Plantagenet
= Lady Isabella of Angouleme
|
King Henry III Plantagenet
= Lady Eleanor dau. of Count
Raymond Berenguer IVof Provence
and Princess Beatrix of Savoy
|
King Edward I Plantagenet
= Princess Eleanor of Castille
|
King Edward II Plantagenet
= Princess Isabella of France
|
Princess Joan Plantagenet
= Gilbert de Clare
Earl of Gloucester
|

Lady Elizabeth de Clare
= Sir Roger D'Amorie
|
Elizabeth D'Amorie
= John Lord Bardolf
|
William Lord Bardolf
= Agnes Poynings
|
Lady Cecilia Bardolf
= Sir Bryan Stapylton
|
Sir Miles Stapylton
= Katherine de la Pole
g. granddaughter of
Geoffrey Chaucer
|
Elizabeth Stapylton
= Sir William Calthorpe
|
Ann Calthorpe
= Sir Robert Drury
|
Anne Drury
= George Waldegrave
|
Sir William Waldegrave
= Juliana Rainsford
|
Sir William Waldegrave II
= Elizabeth Middlemay
|
Mary Waldegrave
= Thomas Clopton
|
Walter Clopton of Fordham
=Anne Thornton
|
Roger Clopton
= Elizabeth Boston
|
Elizabeth Clopton
= James Verdon
|
Elizabeth Verdon
= Samuel Clarke
|
Elizabeth Clarke
= Peter Stoughton
|
Elizabeth Stoughton
= Nicholas Cobb Collison
|
John
(
)
(
Esther

= Reuben Avis
|
Lucy Avis
= Edward Hopgood
|
George Collison Hopgood
= Julia Harding of Godalming
|
Natalie Collison Hopgood (descent from
the Imperial and Royal House of Vere)
= James Weir of Vere of Lewes
|
HI & RH Prince Nicholas de Vere

Collison Imperial Descent from King Vere via Princess Plantina

King Vere 400 BC
Fairy Lord and Dragon King
|
Alternate succession of the Vere
Druid Prophets and Wood Lords
of the Ancient Caledonian
Fairy Forest Kingdom
|
Brude Pont
|
Vere Pont
|
Brude Leo
|
Vere Leo
|
Brude Grant
|
Vere Grant
|
Brude Gnith
|
Vere Gnith
|
Brude Fechir
|
Vere Fechir
|
Brude Cal
|
Vere Cal
|
Brude Cint
|
Vere Cint
|
Vere Feta
Dragon Queen
|
Gartnait Bolg
Priest King of Caledonia

ad 165-169
|
King Vere II
ad 169-178
Ard Righ (High King)
of the Bruithnigh
|
Vipoguenech
|
Fiacha Albus
|
Canutumel
|
Dovernach Vetalec
|
King Vere III Daich Vetla
|
Gartnait Diuperr
Ard Righ (High King)
AD 355
|
Achivir
|
Aniel
|
Giron
|
Mailcon
|
Bridei
High King AD 520
|
Wid I
|
Gartnait
Ard Righ (High King)
|
Ainfrid
|
Talorcan
Ard Righ
|
daughter
= Bile ap Fili
Welsh King of Alcut
at Dumbarton
|
Brude Mac Bile
Ard Righ 693-697
|
Queen Pressina (Bruidhina)
of the Scythian Picts
= King Elinus of Albha, the Dragon
of Berenicia (Northumberland),
descendant of the Uilidian Druid Princes
|
Melusine - Plantina - Meliore
|
The Plantagenista Descent

Torquat b. c. 760	Princess Joan Plantagenet = Gilbert de Clare Earl of Gloucester
Tortulf de Rennes 790	Lady Elizabeth de Clare = Sir Roger D'Amorie
Tertulle Count of Anjou c. 821 = Petronella of France	Elizabeth D'Amorie = John Lord Bardolf
Count Ingelgar of Anjou 845 = Adelais de Rescinde	William Lord Bardolf = Agnes Poynings
Fulk I The Red, Count of Anjou b. 888 = Roscilla de Loches	Lady Cecilia Bardolf = Sir Bryan Stapylton
Fulk II The Good, Count of Anjou b. 920 = Gerberga de Maine	Sir Miles Stapylton = Katherine de la Pole g. granddaughter of Geoffrey Chaucer
Geoffrey Greymantle, Count of Anjou b. 939 = Adele de Vermandois	
Fullk III The Black, Count of Anjou b. 956 = 2. Hildegard of Metz	Elizabeth Stapylton = Sir William Calthorpe
Geoffrey II Martel, Count of Anjou b. 1006 = Agnes of Bourgogne	Ann Calthorpe = Sir Robert Drury
Geoffrey III Le Harbu b. 1040 = Julienne de Langeaise	Anne Drury = George Waldegrave
Geoffrey IV Martel b. 1073 = Bertrade de Montfort	Sir William Waldegrave = Juliana Rainsford
Fulk V The Younger, Count of Anjou b. 1092 = Princess Melisende (Melusine III) of Jerusalem	Sir William Waldegrave II = Elizabeth Middlemay
Count Geoffrey Plantagenet = Princess Mathilda, la Imperatrice daughter of King Henry I and Princess Mathilda of Scotland, daughter of King Malcolm III	Mary Waldegrave = Thomas Clopton
	Walter Clopton of Fordham =Anne Thornton
King Henry II Plantagenet = Countess Eleanor of Aquitaine	Roger Clopton = Elizabeth Boston
King John "Lackland" Plantagenet = Lady Isabella of Angouleme	Elizabeth Clopton = James Verdon
King Henry III Plantagenet = Lady Eleanor dau. of Count Raymond Berenguer IVof Provence and Princess Beatrix of Savoy	Elizabeth Verdon = Samuel Clarke
	Elizabeth Clarke = Peter Stoughton
King Edward I Plantagenet = Princess Eleanor of Castille	Elizabeth Stoughton = Nicholas Cobb Collison
King Edward II Plantagenet = Princess Isabella of France	John (

)
(
Esther
= Reuben Avis
|
Lucy Avis
= Edward Hopgood
|
George Collison Hopgood
= Julia Harding of Godalming
|
Natalie Collison Hopgood (descent from
the Imperial and Royal House of Vere)
= James Weir of Vere of Lewes
|
HI & RH Prince Nicholas de Vere

Collison Descent from King Heinrich of Germany

King Heinrich of Germany
(Henry the Fowler)
|
Princess Gerberga
=King Louis IV of France
936-954
|
Charles Duke of Lower Lorraine 991
|
Lady Gerberga
= Lambert de Louvain
|
Henry of Brussels
|
Maud de Louvain
= Eustace I de Vere d. 1049
Descent from Amelius ("Adolph") de Vere
Comte de Guisnes
|
Eustace II de Vere
= Saint Ida of Ardennes
|
Princess Ida de Vere
= Baudouin de Bourg
Comte de Rethul
|
Prince Hugues I
Comte de Rethul
= Melisende (Melusine II)
dau. Of Bouchard Comte de Corbeil and
Lady Adelaide de Crecy
|
Badouin II de Bourg
King of Jerusalem 1118-1131
= Princess Morfia of Armenia
|

Princess Melisende of Jerusalem (Melusine III)
= Fulke V Plantagenet Count of Anjou
|
Count Geoffrey Plantagenet
= Princess Mathilda, la Imperatrice
daughter of King Henry I and Princess
Mathilda of Scotland, daughter of
King Malcolm III
|
King Henry II Plantagenet
= Countess Eleanor of Aquitaine
|
King John "Lackland" Plantagenet
= Lady Isabella of Angouleme
|
King Henry III Plantagenet
= Lady Eleanor dau. of Count
Raymond Berenguer I Vof Provence
and Princess Beatrix of Savoy
|
King Edward I Plantagenet
= Princess Eleanor of Castille
|
King Edward II Plantagenet
= Princess Isabella of France
|
Princess Joan Plantagenet
= Gilbert de Clare
Earl of Gloucester
|
Lady Elizabeth de Clare
= Sir Roger D'Amorie
|
Elizabeth D'Amorie
= John Lord Bardolf
|
William Lord Bardolf
= Agnes Poynings
|
Lady Cecilia Bardolf
= Sir Bryan Stapylton
|
Sir Miles Stapylton
= Katherine de la Pole
g. granddaughter of
Geoffrey Chaucer
|
Elizabeth Stapylton
= Sir William Calthorpe
|
Ann Calthorpe
= Sir Robert Drury
|
Anne Drury
= George Waldegrave
|
Sir William Waldegrave
= Juliana Rainsford
|

Sir William Waldegrave II
= Elizabeth Middlemay
|
Mary Waldegrave
= Thomas Clopton
|
Walter Clopton of Fordham
=Anne Thornton
|
Roger Clopton
= Elizabeth Boston
|
Elizabeth Clopton
= James Verdon
|
Elizabeth Verdon
= Samuel Clarke
|
Elizabeth Clarke
= Peter Stoughton
|
Elizabeth Stoughton
= Nicholas Cobb Collison
|
John
(
)
(
Esther
= Reuben Avis
|
Lucy Avis
= Edward Hopgood
|
George Collison Hopgood
= Julia Harding of Godalming
|
Natalie Collison Hopgood (descent from
the Imperial and Royal House of Vere)
= James Weir of Vere of Lewes
|
HI & RH Prince Nicholas de Vere

The Jarls (Earls) Collison:
Lords of the Manors in Norfolk

Richard Collison the Elder, Lord of
Litcham Co. Norfolk 1515 AD
|
Richard Collison, Lord of Litcham 1572 AD
= Rose Trumpas
|
Robert Collison the Elder, Lord of Litcham 1573
AD
|
Richard Collison, Lord of Litcham 1611 AD
|
Robert Collison, Lord of Litcham 1650 AD
|
William Collison, Lord of Titteshall 1692 AD
= Elizabeth D'Rosier
|
William Collison, Lord of Titteshall d. 1795
= Mary Cobb
|
Nicholas Cobb Collison b. 1758
= Elizabeth Stoughton
|
John
(
)
(
Esther
= Reuben Avis
|
Lucy Avis
= Edward Hopgood
|
George Collison Hopgood
= Julia Harding of Godalming
|
Natalie Collison Hopgood (descent from
the Imperial and Royal House of Vere)
= James Weir of Vere of Lewes
|
HI & RH Prince Nicholas de Vere

Descent of the Danish
Collison Family of Norfolk

The Collison family have been domiciled
in Norfolk since the age of the Danes and
were Jarls (Danish Earls) in their own right.
The name is mentioned in the "Hundred
Rolls" of 1327. The visitations of Norfolk
make mention of John Collison in 1444,
as receiving seisin from Sir John Clifton
in 1421. Members of the family owned
land in the 1500's in Honingtoft, Ashill,
Newton and Kings Lynn.

Collison Descent from Princess Plantina,
sister of Princess Melusine of the Scythians

King Elinus of Albha, the Dragon
of Berenicia – Northumberland
(descent from the Uilidian Druid Princes)
=Queen Pressina of the Scythian Picts
(descent from King Vere 400 BC)
|

Melusine I - Plantina - Meliore
|
The Plantagenista Descent
|
Torquat b. c. 760
|
Tortulf de Rennes 790
|
Tertulle Count of Anjou c. 821
= Petronella of France
|
Count Ingelgar of Anjou 845
= Adelais de Rescinde
|
Fulk I The Red, Count of Anjou b. 888
= Roscilla de Loches
|
Fulk II The Good, Count of Anjou b. 920
= Gerberga de Maine
|
Geoffrey Greymantle, Count of Anjou b. 939
= Adele de Vermandois
|
Fullk III The Black, Count of Anjou b. 956
= 2. Hildegard of Metz
dau. of Arnulf of Metz
and Princess Oda de Savoy
|
Geoffrey II Martel, Count of Anjou b. 1006
= Agnes of Bourgogne
|
Geoffrey III Le Harbu b. 1040
= Julienne de Langeaise
|
Geoffrey IV Martel b. 1073
= Bertrade de Montfort
|
Fulk V The Younger, Count of Anjou b. 1092
= 1. Ermengarde dau. of Helias Count of Maine
= 2. Princess Melisende (Melusine III) of Jerusalem
|

Count Geoffrey Plantagenet
= Princess Mathilda, la Imperatrice
daughter of King Henry I and Princess
Mathilda of Scotland, daughter of
King Malcolm III
|
King Henry II Plantagenet
= Countess Eleanor of Aquitaine
|
King John "Lackland" Plantagenet
= Lady Isabella of Angouleme
|
King Henry III Plantagenet
= Lady Eleanor dau. of Count
Raymond Berenguer IVof Provence
and Princess Beatrix of Savoy
|

King Edward I Plantagenet
= Princess Eleanor of Castille
|
King Edward II Plantagenet
= Princess Isabella of France
|
Princess Joan Plantagenet
= Gilbert de Clare
Earl of Gloucester
|
Lady Elizabeth de Clare
= Sir Roger D'Amorie
|
Elizabeth D'Amorie
= John Lord Bardolf
|
William Lord Bardolf
= Agnes Poynings
|
Lady Cecilia Bardolf
= Sir Bryan Stapylton
|
Sir Miles Stapylton
= Kathebine de la Pole
g. granddaughter of
Geoffrey Chaucer
|
Elizabeth Stapylton
= Sir William Calthorpe
|
Ann Calthorpe
= Sir Robert Drury
|
Anne Drury
= George Waldegrave
|
Sir William Waldegrave
= Juliana Rainsford
|
Sir William Waldegrave II
= Elizabeth Middlemay
|
Mary Waldegrave
= Thomas Clopton
|
Walter Clopton of Fordham
=Anne Thornton
|
Roger Clopton
= Elizabeth Boston
|
Elizabeth Clopton
= James Verdon
|
Elizabeth Verdon
= Samuel Clarke
|
Elizabeth Clarke
= Peter Stoughton

|
Elizabeth Stoughton
= Nicholas Cobb Collison
|
John
(
)
(
Esther
= Reuben Avis
|
Lucy Avis
= Edward Hopgood
|
George Collison Hopgood
= Julia Harding of Godalming
|
Natalie Collison Hopgood (descent from
the Imperial and Royal House of Vere)
= James Weir of Vere of Lewes
|
HI & RH Prince Nicholas de Vere

Collison Descent from Princess Scota and the High Elves of Ireland - The Tuadha de Danaan - via Princess Plantina

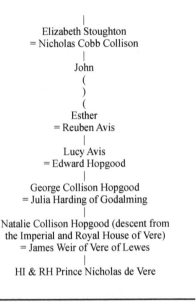

King Tushratta
Dragon Lord of the
Scythian Mittani
|
Tadukhipa
Dragon Queen
= King Fenius Farsaidh
of Scythia
|
Prince Niall of Scythia
Lord of the Region
of Capacyront in Egypt
= Princess Scota of Egypt
Dragon Queen and Princess
of Scythia: Granddaughter
of Pharaoh Amenhotep IV
and cousin of Queen
Kiya Tasherit
|
King Geadheal Glas
(Ancestor of the Scots Gaels)
|
Easru 1300 BC
|
King Sru
|
King Tait
|

King Pamp
|
King Adnoin
|
King Neiheadh
= Princess Macha
|
King Faidh
|
King Iarbhoineol
|
King Beothach
|
King Iobath
|
King Enna
|
King Taborn
|
King Tat
|
King Allaoi
|
King Iondaoi 750 BC
|
King Ned
|
King Partholon (Easar Brec)
Led the Danaan in the Greek
Wars and eventually fled with
his remnant to Ireland.
Partholon was the Great Uncle
of the Legendary Dagdha Mor,
Lord of the Grail Cauldron
of the Danaan in Eire.
|
Lordship of the Elven,
Dragon Kings in Ireland
- The Tuadha de Danaan -
|
King Diancheacht
(Luchtai)
|
Prince Cian
= Princess Eithne, dau. of the
Wizard-King Balor of the Formorians
|
King Bruidhne of the Pict-Sidhes, called by the
Romans "Cruidhne." Flight to Caledonia after
defeat at the hands of the invading Milesians.
|
Cait (Gud/Got),
one of seven sons
|
King Debbecan
|
King Olfinecta
|
King Guididgaedercach

|

King Feth

|

King Gestgurtich

|

King Vere 400 BC
Fairy Lord and Dragon King,
Founder of the Veres in Britain.

|

Alternate succession of the Vere
Druid Prophets and Wood Lords
of the Ancient Caledonian
Fairy Forest Kingdom

|

Brude Pont

|

Vere Pont

|

Brude Leo

|

Vere Leo

|

Brude Grant

|

Vere Grant

|

Brude Gnith

|

Vere Gnith

|

Brude Fechir

|

Vere Fechir

|

Brude Cal

|

Vere Cal

|

Brude Cint

|

Vere Cint

|

Vere Feta
Dragon Queen

|

Gartnait Bolg
Priest King of Caledonia
AD 165-169

|

King Vere II
AD 169-178
Ard Righ (High King)
of the Bruithnigh

|

Vipoguenech

|

Fiacha Albus

|

Canutumel

|

Dovernach Vetalec

|

King Vere III Daich Vetla

|

Gartnait Diuperr
Ard Righ (High King)
AD 355

|

Achivir

|

Aniel

|

Giron

|

Mailcon

|

Bridei
High King AD 520

|

Wid I

|

Gartnait
Ard Righ (High King)

|

Ainfrid

|

Talorcan
Ard Righ

|

daughter
= Bile ap Fili
Welsh King of Alcut
at Dumbarton

|

Brude Mac Bile
Ard Righ 693-697

|

Queen Pressina of the Scythian Picts
= King Elinus of Albha, the Dragon
of Berenicia – Northumberland
(descent from the Uilidian Druid Princes)

|

Melusine I - Plantina - Meliore

|

The Plantagenista Descent

|

Torquat b. c. 760

|

Tortulf de Rennes 790

|

Tertulle Count of Anjou c. 821
= Petronella of France

|

Count Ingelgar of Anjou 845
= Adelais de Rescinde

|

Fulk I The Red, Count of Anjou b. 888

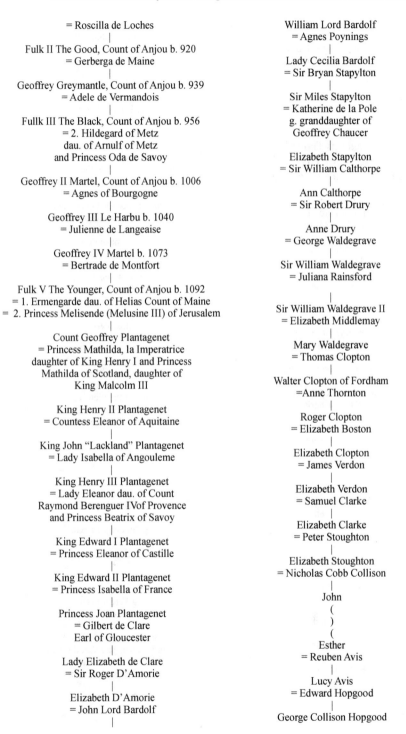

= Roscilla de Loches
|
Fulk II The Good, Count of Anjou b. 920
= Gerberga de Maine
|
Geoffrey Greymantle, Count of Anjou b. 939
= Adele de Vermandois
|
Fullk III The Black, Count of Anjou b. 956
= 2. Hildegard of Metz
dau. of Arnulf of Metz
and Princess Oda de Savoy
|
Geoffrey II Martel, Count of Anjou b. 1006
= Agnes of Bourgogne
|
Geoffrey III Le Harbu b. 1040
= Julienne de Langeaise
|
Geoffrey IV Martel b. 1073
= Bertrade de Montfort
|
Fulk V The Younger, Count of Anjou b. 1092
= 1. Ermengarde dau. of Helias Count of Maine
= 2. Princess Melisende (Melusine III) of Jerusalem
|
Count Geoffrey Plantagenet
= Princess Mathilda, la Imperatrice
daughter of King Henry I and Princess
Mathilda of Scotland, daughter of
King Malcolm III
|
King Henry II Plantagenet
= Countess Eleanor of Aquitaine
|
King John "Lackland" Plantagenet
= Lady Isabella of Angouleme
|
King Henry III Plantagenet
= Lady Eleanor dau. of Count
Raymond Berenguer IVof Provence
and Princess Beatrix of Savoy
|
King Edward I Plantagenet
= Princess Eleanor of Castille
|
King Edward II Plantagenet
= Princess Isabella of France
|
Princess Joan Plantagenet
= Gilbert de Clare
Earl of Gloucester
|
Lady Elizabeth de Clare
= Sir Roger D'Amorie
|
Elizabeth D'Amorie
= John Lord Bardolf
|

William Lord Bardolf
= Agnes Poynings
|
Lady Cecilia Bardolf
= Sir Bryan Stapylton
|
Sir Miles Stapylton
= Katherine de la Pole
g. granddaughter of
Geoffrey Chaucer
|
Elizabeth Stapylton
= Sir William Calthorpe
|
Ann Calthorpe
= Sir Robert Drury
|
Anne Drury
= George Waldegrave
|
Sir William Waldegrave
= Juliana Rainsford
|
Sir William Waldegrave II
= Elizabeth Middlemay
|
Mary Waldegrave
= Thomas Clopton
|
Walter Clopton of Fordham
= Anne Thornton
|
Roger Clopton
= Elizabeth Boston
|
Elizabeth Clopton
= James Verdon
|
Elizabeth Verdon
= Samuel Clarke
|
Elizabeth Clarke
= Peter Stoughton
|
Elizabeth Stoughton
= Nicholas Cobb Collison
|
John
(
)
(
Esther
= Reuben Avis
|
Lucy Avis
= Edward Hopgood
|
George Collison Hopgood

= Julia Harding of Godalming
|
Natalie Collison Hopgood (descent from
the Imperial and Royal House of Vere)
= James Weir of Vere of Lewes
|
HI & RH Prince Nicholas de Vere

Collison Descent from Princess Scota and the High Elves of Ireland -The Tuadha de Danaan -

King Tushratta
Dragon Lord of the
Scythian Mittani
|
Tadukhipa
Dragon Queen
= King Fenius Farsaidh
of Scythia
|
Prince Niall of Scythia
Lord of the Region
of Capacyront in Egypt
= Princess Scota of Egypt
Dragon Queen and Princess
of Scythia: Granddaughter
of Pharaoh Amenhotep IV
and cousin of Queen
Kiya Tasherit
|
King Geadheal Glas
(Ancestor of the Scots Gaels)
|
Easru 1300 BC
|
King Sru
|
King Tait
|
King Pamp
|
King Adnoin
|
King Neiheadh
= Princess Macha
|
King Faidh
|
King Iarbhoineol
|
King Beothach
|
King Iobath
|
King Enna

King Taborn
|
King Tat
|
King Allaoi
|
King Iondaoi 750 BC
|
King Ned
|
King Partholon (Easar Brec)
Led the Danaan in the Greek
Wars and eventually fled with
his remnant to Ireland.
Partholon was the Great Uncle
of the Legendary Dagdha Mor,
Lord of the Grail Cauldron
of the Danaan in Eire.
|
Lordship of the Elven, Dragon
Kings in Ireland – The
Tuadha de Danaan
|
King Diancheacht
(Luchtai)
|
Prince Cian
= Princess Eithne, dau. of the
Wizard-King Balor of the Formorians
|
King Bruidhne of the Picts, called by the
Romans "Cruidhne." Flight to Caledonia after
defeat at the hands of the invading Milesians.
|
Cait (Gud/Got), one
of seven sons
|
King Debbecan
|
King Olfinecta
|
King Guididgaedercach
|
King Feth
|
King Gestgurtich
|
King Vere 400 BC
Fairy Lord and Dragon King
|
Alternate succession of the Vere
Druid Prophets and Wood Lords
of the Ancient Caledonian
Fairy Forest Kingdom
|
Brude Pont
|
Vere Pont

Left lineage:

|
Brude Leo
|
Vere Leo
|
Brude Grant
|
Vere Grant
|
Brude Gnith
|
Vere Gnith
|
Brude Fechir
|
Vere Fechir
|
Brude Cal
|
Vere Cal
|
Brude Cint
|
Vere Cint
|
Vere Feta
Dragon Queen
|
Gartnait Bolg
Priest King of Caledonia
ad 165-169
|
King Vere II
ad 169-178
Ard Righ (High King)
of the Bruithnigh
|
Vipoguenech
|
Fiacha Albus
|
Canutumel
|
Dovernach Vetalec
|
King Vere III Daich Vetla
|
Gartnait Diuperr
Ard Righ (High King)
AD 355
|
Achivir
|
Aniel
|
Giron
|
Mailcon
|

Right lineage:

Bridei
High King AD 520
|
Wid I
|
Gartnait
Ard Righ (High King)
|
Ainfrid
|
Talorcan
Ard Righ
|
daughter
= Bile ap Fili
Welsh King of Alcut
at Dumbarton
|
Brude Mac Bile
Ard Righ 693-697
|
Bruidhina (Pressina)
Dragon Queen, La Fey du
Fontaine: Mermaid, Druidess
= King Elinus (Gille Sidhean:
Elf Servant) of Albha, North Argyll;
The Dragon of Berenicia, Priest King
|
Princess Melusine I
(Maelesanu; Milouziana du Scythes)
La Fey d'Avalon et la Fonteine de Soif
The Fairy Melusine, Neice of Morgan La Fey
= Rainfroy de Vere, Earl of Forez 733
|
Prince Milo de Vere, Duke of Angiers
Count of Anjou,
= Princess Bertha, sister of Charlemagne
(parallel Satanic, Fairy descent via Jesus Christ)
|
Prince Milo II de Vere, Count of Guisnes and Anjou
= Lady Aveline de Nantes
|
Prince Nicassius de Vere, Count of Guisnes
= Lady Agatha de Champagne
|
Prince Otho de Vere, Count of Guisnes
= Lady Constance de Chartres
|
Prince Amelius (Adolph) de Vere Count of Guisnes
= 2. Lady Maud de Ponthieu
|
Prince Gallus (Guy) de Vere, Count of Guisnes
= 2. Lady Gertrude de Clermont de Ponthieu
|
Prince Baldwin de Vere
= Lady Agnes de Jumiege
|
Eustace I de Vere
Comte de Boulogne

d. 1049
= Lady Maud de Louvain
(Descent from Charlemagne)
|
Eustace II de Vere
= Saint Ida of Ardennes
|
Princess Ida de Vere
= Baudouin de Bourg
Comte de Rethul
|
Prince Hugues I
Comte de Rethul
= Melisende (Melusine II)
dau. Of Bouchard Comte de Corbeil and
Lady Adelaide de Crecy
|
Badouin II de Bourg
King of Jerusalem 1118-1131
= Princess Morfia of Armenia
|
Princess Melisende of Jerusalem (Melusine III)
= Fulke V Plantagenet Count of Anjou
|
Count Geoffrey Plantagenet
= Princess Mathilda, la Imperatrice
daughter of King Henry I and Princess
Mathilda of Scotland, daughter of
King Malcolm III
|
King Henry II Plantagenet
= Countess Eleanor of Aquitaine
|
King John "Lackland" Plantagenet
= Lady Isabella of Angouleme
|
King Henry III Plantagenet
= Lady Eleanor dau. of Count
Raymond Berenguer IVof Provence
and Princess Beatrix of Savoy
|
King Edward I Plantagenet
= Princess Eleanor of Castille
|
King Edward II Plantagenet
= Princess Isabella of France
|
Princess Joan Plantagenet
= Gilbert de Clare
Earl of Gloucester
|
Lady Elizabeth de Clare
= Sir Roger D'Amorie
|
Elizabeth D'Amorie
= John Lord Bardolf
|
William Lord Bardolf
= Agnes Poynings

|
Lady Cecilia Bardolf
= Sir Bryan Stapylton
|
Sir Miles Stapylton
= Katherine de la Pole
g. granddaughter of
Geoffrey Chaucer
|
Elizabeth Stapylton
= Sir William Calthorpe
|
Ann Calthorpe
= Sir Robert Drury
|
Anne Drury
= George Waldegrave
|
Sir William Waldegrave
= Juliana Rainsford
|
Sir William Waldegrave II
= Elizabeth Middlemay
|
Mary Waldegrave
= Thomas Clopton
|
Walter Clopton of Fordham
=Anne Thornton
|
Roger Clopton
= Elizabeth Boston
|
Elizabeth Clopton
= James Verdon
|
Elizabeth Verdon
= Samuel Clarke
|
Elizabeth Clarke
= Peter Stoughton
|
Elizabeth Stoughton
= Nicholas Cobb Collison
|
John
(
)
(
Esther
= Reuben Avis
|
Lucy Avis
= Edward Hopgood
|
George Collison Hopgood
= Julia Harding of Godalming
|
Natalie Collison Hopgood (descent from

the Imperial and Royal House of Vere)
= James Weir of Vere of Lewes

HI & RH Prince Nicholas de Vere

Collison Descent from Satan via Prince Milo de Vere

Satan-Lucifer
(Enki; Ea; Khem; Pan; Capricorn:
The Ram of the Shimmering Waters; Leviathan)
=Queen Hawah of Eldar his daughter

Qayin, King of Kish, Son of Satan,
Ancestral Founder of the High Elven
Kings and Queens of the Dragon and the Grail
= Queen Lilith II "Luluwa" (The Pearl)
daughter of Satan by Queen Lilith I
"The Beautiful," mother of all demons:
daughter of Nergal King of the Underworld

Enoch
=Awan

Irad

Mehujael

Methusael

Lamech, Dragon Lord of Ur
= Queen Zillah

Tubal Cain King of Ur
= Ninbanda, d. of Lilith Naamah

King Ham: Chem Zarathustra, Tenth
Archon of Capricorn
=Queen Neelata-Mek

Cush

Nimrod the Mighty Hunter

Boethos/ Hotep Sekhemwy
Pharaoh and founder
of 2nd Dynasty in Egypt
=Queen Bithiah

Pharaoh Raneb/Kalenhkos c. 2800 BC
brought culture of Chem of Capricorn
to Egypt as Khem, the Goat of Mendes
known as Pan in Greece, later the
Sabbatical Goat God of the Witches
and the Baphomet of the Templars

Pharaoh Nynetjer

Pharaoh Sekhemib

Pharaoh Khasekhemwy

daughter
=Pharaoh Sanakhte

daughter
= Pharaoh Sekhemkhet

Pharaoh Khaba 2643-37 BC

Pharaoh Huni 2637-13 BC
= Queen Meresankh I

Pharaoh Sneferu
= Queen Hetep-Heres I

Pharaoh Khufu (Cheops)
= Queen Henutsen

Pharaoh Khefre
= Queen Khamerenebty

Pharaoh Menkaure 2532-04 BC
= Queen Khamerenebty II

Queen Khentkawas
= Pharaoh Userkaf

Pharaoh Neferirkare

Pharaoh Shepsekare

Pharaoh Neferefre

Pharaoh Niuserre

Pharaoh Menkauhor

Pharaoh Djedkare

Pharaoh Unas the Vampire 2375-45 BC
(The Pyramid Texts)

Queen Iput
= Pharaoh Teti

Pharaoh Pepi I
= Queen Ankhnesmerire

Pharaoh Pepi II
= Queen Neith

Pharaoh Merenre II 2184-81 BC
= Queen Nitoctris

Prince Ankhfn-Khonsu

Re-established the Royal
Dragon Court in Egypt
|
Prince Intef I (The Great)
Governor of Thebes
|
Prince Intef II
|
Prince Intef III
|
Pharaoh Mentuhotep I (The Coffin Texts)
= Queen Tem
|
Pharaoh Mentuhotep II
|
Pharaoh Mentuhotep III
|
Queen Tohwait
= Pharaoh Amenhemet
|
Pharaoh Senusret I
= Princess Sarah, d. of Queen Tohwait
(later wife of Abraham)
|
Pharaoh Amenhemet II
-= Queen Keminebu
|
Pharaoh Senusret II
= Queen Nofret
|
Pharaoh Senusret III
= Queen Mereret
|
Pharaoh Amenhemet III
= Queen Aat
|
Pharaoh Amenhemet IV
= Sobeknefru, The Great Dragon Queen of Egypt
(Ratified the Royal Dragon Court)
|
Daughter
= Pharaoh Wegaf

13th Dynasty of Egypt
The Dragon Kings and Queens of
the God Sobekh

Pharaoh Wegaf
|
Pharaoh Ameny Intef c. 1700 BC
|
Pharaoh Sobekhotep III
|
Pharaoh Sobekhotep IV
|
Daughter
= Pharaoh Sobekemsaf
|
Pharaoh Intef VII

|
Daughter
= King Khayan (The Good God)
Dragon King of the Hyksos who
descend from Queen Towait (above)
|
Apepi I
Dragon King of the Hyksos
|
Apepi II
(Apophis the Evil)
|
Senisonb (Dragon Queen)
|
Pharaoh Tuthmosis I
= Queen Mutneferte (Dragon Queen)
|
Pharaoh Tuthmosis II
= Iset
|
Pharaoh Tuthmosis III
(Founded the Rosi-crucis
Therapeutate at Karnak)
= Queen Neferue
|
The Dragon Queen Tio
= Pharaoh Amenhotep II
|
Pharaoh Tuthmosis IV
= Queen Mutemwiya
|
Pharaoh Amenhotep III
= Gilukhipa, Dragon Queen
of the Mitanni
|
Merykhipa (Kiya)
Dragon Queen
= Pharaoh Amenhotep IV
|
Queen Kiya Tasherit 1361 BC
=Prince Rama, descendant of Satan,
Abraham and the Pharaoh Sensuret I
(See above).
Here the direct and unbroken
lines of Satanic descent conjoin
|
Amminadab
|
Nahshon
|
Salma
= Rahab
|
Boaz
|
Obed
|
Jesse
|

The House of David

King David of Israel
=Queen Bath-Sheba
of the Hittites
(Descent from the Hurrians or Aryans)
|
King Solomon, Lord of the Rings
= Sheba Lilith (Venus) his sister
|
Rehoboam
|
Abijah
|
Asa
|
Jehoshephat
|
Joram
|
Azariah
|
Jotham
|
Ahaz
|
Hezekiah
|
Manasseh
|
Amon
|
Josiah
|
Jeconiah
(Exile in Babylon begins)
|
Shealtiel
|
Zerubbabel
|
Abiud
|
Eliakim
|
Azor
|
Zadok
|
Achim
|
Eliud
|
Eleazar
|
Matthan
|
Jacob
|

Joseph
= Mary (Parallel descent
from Satan and the House of David)
|
Jesus Christ The Messiah
(Messach: Anointed of the God Sobekh)
(Yehoshua ben-Joseph, called ben-Panther)
= Mary Magdalene, Priestess of Ishtar (Venus)
|
Josue del Graal
|
Aminadab
= Eurgis d. of King Coel I
sister of Lucius the Great
|
Catheloys
|
Manael
|
Titurel
|
Boaz
(Anfortas)
|
Frotmund
(Frimutel)
|
Faramund 420 AD
Sire of the French Monarchy
= Argotta dau. of Genebaud
of the Sicambrian Franks
|
Clodian of Tournai
= Queen Basina of Thuringia
|
King Meroveus, founder of
the Dynasty of Merovingian
Sorcerer Kings d. 456 AD
= Princess Meira
|
King Childeric of the Franks d. 481 AD
= Queen Basina II of Thuringia
|
King Clovis of the Franks d. 511 AD
= Clotilde of Burgundy
|
King Lothar I d. 561 AD
|
Princess Blitildis
= Prince Ansbert, Great Great Grandson of
King Clodian of Tournai (above) d. 570 AD
|
Lord Arnoald of Scheldt
= Princess Dua of Swabia
|
Arnulf of Metz
= Princess Dobo of Saxony

Lord Ansegis of Brabant (Lower Lorraine)
Margrave of Scheldt d. 685
= Lady Begga, dau of Pepin I, Mayor of Austrasia
|
Lord Pepin II of Heristal, Mayor of the Palaces of
Austrasia, Neustria and Burgundy d. 714
= Lady Alpas
|
Lord Charles Martel (The Hammer) d. 741
|
Pepin the III Brevis, Duke of Lower Lorraine
(Brabant)
Mayor of Neustrasia, King of the Franks
= Lady Leuthergis
|
Princess Bertha
= Prince Milo de Vere, Duke of Angiers
Count of Anjou (son of the Fairy Princess Melusine
I
of the Scythians: parallel descent from Satan via the
Egyptian Kings as above)
|
Prince Milo II de Vere, Count of Guisnes and Anjou
= Lady Aveline de Nantes
|
Prince Nicassius de Vere, Count of Guisnes and
Anjou
Lady Agatha de Champagne
|
Prince Otho de Vere, Count of Guisnes
= Lady Constance de Chartres
|
Prince Amelius (Adolph) de Vere
= Lady Maud de Ponthieu
|
Prince Gallus (Guy) de Vere, Count of Guisnes
= Lady Gertrude de Clermont de Ponthieu
|
Prince Baldwin de Vere
= Adele de Ghent
|
Prince Eustace de Vere
= Lady Maud de Lovain
|
Princess Ida de Vere
= Baudouin de Bourg
Comte de Rethul
(Merovingian descent from
Satan via Charlemagne)
|
Prince Hugues I
Comte de Rethul
= Melisende (Melusine II)
dau. Of Bouchard Comte de Corbeil and
Lady Adelaide de Crecy
|
Badouin II de Bourg
King of Jerusalem 1118-1131

= Princess Morfia of Armenia
|
Princess Melisende of Jerusalem (Melusine III)
= Fulke V Plantagenet Count of Anjou
(Descent from Melusine I's sister Princess Plantina)
|
Count Geoffrey Plantagenet
= Princess Mathilda, la Imperatrice
daughter of King Henry I and Princess
Mathilda of Scotland, daughter of
King Malcolm III
|
King Henry II Plantagenet
= Countess Eleanor of Aquitaine
|
King John "Lackland" Plantagenet
= Lady Isabella of Angouleme
|
King Henry III Plantagenet
= Lady Eleanor dau. of Count
Raymond Berenguer IVof Provence
and Princess Beatrix of Savoy
|
King Edward I Plantagenet
= Princess Eleanor of Castille
|
King Edward II Plantagenet
= Princess Isabella of France
|
Princess Joan Plantagenet
= Gilbert de Clare
Earl of Gloucester
|
Lady Elizabeth de Clare
= Sir Roger D'Amorie
|
Elizabeth D'Amorie
= John Lord Bardolf
|
William Lord Bardolf
= Agnes Poynings
|
Lady Cecilia Bardolf
= Sir Bryan Stapylton
|
Sir Miles Stapylton
= Katherine de la Pole
g. granddaughter of
Geoffrey Chaucer
|
Elizabeth Stapylton
= Sir William Calthorpe
|
Ann Calthorpe
= Sir Robert Drury
|
Anne Drury
= George Waldegrave

Sir William Waldegrave
= Juliana Rainsford
|
Sir William Waldegrave II
= Elizabeth Middlemay
|
Mary Waldegrave
= Thomas Clopton
|
Walter Clopton of Fordham
=Anne Thornton
|
Roger Clopton
= Elizabeth Boston
|
Elizabeth Clopton
= James Verdon
|
Elizabeth Verdon
= Samuel Clarke
|
Elizabeth Clarke
= Peter Stoughton
|
Elizabeth Stoughton
= Nicholas Cobb Collison
|
John
(
)
(
Esther
= Reuben Avis
|
Lucy Avis
= Edward Hopgood
|
George Collison Hopgood
= Julia Harding of Godalming
|
Natalie Collison Hopgood (descent from
the Imperial and Royal House of Vere)
= James Weir of Vere of Lewes
|
HI & RH Prince Nicholas de Vere

Collison Descent from the Dukes of Brittany

Count Frodaldus de Bretagne
|
Count Rivallon de Bretagne
|
Duke Saloman de Bretagne
857-870
= Lady Gimberta

Countess de Bretagne
= Count Garvand de Rennes
|
Count Judicael de Rennes
|
Count Juhel Bereger de Rennes
930-937
= Lady Gerberge
|
Count Conan le Tort de Rennes
= Lady Ermengarde of Anjou
|
Lady Havoise
= Count Geoffrey
|
Duke Alain V de Bretagne
Count de Rennes
= Lady Berta de Blois
|
Lady Judith de Bretagne
= Duke Richard II of Normandy
|
Duke Richard III 1027 AD
|
Duke Robert I 1028 AD
|
King William I of England
= Lady Mathilda van Vlaanderen
dau. of Count Baldwin V of Flanders
|
King Henry I of England
= Princess Mathilda dau. of
King Malcom III Canmore
of Scotland and Margaret,
dau. of Edward the Exile
by Princess Agatha of Bulgaria
|
Princess Mathilda la Imperatrice
(Empress of England and France)
= Count Geoffrey Plantagenet
of Anjou
|
King Henry II Plantagenet
= Countess Eleanor of Aquitaine
|
King John "Lackland" Plantagenet
= Lady Isabella of Angouleme
|
King Henry III Plantagenet
= Lady Eleanor dau. of Count
Raymond Berenguer IVof Provence
and Princess Beatrix of Savoy
|
King Edward I Plantagenet
= Princess Eleanor of Castille
|
King Edward II Plantagenet
= Princess Isabella of France

Princess Joan Plantagenet
= Gilbert de Clare
Earl of Gloucester
|
Lady Elizabeth de Clare
= Sir Roger D'Amorie
|
Elizabeth D'Amorie
= John Lord Bardolf
|
William Lord Bardolf
= Agnes Poynings
|
Lady Cecilia Bardolf
= Sir Bryan Stapylton
|
Sir Miles Stapylton
= Katherine de la Pole
g. granddaughter of
Geoffrey Chaucer
|
Elizabeth Stapylton
= Sir William Calthorpe
|
Ann Calthorpe
= Sir Robert Drury
|
Anne Drury
= George Waldegrave
|
Sir William Waldegrave
= Juliana Rainsford
|
Sir William Waldegrave II
= Elizabeth Middlemay
|
Mary Waldegrave
= Thomas Clopton
|
Walter Clopton of Fordham
=Anne Thornton
|
Roger Clopton
= Elizabeth Boston
|
Elizabeth Clopton
= James Verdon
|
Elizabeth Verdon
= Samuel Clarke
|
Elizabeth Clarke
= Peter Stoughton
|
Elizabeth Stoughton
= Nicholas Cobb Collison
|
John

(
)
(
Esther
= Reuben Avis
|
Lucy Avis
= Edward Hopgood
|
George Collison Hopgood
= Julia Harding of Godalming
|
Natalie Collison Hopgood (descent from
the Imperial and Royal House of Vere)
= James Weir of Vere of Lewes
|
HI & RH Prince Nicholas de Vere

Collison Descent from the Early English Kings

King Egbert
802-839
|
King Aethelwulf
839-858
|
King Alfred the Great
871-899
= Princess Aelhswith
d. 904
|
King Edward the Elder
899-924
|
King Edmund I
939-946
= Princess Aelfgifu
|
King Edgar
959-975
= 2. Princess Aelfthryf
|
King Aelthelred II the Unready
979-1016
= Princess Aelgifu
|
King Edmund II Ironside
d. 1016
= Princess Algitha
|
King (de jure) Edward the Exile
d. 1057
= Princess Agatha of Bulgaria
|
Princess Margaret

= King Malcolm III Canmore
King of Scots

|

Princess Mathilda
= King Henry I of England
1101-1135

|

Princess Mathilda la Imperatrice
(Empress)
= Count Geoffrey Plantagenet

|

King Henry II Plantagenet
= Countess Eleanor of Aquitaine

|

King John "Lackland" Plantagenet
= Lady Isabella of Angouleme

|

King Henry III Plantagenet
= Lady Eleanor dau. of Count
Raymond Berenguer I Vof Provence
and Princess Beatrix of Savoy

|

King Edward I Plantagenet
= Princess Eleanor of Castille

|

King Edward II Plantagenet
= Princess Isabella of France

|

Princess Joan Plantagenet
= Gilbert de Clare
Earl of Gloucester

|

Lady Elizabeth de Clare
= Sir Roger D'Amorie

|

Elizabeth D'Amorie
= John Lord Bardolf

|

William Lord Bardolf
= Agnes Poynings

|

Lady Cecilia Bardolf
= Sir Bryan Stapylton

|

Sir Miles Stapylton
= Katherine de la Pole
g. granddaughter of
Geoffrey Chaucer

|

Elizabeth Stapylton
= Sir William Calthorpe

|

Ann Calthorpe
= Sir Robert Drury

|

Anne Drury
= George Waldegrave

|

Sir William Waldegrave
= Juliana Rainsford

|

Sir William Waldegrave II
= Elizabeth Middlemay

|

Mary Waldegrave
= Thomas Clopton

|

Walter Clopton of Fordham
=Anne Thornton

|

Roger Clopton
= Elizabeth Boston

|

Elizabeth Clopton
= James Verdon

|

Elizabeth Verdon
= Samuel Clarke

|

Elizabeth Clarke
= Peter Stoughton

|

Elizabeth Stoughton
= Nicholas Cobb Collison

|

John

(
)
(

Esther
= Reuben Avis

|

Lucy Avis
= Edward Hopgood

|

George Collison Hopgood
= Julia Harding of Godalming

|

Natalie Collison Hopgood (descent from
the Imperial and Royal House of Vere)
= James Weir of Vere of Lewes

|

HI & RH Prince Nicholas de Vere

Collison Descent from the Early Frankish Kings

Trojan Royal House

|

King Antenor d. 443 BC
Of the Cimmerians of Scythia

|

King Marcomer d. 412 BC
Moved Cimmerians from the Black Sea

To Western Europe and eventually Wales
where they become known as the Cymri
|
King Antenor d. 385 BC
= Princess Cambra of the Sicambrians
|
King Priamus d. 358 BC
|
King Helenus d. 339 BC
Priest-King of the Arcadian God Pallas
|
King Diocles d. 300 BC
Fought the Goths and Gauls
|
Priest-King Bassanus Magnus d. 250 BC
Built Aix la Chapelle
|
King Clodomir d. 232 BC
|
King Nicanor d. 198 BC
|
King Marcomer d. 170 BC
|
King Clodius d. 195 BC
|
King Antenor d. 143 BC
|
King Clodomir d. 123 BC
|
King Merovachus d. 95 BC
|
King Cassander d. 74 BC
|
King Antharius d. 39 BC
|
King Francus d. 11 BC
Changed tribal name from Sicambri to Franks
|
King Clodius d. 20 AD
|
King Marcomer d. 50 AD
|
King Clodomir d. 63 AD
|
King Antenor d. 69 AD
|
King Ratherius d. 90 AD
|
King Richemer d. 114 AD
|
King Odomar d. 128 AD
|
King Marcomer d. 169 AD
Built Marpurg in Hesse
= Princess Athildis of Camelot
|
King Clodomir d. 180 AD
|
King Farabert d. 186 AD

|
King Sunno d. 213 AD
|
King Hilderic d. 253 AD
|
King Bartherus d. 272 AD
|
King Clodius d. 298 AD
|
King Walter d. 306 AD
|
King Dagobert d. 317 AD
|
King Clodomir d. 337 AD
|
King Richemir d. 350
|
King Theodomir d. 360
|
King Clodius d. 378
|
King Dagobert d. 389
|
Lord Genobaud d. 419
|
Princess Argotta
= Lord Faramund of
the Western Franks
419-430
|
King Clodian of Tournai
Priest of Neptune of Arcadia
Lord of the Western Franks 430-446
= Queen Basina I of Thuringia
|
King Meroveus
Founder of the Merovingian Dynasty
of Sorceror Kings d. 456
= Princess Merira dau. of the Quinotaur
|
King Childeric of the Franks d. 481 AD
= Queen Basina II of Thuringia
|
King Clovis of the Franks d. 511 AD
= Clotilde of Burgundy
|
King Lothar I d. 561 AD
|
Princess Blitildis
= Prince Ansbert, Great Great Grandson of
King Clodian of Tournai (above) d. 570 AD
|
Lord Arnoald of Scheldt
= Princess Dua of Swabia
|
Lord Arnulf of Metz
= Princess Dobo of Saxony
|
Lord Ansegis of Brabant (Lower Lorraine)

Margrave of Scheldt d. 685
= Lady Begga, dau of Pepin I, Mayor of Austrasia
|
Lord Pepin II of Heristal, Mayor of the Palaces of
Austrasia, Neustria and Burgundy d. 714
= Lady Alpas
|
Lord Charles Martel (The Hammer) d. 741
|
Pepin the III Brevis, Duke of Lower Lorraine
(Brabant) Mayor of Neustrasia, King of the Franks
= Lady Leuthergis
|
Princess Bertha
= Prince Milo de Vere, Duke of Angiers
Count of Anjou (son of the Fairy Princess Melusine
I
of the Scythians: parallel descent from Satan via the
Egyptian Kings as above)
|
Prince Milo II de Vere, Count of Guisnes and Anjou
= Lady Aveline de Nantes
|
Prince Nicassius de Vere, Count of Guisnes and
Anjou
Lady Agatha de Champagne
|
Prince Otho de Vere, Count of Guisnes
= Lady Constance de Chartres
|
Prince Amelius (Adolph) de Vere
Count of Guisnes
= Lady Maud de Ponthieu
|
Prince Gallus (Guy) de Vere, Count of Guisnes
= Lady Gertrude de Clermont de Ponthieu
|
Prince Baldwin de Vere
= Adele de Ghent
|
Prince Eustace de Vere
= Lady Maud de Lovain
|
Princess Ida de Vere
= Baudouin de Bourg
Comte de Rethul
(Merovingian descent from
Satan via Charlemagne)
|
Prince Hugues I
Comte de Rethul
= Melisende (Melusine II)
dau. Of Bouchard Comte de Corbeil and
Lady Adelaide de Crecy
|
Badouin II de Bourg
King of Jerusalem 1118-1131
= Princess Morfia of Armenia
|

Princess Melisende of Jerusalem (Melusine III)
= Fulke V Plantagenet Count of Anjou
(Descent from Melusine I's sister Princess
Plantina, mother of Lord Torquat of Anjou
and g.mother of Lord Tortulf de Nide de Merle)
|
Count Geoffrey Plantagenet
= Princess Mathilda, la Imperatrice
daughter of King Henry I and Princess
Mathilda of Scotland, daughter of
King Malcolm III
|
King Henry II Plantagenet
= Countess Eleanor of Aquitaine
|
King John "Lackland" Plantagenet
= Lady Isabella of Angouleme
|
King Henry III Plantagenet
= Lady Eleanor dau. of Count

Raymond Berenguer IVof Provence
and Princess Beatrix of Savoy
|
King Edward I Plantagenet
= Princess Eleanor of Castille
|
King Edward II Plantagenet
= Princess Isabella of France
|
Princess Joan Plantagenet
= Gilbert de Clare
Earl of Gloucester
|
Lady Elizabeth de Clare
= Sir Roger D'Amorie
|
Elizabeth D'Amorie
= John Lord Bardolf
|
William Lord Bardolf
= Agnes Poynings
|
Lady Cecilia Bardolf
= Sir Bryan Stapylton
|
Sir Miles Stapylton
= Katherine de la Pole
g. granddaughter of
Geoffrey Chaucer
|
Elizabeth Stapylton
= Sir William Calthorpe
|
Ann Calthorpe
= Sir Robert Drury
|
Anne Drury
= George Waldegrave

Sir William Waldegrave
= Juliana Rainsford
|
Sir William Waldegrave II
= Elizabeth Middlemay
|
Mary Waldegrave
= Thomas Clopton
|
Walter Clopton of Fordham
=Anne Thornton
|
Roger Clopton
= Elizabeth Boston
|
Elizabeth Clopton
= James Verdon
|
Elizabeth Verdon
= Samuel Clarke
|
Elizabeth Clarke
= Peter Stoughton
|
Elizabeth Stoughton
= Nicholas Cobb Collison
|
John
(
)
(
Esther
= Reuben Avis
|
Lucy Avis
= Edward Hopgood
|
George Collison Hopgood
= Julia Harding of Godalming
|
Natalie Collison Hopgood (descent from
the Imperial and Royal House of Vere)
= James Weir of Vere of Lewes
|
HI & RH Prince Nicholas de Vere

Collison Descent from the Fairy House of Salisbury

The descent of Natalie Collison Hopgood from Lord Walter Longspee, Earl of Salisbury, fairy forefather of the Countess of Salisbury in the reign of King Edward III. The Countess, also known as the Fairy Maid of Kent, was Witch Queen of England and the inspiration behind the foundation of the Order of the Knights of the Garter. She was also the inspiration for John Keats' poem, *La Belle Dame Sans Merci*. The Salisbury Crest was the Double Headed Dragon.

King Henry II of England
= Lady Rosamund dau. of Walter de Clifford
Lady of the Labyrinth
|
Lord Walter Longspee Earl of Salisbury
= Ela dau of Lord William de Romara
Later Earl of Salisbury
|
Lord Stephen Longspee – Justiciar of Ireland
= Emilina dau of Walter de Riddlesford
|
Lady Emilina Longspee
= Maurice Fitz Maurice
|
Juliana Fitz Maurice
= Thomas de Clare, Seneschal
of the Forest of Essex
|
Margaret de Clare
= Bartholomew de Badlesmere
|
Margaret de Badlesmere
= Sir John Tiptoft
|
Sir Robert Tiptoft
= Lady Margaret dau.
of William Lord Deincourt
|
Elizabeth Tiptoft
= Phillip Le Spencer
|
Marjorie Le Spencer
= Roger Wentworth of Gosfield
|
Lord Wentworth of Gosfield
= Elizabeth Howard of Essex
|
Marjorie Wentworth
= William Waldegrave
|
George Waldegrave
=Anne Drury
|
Sir William Waldegrave
= Juliana Rainsford
|
Sir William Waldegrave III
= Elizabeth Middlemay
|
Mary Waldegrave

= Thomas Clopton
|
Walter Clopton of Fordham
=Anne Thornton
|
Roger Clopton
= Elizabeth Boston
|
Elizabeth Clopton
= James Verdon
|
Elizabeth Verdon
= Samuel Clarke
|
Elizabeth Clarke
= Peter Stoughton
|
Elizabeth Stoughton
= Nicholas Cobb Collison
|
John
(
)
(
Esther
= Reuben Avis
|
Lucy Avis
= Edward Hopgood
|
George Collison Hopgood
= Julia Harding of Godalming
|
Natalie Collison Hopgood (descent from
the Imperial and Royal House of Vere)
= James Weir of Vere of Lewes
|
HI & RH Prince Nicholas de Vere

Collison Viking Descent from the Norse Kings, Duke William of Normandy and Prince Rhys Ap Tudor of South Wales

King Ingiald The Wicked 600 AD
|
King Olaf of Vermaland, Norway
|
King Halfdan of the Uplanders
|
King Eystein of Raumariki
|
King Halfdan
|
Jarl (Earl) Ivar of the Uplanders

|
Jarl Eystein Glumra
|
Jarl Ranald I the Wise of Orkney
|
Duke Rolf of Normandy 911 AD
|
Duke William I 932 AD
|
Duke Richard I 942 AD
|
Duke Richard II 996 AD
|
Duke Richard III 1027 AD
|
Duke Robert I 1028 AD
|
King William I of England
= Lady Mathilda van Vlaanderen
dau. of Count Baldwin V of Flanders
|
King Henry I of England
= Nesta dau. of Prince Rhys ap
Tudor, Prince of South Wales
(
)
(
)
Lord Herbert Fitzroy Earl of Gloucester
=Lady Mabel dau. of Lord
Robert Fitzhamon, Lord of Corbiel
|
William Fitz Robert Earl of Gloucester
= dau. of Lord Robert Beaumont
Earl of Leicester
|
Lady Amicia Fitz Robert
= Lord Richard de Clare Earl of Hertford
|
Robert De Clare Earl of Gloucester
= Lady Isabel dau. of William Marshall
Earl of Pembrokeshire
|
Lord de Clare Earl of Gloucester
= Lady Mathilda dau. of
John de Lacy Earl of Lincoln
|
Lord Gilbert de Clare
Earl of Gloucester
= Princess Joan Plantagenet
|
Lady Elizabeth de Clare
= Sir Roger D'Amorie
|
Elizabeth D'Amorie
= John Lord Bardolf
|
William Lord Bardolf
= Agnes Poynings

Cecilia Bardolf
= Sir Bryan Stapylton
|
Sir Miles Stapylton
= Katherine de la Pole
g. granddaughter of
Geoffrey Chaucer
|
Elizabeth Stapylton
= Sir William Calthorpe
|
Ann Calthorpe
= Sir Robert Drury
|
Anne Drury
= George Waldegrave
|
Sir William Waldegrave
= Juliana Rainsford
|
Sir William Waldegrave II
= Elizabeth Middlemay
|
Mary Waldegrave
= Thomas Clopton
|
Walter Clopton of Fordham
=Anne Thornton
|
Roger Clopton
= Elizabeth Boston
|
Elizabeth Clopton
= James Verdon
|
Elizabeth Verdon
= Samuel Clarke
|
Elizabeth Clarke
= Peter Stoughton
|
Elizabeth Stoughton
= Nicholas Cobb Collison
|
John
(
)
(
Esther
= Reuben Avis
|
Lucy Avis
= Edward Hopgood
|
George Collison Hopgood
= Julia Harding of Godalming
|
Natalie Collison Hopgood (descent from

the Imperial and Royal House of Vere)
= James Weir of Vere of Lewes
|
HI & RH Prince Nicholas de Vere

Collison Descent from the Scots Kings

King Alpin 839-841
|
King Kenneth I 844-859
King of Picts and Scots
|
King Constantine I 863-877
|
King Donald II 889-900
|
King Malcolm I 942-954
|
King Kenneth II 971-995
|
King Malcolm II 1005-1034

|
Princess Bethoc
= Crinan, Thane of the Isles k. 1045
|
King Duncan I 1034 – 1040 slain by Macbeth
|
King Malcolm III Canmore 1058-1093
= Margaret granddaughter of King Edmund of England
|
Princess Mathilda
= King Henry I
|
King Henry II Plantagenet
= Countess Eleanor of Aquitaine
|
King John "Lackland" Plantagenet
= Lady Isabella of Angouleme
|
King Henry III Plantagenet
= Lady Eleanor dau. of Count
Raymond Berenguer I Vof Provence
and Princess Beatrix of Savoy
|
King Edward I Plantagenet
= Princess Eleanor of Castille
|
King Edward II Plantagenet
= Princess Isabella of France
|
Princess Joan Plantagenet

= Gilbert de Clare
Earl of Gloucester
|
Lady Elizabeth de Clare
= Sir Roger D'Amorie
|
Elizabeth D'Amorie
= John Lord Bardolf
|
William Lord Bardolf
= Agnes Poynings
|
Lady Cecilia Bardolf
= Sir Bryan Stapylton
|
Sir Miles Stapylton
= Katherine de la Pole
g. granddaughter of
Geoffrey Chaucer
|
Elizabeth Stapylton
= Sir William Calthorpe
|
Ann Calthorpe
= Sir Robert Drury
|
Anne Drury
= George Waldegrave
|
Sir William Waldegrave
= Juliana Rainsford
|
Sir William Waldegrave II
= Elizabeth Middlemay
|
Mary Waldegrave
= Thomas Clopton
|
Walter Clopton of Fordham
=Anne Thornton
|
Roger Clopton
= Elizabeth Boston
|
Elizabeth Clopton
= James Verdon
|
Elizabeth Verdon
= Samuel Clarke
|
Elizabeth Clarke
= Peter Stoughton
|
Elizabeth Stoughton
= Nicholas Cobb Collison
|
John
(
)

(
Esther
= Reuben Avis
|
Lucy Avis
= Edward Hopgood
|
George Collison Hopgood
= Julia Harding of Godalming
|
Natalie Collison Hopgood (descent from
the Imperial and Royal House of Vere)
= James Weir of Vere of Lewes
|
HI & RH Prince Nicholas de Vere

Collison Descent from the Spanish Royal Houses via Lady Eleanor of Provence

King Sancho I The Great 970-1035
King of Castile, Navarre and Aragon
|
King Ramiro I, King of Aragon
1035-1063
|
King Sancho-Ramirez
King of Aragon 1063-1094
King of Navarre 1076-1094
|
King Ramiro II (The Monk)
King of Aragon 1134-1137
|
Princess Petronilla
= Count Raymond Berenguer
of Barcelona 1137-1162
|
King Alfonso II 1162-1196
King of Aragon
Count of Barcelona
|
Count Alfonso of Provence
|
Raymond Berenguer IV of Provence
= Princess Beatrix of Savoy
|
Lady Eleanor of Provence
= King Henry III Plantagenet
|
King Edward I Plantagenet
= Princess Eleanor of Castille
|
King Edward II Plantagenet
= Princess Isabella of France
|
Princess Joan Plantagenet

= Gilbert de Clare
Earl of Gloucester
|
Lady Elizabeth de Clare
= Sir Roger D'Amorie
|
Elizabeth D'Amorie
= John Lord Bardolf
|
William Lord Bardolf
= Agnes Poynings
|
Lady Cecilia Bardolf
= Sir Bryan Stapylton
|
Sir Miles Stapylton
= Katherine de la Pole
g. granddaughter of
Geoffrey Chaucer
|
Elizabeth Stapylton
= Sir William Calthorpe
|
Ann Calthorpe
= Sir Robert Drury
|
Anne Drury
= George Waldegrave
|
Sir William Waldegrave
= Juliana Rainsford
|
Sir William Waldegrave II
= Elizabeth Middlemay
|
Mary Waldegrave
= Thomas Clopton
|
Walter Clopton of Fordham
=Anne Thornton
|
Roger Clopton
= Elizabeth Boston
|
Elizabeth Clopton
= James Verdon
|
Elizabeth Verdon
= Samuel Clarke
|
Elizabeth Clarke
= Peter Stoughton
|
Elizabeth Stoughton
= Nicholas Cobb Collison
|
John
(
)

(
Esther
= Reuben Avis
|
Lucy Avis
= Edward Hopgood
|
George Collison Hopgood
= Julia Harding of Godalming
|
Natalie Collison Hopgood (descent from
the Imperial and Royal House of Vere)
= James Weir of Vere of Lewes
|
HI & RH Prince Nicholas de Vere

Collison Descent from the Spanish Royal Houses of Castile, Leon, Aragon and Navarre via Princess Eleanor of Castile

King Sancho I The Great 970-1035
King of Castile, Navarre and Aragon
|
King Ferdinand 1037-1065
King of Castile
|
King Alfonso IV 1072-1109
King of Castile and Leon
|
Queen Uracca 1109-1126
Queen of Castile and Leon
|
King Alfonso VII 1126-1157
King of Castile and Leon
|
King Ferdinand II 1157-1188
King of Leon
|
King Alfonso IX 1188-1230
King of Leon
|
King Ferdinand III
King of Castile 1217-1252
King of Leon 1230-1252
|
Princess Eleanor of Castile d. 1290
= King Edward I of England
|
King Edward II Plantagenet
= Princess Isabella of France
|
Princess Joan Plantagenet
= Gilbert de Clare
Earl of Gloucester

|
Lady Elizabeth de Clare

= Sir Roger D'Amorie

|
Elizabeth D'Amorie
= John Lord Bardolf

|
William Lord Bardolf
= Agnes Poynings

|
Lady Cecilia Bardolf
= Sir Bryan Stapylton

|
Sir Miles Stapylton
= Katherine de la Pole
g. granddaughter of
Geoffrey Chaucer

|
Elizabeth Stapylton
= Sir William Calthorpe

|
Ann Calthorpe
= Sir Robert Drury

|
Anne Drury
= George Waldegrave

|
Sir William Waldegrave
= Juliana Rainsford

|
Sir William Waldegrave II
= Elizabeth Middlemay

|
Mary Waldegrave
= Thomas Clopton

|
Walter Clopton of Fordham
=Anne Thornton

|
Roger Clopton
= Elizabeth Boston

|
Elizabeth Clopton
= James Verdon

|
Elizabeth Verdon
= Samuel Clarke

|
Elizabeth Clarke
= Peter Stoughton

|
Elizabeth Stoughton
= Nicholas Cobb Collison

|
John

(
)

(
Esther
= Reuben Avis

|
Lucy Avis
= Edward Hopgood

|
George Collison Hopgood
= Julia Harding of Godalming

|
Natalie Collison Hopgood (descent from
the Imperial and Royal House of Vere)
= James Weir of Vere of Lewes

|
HI & RH Prince Nicholas de Vere

Collison Descent from the Sacred and Holy Ulidian Archdruid Erc, King of Dalriada

Archdruid Erc, King of Dalriada 450 AD

|
Loarn, King of Dalriada
Appenaged in Dalriada

|
Prince Muiredach

|
Prince Eochaid

|
Prince Bartan
App. In Morvern

|
Prince Colman 590 AD

|
Prince Nechtan

|
Prince Fergus

|
Prince Feradach

|
Prince Ferchar b. c. 660 AD

|
King Melusthainn 680 AD

|
King Elinus (Gille Sidhean:
Elf Servant) of Albha, North Argyll;
The Dragon of Berenicia, Priest King
= Princess Bruidhina (Pressina) Vere
Dragon Queen, La Fey du
Fontaine: Mermaid, Druidess

|
Princess Melusine I Vere
(Maelesanu; Milouziana du Scythes)
La Fey d'Avalon et la Fonteine de Soif
The Fairy Melusine, Neice of Morgan La Fey

= Rainfroy de Vere, Earl of Forez 733

|

Prince Milo de Vere, Duke of Angiers
Count of Anjou,
= Princess Bertha, sister of Charlemagne
(parallel Satanic, Fairy descent via Jesus Christ)

|

Prince Milo II de Vere, Count of Guisnes and Anjou
= Lady Aveline de Nantes

|

Prince Nicassius de Vere, Count of Guisnes
= Lady Agatha de Champagne

|

Prince Otho de Vere, Count of Guisnes
= Lady Constance de Chartres

|

Prince Amelius (Adolph) de Vere Count of Guisnes
= Lady Maud de Ponthieu

|

Prince Gallus (Guy) de Vere, Count of Guisnes
= Lady Gertrude de Clermont de Ponthieu

|

Prince Baldwin de Vere

|

Eustace I de Vere
= Maud de Louvain

|

Eustace II de Vere
Comte de Boulogne
=Saint Ida of Ardennes

|

Princess Ida de Vere
= Baudouin de Bourg
Comte de Rethul

|

Prince Hugues I
Comte de Rethul
= Melisende (Melusine II)
dau. Of Bouchard Comte de Corbeil and
Lady Adelaide de Crecy

|

Badouin II de Bourg
King of Jerusalem 1118-1131
= Princess Morfia of Armenia

|

Princess Melisende of Jerusalem (Melusine III)
= Fulke V Plantagenet Count of Anjou

|

Princess Melisende of Jerusalem (Melusine III)
= Fulke V Plantagenet Count of Anjou

|

Count Geoffrey Plantagenet
= Princess Mathilda, la Imperatrice
daughter of King Henry I and Princess
Mathilda of Scotland, daughter of
King Malcolm III

|

King Henry II Plantagenet

= Countess Eleanor of Aquitaine

|

King John "Lackland" Plantagenet
= Lady Isabella of Angouleme

|

King Henry III Plantagenet
= Lady Eleanor dau. of Count
Raymond Berenguer IV of Provence
and Princess Beatrix of Savoy

|

King Edward I Plantagenet
= Princess Eleanor of Castille

|

King Edward II Plantagenet
= Princess Isabella of France

|

Princess Joan Plantagenet
= Gilbert de Clare
Earl of Gloucester

|

Lady Elizabeth de Clare

= Sir Roger D'Amorie

|

Elizabeth D'Amorie
= John Lord Bardolf

|

Willia} Lord Bardolf
= Agnes Poynings

|

Lady Cecilia Bardolf
= Sir Bryan Stapylton

|

Sir Miles Stapylton
= Katherine de la Pole
g. granddaughter of
Geoffrey Chaucer

|

Elizabeth Stapylton
= Sir William Calthorpe

|

Ann Calthorpe
= Sir Robert Drury

|

Anne Drury
= George Waldegrave

|

Sir William Waldegrave
= Juliana Rainsford

|

Sir William Waldegrave II
= Elizabeth Middlemay

|

Mary Waldegrave
= Thomas Clopton

|

Walter Clopton of Fordham
=Anne Thornton

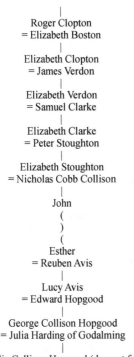

Roger Clopton
= Elizabeth Boston

Elizabeth Clopton
= James Verdon

Elizabeth Verdon
= Samuel Clarke

Elizabeth Clarke
= Peter Stoughton

Elizabeth Stoughton
= Nicholas Cobb Collison

John
(
)
(
Esther
= Reuben Avis

Lucy Avis
= Edward Hopgood

George Collison Hopgood
= Julia Harding of Godalming

Natalie Collison Hopgood (descent from
the Imperial and Royal House of Vere)
= James Weir of Vere of Lewes

HI & RH Prince Nicholas de Vere

Fairy Collison Descent from Satan
via Princess Plantina

Lord Anu and the High Council
of the Anunnaki: The Elohim

Satan-Lucifer
(Enki; Ea; Khem; Pan; Capricorn:
The Ram of the Shimmering Waters; Leviathan)
=Queen Hawah of Eldar his daughter

Qayin, King of Kish, Son of Satan,
Ancestral Founder of the High Elven God
Kings and Queens of the Dragon and the Grail
= Queen Lilith II "Luluwa" (The Pearl)
daughter of Satan by Queen Lilith I
"The Beautiful," mother of all demons:
daughter of Nergal King of the Underworld

Enoch
=Awan

Irad

Mehujael

Methusael

Lamech, Dragon Lord of Ur
= Queen Zillah

Tubal Cain King of Ur
= Ninbanda, d. of Lilith Naamah

King Ham: Chem Zarathustra, Tenth
Archon of Capricorn
=Queen Neelata-Mek

Cush

Nimrod the Mighty Hunter

Boethos/ Hotep Sekhemwy
Pharaoh and founder
of 2nd Dynasty in Egypt
=Queen Bithiah

Pharaoh Raneb/Kalenhkos c. 2800 BC
brought culture of Chem of Capricorn
to Egypt as Khem, the Goat of Mendes
known as Pan in Greece, later the
Sabbatical Goat God of the Witches
and the Baphomet of the Templars

Pharaoh Nynetjer

Pharaoh Sekhemib

Pharaoh Khasekhemwy

daughter
=Pharaoh Sanakhte

daughter
= Pharaoh Sekhemkhet

Pharaoh Khaba 2643-37 BC

Pharaoh Huni 2637-13 BC
= Queen Meresankh I

Pharaoh Sneferu
= Queen Hetep-Heres I

Pharaoh Khufu (Cheops)
= Queen Henutsen

Pharaoh Khefre
= Queen Khamerenebty

Pharaoh Menkaure 2532-04 BC
= Queen Khamerenebty II
|
Queen Khentkawas
= Pharaoh Userkaf
|
Pharaoh Neferirkare
|
Pharaoh Shepsekare
|
Pharaoh Neferefre
|
Pharaoh Niuserre
|
Pharaoh Menkauhor
|
Pharaoh Djedkare
|
Pharaoh Unas the Vampire 2375-45 BC
(The Pyramid Texts)
|
Queen Iput
= Pharaoh Teti
|
Pharaoh Pepi I
= Queen Ankhnesmerire
|
Pharaoh Pepi II
= Queen Neith
|
Pharaoh Merenre II 2184-81 BC
= Queen Nitoctris
|
Prince Ankhfn-Khonsu
Re-established the Royal
Dragon Court in Egypt under
the protection of the God Sobekh,
the Dragon defender of Royalty
|
Prince Intef I (The Great)
Governor of Thebes
|
Prince Intef II
|
Prince Intef III
|
Pharaoh Mentuhotep I (The Coffin Texts)
= Queen Tem
|
Pharaoh Mentuhotep II
|
Pharaoh Mentuhotep III
|
Queen Tohwait
= Pharaoh Amenhemet
|
Pharaoh Senusret I
= Princess Sarah, d. of Queen Tohwait
(later wife of Abraham)

|
Pharaoh Amenhemet II
-= Queen Keminebu
|
Pharaoh Senusret II
= Queen Nofret
|
Pharaoh Senusret III
= Queen Mereret
|
Pharaoh Amenhemet III
= Queen Aat
|
Pharaoh Amenhemet IV
= Sobeknefru The Great Dragon Queen of Egypt,
(Ratified the Royal Dragon Court under Sobekh)
|
Daughter
= Pharaoh Wegaf

13th Dynasty of Egypt
The Dragon Kings and Queens of
the God Sobekh

Pharaoh Wegaf
|
Pharaoah Ameny Intef c. 1700 BC
|
Pharaoh Sobekhotep III
|
Pharaoh Sobekhotep IV
|
Daughter
= Pharaoh Sobekemsaf
|
Pharaoh Intef VII
|
Daughter
= King Khayan (The Good God)
Dragon King of the Hyksos who
descend from Queen Towait (above)
|
Apepi I
Dragon King of the Hyksos
|
Apepi II
(Apophis the Evil)
|
Senisonb (Dragon Queen)
|
Pharaoh Tuthmosis I
= Queen Mutneferte (Dragon Queen)
|
Pharaoh Tuthmosis II
= Iset
|
Pharaoh Tuthmosis III
(Founded the Rosi-crucis
Therapeutate at Karnak)

1469-36 BC
= Queen Neferue
|
The Dragon Queen Tio
= Pharaoh Amenhotep II
|
Pharaoh Tuthmosis IV
= Queen Mutemwiya
|
Pharaoh Amenhotep III
= Gilukhipa, Dragon Queen
of the Mitanni
|
Merykhipa (Kiya)
Dragon Queen
= Pharaoh Amenhotep IV
|
Queen Marytaten
Pharaoh Smenkhkare
|
Princess Scota of Egypt
Dragon Queen and Princess
of Scythia: Cousin of Queen
Kiya Tasherit (descent to Jesus Christ
via Prince Rama and King Solomon)
= Prince Niall of Scythia,
Lord of Capacyront
(Parallel Scythian descent
from Typhoeos – Satan)
|
Lordship of the Elven, Dragon
Kings in Ireland – The
Tuadha de Danaan
|
King Geadheal Glas
(Ancestor of the Scots Gaels)
|
Easru 1300 BC
|
King Sru
|
King Tait
|
King Pamp
|
King Adnoin
|
King Neiheadh
= Princess Macha
|
King Faidh
|
King Iarbhoineol
|
King Beothach
|
King Iobath

King Enna
|
King Taborn
|
King Tat
|
King Allaoi
|
King Iondaoi 750 BC
|
King Ned
|
King Partholon (Easar Brec)
Led the Danaan in the Greek
Wars and eventually fled with
his remnant to Ireland.
Partholon was the Great Uncle
of the Legendary Dagdha Mor,
Lord of the Grail Cauldron
of the Danaan in Eire
|
King Diancheacht
(Luchtai)
|
Prince Cian
= Princess Eithne, dau. of the
Wizard King Balor of the Formorians
|
King Bruidhne of the Picts, called by the
Romans "Cruidhne." Flight to Caledonia after
defeat at the hands of the invading Milesians
|
Cait (Gud/Got), one
of seven sons
|
King Debbecan
|
King Olfinecta
|
King Guididgaedercach
|
King Feth
|
King Gestgurtich
|
King Vere 400 BC
Fairy Lord and Dragon King
|
Alternate succession of the Vere
Druid Prophets and Wood Lords
of the Ancient Caledonian
Fairy Forest Kingdom
|
Brude Pont
|
Vere Pont
|
Brude Leo

Vere Leo	Bridei High King AD 520
Brude Grant	Wid I
Vere Grant	Gartnait Ard Righ (High King)
Brude Gnith	Ainfrid
Vere Gnith	Talorcan Ard Righ
Brude Fechir	daughter = Bile ap Fili Welsh King of Alcut at Dumbarton
Vere Fechir	
Brude Cal	
Vere Cal	Brude Mac Bile Ard Righ 693-697
Brude Cint	Queen Pressina (Bruidhina) of the Scythian Picts = King Elinus of Albha, the Dragon of Berenicia (Northumberland), descendant of the Uilidian Druid Princes
Vere Cint	
Vere Feta Dragon Queen	
Gartnait Bolg Priest King of Caledonia ad 165-169	Melusine - Plantina - Meliore
	The Plantagenista Descent
King Vere II ad 169-178 Ard Righ (High King) of the Bruithnigh (Pict-Sidhes [Pixies] or Elves)	Torquat b. c. 760
	Tortulf de Rennes 790
	Tertulle Count of Anjou c. 821 = Petronella of France
Vipoguenech	
Fiacha Albus	Count Ingelgar of Anjou 845 = Adelais de Rescinde
Canutumel	
Dovernach Vetalec	Fulk I The Red, Count of Anjou b. 888 = Roscilla de Loches
King Vere III "Daich Vetla"	Fulk II The Good, Count of Anjou b. 920 = Gerberga de Maine
	Geoffrey Greymantle, Count of Anjou b. 939 = Adele de Vermandois
Gartnait Diuperr Ard Righ (High King) AD 355	Fullk III The Black, Count of Anjou b. 956 = 2. Hildegard of Metz
Achivir	Geoffrey II Martel, Count of Anjou b. 1006 = Agnes of Bourgogne
Aniel	
Giron	Geoffrey III Le Harbu b. 1040 = Julienne de Langeaise
Mailcon	

Geoffrey IV Martel b. 1073
= Bertrade de Montfort
|
Fulk V The Younger, Count of Anjou b. 1092
= Princess Melisende (Melusine III) of Jerusalem
|
Count Geoffrey Plantagenet
= Princess Mathilda, la Imperatrice
daughter of King Henry I and Princess
Mathilda of Scotland, daughter of
King Malcolm III
|
King Henry II Plantagenet
= Countess Eleanor of Aquitaine
|
King John "Lackland" Plantagenet
= Lady Isabella of Angouleme
|
King Henry III Plantagenet
= Lady Eleanor dau. of Count
Raymond Berenguer IVof Provence
and Princess Beatrix of Savoy
|
King Edward I Plantagenet
= Princess Eleanor of Castille
|
King Edward II Plantagenet
= Princess Isabella of France
|
Princess Joan Plantagenet
= Gilbert de Clare
Earl of Gloucester
|
Lady Elizabeth de Clare
= Sir Roger D'Amorie
|
Elizabeth D'Amorie
= John Lord Bardolf
|
William Lord Bardolf
= Agnes Poynings
|
Lady Cecilia Bardolf
= Sir Bryan Stapylton
|
Sir Miles Stapylton
= Katherine de la Pole
g. granddaughter of
Geoffrey Chaucer
|
Elizabeth Stapylton
= Sir William Calthorpe
|
Ann Calthorpe
= Sir Robert Drury
|
Anne Drury
= George Waldegrave
|

Sir William Waldegrave
= Juliana Rainsford
|
Sir William Waldegrave II
= Elizabeth Middlemay
|
Mary Waldegrave
= Thomas Clopton
|
Walter Clopton of Fordham
= Anne Thornton
|
Roger Clopton
= Elizabeth Boston
|
Elizabeth Clopton
= James Verdon
|
Elizabeth Verdon
= Samuel Clarke
|
Elizabeth Clarke
= Peter Stoughton
|
Elizabeth Stoughton
= Nicholas Cobb Collison
|
John
(
)
(
Esther
= Reuben Avis
|
Lucy Avis
= Edward Hopgood
|
George Collison Hopgood
= Julia Harding of Godalming
|
Natalie Collison Hopgood (descent from
the Imperial and Royal House of Vere)
= James Weir of Vere of Lewes
|
HI & RH Prince Nicholas de Vere

Collison Fairy Descent from Satan via the Tuadha de Danaan

Lord Anu and the High Council

of the Anunnaki: The Elohim

|

Satan-Lucifer
(Enki; Ea; Khem; Pan; Capricorn:

The Ram of the Shimmering Waters; Leviathan)
=Queen Hawah of Eldar his daughter
|
Qayin, King of Kish, Son of Satan,
Ancestral Founder of the High Elven God
Kings and Queens of the Dragon and the Grail
= Queen Lilith II "Luluwa" (The Pearl)
daughter of Satan by Queen Lilith I
"The Beautiful," mother of all demons:
daughter of Nergal King of the Underworld
|
Enoch
=Awan
|
Irad
|
Mehujael
|
Methusael
|
Lamech, Dragon Lord of Ur
= Queen Zillah
|
Tubal Cain King of Ur
= Ninbanda, d. of Lilith Naamah
|
King Ham: Chem Zarathustra, Tenth
Archon of Capricorn
=Queen Neelata-Mek
|
Cush
|
Nimrod the Mighty Hunter
|
Boethos/ Hotep Sekhemwy
Pharaoh and founder
of 2nd Dynasty in Egypt
=Queen Bithiah
|
Pharaoh Raneb/Kalenhkos c. 2800 BC
brought culture of Chem of Capricorn
to Egypt as Khem, the Goat of Mendes,
known as Pan in Greece, later the
Sabbatical Goat God of the Witches
and the Baphomet of the Templars
|
Pharaoh Nynetjer
|
Pharaoh Sekhemib
|
Pharaoh Khasekhemwy
|
daughter
=Pharaoh Sanakhte
|
daughter
= Pharaoh Sekhemkhet
|
Pharaoh Khaba 2643-37 BC

|
Pharaoh Huni 2637-13 BC
= Queen Meresankh I
|
Pharaoh Sneferu
= Queen Hetep-Heres I
|
Pharaoh Khufu (Cheops)
= Queen Henutsen
|
Pharaoh Khefre
= Queen Khamerenebty
|
Pharaoh Menkaure 2532-04 BC
= Queen Khamerenebty II
|
Queen Khentkawas
= Pharaoh Userkaf
|
Pharaoh Neferirkare
|
Pharaoh Shepsekare
|
Pharaoh Neferefre
|
Pharaoh Niuserre
|
Pharaoh Menkauhor
|
Pharaoh Djedkare
|
Pharaoh Unas the Vampire 2375-45 BC
(The Pyramid Texts)
|
Queen Iput
= Pharaoh Teti
|
Pharaoh Pepi I
= Queen Ankhnesmerire
|
Pharaoh Pepi II
= Queen Neith
|
Pharaoh Merenre II 2184-81 BC
= Queen Nitoctris
|
Prince Ankhfn-Khonsu
Re-established the Royal
Dragon Court in Egypt under
the protection of the God Sobekh,
the Dragon defender of Royalty
|
Prince Intef I (The Great)
Governor of Thebes
|
Prince Intef II
|
Prince Intef III
|

Pharaoh Mentuhotep I (The Coffin Texts)
= Queen Tem
|
Pharaoh Mentuhotep II
|
Pharaoh Mentuhotep III
|
Queen Tohwait
= Pharaoh Amenhemet
|
Pharaoh Senusret I
= Princess Sarah, d. of Queen Tohwait
(later wife of Abraham)
|
Pharaoh Amenhemet II
-= Queen Keminebu
|
Pharaoh Senusret II
= Queen Nofret
|
Pharaoh Senusret III
= Queen Mereret
|
Pharaoh Amenhemet III
= Queen Aat
|
Pharaoh Amenhemet IV
= Sobeknefru The Great Dragon Queen of Egypt,
(Ratified the Royal Dragon Court under Sobekh)
|
Daughter
= Pharaoh Wegaf

13th Dynasty of Egypt
The Dragon Kings and Queens of
the God Sobekh

Pharaoh Wegaf
|
Pharaoah Ameny Intef c. 1700 BC
|
Pharaoh Sobekhotep III
|
Pharaoh Sobekhotep IV
|
Daughter
= Pharaoh Sobekemsaf
|
Pharaoh Intef VII
|
Daughter
= King Khayan (The Good God)
Dragon King of the Hyksos who
descend from Queen Towait (above)
|
Apepi I
Dragon King of the Hyksos
|
Apepi II

(Apophis the Evil)
|
Senisonb (Dragon Queen)
|
Pharaoh Tuthmosis I
= Queen Mutneferte (Dragon Queen)
|
Pharaoh Tuthmosis II
= Iset
|
Pharaoh Tuthmosis III
(Founded the Rosi-crucis
Therapeutate at Karnak)
1469-36 BC
= Queen Neferue
|
The Dragon Queen Tio
= Pharaoh Amenhotep II
|
Pharaoh Tuthmosis IV
= Queen Mutemwiya
|
Pharaoh Amenhotep III
= Gilukhipa, Dragon Queen
of the Mitanni
|
Merykhipa (Kiya)
Dragon Queen
= Pharaoh Amenhotep IV
|
Queen Marytaten
Pharaoh Smenkhkare
|
Princess Scota of Egypt
Dragon Queen and Princess
of Scythia: Granddaughter
of Pharaoh Amenhotep IV
and cousin of Queen
Kiya Tasherit
= Prince Niall of Scythia
Lord of Capacyront
(parallel descent from
Satan-Typhoeos)
|
King Geadheal Glas
(Ancestor of the Scots Gaels)
|
Easru 1300 BC
|
King Sru
|
King Tait
|
King Pamp
|
King Adnoin
|
King Neiheadh
= Princess Macha

King Faidh
|
King Iarbhoineol
|
King Beothach
|
King Iobath
|
King Enna
|
King Taborn
|
King Tat
|
King Allaoi
|
King Iondaoi 750 BC
|
King Ned
|
King Partholon (Easar Brec)
Led the Danaan in the Greek
Wars and eventually fled with
his remnant to Ireland.
Partholon was the Great Uncle
of the Legendary Dagdha Mor,
Lord of the Grail Cauldron
of the Danaan in Eire
|
Lordship of the Elven, Dragon
Kings in Ireland – The
Tuadha de Danaan
|
King Diancheacht
(Luchtai)
|
Prince Cian
= Princess Eithne, dau. of the
Wizard-King Balor of the Formorians
|
King Bruidhne of the Picts, called by the
Romans "Cruidhne." Flight to Caledonia after
defeat at the hands of the invading Milesians
|
Cait (Gud/Got), one
of seven sons
|
King Debbecan
|
King Olfinecta
|
King Guididgaedercach
|
King Feth
|
King Gestgurtich
|
King Vere 400 BC

Fairy Lord and Dragon King
|
Alternate succession of the Vere
Druid Prophets and Wood Lords
of the Ancient Caledonian
Fairy Forest Kingdom
|
Brude Pont
|
Vere Pont
|
Brude Leo
|
Vere Leo
|
Brude Grant
|
Vere Grant
|
Brude Gnith
|
Vere Gnith
|
Brude Fechir
|
Vere Fechir
|
Brude Cal
|
Vere Cal
|
Brude Cint
|
Vere Cint
|
Vere Feta
Dragon Queen
|
Gartnait Bolg
Priest King of Caledonia
AD 165-169
|
King Vere II
AD 169-178
Ard Righ (High King)
of the Bruithnigh
|
Vipoguenech
|
Fiacha Albus
|
Canutumel
|
Dovernach Vetalec
|
King Vere III Daich Vetla
|
Gartnait Diuperr
Ard Righ (High King)

AD 355
|
Achivir
|
Aniel
|
Giron
|
Mailcon
|
Bridei
High King AD 520
|
Wid I
|
Gartnait
Ard Righ (High King)
|
Ainfrid
|
Talorcan
Ard Righ
|
daughter
= Bile ap Fili
Welsh King of Alcut
at Dumbarton
|
Brude Mac Bile
Ard Righ 693-697
|
Bruidhina (Pressina)
Dragon Queen, La Fey du
Fontaine: Mermaid, Druidess
= King Elinus (Gille Sidhean:
Elf Servant) of Albha, North Argyll;
The Dragon of Berenicia, Priest King
|
Princess Melusine I
(Maelesanu; Milouziana du Scythes)
La Fey d'Avalon et la Fonteine de Soif
The Fairy Melusine, Neice of Morgan La Fey
= Rainfroy de Vere, Earl of Forez 733
|
Prince Milo de Vere, Duke of Angiers
Count of Anjou,
= Princess Bertha, sister of Charlemagne
(parallel Satanic, Fairy descent via Jesus Christ)
|
Prince Milo II de Vere, Count of Guisnes and Anjou
= Lady Aveline de Nantes
|
Prince Nicassius de Vere, Count of Guisnes
= Lady Agatha de Champagne
|
Prince Otho de Vere, Count of Guisnes
= Lady Constance de Chartres
|
Prince Amelius (Adolph) de Vere Count of Guisnes

= 2. Lady Maud de Ponthieu
|
Prince Gallus (Guy) de Vere, Count of Guisnes
= 2. Lady Gertrude de Clermont de Ponthieu
|
Prince Baldwin de Vere
= Lady Agnes de Jumiege
|
Eustace I de Vere
Comte de Boulogne
d. 1049
= Lady Maud de Louvain
(Descent from Charlemagne)
|
Eustace II de Vere
= Saint Ida of Ardennes
|
Princess Ida de Vere
= Baudouin de Bourg
Comte de Rethul
|
Prince Hugues I
Comte de Rethul
= Melisende (Melusine II)
dau. Of Bouchard Comte de Corbeil and
Lady Adelaide de Crecy
|
Badouin II de Bourg
King of Jerusalem 1118-1131
= Princess Morfia of Armenia
|
Princess Melisende of Jerusalem (Melusine III)
= Fulke V Plantagenet Count of Anjou
|
Princess Melisende of Jerusalem (Melusine III)
= Fulke V Plantagenet Count of Anjou
|
Count Geoffrey Plantagenet
= Princess Mathilda, la Imperatrice
daughter of King Henry I and Princess
Mathilda of Scotland, daughter of
King Malcolm III
|
King Henry II Plantagenet
= Countess Eleanor of Aquitaine
|
King John "Lackland" Plantagenet
= Lady Isabella of Angouleme
|
King Henry III Plantagenet
= Lady Eleanor dau. of Count
Raymond Berenguer IVof Provence
and Princess Beatrix of Savoy
|
King Edward I Plantagenet
= Princess Eleanor of Castille
|
King Edward II Plantagenet

= Princess Isabella of France
|
Princess Joan Plantagenet
= Gilbert de Clare
Earl of Gloucester
|
Lady Elizabeth de Clare
= Sir Roger D'Amorie
|
Elizabeth D'Amorie
= John Lord Bardolf
|
William Lord Bardolf
= Agnes Poynings
|
Lady Cecilia Bardolf
= Sir Bryan Stapylton
|
Sir Miles Stapylton
= Katherine de la Pole
g. granddaughter of
Geoffrey Chaucer
|
Elizabeth Stapylton
= Sir William Calthorpe
|
Ann Calthorpe
= Sir Robert Drury
|
Anne Drury
= George Waldegrave
|
Sir William Waldegrave
= Juliana Rainsford
|
Sir William Waldegrave II
= Elizabeth Middlemay
|
Mary Waldegrave
= Thomas Clopton
|
Walter Clopton of Fordham
=Anne Thornton
|
Roger Clopton
= Elizabeth Boston
|
Elizabeth Clopton
= James Verdon
|
Elizabeth Verdon
= Samuel Clarke
|
Elizabeth Clarke
= Peter Stoughton
|
Elizabeth Stoughton
= Nicholas Cobb Collison
|

John
(
)
(
Esther
= Reuben Avis
|
Lucy Avis
= Edward Hopgood
|
George Collison Hopgood
= Julia Harding of Godalming
|
Natalie Collison Hopgood (descent from
the Imperial and Royal House of Vere)
= James Weir of Vere of Lewes
|
HI & RH Prince Nicholas de Vere

Collison Descent from Joseph of Arimathea and the Archdruid Bran The Blessed

Joseph of Arimathea
=Anna
|
Anna of Arimathea AD 50
= Arch Druid Bran the Blessed
Archetype of the Baphomet of the Knights Templars.
Bran means Raven, Light and Midden or Darkness,
suggesting a mystical, dualist foundation for his
powers as a Druid. His head is buried on Tower Hill
in the Tower of London.
|
Penarden, Iceni Commander
Iceni Commander
=Marius
|
Coel I
|
Lucius
= Gladys
|
Gladys
= Cadwan Prince of Cumbria
|
Coel II of Camulod
|
Cunedd
|
Confer
|
Fer (Vere)
|
Cursalen
|

Clemens
|
Quintinius
|
Cynloyp
|
Ceretic: Guletic of Allt Clud
|
Cinuit
|
Dyfnwal Hen of Strathclyde
|
Ingenach
= Brychan II
|
Lluan
= Gabran King of Scots
|
King Aeden Mac Gabran
The Uther Pendragon
|
King Eochaid Buide
608-630
|
King Donald Brecc
630-643
|
King Domangart
|
King Eochaid
695-696
|
King Eochaid
726-733
|
King Aed Find
748-778
|
King Eochaid
781
= Princess Unuisticc of Fortren
|
King Alpin
King of Scots
839-841
|
King Kenneth I MacAlpin
King of Picts and Scots
844-859
|
King Constantine I
863-877
|
King Donald II
889-900
|
King Malcom I
942-954
|
King Kenneth II

971-995
King Malcom II MacKenneth
1005-1034
|
Princess Bethoc
= Lord Crinan
Thane of the Isles
k. 1045
|
King Duncan I 1035-1040
|
King Malcom III Canmore
1058-1093
= Saint Margaret dau of
Edward the Exile
|
Princess Mathilde
= King Henry I
|
Princess Mathilda la Imperatrice
(Empress of England)
=Geoffrey Plantagenet
Count of Anjou and Maine
|
King Henry II Plantagenet
= Countess Eleanor of Aquitaine
|
King John "Lackland" Plantagenet
= Lady Isabella of Angouleme
|
King Henry III Plantagenet
= Lady Eleanor dau. of Count
Raymond Berenguer IVof Provence
and Princess Beatrix of Savoy
|
King Edward I Plantagenet
= Princess Eleanor of Castille
|
King Edward II Plantagenet
= Princess Isabella of France
|
Princess Joan Plantagenet
= Gilbert de Clare
Earl of Gloucester
|
Lady Elizabeth de Clare
= Sir Roger D'Amorie
|
Elizabeth D'Amorie
= John Lord Bardolf
|
William Lord Bardolf
= Agnes Poynings
|
Lady Cecilia Bardolf
= Sir Bryan Stapylton
|
Sir Miles Stapylton
= Katherine de la Pole

g. granddaughter of

Geoffrey Chaucer
|
Elizabeth Stapylton
= Sir William Calthorpe
|
Ann Calthorpe
= Sir Robert Drury
|
Anne Drury
= George Waldegrave
|
Sir William Waldegrave
= Juliana Rainsford
|
Sir William Waldegrave II
= Elizabeth Middlemay
|
Mary Waldegrave
= Thomas Clopton
|
Walter Clopton of Fordham
=Anne Thornton
|
Roger Clopton
= Elizabeth Boston
|
Elizabeth Clopton
= James Verdon
|
Elizabeth Verdon
= Samuel Clarke
|
Elizabeth Clarke
= Peter Stoughton
|
Elizabeth Stoughton
= Nicholas Cobb Collison
|
John
(
)
(
Esther
= Reuben Avis
|
Lucy Avis
= Edward Hopgood
|
George Collison Hopgood
= Julia Harding of Godalming
|
Natalie Collison Hopgood (descent from
the Imperial and Royal House of Vere)
= James Weir of Vere of Lewes
|
HI & RH Prince Nicholas de Vere

Collison Descent from Queen Mabh, Merlin Taliesin and the Elven House of Pendragon

Queen Mabh
Queen of the Elves of Ireland
(Sword Tutor to Finn MacCool)
|
Merlin Taliesin
Archdruid and Prince Bard
= Princess' Viviane I de Avalon del Acques
|
Princess Ygraine d'Avalon del Acques
= King Aeden MacGabran Pendragon
574-608
|
King Eochaid Buide
608-630
|
King Donald Brecc
630-643
|
King Domangart
|
King Eochaid
695-696
|
King Eochaid
726-733
|
King Aed Find
748-778
|
King Eochaid
781
= Princess Unuisticc of Fortren
|
King Alpin
King of Scots
839-841
|
King Kenneth I MacAlpin
King of Picts and Scots
844-859
|
King Constantine I
863-877
|
King Donald II
889-900
|
King Malcom I
942-954
|
King Kenneth II
971-995
|

King Malcom II MacKenneth
1005-1034
|
Princess Bethoc
= Lord Crinan
Thane of the Isles
k. 1045
|
King Duncan I 1035-1040
|
King Malcom III Canmore
1058-1093
= Saint Margaret dau. of
Edward the Exile and
Princess Agatha of Bulgaria
|
Princess Mathilde
= King Henry I
|
= Princess Mathilda, la Imperatrice
daughter of Princess
Mathilda of Scotland, daughter of
King Malcolm III
= Geoffrey Plantagenet, Count of Anjou
|
King Henry II Plantagenet
= Countess Eleanor of Aquitaine
|
King John "Lackland" Plantagenet
= Lady Isabella of Angouleme
|
King Henry III Plantagenet
= Lady Eleanor dau. of Count
Raymond Berenguer IVof Provence
and Princess Beatrix of Savoy
|
King Edward I Plantagenet
= Princess Eleanor of Castille
|
King Edward II Plantagenet
= Princess Isabella of France
|
Princess Joan Plantagenet
= Gilbert de Clare
Earl of Gloucester
|
Lady Elizabeth de Clare
= Sir Roger D'Amorie
|
Elizabeth D'Amorie
= John Lord Bardolf
|
William Lord Bardolf
= Agnes Poynings
|
Lady Cecilia Bardolf
= Sir Bryan Stapylton
|
Sir Miles Stapylton

= Katherine de la Pole
g. granddaughter of
Geoffrey Chaucer
|
Elizabeth Stapylton
= Sir William Calthorpe
|
Ann Calthorpe
= Sir Robert Drury
|
Anne Drury
= George Waldegrave
|
Sir William Waldegrave
= Juliana Rainsford
|
Sir William Waldegrave II
= Elizabeth Middlemay
|
Mary Waldegrave
= Thomas Clopton
|
Walter Clopton of Fordham
=Anne Thornton
|
Roger Clopton
= Elizabeth Boston
|
Elizabeth Clopton
= James Verdon
|
Elizabeth Verdon
= Samuel Clarke
|
Elizabeth Clarke
= Peter Stoughton
|
Elizabeth Stoughton
= Nicholas Cobb Collison
|
John
(
)
(
Esther
= Reuben Avis
|
Lucy Avis
= Edward Hopgood
|
George Collison Hopgood
= Julia Harding of Godalming
|
Natalie Collison Hopgood (descent from
the Imperial and Royal House of Vere)
= James Weir of Vere of Lewes
|
HI & RH Prince Nicholas de Vere

Collison Imperial Descent from Emperor Louis I

Charlemagne the Great
King of France 771-814
Holy Roman Emperor 800-814
= Princess Hildegarde
|
Emperor Louis I
814-830
=2. Princess Judith of Bavaria
|
Emperor Lothair I
Middle Emperor from 840
King of Western Franks 843-855
|
Emperor Louis II of Italy
855-975
|
Princess Irmengarde
= Count Bouquet VIII of
Provence
|
Lady Kunigund
= Count Sigebert of Verdun
(Bouquet IX of Provence)
|
Duke Gozelo I
Duke of Lower Lorraine
(Descent to the House of Habsburg-Lorraine)
1023-1044
|
Duke Godfrey II
Duke of Upper Lorraine
d. 1069
= Princess Doda
|
Saint Ida of Ardennes
= Eustace II de Vere
Comte de Boulogne
|
Princess Ida de Vere

= Baudouin de Bourg
Comte de Rethul
|
Prince Hugues I
Comte de Rethul
= Melisende (Melusine II)
dau. Of Bouchard Comte de Corbeil and
Lady Adelaide de Crecy
|
Badouin II de Bourg
King of Jerusalem 1118-1131
= Princess Morfia of Armenia
|

Princess Melisende of Jerusalem (Melusine III)
= Fulke V Plantagenet Count of Anjou
descent from Princess Plantina, sister
of the Fairy Princess Melusine I and mother
of Lord Tortulf de Nide de Merle
|
Princess Melisende of Jerusalem (Melusine III)
= Fulke V Plantagenet Count of Anjou
|
Count Geoffrey Plantagenet
= Princess Mathilda, la Imperatrice
daughter of King Henry I and Princess
Mathilda of Scotland, daughter of
King Malcolm III
|
King Henry II Plantagenet
= Countess Eleanor of Aquitaine
|
King John "Lackland" Plantagenet
= Lady Isabella of Angouleme
|
King Henry III Plantagenet
= Lady Eleanor dau. of Count
Raymond Berenguer IVof Provence
and Princess Beatrix of Savoy
|
King Edward I Plantagenet
= Princess Eleanor of Castille
|
King Edward II Plantagenet
= Princess Isabella of France
|
Princess Joan Plantagenet
= Gilbert de Clare
Earl of Gloucester
|
Lady Elizabeth de Clare
= Sir Roger D'Amorie
|
Elizabeth D'Amorie
= John Lord Bardolf
|
William Lord Bardolf
= Agnes Poynings
|
Lady Cecilia Bardolf
= Sir Bryan Stapylton
|
Sir Miles Stapylton
= Katherine de la Pole
g. granddaughter of
Geoffrey Chaucer
|
Elizabeth Stapylton
= Sir William Calthorpe
|
Ann Calthorpe
= Sir Robert Drury

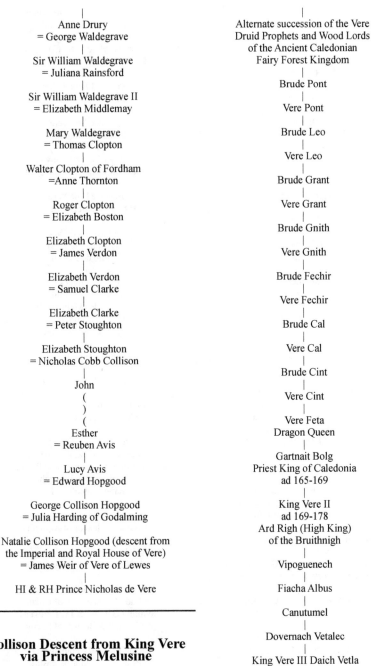

Anne Drury
= George Waldegrave

Sir William Waldegrave
= Juliana Rainsford

Sir William Waldegrave II
= Elizabeth Middlemay

Mary Waldegrave
= Thomas Clopton

Walter Clopton of Fordham
=Anne Thornton

Roger Clopton
= Elizabeth Boston

Elizabeth Clopton
= James Verdon

Elizabeth Verdon
= Samuel Clarke

Elizabeth Clarke
= Peter Stoughton

Elizabeth Stoughton
= Nicholas Cobb Collison

John
(
)
(
Esther
= Reuben Avis

Lucy Avis
= Edward Hopgood

George Collison Hopgood
= Julia Harding of Godalming

Natalie Collison Hopgood (descent from
the Imperial and Royal House of Vere)
= James Weir of Vere of Lewes

HI & RH Prince Nicholas de Vere

Collison Descent from King Vere
via Princess Melusine

King Vere 400 BC
Fairy Lord and Dragon King

Alternate succession of the Vere
Druid Prophets and Wood Lords
of the Ancient Caledonian
Fairy Forest Kingdom

Brude Pont

Vere Pont

Brude Leo

Vere Leo

Brude Grant

Vere Grant

Brude Gnith

Vere Gnith

Brude Fechir

Vere Fechir

Brude Cal

Vere Cal

Brude Cint

Vere Cint

Vere Feta
Dragon Queen

Gartnait Bolg
Priest King of Caledonia
ad 165-169

King Vere II
ad 169-178
Ard Righ (High King)
of the Bruithnigh

Vipoguenech

Fiacha Albus

Canutumel

Dovernach Vetalec

King Vere III Daich Vetla

Gartnait Diuperr
Ard Righ (High King)
AD 355

|
Achivir
|
Aniel
|
Giron
|
Mailcon
|
Bridei
High King AD 520
|
Wid I
|
Gartnait
Ard Righ (High King)
|
Ainfrid
|
Talorcan
Ard Righ
|
daughter
= Bile ap Fili
Welsh King of Alcut
at Dumbarton
|
Brude Mac Bile
Ard Righ 693-697
|
Bruidhina (Pressina)
Dragon Queen, La Fey du
Fontaine: Mermaid, Druidess
= King Elinus (Gille Sidhean:
Elf Servant) of Albha, North Argyll;
The Dragon of Berenicia, Priest King
|
Princess Melusine I
(Maelesanu; Milouziana du Scythes)
La Fey d'Avalon et la Fonteine de Soif
The Fairy Melusine, Neice of Morgan La Fey
= Rainfroy de Vere, Earl of Forez 733
|
Prince Milo de Vere, Duke of Angiers
Count of Anjou,
= Princess Bertha, sister of Charlemagne
(parallel Satanic, Fairy descent via Jesus Christ)
|
Prince Milo II de Vere, Count of Guisnes and Anjou
= Lady Aveline de Nantes
|
Prince Nicassius de Vere, Count of Guisnes
= Lady Agatha de Champagne
|
Prince Otho de Vere, Count of Guisnes
= Lady Constance de Chartres
|

Prince Amelius (Adolph) de Vere Count of Guisnes
= 2. Lady Maud de Ponthieu
|
Prince Gallus (Guy) de Vere, Count of Guisnes
= 2. Lady Gertrude de Clermont de Ponthieu
|
Prince Baldwin de Vere
= Lady Agnes de Jumiege
|
Eustace I de Vere
Comte de Boulogne
d. 1049
= Lady Maud de Louvain
(Descent from Charlemagne)
|
Eustace II de Vere
= Saint Ida of Ardennes
|
Princess Ida de Vere
= Baudouin de Bourg
Comte de Rethul
|
Prince Hugues I
Comte de Rethul
= Melisende (Melusine II)
dau. Of Bouchard Comte de Corbeil and
Lady Adelaide de Crecy
|
Badouin II de Bourg
King of Jerusalem 1118-1131
= Princess Morfia of Armenia
|
Princess Melisende of Jerusalem (Melusine III)
= Fulke V Plantagenet Count of Anjou
|
Count Geoffrey Plantagenet
= Princess Mathilda, la Imperatrice
daughter of King Henry I and Princess
Mathilda of Scotland, daughter of
King Malcolm III
|
King Henry II Plantagenet
= Countess Eleanor of Aquitaine
|
King John "Lackland" Plantagenet
= Lady Isabella of Angouleme
|
King Henry III Plantagenet
= Lady Eleanor dau. of Count
Raymond Berenguer IVof Provence
and Princess Beatrix of Savoy
|
King Edward I Plantagenet
= Princess Eleanor of Castille
|
King Edward II Plantagenet
= Princess Isabella of France

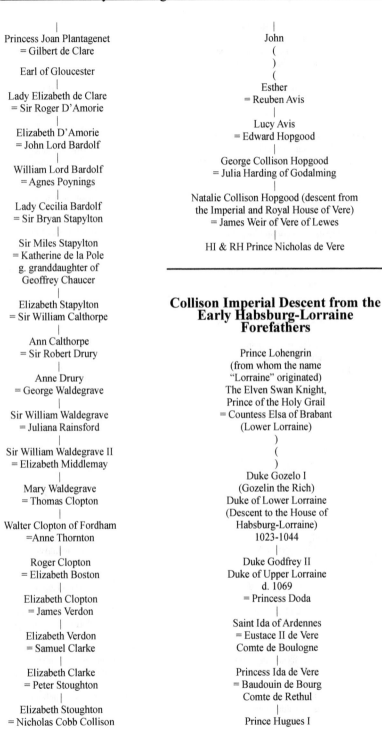

Princess Joan Plantagenet
= Gilbert de Clare

Earl of Gloucester

Lady Elizabeth de Clare
= Sir Roger D'Amorie

Elizabeth D'Amorie
= John Lord Bardolf

William Lord Bardolf
= Agnes Poynings

Lady Cecilia Bardolf
= Sir Bryan Stapylton

Sir Miles Stapylton
= Katherine de la Pole
g. granddaughter of
Geoffrey Chaucer

Elizabeth Stapylton
= Sir William Calthorpe

Ann Calthorpe
= Sir Robert Drury

Anne Drury
= George Waldegrave

Sir William Waldegrave
= Juliana Rainsford

Sir William Waldegrave II
= Elizabeth Middlemay

Mary Waldegrave
= Thomas Clopton

Walter Clopton of Fordham
=Anne Thornton

Roger Clopton
= Elizabeth Boston

Elizabeth Clopton
= James Verdon

Elizabeth Verdon
= Samuel Clarke

Elizabeth Clarke
= Peter Stoughton

Elizabeth Stoughton
= Nicholas Cobb Collison

John
(
)
(
Esther
= Reuben Avis

Lucy Avis
= Edward Hopgood

George Collison Hopgood
= Julia Harding of Godalming

Natalie Collison Hopgood (descent from
the Imperial and Royal House of Vere)
= James Weir of Vere of Lewes

HI & RH Prince Nicholas de Vere

Collison Imperial Descent from the Early Habsburg-Lorraine Forefathers

Prince Lohengrin
(from whom the name
"Lorraine" originated)
The Elven Swan Knight,
Prince of the Holy Grail
= Countess Elsa of Brabant
(Lower Lorraine)
)
(
)
Duke Gozelo I
(Gozelin the Rich)
Duke of Lower Lorraine
(Descent to the House of
Habsburg-Lorraine)
1023-1044

Duke Godfrey II
Duke of Upper Lorraine
d. 1069
= Princess Doda

Saint Ida of Ardennes
= Eustace II de Vere
Comte de Boulogne

Princess Ida de Vere
= Baudouin de Bourg
Comte de Rethul

Prince Hugues I

Comte de Rethul
= Melisende (Melusine II)
dau. Of Bouchard Comte de Corbeil and
Lady Adelaide de Crecy
|
Badouin II de Bourg
King of Jerusalem 1118-1131
= Princess Morfia of Armenia
|
Princess Melisende of Jerusalem (Melusine III)
= Fulke V Plantagenet Count of Anjou
descent from Princess Plantina, sister
of the Fairy Princess Melusine I
|
Count Geoffrey Plantagenet
= Princess Mathilda, la Imperatrice
daughter of King Henry I and Princess
Mathilda of Scotland, daughter of
King Malcolm III
|
King Henry II Plantagenet
= Countess Eleanor of Aquitaine
|
King John "Lackland" Plantagenet
= Lady Isabella of Angouleme
|
King Henry III Plantagenet
= Lady Eleanor dau. of Count
Raymond Berenguer IVof Provence

and Princess Beatrix of Savoy
|
King Edward I Plantagenet
= Princess Eleanor of Castille
|
King Edward II Plantagenet
= Princess Isabella of France
|
Princess Joan Plantagenet
= Gilbert de Clare
Earl of Gloucester
|
Lady Elizabeth de Clare
= Sir Roger D'Amorie
|
Elizabeth D'Amorie
= John Lord Bardolf
|
William Lord Bardolf
= Agnes Poynings
|
Lady Cecilia Bardolf
= Sir Bryan Stapylton
|
Sir Miles Stapylton
= Katherine de la Pole
g. granddaughter of
Geoffrey Chaucer

|
Elizabeth Stapylton
= Sir William Calthorpe
|
Ann Calthorpe
= Sir Robert Drury
|
Anne Drury
= George Waldegrave
|
Sir William Waldegrave
= Juliana Rainsford
|
Sir William Waldegrave II
= Elizabeth Middlemay
|
Mary Waldegrave
= Thomas Clopton
|
Walter Clopton of Fordham
=Anne Thornton
|
Roger Clopton
= Elizabeth Boston
|
Elizabeth Clopton
= James Verdon
|
Elizabeth Verdon
= Samuel Clarke
|
Elizabeth Clarke
= Peter Stoughton
|
Elizabeth Stoughton
= Nicholas Cobb Collison
|
John
(
)
(
Esther
= Reuben Avis
|
Lucy Avis
= Edward Hopgood
|
George Collison Hopgood
= Julia Harding of Godalming
|
Natalie Collison Hopgood (descent from
the Imperial and Royal House of Vere)
= James Weir of Vere of Lewes
|
HI & RH Prince Nicholas de Vere

Collison Descent from the Goddess Venus via the Imperial Roman House of the Julii

The Babylonian Goddess-Queen Tiamat
(The Greek Goddess "Chaos"), Mother of Gaia
|
The Babylonian Goddess-Queen Kishar
(The Greek Goddess Gaia:
Mother Earth)
|
The Babylonian God-King Anu (Chronos-Saturn)
and the High
Council of the Anunnaki: The Jewish Elohim: The
Old Gods
|
The Goddess Venus-Aphrodite
The Bright and Morning Star,
the Jewel in the Crown of Satan
(The Demon Queen Ishtar-Astaroth);
Half-Sister of Queen Lilith.
Jesus consciously equated himself with Venus
as the Bright and Morning Star, the Roman
"Lucifer" in *Revelations,* whilst Jesus' wife Mary
Magdaleine was herself Priestess of the Goddess
Ishtar-Venus (See Chart : "Dragon Descent")
= Typhoeus, (Set-Enki-Satan) God of the Titans;
God-King of the Fairies, father of the Elven
Scythians;
Half-Brother of the God Enlil-Zeus-Jehovah
|
Anchises, Lord of
the Scythians of Troy
|
Lord Aeneas of the Labyrinth
Dragon Prince of Troy
=Princess Creusa
|
Romulus
Founder of Rome
|
Ascanius
|
Julus c. 340 BC
Founder of the Clan of the Julii
|
Numerus Julius Julus
|
Lucius Julus Julius I
|
Caius Julius Julius I
|
Caius Julius Julius II
|
Caius Julius Julius III
|
Lucius Julius Julu

Lucius Julius Julus II
|
Lucius Julius Libo I
|
Lucius Julius Libo II
|
Numerius Julius Caesar
|
Lucius Julius Caesar I
|
Sextus Julius Caesar I
|
Sextus Julius Caesar II
|
Caius Caesar Julius
|
Julius Caesar (Julius Slakten) 120 BC
|
The Lady Julia Julii,
Sister of Emperor Gaius Julius Caesar
(Who was murdered by the Senate of Rome)
|
The Lady Atia of the Julii
=Octavian
|
Octavia Minor
=Marcus Antonius
(Mark Anthony)
|
Antonia Minor
=Emperor Nero
|
Emperor Claudius
= Valeria
|
Genevissa
= Arviragus
|
Marius
|
Coel I
|
Lucius
= Gladys
|
Gladys
= Cadwan Prince of Cumbria
|
Coel II of Camulod
|
Cunedd
|
Confer
|
Fer (Vere)
|
Cursalen
|

Clemens
|
Quintinius
|
Cynloyp
|
Ceretic: Guletic of Allt Clud
|
Cinuit
|
Dyfnwal Hen of Strathclyde
|
Ingenach
= Brychan II
|
Lluan
= Gabran King of Scots
|
King Aeden Mac Gabran
The Uther Pendragon
or Great Dragon of Albany
574-608
Princess Ygraine d'Avalon del Acques
|
King Eochaid Buide
608-630
|
King Donald Brecc
630-643
|
King Domangart
|
King Eochaid
695-696
|
King Eochaid
726-733
|
King Aed Find
748-778
|
King Eochaid
781
= Princess Unuisticc of Fortren
|
King Alpin
King of Scots
839-841
|
King Kenneth I MacAlpin
King of Picts and Scots
844-859
|
King Constantine I
863-877
|
King Donald II
889-900

King Malcom I
942-954
|
King Kenneth II
971-995
|
King Malcom II MacKenneth
1005-1034
|
Princess Bethoc
= Lord Crinan
Thane of the Isles
k. 1045
|
King Duncan I 1035-1040
|
King Malcom III Canmore
1058-1093
= Saint Margaret dau of
Edward the Exile and
Agatha of Bulgaria
|
Princess Mathilde
= King Henry I
|
Princess Mathilda la Imperatrice
(Empress of England)
=Geoffrey Plantagenet
Count of Anjou and Maine
|
King Henry II Plantagenet
= Countess Eleanor of Aquitaine
|
King John "Lackland" Plantagenet
= Lady Isabella of Angouleme
|
King Henry III Plantagenet
= Lady Eleanor dau. of Count
Raymond Berenguer IVof Provence
and Princess Beatrix of Savoy
|
King Edward I Plantagenet
= Princess Eleanor of Castille
King Edward II Plantagenet
= Princess Isabella of France
|
Princess Joan Plantagenet
= Gilbert de Clare
Earl of Gloucester
|
Lady Elizabeth de Clare
= Sir Roger D'Amorie
|
Elizabeth D'Amorie
= John Lord Bardolf
|
William Lord Bardolf
= Agnes Poynings

Lady Cecilia Bardolf
= Sir Bryan Stapylton
|
Sir Miles Stapylton
= Katherine de la Pole
g. granddaughter of
Geoffrey Chaucer
|
Elizabeth Stapylton
= Sir William Calthorpe
|
Ann Calthorpe
= Sir Robert Drury
|
Anne Drury
= George Waldegrave
|
Sir William Waldegrave
= Juliana Rainsford
|
Sir William Waldegrave II
= Elizabeth Middlemay
|
Mary Waldegrave
= Thomas Clopton
|
Walter Clopton of Fordham
=Anne Thornton
|
Roger Clopton
= Elizabeth Boston
|
Elizabeth Clopton
|
= James Verdon
Elizabeth Verdon
= Samuel Clarke
|
Elizabeth Clarke
= Peter Stoughton
|
Elizabeth Stoughton
= Nicholas Cobb Collison
|
John
(
)
(
Esther
= Reuben Avis
|
Lucy Avis
= Edward Hopgood
|
George Collison Hopgood
= Julia Harding of Godalming
|
Natalie Collison Hopgood (descent from

the Imperial and Royal House of Vere)
= James Weir of Vere of Lewes
|
HI & RH Prince Nicholas de Vere

The Collison Descent from the Ancient Welsh Kings 5059 BC–2011 AD

The God-King Satan-Lucifer, son
of Anu and creator of the Elven or Fairy Kings
(Enki; Ea; Khem; Pan; Capricorn:
The Ram of the Shimmering Waters; Leviathan)
=Queen Hawah of Eldar his daughter
|
Qayin, King of Kish, Son of Satan,
Ancestral Founder of the High Elven
Kings and Queens of the Dragon and the Grail
= Queen Lilith II "Luluwa" (The Pearl)
daughter of Satan by Queen Lilith I
"The Beautiful," mother of all demons:
daughter of Nergal King of the Underworld
|
Enoch
=Awan
|
Irad
|
Mehujael
|
Methusael
|
Lamech, Dragon Lord of Ur
= Queen Zillah
|
Tubal Cain King of Ur
= Ninbanda, d. of Lilith Naamah
|
King Ham: Chem Zarathustra, Tenth
Archon of Capricorn
=Queen Neelata-Mek
|
Cush
|
Nimrod the Mighty Hunter
|
Boethos/ Hotep Sekhemwy
Pharaoh and founder
of 2nd Dynasty in Egypt
=Queen Bithiah
|
Pharaoh Raneb/Kalenhkos c. 2800 BC
brought culture of Chem of Capricorn
to Egypt as Khem, the Goat of Mendes
known as Pan in Greece, later the

Sabbatical Goat God of the Witches
and the Baphomet of the Templars
|
Pharaoh Nynetjer
|
Pharaoh Sekhemib
|
Pharaoh Khasekhemwy
|
daughter
=Pharaoh Sanakhte
|
daughter
= Pharaoh Sekhemkhet
|
Pharaoh Khaba 2643-37 BC
|
Pharaoh Huni 2637-13 BC
= Queen Meresankh I
|
Pharaoh Sneferu
= Queen Hetep-Heres I
|
Pharaoh Khufu (Cheops)
= Queen Henutsen
|
Pharaoh Khefre
= Queen Khamerenebty
|
Pharaoh Menkaure 2532-04 BC
= Queen Khamerenebty II
|
Queen Khentkawas
= Pharaoh Userkaf
|
Pharaoh Neferirkare
|
Pharaoh Shepsekare
|
Pharaoh Neferefre
|
Pharaoh Niuserre
|
Pharaoh Menkauhor
|
Pharaoh Djedkare
|
Pharaoh Unas the Vampire 2375-45 BC
(The Pyramid Texts)
|
Queen Iput
= Pharaoh Teti
|
Pharaoh Pepi I
= Queen Ankhnesmerire
|
Pharaoh Pepi II
= Queen Neith
|

Pharaoh Merenre II 2184-81 BC
= Queen Nitoctris
|
Prince Ankhfn-Khonsu
Re-established the Royal
Dragon Court in Egypt
|
Prince Intef I (The Great)
Governor of Thebes
|
Prince Intef II
|
Prince Intef III
|
Pharaoh Mentuhotep I (The Coffin Texts)
= Queen Tem
|
Pharaoh Mentuhotep II
|
Pharaoh Mentuhotep III
|
Queen Tohwait
= Pharaoh Amenhemet
|
Pharaoh Senusret I
= Princess Sarah, d. of Queen Tohwait
(later wife of Abraham)
|
Pharaoh Amenhemet II
-= Queen Keminebu
|
Pharaoh Senusret II
= Queen Nofret
|
Pharaoh Senusret III
= Queen Mereret
|
Pharaoh Amenhemet III
= Queen Aat
|
Pharaoh Amenhemet IV
= Sobeknefru, The Great Dragon Queen of Egypt
(Ratified the Royal Dragon Court)
|
Daughter
= Pharaoh Wegaf

13th Dynasty of Egypt
The Dragon Kings and Queens of
the God Sobekh

Pharaoh Wegaf
|
Pharaoh Ameny Intef c. 1700 BC
|
Pharaoh Sobekhotep III
|
Pharaoh Sobekhotep IV
|

Daughter
= Pharaoh Sobekemsaf
|
Pharaoh Intef VII
|
Daughter
= King Khayan (The Good God)
Dragon King of the Hyksos who
descend from Queen Towait (above)
|
Apepi I
Dragon King of the Hyksos
|
Apepi II
(Apophis the Evil)
|
Senisonb (Dragon Queen)
|
Pharaoh Tuthmosis I
= Queen Mutneferte (Dragon Queen)
|
Pharaoh Tuthmosis II
= Iset
|
Pharaoh Tuthmosis III
(Founded the Rosi-crucis
Therapeutate at Karnak)
= Queen Neferue
|
The Dragon Queen Tio
= Pharaoh Amenhotep II
|
Pharaoh Tuthmosis IV
= Queen Mutemwiya
|
Pharaoh Amenhotep III
= Gilukhipa, Dragon Queen
of the Mitanni
|
Merykhipa (Kiya)
Dragon Queen
= Pharaoh Amenhotep IV
|
Queen Kiya Tasherit 1361 BC
=Prince Rama, descendant of Satan,
Abraham and the Pharaoh Sensuret I
(see above).
Here the direct and unbroken
lines of Satanic descent conjoin
|
Amminadab
|
Nahshon
|
Salma
= Rahab
|
Boaz
|

Obed
|
Jesse
|
The House of David

King David of Israel
=Queen Bath-Sheba
of the Hittites
(Descent from the Hurrians or Aryans)
|
King Solomon, Lord of the Rings
= Sheba Lilith (Venus) his sister
|
King Rehoboam
|
King Abijah
|
King Asa
|
King Jehoshephat
|
King Joram
|
King Azariah
|
King Jotham
|
King Ahaz
|
King Hezekiah
King of Judah 726 BC
= Princess Hephzibah
|
King Mannaseh
King of Judah 697 BC
= Princess Meshullemeth
dau of Haruz of Jotbah
|
King Amon
King of Judah 642 BC
= Princess Jedidah
dau. of Adaiah of Boscath
|
King Josiah
King of Judah 640 BC
= 2. Princess Hamutal
dau. of Jeremiah of Libnah
|
King Zedekiah
King of Judah 598 BC
|
Princess Tamar
= King Eochaid I
High King of Ireland after the
displacement of the remnant
of the Tuadha de Danaan
|
King Irial Faidh

King Eithriall
|
King Follain
|
King Tighernmas
|
King Eanbotha
|
King Smiorguil
|
King Fiachach Labhruine
|
King Aongus Oilbughagah
|
King Maoin
|
King Rotheachta
|
King Dein
|
King Siorna Saoghalach
|
King Oiliolla Olchaoin
|
King Nuadha Fionn Fail
|
King Giallchadh
|
King Simon Breac
|
King Muiriadhach Bolgrach
|
King Fiathadh Tolgrach
|
King Duach Laighrach
|
King Eochaidh Buillaig
|
King Ugaine Mar (The Great)
|
King Cobhtach Caolbreag
|
King Meilage
|
King Jaran Gleofathach
|
King Conla Gruaich
|
King Ceaigach
|
King Oiliolla Caisfhiaclach
|
King Eochaid Foltleathan
|
King Aonghus Tuirimheach
|
King Fiachra Firmara
|

King Feradaig
|
King Fergus I
|
King Maine
(Father of Siadhail: descent to
the O'Shiels of Ireland)
|
King Dornadil
|
King Rowein
|
King Reuther
|
King Eders
|
King Conaire Mor
|
King Admoir
|
King Corbred I
|
King Dare-Dornmoir
|
King Fiachadh
|
King Tuathal Teachtman
|
King Feidhimhioh
|
King Conn of the 100 Battles
|
King Art Aonthir
|
King Cormac Ulfhada Mac Art
|
King Cairbre Liffeachaire
|
King Fiachadh Streabhthuine
|
King Waegdaeg
|
King Sigegart
|
King Saebaid
|
King Siggoth
|
King Saebaid
|
King Saefugel
|
King Sudrtha
|
King Soemil
|
King Westers
|
King Wilgils

King Wyse Frea
|
King Yffe
|
King Aelle of Deira (Northumbria)
559 AD – 588 AD
|
Princess Atha of Berenicia
= King Cadfan of Gwynnedd
625 AD
|
King Cadwallon II of Gwynnedd d. 634
= Princess Helen, granddaughter of Crida
Chief of the Angles
|
King Cadwalladr Pendragon the Blessed 654-664
The last Pendragon of Britain
|
King Edwal of Gwynnedd
|
King Rhodri Molwynog 754 AD
|
King Cinan Tindaethwy 754-816
|
King Gwynnedd
|
Queen Esylth
|
King Merfyn Vrych
|
King Rhodri Mawr (The Great)
of Gwynnedd (North Wales) and
Deheubarth (South Wales)
844-878
= Princess Angharad
|
King Cadell
|
King Hywel Dda
= Princess Elen
|
Prince Owain
|
Prince Einon
|
Prince Cadell
|
Prince Tewdwr
|
King Rhys Ap Tudor of
Deheubarth (South Wales)
|
Princess Nesta of Deheubarth
= King Henry I of England
(
)
(
)

Lord Herbert Fitzroy Earl of Gloucester
=Lady Mabel dau. of Lord
Robert Fitzhamon, Lord of Corbiel
|
William Fitz Robert Earl of Gloucester
= dau. of Lord Robert Beaumont
Earl of Leicester
|
Lady Amicia Fitz Robert
= Lord Richard de Clare Earl of Hertford
|
Robert De Clare Earl of Gloucester
= Lady Isabel dau. of William Marshall
Earl of Pembrokeshire
|
Lord de Clare Earl of Gloucester
= Lady Mathilda dau. of
John de Lacy Earl of Lincoln
|
Lord Gilbert de Clare
Earl of Gloucester
= Princess Joan Plantagenet
|
Lady Elizabeth de Clare
= Sir Roger D'Amorie
|
Elizabeth D'Amorie
= John Lord Bardolf
|
William Lord Bardolf
= Agnes Poynings
|
Cecilia Bardolf
= Sir Bryan Stapylton
|
Sir Miles Stapylton
= Katherine de la Pole
g. granddaughter of
Geoffrey Chaucer
|
Elizabeth Stapylton
= Sir William Calthorpe
|
Ann Calthorpe
= Sir Robert Drury
|
Anne Drury
= George Waldegrave
|
Sir William Waldegrave
= Juliana Rainsford
|
Sir William Waldegrave II
= Elizabeth Middlemay
|
Mary Waldegrave
= Thomas Clopton
|
Walter Clopton of Fordham

=Anne Thornton
|
Roger Clopton
= Elizabeth Boston
|
Elizabeth Clopton
= James Verdon
|
Elizabeth Verdon
= Samuel Clarke
|
Elizabeth Clarke
= Peter Stoughton
|
Elizabeth Stoughton
= Nicholas Cobb Collison
|
John
(
)
(
Esther
= Reuben Avis
|
Lucy Avis
= Edward Hopgood
|
George Collison Hopgood
= Julia Harding of Godalming
|
Natalie Hopgood (descent from

the Collisons of Norfolk and the
Imperial and Royal House of Vere)
= James Weir of Vere
|

HI&RH Prince Nicholas de Vere

Chapter Seventeen

The Nefilim Descent of the House of Collison

The Nephilim Descent of the House of
Collison via the House of Vere
29,628 BC – 2011 AD

The Nephilim were the sons of the Anunnaki Gods and their name as "Nefilim" means "Tree Hewers," "Hewers of Men," and as "Nephilim" their name means "Those who came down." In the Sumerian King Lists it is recorded that the assumption of their Divine Kingship began in Mesopotamia (Iraq) some 31,000 years ago. This time coincides with the demise of the Eljo and Neanderthal races, and the Anunnaki annihilation of the voracious, monstrous Naphidem; sons of those Nephilim who rebelled against the Grand Council of the Anunnaki and bred with human women.

In this respect, acting for the Gods, the Anunnaki sons would have been the hewers or destroyers of men, whilst as the hewers of trees we see them – like their Fairy or Elven descendents - as Lords of the Forests (of Transylvania and Central Europe) practicing early arboriculture, prior to their migration south to Mesopotamia, where there are no forests.

Whilst some commentators have the Nephilim as "Those who came down from Heaven," to the early Mesopotamian inhabitants it might be easier to assume that they meant that the Nephilim were "Those who came down from the north," as their sister Queen Lilith is described as having done. That the Anunnaki themselves came from Heaven is more clearly asserted eslewhere in Sumerian literature, so the foregoing suggestion in no way detracts from the divine or perhaps otherworldly origin of the Anunnaki Gods.

During this period the Cro-Magnon species emerged as a result of genetic hybridisation of the Anunnaki with early Homo Sapiens. In this regard, the Anunnaki Gods are the missing link between early man – the Eljo – and modern Cro-Magnon. No further divine intervention occurred and the Cro-Magnon were left to their own devices and, in the fullness of time kingship was lowered to them by the Gods.

However human kingship was a disaster and was withdrawn by the Anunnaki and invested in their Nephilim sons until 4000 BC. The Nephilim God-Kings left their parents behind in Central Europe – Carpathia, Transylvania and the Bosphorus – and assumed control in Mesopotamia until the reign of the Nephilim King Ubartutu of Shuruppak. King Ubartutu's son King Ziu Sudra left Mesopotamia and reigned in the northern regions of Anatolia (modern Turkey) in 4508 BC, with his centre on the banks of the Black Sea basin, until the Great Flood (the original Biblical inundation) of 4500 BC.

Contrary to the Genesis myth, Adam – The Priest-King Attaba of Kish – was created after the Flood, in 3882 BC, not before. From Adam there are eight recorded generations to Noah who, if he had existed, would have lived 200 years afterwards in the year 3682 BC, which is 818 years after the Biblical Black Sea Flood and 318 years after the Mesopotamian Flood.

The Nephilim Kings of Mesopotamia

King Allulim of Eridu
29, 628 BC
Dynasty descends
|
|
King Alagar of Eridu
Dynasty descends
26,618 BC
|
|
King Enmenluanna of Badtibira
Dynasty descends
23,608 BC
|
|
King Enmengalanna of Badtibira
Dynasty descends
20,598 BC
|
|
King Dumuzi of Badtibira
Dynasty descends
17,598
|
|
King Ensipazianna of Larak
Dynasty descends
14,578
|
|
King Enmenduranna of Sippar

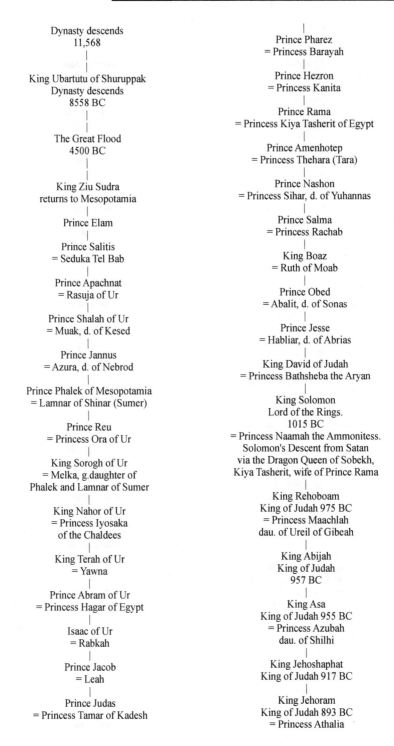

Dynasty descends
11,568
|
King Ubartutu of Shuruppak
Dynasty descends
8558 BC
|
The Great Flood
4500 BC
|
King Ziu Sudra
returns to Mesopotamia
|
Prince Elam
|
Prince Salitis
= Seduka Tel Bab
|
Prince Apachnat
= Rasuja of Ur
|
Prince Shalah of Ur
= Muak, d. of Kesed
|
Prince Jannus
= Azura, d. of Nebrod
|
Prince Phalek of Mesopotamia
= Lamnar of Shinar (Sumer)
|
Prince Reu
= Princess Ora of Ur
|
King Sorogh of Ur
= Melka, g.daughter of
Phalek and Lamnar of Sumer
|
King Nahor of Ur
= Princess Iyosaka
of the Chaldees
|
King Terah of Ur
= Yawna
|
Prince Abram of Ur
= Princess Hagar of Egypt
|
Isaac of Ur
= Rabkah
|
Prince Jacob
= Leah
|
Prince Judas
= Princess Tamar of Kadesh

Prince Pharez
= Princess Barayah
|
Prince Hezron
= Princess Kanita
|
Prince Rama
= Princess Kiya Tasherit of Egypt
|
Prince Amenhotep
= Princess Thehara (Tara)
|
Prince Nashon
= Princess Sihar, d. of Yuhannas
|
Prince Salma
= Princess Rachab
|
King Boaz
= Ruth of Moab
|
Prince Obed
= Abalit, d. of Sonas
|
Prince Jesse
= Habliar, d. of Abrias
|
King David of Judah
= Princess Bathsheba the Aryan
|
King Solomon
Lord of the Rings.
1015 BC
= Princess Naamah the Ammonitess.
Solomon's Descent from Satan
via the Dragon Queen of Sobekh,
Kiya Tasherit, wife of Prince Rama
|
King Rehoboam
King of Judah 975 BC
= Princess Maachlah
dau. of Ureil of Gibeah
|
King Abijah
King of Judah
957 BC
|
King Asa
King of Judah 955 BC
= Princess Azubah
dau. of Shilhi
|
King Jehoshaphat
King of Judah 917 BC
|
King Jehoram
King of Judah 893 BC
= Princess Athalia

dau. of Omri
|
King Ahaziah
King of Judah 885 BC
= Princess Zibiah of Beersheba
|
King Joash
King of Judah 878 BC
Princess Jehoaddan of Jerusalem
|
King Amaziah
King of Judah 840 BC
= Princess Jecoliah of Jerusalem
|
King Uzziah
King of Judah 811 BC
= Princess Jerushah
da. Of Zadok
|
King Jotham
King of Judah 759 BC
|
King Ahaz
King of Judah 742 BC
Princess Abijah
dau of Zechariah
|
King Hezekiah
King of Judah 726 BC
= Princess Hephzibah
|
King Mannaseh
King of Judah 697 BC
= Princess Meshullemeth
dau of Haruz of Jotbah
|
King Amon
King of Judah 642 BC
= Princess Jedidah
dau. of Adaiah of Boscath
|
King Josiah
King of Judah 640 BC
|
King Jehoiakim
King of Judah 609 BC
(Taken Hostage to Babylon)
= Princess Nehushtah
dau. of Elnathan of Judaea
|
King Jechoniah
King of Judah 598 BC
(Taken hostage to Babylon)
|
Prince Shealtiel
|
Prince Pedaiah
|
Prince Zerrubabel

De jure King
of Judah
|
Prince Rhesa
|
Prince Johanan
|
Prince Judah
|
Prince Joseph
|
Prince Semei
|
Prince Mattathias
|
Prince Maath
|
Prince Naage
|
Prince Azallah
|
Prince Nahum
|
Prince Amos
|
Prince Mattathias
|
Prince Joseph
|
Prince Johanan
|
Prince Melchi
|
Prince Levi
|
Prince Matthat
|
Prince Jacob
|
Prince Joseph
|
Jesus Christ The Messiah
(Messach: Anointed of the God Sobekh)
(Yehoshua ben-Joseph, [called ben-Panther])
= Mary Magdalene, Priestess of Ishtar (Venus)

|

Descent to the Fisher Kings of the Grail,
the Merovingian Sorcerer Kings and
the Imperial and Royal House of Vere

|

Jesus and Mary's son - Joseph Ha Rama Theo
|
Josue Del Graal
|
Aminadab

= Eurgis d. of King Coel I
sister of Lucius the Great
|
Catheloys
|
Manael
|
Titurel
|
Boaz
(Anfortas)
|
Frotmund
(Frimutel)
|
Faramund 420 AD
Sire of the French Monarchy
= Argotta dau. of Genebaud
of the Sicambrian Franks
|
Clodian of Tournai
= Queen Basina of Thuringia
|
King Meroveus, founder of
the Dynasty of Merovingian
Sorcerer Kings d. 456 AD
= Princess Meira
|
King Childeric of the Franks d. 481 AD
= Queen Basina II of Thuringia
|
King Clovis of the Franks d. 511 AD
= Clotilde of Burgundy
|
King Lothar I d. 561 AD
|
Princess Blitildis
= Prince Ansbert, Great Great Grandson of
King Clodian of Tournai (above) d. 570 AD
|
Lord Arnoald of Scheldt
= Princess Dua of Swabia
|
Arnulf of Metz
= Princess Dobo of Saxony
|
Lord Ansegis of Brabant (Lower Lorraine)
Margrave of Scheldt d. 685
= Lady Begga, dau of Pepin I, Mayor of Austrasia
|
Lord Pepin II of Heristal, Mayor of the Palaces of
Austrasia, Neustria and Burgundy d. 714
= Lady Alpas
|
Lord Charles Martel (The Hammer) d. 741
|
Pepin the III Brevis, Duke of Lower Lorraine
(Brabant)
Mayor of Neustrasia, King of the Franks

= Lady Leuthergis
|
Princess Bertha
= Prince Milo de Vere, Duke of Angiers
Count of Anjou (son of the Fairy Princess Melusine
I
of the Scythians: parallel descent from Satan via the
Egyptian Kings as above)
|
Prince Milo II de Vere, Count of Guisnes and Anjou
= Lady Aveline de Nantes
|
Prince Nicassius de Vere, Count of Guisnes and
Anjou
Lady Agatha de Champagne
|
Prince Otho de Vere, Count of Guisnes
= Lady Constance de Chartres
|
Prince Amelius (Adolph) de Vere
= Lady Maud de Ponthieu
|
Prince Gallus (Guy) de Vere, Count of Guisnes
= Lady Gertrude de Clermont de Ponthieu
|
Prince Baldwin de Vere
= Adele de Ghent
|
Prince Eustace de Vere
= Lady Maud de Lovain
|
Princess Ida de Vere
= Baudouin de Bourg
Comte de Rethul
(Merovingian descent from
Satan via Charlemagne)
|
Prince Hugues I
Comte de Rethul
= Melisende (Melusine II)
dau. Of Bouchard Comte de Corbeil and
Lady Adelaide de Crecy
|
Badouin II de Bourg
King of Jerusalem 1118 – 1131
= Princess Morfia of Armenia
|
Princess Melisende of Jerusalem (Melusine III)
= Fulke V Plantagenet Count of Anjou
(Descent from Melusine I's sister Princess Plantina,
mother of Lord Tortulf de Nide de Merle)
|
Count Geoffrey Plantagenet of Anjou
= Princess Mathilda of England la Imperatrice
(Empress of England)
|
King Henry II Plantagenet
= Countess Eleanor of Aquitaine
|

King John "Lackland" Plantagenet
= Lady Isabella of Angouleme
|
King Henry III Plantagenet
= Lady Eleanor dau. of Count
Raymond Berenguer IVof Provence
and Princess Beatrix of Savoy
|
King Edward I Plantagenet
= Princess Eleanor of Castille
|
King Edward II Plantagenet
= Princess Isabella of France
|
Princess Joan Plantagenet
= Gilbert de Clare
Earl of Gloucester
|
Lady Elizabeth de Clare
= Sir Roger D'Amorie
|
Elizabeth D'Amorie
= John Lord Bardolf
|
William Lord Bardolf
= Agnes Poynings
|
Lady Cecilia Bardolf
= Sir Bryan Stapylton
|
Sir Miles Stapylton
= Katherine de la Pole
g. granddaughter of
Geoffrey Chaucer
|
Elizabeth Stapylton
= Sir William Calthorpe
|
Ann Calthorpe
= Sir Robert Drury
|
Anne Drury
= George Waldegrave
|
Sir William Waldegrave
= Juliana Rainsford
|
Sir William Waldegrave II
= Elizabeth Middlemay
|
Mary Waldegrave
= Thomas Clopton
|
Walter Clopton of Fordham
=Anne Thornton
|
Roger Clopton
= Elizabeth Boston
|

Elizabeth Clopton
= James Verdon
|
Elizabeth Verdon
= Samuel Clarke
|
Elizabeth Clarke
= Peter Stoughton
|
Elizabeth Stoughton
= Nicholas Cobb Collison
|
John Collison
|
Genetically
Confirmed
|
Esther Collison
= Reuben Avis
|
Lucy Avis
= Edward Hopgood
|
George Collison Hopgood
= Julia Harding
|
Natalie Hopgood, (descent through her father
from the Collisons of Norfolk, the Plantagenet
Kings and the Imperial and Royal House of Vere.
Descent through her mother from Lt. Col
George Butcher of Windsor Castle, Sarah Butcher
of Framlingham and the Huegenot Bourchier
Counts of Versailles, France)
=James Weir of Vere
|
HI&RH Prince Nicholas de Vere

The Nephilim Descent of the House of Collison via King Meroveus 29,628 BC – 2011 AD

The Nephilim Kings of Mesopotamia

King Allulim of Eridu
29,628 BC
Dynasty descends
|
King Alagar of Eridu
Dynasty descends
26,618 BC
|
King Enmenluanna of Badtibira
Dynasty descends
23,608 BC

King Enmengalanna of Badtibira
Dynasty descends
20,598 BC

King Dumuzi of Badtibira
Dynasty descends
17,598

King Ensipazianna of Larak
Dynasty descends
14,578

King Enmenduranna of Sippar
Dynasty descends
11,568

King Ubartutu of Shuruppak
Dynasty descends
8558 BC

The Great Flood
4500 BC

King Ziu Sudra
returns to Mesopotamia

Prince Elam

Prince Salitis
= Seduka Tel Bab

Prince Apachnat
= Rasuja of Ur

Prince Shalah of Ur
= Muak, d. of Kesed

Prince Jannus
= Azura, d. of Nebrod

Prince Phalek of Mesopotamia
= Lamnar of Shinar (Sumer)

Prince Reu
= Princess Ora of Ur

King Sorogh of Ur
= Melka, g.daughter of
Phalek and Lamnar of Sumer

King Nahor of Ur

= Princess Iyosaka
of the Chaldees

King Terah of Ur
= Yawna

Prince Abram of Ur
= Princess Hagar of Egypt

Isaac of Ur
= Rabkah

Prince Jacob
= Leah

Prince Judas
= Princess Tamar of Kadesh

Prince Pharez
= Princess Barayah

Prince Hezron
= Princess Kanita

Prince Rama
= Princess Kiya Tasherit of Egypt

Prince Amenhotep
= Princess Thehara (Tara)

Prince Nashon
= Princess Sihar, d. of Yuhannas

Prince Salma
= Princess Rachab

King Boaz
= Ruth of Moab

Prince Obed
= Abalit, d. of Sonas

Prince Jesse
= Habliar, d. of Abrias

King David of Judah
= Princess Bathsheba the Aryan

King Solomon
Lord of the Rings.
1015 BC
= Princess Naamah the Ammonitess.
Solomon's Descent from Satan
via the Dragon Queen of Sobekh,
Kiya Tasherit, wife of Prince Rama

King Rehoboam
King of Judah 975 BC
= Princess Maachlah

dau. of Ureil of Gibeah
|
King Abijah
King of Judah
957 BC
|
King Asa
King of Judah 955 BC
= Princess Azubah
dau. of Shilhi
|
King Jehoshaphat
King of Judah 917 BC
|
King Jehoram
King of Judah 893 BC
= Princess Athalia
dau. of Omri
|
King Ahaziah
King of Judah 885 BC
= Princess Zibiah of Beersheba
|
King Joash
King of Judah 878 BC
Princess Jehoaddan of Jerusalem
|
King Amaziah
King of Judah 840 BC
= Princess Jecoliah of Jerusalem
|
King Uzziah
King of Judah 811 BC
= Princess Jerushah
da. Of Zadok
|
King Jotham
King of Judah 759 BC
|
King Ahaz
King of Judah 742 BC
Princess Abijah
dau of Zechariah
|
King Hezekiah
King of Judah 726 BC
= Princess Hephzibah
|
King Mannaseh
King of Judah 697 BC
= Princess Meshullemeth
dau of Haruz of Jotbah
|
King Amon
King of Judah 642 BC
= Princess Jedidah
dau. of Adaiah of Boscath
|
King Josiah

King of Judah 640 BC
|
King Jehoiakim
King of Judah 609 BC
(Taken Hostage to Babylon)
= Princess Nehushtah
dau. of Elnathan of Judaea
|
King Jechoniah
King of Judah 598 BC
(Taken hostage to Babylon)
|
Prince Shealtiel
|
Prince Pedaiah
|
Prince Zerrubabel
De jure King
of Judah
|
Prince Rhesa
|
Prince Johanan
|
Prince Judah
|
Prince Joseph
|
Prince Semei
|
Prince Mattathias
|
Prince Maath
|
Prince Naage
|
Prince Azallah
|
Prince Nahum
|
Prince Amos
|
Prince Mattathias
|
Prince Joseph
|
Prince Johanan
|
Prince Melchi
|
Prince Levi
|
Prince Matthat
|
Prince Jacob
|
Prince Joseph
|
Jesus Christ The Messiah

(Messach: Anointed of the God Sobekh)
(Yehoshua ben-Joseph, [called ben-Panther])
= Mary Magdalene, Priestess of Ishtar (Venus)

|

Descent to the Fisher Kings of the Grail,
the Merovingian Sorcerer Kings and
the Imperial and Royal House of Vere

|

Jesus and Mary's son - Joseph Ha Rama Theo

|

Josue Del Graal

|

Aminadab
= Eurgis d. of King Coel I
sister of Lucius the Great

|

Catheloys

|

Manael

|

Titurel

|

Boaz
(Anfortas)

|

Frotmund
(Frimutel)

|

Faramund 420 AD
Sire of the French Monarchy
= Argotta dau. of Genebaud
of the Sicambrian Franks

|

Clodian of Tournai
= Queen Basina of Thuringia

|

King Meroveus, founder of
the Dynasty of Merovingian
Sorcerer Kings d. 456 AD
= Princess Meira

|

King Childeric of the Franks d. 481 AD
= Queen Basina II of Thuringia

|

King Clovis of the Franks d. 511 AD
= Clotilde of Burgundy

|

King Lothar I d. 561 AD

|

Princess Blitildis
= Prince Ansbert, Great Great Grandson of
King Clodian of Tournai (above) d. 570 AD

|

Lord Arnoald of Scheldt
= Princess Dua of Swabia

|

Arnulf of Metz
= Princess Dobo of Saxony

|

Lord Ansegis of Brabant (Lower Lorraine)
Margrave of Scheldt d. 685
= Lady Begga, dau of Pepin I, Mayor of Austrasia

|

Lord Pepin II of Heristal, Mayor of the Palaces of
Austrasia, Neustria and Burgundy d. 714
= Lady Alpas

|

Lord Charles Martel (The Hammer) d. 741

|

Pepin the III Brevis, Duke of Lower Lorraine
(Brabant)
Mayor of Neustrasia, King of the Franks
= Lady Leuthergis

|

Princess Bertha
= Prince Milo de Vere, Duke of Angiers
Count of Anjou (son of the Fairy Princess Melusine
I
of the Scythians: parallel descent from Satan via the
Egyptian Kings as above)

|

Prince Milo II de Vere, Count of Guisnes and Anjou
= Lady Aveline de Nantes

|

Prince Nicassius de Vere, Count of Guisnes and
Anjou
Lady Agatha de Champagne

|

Prince Otho de Vere, Count of Guisnes
= Lady Constance de Chartres

Prince Amelius (Adolph) de Vere
= Lady Maud de Ponthieu

|

Prince Gallus (Guy) de Vere, Count of Guisnes
= Lady Gertrude de Clermont de Ponthieu

|

Prince Baldwin de Vere
= Adele de Ghent

|

Prince Eustace de Vere
= Lady Maud de Lovain

|

Princess Ida de Vere
= Baudouin de Bourg
Comte de Rethul
(Merovingian descent from
Satan via Charlemagne)

|

Prince Hugues I
Comte de Rethul
= Melisende (Melusine II)
dau. Of Bouchard Comte de Corbeil and
Lady Adelaide de Crecy

|
Badouin II de Bourg
King of Jerusalem 1118 – 1131
= Princess Morfia of Armenia
|
Princess Melisende of Jerusalem (Melusine III)
= Fulke V Plantagenet Count of Anjou
(Descent from Melusine I's sister Princess Plantina,
mother of Lord Tortulf de Nide de Merle)
|
Count Geoffrey Plantagenet of Anjou
= Princess Mathilda of England la Imperatrice
(Empress of England)
|
King Henry II Plantagenet
= Countess Eleanor of Aquitaine
|
King John 'Lackland' Plantagenet
= Lady Isabella of Angouleme
|
King Henry III Plantagenet
= Lady Eleanor dau. of Count
Raymond Berenguer IVof Provence
and Princess Beatrix of Savoy
|
King Edward I Plantagenet
= Princess Eleanor of Castille
|
King Edward II Plantagenet
= Princess Isabella of France
|
Princess Joan Plantagenet
= Gilbert de Clare
Earl of Gloucester
|
Lady Elizabeth de Clare
= Sir Roger D'Amorie
|
Elizabeth D'Amorie
= John Lord Bardolf
|
William Lord Bardolf
= Agnes Poynings
|
Lady Cecilia Bardolf
= Sir Bryan Stapylton
|
Sir Miles Stapylton
= Katherine de la Pole
g. granddaughter of
Geoffrey Chaucer
|
Elizabeth Stapylton
= Sir William Calthorpe
|
Ann Calthorpe
= Sir Robert Drury
|
Anne Drury

= George Waldegrave
|
Sir William Waldegrave
= Juliana Rainsford
|
Sir William Waldegrave II
= Elizabeth Middlemay
|
Mary Waldegrave
= Thomas Clopton
|
Walter Clopton of Fordham
=Anne Thornton
|
Roger Clopton
= Elizabeth Boston
|
Elizabeth Clopton
= James Verdon
|
Elizabeth Verdon
= Samuel Clarke
|
Elizabeth Clarke
= Peter Stoughton
|
Elizabeth Stoughton
= Nicholas Cobb Collison
|
John Collison
|
Genetically
Confirmed
|
Esther Collison
= Reuben Avis
|
Lucy Avis
= Edward Hopgood
|
George Collison Hopgood
= Julia Harding
|
Natalie Hopgood, (descent through her father
from the Collisons of Norfolk, the Plantagenet
Kings and the Imperial and Royal House of Vere.
Descent through her mother from Lt. Col
George Butcher of Windsor Castle, Sarah Butcher
of Framlingham and the Huegenot Bourchier
Counts of Versailles, France)
=James Weir of Vere
|
HI&RH Prince Nicholas de Vere

The Nephilim Descent of the House of Collison via Prince Milo de Vere 29,628 BC – 2011 AD

The Nephilim Kings of Mesopotamia

King Allulim of Eridu
29, 628 BC
Dynasty descends

|

King Alagar of Eridu
Dynasty descends
26,618 BC

|

King Enmenluanna of Badtibira
Dynasty descends
23,608 BC

|

King Enmengalanna of Badtibira
Dynasty descends
20,598 BC

|

King Dumuzi of Badtibira
Dynasty descends
17,598

|

King Ensipazianna of Larak
Dynasty descends
14,578

|

King Enmenduranna of Sippar
Dynasty descends
11,568

|

King Ubartutu of Shuruppak
Dynasty descends
8558 BC

|

The Great Flood
4500 BC

|

King Ziu Sudra
returns to Mesopotamia

|

Prince Elam

|

Prince Salitis

= Seduka Tel Bab
|
Prince Apachnat
= Rasuja of Ur
|
Prince Shalah of Ur
= Muak, d. of Kesed
|
Prince Jannus
= Azura, d. of Nebrod
|
Prince Phalek of Mesopotamia
= Lamnar of Shinar (Sumer)
|
Prince Reu
= Princess Ora of Ur
|
King Sorogh of Ur
= Melka, g.daughter of
Phalek and Lamnar of Sumer
|
King Nahor of Ur
= Princess Iyosaka
of the Chaldees
|
King Terah of Ur
= Yawna
|
Prince Abram of Ur
= Princess Hagar of Egypt
|
Isaac of Ur
= Rabkah
|
Prince Jacob
= Leah
|
Prince Judas
= Princess Tamar of Kadesh
|
Prince Pharez
= Princess Barayah
|
Prince Hezron
= Princess Kanita
|
Prince Rama
= Princess Kiya Tasherit of Egypt
|
Prince Amenhotep
= Princess Thehara (Tara)
|
Prince Nashon
= Princess Sihar, d. of Yuhannas
|
Prince Salma
= Princess Rachab
|
King Boaz

= Ruth of Moab
|
Prince Obed
= Abalit, d. of Sonas
|
Prince Jesse
= Habliar, d. of Abrias
|
King David of Judah
= Princess Bathsheba the Aryan
|
King Solomon
Lord of the Rings
1015 BC
= Princess Naamah the Ammonitess.
Solomon's Descent from Satan
via the Dragon Queen of Sobekh,
Kiya Tasherit, wife of Prince Rama
|
King Rehoboam
King of Judah 975 BC
= Princess Maachlah
dau. of Ureil of Gibeah
|
King Abijah
King of Judah
957 BC
|
King Asa
King of Judah 955 BC
= Princess Azubah
dau. of Shilhi
|
King Jehoshaphat
King of Judah 917 BC
|
King Jehoram
King of Judah 893 BC
= Princess Athalia
dau. of Omri
|
King Ahaziah
King of Judah 885 BC
= Princess Zibiah of Beersheba
|
King Joash
King of Judah 878 BC
Princess Jehoaddan of Jerusalem
|
King Amaziah
King of Judah 840 BC
= Princess Jecoliah of Jerusalem
|
King Uzziah
King of Judah 811 BC
= Princess Jerushah
da. Of Zadok
|
King Jotham

King of Judah 759 BC
|
King Ahaz
King of Judah 742 BC
Princess Abijah
dau of Zechariah
|
King Hezekiah
King of Judah 726 BC
= Princess Hephzibah
|
King Mannaseh
King of Judah 697 BC
= Princess Meshullemeth
dau of Haruz of Jotbah
|
King Amon
King of Judah 642 BC
= Princess Jedidah
dau. of Adaiah of Boscath
|
King Josiah
King of Judah 640 BC
|
King Jehoiakim
King of Judah 609 BC
(Taken Hostage to Babylon)
= Princess Nehushtah
dau. of Elnathan of Judaea
|
King Jechoniah
King of Judah 598 BC
(Taken hostage to Babylon)
|
Prince Shealtiel
|
Prince Pedaiah
|
Prince Zerrubabel
De jure King
of Judah
|
Prince Rhesa
|
Prince Johanan
|
Prince Judah
|
Prince Joseph
|
Prince Semei
|
Prince Mattathias
|
Prince Maath
|
Prince Naage
|
Prince Azallah

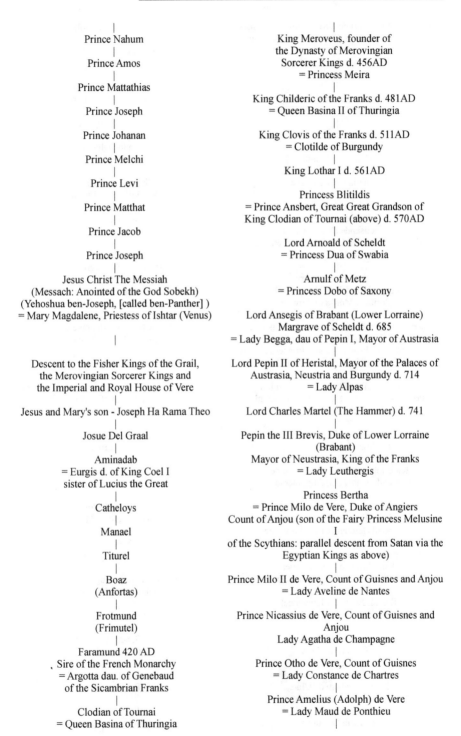

Prince Nahum
|
Prince Amos
|
Prince Mattathias
|
Prince Joseph
|
Prince Johanan
|
Prince Melchi
|
Prince Levi
|
Prince Matthat
|
Prince Jacob
|
Prince Joseph
|
Jesus Christ The Messiah
(Messach: Anointed of the God Sobekh)
(Yehoshua ben-Joseph, [called ben-Panther])
= Mary Magdalene, Priestess of Ishtar (Venus)

|

Descent to the Fisher Kings of the Grail,
the Merovingian Sorcerer Kings and
the Imperial and Royal House of Vere
|
Jesus and Mary's son - Joseph Ha Rama Theo
|
Josue Del Graal
|
Aminadab
= Eurgis d. of King Coel I
sister of Lucius the Great
|
Catheloys
|
Manael
|
Titurel
|
Boaz
(Anfortas)
|
Frotmund
(Frimutel)
|
Faramund 420 AD
, Sire of the French Monarchy
= Argotta dau. of Genebaud
of the Sicambrian Franks
|
Clodian of Tournai
= Queen Basina of Thuringia

|
King Meroveus, founder of
the Dynasty of Merovingian
Sorcerer Kings d. 456AD
= Princess Meira
|
King Childeric of the Franks d. 481AD
= Queen Basina II of Thuringia
|
King Clovis of the Franks d. 511AD
= Clotilde of Burgundy
|
King Lothar I d. 561AD
|
Princess Blitildis
= Prince Ansbert, Great Great Grandson of
King Clodian of Tournai (above) d. 570AD
|
Lord Arnoald of Scheldt
= Princess Dua of Swabia
|
Arnulf of Metz
= Princess Dobo of Saxony
|
Lord Ansegis of Brabant (Lower Lorraine)
Margrave of Scheldt d. 685
= Lady Begga, dau of Pepin I, Mayor of Austrasia
|
Lord Pepin II of Heristal, Mayor of the Palaces of
Austrasia, Neustria and Burgundy d. 714
= Lady Alpas
|
Lord Charles Martel (The Hammer) d. 741
|
Pepin the III Brevis, Duke of Lower Lorraine
(Brabant)
Mayor of Neustrasia, King of the Franks
= Lady Leuthergis
|
Princess Bertha
= Prince Milo de Vere, Duke of Angiers
Count of Anjou (son of the Fairy Princess Melusine
I
of the Scythians: parallel descent from Satan via the
Egyptian Kings as above)
|
Prince Milo II de Vere, Count of Guisnes and Anjou
= Lady Aveline de Nantes
|
Prince Nicassius de Vere, Count of Guisnes and
Anjou
Lady Agatha de Champagne
|
Prince Otho de Vere, Count of Guisnes
= Lady Constance de Chartres
|
Prince Amelius (Adolph) de Vere
= Lady Maud de Ponthieu
|

Prince Gallus (Guy) de Vere, Count of Guisnes
= Lady Gertrude de Clermont de Ponthieu
|
Prince Baldwin de Vere
= Adele de Ghent
|
Prince Eustace de Vere
= Lady Maud de Lovain
|
Princess Ida de Vere
= Baudouin de Bourg
Comte de Rethul
(Merovingian descent from
Satan via Charlemagne)
|
Prince Hugues I
Comte de Rethul
= Melisende (Melusine II)
dau. Of Bouchard Comte de Corbeil and
Lady Adelaide de Crecy
|
Badouin II de Bourg
King of Jerusalem 1118 – 1131
= Princess Morfia of Armenia
|
Princess Melisende of Jerusalem (Melusine III)
= Fulke V Plantagenet Count of Anjou
(Descent from Melusine I's sister Princess Plantina,
mother of Lord Tortulf de Nide de Merle)
|
Count Geoffrey Plantagenet of Anjou
= Princess Mathilda of England la Imperatrice
(Empress of England)
|
King Henry II Plantagenet
= Countess Eleanor of Aquitaine
|
King John 'Lackland' Plantagenet
= Lady Isabella of Angouleme
|
King Henry III Plantagenet
= Lady Eleanor dau. of Count
Raymond Berenguer IVof Provence
and Princess Beatrix of Savoy
|
King Edward I Plantagenet
= Princess Eleanor of Castille
|
King Edward II Plantagenet
= Princess Isabella of France
|
Princess Joan Plantagenet
= Gilbert de Clare
Earl of Gloucester
|
Lady Elizabeth de Clare
= Sir Roger D'Amorie
|
Elizabeth D'Amorie

= John Lord Bardolf
|
William Lord Bardolf
= Agnes Poynings
|
Lady Cecilia Bardolf
= Sir Bryan Stapylton
|
Sir Miles Stapylton
= Katherine de la Pole
g. granddaughter of
Geoffrey Chaucer
|
Elizabeth Stapylton
= Sir William Calthorpe
|
Ann Calthorpe
= Sir Robert Drury
|
Anne Drury
= George Waldegrave
|
Sir William Waldegrave
= Juliana Rainsford
|
Sir William Waldegrave II
= Elizabeth Middlemay
|
Mary Waldegrave
= Thomas Clopton
|
Walter Clopton of Fordham
=Anne Thornton
|
Roger Clopton
= Elizabeth Boston
|
Elizabeth Clopton
= James Verdon
|
Elizabeth Verdon
= Samuel Clarke
|
Elizabeth Clarke
= Peter Stoughton
|
Elizabeth Stoughton
= Nicholas Cobb Collison
|
John Collison
|
Genetically
Confirmed
|
Esther Collison
= Reuben Avis
|
Lucy Avis
= Edward Hopgood

George Collison Hopgood
= Julia Harding
|
Natalie Hopgood, (descent through her father
from the Collisons of Norfolk, the Plantagenet
Kings and the Imperial and Royal House of Vere.
Descent through her mother from Lt. Col
George Butcher of Windsor Castle, Sarah Butcher
of Framlingham and the Huegenot Bourchier
Counts of Versailles, France)
=James Weir of Vere
|
HI&RH Prince Nicholas de Vere

The Nephilim Descent of the House of Collison from the Kings of Ireland
29,628 BC – 2011 AD

The Nephilim Kings of Mesopotamia

King Allulim of Eridu
29, 628 BC
Dynasty descends
|
King Alagar of Eridu
Dynasty descends
26,618 BC
|
King Enmenluanna of Badtibira
Dynasty descends
23,608 BC
|
King Enmengalanna of Badtibira
Dynasty descends
20,598 BC
|
King Dumuzi of Badtibira
Dynasty descends
17,598
|
King Ensipazianna of Larak
Dynasty descends
14,578
|
King Enmenduranna of Sippar
Dynasty descends
11,568
|

King Ubartutu of Shuruppak
Dynasty descends
8558 BC
|
The Great Flood
4500 BC
|
King Ziu Sudra
returns to Mesopotamia
|
Prince Elam
|
Prince Salitis
= Seduka Tel Bab
|
Prince Apachnat
= Rasuja of Ur
|
Prince Shalah of Ur
= Muak, d. of Kesed
|
Prince Jannus
= Azura, d. of Nebrod
|
Prince Phalek of Mesopotamia
= Lamnar of Shinar (Sumer)
|
Prince Reu
= Princess Ora of Ur
|
King Sorogh of Ur
= Melka, g.daughter of
Phalek and Lamnar of Sumer
|
King Nahor of Ur
= Princess Iyosaka
of the Chaldees
|
King Terah of Ur
= Yawna
|
Prince Abram of Ur
= Princess Hagar of Egypt
|
Isaac of Ur
= Rabkah
|
Prince Jacob
= Leah
|
Prince Judas
= Princess Tamar of Kadesh
|
Prince Pharez
= Princess Barayah
|

Prince Hezron
= Princess Kanita
|
Prince Rama
= Princess Kiya Tasherit of Egypt
|
Prince Amenhotep
= Princess Thehara (Tara)
|
Prince Nashon
= Princess Sihar, d. of Yuhannas
|
Prince Salma
= Princess Rachab
|
King Boaz
= Ruth of Moab
|
Prince Obed
= Abalit, d. of Sonas
|
Prince Jesse
= Habliar, d. of Abrias
|
King David of Judah
= Princess Bathsheba the Aryan
|
King Solomon
Lord of the Rings.
1015 BC
= Princess Naamah the Ammonitess.
(King Solomon descends from "Satan"
via the Egyptian Dragon Queen of Sobekh,
Queen Kiya Tasherit, wife of Prince Rama)
|
King Rehoboam
King of Judah 975 BC
= Princess Maachlah
dau. of Ureil of Gibeah
|
King Abijah
King of Judah
957 BC
|
King Asa
King of Judah 955 BC
= Princess Azubah
dau. of Shilhi
|
King Jehoshaphat
King of Judah 917 BC
|
King Jehoram
King of Judah 893 BC
= Princess Athalia
dau. of Omri
|
King Ahaziah

King of Judah 885 BC
= Princess Zibiah of Beersheba
|
King Joash
King of Judah 878 BC
= Princess Jehoaddan of Jerusalem
|
King Amaziah
King of Judah 840 BC
= Princess Jecoliah of Jerusalem
|
King Uzziah
King of Judah 811 BC
= Princess Jerushah
da. Of Zadok
|
King Jotham
King of Judah 759 BC
|
King Ahaz
King of Judah 742 BC
= Princess Abijah
dau of Zechariah
|
King Hezekiah
King of Judah 726 BC
= Princess Hephzibah
|
King Mannaseh
King of Judah 697 BC
= Princess Meshullemeth
dau of Haruz of Jotbah
|
King Amon
King of Judah 642 BC
= Princess Jedidah
dau. of Adaiah of Boscath
|
King Josiah
King of Judah 640 BC
= 2. Princess Hamutal
dau. of Jeremiah of Libnah
|
King Zedekiah
King of Judah 598 BC
|
Princess Tamar of Judah
= King Eochaid I The Milesian.
High King of Ireland after the
displacement of the remnant
of the Tuadha de Danaan
|
King Irial Faidh
|
King Eithriall
|
King Follain
|

King Tighernmas
|
King Eanbotha
|
King Smiorguil
|
King Fiachach Labhruine
|
King Aongus Oilbughagah
|
King Maoin
|
King Rotheachta
|
King Dein
|
King Siorna Saoghalach
|
King Oiliolla Olchaoin
|
King Nuadha Fionn Fail
|
King Giallchadh
|
King Simon Breac
|
King Muiriadhach Bolgrach
|
King Fiathadh Tolgrach
|
King Duach Laighrach
|
King Eochaidh Buillaig
|
King Ugaine Mar (The Great)
|
King Cobhtach Caolbreag
|
King Meilage
|
King Jaran Gleofathach
|
King Conla Gruaich
|
King Ceaigach
|
King Oiliolla Caisfhiaclach
|
King Eochaid Foltleathan
|
King Aonghus Tuirimheach
|
King Fiachra Firmara
|
King Feradaig
|
King Fergus I
|
King Maine

(Father of Prince Siadhail, descent to
the Ua Siadhails or O'Shiels of Ireland)

King Dornadil
|
King Rowein
|
King Reuther
|
King Eders
|
King Conaire Mor
|
King Admoir
|
King Corbred I
|
King Dare-Dornmoir
|
King Corbred II
|
King Luigdig-Ellatig
|
King Modha Lamha
|
King Conaire II
= Princess Saraid
(Migration of the Ulster Horse Lords
to Albany/Scotland c. 200 AD)
|
King Corbred of the Dal Riada
|
King Eochaid
|
King Athirco
|
King Findacher
|
King Thrinklind
|
King Romaich
|
King Angus
|
King Eochaid Muin-Remor
|
King Erc, Archdruid of the sacred
Fir Bolg House of the Ulidian
|
King Fergus Mor
d. 501 AD
|
King Domangart
501-506
|
King Gabran
537-559
|
King Aeden MacGabran Pendragon

574-608
|
King Eochaid Buide
608-630
|
King Donald Brecc
630-643
|
King Domangart
|
King Eochaid
695-696
|
King Eochaid
726-733
|
King Aed Find
748-778
|
King Eochaid
781
= Princess Unuisticc of Fortren
|
King Alpin
King of Scots
839-841
|
King Kenneth I MacAlpin
King of Picts and Scots
844-859
|
King Constantine I
863-877
|
King Donald II
889-900
|
King Malcom I
942-954
|
King Kenneth II
971-995
|
King Malcom II MacKenneth
1005-1034
|
Princess Bethoc
= Lord Crinan
Thane of the Isles
k. 1045
|
King Duncan I 1035-1040
|
King Malcom III Canmore
1058-1093
= Saint Margaret dau of
Edward the Exile and
Agatha of Bulgaria
|

Princess Mathilde
= Henry I of England
|
Princess Mathilde la Imperatrice
(Empress of England)
=Geoffrey Plantagenet
|
King Henry II Plantagenet
= Countess Eleanor of Aquitaine
|
King John 'Lackland' Plantagenet
= Lady Isabella of Angouleme
|
King Henry III Plantagenet
= Lady Eleanor dau. of Count
Raymond Berenguer IVof Provence
and Princess Beatrix of Savoy
|
King Edward I Plantagenet
= Princess Eleanor of Castille
|
King Edward II Plantagenet
= Princess Isabella of France
|
Princess Joan Plantagenet
= Gilbert de Clare
Earl of Gloucester
|
Lady Elizabeth de Clare
= Sir Roger D'Amorie
|
Elizabeth D'Amorie
= John Lord Bardolf
|
William Lord Bardolf
= Agnes Poynings
|
Lady Cecilia Bardolf
= Sir Bryan Stapylton
|
Sir Miles Stapylton
= Katherine de la Pole
g. granddaughter of
Geoffrey Chaucer
|
Elizabeth Stapylton
= Sir William Calthorpe
|
Ann Calthorpe
= Sir Robert Drury
|
Anne Drury
= George Waldegrave
|
Sir William Waldegrave
= Juliana Rainsford
|
Sir William Waldegrave II
= Elizabeth Middlemay

Mary Waldegrave
= Thomas Clopton

Walter Clopton of Fordham
=Anne Thornton

Roger Clopton
= Elizabeth Boston

Elizabeth Clopton
= James Verdon

Elizabeth Verdon
= Samuel Clarke

Elizabeth Clarke
= Peter Stoughton

Elizabeth Stoughton
= Nicholas Cobb Collison

John Collison

Genetically
Confirmed

Esther Collison
= Reuben Avis

Lucy Avis
= Edward Hopgood

George Collison Hopgood
= Julia Harding

Natalie Hopgood (descent from
the Collisons of Norfolk and the
Imperial and Royal House of Vere)
=James Weir of Vere

HI&RH Prince Nicholas de Vere

The Nephilim Descent of the House of Collison via the Welsh Kings 29,628 BC – 2011 AD

The Nephilim Kings of Mesopotamia

King Allulim of Eridu
29, 628 BC
Dynasty descends

King Alagar of Eridu
Dynasty descends
26,618 BC

King Enmenluanna of Badtibira
Dynasty descends
23,608 BC

King Enmengalanna of Badtibira
Dynasty descends
20,598 BC

King Dumuzi of Badtibira
Dynasty descends
17,598 BC

King Ensipazianna of Larak
Dynasty descends
14,578 BC

King Enmenduranna of Sippar
Dynasty descends
11,568 BC

King Ubartutu of Shuruppak
Dynasty descends
8558 BC

The Great Flood
4500 BC

King Ziu Sudra
returns to Mesopotamia

Prince Elam

Prince Salitis
= Seduka Tel Bab

Prince Apachnat
= Rasuja of Ur

Prince Shalah of Ur
= Muak, d. of Kesed

Prince Jannus
= Azura, d. of Nebrod

Prince Phalek of Mesopotamia
= Lamnar of Shinar (Sumer)

Prince Reu
= Princess Ora of Ur

King Sorogh of Ur
= Melka, g.daughter of
Phalek and Lamnar of Sumer
|
King Nahor of Ur
= Princess Iyosaka
of the Chaldees
|
King Terah of Ur
= Yawna
|
Prince Abram of Ur
= Princess Hagar of Egypt
|
Isaac of Ur
= Rabkah
|
Prince Jacob
= Leah
|
Prince Judas
= Princess Tamar of Kadesh
|
Prince Pharez
= Princess Barayah
|
Prince Hezron
= Princess Kanita
|
Prince Rama
= Princess Kiya Tasherit of Egypt
|
Prince Amenhotep
= Princess Thehara (Tara)
|
Prince Nashon
= Princess Sihar, d. of Yuhannas
|
Prince Salma
= Princess Rachab
|
King Boaz
= Ruth of Moab
|
Prince Obed
= Abalit, d. of Sonas
|
Prince Jesse
= Habliar, d. of Abrias
|
King David of Judah
= Princess Bathsheba the Aryan
|
King Solomon, Lord of the Rings
= Sheba Lilith (Venus) his sister
|
King Rehoboam
|
King Abijah

|
King Asa
|
King Jehoshephat
|
King Joram
|
King Azariah
|
King Jotham
|
King Ahaz
|
King Hezekiah
King of Judah 726 BC
= Princess Hephzibah
|
King Mannaseh
King of Judah 697 BC
= Princess Meshullemeth
dau of Haruz of Jotbah
|
King Amon
King of Judah 642 BC
= Princess Jedidah
dau. of Adaiah of Boscath
|
King Josiah
King of Judah 640 BC
= 2. Princess Hamutal
dau. of Jeremiah of Libnah
|
King Zedekiah
King of Judah 598 BC
|
Princess Tamar
= King Eochaid I
High King of Ireland after the
displacement of the remnant
of the Tuadha de Danaan
|
Princess Tamar
= King Eochaid I
High King of Ireland after the
displacement of the remnant
of the Tuadha de Danaan
|
King Irial Faidh
|
King Eithriall
|
King Follain
|
King Tighernmas
|
King Eanbotha
|
King Smiorguil

King Fiachach Labhruine
|
King Aongus Oilbughagah
|
King Maoin
|
King Rotheachta
|
King Dein
|
King Siorna Saoghalach
|
King Oiliolla Olchaoin
|
King Nuadha Fionn Fail
|
King Giallchadh
|
King Simon Breac
|
King Muiriadhach Bolgrach
|
King Fiathadh Tolgrach
|
King Duach Laighrach
|
King Eochaidh Buillaig
|
King Ugaine Mar (The Great)
|
King Cobhtach Caolbreag
|
King Meilage
|
King Jaran Gleofathach
|
King Conla Gruaich
|
King Ceaigach
|
King Oiliolla Caisfhiaclach
|
King Eochaid Foltleathan
|
King Aonghus Tuirimheach
|
King Fiachra Firmara
|
King Feradaig
|
King Fergus I
|
King Maine
(Father of Siadhail: descent to
the O'Shiels of Ireland)
|
King Dornadil
|

King Rowein
|
King Reuther
|
King Eders
|
King Conaire Mor
|
King Admoir
|
King Corbred I
|
King Dare-Dornmoir
|
King Fiachadh
|
King Tuathal Teachtman
|
King Feidhimhioh
|
King Conn of the 100 Battles
|
King Art Aonthir
|
King Cormac Ulfhada Mac Art
|
King Cairbre Liffeachaire
|
King Fiachadh Streabhthuine
|
King Waegdaeg
|
King Sigegart
|
King Saebaid
|
King Siggoth
|
King Saebaid
|
King Saefugel
|
King Sudrtha
|
King Soemil
|
King Westers
|
King Wilgils
|
King Wyse Frea
|
King Yffe
|
King Aelle of Deira (Northumbria)
559 AD – 588 AD
|
Princess Atha of Berenicia
= King Cadfan of Gwynnedd

625 AD
|
King Cadwallon II of Gwynnedd d. 634
= Princess Helen, granddaughter of Crida
Chief of the Angles
|
King Cadwalladr Pendragon the Blessed 654 – 664
The last Pendragon of Britain
|
King Edwal of Gwynnedd
|
King Rhodri Molwynog 754 AD
|
King Cinan Tindaethwy 754 - 816
|
King Gwynnedd
|
Queen Esylth
|
King Merfyn Vrych
|
King Rhodri Mawr (The Great)
of Gwynnedd (North Wales) and
Deheubarth (South Wales)
844 – 878
= Princess Angharad
|
King Cadell
|
King Hywel Dda
= Princess Elen
|
Prince Owain
|
Prince Einon
|
Prince Cadell
|
Prince Tewdwr
|
King Rhys Ap Tudor of
Deheubarth (South Wales)
|
Princess Nesta of Deheubarth
= King Henry Plantagenet I of England
(
)
(
)
Lord Herbert Fitzroy Earl of Gloucester
=Lady Mabel dau. of Lord
Robert Fitzhamon, Lord of Corbiel
|
William Fitz Robert Earl of Gloucester
= dau. of Lord Robert Beaumont
Earl of Leicester
|
Lady Amicia Fitz Robert
= Lord Richard de Clare Earl of Hertford

|
Robert De Clare Earl of Gloucester
= Lady Isabel dau. of William Marshall
Earl of Pembrokeshire
|
Lord de Clare Earl of Gloucester
= Lady Mathilda dau. of
John de Lacy Earl of Lincoln
|
Lord Gilbert de Clare
Earl of Gloucester
= Princess Joan Plantagenet
|
Lady Elizabeth de Clare
= Sir Roger D'Amorie
|
Elizabeth D'Amorie
= John Lord Bardolf
|
William Lord Bardolf
= Agnes Poynings
|
Cecilia Bardolf
= Sir Bryan Stapylton
|
Sir Miles Stapylton
= Katherine de la Pole
g. granddaughter of
Geoffrey Chaucer
|
Elizabeth Stapylton
= Sir William Calthorpe
|
Ann Calthorpe
= Sir Robert Drury
|
Anne Drury
= George Waldegrave
|
Sir William Waldegrave
= Juliana Rainsford
|
Sir William Waldegrave II
= Elizabeth Middlemay
|
Mary Waldegrave
= Thomas Clopton
|
Walter Clopton of Fordham
=Anne Thornton
|
Roger Clopton
= Elizabeth Boston
|
Elizabeth Clopton
= James Verdon
|
Elizabeth Verdon
= Samuel Clarke

Elizabeth Clarke
= Peter Stoughton

Elizabeth Stoughton
= Nicholas Cobb Collison

John Collison

Genetically
Confirmed

Esther Collison
= Reuben Avis

Lucy Avis
= Edward Hopgood

George Collison Hopgood
= Julia Harding

Natalie Hopgood, (descent through her father
from the Collisons of Norfolk, the Plantagenet
Kings and the Imperial and Royal House of Vere.
Descent through her mother from Lt. Col
George Butcher of Windsor Castle, Sarah Butcher
of Framlingham and the Huegenot Bourchier
Counts of Versailles, France)
= James Weir of Vere

HI&RH Prince Nicholas de Vere

Chapter Eighteen

The Elven Collison Descendants of Odin, Lord of the Rings; Princess Plantina, Geoffrey Plantagenet, count of Anjou; the Merovingian Princes, Queen Boudicca and the Ancient Kings of Britian

The Elven Collison Descendants of Odin, Lord of the Rings; Princess Plantina, Geoffrey Plantagenet, Count of Anjou; the Merovingian Princes, Queen Boudicca and the Ancient Kings of Britain

- De Diabolo Venit Et Ad Diabolum Ibid -

Generation No. 1

1. Geoffrey Plantagenet was born 1113, and died 1151. He married Matilda of England, daughter of King Henry and of Matilda. She was born Abt. 1104, and died September 10, 1167.

Notes for Geoffrey Plantagenet:

GEOFFREY, surnamed PLANTAGENET, COUNT d'ANJOU, born 1113, died 1151. King Henry I, of England, in despair over loss of his son, William, Duke of Normandy, who was drowned in the sinking of a ship off the coast of France, sought the aid of GEOFFREY PLANTAGENET, one of the most powerful princes of France, a noble person, with "elegant and courtly manners and a reputation for gallantry in the field." Approving the marriage of his daughter MATILDA with GEOFFREY, King Henry personally invested him with Knighthood, and expressed the hope that all Englishmen would give them full allegiance. The Barons took the oath to uphold the succession of Matilda and Geoffrey and their children after them. Thus Geoffrey heads the line of English kings which bear his Plantagenet name.

The friends of Geoffrey were unaware that their playful nickname for him of Plantagenet would live through the years. Geoffrey was descended from the Elven Princess Plantina, sister of the Fairy Princess Melusine I. Thus he derived his popular title. As eldest son of FULK V, KING OF JERUSALEM, and his wife, Princess Melusine III, Geoffrey was of the House of Angevin Kings, which had been prominent for three centuries. Geoffrey's descent from the House of Angevin Kings follows: From Princess Plantina, sister of the Fairy Princess Melusine – TORQUAT C760. TORTULF C780. THERTULLUS C.800 (Tortulf the Woodman of Nide de Merle), wife PETRONELLA, daughter of Conrad, Count of Paris; (2) INGELERUS I, married Adeline of Challon; (3) FULK, "the red," born 888, died 938, wife Roscilla of Blois; (4) FULK II, The Good, Count of Anjou, died 958, married Gerberga of Catinais; (5) GEOFFREY I, Count of Anjou, died 21 July 987, married Adelaide de Vermandois, also known as Adelaide de Chalons, born 950, died 975-78; (6) FULK III, "the Black" Count of Anjou, born 970, died 21 June 1040, married, second, after 1000, Hildegarde, who died 1 April 1109, married, fifth, Bertrade de Montfort; (9) FULK V, "The Young," Count of Anjou, King of Jerusalem, born 1092; died 10 Nov. 1143, who, as above stated, was the father of GEOFFREY V "PLANTAGENET," Count of Anjou, Duke of Normandy, who, on 3 April 1127, married MATILDA of ENGLAND, daughter of HENRY I, of England. NOTE: Also being given below, is the descent of Geoffrey V of Anjou, (called "Plantagenet") husband of Matilda (Maud), of England, from KING EDWARD THE GREAT.

GENEALOGY OF GEOFFREY PLANTAGENET (born 1113, died 7 Sept. 1151, from Aedd Mawr) (KING EDWARD THE GREAT), who appears to have lived about 1300 B.C. (the line of BOAZ and RUTH) to WILLIAM THE CONQUEROR, whose Genealogy back to ROLLO the DANE, is given: (1) KING EDWARD the GREAT, his son; (2) BRYDAIN, who settled in the island at an early date, and, according to tradition, gave his name to the entire island, which has since been corrupted into "Britain." His son; (3) ANNYN TRO, his son; (4) SELYS HEN, his son; (5) BRWT, his son; (6) CYMRYW, his son; (7) ITHON, his son; (8) GWEYRYDD, his son; (9) PEREDUR, his son; (10) LLYFEINYDD, his son; (11) TEUGED, his son; (12) LLARIAN, in whose day London was a considerable town, having been founded B.C. 1020, or earlier, as some hold, at least 270 years before the founding of Rome; his son; (13) ITHEL, his son; (14) ENIR FARDD, his son; (15) CALCHWYDD, his son; (16) LLYWARCH, his son; (17) IDWAL, his son; (18) RHUN, his son; (19) BLEDDYN, his son; (20) MORGAN, his son; (21) BERWYN, his son; (22) CERAINT FEDWW, an irreclaimable drunkard, deposed by his subjects for setting fire, just before harvest, to the cornfields of Siluris, now Monmouthshire, his son; (23) BRYWLAIS; his son; (24) ALAFON, his son; (25) ANYN, his son; (26) DINGAD, his son; (27) GREIDIOL, his son; (28) CERAINT, his son; (29) MEIRION, his son; (30) ARCH, his son; (31) CAID, his son; (32) CERI, his son; (33) BARAN, his son; (34) LLYR, (KING LEAR).

He was educated in Rome by Augustus Caesar, his son; (35) BRAN, KING of SILURIA. In the year AD 36, he resigned the crown to his son Caradoc, and became Arch-Druid Bran the Blessed of the college of Siluria. Bran married Anna, granddaughter of St. James (Joseph of Aramathea); the neice of Jesus Christ. Jesus and his brother St. James' lineage conjoin with The Uther Pendragon: Aedan Mac Gabran King of Scots, who married Ygraine of Avallon (see Avallon descent). During his seven years in Rome, Bran (St.

Brandon) became the first royal convert to Christianity and was baptized by the Apostle Paul, as was his son, Cardoc, and the latter's two sons, Cyllinus and Cynon (he introduced the use of vellum into England). his son; (36) CARADOC (CARACTACUS), was King of Siluria, (Monmouthshire, etc.), his son; (37) ST. CYLLIN, King of Siluria. He, first of the Cymry (Cimmerians of Scythia), gave infants names, for before, names were not given except to adults.

His brother, Linus the Martyr; his sister Claudia and her husband Rufus Pudens, aided the apostle Paul in the Christian Church in Rome. As recorded in II Timothy 4:21 and Romans 16:13, Rufus Pudens and St. Paul are shown to be half-brothers, children of the same mother, they had different fathers; Paul, by a Hebrew husband and Rufus, by a second marriage with a Roman Christian. His son; (38) PRINCE COEL, son of Cyllin was living AD 120; his son; (39) KING LLEUVER MAWR, (Lucius the Great), the second Blessed Sovereign, married Gladys, whose ancestry for eight immediate past generations is as follows; (a) CAPOIR, whose son was; (b) BELI (HELI) THE GREAT, died B.C. 72, whose son; (c) LUD, died B.C. 62, his son; (d) TENUANTIUS, his son; (e) CYNVELINE (Cymbeline), King of Britain. He was educated in Rome by Augustus Caesar, and later, forestalled the invasion of the island. His eleventh son; (f) AVIRAGUN, King of Britain, lived in Avalon (The Isle of Arran), the renowned enemy of Rome; married VENISSA JULIA, daughter of TIBERIUS CLAUDIUS CAESAR, EMPEROR OF ROME, who was the grandson of MARK ANTONY. The son of Aviragus and Venissa Julia was; (g) MERIC, (Marius,), King of Britain, married the daughter of the GODDESS-QUEEN BOADICEA (VICTORIA.).

They had a daughter; (h) EURGEN, and later a son Coel, who became King of Britain in 125. OLD KING COLE, educated in Rome, built Colchester (Coel-Castra), and died AD 170. (h) EURGEN, (see above), the said daughter of Meric, (Marius) and his wife, the daughter of Boadicea, had, as above stated, Gladys, who became the wife of No. 39 (see above), Lleuver Mawr (Lucius the Great) who is said to have changed the established religion of Britain from DRUIDISM to CHRISTIANITY though this must be patently untrue. The daughter of Lucius the Great and his wife, Gladys, was; (40) GLADYS, who became the wife of Cadvan, of Cambria, Prince of Wales. Their daughter; (41) STRADA, the FAIR, married Coel, a later King of Colchester, living AD 232. Their daughter; (42) HELEN of the CROSS (The Arms of Colchester were a "cross with three crowns"), Helen was born 248, died 328 and became the wife of CONSTANTIUS I, afterward Emperor of Rome, and, in right of his wife, King of Britain. He was born 242, died 306.

The God King of Valhalla: Odin, Lord of the Rings
Their son; (43) CONSTANTINE THE GREAT, born 265, died 336. Of

British birth, he is known as the first CHRISTIAN EMPEROR. The greatest
of all Roman Emperors, he annexed Britain to the Roman Empire, his son;
(44) CONSTANTIUS II, died in 360, his son; (45) CONSTANTIUS III,
married Placida, died in 421, his son; (46) VALENTINIAN III, died in
455. His daughter; (47) EUDOXIA, married Hunneric, who died in 480.
her son; (48) HILDERIC, King of the Vandals in 525, his daughter; (49)
HILDA, married Frode VII, who died 548; her son; (50) HALFDAN, KING
OF DENMARK, his son; (51) IVAR VIDFADMA, KING of DENMARK
and SWEDEN in 660 his son: (52) RORIC SLINGEBAND, KING of
DENMARK and SWEDEN in 700, his son; (53) HARALD HILDETAND,
KING of DENMARK and SWEDEN in 725, his son; (54) SIGURD RING,
living in 750, his son; (55) RAYNER LODBROCK, KING of DENMARK
and SWEDEN, died in 794, married Aslanga.
Aslanga was granddaughter of the one-eyed, hooded God-King ODIN,
Father of Sigfreid and Brunhilde: the Swan Princess and Valkyrie. LORD
OF THE AESIR, Odin was the inspiration for both Tolkien's Gandalf – Grey
Elf – and the one-eyed Sauron Lord of the Rings, from Saur, a Dragon. Odin
was the ancestor of Robert de Vere, the historical Robin Hood or Hoden.
RAYNER LODBROCK'S son; (56) SIGURD SNODOYE, KING of
DENMARK and SWEDEN, died 830, his son; (57) HORDA KNUT,
KING of DENMARK, died in 850, his son; (58) FROTHA, KING of
DENMARK, died 875, his son; (59) GORM ENSKE, married Sida and died
in 890, his son; (60) HAROLD PARCUS, KING of DENMARK, whose
wife was Elgiva, daughter of ETHELRED I, King of England, (a brother
of King Alfred The Great), his son; (61) GORM del CAMMEL, KING
of DENMARK, died in 931. His wife was Thyra, his son; (62) HAROLD
BLAATAND, KING of DENMARK, died in 981, his daughter; (63) LADY
GUNNORA, wife of Richard I, third Duke of Normandy, born 933, died
996. They had (beside their son Richard II ((see later)), a son; (64) ROBERT
d'EVEREUX, the Archbishop, who died in 1087, his son; (65) RICHARD,
Count d'Evereux, died in 1067, his daughter, (66) AGNES EVEREUX, who
became the wife of Simon l de Montfort, her daughter; (67) BERTRADE
MONTFORT, became the wife of FULK IV, Count d'Anjou, born 1043,
died 1109. The said Fulk IV's descent from OLD KING COLE is as follows;

The Frankish Kings

Coel: OLD KING COLE, son of Meric (MARIUS) (g) above mentioned,
was the father of, (1) ATHILDIS, wife of Marcomir IV, King of Franconia,
who died 149. They had (2) CLODOMIR IV, King of the Franks, died
166, married Hasilda, their son; (3) KING FARABERT, died 186, his son;
(4) KING SUNNO, died 213, his son; (5) KING HILDERIC, died 253,
his son; (6) KING PARTHERUS, died 272, his son; (7) KING CLOLIUS
III, died 298, his son; (8) KING WALTER, died 306, his son; (9) KING

DAGOBERT, died 317, his son; (10) GENEBALD I Duke of the East
Franks, died 350, his son; (11) KING DAGOBERT, died 379, his son; (12)
KING CLODIUS I, died 389, his son; (13) KING MARCOMIR, died 404,
his son; (14) KING PHAROMOND, married Argotta, daughter of Genebald,
their son; (15) KING CLODIO, married Basina de Thuringia, and died
455, their son; (16) SIGERMERUS I, married the daughter of Ferreolus
Tomantius, his son; (17) FERREOLUS, married Deuteria, a Roman lady,
their son; (18) AUSBERT, died 570, married Blitheldes, daughter of
Clothaire I, King of France, and his wife Ingonde, and grand-daughter of
CLOVIS THE GREAT, King of France, born 466, baptized at Rheims,
and died 511, and his wife Clothilde, of Burgundy, "The girl of the French
Vineyards."
It was she who led him to embrace Christianity, and mythically three
thousand of his followers were baptized in a single day. When Clovis first
listened to the story of Christ's Crucifixion, he was so moved that he cried,
"If I had been there with my valiant Franks, I would have avenged Him."
Ausbert and Blithildes were the parents of (19) ARNOUL, Bishop of Metz,
died 601, married Oda de Savoy and had (20) ST. ARNOLPH, Bishop of
Metz, died 641, married Lady Dodo and had, (21) ACHISEA, married
Begga of Brabant, who died 698, their son; (22) PEPIN d'HERISTAL,
Mayor of the Palace, died 714, who married Alpais.

PEPIN of HERISTAL made himself conspicuous. His home was near
Spa in the woodland country around Liege. He made the office hereditary
in his family. His heroic son, (23) CHARLES MARTEL, the Hammer,
Mayor of the Palace, King of France, was still more famous, because, in
the decisive Battle of Tours in 732, he utterly routed the Arabs, who had
conquered Spain and the south of France. Charles Martel Married Rotrude
and died in 741. His son, (24) PEPIN THE SHORT (or PEPIN le BREF),
King of France, died in 768, leaving by his wife Bertha, of Laon, a son;
(25) CHARLEMAGNE, Charles the Great, born 2 April 742, probably
at Aix-La-Chapelle, the greatest figure of the Middle Ages, King of the
Franks. Charlemagne and his younger brother, Carloman, succeeded to
equal portions to one of the most powerful of European kingdoms, bounded
by the Pyrenees, the Alps, the Mediterranean and the Ocean. Carloman,
the younger brother, died soon after the death of their father, Pepin The
Short, and with the consent of the great nobles, Charlemagne became King.
Desiderius, the King of Lombardy, had made large encroachments upon the
states of the Roman Pontiff, whose cause was taken up by Charlemagne.
This led to feuds, which Bertha, his mother, endeavored to appease by
arranging a marriage between her son and the daughter of the Lombard.

But the King Lord Charlemagne soon took a disgust to the wife thus
imposed upon him, and repudiated her, that he might marry Hildegarde,

born 757, died 30 April 782, the daughter of a noble family in Suabia. By his wife, Hildegarde, he had a son: (26) LOUIS I, the DEBONAIRE, who by his second wife, Judith, was the father of Gisela, ancestress of Hugh Capet, King of France and of JAMICIA, wife of RICHARD de CLARE, MAGNA CHARTA SURETY. Louis I, by his first wife Ermengarde, who died 818, daughter of Ingram, Count of Basbania, was father of (27) LOTHAIRE, Earl of Germany, who married Ermengarde of Alsace, and had (28) ERMENGARDE, who was the wife of Giselbert. Their son; (29) REGUIER I, Count of Hainault, died 916, who married Albreda, their son; (30) CISELBERT, Duke of Lorraine, married Gerlerga and died 930, their daughter; (31) ALBREDA of LORRAINE, wife of Renaud, Count de Roucy, who died 973, their daughter; (32) ERWENTRUDE ROUCY, married Alberic II, Count de Macon, who died 975, their daughter; (33) BEATRICE MACON, married Geoffrey I de Castenais, their son; (34) GEOFFREY II de CASTINAIS, married Ermengarde de Anjou, their son; (35) FULK IV, Count of Anjou, born 1043, died 1109, married Bertrade de Montfort (no. 67 above), their son (36) FULK V, Count d'Anjou, who, as elsewhere stated (above) was the father of GEOFFREY PLANTAGENET, who married MATILDA of ENGLAND, a great-great-great-grand daughter of RICHARD I, Duke of Normandy and his wife, Lady Cunnora. Matilda's descent from Richard I, Duke of Normandy is as follows: (1) RICHARD I, Duke of Normandy, his son; (2) RICHARD II, Duke of Normandy, died 1026, married Judith de Bretagne, their son; (3) ROBERT the MAGNIFICENT, also known as Robert the Devil, who, by Herleve Falaise, had WILLIAM THE CONQUEROR, father of King Henry I of England, who had Matilda, Wife of Geoffrey Plantagenet.

NOTE: WURTS' MAGNA CHARTA, pp. 158-168 inclusive, gives sixty nine Generations of lineal descent from No. 1, Edward the Great, (Aedd Mawr) to No. 69, Geoffrey Plantagenet. This also shows Geoffrey's descent from the FRANKISH KINGS, Nos. 1, to and including 35; also his descent from No. (6) (HELI) Beli the Great through LUD, through TUANTIUS, through CYNVELIN (CYMBELINE), through AVIRAGUS, through MERIC (MARIUS), through EURGEN, through GLADYS, wife of No. 39, (LLEUVER MAWR) LUCIUS THE GREAT. And page 168 of Wurt's Magna Charta shows that both Geoffrey Plantagenet and his wife, Matilda, or Maud, of England, were descendants of WILLIAM THE CONQUEROR, who, as above stated, was descended from CHARLEMAGNE.
Notes for Matilda of England:

Descent from CHARLEMAGNE to MATILDA, or Maud, of England, wife of GEOFFREY PLANTAGENET; (1) CHARLEMAGNE and wife, Hildegarde had a son; (2) PEPIN, born 776, died 8 July 810, before his father. He was crowned by the Pope in 781, King of Lombardy and Italy, married Bertha, daughter of William, Count of Toulouse, his son; (3) BERNHARD, King of Lombardy, succeeded his father about the year 812, he was deposed by his Uncle Louis, blinded and put to death. By his wife Cunegonde, he had a son; (4) PEPIN, who was deprived of the throne by his Uncle Louis, Emperor, called the Debonair, and received a part of Vermandois and the Seigneuries of St. Quentin and Peronne. His son; (5) PEPIN, Pepin de Senlis de Valois, Count Berengarius, of Bretagne, who was living in 893, the father of (6) LADY POPPA, (puppet or doll), who became the first wife of ROLLO the DANE, first Duke of Normandy. Their son; (7) WILLIAM LONGSWORD, was father of (8) RICHARD the FEARLESS, father of; (9) RICHARD II, "the Good," whose son; (10) ROBERT "THE DEVIL," sixth Duke of Normandy, who, by Herleve de Falaise, daughter of the Tanner, Fulbert de Falaise, had a son; (11) WILLIAM THE CONQUEROR, born at Falaise in 1027, father of HENRY I, KING of ENGLAND, WHO WAS THE LAST OF THE NORMAN KINGS. (Magna Charta 178, 182, 183). She was designated Henry's heir, and on his death (1135), Stephen seized the throne and Matilda invaded England (1139) inuagurating a period of inconclusive civil war. She and her second husband (Geoffrey) captured Normandy and in 1152 the Treaty of Wallingford recognised Henry as Stephen's heir. Burke says she was betrothed in her eighth year (1119) to Henry.

Child of Geoffrey Plantagenet and Matilda England is:
King Henry II Plantagenet, born March 25, 1133 in Le Mans; died July 06, 1189 in Chinon Castle, Anjou.

Generation No. 2
King Henry II Plantagenet. He married (1) Eleanor of Aquitaine May 18, 1152 in Bordeaux, France. She died June 26, 1202. He met (2) Rosamond De Clifford 1160. He met (3) Ida Abt. 1172.
Notes for King Henry II Plantagenet:
KING HENRY II of ENGLAND, son of Matilda, or Maud, of England and her husband, Geoffrey Plantagenet, was born at Le Mans, 25 March 1133 and died at Chinon, 6 July 1189. In 1152 he married Eleanor of Aquitaine, former wife of Louis VII, of France, and daughter of William, Duke of Aquitaine. She survived King Henry nearly three years, dying 26 June 1202. Both were buried at Fontrevaud in Anjou. Their daughter Eleanor married Alphonse IX, King of Castile; their eldest son William, died at the age of four years, their second son, Henry, born 28 Feb. 1155, who on 15 July 1170, by command of his father, was crowned King of England, but died before his father, 11 July 1183, their third son, Richard the Lion Hearted, reigned as King of England from 1189 to 1199. He was the most prominent leader on the Third Crusade to regain Jerusalem for the Christians from the

Mohammedans. He had greater military genius, but less statesmanship than his father.

His great power was in his physical and mental capacity as a soldier, and in his strenuous and irrepressible courage. Richard was proud, cruel and treacherous. He left the government of England in the hands of his Justiciars, and was in his English Kingdom but twice in his reign of ten years; four months at the time of his coronation, and two months, five years later. The Third Crusade was a failure. Richard fell out with the French King, and refused to marry his sister Alice, to whom he had been betrothed since early childhood, but on 12 May 1191, he married Perengaria of Navarre. HE DIED WITHOUT ISSUE. The fourth son of Henry II, Geoffrey, had a son Arthur, who was murdered in 1203, leaving as successor to the throne of England:

Henry II (1154-1189) Born: 5th March 1133 at Le Mans, Maine. Died: 6th July 1189 at Chinon Castle, Anjou. Buried: Fontevrault Abbey, Anjou. Parents: Geoffrey, Count of Anjou and the Empress Matilda. Siblings: Geoffrey, Count of Nantes & William, Count of Poitou. Crowned: 19th December 1154 at Westminster Abbey, Middlesex. Married: 18th May 1152 at Bordeaux Cathedral, Gascony. Spouse: Eleanor, daughter of William X, Duke of Aquitane & divorcee of Louis VII, King of France. Offspring: William, Henry, Matilda, Richard, Geoffrey, Eleanor, Joan & John. Contemporaries: Louis VII (King of France, 1137-1180), Thomas Beckett (Archbishop of Canterbury), Pope Adrian IV, Frederick I (Frederick Barbarossa, Holy Roman Emperor, 1152-1190).

Henry II, first of the Angevin kings, was one of the most effective of all England's monarchs. He came to the throne amid the anarchy of Stephen's reign and promptly collared his errant barons. He refined Norman government and created a capable, self-standing bureaucracy. His energy was equalled only by his ambition and intelligence. Henry survived wars, rebellion, and controversy to successfully rule one of the Middle Ages' most powerful kingdoms. Henry was raised in the French province of Anjou and first visited England in 1142 to defend his mother's claim to the disputed throne of Stephen. His continental possessions were already vast before his coronation: He acquired Normandy and Anjou upon the death of his father in September 1151, and his French holdings more than doubled with his marriage to Eleanor of Aquitaine (ex-wife of King Louis VII of France). In accordance with the Treaty of Wallingford, a succession agreement signed by Stephen and Matilda in 1153, Henry was crowned in October 1154. The continental empire ruled by Henry and his sons included the French counties of Brittany, Maine, Poitou, Touraine, Gascony, Anjou, Aquitaine and Normandy. Henry was technically a feudal vassal of the king of France but, in reality, owned more territory and was more powerful than his French lord.

Although King John (Henry's son) lost most of the English holdings in France, English kings laid claim to the French throne until the fifteenth century. Henry also extended his territory in the British Isles in two significant ways. First, he retrieved Cumbria and Northumbria from Malcom IV of Scotland and settled the Anglo-Scottish border in the North. Secondly, although his success with Welsh campaigns was limited, Henry invaded Ireland and secured an English presence on the island. English and Norman barons in Stephen's reign manipulated feudal law to undermine royal authority; Henry instituted many reforms to weaken traditional feudal ties and strengthen his position. Unauthorized castles built during the previous reign were razed.

Monetary payments replaced military service as the primary duty of vassals. The Exchequer was revitalized to enforce accurate record keeping and tax collection. Incompetent sheriffs were replaced and the authority of royal courts was expanded. Henry empowered a new social class of government clerks that stabilized procedure – the government could operate effectively in the king's absence and would subsequently prove sufficiently tenacious to survive the reign of incompetent kings. Henry's reforms allowed the emergence of a body of common law to replace the disparate customs of feudal and county courts. Jury trials were initiated to end the old Germanic trials by ordeal or battle. Henry's systematic approach to law provided a common basis for development of royal institutions throughout the entire realm.

The process of strengthening the royal courts, however, yielded an unexpected controversy. The church courts instituted by William the Conqueror became a safe haven for criminals of varying degree and ability, for one in fifty of the English population qualified as clerics. Henry wished to transfer sentencing in such cases to the royal courts, as church courts merely demoted clerics to laymen. Thomas Beckett, Henry's close friend and chancellor since 1155, was named Archbishop of Canterbury in June 1162 but distanced himself from Henry and vehemently opposed the weakening of church courts. Beckett fled England in 1164, but through the intervention of Pope Adrian IV (the lone English pope), returned in 1170. He greatly angered Henry by opposing the coronation of Prince Henry. Exasperated, Henry hastily and publicly conveyed his desire to be rid of the contentious Archbishop – four ambitious knights took the king at his word and murdered Beckett in his own cathedral on December 29, 1170. Henry endured a rather limited storm of protest over the incident and the controversy passed.

Henry's plans of dividing his myriad lands and titles evoked treachery from his sons. At the encouragement – and sometimes because of the treatment – of their mother, they rebelled against their father several times, often with Louis VII of France as their accomplice. The deaths of Henry the Young

King in 1183 and Geoffrey in 1186 gave no respite from his children's rebellious nature; Richard, with the assistance of Philip II Augustus of France, attacked and defeated Henry on July 4, 1189 and forced him to accept a humiliating peace. Henry II died two days later, on July 6, 1189. A few quotes from historic manuscripts shed a unique light on Henry, Eleanor. From Sir Winston Churchill Kt, 1675: "Henry II Plantagenet, the very first of that name and race, and the very greatest King that England ever knew, but withal the most unfortunate . . . his death being imputed to those only to whom himself had given life, his ungracious sons. . ."

From Sir Richard Baker, A Chronicle of the Kings of England: Concerning endowments of mind, he was of a spirit in the highest degree generous . . . His custom was to be always in action; for which cause, if he had no real wars, he would have feigned . . . To his children he was both indulgent and hard; for out of indulgence he caused his son Henry to be crowned King in his own time; and out of hardness he caused his younger sons to rebel against him . . . He married Eleanor, daughter of William Duke of Guienne, late wife of Lewis the Seventh of France. Some say King Lewis carried her into the Holy Land, where she carried herself not very holily, but led a licentious life; and, which is the worst kind of licentiousness, in carnal familiarity with a Turk. "King Henry II Plantagenet, had many illegitimate children, one of which was William de Longespee.

More About King Henry II Plantagenet:
Burial: Fontevrault Abbey, Anjou

Notes for Eleanor of Aquitaine:
aka; Rosamond De Clifford

More About Eleanor of Aquitaine:
Burial: Fontevrault Abbey, Anjou
Children of King Henry II, Plantagenet and Eleanor of Aquitaine are:
3 i. Eleanor7. She married Alphonse IX.
4 ii. William, born Abt. 1153; died Abt. 1157.
5 iii. Henry, born February 28, 1154/55; died July 11, 1183.
6 iv. Richard, born Abt. 1157. He married Perengaria May 12, 1191.
Notes for Richard:
Reigned as King of England from 1189 to 1199. He was the most prominent leader on the Third Crusade to regain Jerusalem for the Christians from the Mohammedans. He had greater military genius, but less statesmanship than his father. His great power was in his physical and mental capacity as a soldier, and in his strenuous and irrepressible courage. Richard was proud, cruel and treacherous. He left the government of England in the hands of his Justiciars, and was in his English Kingdom but twice in his reign of ten

years; four months at the time of his coronation, and two months, five years later. The Third Crusade was a failure. Richard fell out with the French King, and refused to marry his sister Alice, to whom he had been betrothed since early childhood, but on 12 May 1191, he married Perengaria of Navarre. HE DIED WITHOUT ISSUE.

+ 7 v. Geoffrey, born Abt. 1160.
+ 8 vi. King John, Lackland, born December 24, 1166 in Beaumont Palace, Oxford, England; died October 19, 1216 in Newark Castle, Newark, Nottinghamshire, England.

Child of King Henry II, Plantagenet and Ida is:
+ 9 i. William De Longespee, born 1173 in England; died March 07, 1225/26 in Salisbury, Wilts, England.

Generation No. 3
7. Geoffrey (King Henry II Plantagenet, Geoffrey, Fulk V, Fulk IV, Geoffrey II de Castinais, Geoffrey I de1) was born Abt. 1160.
Child of Geoffrey Plantagenet is:
10 i. Aurthur8, born Abt. 1185; died 1203.
8. King John, Lackland (King Henry II Plantagenet, Geoffrey, Fulk V, Fulk IV, Geoffrey II de Castinais, Geoffrey I de1) was born December 24, 1166 in Beaumont Palace, Oxford, England, and died October 19, 1216 in Newark Castle, Newark, Nottinghamshire, England. He married Isabell August 24, 1200 in Bordeaux, daughter of Aymer de Tallifer and Alice. She was born Abt. 1188 in Angouleme, and died May 31, 1246 in Fontevraud.

Notes for King John, Lackland:
KING JOHN, LACKLAND, the fifth son of Henry II and Eleanor of Aquitaine, born at Oxford, 24 Dec. 1166, died at Newark Castle, Notts, 19 Oct. 1216, married, first on 29 August 1189, Isabel, daughter of William, Earl of Gloucester; married, second, in 1200, Isabel, daughter of Aymer de Taillefer, the Swordsmith. She was the mother of all his children. John S. Wurts, in his Magna Charta, pages 6 to 17, inclusive. Page 6; "In case we have forgotten our English history, let us be reminded that King John was a horrid person, an arbitrary and mercenary ruler, who threw people into dungeons at the drop of a hat; married off wards of the crown, young widows and pretty girls, to foreign adventurers and then collected a nice percentage of the ward's fortunes from their husbands... he greatly increased the royal taxes and replenished his exchequer with the confiscated property of the clergy."
Shortly after he became King, he quarreled with the Pope, who deposed him and proclaimed him no longer King. John ignored the deposing, and made a gift to the Pope of all the realm, crown and revenue, by written

indenture, dated Monday, 13 May 1213. John then received the crown back as the Pope's tenant and vassal, at a rental of a thousand marks for the whole kingdom, 700 for England and 300 for Ireland.

Under this condition the Barons of England were only yeoman, or free-holders, or copy-holders of King John, the free-holder of the Pope, and tiring of John's tyranny, they called a conference after King John had left the Abbey at Saint-Edmundsbury (where he had been asked to attend the conference, which had been called by Stephen Langston, Archbishop of Canterbury), at which meeting nothing was accomplished, the barons took a solemn oath on the high altar, that they would stand united until they could compel the King to confirm their liberties, or they would wage war against him to the death. They did wage war, "a holy crusade against John to recover the liberties their forefathers had enjoyed." Virtually powerless, and with nearly his whole Baronage and the majority of his subjects of all degrees in arms against him, he finally called his Barons to a conference. They said, "let the day be the 15th of June and the place Runnemede" (which is in sight of Windsor Castle, and was used as "the field of council").

In this way was brought about the GREATEST EVENT OF KING JOHN'S REIGN, the veritable wresting from him of MAGNA CARTA, granting rights to the people of his realm, "an expression in written words of the principles of human life," which had been either grossly neglected or altogether forgotten by the king. Section 61 of the Charter authorized the election of twenty five Surety Barons, who would see that the previsions of the Charter were carried into effect. Their names are not recorded in the Magna Carta, "but we learn them from Matthew Paris' "Chronilca Majora.'"" These Barons were astonishingly inter-related. Among them were several instances of father and son, of father-in-law and son-in-law, of brothers and cousins. Twenty of the twenty-five were related in the degree of second cousin, or nearer. Of these twenty-five, only seventeen have descendants surviving to the present day. They had a common descent from Charlemagne. On the 15th day of June, 1215, more than two thousand knights and barons were encamped on the field of Runnemede to await the coming of King John and secure from him the rights of the people of England, although John had previously sworn by "God's teeth," his favorite oath, that he would never agree to such demands or any part of them. Runnemede was the "ancient meadow of council," and is within sight of Windsor Castle. For ages, this had been crown land and rented for pasturage. When it was proposed a few years ago (from the Crown Edition of Magna Carta, reprint 1945), to sell the field of Runnemede to the highest bidder, a great outcry arose. (The former Cara Rogers, now Lady Fairhaven, an American girl, a member of the "Magna Carta Dames," bought and presented to the British people the field of Runnemede as a memorial to her husband, to be kept for all time as a sacred, historic spot).

On 15 June 1215, before the day passed, the king affixed his seal to the original, but preliminary draft known as the "Articles of the Barons," which contained forty-nine articles, setting forth the principles of the Charter. The exact terms of the Charter were decided upon during the four days that followed. On the 19th of June 1215, the great seal was affixed, presumably to twenty-five duplicate copies, perhaps one for each of the twenty-five Surety Barons, who were to see that King John kept his promises. Neither the king, the barons, nor the knights could read or write, except a few, but a scholar, who was the Secretary of the Baron of Kendal, had accompanied him to Runnemede.

DESCENT OF ISAREL DE TAILLEFUR, second wife of KING JOHN OF ENGLAND from CHARLEMAGNE:
More About King John, Lackland:
Burial: Worcester, Cathedral
Notes for Isabell: She was the mother of all his children. John S. Wurts, in his Magna Charta, pages 6 to 17, inclusive.
More About Isabell:
Burial: Fontevraud Abbey
Child of King John and Isabell is:

King Henry III, born October 01, 1207 in Winchester, England; died November 16, 1272 in Westminster, Palace, London, England.
William De Longespee was born 1173 in England, and died March 07, 1225/26 in Salisbury, Wilts, England. He married Ela Fitzpatrick. She was born 1191 in Amesbury, Wiltshire, England, and died August 24, 1261 in Lacock, Wiltshire, England.
Notes for William De Longespee: According to Gary Boyd Roberts' Royal Descents of 500 Immigrants..., pp. 345-347, the mother of William LONGESPEE (natural son of King Henry II of England) was Ida, who married Roger BIGOD, 2nd Earl of Norfolk. One source of this is evidently a charter of William LONGSWORD published in the Cartulary of Bradenstoke Priory, ed. Vera C. M. Longdon, in which Countess Ida is explicitly named as his mother. The fact that William named a daughter Ida does lend credence to this, of course.

Child of William Longespee and Ela Fitzpatrick is:
Stephen De Longespee, born Abt. 1216 in Sutton, Co.
Northampton, England; died 1260 in Sutton, Co. Northampton, England.
Generation No. 4
King Henry III was born October 01, 1207 in Winchester, England, and died November 16, 1272 in Westminster, Palace, London, England. He married Queen Eleanor of Provence January 04, 1235/36 in England. She was

born Abt. 1217 in Aix-en-Provence, and died June 24, 1291 in Amesbury, Wiltshire.

Notes for King Henry III:

Brother of King Richard. King of England. He was crowned king 28 Oct. 1216, when only nine years of age. On 14 January 1236, he married Eleanor of Provence. A Plantagenet King; House of Anjou.

Notes for Queen Eleanor of Provence:

Queen Eleanor took the veil at Amesbury in Wiltshire, and died there 24 June 1291. Their elder sons, John and Henry, died young.

QUEEN ELEANOR'S GENEALOGY (1) CLOVIS, King of the Franks, married Clothilde, his son; (2) Clothaire I, born 497, died 561, married Ingolde, their son; (3) Chilperice I, born 523, died 584, married Fredegonde, born 543, died 598, his son; (4) Clothaire II, born 584, died 628, married Bertrude, who died 618, his son; (5) Claribert II, born 608, died 631, married Gisela, daughter of Arnoud, of Gascony, his son; (6) Boggis, Duke of Aquitaine, died 688, married Oda, his son; (7) Eudes, Duke of Aquitaine, married Valtrude, daughter of Valtrude and her husband, Walchigise, Count of Verdon, son of St. Arnolph, Bishop of Metz and his wife, Dodo, his son; (8) Hunold, Duke of Aquitaine, died 774, his son; (9) Waifir, Duke of Aquitaine, died 768, married his cousin, Adele, daughter of Loup I, Duke of Gascony, his son; (10) Loup II, Duke of Gascony, died 778, his son; (11) Adelrico, Duke of Gascony, died 812, his son; (12) Ximeno, Duke of Gascony, died 816, married Munia, his son; (13) Inigo Arista, first King of Navarre married Iniga Ximena, his son; (14) Careia II, of Navarre, married Urracca of Gascony, daughter of a cousin, Sancho II, his son; (15) Sancho I, became King of Navarre in 905, married his cousin Toda, daughter of Aznzr Galindez, Count of Aragon, his son; (16) Garcia III, became king in 921, died 970, married Teresa Iniquez of Aragon, and had (17) Sancho II Abarca, died 994.

He married Urracca Clara, daughter of Fortuna Ximenez, of Navarre, his second cousin, his son; (18) Garcia V, King of Navarre, died 999, married Ximena, daughter of Consslo, Count of Asturias and his wife, Teresa. They were the parents of the earlier of the two kings, both called Sancho III, this one; (19) Sancho III King of Navarre from 1000 to 1035, married Munia, daughter of Sancho of Castile, and thus united the two important Houses of Castile and Navarre, to which that of Aragon was later added, his son; (20) Ramirez I, founded the kingdom of Aragon, was killed in battle by the Moors, 8 May 1063. By his wife Gisberge, he had; (21) Sancho-Ramirez, died 4 June 1094, King of Aragon, married, first, Felice, who died 14 April 1086, daughter of Hildouin, Count of Rouci, his son; (22) Ramirez II, King of Aragon, married Agnes, daughter of William IX, Duke of Aquitaine.

His daughter; (23) Petronella was only two years old when her father abdicated the throne in her favor. He had arranged that Raymund Berenger V, Count of Barcelona, should govern the realm as Prince of Aragon, and that he should, at the proper time, marry Petronella. This was accomplished in accordance with his wish. Petronella died 18 October 1172, their son; (24) Alphonse II, King of Aragon, born 1151, died 25 April 1196, married his cousin Sanchia, who was descended as follows; KING SANCHO III (Navarre) and his wife Munia, as stated above, were the parents of (1) Ferdinand I, King of Castile from 1033 to 1065, died in battle 27 Dec. 1065. In 1035, he married Sanchia, daughter of Alphonso V, King of Leon, and thus united the latter kingdom to his own; (2) Alphonso VI, King of Castile and Leon, married a daughter of Robert, Duke of Burgundy, his daughter; (3) Urracca, married first, Raimond of Burgundy, who died in 1108, after which, Urracca married Alphonso I, King of Aragon. Her only child, son of Raimond, was; (4) Alphonso-Raimond VII, born 1103, died 1157. By his first wife, Berenguela, he had two sons, Sancho III (or Alphonso), and Ferdinand II, King of Leon, died 1188. By his second wife, Richilda of Poland, he had; (5) Sanchia, wife of Alphonso II, King of Aragon, as stated above. Her son; (6) Alphonso II, King of Provence, who reigned from 1196 to 1209, his son; (7)

Raimond-Berenger IV, King of Provence, married Beatrice (Beatrix), daughter of Thomas, Count of Savoy, his daughter; (8) ELEANOR OF PROVENCE, became the wife of HENRY III KING OF ENGLAND as stated above.

Child of King Henry and Queen Eleanor of Province is:
King Edward I, born June 17, 1239 in Westminster, Palace, London, England; died July 07, 1307 near Carlisle, England. He married Princess Eleanor of Castile in Las Huelgas, daughter of King Ferdinand III. She was born abt. 1244 in Castile, and died November 24, 1290 in Herdeby, Near Grantham, Lincolnshire.
Notes for King Edward I:
EDWARD I, KING OF ENGLAND, (called Longshanks), Earl of Chester, born at Westminster 17 June 1239, married Eleanor of Castile. In 1272 he went on a Crusade as far as Acre, where his daughter JOAN (see later) was born, and although he inherited the crown that year, he did not return to England until 1274, being crowned on August 19th. He was eminent as a ruler and as a legislator, and succeeded in enacting many new laws. He determined to authorize no new legislation without the counsel and acquiescence of those who were most affected by it. Not until late in his reign did he call a whole Parliament together. Instead he called the Barons together in any matter that affected the Barons, and the representatives of the townsmen together in any matter that affected the townsmen, and so

with other classes. Edward's first wife, ELEANOR OF CASTILE, whom he married in 1254, died 20 Nov. 1290. Reign: 1272-1307; Of the Plantagenets, House of Anjou. In 1270 Edward left England to join the Seventh Crusade. The first years of Edward's reign were a period of the consolidation of his power.

He suppressed corruption in the administration of justice, restricted the jurisdiction of the ecclesiastical courts to church affairs, and eliminated the papacy's overlordship over England. In 1290 Edward expelled all Jews from England. In 1296, after invading and conquering Scotland, he declared himself king of that realm. The conquest of Scotland became the ruling passion of his life. He was, however, compelled by the nobles, clergy and commons to desist in his attempts to raise by arbitrary taxes the funds he needed for campaigns. In 1307 Edward set out for the third time (at age 68) to subdue the Scots, but he died en route near Carlisle on 7 Jul 1307.

More About King Edward I:
Burial: Westminster, Abbey, London, England
 Notes for Princess Eleanor of Castile:
Of Castile and Leon Spain. Eleanor was only about ten years old when married to the 15-year-old Edward of Westminster at Las Huelgas in 1254. Such child marriages were commonplace in Europe in the Middle Ages and the brides were usually consigned to their husbands' families to complete their education. The marriages were not consummated until the bride reached a suitable age (usually 14 or 15) and in Eleanor's case it seems to have been 18 or 19.
More About Princess Eleanor of Castile:
Burial: Westminster, Abbey, London, England
Children of King Edward and Princess Eleanor of Castile are:
Edward II, born April 25, 1284 in Caernarvon, Castle, Wales; died September 21, 1327 in Berkeley Castle, Gloucestershire.

|

King Edward II Plantagenet
= Princess Isabella of France

|

Princess Joan Plantagenet
= Gilbert de Clare
Earl of Gloucester

|

Lady Elizabeth de Clare
= Sir Roger D'Amorie

|

Elizabeth D'Amorie
= John Lord Bardolf

|
William Lord Bardolf
= Agnes Poynings
|
Lady Cecilia Bardolf
= Sir Bryan Stapylton
|
Sir Miles Stapylton
= Katherine de la Pole
g. granddaughter of
Geoffrey Chaucer
|
Elizabeth Stapylton
= Sir William Calthorpe
|
Ann Calthorpe
= Sir Robert Drury
|
Anne Drury
= George Waldegrave
|
Sir William Waldegrave
= Juliana Rainsford
|
Sir William Waldegrave II
= Elizabeth Middlemay
|
Mary Waldegrave
= Thomas Clopton
|
Walter Clopton of Fordham
=Anne Thornton
|
Roger Clopton
= Elizabeth Boston
|
Elizabeth Clopton
= James Verdon
|
Elizabeth Verdon
= Samuel Clarke
|
Elizabeth Clarke
= Peter Stoughton
|
Elizabeth Stoughton
= Nicholas Cobb Collison
|
John Collison

|
Genetically
Confirmed
|
Esther Collison

= Reuben Avis
|
Lucy Avis
= Edward Hopgood
|
George Collison Hopgood
= Julia Harding
|
Natalie Hopgood, (descent through her father
from the Collisons of Norfolk, the Plantagenet
Kings and the Imperial and Royal House of Vere.
Descent through her mother from Lt. Col
George Butcher of Windsor Castle, Sarah Butcher
of Framlingham and the Huegenot Bourchier
Counts of Versailles, France)
=James Weir of Vere
|
HI&RH Prince Nicholas de Vere

Chapter Nineteen

The House of Collison European Descents

Collison Descent from the Royal Dynasty of Luxembourg

Merovech, born 415, King of the Franks, deceased 456
Married
Verica, born 419.
|
Chilperik I, King of the Salian Franks
Married
Andovera
|
Clovis, born 466, deceased 511
Married
Arnegundis
|
Chlotarius II, deceased 628
Married
Arnegundis
|
Chilperik II, deceased 584
Married
Fredegonde
|
Clotarius II de Grote, deceased 628
|
Dagobert I, born 602, deceased 639
Married
Nanthild
|
Clodowech II, born 631, deceased 657
|
Arnulf van Metz, born 582, deceased 641
Married
Oda, deceased 581
|

Thedoric III, King of the Franks, deceased 690
Married
Clotilde, deceased 692
|
Angesil
Married
Begga, deceased 692
|
Bertrade Prum....
|
Pippijn van Herstal, deceased 714
Married
Chalpais, deceased 705
|
Hnabi, Count of Alamannen
|
Heribert van Laon, Count of Laon
Married
Gisele Bertrade
|
Karel Martel, deceased 741
Married
Rothude of Chrotud, deceased 724
|
Gerold I, Count of the Franks [Vinzgouw]
Married
Imma
|
Pippijn de Korte, deceased, 768
Married
Bertrada van Laon, born 742, deceased 783
|
Welf I, Count of Beieren
Married
Eigilwich
|
Ingram, Count of Haspengouw
Married
Ava
|
Karel de Grote, Emperor, born April 2 742,
deceased Jan. 28 814
Married
Hildegard, born 758, deceased April 30 783
|
Odo van Orleans
Judith Welf, deceased 843
|
Hugo van Tours
Married
Ava
|
Lodewijk I, Emperor, born 778 te Chassenneuil,
deceased June 20 840 Ingelheim
Married

Irmingard, deceased Oct. 3 818

Karel II , Emperor, born June 13 823, Frankfurt,
deceased Oct. 6 877 te Maurienne
Married
Ermentrudis van Orlsans, born 830, deceased Oct.
6 869
|
Adalhard, Count of Paris
|
Lotharius I, King of the Franks, born 795,
deceased,Sept. 29 855
Married
Ermentrudis van OrlSans, born 830, deceased 869
|
Boudewijn II, Count of Flanders , born 865,
deceased Sept. 10 918
Married
Judith of West France, born 844
|
Edward I, King of England
Married
Aelfleda van Bernicea
|
Lodewijk II , born nov,1 846, deceased, April 10
879
Married
Adelheid van Paris
|
Gijsbrecht I van Leuven, Count of Darnau
|
Boudewijn II , Count of Flanders, born 865,
deceased Sept. 918
Married
Aelftryth of Wessex , deceased june 7 929
|
Hendrik I van Saksen, King of Germany
Married
Mathilde van Westfalen
|
Karel III, King of Franks, born Sept.17 879,
deceased Oct. 7 929
Married
Eadgfu of England, born 869
|
Renier I van Hehegouwen, deceased 915
Married
Alberda
|
Arnulf I, Count of Flanders, deceased 965
Married
Adela van Vermandios, born 912. deceased 960
|
Dirk I of Holland, deceased 939
Married

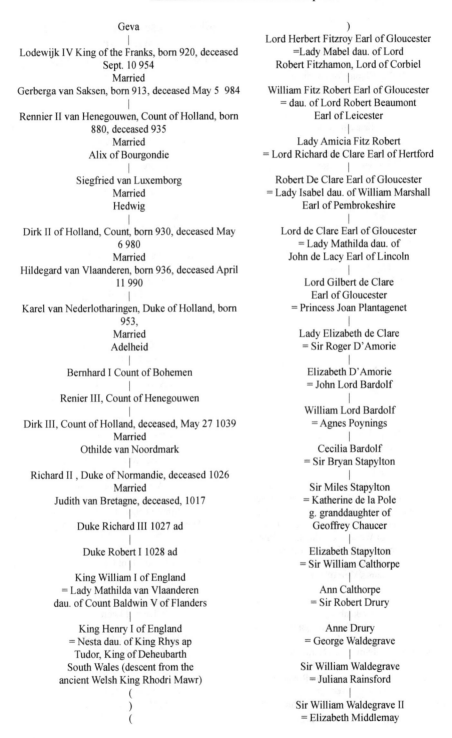

Geva
|
Lodewijk IV King of the Franks, born 920, deceased
Sept. 10 954
Married
Gerberga van Saksen, born 913, deceased May 5 984
|
Rennier II van Henegouwen, Count of Holland, born
880, deceased 935
Married
Alix of Bourgondie
|
Siegfried van Luxemborg
Married
Hedwig
|
Dirk II of Holland, Count, born 930, deceased May
6 980
Married
Hildegard van Vlaanderen, born 936, deceased April
11 990
|
Karel van Nederlotharingen, Duke of Holland, born
953,
Married
Adelheid
|
Bernhard I Count of Bohemen
|
Renier III, Count of Henegouwen
|
Dirk III, Count of Holland, deceased, May 27 1039
Married
Othilde van Noordmark
|
Richard II , Duke of Normandie, deceased 1026
Married
Judith van Bretagne, deceased, 1017
|
Duke Richard III 1027 ad
|
Duke Robert I 1028 ad
|
King William I of England
= Lady Mathilda van Vlaanderen
dau. of Count Baldwin V of Flanders
|
King Henry I of England
= Nesta dau. of King Rhys ap
Tudor, King of Deheubarth
South Wales (descent from the
ancient Welsh King Rhodri Mawr)
(
)
(

)
Lord Herbert Fitzroy Earl of Gloucester
=Lady Mabel dau. of Lord
Robert Fitzhamon, Lord of Corbiel
|
William Fitz Robert Earl of Gloucester
= dau. of Lord Robert Beaumont
Earl of Leicester
|
Lady Amicia Fitz Robert
= Lord Richard de Clare Earl of Hertford
|
Robert De Clare Earl of Gloucester
= Lady Isabel dau. of William Marshall
Earl of Pembrokeshire
|
Lord de Clare Earl of Gloucester
= Lady Mathilda dau. of
John de Lacy Earl of Lincoln
|
Lord Gilbert de Clare
Earl of Gloucester
= Princess Joan Plantagenet
|
Lady Elizabeth de Clare
= Sir Roger D'Amorie
|
Elizabeth D'Amorie
= John Lord Bardolf
|
William Lord Bardolf
= Agnes Poynings
|
Cecilia Bardolf
= Sir Bryan Stapylton
|
Sir Miles Stapylton
= Katherine de la Pole
g. granddaughter of
Geoffrey Chaucer
|
Elizabeth Stapylton
= Sir William Calthorpe
|
Ann Calthorpe
= Sir Robert Drury
|
Anne Drury
= George Waldegrave
|
Sir William Waldegrave
= Juliana Rainsford
|
Sir William Waldegrave II
= Elizabeth Middlemay

Mary Waldegrave
= Thomas Clopton

Walter Clopton of Fordham
=Anne Thornton

Roger Clopton
= Elizabeth Boston

Elizabeth Clopton
= James Verdon

Elizabeth Verdon
= Samuel Clarke

Elizabeth Clarke
= Peter Stoughton

Elizabeth Stoughton
= Nicholas Cobb Collison

John Collison

Genetically
Confirmed

Esther Collison
= Reuben Avis

Lucy Avis
= Edward Hopgood

George Collison Hopgood
= Julia Harding

Natalie Hopgood, (descent through her father
from the Collisons of Norfolk, the Plantagenet
Kings and the Imperial and Royal House of Vere.
Descent through her mother from Lt. Col
George Butcher of Windsor Castle, Sarah Butcher
of Framlingham and the Huguenot Bourchier
Counts of Versailles, France)
= James Weir of Vere

HI&RH Prince Nicholas Tarnawa-de Vere von
Drakenberg
KGC., KCD., KT.St.A.S. Sovereign Prince and
Grand Duke of
the Incorporeal Sovereign Nation State of
Drakenberg. Sovereign
Grand Master of the Imperial and Royal Dragon
Court, Sovereign
Grand Master and Commander-in-Chief of the
Order of Knights Templars

Collison Descent from the Pagan Magyar
Kings and Princes of Hungary

Prince Almos of Hungary d. 895

Prince Arpad of Hungary d. 907

Prince Zoltan of Hungary d. 947

Prince Taksony of Hungary d. 972

Duke Mihaly of Poland d. 976
= Princess Adelajda of Poland

Prince Vasul (Pagan Magyar) d. 1037

King Bela I of Hungary d. 1063
= Princess Rixa of Poland d. of
King Miezsko and Queen Rixa
of Poland

King Andrew I of Hungary
= Princess Anastasia d. of
Grand Duke Iaroslav I and
Princess Ingeborg of Sweden

Princess Adelaide of Hungary
= King Wratislav II of Bohemia

King Bodeslas III of Poland
= Princess Zbyslava of Kiev d. of

Grand Prince Michael II of Kiev

King Vladislas II of Poland
= Princess Agnes de Babenberg
d. of Prince Leopold III and Princess
Agness Hohenstauffen of Franconia

Princess Richilde of Poland
= King Alfonso VII of Castile - Galicia

King Ferdinand II 1157-1188
King of Leon

King Alfonso IX 1188-1230
King of Leon

King Ferdinand III
King of Castile 1217-1252
King of Leon 1230-1252

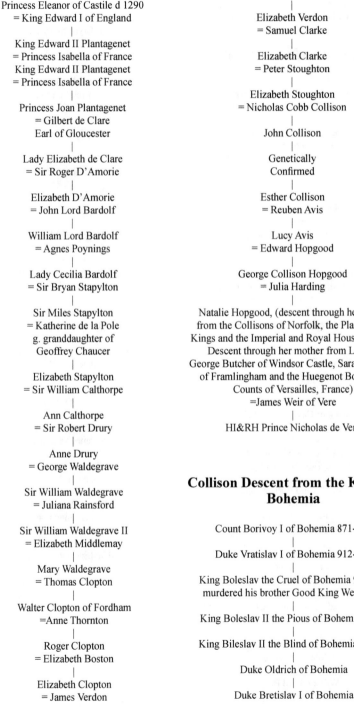

Princess Eleanor of Castile d 1290
= King Edward I of England

King Edward II Plantagenet
= Princess Isabella of France
King Edward II Plantagenet
= Princess Isabella of France

Princess Joan Plantagenet
= Gilbert de Clare
Earl of Gloucester

Lady Elizabeth de Clare
= Sir Roger D'Amorie

Elizabeth D'Amorie
= John Lord Bardolf

William Lord Bardolf
= Agnes Poynings

Lady Cecilia Bardolf
= Sir Bryan Stapylton

Sir Miles Stapylton
= Katherine de la Pole
g. granddaughter of
Geoffrey Chaucer

Elizabeth Stapylton
= Sir William Calthorpe

Ann Calthorpe
= Sir Robert Drury

Anne Drury
= George Waldegrave

Sir William Waldegrave
= Juliana Rainsford

Sir William Waldegrave II
= Elizabeth Middlemay

Mary Waldegrave
= Thomas Clopton

Walter Clopton of Fordham
=Anne Thornton

Roger Clopton
= Elizabeth Boston

Elizabeth Clopton
= James Verdon

Elizabeth Verdon
= Samuel Clarke

Elizabeth Clarke
= Peter Stoughton

Elizabeth Stoughton
= Nicholas Cobb Collison

John Collison

Genetically
Confirmed

Esther Collison
= Reuben Avis

Lucy Avis
= Edward Hopgood

George Collison Hopgood
= Julia Harding

Natalie Hopgood, (descent through her father
from the Collisons of Norfolk, the Plantagenet
Kings and the Imperial and Royal House of Vere.
Descent through her mother from Lt. Col
George Butcher of Windsor Castle, Sarah Butcher
of Framlingham and the Huegenot Bourchier
Counts of Versailles, France)
=James Weir of Vere

HI&RH Prince Nicholas de Vere

Collison Descent from the Kings of Bohemia

Count Borivoy I of Bohemia 871-894

Duke Vratislav I of Bohemia 912-926

King Boleslav the Cruel of Bohemia 935-967
murdered his brother Good King Wenceslas

King Boleslav II the Pious of Bohemia d.999

King Bileslav II the Blind of Bohemia d.1035

Duke Oldrich of Bohemia

Duke Bretislav I of Bohemia

= Countess Judith von Schweinfurt
dau. of Count Heinrich, Graf von
Schweinfurt
|
King Wratislav III of Bohemia
= Princess Adelaide of Hungary
|
Princess Judith of Bohemia
= King Vladislav I of Poland
|
King Bodeslas III of Poland
= Princess Zbyslava of Kiev
dau. of Grand Prince Michael II
of Kiev
|
King Vladislas II of Poland
= Countess Agnes von Babenberg
dau. of Duke Leopold III Hohenstauffen
of (Franconia) Austria
|
Princess Richilde of Poland
= King Alfonso VII of Castile-Galicia
|
King Ferdinand II 1157-1188
King of Leon
|
King Alfonso IX 1188-1230
King of Leon
|
King Ferdinand III
King of Castile 1217-1252
King of Leon 1230-1252
|
Princess Eleanor of Castile d. 1290
= King Edward I of England
|
King Edward II Plantagenet
= Princess Isabella of France
King Edward II Plantagenet
= Princess Isabella of France
|
Princess Joan Plantagenet
= Gilbert de Clare
Earl of Gloucester
|
Lady Elizabeth de Clare
= Sir Roger D'Amorie
|
Elizabeth D'Amorie
= John Lord Bardolf
|
William Lord Bardolf
= Agnes Poynings

|
Lady Cecilia Bardolf
= Sir Bryan Stapylton
|
Sir Miles Stapylton
= Katherine de la Pole
g. granddaughter of
Geoffrey Chaucer
|
Elizabeth Stapylton
= Sir William Calthorpe
|
Ann Calthorpe
= Sir Robert Drury
|
Anne Drury
= George Waldegrave
|
Sir William Waldegrave
= Juliana Rainsford
|
Sir William Waldegrave II
= Elizabeth Middlemay
|
Mary Waldegrave
= Thomas Clopton
|
Walter Clopton of Fordham
=Anne Thornton
|
Roger Clopton
= Elizabeth Boston
|
Elizabeth Clopton
= James Verdon
|
Elizabeth Verdon
= Samuel Clarke
|
Elizabeth Clarke
= Peter Stoughton
|
Elizabeth Stoughton
= Nicholas Cobb Collison
|
John Collison
|
Genetically
Confirmed
|
Esther Collison
= Reuben Avis
|
Lucy Avis
= Edward Hopgood

George Collison Hopgood
= Julia Harding
|
Natalie Hopgood, (descent through her father
from the Collisons of Norfolk, the Plantagenet
Kings and the Imperial and Royal House of Vere.
Descent through her mother from Lt. Col
George Butcher of Windsor Castle, Sarah Butcher
of Framlingham and the Huegenot Bourchier
Counts of Versailles, France)
=James Weir of Vere
|
HI&RH Prince Nicholas de Vere

Collison Descent from the Early Dukes of Saxony

Duke Hadugato of Saxony c 531
|
Duke Berthoald of Saxony c 627
|
Duke Theoderic of Saxony 743-744
|
Duke Widukind of Saxony 777-810
|
Duke Abo of Saxony 785-811
|
Hattonid Dynasty
|
Duke Banzleib of Saxony 830
|
Ottonian Dynasty
|
Duke Liudolf of Saxony 850
|
Duke Bruno of Saxony 852-880
|
Duke Otto the Illustrious of Saxony 880-912
=Princess Hedwiga of Franconia dau. of
Duke Henry of Franconia and Princess
Ingeltrude of Fruili
|
King Henry the Fowler of Germany
= St. Matilda of Ringelheim
|
Princess Gerberga
=King Louis IV of France
936-954
|
Charles Duke of Lower Lorraine 991
|
Lady Gerberga

= Lambert de Louvain
|
Henry of Brussels
|
Maud de Louvain
= Eustace I de Vere d. 1049
Descent from Amelius ("Adolph") de Vere
Comte de Guisnes
|
Eustace II de Vere
= Saint Ida of Ardennes
|
Princess Ida de Vere
= Baudouin de Bourg
Comte de Rethul
|
Prince Hugues I
Comte de Rethul
= Melisende (Melusine II)
dau. Of Bouchard Comte de Corbeil and
Lady Adelaide de Crecy
|
Badouin II de Bourg
King of Jerusalem 1118-1131
= Princess Morfia of Armenia
|
Princess Melisende of Jerusalem (Melusine III)
= Fulke V Plantagenet Count of Anjou
|
Count Geoffrey Plantagenet of Anjou
= Princess Mathilda of England la Imperatrice
(Empress of England)
|
King Henry II Plantagenet
= Countess Eleanor of Aquitaine
|
King John 'Lackland' Plantagenet
= Lady Isabella of Angouleme
|
King Henry III Plantagenet
= Lady Eleanor dau. of Count
Raymond Berenguer IVof Provence
and Princess Beatrix of Savoy
|
King Edward I Plantagenet
= Princess Eleanor of Castille
|
King Edward II Plantagenet
= Princess Isabella of France
|
Princess Joan Plantagenet
= Gilbert de Clare
Earl of Gloucester
|
Lady Elizabeth de Clare

= Sir Roger D'Amorie
|
Elizabeth D'Amorie
= John Lord Bardolf
|
William Lord Bardolf
= Agnes Poynings
|
Lady Cecilia Bardolf
= Sir Bryan Stapylton
|
Sir Miles Stapylton
= Katherine de la Pole
g. granddaughter of
Geoffrey Chaucer
|
Elizabeth Stapylton
= Sir William Calthorpe
|
Ann Calthorpe
= Sir Robert Drury
|
Anne Drury
= George Waldegrave
|
Sir William Waldegrave
= Juliana Rainsford
|
Sir William Waldegrave II
= Elizabeth Middlemay
|
Mary Waldegrave
= Thomas Clopton
|
Walter Clopton of Fordham
=Anne Thornton
|
Roger Clopton
= Elizabeth Boston
|
Elizabeth Clopton
= James Verdon
|
Elizabeth Verdon
= Samuel Clarke
|
Elizabeth Clarke
= Peter Stoughton
|
Elizabeth Stoughton
= Nicholas Cobb Collison
|
John Collison
|
Genetically

Confirmed
|
Esther Collison
= Reuben Avis
|
Lucy Avis
= Edward Hopgood
|
George Collison Hopgood
= Julia Harding
|
Natalie Hopgood, (descent through her father
from the Collisons of Norfolk, the Plantagenet
Kings and the Imperial and Royal House of Vere.
Descent through her mother from Lt. Col
George Butcher of Windsor Castle, Sarah Butcher
of Framlingham and the Huegenot Bourchier
Counts of Versailles, France)
=James Weir of Vere
|
HI&RH Prince Nicholas de Vere

Collison Descent from the Babenberg Dynasty of Austria

Count Adalbert I von Babenberg d. 997
= Brunehilde of Saxony dau. Of Duke Otto
the Illustrious of Saxony and Princess Hedwig
|
Count Adalbert II von Babenberg 901-933
|
Count Leopold I von Babenberg 923-994
= Lady Richenza
|
Count Albert I von Babenberg 983-1065
= Lady Adela of Venice
|
Count Ernest I von Babenberg 1027-1075
= Lady Maud of Lausnitz
|
Count Leopold II von Babenberg "The Fair" 1050-1136
= Princess Ida of Germany dau. of King Henry III
"The Black" of Germany and Princess Agnes of
Poitou
|
Duke Leopold III von Babenberg 1073-1110
= Princess Agnes of Franconia dau. of King Henry
IV of Germany and Princess Bertha von
Hohenstauffen of Maurienne
|
Princess Agnes von Babenberg-Hohenstauffen

= King Vladislas III of Poland
|
Princess Richilde of Poland
= King Alfonso VII of Castile-Galicia
|
King Ferdinand II 1157-1188
King of Leon
|
King Alfonso IX 1188-1230
King of Leon
|
King Ferdinand III
King of Castile 1217-1252
King of Leon 1230-1252
|
Princess Eleanor of Castile d 1290
= King Edward I of England
|
King Edward II Plantagenet
= Princess Isabella of France
|
Princess Joan Plantagenet
= Gilbert de Clare
Earl of Gloucester
|
Lady Elizabeth de Clare
= Sir Roger D'Amorie
|
Elizabeth D'Amorie
= John Lord Bardolf
|
William Lord Bardolf
= Agnes Poynings
|
Lady Cecilia Bardolf
= Sir Bryan Stapylton
|
Sir Miles Stapylton
= Katherine de la Pole
g. granddaughter of
Geoffrey Chaucer
|
Elizabeth Stapylton
= Sir William Calthorpe
|
Ann Calthorpe
= Sir Robert Drury
|
Anne Drury
= George Waldegrave
|
Sir William Waldegrave
= Juliana Rainsford
|
Sir William Waldegrave II

= Elizabeth Middlemay
|
Mary Waldegrave
= Thomas Clopton
|
Walter Clopton of Fordham
=Anne Thornton
|
Roger Clopton
= Elizabeth Boston
|
Elizabeth Clopton
= James Verdon
|
Elizabeth Verdon
= Samuel Clarke
|
Elizabeth Clarke
= Peter Stoughton
|
Elizabeth Stoughton
= Nicholas Cobb Collison
|
John Collison
|
Genetically
Confirmed
|
Esther Collison
= Reuben Avis
|
Lucy Avis
= Edward Hopgood
|
George Collison Hopgood
= Julia Harding
|
Natalie Hopgood, (descent through her father
from the Collisons of Norfolk, the Plantagenet
Kings and the Imperial and Royal House of Vere.
Descent through her mother from Lt. Col
George Butcher of Windsor Castle, Sarah Butcher
of Framlingham and the Huegenot Bourchier
Counts of Versailles, France)
=James Weir of Vere
|
HI&RH Prince Nicholas de Vere

Collison Descent from the Ancient Kings of Poland

The Kings of Poland originated with Lech, who was one of three Varangian brothers (including Rurik or Rus who founded the Russian state and Cech or Czech who founded Bohemia).

Duke Piast (Founder of the Piast dynasty)
|
Duke Siemowit I c. 890 AD
|
Duke Lestko c. 920 AD
|
Duke Siemosyl
|
Duke Mieszko I 960-992
|
Duke Boleslaw I the Brave
First King of Poland in 1025
|
King Mieszko II 1025-1031
|
King Casimir I 1039-1058
= Princess Dobroniega of Kiev
dau. of Grand Prince Vladimir of Kiev
|
King Vladislav I
= Princess Judith of Bohemia dau. of
King Wratislav II of Bohemia and
Princess Adelaide of Hungary
|
King Vladislav II
= Princess Agness Hohenstauffen of
Babenberg dau. of Duke Leopold
Hohenstauffen of Austria-Franconia
|
Princess Richilde of Poland
= King Alfonso VII of Castile-Galicia
|
King Ferdinand II 1157-1188
King of Leon
|
King Alfonso IX 1188-1230
King of Leon
|
King Ferdinand III
King of Castile 1217-1252
King of Leon 1230-1252
|
Princess Eleanor of Castile d 1290
= King Edward I of England

|
King Edward II Plantagenet
= Princess Isabella of France
King Edward II Plantagenet
= Princess Isabella of France
|
Princess Joan Plantagenet
= Gilbert de Clare
Earl of Gloucester
|
Lady Elizabeth de Clare
= Sir Roger D'Amorie
|
Elizabeth D'Amorie
= John Lord Bardolf
|
William Lord Bardolf
= Agnes Poynings
|
Lady Cecilia Bardolf
= Sir Bryan Stapylton
|
Sir Miles Stapylton
= Katherine de la Pole
g. granddaughter of
Geoffrey Chaucer
|
Elizabeth Stapylton
= Sir William Calthorpe
|
Ann Calthorpe
= Sir Robert Drury
|
Anne Drury
= George Waldegrave
|
Sir William Waldegrave
= Juliana Rainsford
|
Sir William Waldegrave II
= Elizabeth Middlemay
|
Mary Waldegrave
= Thomas Clopton
|
Walter Clopton of Fordham
=Anne Thornton
|
Roger Clopton
= Elizabeth Boston
|
Elizabeth Clopton
= James Verdon
|
Elizabeth Verdon

= Samuel Clarke

Elizabeth Clarke
= Peter Stoughton

Elizabeth Stoughton
= Nicholas Cobb Collison

John Collison

Genetically
Confirmed

Esther Collison
= Reuben Avis

Lucy Avis
= Edward Hopgood

George Collison Hopgood
= Julia Harding

Natalie Hopgood, (descent through her father
from the Collisons of Norfolk, the Plantagenet
Kings and the Imperial and Royal House of Vere.
Descent through her mother from Lt. Col
George Butcher of Windsor Castle, Sarah Butcher
of Framlingham and the Huegenot Bourchier
Counts of Versailles, France)
=James Weir of Vere

HI&RH Prince Nicholas de Vere

Collison
Descent from the Dynasty of
Hohenstauffen

Count Frederick of Buren 1036-1146
= Lady Hildegarde

Count Frederick I von Hohenstauffen 1050-1105
= Princess Agnes of Franconia
dau. of King Henry IV of Germany
and Princess Bertha of Maurienne

Princess Agnes II of Franconia
= Duke Leopold III of Austria

Countess Agnes von Babenberg
dau. of Duke Leopold III of Austria
=King Vladislas II of Poland

Princess Richilde of Poland
= King Alfonso VII of Castile-Galicia

King Ferdinand II 1157-1188
King of Leon

King Alfonso IX 1188-1230
King of Leon

King Ferdinand III
King of Castile 1217-1252
King of Leon 1230-1252

Princess Eleanor of Castile d 1290
= King Edward I of England

King Edward II Plantagenet
= Princess Isabella of France
King Edward II Plantagenet
= Princess Isabella of France

Princess Joan Plantagenet
= Gilbert de Clare
Earl of Gloucester

Lady Elizabeth de Clare
= Sir Roger D'Amorie

Elizabeth D'Amorie
= John Lord Bardolf

William Lord Bardolf
= Agnes Poynings

Lady Cecilia Bardolf
= Sir Bryan Stapylton

Sir Miles Stapylton
= Katherine de la Pole
g. granddaughter of
Geoffrey Chaucer

Elizabeth Stapylton
= Sir William Calthorpe

Ann Calthorpe
= Sir Robert Drury

Anne Drury
= George Waldegrave

Sir William Waldegrave
= Juliana Rainsford

Sir William Waldegrave II
= Elizabeth Middlemay

Mary Waldegrave
= Thomas Clopton

Walter Clopton of Fordham
=Anne Thornton

Roger Clopton
= Elizabeth Boston

Elizabeth Clopton
= James Verdon

Elizabeth Verdon
= Samuel Clarke

Elizabeth Clarke
= Peter Stoughton

Elizabeth Stoughton
= Nicholas Cobb Collison

John Collison

Genetically
Confirmed

Esther Collison
= Reuben Avis

Lucy Avis
= Edward Hopgood

George Collison Hopgood
= Julia Harding

Natalie Hopgood, (descent through her father
from the Collisons of Norfolk, the Plantagenet
Kings and the Imperial and Royal House of Vere.
Descent through her mother from Lt. Col
George Butcher of Windsor Castle, Sarah Butcher
of Framlingham and the Huegenot Bourchier
Counts of Versailles, France)
=James Weir of Vere

HI&RH Prince Nicholas de Vere

The Collison Cousins of King Sigismund of Hungary Founder of Societas Draconis (The Dragon Court), Husband of the Vampire Queen Barbara Cille

Origins with the Early Kings of Poland

The Kings of Poland originated with Lech, who was one of three Varangian brothers (including Rurik or Rus who founded the Russian state and Cech or Czech who founded Bohemia).

Duke Piast (Founder of the Piast dynasty)

Duke Siemowit I c. 890 AD

Duke Lestko c. 920 AD

Duke Siemosyl

Duke Mieszko I 960-992

Duke Boleslaw I the Brave
First King of Poland in 1025

King Mieszko II 1025-1031

King Casimir I 1039-1058
= Princess Dobroniega of Kiev
dau. of Grand Prince Vladimir of Kiev

King Vladislav I
= Princess Judith of Bohemia dau. of
King Wratislav II of Bohemia and
Princess Adelaide of Hungary

King Vladislav II
= Princess Agness Hohenstauffen of
Babenberg dau. of Duke Leopold
Hohenstauffen of Austria-Franconia

Prince Zibigniew-Princess Richilde
(Descent to the House of Collison)

Boleslas III

Ladislas II

Boleslas IV

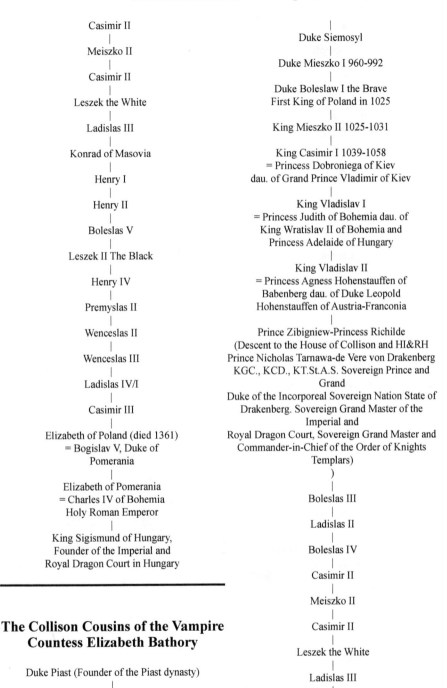

Casimir II
|
Meiszko II
|
Casimir II
|
Leszek the White
|
Ladislas III
|
Konrad of Masovia
|
Henry I
|
Henry II
|
Boleslas V
|
Leszek II The Black
|
Henry IV
|
Premyslas II
|
Wenceslas II
|
Wenceslas III
|
Ladislas IV/I
|
Casimir III
|
Elizabeth of Poland (died 1361)
= Bogislav V, Duke of
Pomerania
|
Elizabeth of Pomerania
= Charles IV of Bohemia
Holy Roman Emperor
|
King Sigismund of Hungary,
Founder of the Imperial and
Royal Dragon Court in Hungary

|
Duke Siemosyl
|
Duke Mieszko I 960-992
|
Duke Boleslaw I the Brave
First King of Poland in 1025
|
King Mieszko II 1025-1031
|
King Casimir I 1039-1058
= Princess Dobroniega of Kiev
dau. of Grand Prince Vladimir of Kiev
|
King Vladislav I
= Princess Judith of Bohemia dau. of
King Wratislav II of Bohemia and
Princess Adelaide of Hungary
|
King Vladislav II
= Princess Agness Hohenstauffen of
Babenberg dau. of Duke Leopold
Hohenstauffen of Austria-Franconia
|
Prince Zibigniew-Princess Richilde
(Descent to the House of Collison and HI&RH
Prince Nicholas Tarnawa-de Vere von Drakenberg
KGC., KCD., KT.St.A.S. Sovereign Prince and
Grand
Duke of the Incorporeal Sovereign Nation State of
Drakenberg. Sovereign Grand Master of the
Imperial and
Royal Dragon Court, Sovereign Grand Master and
Commander-in-Chief of the Order of Knights
Templars)
)
|
Boleslas III
|
Ladislas II
|
Boleslas IV
|
Casimir II
|
Meiszko II
|
Casimir II
|
Leszek the White
|
Ladislas III
|
Konrad of Masovia
|

The Collison Cousins of the Vampire
Countess Elizabeth Bathory

Duke Piast (Founder of the Piast dynasty)
|
Duke Siemowit I c. 890 AD
|
Duke Lestko c. 920 AD

Henry I
|
Henry II
|
Boleslas V
|
Leszek II The Black
|
Henry IV
|
Premyslas II
|
Wenceslas II
|
Wenceslas III
|
Ladislas IV/I
|
Casimir III
|
Louis I
|
Ladislas II
|
Ladislas III
|
Casimir IV
|
John I AlbertAlexander
|
Sigismund I
|
Sigismund II
|
August I
|
Henry III
|
Maximilian I
|
Stephen I Báthory
(Brother of Elizabeth Bathory,
the mother of Elizabeth Bathory of Escid,
The Vampire Countess of Transylvania)

Chapter Twenty

Collison Descent from the Ostrogoths

**Royal Descent of the House of Collison from the Kings
of the Ostrogoths via the Royal House of Vere**

The Ostrogoths of Romania

King Vultwulf 350 AD
|
King Valaravaus 380 AD
|
King Winithar 400 AD
Conquered Vanadi-Slavs
|
King Wandalar d. 459 AD
|
King Theodemer d. 475 AD
|
King Theoderic The Great of Italy
King of Macedonia
King of the Visigoths d. August 30th 526 AD
|
Princess Theodora
= Count Severinus of Cartegena
|
Princess Theodosia
= Leovigild of Spain
|
St. Hermengild d. 585
= Princess Ingunda of France
dau. of King Sigebert of France
and Princess Brunchildis of Spain
|
King Athanagildo
= Princess Flavia Juliana
of Byzantium
|
King Ardebasto

403

= Princess Godo
|
King Ervigo of Spain
= Princess Liubigotona
Descent from King Clovis of France
|
Duke Pedro of Cantabaria
|
Princess Aupais of the Goths
= Duke Pepin of Heristal of France
Mayor of the Palaces of
Austrasia, Neustria and Burgundy
|
Lord Charles Martel (The Hammer)
|
Pepin the III Brevis, Duke of Lower Lorraine
(Brabant)
Mayor of Neustrasia, King of the Franks
= Lady Leuthergis
|
Bertheld, dau of King Pepin of the
Franks, sister to Charlemagne.
Prince Milo I de Vere, Sovereign Duke
of the State of Angiers, Count of Anjou
|
Descent from the Dragon Queens of Egypt,
King Solomon, Christ and King Meroveus,
Founder of the Merovingian
Royal Dynasty of the Franks
(See chart - Jesus' descent from Satan)
|
Prince Milo II de Vere
= Lady Aveline de Nantes
|
Prince Nicassius de Vere, Count of Guisnes and
Anjou
=Lady Agatha de Champagne
|
Prince Otho de Vere, Count of Guisnes
= Lady Constance de Chartres
|
Prince Amelius (Adolphus) de Vere Count of
Guisnes
2. = Lady Maud de Ponthieu
|
Prince Gallus (Guy) de Vere, Count of Guisnes
2. = Lady Gertrude de Clermont de Ponthieu
|
Prince Baldwin de Vere de Boulogne
= Adele de Ghent
|
Prince Eustace de Vere
= Lady Maud de Lovain
|
Princess Ida de Vere

= Baudouin de Bourg
Comte de Rethul
(Merovingian descent via Charlemagne)
|
Prince Hugues I
Comte de Rethul
= Melisende (Melusine II)
dau. Of Bouchard Comte de Corbeil and
Lady Adelaide de Crecy
|
Badouin II de Bourg
King of Jerusalem 1118 – 1131
= Princess Morfia of Armenia
|
Princess Melisende of Jerusalem (Melusine III)
= Fulke V Plantagenet Count of Anjou
|
Count Geoffrey Plantagenet of Anjou
= Princess Mathilda of England la Imperatrice
(Empress of England)
|
King Henry II Plantagenet
= Countess Eleanor of Aquitaine
|
King John 'Lackland' Plantagenet
= Lady Isabella of Angouleme
|
King Henry III Plantagenet
= Lady Eleanor dau. of Count
Raymond Berenguer I Vof Provence
and Princess Beatrix of Savoy
|
King Edward I Plantagenet
= Princess Eleanor of Castille
|
King Edward II Plantagenet
= Princess Isabella of France
|
Princess Joan Plantagenet
= Gilbert de Clare
Earl of Gloucester
|
Lady Elizabeth de Clare
= Sir Roger D'Amorie
|
Elizabeth D'Amorie
= John Lord Bardolf
|
William Lord Bardolf
= Agnes Poynings
|
Lady Cecilia Bardolf
= Sir Bryan Stapylton
|
Sir Miles Stapylton

= Katherine de la Pole
g. granddaughter of
Geoffrey Chaucer
|
Elizabeth Stapylton
= Sir William Calthorpe
|
Ann Calthorpe
= Sir Robert Drury
|
Anne Drury
= George Waldegrave
|
Sir William Waldegrave
= Juliana Rainsford
|
Sir William Waldegrave II
= Elizabeth Middlemay
|
Mary Waldegrave
= Thomas Clopton
|
Walter Clopton of Fordham
=Anne Thornton
|
Roger Clopton
= Elizabeth Boston
|
Elizabeth Clopton
= James Verdon
|
Elizabeth Verdon
= Samuel Clarke
|
Elizabeth Clarke
= Peter Stoughton
|
Elizabeth Stoughton
= Nicholas Cobb Collison
|
John Collison
|
Genetically
Confirmed
|
Esther Collison
= Reuben Avis
|
Lucy Avis
= Edward Hopgood
|
George Collison Hopgood
= Julia Harding
|
Natalie Hopgood, (descent through her father

from the Collisons of Norfolk, the Plantagenet
Kings and the Imperial and Royal House of Vere.
Descent through her mother from Lt. Col
George Butcher of Windsor Castle, Sarah Butcher
of Framlingham and the Huegenot Bourchier
Counts of Versailles, France)
=James Weir of Vere
|
HI&RH Prince Nicholas de Vere

Chapter Twenty One

Ancient Royal Gothic Descents of the House of Collison

The Gothic Balthae Dynasty

King Boiorix of the Goths d. 101 BC
Line descends
|
King Etepamara of the Goths c. 90 AD
Line descends
|
King Nidad of the Visi-Goths (Tervingi)
218-249
|
King Ovida of the Visi-Goths 249-273

King Ascaric of the Visi-Goths
Line descends
|
King Vidigoia of the Visi-Goths
|
King Wihturic of the Visi-Goths c. 376
|
King Athanaric of the Visi-Goths 383
= Queen Gaatha of the Visi-Goths
dau. of King Fridigar of the Goths
|
King Alaric of the Visi-Goths
Sacked Rome in 410 AD
|
King Teodoredo 1st Gothic King of Spain 418-451
|
King Evarix of the Visi-Goths
Gothic King of Spain 466-484
= Princess Ragnahilde
|
King Alaric II Gothic King of Spain
= Princess Arevagna
|
King Giselac Gothic King of Spain 507-511
|
King Amalaric Gothic King of Spain 511-531
|
King Tribigildo Gothic King of Spain 531-548
= Princess Gisela of the Goths
|
King Thiudigisclus Gothic King of Spain 548-549
|

King Theodimir Gothic King of Spain 567-571
|
King Leova Gothic King of Spain 571-572
= Princess Theodosia
|
King Hermenegild II Gothic King of Spain
Murdered 586
|
King Recaredo I Gothic King of Spain 586-601
= Princess Clotsvinth of France
|
King Leova Gothic King of Spain 601-603
|
King Witeric Gothic King of Spain 603-610
|
King Gundemar Gothic King of Spain 610-612
|
King Sisebuto Gothic King of Spain 612-621
|
King Suintila Gothic King of Spain 621-631
|
King Sisenande Gothic King of Spain 631-636
|
King Chintila Gothic King of Spain 636-640
Son of King Fritgarde and Queen Chinterico
|
King Tulga Gothic King of Spain 640-642
|
King Chindasuinto 642-649
= Princess Reciberga
|
King Reccesvinto Gothic King of Spain 649-672
|
King Ervigio Gothic King of Spain 680-687
= Princess Liubigotona
|
King Rodrigo Gothic King of Spain 709-711
|
King Pelayas 1st King of Asturias 718-737
= Princess Ingunde of France
|
King Atanagildo Gothic King of Spain
= Princess Flavia Juliana of Byzantium
|
King Atanagildo Gothic King of Spain
= Princess Goto of Burgundy
|
King Ervigio Gothic King of Spain
= Princess Liubigotona of the Goths
|
King Pedro of Spain
|
Princess Aupais of the Goths
= Duke Pepin II of Heristal, Mayor of the
Palaces of Austrasia, Neustria and Burgundy
|
Lord Charles Martel (The Hammer)
|
Pepin the III Brevis, Duke of Lower Lorraine

(Brabant)
Mayor of Neustrasia, King of the Franks
= Lady Leuthergis
|
Charlemagne the Great
King of France 771-814
Holy Roman Emperor 800-814
= Princess Hildegarde
|
Emperor Louis I
814-830
=2. Princess Judith of Bavaria
|
Emperor Lothair I
Middle Emperor from 840
King of Western Franks 843-855
|
Emperor Louis II of Italy
855-975
|
Princess Irmengarde
= Count Bouquet VIII of
Provence
|
Lady Kunigund
= Count Sigebert of Verdun
(Bouquet IX of Provence)
|
Duke Gozelo I
Duke of Lower Lorraine
(Descent to the House of Habsburg-Lorraine)
1023-1044
|
Duke Godfrey II
Duke of Upper Lorraine
d. 1069
= Princess Doda
|
Saint Ida of Ardennes
= Eustace II de Vere
Comte de Boulogne
|
Princess Ida de Vere
= Baudouin de Bourg
Comte de Rethul
|
Prince Hugues I
Comte de Rethul
= Melisende (Melusine II)
dau. Of Bouchard Comte de Corbeil and
Lady Adelaide de Crecy
|
Badouin II de Bourg
King of Jerusalem 1118-1131
= Princess Morfia of Armenia
|
Princess Melisende of Jerusalem (Melusine III)
= Fulke V Plantagenet Count of Anjou
descent from Princess Plantina, sister

of the Fairy Princess Melusine I and mother
of Lord Tortulf de Nide de Merle
|
Count Geoffrey Plantagenet of Anjou and Maine
= Princess Mathilda of England la Imperatrice
(Empress of England)
|
King Henry II Plantagenet
= Countess Eleanor of Aquitaine
|
King John 'Lackland' Plantagenet
= Lady Isabella of Angouleme
|
King Henry III Plantagenet
= Lady Eleanor dau. of Count
Raymond Berenguer IVof Provence
and Princess Beatrix of Savoy
|
King Edward I Plantagenet
= Princess Eleanor of Castille
|
King Edward II Plantagenet
= Princess Isabella of France
|
Princess Joan Plantagenet
= Gilbert de Clare
Earl of Gloucester
|
Lady Elizabeth de Clare
= Sir Roger D'Amorie
|
Elizabeth D'Amorie
= John Lord Bardolf
|
William Lord Bardolf
= Agnes Poynings
|
Lady Cecilia Bardolf
= Sir Bryan Stapylton
|
Sir Miles Stapylton
= Katherine de la Pole
g. granddaughter of
Geoffrey Chaucer
|
Elizabeth Stapylton
= Sir William Calthorpe
|
Ann Calthorpe
= Sir Robert Drury
|
Anne Drury
= George Waldegrave
|
Sir William Waldegrave
= Juliana Rainsford
|
Sir William Waldegrave II
= Elizabeth Middlemay

|
Mary Waldegrave
= Thomas Clopton
|
Walter Clopton of Fordham
=Anne Thornton
|
Roger Clopton
= Elizabeth Boston
|
Elizabeth Clopton
= James Verdon
|
Elizabeth Verdon
= Samuel Clarke
|
Elizabeth Clarke
= Peter Stoughton
|
Elizabeth Stoughton
= Nicholas Cobb Collison
|
John Collison
|
Genetically
Confirmed
|
Esther Collison
= Reuben Avis
|
Lucy Avis
= Edward Hopgood
|
George Collison Hopgood
= Julia Harding
|
Natalie Hopgood, (descent through her father
from the Collisons of Norfolk, the Plantagenet
Kings and the Imperial and Royal House of Vere.
Descent through her mother from Lt. Col
George Butcher of Windsor Castle, Sarah Butcher
of Framlingham and the Huegenot Bourchier
Counts of Versailles, France)
=James Weir of Vere
|
HI&RH Prince Nicholas de Vere

Chapter Twenty Two

Collison Cousin Descent from Vlad III Dracula Tepes

Collison Cousin Descent from Vlad III Dracula

Prince Almos of Hungary
Prince of Transylvania
d. 895

|

Prince Arpad of Hungary
Prince of Transylvania
d. 907

|

Prince Zoltan of Hungary
Prince of Transylvania
d. 947

|

Prince Taksony of Hungary
Prince of Transylvania
d. 972

|

Duke Mihaly of Poland
Prince of Transylvania
d. 976
= Princess Adelajda of Poland

|

Prince Vasul (Pagan Magyar)
Prince of Transylvania
d. 1037

|

King Bela I of Hungary
King of Transylvania
d. 1063
= Princess Rixa of Poland d. of
King Miezsko and Queen Rixa
of Poland
(Descent to the House of Collison and
HI&RH Prince Nicholas Tarnawa-de Vere von Drakenberg KGC., KCD.,
KT. St. A.S. Sovereign Prince and Grand Duke of the Incorporeal Sovereign

Nation State of Drakenberg. Sovereign Grand Master of the Imperial and Royal Dragon Court, Sovereign Grand Master and Commander-in-Chief of the Order of Knights Templars).

|

Solomon (Salamon) August 1063 28 October 1074 son of Andrew I

|

Géza I, 28 October 1074, 25 April 1077 son of Béla I

|

St. Ladislaus (Szent László) 25 April 1077, 29 July 1095 son of Béla I

|

Coloman (Könyves Kálmán) 29 July 1095 3 February 1116 son of Géza I.

|

Stephen II 3 February 1116, 3 April 1131 Son of Kálmán

|

Árpáds Béla II the Blind (Vak Béla) 3 April 1131, 13 February 1141 grandson of Géza I., son of Álmos, Kálmán's executed younger brother

|

Géza II, 13 February 1141, 31 May 1162 son of Béla II

|

Stephen III, 31 May 1162, 4 March 1172 son of Géza II

|

Ladislaus II, 31 May 1162, 14 January 1163 rebel anti-king, younger brother of Géza II.

|

Stephen IV, 14 January 1163 June 1163 rebel anti-king, younger brother of Géza II.

|

Béla III, 4 March 1172, 13 April 1196 younger brother of Stephen III.

|

Emeric (Imre) 13 April 1196, 30 November 1204 son of Béla III.

|

Ladislaus III, 30 November 12047 May 1205 son of Imre, crowned and died as a child

|

Andrew II, 7 May 1205, 21 September 1235 brother of Imre

|

Béla IV, 14 October 1235, 3 May 1270 son of Andrew II., the "second founder" after the First Mongol invasion (1241-42)

|

Stephen V, 3 May 1270, 6 August 1272 son of Béla IV.

|

Ladislaus IV the Cuman (Kun László) 6 August 1272, 10 July 1290 son of Steven V.; unsuccessful

Mongol invasion; lived with the nomad Cuman tribes

|

Andrew III, 4 August 1290, 14 January 1301 grandson of Andrew II., born in Venice last of the Árpád dynasty

|

Wenceslaus of Bohemia (Vencel) 1301-1305 King of Bohemia, elected as King of Hungary but not universally recognized

|

Otto of Bavaria (Béla V) (Ottó) or Béla V, 6 December 1305-1308 Duke of Lower Bavaria, was not universally recognized

|

Charles Robert I (Károly Róbert) 20 August 1310, 16 July 1342 established the Angevin dynasty in Hungary.

|

Louis I the Great (Nagy Lajos) 16 July 1342, 11 September 1382 also King of Poland

|

Maria I (I. Mária) 11 September 1382, 17 May 1395 married Sigismund of Luxemburg

|

Charles II the Small (Kis Károly) 31 December 1385, 24 February 1386, also King of Naples, in opposition to Mary

|

Sigismund (Zsigmond) 31 March 1387, 9 December 1437, later also Roman-German King (since 1410), King of Bohemia (since 1419), Holy Roman Emperor (since 1433)

|

Albert 1, January 1438, 27 October 1439 son-in-law Sigismund, also Roman-German King, King of Bohemia, Duke of Austria Kingship disputed between Ulászló I and Ladislaus Posthumus

Jagiellon Ulászló I, 15 May 1440, 10 November 1444 also King of Poland

|

Ladislaus V Posthumus, 15 May 1440, 23 November 1457 born in 1440 after his father's death, spent most of his life in captivity.

|

János Hunyadi, 1446-1453 ruled as regent. Fought with great success against the Ottomans

|

Matthias Corvinus (Corvin Mátyás) 24 January 1458, 6 April

|

Ilona Szilagyi, Daughter of Stephen Szilagyi; cousin of Matthias Corvinus = Vlad III Dracula

APPENDIX A

The Senior Descent of the House of Vere in Ireland

Descent of the House of Vere to H.E.
Count Clive Weir of Vere of Enniskillen

Lady Euphemia Hamilton
(descent from the High Elves of Ireland,
Princess Melusine and the Scots Kings)
= Lord James Weir of Vere,
Baron Blackwood d. 1599
|
James (d.sp.) – William – Robert (moved to Fermanagh)
|
Alexander Weir of Vere
|
Alexander Weir of Vere
= Sarah Goodwin
|
Robert Weir of Vere
= Anne Carlton
|
John Weir of Vere
|
Captain Noble Weir of Vere
Of Enniskillen
|
Robert Weir of Vere
= Frances Weir of Vere
|
Lancelot Weir of Vere b. 1834
|
Robert Weir of Vere
|
Lancelot Weir of Vere
|
Ivan Weir of Vere
|
Count Clive Weir of Vere von Drakenburg
= Countess Sharon Marrs
|
Countess Hannah – Countess Deborah – Count Robert – Count Harry Alexander

APPENDIX B

The Descent of the Baronial House of Weir of Vere of Kildress Ulster, in Western Australia

The prince James Weir of Vere,
Baron Blackwood d. 1595
= Lady Euphemia Hamilton
|
Sir William Vere of Stanebyres Castle
= Elizabeth Hamilton, his cousin
(descent from the High Elves of Ireland,
Princess Melusine and the Scots Kings)
|
Lord Thomas Weir of Vere, Baron Kirkton
= Lady Jane Somerville, the hereditary Witch of
the Dragon House of the Earls Somerville
|
Major Thomas Weir of Vere of Edinburgh,
Baron Kirkton of Mid-Lothian
The hereditary Witch King of Mid-Lothian
= Margaret Bourdon
|
Lord Thomas Weir of Vere,
Baron Kirkton of Mid-Lothian,
Hereditary Witch King in Ireland
= Mary Robison of Cookstown Ulster
(
)
John Weir of Vere
|
Andrew Weir of Vere
|
Margaret Weir of Vere of Kildress
|
Archibald Weir of Vere of Kildress
= Rachel Stewart of Desertcreat
|
Robert Weir of Vere of Kildress
|
John Weir of Vere of Ardwell, Logan Manor
= Mary Logan dau. of Thomas Logan of
Ardwell, Logan Manor, Galloway
|
William Weir of Vere
= Susan Helen Craw
of Kirkmaiden, Scotland
1910

|
Baron William Ian Weir of Vere von Drakenberg of
Leeming
Western Australia
= Coral Morwyn Thomas
|
Coral Anne Weir of Vere of Leeming
= William Doney
|
Martin Paul – Kaaron – Naomi - Adam
|
Emma – Maree – Philip

Vere of Lewes

Thomas Weir of Vere
= Mary Robison
|
John Weir of Vere
|
Margaret Weir of Vere
=Archibald Thompson of MacTammais (MacTavish)
|
Archibald Weir of Vere
=Rachel Stewart
|
Robert Weir of Vere
=Sarah Graham
|
John Weir of Vere
=Mary Logan
|
Thomas Weir of Vere
=Anne Grant MacDonald
|
Alan Weir of Vere of Lewes
=Elizabeth Dahlmann
|
Jamie and Mandy de Vere von Drakenberg

APPENDIX C

The Meaning of the Vere name in Eurasia

Simple Introduction

The Vere name appears first in Sanskrit, which originated with the Aryan-Scythians of the Iranian Plateau and Greater Scythia in 1800 Bc. It has correlates in numerous Indo-European language branches, in which the name means exactly the same thing.

In Gallic we have the situation where the letters "P" and "B" are interchangeable, and where "Bh," "B" and "Mh" translate as "V," as does the letter "F." In Russian Cyrillic "B" also translates as "V."

Sanskrit: Vira = Man, Hero (mighty overlord). Broken into its component syllables: Vi = High; Ra (from Ri/Rig) = Royal/King.

Avestan (Old Eastern Scythian): Vira = Man, Hero (mighty overlord) Broken into its component syllables: Vi = High; Ra (from Ri/Rig) = Royal/King.

Kushan (Old Western Scythian), Danaan and Pictish Scythian (Ireland and Scotland): Fer/Ver/Vere = High King. (cf; Irish Gaelic – Fir = Man). Broken into its component syllables: Ve = High; Re (from Ri/Righ) = Royal/King. Cf: Ardrigh = Gaelic; High King.

Roman: Viri = Mighty, Great, Overlord (as in the Latin "Virideus": Mighty God or Chief God).Broken into its component syllables: Vi = High; Ri (from Ri/Regis) = Royal/King.

Old German: Ver/Vor/Uber or Wer = Man, Truth, Over. (as in Waerloga or Warlock where Waer = Truth and Loga = to lie. Waerloga means to present lies as the truth. It refers to a traitor and has no connection with witchcraft). Cf: Uberherr = Overlord.

413

Old French: Ver = Green/Spring (fairy and witch associations with the forests and fertility, see: Melusine de Vere, the Dragon/Fairy Witch of the forest maze of Angiers), Truth/Glass/Crystal (transparency or truth, cf; "The crystal womb of the Virgin from whence shone the light of Christ").

Old Romano-British – Ver/Vor = Overlord (Ver/Vortigherna - "Vortigern": Overlord or High King).

Old Anatolian (Turkey): Vere (Over/lord) directly related to Vber/Uber (over/lord), meaning Witch (Archdruid)/Vampire. From thence to Romania and Transylvania where vampire/overlord is "Oupire," on to Russia where vampire/overlord is "Upiore."

Because of the interchangeable nature of the letters P, B, Bh, Mh and V in ancient Europe, the following applies.

Anatolia was originally a Gaelic-Scythian district controlled by the druids. The word Vber (vampire-witch-druid-overlord) would therefore have translated as V-Ver.

In Scythian (Gallic) Transylvania Oupire (vampire) would have originally been "Ou – Vir – E."

In Scythian Bulgaria (and later Eire) Fir is pronounced VIR; meaning "Man." Our early ancestors: The Fir Bolg predecessors of the Tuadha de Danaan in pre-Christain Ireland, originated in Bulgaria. Scholars have stated that the word "Bolg" means bag and, because of this somewhat tenuous translation, others have assumed that the name Fir Bolg meant "Men of the bags" and have attributed the epithet to a time when they claim that the Fir Bolg were enslaved and forced to carry bags of earth from point a, to point b, by their captors.

In The Dragon Legacy I specifically pointed out that the word "Bolg" meant "God" (as does the British "Bog" syllable in the word "Boggart" or "Fairy"). In particular Bolg is the male component of the Gallic God of Lightning and has a direct linguistic and deific correlation with the Sumerian/Babylonian Anunnaki-Dragon God of Lightning and Storms: Baal.

Consequently the name "Fir/Vir/Ver Bolg" actually means "Men of God," specifically the God of Lightning (and Storms). In the Gothic, Shamanic and Kabbalistic Traditions Lightning becomes the Great Serpent or Dragon which descends the Tree of Life from Heaven to Earth as inspiration from the Gods.

Therefore "Fir/Vir/Ver Bolg" means specifically: "Priests/Overlords of the Dragon"; inspired from, and directly connected to, the Gods. Likewise, as with "Bolg," its British counterpart "Bog" meaning both "god" and "fairy" (Vey or Vere), indicates our ancient and continuing union with Godhead and the divine knowledge, wisdom and inspiration (Dragon Fire/Lighning) residing within our holy, royal blood.

In Siberia, the Shamans carried magical bags made from the skins of the Crane, which bird (formerly a sacred symbol of the Gallic Druids) is still sacred to the Hokkaido shamans of the Ainu of Northern Japan today.

The meaning of the name "Fir Bolg" as "Men of the Bags" is therefore purely incidental, and the carrying of the earth of one's motherland in bags when one migrated to a new land, was a tradition which was Scythian in origin, and stretched from as far afield as Transylvania to Scotland.

In this we are reminded that vampires generally, (and mythically Dracula in particular), covered the bottom of their coffins with native soil. In the 19th century, displaced Scots (Scythians) who suffered the Highland Clearances, migrated with Scottish soil in their boots and shoes, so they would always be walking on the sacred earth of their homeland. This ancient tradition relates to the belief that the sovereignty of the earth where one is born carries power.

In Russia the word Upiore (vampire) would have translated "U – VI – ORE."

In Old German Uber translates as "U- VER." Hence Uberherren: Uverherren = Overlords.

In Old French, Fairy also appears as Fey or Vey. This is a Gallic leftover where the letter "F" translates as the letter "V." This tradition still abides in the modern Welsh language. Consequently the name (Title) Vere is also synonimous with Vey or Fey.

In all instances the word "witch" (a clear seer) and the word "dragon" (a clear seer) are synonymous. Vere therefore also means "Dragon" and "Witch" (Druid/Fairy). Vere = Fairy King, via "fairy" which in Latin means Controller of Fate or Overlord. As above.

The direct linguistic and terminological links and relationships between these noun-verbs is utterly apparent and obvious, representing the transmigration and corruption of loan words and root meanings across Eurasia.

In summary the noun-verb "Vere" has justifiably been surrounded in an aura of magic, mystery and holy blood traditon for millenia and acquired a certain mystique arising from the myths and legends which have become the accretions attaching themselves to the historical, socio-political fact of Vere High Dragon Kingship. Consequently, the name Vere, contrary to the opinion of some authors, is not Norman-French in origin, and was not adopted by the Veres from the names of their estates. Rather, these estates, villages and towns derived their names from their Vere overlords.

Cyngor Sir **CEREDIGION**   **CEREDIGION** County Council

Miss Bronwen Morgan, LL.B.
Prif Weithredwr
Chief Executive

SWYDDOG COFRESTRU ETHOLIADOL

Neuadd Cyngor Ceredigion, Penmorfa, Aberaeron, SA46 0PA

☎   01545 572000
Ffacs/Fax   01545 572029
bronwenm@ceredigion.gov.uk
www.ceredigion.gov.uk
DX 92401 ABERAERON

HI & RH Prince N. de Vere von Drakenberg
Rathdragun Mor

SY23 4BA

Dyddiad
Date

Gofynnwch am
Please ask for

Llinell Uniongyrchol
Direct Line

Fy nghyf
My ref

Eich cyf
Your ref

Dyddiad Fel y Marc Post
Date as Postmark

EL/DWJ/CMT

☎ 01545-572033/572035

Dear Sir

REGISTER OF ELECTORS

I refer to our recent telephone conversation on the 14th of August and your letter dated the 1st of August, and firstly would like to apologise for the delay. I can confirm that your name of HI & RH Prince Nicholas de Vere von Drakenberg, appears on the Ceredigion Register of Electors, under the address of Rathdragun Mor, Llanafan, Aberystwyth, Ceredigion, SY23 4BA.

If you require any further information or assistance, then please do not hesitate to contact me.

Yr eiddoch yn gywir
Yours faithfully

CANFASIO BLYNYDDOL O ETHOLWYR 2009	CYNGOR SIR CEREDIGION		CEREDIGION COUNTY COUNCIL	ANNUAL CANVASS OF ELECTORS 2009

Dyddiad Cymhwysol 15fed Hydref 2008

Qualifying Date 15th October 2008

Llinell Gymorth
Helpline ☎ (01545) - 572033 / 572035

Peidiwch â Cholli'ch Hawl i Bleidleisio

Don't Lose your Right to Vote

Cyfeiriad	Address

RATHDRAGUN MOR

▉▉▉▉▉▉▉

SY23 4BA

‖‖‖‖‖‖‖‖‖‖‖‖‖‖‖‖
* 1 0 2 8 0 5 8 8 0 3 *

ENWAU'R TRIGOLION SYDD Â'R HAWL I BLEIDLEISIO / NAMES OF RESIDENTS ELIGIBLE TO VOTE		**3** Cenedligrwydd / Nationality	**4** Eithriad Gwasanaeth Rheithgor / Jury Service Exemption	**5** Cofrestr a Olygwyd / Edited Register	**6** Pleidlais Bost / Postal Vote

MELER Y NODIADAU ISOD - OS OES UNRHYW ENW WEDI EI GOFNODI YN ANGHYWIR, DILEWCH EF I YSGRIFENNWCH YR ENWAU) CYWIR. PEIDIWCH AG ANGHOFIO CYNNWYS ENWAU Y RHAI SYDD I 16/17 MLWYDD OED, A'U DYDDIADAU GENI. OS NAD OES NEB SYDD YN GYMWYS, CWBLHEWCH RHANNAU 9 A 10 YN UNIG.

SEE NOTES BELOW - IF ANY NAME IS ENTERED WRONGLY, CROSS OUT AND WRITE IN CORRECT NAME(S). DON'T FORGET TO INCLUDE 16/17 YEAR OLDS AND THEIR DATES OF BIRTH. IF NOBODY IS ELIGIBLE, JUST COMPLETE PARTS 9 AND 10.

Os byddwch yn 70 oed neu'n hŷn ar 15 Hydref 2008, ticiwch yma. If you will be 70 or over on the 15th October 2008, then tick here.

Os NAD ydych am ymddangos ar y Gofrestr a Olygwyd, ticiwch yma (gweler y nodyn). If you do NOT want to appear on the Edited Register then tick here (see note).

Ticiwch yma os hoffech gael ffurflen gais am Bleidlais Bost. (NID oes rhaid i chi ddo'r blwch hwn os ydych sieces yn pleidleisio drwy'r post). Tick here if you would like a Postal Vote Application form. (You do NOT need to tick this box if you are already a Postal Voter).

Enw (LLYTHRENNAU BRAS) / name (BLOCK LETTERS PLEASE)

Enw cyntaf a llythrennau canol yr enw (LLYTHRENNAU BRAS) / First name and middle initials (BLOCK LETTERS PLEASE)

BROOKS	JOHN A.		✓		
DE VERE VON DRAKENBERG	HI&RH PRINCE N				

Oes yna unrhyw un 16 neu 17 oed yn byw yn y cyfeiriad yma? / **Are there any 16 and 17 year olds living at this address?**

owch enwau a dyddiad geni pobl 16/17 oed. Please give names and dates of birth of 16/17 year olds		Cenedligrwydd / Nationality	Dyddiad geni llawn / Full date of birth	Gofrestr Olygedig / Edited Register	Pleidlais Bost / Postal Vote

enw (LLYTHRENNAU BRAS) / name (BLOCK LETTERS PLEASE)

Enw cyntaf a llythrennau canol (LLYTHRENNAU BRAS) / First name and middle initials (BLOCK LETTERS PLEASE)

					✓

Os ydych wedi symud tŷ o fewn CEREDIGION yn ystod y deuddeg mis diwethaf, nodwch y cyfeiriad blaenorol, os gwelwch yn dda / **If you have moved house within CEREDIGION in the last twelve months, please state previous address**

Os yw unrhyw rai o ganlynol yn gymwys rhowch ✓ yn y bocs perthnasol	**If any of the following apply put a ✓ in the relevant box**	**10**	**Datganiad**	**Declaration**

MAE'N DROSEDD I ROI GWYBODAETH FFUG WRTH LENWTR FFURFLEN HON. IT IS AN OFFENCE TO GIVE FALSE INFORMATION IN COMPLETING THIS FORM.

Yr wyf yn datgan hyd eithaf fy ngwybodaeth a'm cred bod y manylion a roddwyd yn wir a chywir.

I declare that to the best of my knowledge and belief the particulars given are true and accurate.

Iddo'n wag ar 15fed Hydref 2008 roperty empty on 15th October 2008 — Dinasyddion Gwledydd Tramor / Foreign Nationals ☐

Iddo Busnes/Gwyliau usiness/Holiday Premises — Cofrestrwyd Rywle arall / Registered Elsewhere ☐

Llofnod: / Signature: **X DE VERE** 〰️

Dyddiad: / Date: **19-08-08**

Rhif ffôn yn vstod y dydd (ddim yn orfodol)

ETHOLIAD SENEDDOL EWROPEAIDD
EUROPEAN PARLIAMENTARY ELECTION

ROYAL MAIL
Talwyd Y Cludiant
Postage Paid
HQ 16697

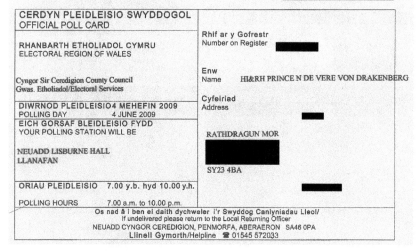

CERDYN PLEIDLEISIO SWYDDOGOL
OFFICIAL POLL CARD

RHANBARTH ETHOLIADOL CYMRU
ELECTORAL REGION OF WALES

Cyngor Sir Ceredigion County Council
Gwas. Etholiadol/Electoral Services

DIWRNOD PLEIDLEISIO 4 MEHEFIN 2009
POLLING DAY   4 JUNE 2009
EICH GORSAF BLEIDLEISIO FYDD
YOUR POLLING STATION WILL BE

NEUADD LISBURNE HALL
LLANAFAN

ORIAU PLEIDLEISIO   7.00 y.b. hyd 10.00 y.h.

POLLING HOURS   7.00 a.m. to 10.00 p.m.

Rhif ar y Gofrestr
Number on Register

Enw
Name   HI&RH PRINCE N DE VERE VON DRAKENBERG

Cyfeiriad
Address

RATHDRAGUN MOR

SY23 4BA

Os nad â i ben ei daith dychweler i'r Swyddog Canlyniadau Lleol/
If undelivered please return to the Local Returning Officer
NEUADD CYNGOR CEREDIGION, PENMORFA, ABERAERON SA46 0PA
Llinell Gymorth/Helpline ☎ 01545 572033

UK Passport Service

Newport Passport Office Upper Dock Street Newport NP20 1XA
Swyddfa Basport Casnewydd Stryd y Doc Uchaf Casnewydd NP20 1XA

PLEASE AFFIX CORRECT POSTAGE

HI&RH PRINCE NICHOLAS DE VERE VON DRAKENBERG

DE VERE VON DF
N

PO Box 175
Newport
NP20 1XA

7

SY23 4BA

P STOWELL

REF:

PLEASE USE THIS LABEL ON YOUR REPLY ENVELOPE

20 March 2007

Dear SIR

RE: PASSPORT APPLICATION FOR HI&RH PRINCE NICHOLAS DE VERE VON DRAKENBERG

Thank you for your passport application for the above named. However:

- You have omitted to enclose two recent photographs.

Please forward two recent duplicate photographs (i.e taken in the last month).

Please stick the attached label to the outside of your reply envelope with the correct postage.
Please do not phone us unless it is absolutely necessary. Repeated phone calls and
correspondence affect our ability to process applications. For information on how long we take to
process passport applications you may visit our web site www.passport.gov.uk or phone 0870 521
0410.

Yours sincerely

MRS P STOWELL   TEL 01633 477766 TEAM 7

info@passport.gov.uk www.passport.gov.uk

An Executive Agency of the Home Office
Un o Asiantaethau Gweithredol y Swyddfa Gartref

INVESTOR IN PEOPLE

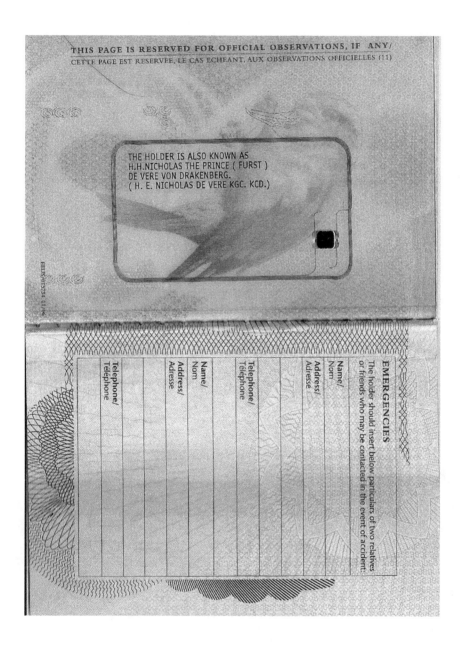

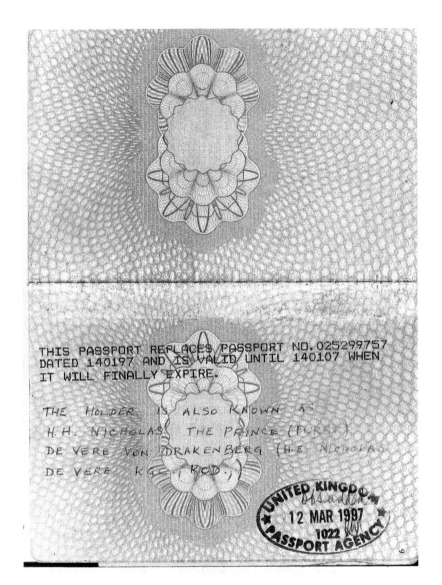

THIS PASSPORT REPLACES PASSPORT NO. 025299757
DATED 140197 AND IS VALID UNTIL 140107 WHEN
IT WILL FINALLY EXPIRE.

THE HOLDER IS ALSO KNOWN AS
H.H. NICHOLAS THE PRINCE (FÜRST)
DE VERE VON DRAKENBERG (H.E. NICHOLAS
DE VERE KGC (KCD.))

UNITED KINGDOM
12 MAR 1997
1022
PASSPORT AGENCY

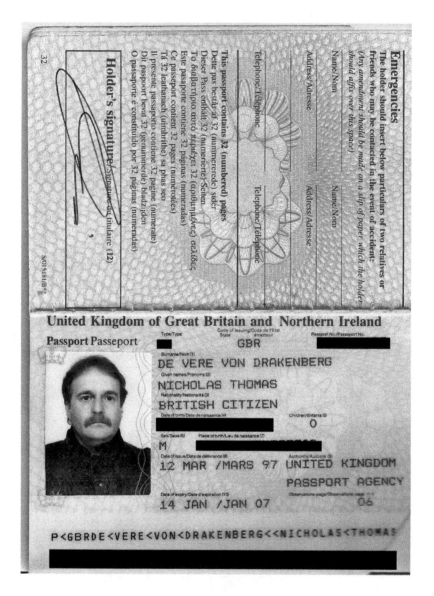

Holder's signature/Signature du titulaire (12).

This passport contains 32 (numbered) pages
Dette pas bestâr af 32 (nummererede) sider
Dieser Pass enthält 32 (numerierte) Seiten
Tò διαβατήριο αυτό περιέχει 32 (αριθμημένες) σελίδες
Este pasaporte contiene 32 páginas (numeradas)
Ce passeport contient 32 pages (numérotées)
Tá 32 leathanach (uimhrithe) sa phas seo
Il presente passaporto contiene 32 pagine (numerate)
Dit paspoort bevat 32 (genummerde) bladzijden
O passaporte é constituído por 32 páginas (numeradas)

Emergencies
The holder should insert below particulars of two relatives or
friends who may be contacted in the event of accident.
(Any amendment should be made on a slip of paper which the holder
should affix over this space)

Name/Nom
Address/Adresse
Telephone/Téléphone

Name/Nom
Address/Adresse
Telephone/Téléphone

United Kingdom of Great Britain and Northern Ireland

Passport Passeport

Type/Type	Code of Issuing/Code de l'État State émetteur	Passport No./Passeport No.
	GBR	

Surname/Nom (1)
DE VERE VON DRAKENBERG

Given names/Prénoms (2)
NICHOLAS THOMAS

Nationality/Nationalité (3)
BRITISH CITIZEN

Date of birth/Date de naissance (4)   Children/Enfants (5)
                                          0

Sex/Sexe (6)   Place of birth/Lieu de naissance (7)
M

Date of issue/Date de délivrance (8)   Authority/Autorité (9)
12 MAR /MARS 97   UNITED KINGDOM
                    PASSPORT AGENCY

Date of expiry/Date d'expiration (10)   Observations-page/Observations-page (11)
14 JAN /JAN 07   06

P<GBRDE<VERE<VON<DRAKENBERG<<<NICHOLAS<THOMAS

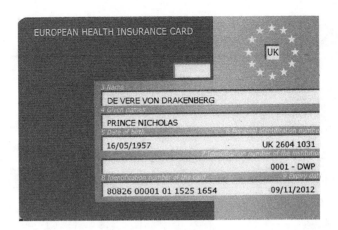

DRIVING LICENCE

1. DE VERE VON DRAKENBERG
2. PRINCE NICHOLAS

3. 16–05–57 GREAT BRITAIN
4a. 08–03–05 4b. 07–03–15 4c. DVLA

5.
7. Von Drakenberg

8. HILL HOUSE, 94 NORTH STREET, TURNERS HILL, CRAWLEY, RH10 4NS

9. A,B,BE,B1,C1,C1E,D1,D1E,*f,k,l,n,p,h*

Keep this safe

Counterpart Driving Licence

DVLA
Driver and Vehicle
Licensing Agency

Important Document – The photocard and paper counterpart should be kept together. Both must be produced when required.

C 7182996 **D740**

PRINCE NICHOLAS DE VERE VON
DRAKENBERG
HILL HOUSE
94 NORTH STREET
TURNERS HILL
CRAWLEY
RH10 4NS   73841

2450630300
Driver number

Issue number

45A

Von Drakenberg

Provisional Entitlement *(see booklet INS57P for category details)*

Category	From	Until	Codes	Category	From	Until	Codes
G	16 05 74	15 05 27					

Entitlement History *(see Section 3 overleaf)*

Category	From	Codes

Endorsements *(as supplied by convicting Court) See booklet INS 57P for offence codes*

Convicting Court code	Date of conviction			Offence code	Date of offence			Fine £	Disqual. period	Other	Penalty points
	Day	Month	Year		Day	Month	Year				

NOTE: < means "earlier than"

You may only drive the above if you hold current entitlement for a higher category.

Official Use

Changes to your permanent address, please write clearly in the boxes using CAPITAL LETTERS IN BLACK INK. *(See Section 5 overleaf)*

New house No.   New Post Code

New address

This document must not be used for change of name. For change of name please refer to the D1, which can be obtained from Post Office® branches.

Send the completed form with your photocard licence to DVLA, Swansea, SA99 1BN

Sign in the
white box to
confirm changes   Date _____

C 7182996

An executive agency of the
Department for
Transport

7/04

NATIONAL INSURANCE NUMBERCARD

DEPARTMENT FOR WORK AND PENSIONS / INLAND REVENUE

N.I number

PRINCE NICHOLAS DE VERE

THIS IS NOT PROOF OF IDENTITY

SOCIAL SERVICES CARD
CÁRTA SEIRBHÍSÍ
SÓISIALACHA

IRL

6OO713 8392678030 OO3

PRINCE NICHOLAS DE VERE

PPS (RSI) NUMBER/UIMHIR

ISSUE DATE/DÁTA EISIÚNA
07/04/2005

The Map of World Government and the Descending Seniority of Global Royal Families

– University of Heidelberg 2006 –

http://www.scribd.com/doc/22622835/World-Government-Schematic

Organisations rendered in parentheses indicate non
Royal corporations or individuals

(The World Trade Organisation)

(The Bilderberg Group)

The Imperial and Royal House of Tarnawa
De Vere von Drakenberg and the Imperial
and Royal Dragon Court of the Sovereign
Grand Duchy of Drakenberg

And

The Earl of Rothmere and the Baron von Worms

The House of Rothschild

(The United States Government including

The CIA and the NSA Intelligence Agencies)

(NATO)

(The European Union)

(Le Republique de France)

(The Holy See and Pope Benedict VI)

The House of Windsor

The Sovereign Military Order of Malta

The House of Lichtenstein

The Houses of Wurtemburg, Westminster and Stewart

(BarclaysBank PLC)

(The Bank of England)

The European Council of Princes

(President: Mr. Michael La Fosse de Chatrie

a.k.a. Prince Michael Stewart of Albany)

(BP Amoco PLC and Royal Dutch Shell Oil)

Baroness Dunn

(Ford Motor Company)

APPENDIX E

Krupa Shield

The Descent of the Imperial and Royal Dragon Princes of Tarnawa-Krupa de Vere von Drakenberg, and the Amalgamation of the Western and Eastern Dragon Dynasties

Imperial Proclamation
The Scythian-Merovingian and Khazarian-Ashina Elven, Cousin Imperial and Royal Families of de Vere von Drakenberg and Tarnawa-Krupa are amalgamated, abiding in perpetuity as one family indivisible – under the suzerainty of the former – to become the greater Eurasian Dynasty of Tarnawa (-Krupa) de Vere von Drakenberg, a dynasty encompassing the Kuchan Province of China in the east; to Southern Gothic Spain in the west.

DESCENT TO THE ROYAL HOUSE OF TARNAWA-KRUPA DE VERE VON DRAKENBERG OF ASHINA OF KHAZARIA THE CENTRAL ASIAN TRIBE AND DYNASTY OF THE WOLF AND THE DRAGON
«…son of a Wolf and a Sea Goddess..»
(genetic-genealogy ancestral pool)

SUMERIAN-TURKO HUNNIC LINGUISTIC/SYMBOLIC CONNECTION
F.Hommel in the Sumerian texts found 200 words coinciding with Türkic words [Hommel F. , 1915].
Olyas Suleymenov observed 60 Sumerian words similar to the Türkic words: ada "father," ama "mother," tu "to give birth," ere "man," "soldier," ugu "arrow," tag "fasten," zag "side," bilga "wise, ancestor," me "I,"

ze "you," ane "here, now," gud "bull," gash "bird," kir "dirt, soil," ush "three," u "ten," ken "wide," uzuk "long," tush "descend," ud "fire," udun "tree, firewood," dingir "god, sky," tengir "god, sky," etc. O.Suleymenov [Suleymenov O., 1975, 230-242] subjects each word to research, proves the Sumero-Türkic concurrences.

A Russian scientist, I.M.Diyakonov, comparing the Sumerian words with the Indo-European, does not find a single case of coincidence [Diyakonov I.M., 1954, 84].

O.N. Tuna suggests that the Türkic language 5,500 years b.p. already had a logically developed by its carriers phonetical set and grammatic system. Allowing another 5500 years before that for the development of this system, the age of the Türkic language appears to be 11,000 years. As to time of the recording of the Türkic language in writing (Sumerian cuneiform writing), it was 8,000-8,500 years ago [Tuna O.N., 1990, 49].

A sample of Gokturk Inscriptions, commissioned by Gokturk Khans (Royal Ashina Dynasty), one of several in Mongolia, near river Orkhun, dated 732-735;

(from Bilge Khan):

"He (Sky God or "Gok Tanri") is the one who sat me on the throne so that the name of the Turkish Nation would live forever."

Tanri, Tengri or Tengeri means in Turkic language - Sky, God, Sky-God.
Tengir or Dingir is in Sumerian language - Sky, God, Sky-God.
Sky God is EL-ENLIL-YHWH-TENGRI-LORD OF THE AIR AND EARTH.

In ancient Turkic mythology symbol for Tengri - the Sky God is a Dragon.
KINGS OF TURKS - TURKISH ROYALTY Descent-Lines
Part 0: Descent of Tiamat (the very same as of The House of Vere of Anjou)
Part 1: Kings of Turks (Note; list should be considered as Krupa ancestral genealogical „pool")
Part 2: Kings of Khazars (Note; list from no.01-26th should be considered as Krupa ancestral genealogical „pool")
Part 3: Q1b Ashkenazi Jewish families/Krupa family list (PARTIAL)
Part 0.: Descent of Tiamat (Mother Queen)
Dragon Queen of the Annunaki
– refer to the «Descent of the Royal House of Vere of Anjou» chart
Part 1:The Turkish Royalty Descent-Line-ASIA

SCYTHIAN SKHILTY DYNASTY
DRAGON KINGS

01. Abtin (800 BC), chief/king of the Hyrkanians [Scythians] in Central Asia, claimed descent from the semi-mythological Skhilti Dynasty of Scythia, which claimed descent from Targitaus, called "1st" King of Scythia, the ancestor-deity of the Scythians and mythological eponymous ancestor of the Turks, the son of the Nephilim Zuisundra (descendant of Enki) and a mortal-woman, the sis of Thoas, King of Scythia, &, dau
of Borysthenes, King of Lemnos

[note: another myth says the dynasty
descended from one of the sons of the epic Greek hero Hercules
begotten of the "monstrous" half-human/half-reptile Scythian queen,
circa 1200 BC]
02. Faridun, last chief/king of the Hyrkanians, settled in the Iranian
province of Baluchestan

SHAMAN (TENGRIST) ROYAL AFRASIYAB DYNASTY DRAGON KINGS

03. Tur, 1st King of Turan, bro of Salm & Erij [the father of
Manuchehr, father of Nowzar], c. 750 BC
04. Duraushasp, King of Turan
05. Spaenyasp, King of Turan 700 BC
06. Turak, King of Turan
07. Zadsham, King of Turan, contemporary of Ariantas, King of Scythia
(650 BC) [Scythia's Paralat Dynasty, conquered by Sarmatians circa
100 BC]
08. Pashang, King of Turan 600 BC
09. Afrasiyab, last King of Turan, gave name to Turkish Royalty, which
called itself the House of Afrasiyab; conquered by Cyrus "The Great,"
Shah of Persia [identified with Kei-Khusru of Persian saga], who
annexed Turan to Persia, c. 550 BC
10. Phrada, first King of proto-Turks [were refugees from Turan on the
move], 522BC, migrated and settled in Turkestan [modern Turkmenistan]
in Central Asia
from whom descends: about 17 generations
[vassals successively of the Persians (c 500-330 BC), Greco-Macedonians
(330-312BC), the Seleucids of Syria (312-256 BC), and the Hellenic
Kingdom of Bactria (256-58 BC) until at length achieving independence]
28. Bonon, King of Margiana [Margush] [modern Merv region] located in
Turkestan [modern Turkmenistan], 58-20 BC
29. Spalyris, King of Margiana [Turkestan] 20-1 BC
30. Ortagan, King of Margiana [Turkestan] 1 BC-AD 20
31. Gondophar, King of Margiana [Turkestan] AD 20-50
32. Pacorus, King of Margiana [Turkestan] 50-60
33. Kanaban, King of Margiana [Turkestan] 60-80
from whom descends: about 11 generations
[vassals successively of the Kushans (80 BC-AD 240), Persians
(240-350), and Chinese (350-406)]
45. Liu Tsugu, a Turkish prince (d398), whose parents migrated and
settled in China's northern Liang
province along with the other Turks

46. Ashina [Ashihna] [Asena], revolted against Chinese vassalage and
broke free achieving independence for China's northern Liang province;
duke of the Turks [or Liang] 398, chief/king 406 (d433), eponym of the
Assena/Ashina clan

issue:
a. Apangpu [Tsugu-Pieng-Sun], descends chiefs/kings of the Turks, and,
ancestor of Bumin Khan, their first king (552), who founded the
Turkish Kingdom, centered at first in the Altai Mountains of Central
Asia (below)
b. Ichichni Shihtu, descends chiefs/kings of the Uighurs, and, father
of Asyana Shad, father of [?] Ay Uzhru, their first king (487), who
founded the Uygur [Uighurite] Empire centered in Central Asia between
the Mongols, Huns, and Chinese
c. Nothuliu, descends chiefs/kings of the Avars, and, grandfather of
Saroshu, Duke of Ukraine, grandfather of Kanadik, father of Bayar
Khan, their first king (562), who founded the Avarite Khanite centered
in the area between the Russia, Hungary, and Bessarabia
47. Apangpu [Tsugu-Pieng-Sun], chief/king of the Turks 433-461, led
migration of the Turks from China's northern Liang province to China's
western Xinjiang province, and settled in Kan-suh, near the modern
city of Shan-Tan, where the Turkish royal citadel was built on the
near-by hill so-called "Turku," "Diirkii," or "T'u-chueh" for the
tribe's national name, onetime the Turks' capital-city, and, ancestor
state of the later Avarite Khanate (562-796) [vassals of the powerful
Juan-Juan empire (c450-545)]
48. Hsien I, chief/king of the Turks 461-490

issue:
a. Pusun, chief/king of the Turks 490-491, father of Hsien II,
chief/king of the Turks 511-521
b. Kulapan, chief/king of the Turks 491-496
c. Liangu (below), father of Mengen (below)
49. Liangu, chief/king of the Turks 496-511
50. Mengen, chief/king of the Turks 521-523
51. Tuwu Tayehu [Tsugu T'u-u Mengen], chief/king of the Turks 523-545
issue:
a. Bumin, chief 545/king 552 of the Turks, below
b. Istemi (d576), below
c. Tardu, (d573), below
----
note: the descent-line above is continued below, see
----
note: issue of Bumin (above)
[a] Bumin, tribal chief of the Turks 545, reck'd 1st King of Turks;
revolts versus the Juan-Juan empire and migrates westwards; repulsing
attacks by the [H]Ephthalies [a Hunnish tribe] upon the Turks
migrating through the Russian
steppes; made an astonishing advance;
and establishes another settlement in Turkestan, founding [another]
Turkish state [the Tu-Kiu kingdom] in Central Asia, Year 552 (d553)
= Chang-Lo[-Kung-Cho], dau of Xi-Wei Wen-Ti, Emperor of China [N Wei]
535-552, & wife, dau of Anahuai [Anakai], King of Juan-Juan
issue:

a. Kholo [Kara Khan], # 2
b. Kushu Mugan, # 3
c. Tapur [Taspar], # 5

---

note: issue of Istemi [Iski Khan], bro of Bumin (above)
[b] Istemi [Shetimi] [Stembis] [Silzibul] [Iski Khan] (d576)
issue:
a. Shaporo, # 8B
b. Khulagu, # 10 B
c. Anghis Jabgu (d590)
d. dau [name], 1st wife of Khusru I [Xusrau], Shah of Persia (d579)

---

note: issue of Tardu, bro of Bumin (above)
[c] Tardu [Sukhaili] [Dardo] (d573)
issue:
a. Turruk Khan (d598) (below)
b. Togrul Khan (below)
issue of Turruk Khan (above):
a. Shabolo [I], # 12B
b. Saba, kld 589
c. Shifkwi [I], # 13B
issue of Togrul Khan, bro of Turruk Khan (above):
a. Tuli Khan, aka Koran Kagan, # 15B

regnal-list of Turkish rulers
[dates are approximate: there are
variations of this genealogy, each of which give a different
chronology]
According to the New Book of Tang, the Ashina were related to the northern
tribes of the Xiongnu. As early as the 7th century, four theories about their
mythical origins were recorded by the Book of Zhou, Book of Sui and
Youyang Zazu:
- Ashina was one of ten sons born to a grey she-wolf (see Asena) in the north
of Gaochang.
- The ancestor of the Ashina was a man from the Suo nation, north of
Xiongnu, whose mother was a wolf, and a season goddess (Persephone?).
- The Ashina were mixture stocks from the Pingliang commandery of
eastern Gansu.
- The Ashina descended from a skilled archer named Shemo, who had once
fallen in love with a sea goddess (Amphitrite?) west of Ashide cave.
These stories were sometimes pieced together to form a chronologically
narrative of early Ashina history. However, as the Book of Zhou, the Book
of Sui, and the Youyang Zazu were all written around the same time, during
early Tang Dynasty, whether they could truly be considered chronological
or rather should be considered competing versions of the Ashina's origin is
debatable. These stories also have parallels to folktales and legends of other
Turkic peoples, for instance, the Uyghurs and the Wusun.

SHAMAN (TENGRIST) ROYAL ASHINA DYNASTY
DIVINE HEROES, AK-JANG;HERO-MESSIAH-KING
DRAGON KINGS

01. Bumin [T'u-min] Khan, tribal chief of the Turks 545, reck'd 1st
King of Turks, founds [another] Turkish state 552 (d553), changed
family-name from "Tsugu" to "Assena"(Ashina)

The name Tujué (like that of Ashina) appeared in Chinese sources relatively
late, the first record being dated 542 meaning "strong" or "powerful."
Göktürk is said to mean "Celestial Turks." This is consistent with "the
cult of heavenly ordained rule" which was a pivotal element of the Altaic
political culture before being imported to China.
Similarly, the name of the ruling Ashina clan probably derives from the
Khotanese Saka term for "deep blue," aššina.
The name might also derive from a Tungusic tribe related to Aisin.
issue: see above
02. Kholo Kagan [Kara Khan] [Qara Issyk Khan] [Kelou Irksi Kagan],
King 553 (above)
issue:
a. Yandu Muchu Kagan, # 4
b. Kiuli Tegin [Mohotou]
c. [Y]Angsu Tegin [Yang-Su Tuliu]
----
note: issue of "Prince" [Y]Angsu Tegin (above), the son of Kholo
Kagan [Kara Khan], was:
a. Nivar Kagan [Neri Khan], # 8A
b. Zhangar, # 9A
c. Basyu Tegin [Boshir Teghin], # 11A
----
03. Muqan [Kushu Mugan Kagan] [Mukan; Mogan] [Djigin], King 553-572
issue:
a. Apa Qagan, # 7
b. Kayen (dau), 2nd wife of Khusru I [Khosroe], Shah of Persia (d579)
c. [name] (dau), wife of Pei-Chou Wu-Ti, Emperor of China [N Chou]
(d578)
04. Yandu Muchu Kagan, King 572
05. Tapur Qagan [Taspar] [Thopo Kagan] [To-Pei] [Arslan Tabo Khan],
King 572-578
issue:
Amrak, # 6
06. Amrak [Amro Khan][Anlo Khan], King 578
07. Apa Qapan [Apoukia Kagan] [Dizabul] [Ta-lo-pien], King 578-581
[note: his reign marks the first brilliant epoch of early Turkish
history]
issue:
a. Danao Tegin (d638)
b. Asena Tegin, father of Yasir Bulsa Kapan, father of Chuja Yabgu

(d644), father of Ghora Jabgu [Shaporo VII], # 21A

581: kingdom split into halves, west and east [A & B][dates are
approximate: there is another chronology that puts this event in Year
578 rather than Year 581; and the dates of the Turkish khans are
adjusted to that year]

8A Nivar Kagan [Neri Khan], King 581-597
issue:
a. Pio-She Tegin, kld 589
b. Nikul Chula [Nili Khan], # 10A
c. Shifkwi [II], # 13A
d. Tong Jabgu Khan, # 14A
e. Moho Shad

---

note: issue of "Prince" Moho Shad (above), the son of Nivar Kagan [#
8A], was:
a. Shapolo [II] Tielishe Kaghan [Tongngo] (d639), # 18B
b. Nichu Kagan [Hilipi Khan] (639-641 dep, d653), # 19B
c. Kian Shad, father of Pihotu Kaghan (d641), # 21B
d. Kieyue Khan [Puli Shad], King of Khazars (640)

---

note: issue of Kieyue Khan, King of Khazars (above), was:
a. Ashena Holo [Shapolo Kagan] (d657), father of Tiyun Shehu, # 23A, &
Kaban Kagan, King of Khazars (670)
b. Khalge Kaghan [Harbis II], King of Khazars (650), below

9A Zhangar, King 597-599
issue:
a. Bagatur [I], # 15A
10A Nikul Chula [Nili Khan], King 599-603
issue:
a. Nipo Taman Khan, # 12A
b. Kiue Tatu, aka Kwoupe Kaghan, # 17A
11A Basyu Tegin [Boshir Teguin], King 603
12A Nipo Taman Khan [Hsien III], King 603-615 dep, d618
13A Shifkwi [II] [Shih Kuei] [Che-Kuei], King 615-618
14A Tong Yabghu Khan, King 618-627 [identified with Ziebel, King of
the Khazars]
issue:
a. Tili Tegin [Ipipolo], aka Shaporo IV, # 16A
b. Tatu Shad, father of Yiwu Khan, # 19A
c. Harbis I [Irbis], King of Khazars (630), who, by his wife,
Epiphania [dau of Heraclius, Byzantine Emperor], begot Anastasia
(dau), wife of Khalga Kaghan [Harbis II], see part 2 (below)
d. Tien Kiue
e. Yasu Tegin
15A Bagatur [I] Kiuliug, King 627

issue:
a. Ilvi Shifkwi Khan, # 20A
16A Tili Khan [Ipipolo] aka Shaporo IV, King 627-632
issue:
a. Symo Khan, # 18A
17A Kwoupe Khagan, King 632-639
18A Symo Khan, King 639-641

18B Shapolo [II] [Tielishe Khan] [Tongngo], King 639
issue:
a. Ikilishe Khan, # 20 B
19B Nichu Kagan [Hilipi Khan], King 639-640 dep, d653
20 B Ikilishe [Mohotou] Khan, King 640
issue:
a. Shifkwi, # 22B
21B Pihotu Khan, King 640-641
22B Shifkwi [Shekwei] Khan, King 641-?

19A Yiwu Khan, King 641-646
20A Ilvi Shifkwi Khan, King 646-653
21A Ghora Jabgu, aka Shaporo VII, King 653-657, deposed by Chinese
issue:
a. Mishe
22A Mishe, anti-king [in exile] 657-664
issue:
a. Yong Khan
23A Tiyun Shehu, anti-king [in exile] 664-677
24A Yong Khan, anti-king [in exile] 677-693
issue:
a. Suizi
25A Suizi, anti-king [in exile] 693-4 deposed by Chinese, ancestor of
Huang Tsung, Emperor of China 923-926

8B Shaporo [III] [Shetu Yabgu] [Che-Thu] [Yshbar Khan], King 581-587
[son of Istemi, bro of Bumin] (above),
issue:
a. Rudan Kagan, # 9B
9B Rudan Kagan [Buli Khan], King 587
10 B [K]Hulagu [Chulo-Khan; Tolos-Shad] [Tchu-lo-heu], King 587-588
issue:
a. Tulan [Dolan] Kagan, # 11B
b. Tateu [Datou] Kagan, # 14B
11B Tulan Kagan [Dolan] [Tiduin] [Yong Yulu Khan] King 588-598
= Yang-Ling, dau of Sui-Wenti, Emperor of China 581-604
issue:
a. Shipi, # 17B
b. Chulo, # 18C
c. Kieli, # 19C

12B Shabolo Khan, King 598
13B Shifkwi [I], King 598-599
14B Tateu Kagan [Datou] [Tatu Khan] [Bogiu Tardush Kagan] [Puchi],
King 599-603
issue:
a. Qimin Kagan, # 16B
15B Koran Kagan [Tuli Khan], King 603
issue:
a. Nishu Kutlo Kagan, # 24B
b. Khilash Khan, aka Shaporo V, # 26W
c. Irbis Kagan [Il-Kiuliug Shad] [Huo-Hsien], # 27W
d. Bagadur II Irbis [Khu-Mo-Khe], # 26E
e. Ilviro [Shaporo VI] Khan [Yshbar Jabghu], # 27E
16B Qimin Kagan [Chi-Min] [Duli I Khan], King 603-609
17B Shipi [Shih-Pi] [Dugi Shibir Khan] [Tujieli], King 609-619
issue:
a. Toli [Duli II] Khan, # 22C
b. Sirin (dau), wife of Khusru II "Parvez," Shah of Persia (d628)
18C Chulo [Tchu-Lo] Kagan, King 619-620
issue:
a. Ochir Tegin, father of Wen Tchuen Assete [# 34], Nichofu [# 35], &
Baz Kagan [# 37]
19C Kieli Khan [Xieli Khan] [Hsieh-Li] [Illig] [Kat il-Khan Tugbir],
King 620-629 dep, d633
issue:
a. Tupi Khan, # 20C
b. Szelipi [Li-Su-Mo], # 29
c. Hopo Khan [Ho-Pei] [Khepi Kagan], # 32
20C Tupi Khan, King 629
21C Schehu Khan, King 629-630
issue:
a. Kari Khan (d639), father of Mizif Kagan, [1st] King of Eastern
Turkestan 657-679, father of Yuan Ching Khan [Husehelo] , [2nd] King
of Eastern Turkestan
b. Aldo Yabghu Khan (d645), father of Buchin Khan, [3rd] King of
Eastern Turkestan 697-?, father of Khusere Khan, [4th] King of
Eastern Turkestan ?-703
c. Kayi, father of "Prince" Ochir, father of Wuchile [Utehele] Khan,
[5th] King of Eastern Turkestan 703-706, father of Sokho Khan, [6th]
King of Eastern Turkestan 706-711, & [his bro] Mecho [Mochuo] Khan,
[7th] King of Eastern Turkestan 711-716, father of Sughlu Khan, [8th]
King of Eastern Turkestan 716-738, father of Tu-Ho Khan, [9th] King of
Eastern Turkestan 738-739, & [his bro] Mo-Ho Bagan, [10th] King of
Eastern Turkestan 739-744, deposed by the Chinese
22C Toli [Duli II] Khan, King 630-631
issue:
a. Dudu Ghologur Khan, # 25B
23B Telige Teguin [Irbis Bolun Yabgu Kagan], King 631-633

24B Nishu Kutlo Kagan, King 633
25B Dudu Ghologur Khan, King 633-639 dep
26W Khilash Kagan, aka Shaporo V, King 633-639
26E Bagadur II [Khu-Moe-Khe], King 633-639
27W Irbis Kagan [Huo Hsien], King 639-641
issue:
a. Torak Han, # 28
27E Ilviro Shaporo VI Khagan [Yshbar Jabghu], King 639-641
28. Torak Han, King 641-644, dep, d656
issue:
a. Ay Kutlug Khan, # 33
29. Szelipi Khan [Li-Su-Mo], King 644-646
issue:
a. Hollyg Yshbar Khan # 30
b. Jenchu Shibir Khan, # 31
30. Hollyg Yshbar Khan , King 646-648
31. Jenchu Shibir Khan, King 648-653
32. Hopo Khan [Ho-Pei] [Khepi Kagan], King 653-664
33. Ay Kutlug Khan, King 664 dep (d685), the father of Qimin Tur
(d724), father of Yasak (d768), father of Tok Temur (d810), father of
Sungur (d865), father of Bulgai (d906), father of Sakur, father of
Batur, father of Togrul Khan (d1058), father of Ay Kutluq (d1097),
father of Baz Temur (d1165), father of Kizil Beg (1200), father of
Qia-Alp (1225), ancestor of Turkey's Ottoman Dynasty
--664:
reunion of Turkish tribes
----
34. Wen-Tchuen-Assete, King 657/664-679
issue:
a. Qutlugh Khan, # 39
b. Mokor Kapagan Kagan, # 40
c. Zieghu (683), father of Asena Tegin, father of Ghora Kagan, # 52
35. Nichofu [Nishu-Beg], King 679-681
issue:
a. Funian, # 36
36. Funian, King 681-2
37. Baz Kagan, King 682
issue:
a. Toghu Che, # 38
38. Toghu Che, King 682 dep (d715)
issue:
a. Utibeg
39. Qutlugh Khan [Kutluqh Ilteres Khan] [Idat Khan], King 682-691
issue:
a. Bilghe Khan, # 42
b. Tengri Kul, # 45
40. Mokor Kapagan Kagan, King 691-716
issue:

a. Fugiuy Bogiu, # 41
41. Fugiuy Bogiu [Kuchuk Khan] [Inal Khan], King 716
42. Bilghe Khan, King 716-731
issue:
a. Igen Khan, # 43
b. Duzhi Khan, # 46
c. Koto Khan, # 47
d. Kiethi Khan , # 48
e. Ozmish Khan, # 49
43. Igen Khan [I-Jan], King 731-735
44. Yollug Khan, King 735-739
45. Tengri Kul [Kul Tegin], King 739-742
46. Duzhi Khan, King 742
47. Koto [Ku-Tu] [Siuan] Khan, King 742-743
48. Kiethi Khan [Tieh Shih], King 743
49. Ozmish Khan, King 743-744
= [name], queen-regent 744-745
issue:
a. Pomei [Baimei] Khan, # 35
50. Pomei [Pei-Mei] [Baimei] Khan, King 744-745, dep

745: the Turkish state was conquered by the Uighurs, who established
an empire in Central Asia (487-1335)

----

51. Etimis [Il-Itmish] Khan, King [in exile] 745-748
52. Ghora Kagan, King [in exile] 748-?, the ancestor of later Turkish
rulers

----

descent-line continued from above, see
52. Istemi [Silzibul] [Iski Khan] (d576), bro of Bumin, 1st King 552
(above)
53. [K]Hulagu, King 587-588
54. Tulan Kagan, King 588-599
55. Chulo Kagan, King 619-620
56. Ochir Tegin, prince
57. Wen-Tchuen-Assete, King 657/664-679
58. Zieghu (683)
59. Asena Tegin
60. Ghora Kagan, King 748-? [note: Formhals says in his "Royal Race
of Deuman" that Seljuk was his 6th great-grandson]
61. Oghuz Khan, Prince of Basmils [union of 24 Turkish tribes] (775),
migrated into northern and western Khwarazm, made the fortress at
Enikert his residence; may possibly be identified with [?] Kerekuci
Hoci in the "traditional pedigree"
62. Asena Tegin, possibly id. with [?] Toksurmu Ilci in the
"traditional pedigree" [grandson]
63. Ucoko Kagan, possibly id. with [?] Lokman Assena in the
"traditional pedigree" [1st gt-grandson]

issue:
a. Kamgu Kagan, Turkish-King
b. Bayindir Khan, Turkish-King (below)
c. Kazan Yabgu, Turkish-King
64. Bayindir Khan, possibly id. with [?] Ertugrul in the "traditional
pedigree" [2nd gt-gdson]
65. Qiniq Qagan [3rd gt-gdson]
66. Shaghri Beg [4th gt-gdson]
67. Duqaq [Dukak] [Tuquq] "Iron-Bow"[5th gt-gdson]
68. Seljuk [6th gt-gdson], founded the Seljuk Dynasty (900); in the
"traditional pedigree" he is said to have been "X" number of
generations from Afrasiyab, King of Turan (above), whom the Seljuk
Dynasty apparently regarded as its "official ancestor." He converted
to Islam.

Part 2:
Kings of Khazaria [the Khazars]-EUROPE

„Know that we are descended from Japhet (son of Noah/?/, grandson of
Lamech), through his son Togarmah. [In Jewish literature Togarmah is
the father of all the Turks.] I have found in the genealogical books of my
ancestors that Togarmah had ten sons. These are their names: the eldest
was Ujur, the second Tauris, the third Avar, the fourth Uauz, the fifth Bizal,
the sixth Tarna, the seventh Khazar, the eighth Janur, the ninth Bulgar, the
tenth Sawir. [These are the mythical founders of tribes that once lived in the
neighborhood of the Black and Caspian Seas.] I am a descendant of Khazar,
the seventh son."

JOSEPH THE KING, SON OF AARON THE KING, THE TURK – MAY
HIS CREATOR PRESERVE HIM TO THE HEAD OF THE ASSEMBLY,
HASDAI, THE SON OF ISAAC, SON OF EZRA. –about 960

Note; for clarification of Japhet ancestry check «The Descendancy of Royal
House of Vere of Anjou» chart

regnal-list

SHAMAN (TENGRIST) ASHINA (ANSA) DYNASTY OF KHAZARIA
DIVINE HEROES, AK-JANG;HERO-MESSIAH-KING
DRAGON KINGS

01. Ziebel, [1st] King (620), identified with Tong Yabghu Khan, King
of Turks 618-627 (above)
02. Harbis [I] [Irbis], King (630), son
= Epiphania, dau of Byzantine Emperor Heraclius
issue:
a. Anastasia (dau), wife of Khalge Kaghan [Harbis II], King # 4
(below)

03. Kieyue Khan, King (640), cousin
son of Moho Shad, bro of 1st King Ziebel (above)
issue:
a. Khalge Kaghan [Harbis II], King # 4
b. Ashena Holo, father of Kaban Kagan, King # 5
04. Khalge Kaghan, aka Harbis II], King (650), son
= Anastasia, dau of Harbis I (above)
issue:
a. Ibuzir Glavan, King # 6
b. Theodora (dau), wife of Justinian II, Byzantine Emperor
659 additional unnamed members of Western Türkic Kaganate (ONOQ)
Royal Ashina clan move to western ulus E of Itil-Capitol of Khazaria,
forming large royal group (class)
05. Kaban Kagan, King (670), nephew
06. Ibuzir Glavan, King 690-715, cousin
07. Barjik [Bardzhik], King 715-731, son
= Prisbit, regent 731-737 dep, sis of Hazer Tarkman, Khan of the Beks
issue:
JEWISH ASHINA KINGS (EMPERORS) OF KHAZARIA
DRAGON HEBREW KINGS

a. Bulan Sabriel, King # 8
b. Bihar, King # 9

08. Bulan (Sabriel), King (740), CONVERTED TO JUDAISM TOGETHER
WITH 4000 ROYALS/NOBLES,
"Babylonian" DRAGON Levit/Aaronite genetic "input" trough marriages
onward

issue:
a. Bagatur, King # 10
09. Bihar [Bizar], King (750), bro
issue:
a. Tzitzak (Chichak), aka Irene, wife of Constantine V, Byzantine
Emperor 741-775
b. Dau, wife of Constantine II, King of Abasgia
10. Bagatur, King (760), nephew
issue:
a. Obadiah, King # 11
b. Hanukkah, King # 14
c. Zebulun, King # 16
11. Obadiah (Ovadiya), King 786-809, son
12. Hezekiah (Hizkiah), King 809-?, son
13. Manasseh I, son
14. Hanukkah, great-uncle
15. Yitzchak (Isaac), son
16. Zebulun, uncle
17. Manasseh II, great-nephew

18. Nisi, son
19. Aaron I, King (900), son
issue:
a. Menahem, King # 20
b. Benjamin, King # 21
20. Menahem, son
21. Benjamin, bro
22. Aaron II, son
23. Hakan Yusuf (Joseph), King 940-965, son
24. David, King 965-969, son, deposed by Russians, who overran and conquered Khazaria in 969; died an exile in Taman 986/8
25. George Tzula, royal heir, son, an exile in Kerch; was acknowledged king by the scattered remnant of the Khazars (Royals remained in majority in Ukraine /Western Khazaria/, some escaped elsewhere; Spain,etc.); was defeated and taken prisoner in 1016 [last one]

Part 3.;
Royal Ashina-Levit Hebrew descendants after fall of Khazaria

26. 11th-18th cent.; GRADUAL AND COMPLETE ASSIMILATION INTO ASHKENAZI JEWISH RELIGIOUS AND CULTURAL IDENTITY, RUSSIAN EMPIRE, POLISH-LITHUANIAN COMMONWEALTH, HUNGARY, ROMANIA etc.. Last known mention of Khazars as nation in 13th century, as Khazar Jews (descendants of royal converts).

Partial list of Jewish (Y-DNA Central Asian haplogroup Q1b/M-378) families (Levits);
Leki(Schweitzer), Levy,Rotschild, Abelman, Mink(ovsky), Costin(sky), Black, Porter, Horwitz, Marks, Shakinovsky, Sherman, Brandt, Backalenick, Goldman, Zwick, Kushner, Liebman, Silver, Krupa, Rosenberg, Shainis, Friedman, Goldfoot, Geber, Farkas, Jaron, Podolski, Palmer, Howard, Rosenstraus, Tober, Thaler, Zeidman, Altshuler, Fogle, Baraban, Blueglass, Frank, Loebman, Abrams, Borrus, Lewis, Kochman, Orlen, Naviasky and others.
Note; due to centuries of constant persecution and attempts to annihilate Jewish populations it is often very hard (impossible) to locate longer paper trails as genealogical proofs, therefore extensive and detailed genetic-genalogy research has been undertaken in this matter)
27. Krupa family converts to Roman Catholicism – Polish Nobility of Jewish Extraction
28. Jan Krupa (d.1919) (wife; Anastasia Krupa born Podkowa) issue;
a)   Jan Krupa
b)   Alfred Krupa
c)   Engelbert Krupa (d.II WW)
d)   Hilde Krupa (d.II WW)
29. Jan Krupa
issue;

a) Janusz Krupa
b) Ilonka Krupa
30. Alfred Krupa (b.1915-d.1989.) (wife; Štefica Krupa born Ozbolt)
issue;
a)   Mladen Krupa
31. Mladen Krupa (b.1949) (wife; Durdica Krupa born Bencic´)
issue;
a)   Alfred Krupa – Freddy
b)   Margareta Krupa
c)   Magdalena Krupa (b.1980)
d)   Mladen Krupa (b.1983)
32. Alfred Krupa – Freddy (b.1971) (wife; Ljiljana Krupa born Jakšetic´)
issue;
a)   Gabriel Alfred Krupa (b.1999)
b)   Eleonora Krupa (b.2005)
33. Margareta Krupa (b.1978) (housband;Dario Juric´)
issue;
a)   Emanuel Krupa (Juric´) (b.1999)
b)   Noah Krupa (Juric´) (b.2005)
(material under constant update and expansion)

References;

Davis Hughes, hughrdave@aol.com (2004)
New Standard Jewish Encyclopedia
Tarnawa-Krupa family archive
FamilyTreeDNA Houston Y-DNA testing results and records for Alfred
Krupa (2007, 2008)
http://starnarcosis.net/obsidian/siberia.html
HIRH Nicholas Tarnawa- De Vere von Drakenberg archive, 2009
Mirfatyh Zakiev
http://en.wikipedia.org/wiki/Ashina_%28clan%29
iGENEA-Zurich Ancestral analyse certification,2009
http://en.wikipedia.org/wiki/Mythology_of_the_Turkic_and_Mongolian_
peoples
http://www.turkishculture.org
http://www.familytreedna.com/public/AshinaRoyalDynasty/default.aspx
http://en.wikipedia.org/wiki/G%C3%B6kt%C3%BCrks

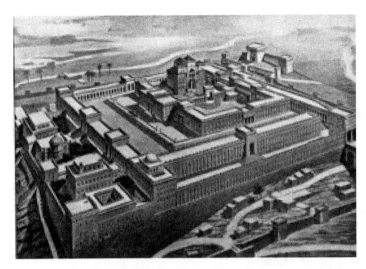

Temple of Jerusalum

ASHKENAZI LEVI'IM AND COHANIM DNA LINK FOR THE KRUPA FAMILY

H.I.RH. PRINCE ALFRED TARNAWA KRUPA–DE VERE VON DRAKENBERG HA-LEVI

Descendant of Hebrew Levi-Aaron line through fusion with Royal Tengrist Ashina of Khazaria line

Levite — in Jewish tradition, a Levite, Modern *Levi* Tiberian *Lewî* ; "Attached") is a member of the Hebrew Tribe of Levi. When Joshua led the Israelites into the land of Canaan, the Levites were the only Israelite tribe who received cities but no tribal land "because the Lord the God of Israel himself is their possession." The Tribe of Levi served particular religious duties for the Israelites and had political responsibilities as well. The tribe is named after Levi, one of the twelve sons of Jacob (also called Israel). Levi had three sons: Gershon, Kohath, and Merari (Genesis 46:11). (extracts from http://en.wikipedia.org/wiki/Levite)

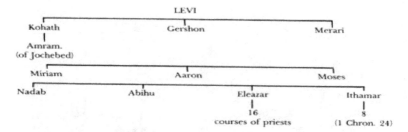

Levi tribe initial genealogy *(http://www.biblecentre.org/images/commentaries/chart_levi.JPG)*

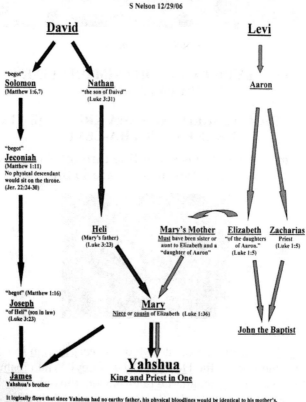

From The Book of Hebrews (http://www.judaismvschristianity.com/hebrews.htm)

"Talmudic sources may possibly be interpreted to support the notion of differences in the social, religious, and legal barriers that relate to the assumption of Cohen and Levite status. These include descriptions of the possible assumption of Levite status other than through patrilineal descent, in a Talmudic passage describing a debate regarding the potential assignment of Levite status to a man (and his descendants) whose father was a non-Jew and whose mother was the daughter of a Levite. Such differences could have provided the backdrop for the sanctioned acceptance of Levite status other than through patrilineal descent." (*Multiple Origins of Ashkenazi Levites: Y Chromosome Evidence for Both Near Eastern and European Ancestries* – Doron M. Behar, Mark G. Thomas, Karl Skorecki,1 Michael F. Hammer, Ekaterina Bulygina, Dror Rosengarten, Abigail L. Jones, Karen Held, Vivian Moses, David Goldstein, Neil Bradman, and Michael E. Weale Bruce Rappaport Faculty of Medicine and Research Institute, Technion and Rambam Medical Center, Haifa, Israel; The Centre for Genetic Anthropology and The Centre for Population Genetics and Human Health, Department of Biology, University College London, London; and Division of Biotechnology, University of Arizona, Tucson, AZ).

DNA Y chromosome tests, performed by FTDNA-University of Arizona , showed and CONFIRMED direct patrilineal connection with growing number of families with Levit tradition (oral tradition, material artifacts, grave inscriptions, etc.).

That means that we share common male Levit ancestor, further it means that we are all rightfull Levites (descendants of the same Levi,Aaron and Moses family) trough female genetic inflow /the Annunaki way/, which is sanctioned – approved by Talmud. Our calculation is that we have branched from one person before some 700-1000 years ago, most probably on territory of The Kingdom of Poland (The Polish-Lithuanian Commonwealth).

Those **Levit** families within **KRUPA** male lineage are ;

1. **Levy** (*37 Marker /Genetic Distance* – 3)

2. **Goldsmith-Levy** (*37 Marker/Genetic Distance* -3)

3. **Zwick** (*37 Marker /Genetic Distance* – 3)

4. **Brandt**

5. **Loebman**

6. **Friedman** (*37 Marker /Genetic Distance* – 4)

7. **Kushner** (*25 marker/Genetic Distance* -3)

8. **Marks** (*67 Marker/ Genetic Distance* – 4)

9. **Sherman** (*37 Marker /Genetic Distance* – 3)

10. **Howard** (Horwitz) (*37 Marker /Genetic Distance* – 4)-RABBINICAL *family*

http://horwitzfam.org/horwitz_home.htm

11. **Frank**

12. **Sooper** (*12 marker/Genetic Distance* -1) -possible Cohanim

13. **Liebman**

14. **Bekhor**

15. **Horwitz**

16. **Tober**

The **Cohanim** (High Priests) tradition families are;

1. **Blueglass**

2. **Bluglass**

3. **Black** *(67 Marker/Genetic Distance -11) (maternal side)*

4. **Porter** (*67 Marker/ Genetic Distance* – 5)

Most likely there is much more, but so far we didnt find out did they claim Levit origin – or perhaps some of them lost oral tradition (knowledge) due to the centuries of constant hardships and relocations, or they just didn't not take DNA tests yet.

Genetic distances expressed in here depends also on how extended test of Y-chromosome mutations (current options are; 12, 25, 37 or 67 genetic markers) has been ordered by certain family. Also, values for the Autosomal DNA tests has not been included, due to small size databases at present time.

Dr. Bennet Greenspan confirmed, president of FTDNA-Houston, that our DNA matches one Levit from Israel.

Language: FR IT DE ES   Currency: EUR GBP CHF   » Search   Logout

DISCOVER
YOUR HISTORY »

«This was my only real chance to find a
trace going back to the 17th Century.»
Dieter Finkhäuser, Deutschland
» more customer reviews

iGENEA

Welcome, Alfred Krupa!

Sign out

This page contains the result of your iGENEA test.

Result 89372, Alfred Krupa

Your iGENEA-result refers to 3 different epochs. The **haplogroup** shows your origins
in Pre-history. We would like to help you interpret your DNA results by defining your
primal people and region of origin. The **Primal people** shows your ancient ethnicity
(900 BC to 900 AD). The **Region of origin** shows the area in which your profile is
typical. A line has to have lived in a region for at least 500 years for a profile to be
typical for that region. There is a possibility that your DNA profile cannot be attributed
to one primal people or region unambiguously. In this case, several possible primal
peoples and/or regions are listed. This means that you belong to one of these primal
peoples and come from one of these regions.

PLEASE INSTALL
ADOBE FLASH PLAYER

Get ADOBE®
FLASH® PLAYER

Paternal lineage:	Haplogroup	Q ■
	Antic tribe	Jews
	Region of origin	Eastern Europe

Upgrades:	Upgrade from YDNA to mtDNA-Starter	CHF 109.-
	Upgrade from YDNA to mtDNA-Plus	CHF 169.-
	Upgrade from YDNA to mtDNA-Super	CHF 339.-
	» Overview Deep Clades	

Explanations:	What is DNA-Genealogy?
	How do I use DNA-genealogy?
	Surprised by your Result?
	iGENEA-security
	Methods of Analysis
	Haplogroups by Country
	FAQ: Frequently Asked Questions
	Forum

Genetic values 89372

Paternal lineage

Locus	1	2	3	4	5	6	7	8	9	10
DYS#	393	390	19*	391	385a	385b	426	388	439	389-1
Allele	14	22	13	10	14	16	12	12	12	13
Locus	11	12	13	14	15	16	17	18	19	20
DYS#	392	389-2	458	459a	459b	455	454	447	437	448
Allele	15	29	17	9	9	11	11	24	14	19

Locus	21	22	23	24	25	26	27	28	29	30
DYS#	449	464a**	464b**	464c**	464d**	460	GATA H4	YCA II a	YCA II b	456
Allele	29	14	15	15	16	10	9	19	19	15
Locus	31	32	33	34	35	36	37	38	39	40
DYS#	607	576	570	CDY a	CDY b	442	438	531	578	395S1a
Allele	14	17	16	33	38	12	11	11	8	15
Locus	41	42	43	44	45	46	47	48	49	50
DYS#	395S1b	590	537	641	472	406S1	511	425***	413a	413b
Allele	19	8	11	10	8	11	11	0	22	22
Locus	51	52	53	54	55	56	57	58	59	60
DYS#	557	594	436	490	534	450	444	481	520	446
Allele	16	11	12	12	18	8	12	24	16	13
Locus	61	62	63	64	65	66	67			
DYS#	617	568	487	572	640	492	565			
Allele	12	11	13	10	12	13	13			

Other free services   Instructions

» Napoleon project
» Surname projects (currently active: 5'653 Projects)
» Geographische Projekte
» Ysearch.org
» Mitosearch.org

Data related to test 89372   Y-DNA-67 Test

Set sent: 04.11.2009   Samples returned: 04.11.2009
Test paid: 05.11.2009   Written report sent: 26.11.2009

FamilyTreeDNA Database

» Instructions

FamilyTreeDNA was founded in 2000 and was the first company in the world to carry out DNA-genealogy tests that concentrated on genealogical research. Today, FamilyTreeDNA possesses the largest genealogical DNA database in the world.

iGENEA has specialised in the origins of Europeans, especially on antic people groups of Europe. In order to give all iGENEA-clients access to the world's largest data base through FamilyTreeDNA, iGENEA works together closely with FamilyTreeDNA.

Since the FamilyTreeDNA-database is mostly in English, we recommend that you Instructions read

To reach the FamilyTreeDNA database please click on the "FamilyTreeDNA Login". Your FamilyTreeDNA result will be opened in a new window. **Close this page again** and use the links you will find in the following aprons to get directed in specific pages of your result in the database. » FamilyTreeDNA Login

Find genetic cousins   Instructions

Under the following link you can view the names and E-mail addresses of people with whom you are genetically matched along the paternal line. The database is regularly updated; this means that over time more and more persons will match you genetically.

» Y-DNA matches   Determine degree of kinship

Information on Y-DNA matches
If, for example, you compare the matches of a 12 marker result, you may find people with whom you share your surname. An exact match of 12 markers with this person means that with a probability of 99%, the last shared ancestor goes back no further than 29 generations. Correspondingly, a 25, 37 or 67 marker match indicates a closer relationship. If 67 of 67 markers of two men match, this indicates with a probability of 90% that the last joint ancestor goes back no further than 4 generations. The higher the number of matching markers, the greater the probability of a relationship and the closer the relationship is.

» Show genetic relatives on a world map NEW!   Instructions

Directions to "Show genetic relatives on world map."

My Maps is a new tool in your online-result which allows you to localize your genetic relatives on a world map. Every genetic relative is represented as a single dot. Different colors represent the genetic distance.

1. Click on the rubrik „User Preferences"
2. Enter under "paternal/maternal side" the name, birthplace, date of birth, date of death, and place of origin for your last known ancestor. The information that you enter can be chosen and changed at any time.
3. Under „paternal/maternal origin" you have to enter the latitude and longitude of their georgraphic place of origin.
4. Click below on „Update" to save the information you just entered.
5. Return to "MyMaps". You can already see your personal Global Family Map!
6. Under „Display", you can choose the genetic rubric that you want displayed.

More special offers

The following iGENEA tests are discounted this month. (Why not use this opportunity to tell a friend about this limited special offer?)
» Y-DNA-37 Test   CHF 249.- instead CHF 299.- (Discount until 30.11.2009)
» Y-DNA-67 Test   CHF 379.- instead CHF 399.- (Discount until 30.11.2009)
» Super-Combination CHF 849.- instead CHF 899.- (Discount until 30.11.2009)

By the way, all iGENEA tests are also available as gift vouchers.

Do you operate a web site? If so, become an affiliate of iGENEA and easily earn € 10.00 with each iGENEA product that is sold via your web site. Information can be found under www.igenea.com/affiliate

Are you satisfied with iGENEA and would you like to recommend us? If so, send your friends an E-mail and tell them about iGENEA: » Tell a friend about iGENEA.

Bonus Program

Give yourself a gift and refer a friend to iGENEA! For every successful referral, you will receiveCHF 15.- a reward in the form of iGENEA coupons. You can save the up to use toward another analysis, or you can redeem them for gift certificates.

People you refer to us enter **your lab number '89372'** when they place their orders. As soon as the order is paid, the reward is credited to your account.

By the way: Clients, who include your laboratory number with their order will receive a **discount of 5% immediately**! » Tell a friend about iGENEA

Your open referrals:
No open referrals.

Your paid referrals:
No referrals paid yet.

Telephone:	GB: 0808 101 34 20 (C&W)
	GB: 0808 234 26 07 (BT)
	EU: 0041 43 817 13 91
E-Mail:	info@igenea.com
Address:	Gentest.ch GmbH
	iGENEA
	Schlossgasse 9
	Postfach 7179
	CH-8023 Zürich

Home
About the Test
Origins analysis
Ancestor research
Customer reviews
Tests & Prices DISCOUNT
Result
Order now

Support:

The International Commission and Association on Nobility
Commisione e Associazione Internazionale sulla Nobiltá
Comisión e Asociación Internacional sobre la Nobleza

NOBILITY RECOGNITION

We do here certify that

MLADEN KRUPA

by thorough verification of evidence is herby Recognized as a inguished true noble member of the House of Ashina Royal Clan and such is a member of the high nobility of Europe.

In witness therefore we do hereby set Our hand and Seals.

Sept. 11, 2009
_____
Date

_____
President Signature

MEANING OF THE KRUPA AND TARNAWA NAMES

A SHORT INTRODUCTION WITH SOME HISTORICAL, GEOGRAPHICAL AND GENEALOGICAL INFORMATIONS INSERTED

1. Krupa is the Polish-Russian/Slavic form of older Turkic ARPA or ARPAG, with the same meaning; barley, barley grain, barley fruits, – according to *Jewish Family Names and Their Origins*, by Heinrich Walter Guggenheimer, Eva H., but it is also found in Pakistan, north-west India/Bangladesh (E.Pakistan), unchanged – as Krupa.

2. Krupa on Sanskrit means "compassion" (grace) according to the "Apte's Sanskrit -English Dictionary." http://www.indiadivine.org/audarya/shakti-sadhana/121148-krupa-prasada-kataxa.html

3. Krupa, a Hindu name for a female meaning grace, mercy, favor, love, passion, compassion, forgiveness, blessings, and hope http://en.wikipedia.org/wiki/Krupa

4. Form of address for European Duke (lat. Dux), military warlord and ruler, considered as equal to Turkic Beg (Bek,Beig etc.), is "His Grace" (Grace, compassion=Krupa). The regions or provinces where Beys (the equivalent of Duke in Europe) ruled or which they administered were called Beylik, roughly meaning "emirate" or "principality" in the first case, "province" or "governorate" in the second (the equivalent of duchy in Europe). Bey or a variation has also been used as an aristocratic title in various Turkic states, such as Bäk in the Tatar Khanate of Kazan, in charge of a Beylik called Bäklek. The Balkar princes in the North Caucasus highlands were known as taubiy (taubey), meaning the "mountainous chief." (From Wikipedia, the free encyclopedia.)

5. Tarnawa is the SHIELD (CoA) and the CLAN of Poland traditionally associated /in old Polish-Lithuanian armorials/with the Krupa noble family (among other families), and it is labeled as a shield of "szlachta odwieczna" – "Uradel" (a nobility from ever, self-rooted nobility, ancient nobility,root nobility). http://en.wikipedia.org/wiki/Tarnawa coat of arms

6. The Polish Nobility emerged as a clan (family or tribe) system before 1000 A.D. Each clan had its own mark, a tamga, which eventually evolved into the symbols found on Polish coats of arms. http://www.angelfire.com/mi4/polcrt/PolNobility.html Crown used on Krupa-Tarnawa CoA (like on other Polish arms) are often described, in heraldic terminology, as "Ducal."

7. The oldest, original latin text of J.Dlugosz speaks about Petrus Krupa de Tarnawa family. Krupa de Tarnawa in translation from Latin means "Krupa of Tarnawa" or "Krupa from Tarnawa," designating Tarnawa as a place/location. Krupa herb Tanawa in translation from Polish means just Krupa – Coat of Arms Tarnawa.

8. Tarnawa is a name of several places on territory of the Polish-Lithuanian Commonwealth (Kingdom), mainly in Galicia.There is also an example in Bulgaria.

9. Tarnawa is the city in Northern Pakistan in Hazara region (in Karakorum Mtns. region), and the place in Hazarajat (Hazaristan) in Afghanistan (in Hindu Kush Mountains). http://wikimapia.org/10055074/Tarnawa-Dogah-Edited-by-Shahzad-Satti http://www.fallingrain.com/world/AF/28/Tarnawa.html

10. Tarnawa name AS EXACT SPELLING (name of places, nickname, personal name, label, etc.) is not recorded anywhere else in the world, except in northern Pakistan and Afghanistan, and in former Polish-Lithuanian Commonwealth (Eastern Europe), and no "other" Krupa family "emerged" with "noble" ancestry claimed (very important fact, as Krupa in exact spelling is often surname among Roman Catholics, Greek-Byzantine Catholics and Jews, throughout Eastern Europe, and as name in Indian subcontinent).

11. The Indian Kushan Empire (c. 1st–3rd centuries) among other covered areas / earlier Indo-Greek BACTRIA / currently inhabited with the Hazara and Sindhi population, only noted carrier of the Q1b SNP mutation, beside Ashkenazi Jews of Eastern Europe (except in some other individual cases).

12. The Indian Kushan Empire covered area of northern Afghanistan, the whole of Pakistan, northern India, southern Uzbekistan and Tajikistan and area of North-West China (Xinjiang-Turkestan) – the ultimate home of the Ashina Royal Tribe of Turks ("original 500 families"). We assume that the legacy and heritage of the Indian Kushan Empire (Royal Yuezhi) is responsible for original association of Krupa name/form of address with White Hun-Turkic bloodline, later the Krupa family.

13. The very same case, as with The Kushan Empire, is with The White Hun Empire. The Hephthalites or White Huns were a Central Asian nomadic confederation whose precise origins and composition remain obscure. They were called Sveta Huna ("White Huns") by the Indians. According to Chinese chronicles, they were originally a tribe living to the north of the Great Wall and were known as Hoa or Hoa-tun. Elsewhere they were called White Huns. They had no cities or system

of writing, and lived in felt tents. For many years, scholars suggested that they were possibly of Turkic stock, and it seems likely that at least some groups amongst the Hephthalites were Turkic-speakers. Chinese chronicles state that they were originally a tribe of the Yuezhi, living to the north of the Great Wall, and subject to the Rouran (Jwen-Jwen), as were some Turkic peoples at the time. Their original name was Hoa or Hoa-tun; subsequently they named themselves Ye-tha-i-li-to, after their royal family, which descended from one of the five Yuezhi families, which also included the Kushan. (From Wikipedia, the free encyclopedia.)

14. "With the discovery of haplogroup Q among Ashkenazi Jews, DNA researchers may have found the "smoking gun" of Khazarian ancestry." (*A MOSAIC OF PEOPLE: The Jewish Story and a Reassessment of the DNA Evidence*, by Ellen Levy-Coffman.)

15. "...I agree that it is likely that the presence of haplogroup Q among Ashkenazic Jews could come from descent from the Khazars."
(Kevin Brook, author of *The Jews of Khazaria* (Second Edition: Rowman & Littlefield, 2006) in open response to D.Howard, administrator of the Ashkenazi-Q Yahoo group.

16. Astrakhan State University (Dmitry Vasilyev) trough excavations funded by the Russian-Jewish Congress, proven that conversion of Khazars to Judaism was indeed limited only to a very narrow circle-ruling imperial class. (The Associated Press, "Scholar Says Ruins Are Medieval Jewish Capital," Published September 21, 2008.)

17. One 6-letter Khazar runic word means "I have read [it]." It was written on the bottom of the Kievan Letter, a document written by the (possibly-Khazar) Jews of Kiev in the early 10th century. The signatures on the Kievan Letter are of mixed Hebrew (ex: Yitzhak, Sinai, Yehudah) and Turkic/Slavic (ex: Manas, Gostata) origins, apparently indicating an environment of rich and diverse linguistic heritage of the Khazarian/Turkic society, certainly allowing survival of the words "Krupa" (Arpa) and "Tarnawa" (and 4-equal barr cross as tamga/shamanic seal).

18. This Krupa family is of Ashkenazi Jewish ancestry (mainly of former Polish-Lithuanian Commonwealth and Russia), as visible in lists of 12, 25, 37 and 67 Y-DNA matches, within containing significant number of matches with Levit tradition (and some of Cohanim tradition). In some other lines-branches of this Ashkenazi Q1b family, Levit status has been obviously remembered and preserved, in this particular branch, that was case with "Krupa-Grace" ("lordship") identity. The Krupa family Y-DNA has been tested at the FamilyTree DNA, Houston, Texas; the pioneer and the world's largest DNA testing company in the new field of genetic genealogy. Jewish comparative databases in FTDNA are the largest in the world, containing records for Ashkenazim and Sephardim, as well as Levites and Cohanim.

19. "…szlachta simply addressed each other by their given name or as 'Sir Brother' (Panie bracie) or the feminine equivalent. The other forms of address would be 'Illustrious and Magnificent Lord,' 'Magnificent Lord,' 'Generous Lord' or 'Noble Lord' (in decreasing order) or simply 'His/Her Grace Lord/Lady XYZ.'" (Wikipedia about Szlachta.)

20. This Krupa family is carrier of a rare haplogroup Q1b (M378) mutation, as subclade of Q (M242) "asiatic" or "mongolic" haplogroup. http://m242.haplogroup.org/?do=search&id=krupa

21. Q1b (M378) found in 5% of Ashkenazi Jews and at low frequency among samples of Hazara, Sindhis, and nowhere else so far (except in some individual cases)-meaning in south-western Central Asia. ("Sengupta 2006" – Sanghamitra Sengupta, Lev A. Zhivotovsky, Roy King, S.Q. Mehdi, Christopher A. Edmonds, Cheryl-Emiliane T. Chow, Alice A. Lin, Mitashree Mitra, Samir K. Sil, A. Ramesh, M.V. Usha Rani, Chitra M. Thakur, L. Luca Cavalli-Sforza, Partha P. Majumder, and Peter A. Underhill, "Polarity and Temporality of High-Resolution Y-Chromosome Distributions in India Identify Both Indigenous and Exogenous Expansions and Reveal Minor Genetic Influence of Central Asian Pastoralists," "The American Journal of Human Genetics", Volume 78, Issue 2, 202-221, 1 February 2006.) The Hazara are a Persian-speaking people residing in the central region of Afghanistan (referred to as Hazarajat) and northwestern

Pakistan. The Hazara are predominantly Shi'i Muslims and are the third largest ethnic group in Afghanistan, composing ca. 10% of the population. Hazaras can also be found in large numbers in neighboring Iran and Pakistan, primarily as refugees, and as diaspora around the world. http://en.wikipedia.org/wiki/Hazara_people

The Sindhis are a Sindhi speaking socio-ethnic group of people originating from Sindh, a province of Pakistan. Today Sindhis that live in Pakistan belong to various religious denominations including but not limited to Muslim, Zorastrian, Hindus and Christians. After the Partition of India in 1947, a large number of Indian Muslim refugees (Muhajirs) flocked into Pakistan and settled in the prosperous Sindh region. At the same time Sindhi Hindus migrated to India in large numbers. (From Wikipedia, the free encyclopedia.)

22. There is located a distant Q1b match from India from the Brahman Caste (hereditary Hindu priestly caste, alike Levit caste in Hebrews). http://m242haplogroup.org/?do=search&id=krupa

23. Q1b matches from Central Asia/most distant known ancestral origins from Pakistan, Afghanistan, Uzbekistan etc.,visible in Q-DNA Project and in the Ashina Royal Dynasty DNA Project, clearly shows our Silk Road/Lazurite route path from Afghanistan/Pakistan, North-West China/South Siberia to Eastern Europe. Those matches are not so close to us, Krupa Ashkenazi Q1b, but still relat.gen. close, and not Jews(!), meaning that there was religious conversion and that conversion took place at some point after our ancestors branched. One group remained in Central Asia, others (the Krupa family ancestors among them) moved to China (Xinjiang), after that to Europe (future Khazaria) via the Altai Mountains area (here the migrants joined the ranks of the Turk tribal unit) and accepted Judaism in, what is today, South Russia. From the Kushan Empire, the White Hun Empire, the Xiongnu Empire, the Gok-Turk Empire, then through the Khazarian Empire, to the old Kingdom of Poland. Total Khazar story and 1st millennium story.

24. Q1b IS FOUND IN EUROPE ALMOST ONLY WITHIN ASHKENAZI GENETIC POOL, CREATING SPECIFIC

ASHKENAZI Q1b HAPLOTYPE, WHICH MEANS THAT PRESENCE IN EUROPE IS ALMOST 0% (DISTRIBUTION OF HAPLOGROUP Q WITH ALL KNOWN SUBCLADES IN EUROPE IS 0.61%).

Conclusion: There is a complete, exact and full match of the surname, the noble clan/shield name, the town and places names, legal basis for nobilitation, ancestral geographical locations and locations of restricted distribution of specific and rare Y-DNA (haplogroup), plus confirming TMRCA* calculations – in places where we see Q1b's examples we find both names Krupa and Tarnawa, as well having several options for possible origins of heraldic Tarnawa, including a number of old Runic and Indian scriptures (Brahmi, Kharoshti etc.) and original meaning of the word Krupa (applicable to the Krupa family in question), all in the very same places.

Suggested origin: Yuezhi Royal families of Old Turkic/Hunnic stock ruled over Indian Kushan Empire and Turkic White Hun Empire (Hepthalites). Remnants later joined diverse Ashina Royal Tribe (constituted of 500 families) as part of the Xiongnu (Hun) confederation, and after that, of the Gok-Turks (Celestial Turks) and consequently of Khazars in southeastern Europe. "Tarnawa" seal was possibly just one of the seals of this blood line (together with Trident, Water Dragon, Mountain Goat/Ram and others), with origin in Central Asian area of Hindukush-Altai-Pamir-Karakoram, but with its' very beginning within the ancient Annunaki Sumerian civilisation.

APPENDIX F

The Sovereign Nation of Drakenberg

Public Register of the Dragon Families and Members of the Dragon Court

Wales:

Nicholas Sanada Tarnawa-de Vere von Drakenberg

Sovereign, Grand Master and Commander in Chief.

The Lady Julianne Sanada-de Vere von Drakenberg,

The Princess Anam Cara of the House of Vere.

Mandy, Laura and Jay de Vere von Drakenberg

England:

Michael Hunter von Drakenberg RAD., SDR

Dragon King of Arms

Scotland:

Jamie de Vere von Drakenberg, SDR.

Eloise de Vere von Drakenberg

Eleanor de Vere von Drakenberg

Ireland:

Clive de Vere von Drakenberg, SDR.

Sharon de Vere von Drakenberg

Hannah de Vere von Drakenberg

Deborah de Vere von Drakenberg

Robert de Vere von Drakenberg

Harry Alexander de Vere von Drakenberg

Australia:

William Ian de Vere von Drakenberg

Anne de Vere von Drakenberg

Martin de Vere von Drakenberg

Geoffrey de Vere von Drakenberg

Stephanie de Vere von Drakenberg

Kaaron Mitchell de Vere von Drakenberg

Emma Mitchell de Vere von Drakenberg

Maree Mitchell de Vere von Drakenberg

Philip Mitchell de Vere von Drakenberg

Brady Mitchell de Vere von Drakenberg

Adam Doney de Vere von Drakenberg

Mitchell de Vere von Drakenberg

Riley de Vere von Drakenberg

Grace de Vere von Drakenberg

Naomi Scott de Vere von Drakenberg

America; Illinois:

-Clannad An MacTamhais -

Gregory Thompson de Vere von Drakenberg

Teresita Thompson de Vere von Drakenberg

Sarah Thompson de Vere von DrakenbergTiffany Thompson Spencer de Vere von Drakenberg

America; Michigan:

Mary Alber de Vere von Drakenberg
Michael Alber de Vere von Drakenberg
Andrew Alber de Vere von Drakenberg

America; Hawaii:

Daniel Alber de Vere von Drakenberg

Senior Dragon Families in Eastern Eurasia:

Croatia:

Major Mladen Tarnawa Krupa-de Vere von Drakenberg Sr.

Colonel-in-Chief of the Order of Knights Templars

within the Imperial and Royal Dragon Court

Alfred Tarnawa Krupa-de Vere von Drakenberg:

Dragon Grand Master in Eastern Europe.

Gabriel Tarnawa Krupa von Drakenberg

Eleanor Tarnawa-Krupa von Drakenberg

Mladen Tarnawa-Krupa von Drakenberg Jr.

Magdalena Tarnawa-Krupa von Drakenberg

Margareta Tarnawa-Krupa Juric von Drakenberg

Noah Tarnawa-Krupa von Drakenberg

Emanuel Tarnawa-Krupa von Drakenberg

Seneschals of the Dragon Court; SDR:

Michael Hunter von Drakenberg RAD., SDR: Seneschal of England

Jamie de Vere von Drakenberg SDR: Seneschal of Scotland

Clive de Vere von Drakenberg SDR: Seneschal of Ireland and Chief Archivist

The Hon. Lady Twyman SDR

The Hon. Lady Peters SDR

H.E. Baron Robert Quinn SDR

The Seneschals of the Knights Templars in Eastern Eurasia (Sub Rosa)

Court of Honourable Companions
-Spouses, Friends and Supporters-

Alexandre Bathoru – Bathory CDR.

Nicolas Kropacek von Sachsentein CDR.

Dr. Felicity Smart CDR.

Djurdjica Tarnawa-Krupa CDR.

Lilian Tarnawa-Krupa CDR.

Linda Weir CDR.

Lorna Green CDR.

Eugene Paul Alber CDR.

Vivian Lindfield Hunter CDR

The Baron Scott Mitchell CDR.

Sandy Doney CDR.

David Scott CDR.

Heather Nobriga Alber CDR.

Michelle Alber CDR.

Joshua Free CDR.

Arif Hasan Khan CDR.

Matthew Collison CDR.

Guadalupe Collison CDR.

Jacob Collison CDR.

Isabella Collison CDR.

Luke Collison CDR.

Charles Johnson CDR.

Paul Tice CDR.

Anthony Hanlon CDR.

Kim Hanlon CDR.

Mark Pinkham CDR.

Oisin Mulcahy CDR.

Lisa Palmer CDR.

Christina Paul CDR.

Anne Furnaris CDR.

William Furnaris CDR.

Andrew Dixon CDR.

David Schweitzer CDR.

Eric Schweitzer CDR.

Ryan Schweitzer CDR.

Shannon Schweitzer CDR.

Jonah Schweitzer CDR.

Karen Schweitzer CDR.

Michael Power CDR.

Shiela Power CDR.

Oliver Garcias CDR.

Vere Genealogical Index

Collison Genealogical Index

Vere and Collison Primary Genealogical Sources

Classical Sources:

Sumerian Anunnaki King Lists – Library of Ninevah, northern Iraq and the Library of King Nebuchadnezzar of Babylon.

Egyptian Kings Lists, by Dr. David Rohl.

Egyptian Hyksos King Lists by the Dynastic Priest and Historian Manetho of Egypt.

Scythian Mittani King Lists for Syria researched and collated for the House of Vere by Sir Laurence Gardner.

Scythian Martial Custom and Practice, Heroditus, 400 BC.

Scythian Pictish King Lists for Scotland and France, researched and collated for the House of Vere by Sir Laurence Gardner.

Historia Britonum, Nennius, 800 AD.

Medieval Scottish Manuscripts:

Bain I, 174.

Panmure II, 126.

Colne Priory MSS.

Kelso Abbey MSS

Paisley Abbey MSS.

Arbroath Abbey MSS.

Charter "De Decimus Episcopatus," 1100 AD, Moray.

Medieval and Post-Reformation Sources:

Family Archives of the House of Vere of Oxford, Lanark, Fermanagh and Clare.

Collison Royal Genealogies, House of Vere, Co. Clare, Ireland.

The Plantagenet Chronicles, Thomas de Loche (1130) and Jean de Mortimer (1164-1173).

Transcript of the trial of Major Thomas Weir, Edinburgh, April 10th 1670. House of Vere.

Sir Randolph Crew's summary - House of Lords Archives.

Roll of Arms of the Lord Lyon King of Arms of Scotland, Lyon Court, Edinburgh, Scotland.

Arden, St. George and Glover Rolls of Arms, ref: College of Arms, London, England.

Victorian Government Documents:

Parish Records and Census Returns for County Tyrone – Public Records Office, Belfast, Northern Ireland.

Griffith's Valuations for Tyrone – Public Records Office, Belfast, Northern Ireland.

Parish Tithe Records for County Tyrone – P.R.O. Belfast.

Post Great War Government Documents:

Parish Records and Census Returns for Wigtonshire – Scottish Records Office, New Register House, Edinburgh, Scotland.

Post Second World War Government Documents:

Registry for Births, Marriages and Deaths for Cumbria, Kent, East Sussex, Hertfordshire and West Sussex – St. Catharine's House Records, Preston, Lancashire, England.

Official Government Documentary Proofs of Identity and Title:

British Government's Home Office Identity and Passport agency.

Government Register of Electors for West Sussex and Carmarthenshire up to 2009.

Department for Work and Pensions (National Insurance Identity Division).

Department of Transport. (Licensing and Identity Agency).

European Union Health Services Department. (Medical Identity Card Division).

Republic of Ireland Financial Services Department (Identity Card Division).

Department of Genetics and Haematology, London University, U.K.

Secondary Sources for Genealogies

Histories of England – Baron Thomas Babington Macaulay, Lord Macaulay of Rothley Temple, (1800-1859). Politician and historian. Educated at Trinity College, Cambridge, he became one of the acknowledged intellectual pundits of his age. He entered the Supreme Council for India in 1834 where his famous *Minutes on Law and Education* had a decisive influence on the development of the sub-continent. He was Secretary-At-War 1839-41 and went on to write his acclaimed, best-selling *Histories of England* between 1849-1855. "He used a wide range of manuscript sources with great skill, and modern historians neglect his reconstruction of events at their peril": Margaret Drabble CBE, Morley College.

The Dictionary of National Biography – designed and published by George Smith (1824-1901). *The Dictionary* was first published in 1882 with Sir Leslie Stephen (1832-1904) as editor. The *DNB* in its original form included biographies of all the national notabilities from the earliest time to 1900. The work has been continued by the publishing of decennial supplements. Stephen was succeeded as editor by Sir Sydney Lee and their names appear jointly on the title pages of volumes XXII to XXVI (1890). In 1917 the *Dictionary* was transferred to Oxford University.

Myths of the Middle Ages – Reverend Father Sabine Baring Gould, Lord of Lew Trenchard, Devon, (1834-1924). Baring-Gould travelled the Continent extensively and was educated at Clare College, Cambridge. An antiquarian and folklorist, Baring-Gould, a prolific writer, was the author of numerous works including *Mehalah*, which Swinburne compared to *Wuthering Heights*.

Burke's Peerage – properly *A Genealogical and Heraldic History of the Peerage and Baronetage of the United Kingdom*, 1826-1947, first compiled by John Burke in 1826 and published anually after 1947.

Burke's Irish Landed Gentry – Published 1897.

The Itinerary – Reverend John Leland, (1503-1552). "The earliest of modern antiquaries," Leland was educated at St. Paul's School and Christ's College, Cambridge. He studied in Paris, took holy orders and by 1530 was involved with the Royal Libraries. From 1533 he received a commission from King Henry VIII to search the monastic and collegiate libraries for old authors. He made a tour through England between 1535 and 1543 intending his researches to be the basis of an opus magna on the *Histories and Antiquities of the Nation*. His notes were first published at Oxford University by the historian Thomas Hearne (1678-1735) as *The Itinerary* in nine volumes in 1710-12. Lucy Toulmin Smith produced an edition of *The Itinerary* in 1906-10 in which she noted that the descent of Vere was included as an extract from Folio 42 of the original work, which was formerly preserved in Stow's original collection.

Stow MSS – John Stow (1525-1605). A collection of manuscripts first collated in 1564. Stow transcribed manuscripts and was the first person to compose historical works based on a systematic study of Public Records. He assisted Parker with editing historical texts and his chief publications were *The Workes of Geoffrey Chaucer* (1561); *Summary of English Chronicles* (1565); *The Chronicles of England* (1580) and *A Survey of London*. An edition of the collection was published by Strype in 1720 and the fullest edition of the original work was C.L. Kingsford's, which was published in 1908.

Complete Peerage of England, Scotland, Ireland, Great Britain and the United Kingdom, Extant, Extinct or Dormant – George Edward Cokayne MA, born in Russell Square, London in 1825; the son of Dr. William Adams LLD and The Hon. Mary Anne Cokayne, neice and co-heiress of Borlase, 6th Viscount Cullen. Complying with his mother's wishes Cokayne changed his name by royal license on 15th August 1873. Cokayne was educated at Exeter College, Oxford. Barrister; Lincoln's Inn (1853); Rouge Dragon Pursuivant-of-Arms (1859-1870), Lancaster Herald (1870-1882); Norroy King-of-Arms (1882-1894) Clarenceux King of Arms from 1894. *His Complete Peerage of the United Kingdom...* in 8 volumes was compiled between 1887-98 and published by George Bell. Holding Library: Trinity College Dublin.

Royal Genealogies or *The Genealogical Tables of Emperors, Kings and Princes from Adam to These Times*, by Dr. James Anderson DD., MA., (1680-1739). Anderson was born in Aberdeen where he was also later educated and took his degrees. He was appointed Presbyterian Minister for Swallow Street and Lisle Street, Leicester Fields in London between 1710 and 1734. Described as "a learned man" Anderson, who was a Freemason, was assigned the task, in 1721, of compiling an authoritative digest of the *Constitutions* of the fraternity (see Entick's edition of 1747; page 194 et seq). As Grand Warden of the Grand Lodge in London he presented his work to the Order in 1723.

It has appeared in numerous subequent editions and has been long recognised by English Freemasons as the standard code on its subject. Editions were translated into German and also appeared in America in 1855, as facsimiles of the earlier English version. The work by which Anderson is chiefly remembered, *The Royal Genealogies*, was first published in 2 volumes in London in 1732. Anderson based this work on the earlier *Genealogische Tabellen* of Johann Hubner (see below). The relatively later tables of the *Genealogies* were considered by Sir Stephen Leslie (*Dictionary of National Biography*) "to be of use (i.e. a valid historical source work) in relation to the genealogies of continental dynasties and houses" (Re: Vere). *Royal Genealogies*: Holding Library; Cambridge University.

Genealogische Tabellen – Johann Hubner. Properly: *Der Genealogische Tabellen zur erlauterung der politische historie vom anfange biss auf diesen tag continuiret*, published in one volume, Leipzig 1719. Holding library: Glasgow.

The Collections – Sir James Dalrymple. *Collections concerning the Scottish history, preceeding the death of King David the First, in the year 1153. Wherein the soveraignity of the crown and independency of the church are cleared; and account given of the antiquity and purity of the Scottish-British church, and the novelty of popery in this kingdom. With an appendix containing the copies of charters of foundation of some churches; with genealogical accounts of the donors and witnesses.* First published in Edinburgh in 1705 by the heirs and successors of Andrew Anderson; sold by John Vallange and Mrs. Ogstoun ...[8], LXXXVI, [4], 432, [4] p. (80) Holding Library: Durham.

The Surnames of Scotland, Their Origin, Meaning, and History, by Dr. George Fraser Black. Published in New York in 1946: The New York Public Library. Holding Libraries: Cambridge; Edinburgh; Leeds; Liverpool; Nottingham ; SAS ; Sheffield.

The Scottish Hazard – Beryl Platts: British Library.

The Bloodline of the Holy Grail – Sir Laurence Gardner: Element Books 1997.

Genesis of the Grail Kings – Sir Laurence Gardner: Bantam Press 1999.

The True Elves of Europe – an essay by Leonid Korablev.

God of the Witches – Prof. Margaret Murray: Rider and Co.

The Witch Cult in Western Europe – Prof. Margaret Murray: Rider and Co.

The Veres of Hedingham Castle – Miss Verily Anderson.

The Madness of Kings – Prof. Vivian Green.

Lady Pembrokeshire's Genealogies – Reference Section, City of Brighton Library.

Jesus: Last of the Pharoahs - Ralph Ellis. The Egyptian descent of Jesus Christ.

The Secret Gospel of Mark – Prof. Morton Smith.

Scio Cui Credido

She Messiah

She-Messiah – *La Messie* – written by my beloved cousin Prince Alexandre de Bothuri-Bàthory, is published by Cogito group media ISBN/EAN 978-29238650-03-3 and was first released in France and in all the French-speaking countries in November, 2010; then in Spanish in Spring 2011, and also in its English version on the same date. Critics are comparing Alexandre's work with the novel *Zanoni* by the Victorian Occultist Lord Bulwer-Lytton of Knebworth. It is a novel which is also catalogued as an esoteric thriller, wherein an American top model of French- Scottish origins has her whole life turned upside down on account of a strange diamond jewel labeled the "Southern Cross," which she had bought at Sotheby's in New York. The talisman is gifted with supernatural powers, which will guide her to achieve her prophesied Messianic status, but she will have to battle evil persons who are intent on stopping her transformation and who are determined to steal this famous diamond, also known as the "Light of Luxor" by the Secret Royal Order of the Trinity of Luxor. Famous French composer prodigy Stéphane Blet created a sonata no. 9 opus 213 for *She-Messiah*.

The author is an accomplished Magus, Scholar and Philosopher who currently lives in Florida with his noble lady wife, Elaine Bédard. They are very much involved with European arts and travel extensively.

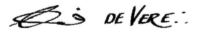

HI&RH Prince Nicholas Santa
Tarnawa-de Vere von Drakenberg,
KCD., Sov. GM KTStA, Sov KTSH., Sov. IRDC.,
HG The Grand Duke Nicholas of Khazaria

Printed in the USA
CPSIA information can be obtained
at www.ICGtesting.com
LVHW022315081223
765728LV00005B/142